HOUGHTON MIFFLIN SOCIAL STUDIES

# A Message of Ancient Days

*H*istory truly bears witness
to the passage of time,
sheds light upon the truth,
breathes life into the power
of memory, provides instruction
for daily life, and carries
**a message of ancient days.**

**Cicero**

Beverly J. Armento
Gary B. Nash
Christopher L. Salter
Karen K. Wixson

# A Message of Ancient Days

Houghton Mifflin Company • Boston

Atlanta • Dallas • Geneva, Illinois • Princeton, New Jersey • Palo Alto • Toronto

## Consultants

*World History Consultant*
Scott Waugh
Associate Professor of History
University of California—Los Angeles
Los Angeles, California

*Program Consultants*
Edith M. Guyton
Associate Professor of Early
  Childhood Education
Georgia State University
Atlanta, Georgia

Gail Hobbs
Associate Professor of Geography
Pierce College
Woodland Hills, California

Charles Peters
Reading Consultant
Oakland Schools
Pontiac, Michigan

Cathy Riggs-Salter
Social Studies Consultant
Hartsburg, Missouri

Alfredo Schifini
Limited English Proficiency Consultant
Los Angeles, California

George Paul Schneider
Associate Director
  of General Programs
Department of Museum Education
Art Institute of Chicago
Chicago, Illinois

Twyla Stewart
Center for Academic Interinstitutional
  Programs
University of California—Los Angeles
Los Angeles, California

## Teacher Reviewers

David E. Beer (Grade 5)
Weisser Park Elementary
Fort Wayne, Indiana

Jan Coleman (Grades 6–7)
Thornton Junior High
Fremont, California

Shawn Edwards
  (Grades 1–3)
Jackson Park Elementary
University City, Missouri

Barbara J. Fech (Grade 6)
Martha Ruggles School
Chicago, Illinois

Deborah M. Finkel
  (Grade 4)
Los Angeles Unified
  School District,
  Region G
South Pasadena,
  California

Jim Fletcher (Grades 5, 8)
La Loma Junior High
Modesto, California

Susan M. Gilliam
  (Grade 1)
Roscoe Elementary
Los Angeles, California

Vicki Stroud Gonterman
  (Grade 2)
Gibbs International
  Studies Magnet School
Little Rock, Arkansas

Lorraine Hood (Grade 2)
Fresno Unified School
  District
Fresno, California

Jean Jamgochian
  (Grade 5)
Haycock Gifted and
  Talented Center
Fairfax County, Virginia

Susan Kirk-Davalt
  (Grade 5)
Crowfoot Elementary
Lebanon, Oregon

Mary Molyneaux-Leahy
  (Grade 3)
Bridgeport Elementary
Bridgeport, Pennsylvania

Sharon Oviatt
  (Grades 1–3)
Keysor Elementary
Kirkwood, Missouri

Jayne B. Perala (Grade 1)
Cave Spring Elementary
Roanoke, Virginia

Carol Siefkin (K)
Garfield Elementary
Sacramento, California

Norman N. Tanaka
  (Grade 3)
Martin Luther King Jr.
  Elementary
Sacramento, California

John Tyler (Grades 5, 8)
Groton School
Groton, Massachusetts

Portia W. Vaughn
  (Grades 1–3)
School District 11
Colorado Springs,
  Colorado

Printed in the U.S.A.

ISBN: 0-395-52729-5
FGHIJ-VH-9987654321

Development by Ligature, Inc.

## Acknowledgments

Grateful acknowledgment is made
for the use of the material listed below.
The material in the Minipedia is
reprinted from *The World Book*
*Encyclopedia* with the expressed permission of the publisher. © 1990 by World
Book, Inc.

*–Continued on page 541.*

# From Your Authors

*T*hrough the tall cedar trees of the Forbidden Forest appeared the terrifying giant Huwawa. The towering creature had a head like a lion's and the teeth of a fierce dragon. His fiery breath struck fear into the hearts of all his enemies.

*So begins one of the stories in* Gilgamesh, *a long poem first written down more than 4,000 years ago. In the poem, Gilgamesh appears as a superhero with magical powers. But the real Gilgamesh was the king of an ancient city in present-day Iraq. In Chapter 6 of this book, you will read more about both the legendary Gilgamesh and the amazing Sumerian civilization in which the real Gilgamesh lived.*

*Most of the people you will meet in this book lived long ago in places that may seem very far away from your home. But they all had feelings just like yours and faced many of the same challenges you will face in your life. And whether they were great leaders or ordinary people, their actions helped shape the world you live in now.*

*As you read about these people, places, and events, we hope you will ask many questions. Some questions may be about history: "What caused these people to make the decisions they did?" or "How do we know about these events?" Other questions may be about geography: "What are the land and weather like in that place?" or "Why did people choose to settle there?" Still other questions may be about economics: "How did people meet their needs for food and shelter?" or "How did people work out ways for using scarce resources?"*

*Most of all, we hope you catch the excitement of thinking, questioning, and discovering answers about your world— now and in the 21st century.*

Beverly J. Armento
Professor of Social Studies
Director, Center for Business and
Economic Education
Georgia State University

Christopher L. Salter
Professor and Chair
Department of Geography
University of Missouri

Gary B. Nash
Professor of History
University of California—Los Angeles

Karen K. Wixson
Associate Professor of Education
University of Michigan

# Contents

# Exploring

*The story of the past is hidden all around you in the world of the present. "Exploring" pages tell you the secrets of how to find it.*

# Literature

*Throughout history people have expressed their deepest feelings and beliefs through literature. Reading these stories, legends, poems, and shorter passages that appear in the lessons will help you experience what life was like for people of other times and places.*

# Primary Sources

*Reading the exact words of the people who made and lived history is the best way to get a sense of how they saw themselves and the times in which they lived. You will find more than 50 primary sources throughout this book, including the following:*

# A Closer Look

*Take a closer look at the objects and pictures spread out on these special pages. With the clues you see, you'll become a historical detective.*

# A Moment in Time

*A person from the past is frozen at an exciting moment. You'll get to know these people by reading about where they are, what they're wearing, and the objects around them.*

# Charts, Diagrams, and Timelines

*These visual presentations of information help give you a clearer picture of the people, places, and events you are studying.*

# Maps

*The events of history have been shaped by the places in which they occurred. Each map in this book tells its own story about these events and places.*

# Starting Out

*What makes this textbook so much more interesting than others you've used? In this book, the people of the past speak directly to you, through their actual words and the objects they used. You'll walk inside their houses and look inside their cooking pots. You'll follow them as they go to school, build cities, fight wars, work out settlements for peace.*

753 B.C.      A.D. 476

49 B.C.      A.D. 235

**When and where?** The timeline at the beginning of each lesson and the lesson title tell you the time and place.

**From unit to chapter to lesson**—each step lets you see history in closer detail. The maps and photos show you where events happened. The art introduces you to the people.

**Right from the beginning** the lesson opener pulls you into the sights, the sounds, the smells of what life was like at that time, in that place.

**Like a road sign,** the question that always appears here tells you what to think about while you read the lesson.

**Look for these key terms.** They are listed here so that you can watch for them. The first time they appear in the lesson they are shown in heavy black print and defined. Key terms are also defined in the Glossary.

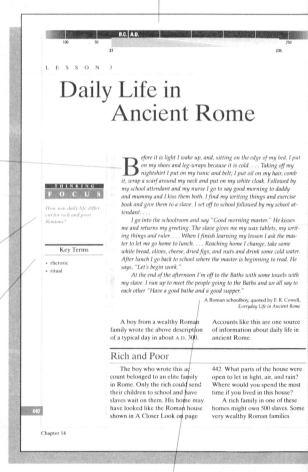

B.C. | A.D.
100   50   27          750   235

L E S S O N   3

# Daily Life in Ancient Rome

**THINKING FOCUS**

*How was daily life different for rich and poor Romans?*

**Key Terms**

• rhetoric
• ritual

Before it is light I wake up, and, sitting on the edge of my bed, I put on my shoes and leg-wraps because it is cold. . . . Taking off my nightshirt I put on my tunic and belt; I put oil on my hair, comb it, wrap a scarf around my neck and put on my white cloak. Followed by my school attendant and my nurse I go to say good morning to daddy and mummy and I kiss them both. I find my writing things and exercise book and give them to a slave. I set off to school followed by my school attendant. . . .

I go into the schoolroom and say "Good morning master." He kisses me and returns my greeting. The slave gives me my wax tablets, my writing things and ruler. . . . When I finish learning my lesson I ask the master to let me go home to lunch. . . . Reaching home I change, take some white bread, olives, cheese, dried figs, and nuts and drink some cold water. After lunch I go back to school where the master is beginning to read. He says, "Let's begin work."

At the end of the afternoon I'm off to the Baths with some towels with my slave. I run up to meet the people going to the Baths and we all say to each other "Have a good bathe and a good supper."

A Roman schoolboy, quoted by F. R. Cowell,
*Everyday Life in Ancient Rome*

A boy from a wealthy Roman family wrote the above description of a typical day in about A.D. 300.

Accounts like this are one source of information about daily life in ancient Rome.

## Rich and Poor

The boy who wrote this account belonged to an elite family in Rome. Only the rich could send their children to school and have slaves wait on them. His home may have looked like the Roman house shown in A Closer Look on page

442. What parts of the house were open to let in light, air, and rain? Where would you spend the most time if you lived in this house?

A rich family in one of these homes might own 500 slaves. Some very wealthy Roman families

440

Chapter 14

**Letters, diaries, books**—short passages from these primary sources let people from the past speak to you. When you see a tan background, a red initial letter, and a gray bar, you know that the quotation is a primary source.

**Take a closer look**, in this case at a Roman house. Look at the couches in the dining room, the pictures on the floors.

## A CLOSER LOOK

# A Roman House

*Imagine living in a home that was also your parents' work place. Relatives, friends, servants, and clients would always be coming and going. There might be a vegetable garden and a couple of stores under your roof, too.*

**Would you walk** on your artwork? The Romans did. Romans decorated their floors with mosaics like this one.

**If you put** out this dog-shaped oil lamp, your bedroom would be totally dark—even during the day! That's because bedrooms rarely had windows.

**The father of the family** sits here, where he can see all the action.

Back yard

Garden

Kitchen

Statue of great-grandfather

Stores

Door, open all day

Reading room

**Like a living room today,** the atrium was the place where Roman families entertained their guests. But the Roman living room had a hole in its roof. Rainwater poured into a pool where it was stored for drinking and washing.

Bedroom

**Can you eat lying down?** Romans held dinner parties in a room called the *triclinium*, which means "three-couch place." The room had three couches, and dinner guests ate while lying on their sides.

**Only the rich** could afford glass pitchers and bowls like these.

442

Chapter 14

### Family Life in the Empire

By the time Rome had become the center of an empire, family life was changing. In the days of the Republic, the father was the undisputed head of the family. He could even sell his children as slaves. He could arrange marriages for his daughters when they were only 12 to 15 years old. He would do this for the political and economic benefits it would bring to the family. The young bride and groom had little to say about it.

By the A.D. 100s, however, family discipline had become less harsh, and the father's power had been reduced. A father no longer had the right to sell his children or to force marriages. In addition, women had more freedom. Unlike women in other ancient cultures such as Greece, Roman women were independent under the law. They could have their own property and slaves.

Families that could afford the cost of private education sent their children and even household slaves to school beginning at about age seven. These children studied basic reading, writing, and arithmetic. The schools were small, and one teacher was responsible for all subjects. Teachers followed the rule of the Greek playwright Menander: "A man who has not been flogged [beaten] is not trained."

Girls usually did not have any formal education after age 15. Usually at 15, the sons of wealthy parents continued their education by taking classes in Latin and Greek literature and **rhetoric**—the art of effective writing and speaking. Students needed to learn rhetoric in order to enter law or politics. Romans believed that skill in rhetoric was the mark of a gentleman.

The Roman schools rarely had classes in science, engineering, or complex mathematics. The few professional people—engineers, doctors, or lawyers, for example—learned through apprenticeships, not through formal education. ∎

◄ *Some people in Pompeii were eating their midday meal when Vesuvius erupted. (See How Do We Know? on page 444.) Several foods, preserved intact under the ashes, can be seen today in the Pompeii Museum, including this loaf of bread.*

◄ *This young Roman student looks thoughtful. Is she thinking about the day's lesson?*

∎ *What were family life and schooling like for young people growing up in the Roman Empire?*

### Benefits of Life in Rome

The city of Rome was a crowded, busy, thriving place—the center for the best and worst of the Mediterranean world. Disease, crime, and fires raged there. But life in Rome also had its benefits. The emperors made a point of trying to keep the city people happy.

443

The Roman Empire

---

...emperor might command a personal slave population of 20,000. Household slaves did just about every job imaginable. They cooked, served meals, cleaned, and took care of the children. Each slave might have only one job—folding the master's clothes or fixing the mistress's hair, for example.

In contrast, the vast majority of those who lived in the city had tiny apartments in five-story apartment buildings called *insulae* (IHN suh ly). In some cases, an entire family would crowd into a single room.

For every wealthy home in Rome, there were 26 blocks of *insulae*. Most *insulae* were dark from public roads...

The Roman writer Juvenal described the poorer neighborhoods of Rome in the A.D. 100s:

M ost of the city [is] propped up with planks to stop it collapsing. Your landlord stands in front of cracks that have been there for years and says, "Sleep well!" although he knows that the house itself may not last the night. I wish I lived where there were no fires, no midnight panics.

In these crowded conditions, fires and crime were serious problems. Lack of sanitation also contributed to the spread of disease. The problem was so severe that about one-fourth of the babies born in Rome did not live through their first year. Half of all Roman children did not live to be 10 years old. ∎

*...in the darkness, may be answering the age-old question; "What did you learn in school today?"*

◄ *This make-up box and the hairpin shown with it once belonged to a wealthy Roman woman.*

∎ *How did the housing of the rich Romans compare with the housing of the poor?*

441

The Roman Empire

---

**Every age has its great storytellers.** Each chapter includes short examples of fine writing from or about the period. The literature is always printed on a tan background with a blue initial letter and a multicolored bar.

---

**Frozen at a moment in time,** this Roman engineer transports you back to the past. You learn all about him, through his equipment, his clothes, the place he's working.

## A MOMENT IN TIME

# A Roman Engineer

*8:42 A.M., August 28, 109 B.C.
On what will be the Via Aemilia Scauri outside Pisa*

**Crossbars**
Now that the top of his surveying instrument is level, he can look ahead to where his assistant is standing. He shouts directions to the assistant, who marks the ground where the road should go.

**Ear**
Our engineer can hear the shouts of slaves and praetors digging half a mile away. The diggers are already working on the stretch of road he planned just days ago.

**Robe**
He's wearing his finest today despite the heat. The official in charge will come by soon to inspect. Our engineer wants to look his best.

**Clasp**
This gift was sent by his wife in Rome. Because of the excellent roads, it reached him in only three days.

**Measuring Cord**
Besides the mathematics he needs to make accurate measurements, our engineer has studied music, astronomy, and medicine. The best engineers know all the arts and sciences.

**Mental Point**
He likes the moments each day when he moves his equipment ahead and plants it in a new place. The army is anxious to have this road finished, and movement means progress.

# Continuing On

*As you get to know the people of the past, you'll want ways of understanding and remembering them better. This book gives you some tools to use in learning about people and places and remembering what you've learned.*

**Giving you the inside story** is the purpose of two special paragraphs. How Do We Know? tells you where information about the past comes from. Its companion, Across Time & Space, connects what you're reading to things that happened centuries ago or continents away. (See page 417 for an example.)

**The titles outline the lesson.** The red titles tell you the main topics discussed in the lesson on "Daily Life in Ancient Rome." The blue titles tell you the subtopics.

**A picture is worth a thousand words.** But just a few words in a caption can help you understand a picture, a photograph, a map, or in this case, an illustration of a Roman circus.

---

### How Do We Know?

HISTORY *In A.D. 79, Mount Vesuvius, a volcano in southern Italy, erupted. Afterward, nearly 13 feet of ash and stone covered the nearby town of Pompeii. During the past two centuries, archaeologists have rediscovered the town. Studying what remains of Pompeii has given archaeologists a clear picture of daily life in the Roman Empire.*

### Public Services

The government gave free wheat to male citizens on a regular basis. This gift of food was important to the poor people of Rome, who often went hungry. On special occasions, the emperor also gave money to the citizens of Rome. The wheat and money came from taxes that farmers and other people in the provinces paid.

Another benefit of living in Rome was the plentiful water supply. The system of aqueducts carried 200 million gallons of water to Rome daily. With so much water available, the city built public baths where residents, rich and poor, could bathe and swim for a small fee. These baths became important gathering places.

### Entertainment

The emperors spent enormous sums of money to entertain the people. In fact, 159 days each year

had been declared holidays by the A.D. 50s. Later emperors found it necessary to limit the number of holidays each year. Still, nearly one-third of the days of each year remained holidays throughout the A.D. 100s.

On these holidays the emperors provided elaborate circuses and games to keep the people content. The Circus Maximus was a gigantic Roman arena that could hold nearly 200,000 spectators. There, spectacular daredevil chariot races took place. "All Rome today is in the circus," wrote Juvenal. "Such sights are for the young, whom it befits to shout and make bold wagers with a smart damsel by their side."

Chariot racing was also popular at the Colosseum, but so were some of the more bloody sports. Wild beasts were hunted and killed by the hundreds. Gladiators fought each other to the death. During

the years A.D. 106 to 114, 23,000 gladiators fought to entertain the citizens. The Romans were so fond of bloody events that during the intermissions, Roman officials executed condemned criminals for the entertainment of the audience.

However, the benefits of life in Rome such as free food and spectacular entertainment did not appeal to all Romans. Some claimed that the citizens took too much interest in those things and not enough interest in their government. Even members of the elite class, who benefited the most, saw problems. The Roman historian

Tacitus said that the empire made slaves of free men. The Roman writer Juvenal also complained that the public "longs for just two things—bread and circuses." ■

▲ *Circuses were a major form of entertainment in the Roman Empire. This "Mosaic of the Circus Games" was found in Roman Gaul. It dates from about A.D. 175.*

### Religious Practices

Many Romans believed that they had been able to build their empire and find peace because they had kept their gods happy. Like many other ancient peoples, the Romans had gods for every act and event in their lives.

### The Many Gods of the Romans

The great gods of the Roman state were Jupiter, Juno, and Minerva. Jupiter was the supreme god. He controlled the thunder and lightning and was the special guardian of Rome. Juno was his wife. She was the queen of the gods and the protector of women. Minerva was the goddess of wisdom and guardian of craftworkers. The Romans joined together on specific days to worship these gods. In this way they showed their unity and their loyalty to the state.

At home, the Romans worshiped household gods, such as Vesta, Lares (*LAIR eez*), and Penates (*puh NAY teez*). Vesta guarded the fireside, where people

cooked and kept warm. Lares guarded the land, and Penates watched over the stored food. Family members made daily offerings to these gods and asked for protection in exchange.

Many of these Roman gods had been borrowed from the Greeks at an earlier time. For example, Jupiter was the Greek god Zeus, and Juno was the Greek goddess Hera. Diana, the Roman goddess of the hunt, was the Greek goddess Artemis. Mars, the Roman god of war, was the Greek god Ares.

In A.D. 126, the Romans erected a magnificent temple called the Pantheon (*PAN thee uhn*) to honor all the Roman gods and goddesses. They built it in the shape of a drum, with a dome rising 14 stories above the ground. They covered the dome with gleaming brass so that people could see it

■ *How did the emperors provide bread and circuses for the people of Rome?*

▼ *Found in the ruins of Pompeii, this household shrine contains small statues that include one of Lares, the guardian of houses.*

▼ *The Roman public baths were complex structures. (1) A furnace heated (2) a tank of water. (3) Pipes carried the hot water to the pools. The Romans began their bath in a hot-water pool, continued it in (4) a warm-water pool, and ended it in (5) a cool-water pool.*

444

Chapter 14

---

**Cutaway diagrams show you** what's under the roof—in this case, the famous Roman baths. Other illustrations, charts, and graphs tell you how things work and how one bit of information relates to another.

**You're in charge of your reading.** See the red square at the end of the text? Now find the red square over in the margin. If you can answer the question there, then you probably understood what you just read. If you can't, perhaps you'd better go back and read that part of the lesson again.

**Some tools you'll always use.** The Understanding pages walk you through skills that you will use again and again, as a student and later on in life.

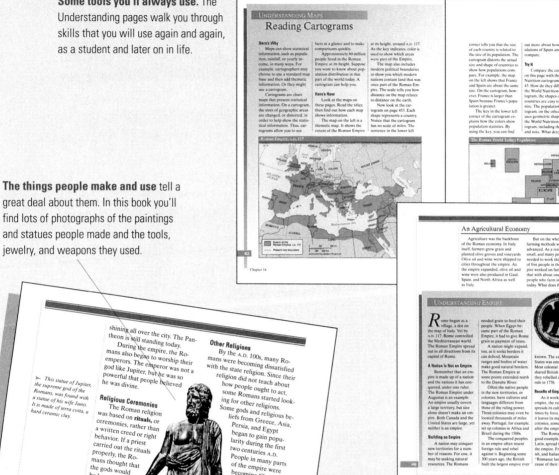

**The things people make and use** tell a great deal about them. In this book you'll find lots of photographs of the paintings and statues people made and the tools, jewelry, and weapons they used.

**A special kind of Understanding** page looks at concepts—the big ideas that help put all the pieces together. This section helps you understand ideas like the Family, Democracy, and in this case, an Empire.

**After you read the lesson,** stop and review what you've read. The first question is the same one you started out with. The second question connects the lesson to what you've studied earlier. Other questions and an activity help you think about the lesson you've read. Chapter Review questions help you tie the lessons together. (See pages 456 and 457 for an example.)

**Every map tells a story,** The maps in this book tell the story of where people like Hannibal and his army went and what the land was like.

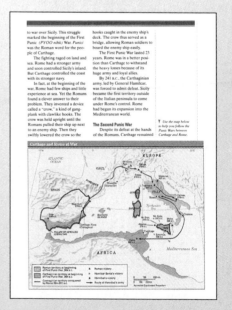

# Also Featuring

*Some special pages show up only once in every unit, not in every lesson in the book. These features continue the story by letting you explore an idea or activity, or read a story about another time and place. The Time/Space Databank in the back of the book brings together resources you will use again and again.*

**School isn't the only place** where you can learn social studies. This feature gives you a chance to explore history and geography outside the classroom—at home or in your own neighborhood.

EXPLORING

## Greek Architecture in Your Community

*This scale model of Buckingham Palace is entirely made up of interlocking plastic bricks. What elements of Greek architecture can you identify?*

▲ *The three classical types of Greek capitals are Doric (top), Ionic (middle), and Corinthian (bottom).*

Chapter 12

368

MAKING DECISIONS

## Public Policy: Spend Less? Raise Taxes?

*U ncontrolled prices are widespread in the sales taking place in the markets and in the daily life of the cities . . . we have decided that maximum prices of articles for sale must be established . . . Thus, when the pressure of high prices appears anywhere . . . [greed] will be checked by the limits . . . of the law.*

Emperor Diocletian, Edict on Prices, A.D. 301

*W hen . . . he brought about enormously high prices, he attempted to legislate the prices of [goods]. Then much blood was spilled . . . nothing appeared on the market because of fear, and prices soared much higher. In the end, after many people had lost their lives, it became absolutely necessary to repeal the law.*

Lactantius, Christian writer living in Rome, A.D. 245-325

▼ *Diocletian and his co-emperor Maximian ruled the empire together.*

### Background

When Diocletian became emperor of Rome in A.D. 284, he faced an empire in crisis. Enemies along the empire's borders were constantly waging war against Rome. The once-powerful Roman army was no longer strong enough to fight off their attacks. Warfare left the cities and countryside in ruins.

In addition, the empire had grown so large that the government in Rome wasn't able to rule it efficiently. Lawsuits in distant provinces were often left unsettled because there were no government officials to hear them.

Closer to home, arguments and civil wars broke out each time an emperor died or retired: Who would follow him to the throne? Prices were also rising rapidly, making it harder for people to survive.

Finally, the treasury—the money used to pay for the government and army—was running out. The empire was falling apart. What could Diocletian do to save it?

Chapter 15

402

Diocletian began by making a number of decisions. First he reorganized the government. He appointed a co-emperor and two junior emperors. Each of these men ruled a portion of the empire. In this way a local problem could be quickly brought to the attention of one of the rulers. This same system would help ensure a peaceful transfer of power at the end of an emperor's reign.

The four regions of the empire were further divided into more than a hundred provinces—double the number that had existed before. Each province was run by a governor and hundreds of government officials.

To safeguard the borders, Diocletian increased the size of the army. In addition to the troops stationed along the empire's frontiers, he created specially trained troops stationed in cities nearby. These troops stood ready to move quickly to any point along the border in case of enemy attack.

To fight rising prices, Diocletian issued his Edict on Prices, setting the top price to be charged or paid for any item. He also introduced a new system of coins.

*What should be done about attacks on the empire?*

**Decision**
Increase size of army

**Outcomes**
- More soldiers
- Borders defended
- Cities, countryside safe
- Empire strong, unified
- Fewer workers
- More money spent on army
- Increased taxes
- Unhappy taxpayers

### The Cost of Decisions

What did Diocletian hope to achieve with these changes? He wanted to bring peace and make the empire secure. He also wanted to make government more effective and efficient and to keep the economy stable.

Though many Romans agreed that these were worthy goals, some of the decisions Diocletian made based on these goals were not so popular. All of these changes cost money, and that meant higher taxes. Now there were four royal courts to pay for, not just one. There were nearly three times the number of government workers as before, and all of these workers had to be paid. As the army increased in size, more money had to be spent on soldiers' salaries, training, and supplies.

▲ *What were the goals behind Diocletian's decision to increase the size of the army? Did the outcome of that decision support his goals?*

483

Christianity and the Fall of Rome

**What would you do?** The Making Decisions pages show you an important decision from the past. Then you practice the steps that will help you to make a good choice.

**Stories have always been important** parts of people's lives. Each unit in the book has at least one story about the time and place you're studying. In this case, it's a retelling of a Roman tale. Roman schoolboys and girls probably read this story, too.

LITERATURE

## The War over Latium

*Alfred J. Church*

*After Troy was destroyed by the Greeks, the hero Aeneas and the other Trojan survivors left to find a new home in Italy. In this story from The Aeneid for Boys and Girls, the goddess Juno, who hates Aeneas, is determined to keep the Trojans from settling in the Latium Plain. She decides to seek help from the underworld.*

*The Roman poet Virgil wrote the Aeneid (ih NEE uhd), an epic poem about the beginnings of Rome. Here is a retelling of parts of the Aeneid.*

**Aeneas** (ih NEE uhs )

**treachery** betrayal

J uno went down into the lower parts of the earth, and called to her Alecto, who was one of the Furies, who loved anger and war and treachery, and all evil and hateful things. Even her own sisters, the Furies, could not bear to look on her, so dreadful was she to behold. Juno said to her: "Daughter of Night, I have suffered a great wrong and disgrace, and I want you to help me. A man whom I hate, Aeneas by name, desires to have a kingdom in Italy; keep him from it. He wishes to have Lavinia, the daughter of King Latinus, to wife: see that he does not. You can set brother against brother; you can bring . . .

**The Time/Space Databank** is like a reference section of a library at your fingertips. It's the place to go for more information about the places, people, and key terms you meet in this book.

**What's a minipedia?** It's a small version of an encyclopedia, one that you don't have to go to your library to use. It's bound right into the back of your book so you can quickly look up its articles, charts, and graphs.

**The Atlas maps out the world.** Special maps tell you about the languages, religions, climates, and resources of the world. Historical maps let you compare what was going on at the same time in different places.

should have Lavinia for his wife? You say that she must marry a stranger. Is he not a stranger? Are not all who are not subjects of your kingdom strangers? This, and this only, is what the gods demand. Further, if you look into the matter, you will see that this stranger also in race, for he is of the family of Inachus, and Inachus was a Greek."

But when she saw that her husband was not moved at all by her words, the madness altogether overcame her. She rushed out of the palace, and through the streets of the city, taking her daughter with her. And, as she went, she called to the other women to follow her, so that a whole multitude went after her. And many wild creatures, they ran through the woods, the mother leading them, holding a burning torch in her hand, and as though the marriage song of her daughter and Turnus.

The next thing that the Fury did was that she went to the city where Turnus lived. He was asleep, and the Fury went in and stood by his bedside. She had taken the shape of an old woman, a priestess of the Temple of Juno, and she said: "Turnus, are you content that you should lose that which is your right, and that the kingdom should be taken from you? King Latinus takes from you the wife that he had promised, and is about to hand over his kingdom to a stranger from over the sea. Juno bade me come and tell you this. Arm your people; drive these strangers out of the land, and burn their ships with

*Inachus* (IHN uh kuhs)

# Unit 1
## The World Past and Present

*Like a snapshot in a family album, this sculpture records a moment in time. The happy husband and wife lived 2,500 years ago in what is now Italy. They are shown seated together at a grand banquet. What could their lives have been like? Certainly, they lived in a world that was different from ours. Yet the people of the past shared many of our feelings and needs. Their experiences helped shape our world.*

# 6500 B.C.

*Terra cotta sarcophagus from an Etruscan tomb at Cerveteri, Italy, c. 600 B.C. Louvre, Paris*

Today

# Chapter 1

## *Peoples of Our World*

*A child gently sways back and forth in a swing. Other children shout and laugh as they toss a ball. Still others scamper to launch kites in the afternoon breeze. These are familiar scenes of daily life. The time could be the present, but it also could be thousands of years ago. In ancient Greece, children swung in swings. In Rome they played catch. The Chinese flew kites. In many ways, the lives of the people of the past were not so different from our own.*

Just as we play board games today, the ancient Egyptians used this game board and these "throwing sticks" about 1400 B.C.

# 1500 B.C.

In some parts of the world, people have been writing down their thoughts and feelings for more than 5,000 years. This message was written on the walls of a cave in southern China about 1100 B.C.

This might have been a toy or a religious object. It was made about 700 B.C. by the Etruscans, a people who lived in what is now Italy.

Today

# Links with the Past

**Key Term**

- history

The Romans called him "the Scourge of God." Attila the Hun and his men swept across Europe 1,500 years ago and conquered the cities of the once-proud Roman Empire. The Romans, who thought these invaders were uncivilized, called them barbarians. Yet one Roman had a different view of the leader of the Huns. After one dinner with Attila and his captains, the Roman historian Priscus wrote the following:

A lavish meal, served on silver trenchers [platters], was prepared for us and the other barbarians, but Attila just had some meat on a wooden platter. . . . Gold or silver cups were presented to the other diners, but his own goblet was made of wood. His clothes, too, were simple, and no trouble was taken except to have them clean. The sword that hung by his side, the clasps of his barbarian shoes and the bridle of his horse were all free from gold, precious stones or other valuable decorations. . . .

As twilight came on torches were lit, and two barbarians entered before Attila to sing some songs they had composed, telling of his victories and valor in war. . . . After the songs a Scythian entered, a crazy fellow who told a lot of strange and completely false stories, not a word of truth in them, which made everyone laugh . . . all that is except Attila. He remained impassive, without any change of expression, and neither by word or gesture did he seem to share in the merriment except that when his youngest son, Ernas, came in and stood by him, he drew the boy towards him and looked at him with gentle eyes.

Priscus, *History*, c. A.D. 448

➤ *What impression of Attila the Hun does this portrait give you?*

# The People of the Past

People of ancient times may seem like distant mysteries to us. Yet descriptions like Priscus's account of his dinner with Attila help us see them more clearly. We can begin to understand what kind of people they were.

Think about the portrait of Attila that Priscus presents. For example, Priscus notes that Attila eats from a wooden tray and drinks from a wooden goblet, or cup. Attila was the leader of the Huns. Why didn't he eat off the silver platters like the rest of his guests?

He and his men took great treasures from the cities they conquered. Why did Attila dress so plainly? Think about the way that he looked at his son. Can't you almost see the tender expression on his face?

The Romans saw Attila as a fierce warrior, but as this portrait shows, he was more than that. He was also a man with a unique personality and a family, just like people today.

*◄ The Egyptians painted portraits of the dead on the wrappings of mummies, like this portrait of a child from about A.D. 100.*

## Lives of the Past

Studying the past allows you to "see" the faces of the famous and the nameless people who lived thousands of years before you. It helps you understand what their lives were like.

In Boston's Museum of Fine Arts, for example, you can see the 1,800-year-old mummy of a young Egyptian girl. Her portrait was painted where the wrappings cover her face.

The portrait shows that her hair is bobbed short in the style of the Roman emperor's court (Egypt was ruled by Rome during her lifetime). Her large, round eyes, dark brown, look out at you. Her lips are colored gold with something like lipstick.

The same sun you play under once warmed her skin. The same earth spun her through space. The light you see from a nearby star was just leaving the star when she laughed in the night.

Surely children like this Egyptian girl lived in a world that was much different from ours. Yet in many ways it was the same. Think about how people treat their pets today. Now look at A Moment in Time on the next page.

*▼ A young girl in ancient Egypt might have used a bronze and gold make-up kit like this one.*

5

# A Nubian Princess

*9:11 A.M., May 10, 1341 B.C.*
*In a house in Nubia, an ancient African*
*kingdom south of Egypt*

**Makeup**
Her mother helped her grind the colors and put them on in the cool air of early morning. Our princess wants to look as grown-up and royal as she feels.

**Hand**
The princess is directing her servants. They are loading her boat with ivory, rare African wood, and other gifts for the king of Egypt. She'll be leaving for Egypt in a few minutes.

**Earrings**
She has never worn such long earrings, but her older sister told her that Egyptian teen-agers wear even longer ones. The king is a teen-ager, too. She wonders what he looks like.

**Jewel Box**
Carved from white stone, this is the gift that she will hand to the king of Egypt. Her parents asked her to pick the best jewelry from local crafts-people. She did, but not before she hid her favorite ring in her room.

**Gown**
Late last night servants finally got the folds of her new linen dress to fall perfectly. The wooden ma-chine that presses the folds broke last week and wasn't repaired until yesterday.

**Cat**
Her shy pet, named Miu, has been rushing around the house with her all morning. All the princess's friends have cats, too.

**Sandals**
She's wearing leather sandals for this special occasion. Her everyday sandals are made from the same plant used to make paper.

## The Golden Rule

**Aristotle, 384–322 B.C., ancient Greece:**
"We should behave to our friends as we would wish our friends to behave to us."

**Confucius, 551–479 B.C., ancient China:**
"What you do not want done to yourself, do not do to others."

**Jesus, c. 4 B.C.–A.D. 29, ancient Israel:**
"So whatever you wish that men would do to you, do so to them."

500 400 300 200 100 B.C. A.D. 100

---

*B*ecause of one throw of the dice I have driven away a devoted wife. My wife's mother hates me, and my wife pushes me away; the man in trouble finds no one with sympathy. They all say, "I find a gambler as useless as an old horse that someone wants to sell."

The sad story told above is more than 3,000 years old. It is part of the Vedas, a collection of sacred poems from what is now the country of India.

### The Story of the Past

The study of the past is called **history.** When we set out to study history, we are able to draw the people and events of ancient times closer to us.

We can see how our lives are similar to theirs and also how they are different. We can see how people of the distant past had to face some of the very same problems we face today. And we can appreciate the connections that bind together people of all time periods and all areas of the world. ■

▲ *Notice how people from different time periods and different parts of the world have expressed similar ideas.*

■ *What are two examples of written sources that tell us about daily life in ancient times?*

---

## R E V I E W

1. **FOCUS** What do we have in common with the people of the past?
2. **CONNECT** What are some ways American history has been affected by the experiences of people of ancient times?
3. **SOCIAL SYSTEMS** What are two concerns people faced in the past that we still face today?
4. **CRITICAL THINKING** You have read about how people today are similar to the people of the past. In what ways are we different?
5. **WRITING ACTIVITY** Imagine that you could have a conversation with a 12-year-old child who lived 2,000 years ago. What kinds of common experiences do you think you could talk about? Write the dialogue of your conversation.

9

# Making Hypotheses

### Here's Why

Some maps provide geographical information about the modern world. Others provide geographical information about the past, such as the sea routes used by Greek traders or the extent of empires in ancient Africa. These are called historical thematic maps because they show specific historical information.

Historical thematic maps can help you see links between events that happened in different places and at different times. Using your observations, you can form a

hypothesis. The hypothesis, or explanation based on available facts, may be about what has occurred or is likely to occur.

As you have read, the present is connected to the past. For example, many Europeans today speak Romance languages, such as French, Italian, Portuguese, Romanian, and Spanish. Romance languages come from Latin, which was the language spoken by early Romans. By studying historical thematic maps, you may be able to form a hypothesis about the spread of languages.

### Here's How

Look at the map that shows where Romance languages are spoken in Europe today. Next study the map that shows the roads linking the Roman Empire. Compare the two maps.

Notice how well developed the roads are that connect Rome to the territories that are now Spain and Portugal. From these maps, you can form a hypothesis that Rome had a strong influence on these territories. Through this network of roads, the Roman army was able to move soldiers and supplies.

## Romance Languages in Modern Europe

Roman traders used the roads to transport goods.

Roman soldiers and traders probably spread the Latin language throughout these territories as they traveled the roads. The fact that two Romance languages, Spanish and Portuguese, are still spoken there seems to support this hypothesis.

Where else is the road system well developed? In the second map, you can see that a complex system of roads links France to Rome.

Now look at Germany. The Romans built fewer roads into Germany. From the lack of roads, you might hypothesize that the Romans had less influence here. Look at the map of Romance languages. Does it support your hypothesis? Is German a Romance language?

After studying these two maps, you can form a hypothesis. The Romance languages spread through Europe by means of the road and trade network that was part of the Roman Empire.

## Try It

Find the map of major languages of the world on page 515 in the Atlas. Where is English spoken? Why do you think English is spoken in both the United States and Australia? Why do you think Portuguese is spoken in Brazil?

## Apply It

Look at the map of World Religions on page 515 of the Atlas. Which religion has spread the least? The most? Knowing what you do about how cultures, languages, and ideas spread, what hypothesis can you form about these two religions?

Look again at the map. Try to find other patterns of information on the map. What hypothesis can you form from these patterns?

## Roman Roads, A.D. 117

L E S S O N   2

# Building on the Past

### Key Terms

* myth
* culture

*I*carus, beating his wings in joy, felt the thrill of the cool wind on his face and the clear air above and below him. He flew higher and higher into the blue sky until he reached the clouds. His father called out in alarm. He tried to follow, but he was heavier and his wings would not carry him. Up and up Icarus soared, through the soft moist clouds and out again toward the glorious sun. He was bewitched by a sense of freedom; he beat his wings frantically so that they would carry him higher and higher to heaven itself.

Greek myth, "The Flight of Icarus," retold by Sally Benson

Did you ever wish you could fly? The idea of flight has intrigued people throughout the ages. Three thousand years ago the ancient Greeks told the story of a boy named Icarus who wanted to fly. Icarus flew toward the sun on wings made of feathers and wax. But he flew too close to the sun, and the wax melted. He fell from the sky to his death.

The story of Icarus is not true. It is a **myth,** a story told by people to explain their past. Nevertheless, it shows that people long ago were also fascinated with flight.

People have been experimenting with flying machines since the days of the ancient Greeks. In the 300s B.C., a Greek named Archytas *(ahr KY tuhs)* built a "wooden pigeon" that moved through the air. Around the same time, the Chinese discovered how to make kites. Today, we have learned to make machines that let us fly. But like Icarus, we still try to fly higher, now reaching toward the stars.

## Learning from the Past

The dream of flight is one of the many ideas we share with the people who came before us. In fact, we owe much to the inventions and accomplishments of people of the past.

Many things we take for granted today were made possible by the achievements of the people who came before us. Take, for example, something as simple as a bicycle. The bicycle as we know it dates back only to about 1790, when a Frenchman invented a two-wheeled wooden scooter. On the next page, A Closer Look shows some of the inventions that had to come first. ■

■ *In what way do modern inventions depend on the past?*

12

# Bicycle Technology

*When you ride a bicycle, you are pedaling a machine that took thousands of years to create. Each part of a bicycle has a long history.*

**How do you make a faster wheel?**
That's what people in Mesopotamia were wondering about 2,000 B.C. They came up with the idea of spokes to lighten the heavy, solid wheels on their chariots (below). With spokes the chariots rolled faster.

**Life didn't have much bounce** before rubber was discovered in Mexico 2,000 years ago. The statue below shows an ancient Mexican athlete playing a sport that used a rubber ball. Spanish explorers brought rubber back to Europe. In 1888, an Englishman made the first inflatable rubber tires.

**Italian inventor Leonardo da Vinci** drew this chain drive around A.D. 1500. In 1770, a European inventor used a chain drive in silk-making machinery. From that idea the chain drive was adapted for use in bicycles in 1869.

13

Peoples of Our World

# Learning from Other Cultures

As the example of the bicycle shows, we have built on inventions from many different periods of time and from many different cultures. A **culture** consists of the behaviors, beliefs, customs, and attitudes of a group of people. It is reflected in the artwork, the literature, the language, the inventions, and traditions of the people. It is affected by the geography and climate where people live.

We have benefited from the accomplishments of human cultures reaching back millions of years. Throughout this book you will learn about the many contributions of these ancient cultures. You will also recognize how the decisions and actions of people in the past affect our lives today.

## The Earliest Cultures

The first human cultures began developing about two million years ago. One of the first accomplishments of these cultures was learning to make and use crude stone tools. With simple tools such as sharp-edged rocks, people could hunt animals for food. They also learned to work together to go after large animals. These groups of people then developed rules of behavior for members to obey.

A second important accomplishment of early cultures was learning to farm. About 9000 B.C., people in some parts of the world began to settle down in one place for long periods and produce their own food. Once farmers could produce enough crops to feed other people, some people had time to develop other skills, such as pottery making or weaving.

Another important development was the rise of cities in some

*▼ Notice the different wedding traditions of cultures found in the United States, China, and Indonesia.*

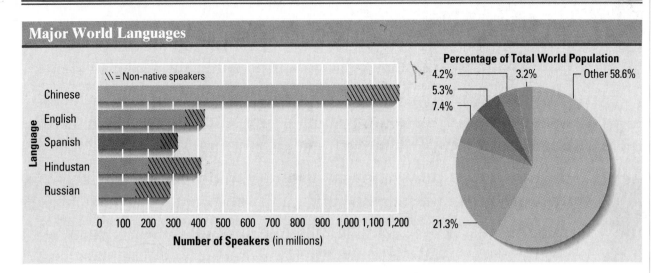

## Major World Languages

**Number of Speakers** (in millions)

\\\ = Non-native speakers

Language:
Chinese
English
Spanish
Hindustan
Russian

0  100  200  300  400  500  600  700  800  900  1,000  1,100  1,200

**Percentage of Total World Population**

4.2%
5.3%
7.4%
3.2%
Other 58.6%
21.3%

parts of the world beginning about 3500 B.C. As larger groups of people gathered together in cities, more opportunities for specialized workers, such as builders, bakers, and artists were created. In addition, city life resulted in the need for more extensive systems of government. And bringing people together also meant a greater exchange of ideas.

### Changes in Cultures

What causes cultures to change? New ideas and inventions often lead people to develop new ways of doing things. For example, the invention of writing systems allowed people to record their thoughts and discoveries and to communicate them to other people.

Changes in the environment also cause cultures to change. Over time, the climate in an area can change. Also, natural disasters such as floods and earthquakes can alter the landscape. People must then move or learn to adjust to new living conditions.

Another major source of change is contact with other cultures. When people from different cultures meet, they are exposed to the ways of life of each culture.

Cultures change from within as well. Factors such as population growth and conflicts between groups within a culture can bring about new ways of doing things.

### The Cultures of Today

Today we live in a world of many cultures—a multicultural world. We have learned from cultures of all parts of the world, and we continue to interact with other cultures. We are linked to the cultures of the past, just as cultures of the future will be linked to us. ■

▲ *Languages often vary from one culture to another. Turn to the map of world languages on page 515 of the Atlas to see where these languages are spoken.*

### Across Time & Space

*When cultures come in contact, they learn from each other. For example, Native Americans taught European settlers how to grow corn and sweet potatoes. The settlers passed the information back to Europe. Now these foods are cultivated all around the world.*

■ *What is a culture?*

## R E V I E W

1. **FOCUS** How have we learned from the past?
2. **CONNECT** What do cultures of today have in common with cultures of the past?
3. **SOCIAL SYSTEMS** How are cultures different from each other?
4. **CRITICAL THINKING** What will the cultures of the future be able to learn from the cultures of today?
5. **ACTIVITY** Select an everyday object and investigate how it is connected to the past. Make a list showing at least three inventions that are linked to the object you selected.

**TODAY**

L E S S O N   3

# Moving into the Future

**THINKING**
**FOCUS**

*How will our decisions affect the lives of people in the future?*

### Key Terms

- rain forest
- deforestation

A
ntisiranana, Madagascar—The rain forest that crowns Amber Mountain still echoes like a cathedral with the strange cries of creatures that exist no place else on Earth.

As they have for centuries, sorcerers from the local Antakarena tribe climb into the hills to bathe beneath sacred waterfalls, strictly observing taboos aimed at pleasing the spirits of ancestors buried there. . . .

The mountain is besieged, however, by others driven by hunger or greed to plant crops in the forest, burn off areas for grazing, cut firewood or drag away massive rosewood logs to sell as lumber.

"Enchanting Forest," by Tom Masland, *Chicago Tribune*, May 31, 1989

What will become of the rain forests of Madagascar, an island nation off the coast of East Africa? **Rain forests** are lush green regions, brimming with plant and animal life, that receive more than 140 inches of rain a year. Today the rain forests throughout the world are in danger.

Issues such as the fate of rain forests have faced people throughout the ages. And just as the decisions of the past have affected our lives, the decisions made today will affect people for ages to come.

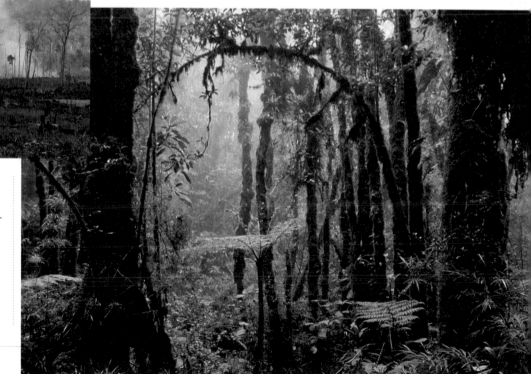

➤ *Rain forests, like the one at the right, are sometimes cleared using a method called slash and burn, shown above.*

# An Age-Old Problem

As long as people have settled in groups, they have cut down or cleared away forests. This process is called **deforestation.** People cut down trees for lumber. They use the land for grazing animals, growing crops, or building settlements.

Nevertheless, the loss of forest land has caused problems throughout time. For example, 2,300 years ago an important Greek teacher named Plato complained about the deforestation of his homeland.

> *T here are mountains in Attica which now can keep nothing but bees, but which were clothed not so long ago with fine trees, producing timber suitable for roofing the largest buildings.*
>
> Plato, *Critias,* c. 360 B.C.

Plato said that without the forest cover, rain just flowed over the mountains to the sea. The water supply from mountain streams that the Greeks once depended upon dried up.

In ancient Rome, deforestation caused flooding. A Roman scholar, Pliny the Elder, wrote 2,000 years ago that, "Indeed devastating torrents unite when the wood that used to hold the rivers and absorb them has been cut away from hills."

Much of the United States was once covered with forests. But as the European settlers moved westward, they cleared vast areas to

*This drawing, called* Plan of an American New Cleared Farm, *shows how European settlers cut down the forests of America.*

*Find the areas where rain forests are expected to remain in the year 2000.*

## Destruction of Tropical Rain Forests

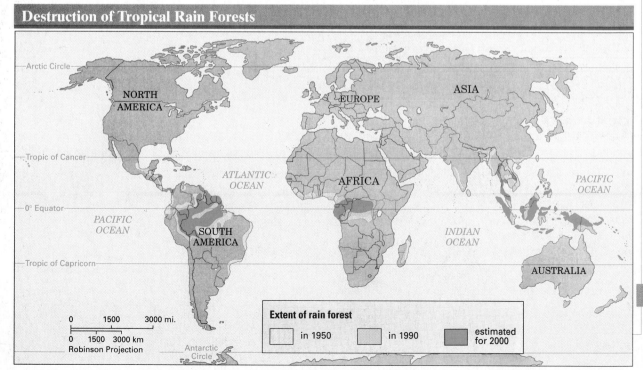

Arctic Circle

NORTH AMERICA

EUROPE

ASIA

Tropic of Cancer

ATLANTIC OCEAN

AFRICA

PACIFIC OCEAN

0° Equator

PACIFIC OCEAN

SOUTH AMERICA

INDIAN OCEAN

Tropic of Capricorn

AUSTRALIA

0   1500   3000 mi.

0   1500   3000 km
Robinson Projection

Antarctic Circle

**Extent of rain forest**

in 1950      in 1990      estimated for 2000

build towns, graze animals, and grow crops. Logging operations continue to reduce the size of American forests.

Today, deforestation is a global problem. Look at the map on page 17. How has the area covered by rain forests changed from 1950 to 1990? The United Nations predicts that at the present rate, one-fifth of the remaining rain forests will be cleared by the year 2000. ■

■ What is deforestation?

## A Current Problem

In Madagascar, an island about the size of Texas 300 miles off the coast of East Africa, 80 per cent of the rain forests have been destroyed already. If deforestation continues at the present rate, the rain forests will be gone entirely in 15 years.

As has happened in the past, Madagascar faces strong pressures to clear the land of the rain forests. Cutting down the trees for lumber and other wood products helps Madagascar's economy. Clearing the land for farming helps Madagascar feed its people.

Nevertheless, the destruction of the rain forests causes serious problems. The chart below shows the effects of deforestation. How does it affect the world's atmosphere? How does it contribute to flooding?

If the rain forests of Madagascar disappear, so will their unique plant and animal species. Scientists

▼ What are the effects of deforestation?

Rare plant and animal species that rely on the unique habitats found in rain forests become extinct.

The livelihoods of native people, such as those who extract material from rubber trees for making rubber, are destroyed.

The slash and burn method pollutes the air and may contribute to the "greenhouse effect," the gradual warming of the earth's atmosphere.

When logging operations clear vast areas, topsoil is washed away, so nothing will grow.

When the roots of trees and plants that soak up water are removed, flooding can result.

estimate that 86 per cent of the plants, 95 per cent of the reptiles, and 65 per cent of the birds in Madagascar's rain forests exist nowhere else. Destruction of the rain forests would also ruin the homelands of native cultures.

The rivers that run from these lush forests will also dry up. Without this water, the farmers in Madagascar will suffer. Finally, the long-term effects of deforestation on the earth's atmosphere could cause problems far beyond the borders of Madagascar. ■

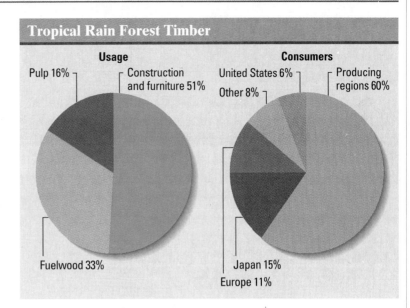

**Tropical Rain Forest Timber**

**Usage**
Pulp 16%
Construction and furniture 51%
Fuelwood 33%

**Consumers**
United States 6%
Producing regions 60%
Other 8%
Japan 15%
Europe 11%

*▲ How much of the timber from rain forests does the United States use?*

# Looking for Answers

What can the past tell us about the problems of today? By studying the past, we can see how previous cultures dealt with similar problems. We can understand the effects of their actions, and we can make judgments about how our actions might affect the future.

## Examining the Past

In the case of deforestation, people have recognized its effects for centuries. Yet in the past, people did not choose to conserve the forests. They made other choices. Those choices affected their lives and the lives of the generations that followed.

Today, we can examine the choices made in the past as we make new choices. What choices will we make about deforestation?

## Learning from the Past

Deforestation is a global problem. Dealing with it will take an international effort. In our multicultural world, we must understand the history of other cultures in order to solve problems together. By studying the past, we can see the roots of the present and we can better understand our world neighbors.

Learning about the past gives us a framework for making decisions about the issues that we face today. It also helps us understand how our actions will affect the people of tomorrow. ■

*■ Why does Madagascar face pressure to clear its rain forests?*

*■ How can learning about the past help us understand the problems of today?*

## REVIEW

1. **FOCUS** How will our decisions affect the lives of people in the future?
2. **CONNECT** Why might people from different cultures have differing views on the problem of deforestation?
3. **CITIZENSHIP** What are two ways that learning about the past helps us make decisions today?
4. **CRITICAL THINKING** You have read that Plato and Pliny warned of the effects of deforestation more than 2,000 years ago. Why did people continue to destroy rain forests?
5. **WRITING ACTIVITY** Imagine someone said to you, "Why should I care about the rain forests of Madagascar?" How would you answer that person? Write an essay that gives your response.

19

# Rain Forests: Preserve Them? Use Them?

W e simply cannot replace this invaluable resource once it is gone. The rain forests . . . once lost, can never be regained. Every second of every day, we are losing a tropical forest the size of a football field.

Hon. John E. Porter
U.S. Representative, Illinois

H ow can Brazil be expected to control its economic development, [Brazil's President José Sarney] asks, when it is staggering under a $111 billion foreign debt load? By what right does the U.S. . . . lecture poor countries like Brazil on their responsibilities to mankind?

Time,
September 18, 1989

## Background

From the air, Brazil's great forests look like a giant green cushion. Once the earth nourished many such rain forests. Now only a few remain. The loss of these rain forests affects the entire world.

How? Like all plants, the huge trees of the forest take in carbon dioxide from the air. They use this gas to make their food. The enormous forests, therefore, help balance the carbon dioxide and oxygen in the earth's atmosphere. When trees are cut down, we reduce the amount of carbon dioxide taken from the air. At the same time, we are burning more gasoline and other fossil fuels, releasing more carbon dioxide

into the air. Some scientists predict that this build-up of carbon dioxide in the atmosphere will cause the world's climate to grow warmer and warmer. We cannot foresee all the results of this global warming. One possibility, though, is that fertile farmland could someday become barren desert.

A close look at the rain forests reveals bare patches, some as big as the state of Connecticut. Other effects of deforestation are more difficult to see. When trees go, so do animals, plants, insects, and birds. Species as unique as the frogs shown here may become extinct if this trend continues. Such extinctions could have far-reaching effects. For example, many of our

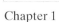

medicines come from plants. What if a plant growing in a rain forest today contains a cure for a form of cancer? What if the plant becomes extinct as the forest shrinks?

## Roots of the Problem

If you look only at the effects of this loss of rain forests, the solution may seem clear: Put a stop to it. To see how complicated the problem really is you have to study the causes—the reasons for clearing the rain forests.

Brazil has a large and rapidly growing population. Providing jobs and housing requires space. Some forests are cleared to build homes, factories, roads, and bridges.

Like most countries, Brazil wants to keep a balance of trade. This means that Brazil tries to sell to other nations as much as it buys from them. Brazil imports steel and other products. It exports beef and lumber. Forests are cleared to provide grazing land for cattle. Lumber, of course, comes from the forests.

In addition, Brazilian miners bring nearly 70 tons of gold a year out of the rain forests. Some areas are cleared to give the miners room to work.

Brazilians want to raise their standard of living. If the rain forests can be useful, why should they not benefit the nation in which they grow?

## Decision Point

1. After reading about the problem of the rain forests, what questions do you have?
2. Where would you look for more information about global warming? About Brazil's economy?
3. Are there ways to both preserve and use the rain forests? How can you find out?
4. Choose one topic related to the rain forest problem. What more do you need to know about it? Find the information in newspapers and magazines.
5. Discuss the new information you and your classmates found. Based on this very limited information, what ideas and alternatives can you suggest?

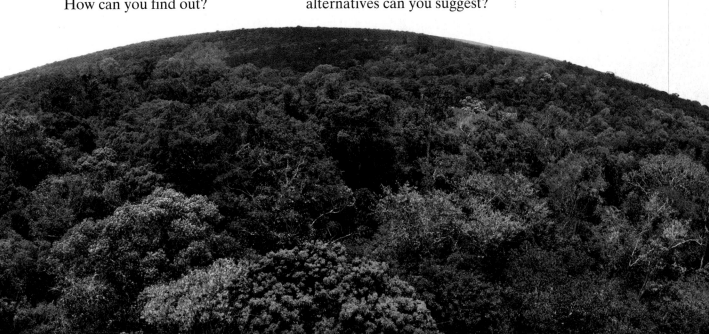

# Chapter Review

## Reviewing Key Terms

culture (p. 14)          myth (p. 12)
deforestation (p. 17)    rain forest (p.16)
history (p. 9)

**A.** Imagine you are playing a game in which your partner tries to guess the key term you are thinking of. For each of the four key terms below, think of a phrase you could give to your partner as a clue. Write each phrase on your own paper. An example has been done for you.
  1. rain forest: huge numbers of different plants and animals
  2. deforestation
  3. culture
  4. history

**B.** Be sure you understand the meanings of the five key terms. Then answer each question by writing one or more sentences.
  1. Was the reading by Priscus an example of history or of myth? Explain why you think so.
  2. What is one way in which culture and history are related?
  3. In the selection entitled "Enchanting Forest," what do we learn about the Antakarena culture?
  4. What do we learn about Madagascar's rain forest in that selection?
  5. What examples from history of deforestation are given in the chapter?

## Exploring Concepts

**A.** On your own paper, copy and complete the outline below. Then use it to write a summary of the chapter. For each main idea, write a short paragraph.

  I. The present is like the past.
     A.
        1. Playing with toys
        2. Eating snacks
        3.
     B. Problems of daily life
  II. The present builds on the past.
     A.
     B. Accomplishments of early cultures
        1.
        2.
  III. The present affects the future.
     A. An old and new problem
     B. Ways of solving the problem
        1.
        2.

**B.** Answer each question with information from the chapter.
  1. What are three ways in which the lives of people from the past were similar to our lives today? List specific examples.
  2. How do the examples of the flight of Icarus, the wooden pigeon, and the invention of the bicycle show how people build on the past?
  3. What messages from the past can help us understand the problem of deforestation today? How do these messages help us to understand the problem?
  4. How is cultural development seen in the daily lives of the people of a culture?
  5. What accomplishments led to people's jobs being specialized? What were some important results of building cities?
  6. Why might a very important part of the Antakarena culture disappear if all of the rain forests of Madagascar are destroyed?

# Reviewing Skills

1. Compare the Africa rainfall map on this page and the world vegetation map on page 516 in the Atlas. What hypothesis might you make about the relationship between vegetation and rainfall amount?
2. What observations based on these maps support your hypothesis?
3. Looking only at the rainfall map, if your hypothesis is accurate, in what part of Madagascar would you expect to find rain forests?
4. Now look at the vegetation map. What part of Madagascar is covered by rain forests? Compare this information with your answer to question 3.
5. Suppose you wanted to write a report on why deforestation has occurred throughout history to the present. The only information you have to begin with is two maps: a map showing world deforestation, and a world land-use map. How would you begin?

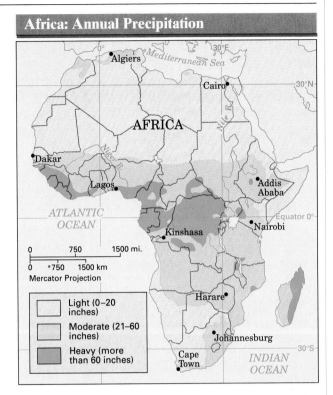

**Africa: Annual Precipitation**

Light (0–20 inches)

Moderate (21–60 inches)

Heavy (more than 60 inches)

Mercator Projection

## Using Critical Thinking

1. In the chapter, you got a glimpse of the attitudes of Sumerian children and parents toward each other around 600 B.C. What might historians of the future learn about your culture from things that you have written? Write a short paragraph describing how your attitudes are reflected in the clothes you wear as well as in things you say and do.

2. A people's culture is partly reflected in its inventions. The personal computer was invented in the United States in the 1970s. Suppose you are a historian in the future. What would you say the use of the personal computer represented about our culture? Make a list of behaviors, beliefs, and attitudes you think are reflected in the use of the personal computer.

## Preparing for Citizenship

1. **WRITING ACTIVITY** Describe the setting and main character for the beginning of a story about an Antakarena child. Learn as much as you can about Madagascar's rain forests and the people who live there. Find out about the culture and the plant and animal life of Madagascar. Use that information in your description.

2. **COLLABORATIVE LEARNING** The people of the past were in many ways very much like the people of the present. Team up with three other people. Each person in the group should research a well-known person of the distant past. As a group, decide who of the four historical figures interests you most. Choose one important event in that person's life. Work together to create a short scene about that event. Set the scene in modern times without changing the historical figure's attitudes, beliefs, or behavior.

# Chapter 2
## *People and Places*

Today astronauts explore new frontiers, just as ancient sea captains once did. Modern builders change the face of the earth with their skyscrapers and freeways, just as early people changed the land with their fields and villages. Settlers still seek gentle landscapes and mild climates, while they avoid rugged mountain ranges and harsh climates. Throughout time, the world has shaped the way people live. And the actions of people have reshaped the world.

# 3000 B.C.

The people of ancient Egypt used the waters of the Nile River to make the desert bloom. This model of farmers plowing a field was made in about 2000 B.C.

About A.D. 100, the Greek astronomer Ptolemy published a map of the known world. His map was accepted for nearly 1,400 years, until explorers found a "New World" in the Americas. This version of Ptolemy's map was printed in A.D. 1482.

The wonders of foreign lands fascinated Roman travelers. This Roman mosaic from about 80 B.C. shows the sights Romans saw when they visited the Nile River Valley in Egypt.

# Today

L E S S O N   1

# Interacting with the World

## THINKING
## F O C U S

*How do climate and topography affect human life?*

### Key Terms

- topography
- climate
- diffusion
- region

*The day had turned very hot. It was now in the nineties. I saw eighteen sheep crowded into a little blot of shade under a frail hawthorn tree. Children cooled themselves by kicking water in a ditch. Farmers with lamp shade hats planted crops by pushing one sprout at a time into the ground, in a process that had a greater affinity to needlepoint than to farming, as though they were stitching a design into the furrows. And though there were black peaks and mountain ranges on both sides of the train, the land fell away, and it was as if we were approaching the ocean—the land dipped and had the smooth, stony look of the seashore. It was the hottest part of the day, but even so the land was full of people. Hours later, in an immense and stony desert I saw a man in a faded blue suit, bumping over the stones on his bike.*

*Then there were sand dunes near the track—big soft slopes and bright piles; but the snowy peaks in the distance still remained. I had not realized that there was anything so strange as this on this planet.*

Paul Theroux, *Riding the Iron Rooster*

In 1988, Paul Theroux, an American writer, wrote about his travels across China by train. As he traveled, Theroux observed many people and places. He noticed how certain kinds of places affected people and their ways of life.

Theroux boarded the train in Lanzhou *(lahn joh)* at about midnight the night before his account above. The next evening, from

➤ *In some parts of China, farmers have conquered the mountains by carving out terraces for their crops.*

the window of the dining car, he could see the town of Jiayuguan (*jyuh yoo kwahn*). It lay "glowing in the sand" of the Gobi, an immense desert. Trace his journey on the map of China below.

## Living in the World

Like Paul Theroux, geographers study the relationships between people and their world. They study the factors that influence where people settle and how they live. Among these are topography and climate.

**Topography** refers to the surface, or physical, features of an area. These include mountains and valleys, rivers and lakes, sandy shores and grassy plains. Examine the map of China below.

China is a land of topographic extremes. Mount Everest, the highest peak in the world, soars 29,028 feet above sea level. That's more than five miles high! The Turfan Depression, a fertile area in the middle of a desert, lies 505 feet below sea level. Vast dry plains stretch across parts of western China. Limestone hills in the southeast shoot almost straight up, 100 to 600 feet from the ground. Two rivers rise in the highlands of

▼ *Why do you think fewer people live in the Plateau of Tibet than in eastern China?*

### China: Topography and Population Density

**POPULATION**

| Per sq. mi. | Per sq. km |
|---|---|
| Less than 2 | Less than 1 |
| 2–25 | 1–10 |
| 25–60 | 10–25 |
| 60–125 | 25–50 |
| 125–250 | 50–100 |
| More than 250 | More than 100 |

0    250    500 mi.

0    250    500 km

Polyconic Projection

27

People and

western China. They are the Chang Jiang *(chahng jyahng)* and the Huang He *(hwahng hay)*. They water the hilly, fertile fields to the east. In the words of Paul Theroux, China is "more like a whole world than a mere country."

The climates of China are as varied as its topography. **Climate** is the general pattern of weather in an area over time. The most important elements of climate are precipitation and temperature. Precipitation is water or ice that falls to the earth, such as rain, snow, or sleet.

The Tibetan Highlands of southwest China are dry and cold. They get less than 20 inches of rain annually, and July temperatures average less than 45° F. But parts of southeast China along the coast are rainy and hot. Some areas get more than 80 inches of rainfall a year, with January temperatures averaging more than 60° F.

## Where People Live

Look at the map on page 27. Note that China's 1.08 billion people are spread unevenly over the country's 3.7 million square miles. Which areas are most densely populated? Many people live in the southeast and along the east coast. Fewer live in the north and west.

To understand settlement patterns, first examine China's topography. How does the topography of the southeast differ from that of the north and west? Some parts of eastern China and the coast are hilly, but they are not as mountainous as the north and west. Also, southeastern China has plenty of rivers for water and transportation. For example, trace the Chang Jiang River and its tributaries.

► *Compare this map to the map on page 27. In what climate region of China do most people live?*

**China: Climate**

**Climate regions**

Tropical wet and dry (hot, with rainy and dry seasons)

Desert (dry, either hot or cold)

Semiarid (short rainy season)

Humid subtropical (hot, rainy summer and mild, rainy winter)

Continental (hot summer, cold winter)

Highland (climate varies with elevation)

The north and west, however, lack sources of water and are covered by vast areas of desert instead of fertile fields. What is the population density of the desert area known as the Gobi?

China's climate also affects settlement patterns. Look at the map on page 28. The climate along China's coast is mild—warmer in the winter and cooler in the summer than the climate farther inland. The coast also receives a great deal of rain. Most people in China are farmers. Think about what farmers need—fertile land, water, and a long growing season. Can you see why most of the people in China live in the eastern part of the country?

Throughout the world, people's choices of where they live are influenced by topography and climate. The first human settlements, farms, and cities developed in places where the climate and topography made farming possible.

For the most part, people are still drawn to places where the land is level and climates are warm or mild with plenty of rain. Study the world physical map on pages 504 and 505 and the world climate map on page 516 of the Time/Space Databank. Besides eastern China, other areas with this favorable mix of nature include western Europe, northern India, and much of the eastern United States, as well as its West Coast. You won't be surprised to learn that these areas are some of the most heavily populated in the world.

## How People Live

Not all places in the world have mild temperatures, rivers suited for transportation, and level land. Find the Sichuan *(SEE shwahn)* Basin on the map on page 28. It is cut off from the rest of China by high mountains. The climate is good for farming, but the topography is not. The area is far too hilly. Even so, the Sichuan Basin is an important farming area. People have dug into the sides of the hills to create level strips of land, or terraces, that they can farm. These people have modified their environment to suit their needs as farmers.

Now find the Plateau of Tibet on the map. Here both the climate and the topography of the plateau make farming difficult. The temperatures are very cold, and little rain falls. Most of the plateau is a rocky wasteland. But in some areas, people can live by herding the yak, a tough animal capable of surviving the cold.

These herders depend upon the yak for their survival. They live in tents made of yak hair. They use yak hides to make their shoes. The yak also provides the Tibetans with milk, meat, and transportation. ■

*Amid the highest mountains and plateaus in the world, these Tibetans are yak herders. The yak, a sort of hairy buffalo, provides the Tibetans with nearly everything they need, from milk to rope.*

■ *Where do humans tend to settle and why?*

# Moving Through the World

Faced with an environment that makes farming difficult, the people of the Sichuan Basin came up with an answer— they decided to modify their environment. The people of Tibet chose another answer. They adapted to their environment by developing other means of getting food—herding yaks. But sometimes people are unable to modify or adapt. In these cases, people may choose to move to a different environment.

### Kinds of Movement

People move to other areas for a variety of reasons. One type of movement is only temporary. You, for example, travel to and from school every day. Many adults are daily commuters, going to and from their work. This type of movement happens over and over in a cycle. Thus, it's called cyclic movement.

A second type of movement is periodic. It's when you move to a new place and stay for a period of time. For example, you might spend summer vacations at camp. But, eventually, you return home.

Periodic movement is a part of life for the Mongols and Kozakhs of northern China. These people herd sheep and goats. They move often, whenever their herds have eaten all the grass in a place. They move periodically, never staying permanently in one place.

A third type of movement is called migration. When people migrate, they leave their homeland to live permanently in another place. Your ancestors probably migrated to the United States. Archaeological evidence shows that people first migrated to the Americas from Asia between 20,000 and 40,000 years ago, across the Bering Strait.

### One Effect of Movement

Whenever people move from place to place, they discover new ideas, values, languages, and inventions. Sometimes they adopt elements of a new culture, changing them if necessary to fit their own needs. **Diffusion** is the spread of the ideas, values, and inventions of one culture into another culture.

The spread of the yo-yo is one example of diffusion. You've probably played with a yo-yo at one time or another. But did you know that the yo-yo has a worldwide reputation? At left is a map that

*▼ This world map is centered on the North Pole. Compare it to the world political map on pages 502 and 503 in the Atlas. What differences do you notice?*

## The Yo-yo Around the World

**CHINA**
Chinese spin ivory yo-yos by 1000 B.C.

**GREECE**
Greek children play with yo-yos by 500 B.C.

**PHILIPPINES**
Philippine hunters use stone yo-yos as weapons as early as 5000 B.C.

**FRANCE**
Yo-yos become a favorite toy of the French nobility in the 1780s.

**UNITED STATES**
Donald Duncan founds Duncan Toy Co. and introduces the yo-yo to the American public in 1929.

**ENGLAND**
British nickname the yo-yo the "Prince of Wales' Toy" after an artist shows King George IV (the Prince of Wales) playing with a yo-yo in 1791.

```
0        2000    4000 mi.
0   2000  4000 km
Polar Equidistant Projection
```

shows the cultures where the yo-yo has appeared over the years. As the yo-yo moved from culture to culture, it changed. In prehistoric times, Philippine hunters used stone yo-yos as weapons. Later, the Chinese used ivory yo-yos as toys. Many centuries later, the yo-yo became a fad among the French nobility, who called the yo-yo *l'emigrette* or "the migrant." Inspired by the Philippine yo-yo, American inventor Donald Duncan began producing yo-yos in the 1920s. Duncan introduced the first plastic yo-yo in 1957. In its diffusion, the yo-yo has changed from a weapon to a toy and from stone to plastic.

The story of the alphabet is another case of diffusion. About 4,000 years ago, the Phoenicians *(fih NIHSH uhns)*, who lived in what is now Lebanon, developed an alphabet. When Phoenician merchants traded with the Greeks, the alphabet traveled to many Greek-speaking areas. Through exploration, trade, and war, the Greeks carried the alphabet even farther, eventually to the Italian peninsula. There, the Romans dropped several letters and gave the rest of the letters Latin names. When Roman soldiers marched into Britain, their alphabet went with them. Over time, this alphabet was transported to the New World. The alphabet in use today by English-speaking peoples is known as the Roman alphabet. You can learn more about it and other common alphabets on pages 488 and 489 in the Minipedia.

All cultures owe much to other cultures. For example, people played a game similar to modern football 5,000 years ago in Egypt. What examples of cultural diffusion can you see in your daily life—in your music, food, and clothes? ■

▲ *The word* yo-yo *means "to return" in Tagalog, a Philippine language.*

■ *Why do large groups of people sometimes move from their homeland?*

▼ *These farmers live in one of China's farming regions. They're harvesting grain.*

## Looking at the World

Geographers study the world and how people relate to it. They need to find ways of making sense of all the information they gather.

One way to better understand it all is to think about the world in terms of regions. Areas having similar characteristics that differ from surrounding areas are called **regions.** Geographers divide the world into various kinds of regions—language regions, topographic regions, religious regions, and even sports regions. For example, geographers divide China into several climate regions.

31

As Paul Theroux traveled through China, he crossed several boundaries. He crossed one boundary as he entered China. He crossed others as he passed from one climate region to another. A boundary is a dividing line between regions, countries, or other areas of the world.

## Two Kinds of Boundaries

Boundaries may be natural or artificial. Natural boundaries are geographical features of the earth such as mountains or rivers. For example, the Heilong Jiang (*hay lung chyahng*) River runs along part of the border between the U.S.S.R. and China. This powerful river serves as an unmistakable boundary between the two countries.

Artificial boundaries are those created by humans. While natural boundaries like a river are easily recognized, artificial boundaries are not always so easy to find in the real world. Some kinds of artificial boundaries, such as the borders between countries, are indicated only by signs. The border between Canada and the United States is marked by signs across major highways that pass between the two countries. In less-traveled areas, however, the U.S.-Canada border is unnoticeable. It even passes through some people's back yards.

## The Effect of Boundaries

The main purpose of boundaries is to show the extent of a state, country, or region. If there were no boundary between Canada and the United States, how would each government know who could vote?

Another purpose of boundaries is to prevent passage. Chinese rulers ordered the building of the Great Wall of China between the 400s B.C. and A.D. 1600. They hoped that the 4,000 mile wall would keep the Mongols from invading China and also keep Chinese farmers from leaving their farms.

Boundaries serve a purpose but they can also cause problems. People don't always agree on artificial boundaries. In 1846, the United States and Mexico went to war, partly over a dispute about their border.

But even natural boundaries can lead to disagreements. Mexico and the United States finally agreed that the Rio Grande would represent part of the boundary between the two countries. Since that agreement, however, the Rio Grande has constantly shifted its course, forcing the two countries to adjust the border often.

So boundaries can be walls, preventing the movement of people and ideas. Or they can be doorways. Since boundaries mark the places where two countries or regions meet, they provide an opportunity for contact between people and the spread of ideas.

## China: Economic Use

**Legend:**
- Farming
- Grazing
- Forests
- Urban and industrial
- Little land use
- Fishing
- Mining
- Drilling
- Canal

*0  500  1000 mi.*
*0  500  1000 km*
Mercator Projection

*How do the people of Guangzhou use the land?*

Geographers also divide China into regions according to the ways people use the land to make a living. The map on this page shows China's economic use regions. Where are China's forest regions? Where are China's industrial regions?

Compare the climate map with the economic use map, focusing on the continental climate region in northeastern China. This region has hot summers and cold winters. According to the economic use map, how is the land in this region used? What connection do you notice between the area's climate and economic use of the land?

Now, for contrast, examine the northern and western regions. In these areas climate and terrain make life rugged. What do the people do for a living?

Geographers use regions to help them understand the ways in which people interact with the world. But there is also another way that geographers learn about the world. They create and study maps. ■

■ *Why do people divide the world into regions?*

R E V I E W

1. **FOCUS** How do climate and topography affect human life?

2. **CONNECT** What examples of diffusion can you find in Chapter 1?

3. **ECONOMICS** Examine the world maps in the Time/Space Databank. How do climate and topography affect the use of land in some countries? Consider Greece, Saudi Arabia, and Brazil as examples.

4. **CRITICAL THINKING** Climate and topography clearly affect human life. But how do humans affect the climate and topography of the areas where they live? How do these effects in turn end up affecting human life?

5. **ACTIVITY** Draw a map of your city, town, or neighborhood. Then divide it into regions. Explain what distinguishes each region.

33

People and Places

L E S S O N   2

# Understanding a Map

**THINKING**
**F O C U S**

*What do you need to know in order to use a map?*

## Key Terms

- scale
- cartographer
- legend
- inset

▼ *A map at this angle is often called a bird's-eye view.*

You're standing at the foot of one of the world's tallest buildings—the Sears Tower in Chicago, Illinois. Your neck aches as you strain to see the top of the building—110 stories—1,454 feet above you.

You walk inside, board the elevator, and zoom to the observation deck on the 103rd floor. Through floor-to-ceiling windows, you look at the city, which spreads out in all directions below you.

Looking east, you see Lake Michigan dotted with boats. Looking west, you see the University of Illinois and a tangle of streets and freeways. Elsewhere are high-rise buildings, factories, schools, parks, churches, parking lots, and train tracks. Bright blue swimming pools gleam from a few apartment rooftops.

From 103 stories up, the city looks flat—something like a map. Of course, you can't lift the edges of the city, fold it into a small packet, and stick it into your pocket. However, the view from the observation deck is quite similar to a city map, for a map is like a picture of a place taken from above. In fact, mapmakers often use aerial photos—photos taken from the air—to help them make accurate maps.

Look closely at the photograph and the map below. Both show portions of the city of Chicago. What are the differences between the photo and the map?

Sears
Tower

# The Extent of a Map

How does the view from the observation deck differ from a map of the city? One obvious difference is size.

### Scale

A map is a flat representation of the earth's surface. But a map is usually much smaller than the area it represents. A map must be drawn to scale in order to accurately represent the area shown. **Scale** is the relationship between distance on a map and actual distance on the earth.

Examine the illustration on this page. Look at the bottom layer. It shows a portion of a city. Find the museum in the city. Now look at the layer above. It shows only the museum and the sidewalks around it. The third layer shows the layout of the museum's rooms. Finally, the top layer shows one room in the museum.

Each drawing is the same size. But each one shows a different area. The bottom layer shows the largest area—a part of the city. The top layer shows the smallest area—a room in the museum.

Each layer is drawn to a different scale. Compare the scale bars beside each layer. The bottom layer is drawn to the smallest scale. A half inch on this layer represents 60 feet in the real world. That half inch covers the distance from the street corner to the sidewalk leading to the museum entrance. The top layer is drawn to the largest scale. According to the scale bar, a half inch on this layer represents five feet in the real world. This half inch takes you only a short distance, from the cat display to the mummy. The top layer is drawn closer to actual size than the bottom layer. In general, a large-scale map shows a small area, and a small-scale map shows a large area.

In A Closer Look on pages 36 and 37, you'll find several maps of the same area, some even drawn at the same scale. But each map looks different because each was created for a different purpose.

0      5 ft.

0      15 ft.

0      30 ft.

0      60 ft.

*Use the scale in the top layer. How many feet long is the mummy case on the left side of the room?*

35

# Many Kinds of Maps

*If you have a question about a place, there's probably a map that will answer it. The most common maps give the location of cities, roads, lakes, rivers, and political boundaries. But more specialized maps can also give you information on temperature, rainfall, and even history. If you have a question about Italy, look at these maps for an answer.*

*Compass*

**Italy**
**political map**

National park (N.P.)
International boundary
Regional boundary
Expressway
Other road
Railroad
⊛ National capital
★ Regional capital
• Other city or town

WORLD BOOK map

**Holy Roman Empire**

Boundary of present-day Italy

**Italy c. A.D. 1500** is the subject of the historical map above. The map reveals how the area was split into many small, independent states at that time.

## Italy
### terrain map

- ▬▬ International boundary
- ▬ Land region boundary
- • City
- + Elevation above sea level
- )( Mountain pass
- ∴ Ruins

WORLD BOOK map

**What's up?** This map illustrates the ups and downs of Italy's rugged landscape. Five hundred years ago, these mountains helped divide Italy into more than a dozen small states. Compare this map with the ones below to see how Italy's weather patterns follow the mountain ranges.

| Inches | Centimeters |
|---|---|
| More than 60 | More than 150 |
| 40 to 60 | 100 to 150 |
| 30 to 40 | 75 to 100 |
| Less than 30 | Less than 75 |

| Degrees Fahrenheit | Degrees Celsius |
|---|---|
| Above 75 | Above 24 |
| 68 to 75 | 20 to 24 |
| 61 to 68 | 16 to 20 |
| Below 61 | Below 16 |

**Italy's annual rainfall** is the subject of this map. In which city are you more likely to need an umbrella: Florence or Bari?

**Italy's average July temperatures** are shown on this map. Study it, and you'll know why beaches up and down Italy's coasts are so crowded in the summer.

*Thermometer*

People and Places

**Northern Hemisphere**

**Southern Hemisphere**

**Eastern Hemisphere**

**Western Hemisphere**

▲ *Find the equator and the prime meridian on the globe above. Which of the four hemispheres at the right looks most familiar to you? Why?*

## Latitude and Longitude

Mapmakers and geographers use scale to measure distances on a map. They use another system—an imaginary grid—to locate places on a map. This grid is made up of intersecting lines of latitude and longitude.

The idea of using a grid to pinpoint certain places on the earth is not new. In 300 B.C., in what is now Turkey, a mapmaker named Hipparchus (*hih PAHR kuhs*) drew a grid of equally spaced, parallel lines over his maps. Then he identified the locations of places in the world by referring to their locations on the grid.

Examine the globe on the far left above. It shows lines of latitude and longitude. Lines of latitude, or parallels, run east and west around the globe. All lines of latitude are parallel to the equator. They never meet.

Lines of longitude, or meridians, run north and south from the North Pole to the South Pole. They're not parallel. As you can see on the globe, lines of longitude are farthest apart at the equator. As they move northward and southward away from the equator, these lines become closer together until finally they meet at the North and South poles.

Mapmakers measure latitude and longitude in units called degrees. Latitude is measured in degrees north and south of the equator. The equator is 0 degrees latitude. Longitude is measured east and west of the prime meridian. The prime meridian is 0 degrees longitude. Look at the globe at the top left of the page. Where do the equator and the prime meridian meet?

The four smaller globes on this page show the earth's four hemispheres. The word *hemisphere* comes from a Greek word, which means "half of a sphere." The equator divides the earth into two equal halves—the northern and southern hemispheres. The prime meridian and the longitude line opposite it at 180 degrees divide the earth into the eastern and western hemispheres.

The small globes show you that North and South America are found in the western hemisphere. Can you name three continents in the eastern hemisphere?

If you wanted to visit Asia, would you start out for the northern or southern hemisphere? In which of the four hemispheres is Africa found? ■

■ *What do you need to know about a place in order to locate it on a map?*

## The Content of a Map

In order to read a map, you need to know more than just how to use scale and lines of latitude and longitude. **Cartographers,** or mapmakers, also use symbols to communicate information. To read a map, you need to know how to decode these symbols.

### Understanding Symbols

Take a look at the map on this page. This map shows the Iberian Peninsula, which includes modern-day Spain and Portugal. In ancient times, the Romans ruled this area. Now examine the legend in the lower left corner. A **legend** explains the symbols used on a map.

Can you find the tiny symbol of an aqueduct, a structure built to transport water? These symbols show where the ancient Romans built aqueducts centuries ago. The famous aqueduct at Segovia still stands in Spain today. Can you find it near the center of the peninsula? How many other aqueducts can you find on this map?

The Romans also built roads to help them move troops and supplies quickly from town to town. A red line on the map stands for their roads on the peninsula.

The orange area on the map represents a senatorial province. Roman senators were expected to oversee this area. The yellow areas were provinces under the control of the Roman emperor. What are the names of the imperial provinces? In which province is Carthago Nova located?

### Using Insets

The map shows you where the Romans built aqueducts and roads and how they organized their rule

*The Romans named the temples at Carthago Nova after gods or heroes. Hercules was a hero of superhuman strength, and Mercury was the god of commerce and travel. What does this information tell you about the ancient Romans of Carthago Nova?*

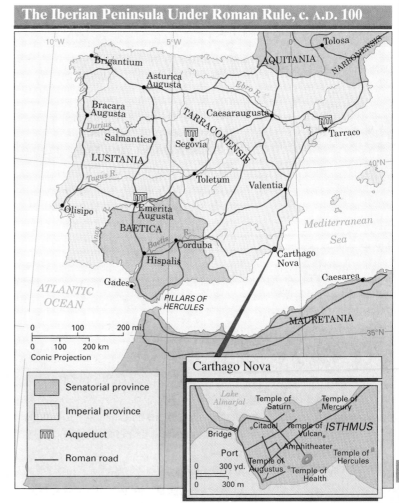

The Iberian Peninsula Under Roman Rule, c. A.D. 100

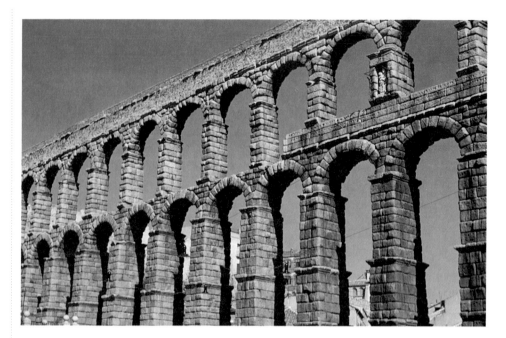

*The Romans used many arches to build this aqueduct at Segovia, Spain. The water flowed through a channel along the top.*

over the Iberian Peninsula. But the map offers even more information. In the bottom right corner there is another, smaller map. What does this map tell you?

The smaller map is called an **inset,** or a map that appears within a larger map and shows some of the same area. Usually the inset shows a small but important part of the area in greater detail. The inset on page 39 shows Carthago Nova, a city on the peninsula's southeastern coast. Compare the scale of the inset with the scale of the map of the Iberian Peninsula. Which map is drawn to a larger

scale? What distance does one-fourth of an inch represent on the inset? What distance does it equal on the larger map? Using the scale on the inset, how far is it from the bridge to the amphitheater?

Lines of latitude and longitude, legends, symbols, insets, and scale make up the basic language of most maps. Once you understand this language, you're ready to begin putting maps to work.

Maps can be valuable tools whether you're learning about an ancient culture or simply trying to find an unfamiliar street in your own hometown. ■

*■ What is the purpose of an inset map?*

1. **FOCUS** What do you need to know in order to use a map?
2. **CONNECT** What effect of human movement discussed in Lesson 1 is illustrated by the map of the Iberian Peninsula?
3. **GEOGRAPHY** Based on what you know about patterns of human settlement, why do you think the Romans settled in Carthago Nova?
4. **CRITICAL THINKING** Imagine two maps that are exactly the same size. One of the maps is a map of world cli-

mate regions. The other map is a map of national parks in the United States. Which map is made at a larger scale?

5. **CRITICAL THINKING** What hemisphere would you expect to be shown at the center of most world maps made in the United States? Why?

6. **ACTIVITY** Draw a map of the neighborhood around your school. Include a legend with the map. Don't forget symbols for stop lights, crosswalks, stores, and any special buildings.

Chapter 2

# Locating Places

## Here's Why

Suppose someone asked you the location of a city. You could go to the map and help the person find the city. Or you could provide the person with the latitude and longitude of the city. How would you figure out the latitude and longitude of Chongqing, China?

## Here's How

As you know, latitude and longitude are used to tell the exact location of places on the earth. Look at the map on this page. Notice that the grid on this map has latitude and longitude lines every 10 degrees. Chongqing is just below the 30 degree line of latitude, so it is about 29°N. Now look at the lines of longitude. Chongqing is between 100°E and 110°E. To get a more exact location, imagine a line of longitude at 105°E, halfway between 100°E and 110°E. Chongqing is about halfway between 105°E and 110°E, at about 107°E. The location of Chongqing, China, is 29°N, 107°E. Note that latitude is always given first, then longitude.

## Try It

Look at the map again. Identify the cities that are found at these locations:

1. 25°N, 67°E
2. 36°N, 140°E
3. 44°N, 88°E

Give the latitude and longitude for these cities:

4. Colombo, Sri Lanka
5. Manila, Philippines
6. Harbin, China

## Apply It

Turn to the Eurasia map on pages 508-509 in the Atlas. Write the latitude and longitude of five cities or islands. Then play the "Where am I?" game with a partner. For example, one person says, "I am visiting a place at 29°N, 50°E. Where am I?" The other person then uses the map to find the answer.

## Southern Asia

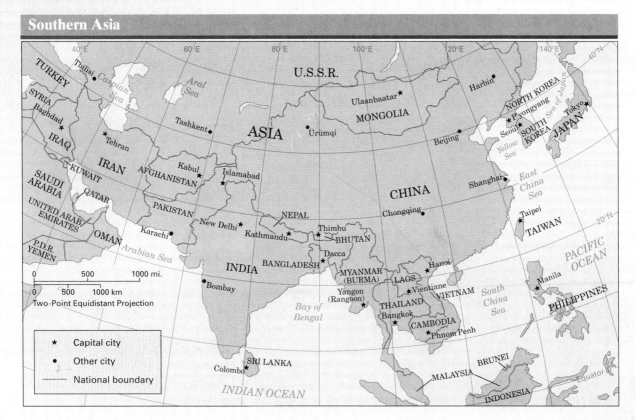

- ★ Capital city
- • Other city
- — National boundary

41

People and Places

L E S S O N   3

# Putting Maps to Work

*What decisions must cartographers make?*

## Key Terms

- thematic map
- projection

➤ *How many cholera deaths were recorded near the Oxford Street water pumps? The Piccadilly pump?*

A cholera epidemic! In the 1820s, these words were enough to strike fear into the bravest heart. Cholera *(KAHL ur uh)* was usually fatal, killing its victims in less than seven days.

The epidemic spread quickly from India to Russia and then through central Europe, reaching Scotland by 1832. In 1849, severe outbreaks hit Paris and London. Today, doctors know how to treat and prevent cholera. But in the early 1800s, no one knew much about the disease.

John Snow, a doctor in the London neighborhood of Soho, grew discouraged. By 1854, cholera had claimed the lives of 500 people in Soho, and there was no sign that

things would improve. Dr. Snow tried everything he knew, but none of his cholera patients recovered.

But Dr. Snow had an idea. He'd had some training in geography, and he decided to use his training to track down the source of the disease. One night he listed the addresses of all the cholera victims in Soho. Then he took a street map and marked each victim's address with a dot.

Before you read on and learn what happened, look at Dr. Snow's map on this page. Do you see any pattern in the dots? Dr. Snow did. The map revealed that almost all of the cholera victims lived near a public well, known as the Broad Street Pump. The map supported what Dr. Snow suspected—the epidemic was somehow related to the city's water supply.

Dr. Snow contacted city officials. Workers quickly removed the handle from the Broad Street Pump, forcing people to go elsewhere for water. Almost immediately, the number of new cholera cases dropped to zero.

Today, few people contract cholera where there are working sewage systems. Even fewer die from it where there is medical care. In the 1850s, Dr. Snow's map provided a needed clue to the source of this disease—bad water.

### Dr. Snow's Cholera Map, 1854

Cholera death · × Water pump     0 ____ 100 yd.

# Maps for Different Purposes

Dr. Snow's purpose was to find a link between the addresses of cholera victims and the location of Soho water supplies. For his base map, he chose a general map of Soho, showing people's houses. By marking victims' addresses and the water pumps, he created a thematic map. A **thematic map** shows information on a special theme or subject.

Like Snow, all mapmakers choose base maps and thematic information to fit their needs. Both maps on this page are thematic, but each has a different purpose.

The map at the right shows the London subway system. What's the purpose of this map? Who would use it? Shoppers, tourists, and workers might use it to find their way around the city. In this map, cartographers limited their thematic information to subway stops and routes.

The second map is a cartogram, a type of map that shows statistical information. Compare

the cartogram with the world political map on pages 502–503 of the Atlas. What differences do you notice in the size of the countries? On the cartogram, scale isn't used to measure distance. Instead, it gives information about populations. The size of each country on the cartogram is related to the size of its population. For example, a heavily populated country like

*The London subway is known as the Under-ground or the Tube. How would you use a map like this?*

*Which countries with large populations suffer serious malnutrition?*

## World Nutrition

**Calorie supply per person**

- Well above requirements
- Above requirements
- Adequate nutrition
- Some malnutrition
- Serious malnutrition
- No information available

Note: The size of each country is proportional to its population.

43

■ *On what do cartographers base their decisions when choosing types of maps?*

India appears to be larger than it actually is. A less-populated country like Canada appears smaller than it actually is. What is the purpose of this map? Who might use it?

Organizations working to combat world hunger might find this map useful. With it, they could identify countries where poor nutrition is a problem. ■

## The Shape of the Earth

▼ *Compare the size of Greenland, which is highlighted in red, on the four projections.*

Whether a map shows world nutrition or subway routes, it's a means of giving information about the earth. But as cartographers try to make accurate maps, they face one serious problem: the shape of the earth. The earth is a sphere, and a map is flat. It's impossible for cartographers to accurately show the earth's curved surface on the flat surface of a map.

Imagine trying to flatten a basketball. No matter how you do it, some parts will tear, and other parts will stretch. Mapmakers face the same kind of problem when they try to map the earth.

Over time, however, cartographers have developed different map **projections,** or ways of transferring the curved surface of the earth onto a flat map. All projections are compromises, though, because they all distort distance, direction, size, or shape.

Each world map on this page and the facing page is based on a different projection. Notice how the shapes and sizes of continents vary from map to map. Also notice differences in the way lines of latitude and longitude are shown on each map.

The first map is a Mercator projection. It is named for the German cartographer Gerhardus Mercator, who first published the projection in 1569. On a Mercator projection, the shapes of the continents are fairly accurate, but their sizes are greatly distorted, especially near the poles. For example, on a Mercator projection, Greenland appears to be huge. But it's not. Actually, Greenland is about the size of Mexico.

### Mercator Projection

### Peters Projection

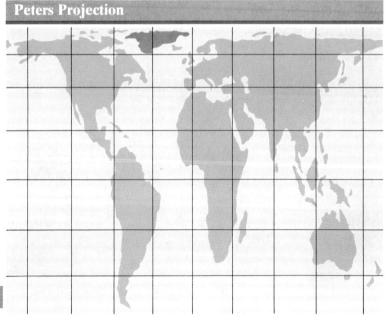

Over time, Hanno's fleet settled several Phoenician colonies on Africa's west coast. With that mission completed, he and his crew sailed on. Hanno and his crew explored the coast as far south as present-day Sierra Leone and possibly even farther. Look at the map on page 46. Trace the route of Hanno and his crew.

## Exploring the World

Centuries ago, missions like Commander Hanno's provided most of the information about the world. As people began to travel farther and farther from their homelands, their geographic knowledge grew. Why did people begin to reach out beyond their borders? One reason was the desire to trade.

### The Drive to Trade

Before Hanno's time, Phoenicia was just a narrow strip of land between the Mediterranean Sea and the Lebanon Mountains. It was slightly more than 100 miles long and only 16 miles wide in places.

The Phoenicians weren't able to grow enough food to feed their population. But they discovered other ways to meet their needs. They were expert traders who made use of the resources in their environment. Tall trees blanketed the surrounding mountains. They cut these down for lumber. From the sea, they gathered a special type of shellfish. They crushed the shells to make a purple dye. They used the dye to color their finely woven cloth, which was highly prized in the ancient world.

The Phoenicians traded their lumber and purple-dyed cloth for food and other necessities. As their trade increased, the Phoenicians expanded their territory by building ports in southern Spain and northern Africa. One of these ports was Carthage, founded about 750 B.C.

### Trade with India

In those days, trading and exploring seemed to go hand-in-hand. Traders were always looking for new markets and faster routes. In their search, they brought back knowledge of distant lands.

About 2,000 years ago, Mediterranean traders dreamed of far-off India and its treasures. India offered rare spices, gems, perfumes, sugar, woods, gold, brass, and iron to any traders brave enough to risk the difficult trip.

The journey from the shores of the Mediterranean to Indian markets was a rough one. On land, traders faced muddy roads, thick jungles, huge mountain ranges, and bandits. Sea travel was also risky. After crossing the Red Sea or the Persian Gulf, sailors faced the dangers of the Arabian Sea. Powerful, seasonal winds called monsoons swept across these waters. The **monsoon** is a wind system that has an effect on the climate in southern Asia. These powerful winds blow from the southwest from April to October, bringing heavy rain much of

*This is one type of shellfish the Phoenicians crushed to make their purple dye. The Greeks named the Phoenicians after the purple-dyed goods they traded. The Greek word* phoinix *means "red-purple."*

➤ *Using the scale, find the round-trip mileage from Rome to Patala, India. Take the route that goes to Alexandria, through the Red Sea, then follows the coast.*

## How Do We Know?

**HISTORY** *We know about ancient trade partly from written records. The oldest remaining record of a voyage refers to an Egyptian trading mission. According to the record, around 3200 B.C., Egyptian traders sailed "forty ships of one hundred cubits with cedar wood from Byblos (BIHB luhs)," one of Phoenicia's cities.*

■ *What areas of the world did Mediterranean peoples learn about?*

the time. From November to March, the winds are dry and blow from the northeast.

Ancient ships hugged the coast so they could seek shelter from the fierce winds. Those who braved the open seas for a direct route to India were often shipwrecked.

Around A.D. 37, a Greek named Hippalus used his knowledge of geography and monsoons to sail from the Red Sea directly across the Arabian Sea to India. He used the monsoons to work in his favor. On the way to India, his ship was pushed by the monsoon blowing from the southwest. On the return voyage, it was helped by the monsoon blowing from the northeast. Use the scale on the map above to compare Hippalus's trade route with the older sea routes. How much shorter was Hippalus's route? ■

## Learning About the World

Early explorers and traders knew the importance of keeping careful records of their journeys so that more accurate maps might be made. In some cases, they took along historians and geographers to help them keep track of their travels.

Some early maps were based on records made during the conquests of Alexander the Great, one of history's most famous military leaders. Alexander ruled Macedonia, a kingdom that lay to the north of Greece. He had maps made as his huge army battled to victory from Egypt to India between 334 and 326 B.C. On his marches, Alexander took geographers, a historian, and astronomers—scientists who study stars and planets. He also took *bematistae (buh MAH tees ty)* or "steppers," who measured distance by the steps they took. This army of soldiers and scholars covered 20,000 miles, fighting and conquering, but also recording and mapping.

### Written Records

As people traveled and learned about the world, they recorded their knowledge in writing, as well as on maps. For example, Chinese scholars spent some 800 years, between 1122 and 256 B.C., putting together a guide to China's geography called *Shan Hai Chung.*

Ancient historians also noted geographic information when recording events. Herodotus, for example, was a Greek historian and geographer. In the 400s B.C., he included geographic descriptions in his history of the world. Gaius Fannius Strabo was a Roman historian. In A.D. 18, he wrote a 17-volume work called *Geography,* in which he described every place known to the Greeks and Romans. Claudius Ptolemy, a Greek geographer and astronomer, published his *Guide to Geography* in A.D. 100. In his work he included the latitudes and longitudes of 8,000 places, 26 maps of parts of the world, and one map of the entire known world.

### Ancient Maps

People have been making maps for thousands of years. One of the oldest existing maps is a clay map found in northern Iraq. It dates to around 2300 B.C. and shows rivers, hills, and settlements with measurements of farm plots.

Ancient mapmakers were able to make fairly accurate maps of areas they knew well. When dealing with unknown lands, however, they often left unexplored areas blank or filled them in with their imaginations. An ancient "world map" made of clay was also found in Iraq, in an area that was once known as Mesopotamia. In this map, shown below, the world was pictured through the eyes of the Assyrians, who ruled Mesopotamia between about 722 and 626 B.C. They saw the world as round and flat. Can you find the Euphrates River that flowed through the middle of their world?

### Advances in Cartography

Information from explorers and traders helped early cartographers improve their maps. Technological developments also led to more accurate mapmaking.

About 2,000 years ago, the Chinese discovered a way to find direction with a piece of magnetized iron ore called a lodestone. They placed the lodestone on wood or reeds, then floated it in water. The lodestone always swung around to point toward the north. The Chinese had created a simple compass.

**Across Time & Space**

*In his map of the world, Claudius Ptolemy showed Asia much closer to Europe than it actually is. This mistake led Christopher Columbus to attempt to reach Asia by sailing west from the coast of Spain in 1492. Columbus never reached Asia. Instead, he landed in the "New World" of the Americas.*

▼ *Can you locate the sea that encircles the earth in this ancient map of the "world"?*

➤ *The earliest astrolabes probably date back to the 200s B.C. in Greece. Sailors used astrolabes like the one shown here to help them navigate.*

A gnomon is the blade that stands upright in the center of a sundial. When the sun shines, the gnomon casts a shadow, pointing to the hour. Early scholars learned they could use gnomons to find the height of the sun at different times during the day. They then used this information to help them figure out the distance between two points. Around 240 B.C., the Greek mathematician Eratosthenes *(ehr uh TAHS thuh neez)* used a gnomon to help him figure out the earth's circumference.

Through the centuries, technological advances have continued to help cartographers improve their maps. In the A.D. 1400s, for example, improvements in navigational equipment allowed European sailors to explore much of the world. Their explorations provided valuable information for mapmakers.

Today's cartographers rely on space-age technology. Like the ancient sailing ships, satellites now circle the earth, sending back information and adding to our knowledge of the world. Aerial photography, using infrared film, allows mapmakers to record information not visible to the eye. Computers and radar also make the mapmaker's job easier. ■

Ancient people also learned how to use the planets and stars to help them determine location and distance on the earth. Two early scientific instruments that helped them were the astrolabe *(AS truh layb)* and the gnomon *(NOH mahn)*.

An astrolabe is a disk with marks around its edge like a ruler. Scholars and sailors used the astrolabe to sight the positions of the sun and stars and to figure out their height in the sky. This information aided them in determining latitude.

■ *What technologies helped early mapmakers figure out direction, location, and distance?*

R E V I E W

1. **FOCUS** How did people begin to learn about the world?
2. **CONNECT** In Chapter 1 you learned how the present is built on the past. Give three examples of ways in which present geographical knowledge is built on past developments.
3. **ECONOMICS** Why were the Phoenicians willing to make the effort to settle the west coast of Africa?
4. **CRITICAL THINKING** What might historians learn about the Assyrians from their map of the ancient world on page 49?
5. **CRITICAL THINKING** What advantages do aerial and satellite cameras offer mapmakers?
6. **WRITING ACTIVITY** Imagine that you traveled with Commander Hanno from Carthage to Africa or with Hippalus from the Mediterranean shores to India. Write a page about one of your experiences in diary form.

# Locating Cities on a Map

### Here's Why

You know that maps can help you understand history. Suppose you wanted to find the location of Carales, a Phoenician port city. You could look in a historical atlas.

### Here's How

An atlas is a book of maps and geographical facts. Historical atlases contain maps that show geographical information about the past. For example, a historical world atlas might have maps showing China in A.D. 200, trade routes of the Roman Empire, or the kingdoms of ancient Egypt. Usually an atlas has an index in the back of the book that lists place names and the pages on which you can find them.

Look at the sample index page below. Find "Carales." Notice the letter-number combination "B1" following the entry "Carales." Next to B1 is the listing for a page number. If this was a real atlas, you would turn to page 51. Instead, just look at the map below. The grid location B1 can help you find Carales on the map.

First find the letter "B" along the right side of the map. Next find the number "1" at the top. With your finger, trace a line across from the B, meeting another line coming from the 1. Carales is located in the square formed by the grid lines.

Grid lines sometimes appear only along the sides of the map with the reference letters and numbers. In such cases it is up to you to follow the imaginary lines across the map as if they were actually present.

### Try It

Look again at the sample index below. Find Cyrene. What are the grid references for Cyrene? Find Cyrene on the map. Where is Cyrene located in relationship to the grid lines? What are the grid references for Crete? Find Crete on the map.

### Apply It

Find the location of the earliest cities in your state. What cities already existed at the time your state joined the union? Give the grid location for these cities.

## The Eastern Mediterranean in the 600s B.C.

The Eastern Mediterranean in the 600s B.C.

Greek settlements
Assyrian Empire
Phoenician colonies
Etruscan settlements

0 150 300 mi.
0 150 300 km
Azimuthal Equidistant Projection

# Chapter Review

## Reviewing Key Terms

cartographer (p. 39)     projection (p. 44)
climate (p. 28)          region (p. 31)
diffusion (p. 30)        scale (p. 35)
inset (p. 40)            thematic map (p. 43)
legend (p. 39)           topography (p. 27)
monsoon (p. 47)

**A.** Which key term can be defined by using one of these word groups? Include the words in a sentence that defines the term.
1. smaller, details
2. powerful, seasonal
3. adopt, culture
4. purpose, represent
5. shape, round, flat
6. mountains, valleys, rivers, lakes

**B.** Some of the following statements are true and some are false. Write *True* or *False* for each statement. Then rewrite the false statements to make them true.
1. Diffusion occurs when people change their land to make farming easier.
2. The climate region of northeastern China is heavily populated.
3. All maps have the same scale so people can see the distance between two cities.
4. Ancient cartographers had difficulty making maps of areas that were far away from their homelands.
5. The legend on a map explains how the world is divided into hemispheres.

## Exploring Concepts

**A.** Each of the six groups of words below have something in common. They are also different in important ways. For each group, answer the following questions on your own paper. What do these things have in common? How are they different?
1. farming
   herding
   fishing
2. cyclic
   periodic
   migratory
3. natural boundary
   artificial boundary
4. latitude
   longitude
5. Mercator projection
   Peters projection
   Goode's interrupted homolosine projection
   Robinson projection
6. gnomon
   astrolabe

**B.** Support each statement with facts and details from the chapter.
1. Geographers divide the world into various kinds of regions.
2. Sometimes large groups of people move from their homeland to another place.
3. Most of China's people live in the eastern part.
4. People sometimes change an invention from one culture to fit the needs of their own culture.
5. Cartographers still use map grids to locate places on the world.
6. Dr. Snow's map showed the reason for the cholera epidemic.
7. Mediterranean traders traveling to India needed to know topography and climate.
8. Both the Mercator projection and the Peters projection distort the appearance of the continents.
9. Ancient historians included geographic information in their records.

# Reviewing Skills

1. Look at the latitude and longitude lines on the map of the Iberian peninsula on this page. What is located at 36° N, 5° W?
2. Using the map, give the latitude and longitude of these cities:
   a. Toledo, Spain
   b. Cartagena, Spain
   c. Segovia, Spain
   d. Tarragona, Spain
3. Use the map on page 51. Find Damascus, Leptis, and Athens. Give the grid references for each as they would appear in their atlas index entries.
4. Study the world nutrition map on page 43. What general information about hunger can you learn from the map?
5. What terms does a navigator use to give the exact location of the ship?

Iberian Peninsula

# Using Critical Thinking

1. How do topography and climate influence the kinds of sports played in a particular region? Give examples to explain your answer.
2. Imagine you could choose another country to live in for one year. Before you make your final choice, what things would you be interested in finding out? What kinds of maps would you need to consult?
3. Some animals, such as the yak in Tibet, help people to survive in the environment. Would people in the desert and arctic climates have difficulty surviving without the help of animals? Name specific animals and tell how they are useful. Which animals make life in your climate region easier? How would your life be different without those animals?

# Preparing for Citizenship

1. **WRITING ACTIVITY** Cut out a weather map from a recent newspaper. Study the content of the map, including the symbols. Write a brief weather report based on information on the map. Compare your report with others in the class.
2. **GROUP ACTIVITY** Meet with a small group of classmates to discuss what you have learned about cyclic movement. Make a chart listing the cyclic activities of five people. Use examples based on people in your neighborhood. For instance, your postal carrier travels the same route every working day.
3. **COLLABORATIVE LEARNING** Working in groups of four, create a map of your school. Each person in the group should be in charge of one of the following four tasks:
   a. drawing a general map of the school building and school grounds
   b. making a legend for the map
   c. figuring out the scale of the map
   d. creating an inset of a particular school area (gym, lunchroom, library)
   Exchange maps with another group. Measure the distance between where you are now and the area shown in the inset.

# Chapter 3

# Learning About the Past

A fleck of gold flashes in the dust. Could it be the clue that leads researchers to the tomb of an ancient king? A farmer stumbles upon a broken piece of pottery. Could this be evidence of a city that disappeared thousands of years ago? Children exploring a cave find strange writing on the walls. Could these words unlock the secrets of a lost civilization? Learning about the past is a search for clues to hidden worlds.

In 1822, a French scholar figured out how to read the strange writing of the ancient Egyptians. Historians could then finally understand Egyptian records, like this list of Egyptian kings from about 1270 B.C.

Fascinated by tales of the ancient Greeks, German businessman Heinrich Schliemann dug beneath the ruins of Mycenae, an ancient Greek city. In 1876, he unearthed treasures like this gold lion's head from about 1570 B.C.

# 6500 B.C.

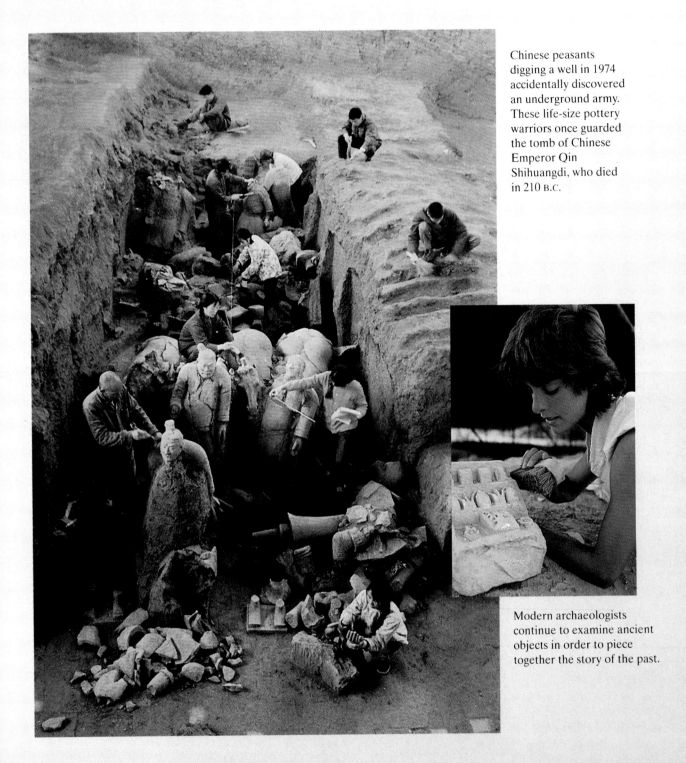

Chinese peasants digging a well in 1974 accidentally discovered an underground army. These life-size pottery warriors once guarded the tomb of Chinese Emperor Qin Shihuangdi, who died in 210 B.C.

Modern archaeologists continue to examine ancient objects in order to piece together the story of the past.

Today

L E S S O N   1

# Understanding History

### THINKING FOCUS

*How do historians learn about the past?*

*My mother now began to beg, urge, and command me to escape as best I could. . . . I replied that I would not be saved without her. Taking her by the hand, I hurried her along. . . . And now came the ashes, but at first sparsely. I turned around. Behind us, an ominous thick smoke, spreading over the earth like a flood, followed us. . . . To be heard were only the shrill cries of women, the wailing of children, the shouting of men. Some were calling to their parents, others to their children, others to their wives—knowing one another only by voice.*

Pliny the Younger, from letters written to the historian Tacitus

### Key Terms

- prehistory
- fossil
- artifact
- oral tradition
- primary source
- secondary source

➤ *During the eruption, many people were buried in volcanic ash. The bodies later decayed, but the impressions left were preserved in the hardened ash. Archaeologists then filled the impressions with plaster to make casts of the victims, like the one shown here.*

Pliny the Younger wrote this about the eruption of the volcano Mount Vesuvius in A.D. 79, when he was just 18 years old. His letters give valuable information about the disaster that destroyed the Roman cities of Pompeii and Herculaneum. However, written records like these aren't the only sources of information about the eruption. Volcanic lava and ash sealed Pompeii and Herculaneum exactly as they were almost 2,000 years ago, so the cities are like time capsules. Archaeologists *(ahr kee AHL uh jihsts)* have uncovered many clues that tell how the people of Pompeii and Herculaneum lived.

For example, one wall painting in Pompeii shows the games that were being held in the local sports arena. Campaign slogans on other walls within the city show that, at the time of the volcano's eruption, Pompeii was getting ready for elections. Other evidence shows that, like us, the Romans kept watchdogs. Colored tiles on a floor uncovered at Pompeii spell out the message *cave canem*. This means, "Beware of the dog." Archaeologists even have an idea of what ancient Romans ate. Sealed in the ash were loaves of bread, eggs, nuts, and lentils.

# Historical Evidence

Pliny's letter and the wall paintings at Pompeii are examples of the two kinds of sources historians use to study the past: written sources and nonwritten sources. To learn about the past, historians must seek out as many different sources as they possibly can, both written and nonwritten, and then try to find out what they mean.

## Kinds of Sources

To most people, written sources mean books. But to historians, written sources might also be letters, diaries, speeches, popular songs, poems, business records, or campaign slogans. They could be the marks on ancient tombs or old calendars and maps—anything with writing on it.

Anything written down can give historians clues about the people and events of the past. However, written sources only go back to about 3000 B.C. That's

when writing developed in Mesopotamia, an ancient country in what is now the Middle East. History before the development of writing is called **prehistory.** To learn about prehistoric times, historians must rely completely on nonwritten sources.

Nonwritten sources include **fossils**—the remains or imprints of once-living plants or animals. Dinosaur fossils, for example, can tell about the kinds of dinosaurs that lived in a certain time and place.

Other nonwritten sources are **artifacts,** or objects made by humans. Ancient jewelry, tools, coins, and toys teach about the customs and beliefs of people of the past.

Still other nonwritten sources are tombs, monuments, and even entire cities. The streets and buildings of Pompeii, preserved beneath the ashes, give a picture of life as it was in A.D. 79.

Another important nonwritten source is a culture's **oral tradition,**

*◄ This ancient carving of Egyptian scribes is a nonwritten source. The carving shows that the Egyptians wrote with penlike instruments.*

*▲ The pages above from a French songbook of 1470 are a valuable written source. They show how music was written down at the time.*

*◄ Will today's compact discs like the one at left be a nonwritten source for historians of the future?*

57

the legends, myths, and beliefs passed on by word of mouth from generation to generation. Over time, many myths and legends have been written down. For example, the legend of King Odysseus was part of the ancient Greek oral tradition. It was finally written down by the Greek poet Homer between 800 and 700 B.C., and it is Homer's version that is known today.

## The Historian's Job

Historians do not just collect facts. They also must examine the information they collect and then decide how to interpret it. Doing this carefully often can take a long time. For example, in the 400s B.C., a Greek historian named Thucydides (*thoo SID ih deez*) spent 27 years studying the war between the Greek city-states of Athens and Sparta. Here is how Thucydides

## UNDERSTANDING ORAL TRADITION

*L*ong before Homer wrote the *Odyssey* (*AHD ih see*), people kept the adventures of King Odysseus alive by word of mouth. The legends, stories, ideas, customs, and beliefs that a culture passes on by word of mouth make up its oral tradition.

### Word of Mouth

Once something is written down it remains in that form without changing. An oral tradition, on the other hand, may change constantly from generation to generation. It changes as the interests, opinions, fears, and needs of each generation change.

How useful is oral tradition to historians if accounts told by word of mouth change and become inaccurate? Historians can't be sure that an oral tradition portrays events from long

ago accurately. However, oral traditions do tell about the kinds of things that were important to people of the times.

### A Source of Information

Ancient cultures that existed before the development of writing depended on oral tradition to communicate their ideas and record events. Through oral traditions the elders taught the younger members of the society about their culture. This is why historians are interested in ancient oral traditions.

India and China are two places where ancient oral traditions are still remembered and passed on. But in many places oral traditions have been forgotten. Historians can only learn about

the oral traditions of most ancient cultures if someone along the way bothered to record them in writing.

The oral tradition still exists in some modern societies, side by side with written records. Among West Africans, for example, the storyteller is an important member of society. He records family histories and recites them on special occasions.

Historians must be careful when interpreting oral tradition. Nevertheless, oral tradition can be a useful source for information about people of the past.

Chapter 3

described the difficult job of the historian:

> He must not be misled by the exaggerated fancies of the poets, or by the tales of chroniclers who seek to please the ear rather than speak the truth. . . . At such a distance of time he must make up his mind to be satisfied with conclusions resting upon the clearest evidence which can be had. . . . Of the events of the war I have not ventured to speak from any chance information, nor according to any notion of my own; I have described nothing but what I either saw myself, or learned from others of whom I made the most careful and particular enquiry. The task was a laborious one, because eye-witnesses of the same occurrences gave different accounts of them, as they remembered or were interested in the actions of one side or the other.
>
> Thucydides, 400s B.C.

## The Interpretation of Sources

As Thucydides says, sources are open to interpretation. Has one of your teachers ever asked you to tell your side of the story after a disagreement with another student? Did your version differ from your friend's?

Now consider two written records of a war—one from the winner's point of view; one from the loser's. How might the two be different?

Historians must keep in mind that everyone has his or her own point of view. Whether or not the author of a source is a man or a woman, rich or poor, or young or old will affect the way he or she sees and describes an event.

Nonwritten sources are, of course, also open to interpretation. Suppose, for example, that archaeologists uncover the remains of an ancient walled structure. Some historians might think it is a fort. Others, however, might argue it is a cattle corral. ■

▲ Can you identify the modern-day artifacts shown above? Imagine the difficulty interpreting ancient artifacts.

■ What kinds of sources do historians use to learn about the past?

## The Evaluation of Sources

Historians ask questions about a source to determine how accurate and useful it is. A historian studying Pliny's account of the eruption would start by asking these questions:

*Who was the writer?* Pliny was a well-educated young man from a wealthy family. He had studied science under his uncle. As a result, his description of the process of the eruption is very valuable to historians. They want to know how the writer's background might affect his or her account.

*What kind of source is it?* Pliny's account was one of many letters he wrote about life in the Roman Empire. His letters have given historians valuable information about the life and politics of the Roman Empire.

Different kinds of sources offer different kinds of information. Letters or diaries, for example, may tell a great deal about people's daily lives. Political speeches, on the other hand, might help explain a government's policies.

*When was the source produced?* Pliny wrote his description of the eruption shortly after it happened. Sources produced during the same time period as the events

### Across Time & Space

*In the early 1800s, the British artist Sir William Gell visited and sketched the houses of Pompeii as they might have looked before the eruption of Vesuvius. His drawings helped make Pompeii popular. In fact, people began building new houses in the Pompeiian style.*

59

*Compare the photo above with the painting on the next page. Both depict eruptions of Mt. Vesuvius. What can you learn from each?*

■ *Why do historians ask questions about their sources?*

are secondary sources. They are likely to be more accurate because they were recorded when the event was fresh in people's minds.

*Where was the source produced?* Pliny's account was an eyewitness account. Therefore, it is more valuable to historians than one written by someone who merely heard about the disaster. Even if a source was produced during the time period of the event, historians want to know if the author was actually at the event.

*Why was the source produced?* Pliny wrote about the eruption in letters to the Roman historian Tacitus. Most of Pliny's letters were a mix of historical information and literature. Writing such letters was a fashionable thing for wealthy young Roman men to do.

Writers have many different reasons for writing. One writer may just want to describe an event. Another might want to prove a point, impress someone, or make someone else look bad. Understanding why a source was produced helps historians judge the accuracy of the information that is presented. ■

they describe are called **primary sources.** Materials that were created later by people who studied the original sources are called **secondary sources.** The photo at the top of this page shows the eruption of Mt. Vesuvius in 1944. Because the photo records an event at the time of the event, it is a primary source. The painting of Mt. Vesuvius on the next page shows the eruption of A.D. 79. However, the painting wasn't made until 1785, so it's a secondary source.

Primary sources are generally more valuable to historians than

## The Puzzle of History

History has been called a conversation between the present and the past. People of the past communicate with people of today through the writing, artifacts, and structures they leave behind.

Each generation has historians who gather and evaluate sources of information about the past. However, the way these historians interpret the sources they find varies from generation to generation.

60

After all, every generation sees the world differently. And because each generation and each individual looks at things from a new point of view, history is always open to different interpretations.

History also has been compared to a jigsaw puzzle. Some pieces of the puzzle have been lost forever. Pieces once considered lost have now been found. The available pieces can be fitted together in many ways. Each generation of historians tries to put together the available pieces of the puzzle and to interpret the picture that emerges. In doing so, they hope to understand not only what happened in the past, but how it happened, and why it happened. ■

▲ *In 1785, artist Angelica Kauffmann painted the A.D. 79 eruption of Mt. Vesuvius. Pliny the Younger studies with his mother at Misenum as they learn of the eruption.*

■ *Why do historians study the past?*

## REVIEW

1. **FOCUS** What methods and sources do historians use to learn about the past?
2. **CONNECT** Is the map on page 39 a primary source or a secondary source? Why?
3. **HISTORY** Why do historians ask questions about their sources?
4. **CRITICAL THINKING** In ancient Rome fewer women than men left behind written sources. How might this have affected historians' knowledge of the history of Rome?
5. **WRITING ACTIVITY** Look around your home. What written and nonwritten sources do you see? Make a list of the sources. Then, using one or two of the sources on your list, try to write a history of your family. Follow Thucydides' advice as you write and evaluate your sources carefully.

Learning About the Past

# Evaluating Information

### Here's Why

People learn about the past in many ways. Written records, fossils, artifacts, and oral traditions are all keys to understanding the past. By gathering and evaluating these sources, historians form their ideas about past events.

As you study the past, you also need to evaluate historical evidence. To do this, you must be able to tell the difference between facts, reasoned judgments, and opinions.

Look at the picture below of the gigantic stone statues found on Easter Island. This island is located in the eastern Pacific Ocean, 2,300 miles west of Chile. The Polynesian name for Easter Island is Rapa Nui *(rap uh NOO ee)*. Its Chilean name is Isla de Pascua *(EEZ lah thay PAHS kwah)*.

The statues, called moai *(MOH eye)*, were made hundreds of years ago. Suppose you read an account of how these statues were made. How would you know whether or not to believe the account?

### Here's How

To decide whether information is accurate, look for facts, reasoned judgments, and opinions. An interpretation that depends on facts and reasoned judgments is likely to be correct. An explanation that offers only opinions has little value.

Read "The Easter Island Story" on

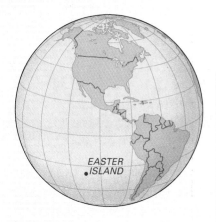

EASTER
·ISLAND

this page. It contains facts, reasoned judgments, and opinions.

A fact is a statement that can be proven. There are many forms of proof. The findings of archaeologists can be proof, or proof can come from written sources or direct observation.

Find the statement highlighted in blue in "The Easter Island Story." This statement is a fact because there is proof that it is true. Photographs and other records show the statues and stone picks that archaeologists found at the volcano.

A reasoned judgment is a statement that is based on fact but has not been proven. Key words like *probably*, *perhaps*, and *possibly* can help you to identify reasoned judgments.

The statement highlighted in purple is a reasoned judgment. It explains how the statues may have been lifted onto their platforms. Can you find the facts that support this idea? They directly follow the reasoned judgment. People on Easter

Island tested this idea in the 1950s. Using two logs as levers, they lifted a 25-ton statue. Yet it has not been proven that the statues' makers used logs as levers. It only has been shown that this is possible.

An opinion is a statement of personal preference, feelings, or ideas. Words such as *think* and *feel* often indicate that a statement is an opinion. The statement highlighted in green is an opinion. It tells you how the writer feels about the statues.

## Try It

Look again at "The Easter Island Story." Find a fact, a reasoned judgment, and an opinion. Be sure to choose examples that have not been discussed already.

## Apply It

Listen to a newscast or read a newspaper or magazine article. Record one fact, one reasoned judgment, and one opinion. Point out any key words that helped you identify the types of statements.

### The Easter Island Story

I think the moai of Easter Island are exciting artifacts. They are certain to interest people in the future.

Islanders used stone picks to carve the moai from the rock of the extinct volcano Rano Raruku. Both inside and outside of the crater, archaeologists have found many unfinished statues and thousands of stone picks. All of the moai are made of a yellow-gray stone called tuff. The tuff comes from the crater walls of Rano Raruku.

The islanders probably dragged the statues from the volcano to the places where they stand now. In the 1950s, people from Easter Island tested this idea. They found that it took 180 people to pull a medium-sized statue!

The people who built the statues probably used log levers to lift the statues onto their platforms. Trees grow on the island today. And by studying pollen deposits, scientists have learned that there were trees on the island in the past. Also, people in other times and places have used logs for the same purpose.

Learning About the Past

L E S S O N   2

# Examining Sources

**THINKING
FOCUS**

*How do archaeologists
investigate ancient
cultures?*

### Key Terms

- archaeology
- excavation
- radiocarbon dating

➤ *Tollund man was
found in a Danish peat
bog like the one shown
here. After scientists determined what Tollund
Man ate for his last meal,
they prepared a similar
meal of seeds and grain.
The resulting mixture
tasted quite bitter.*

The dead man lay on his side in a swampy area called a peat bog. His face was so calm that he appeared to have died in his sleep. But it was clear that he hadn't; a rope was wound tightly around his neck.

Two Danish workers discovered the man's body in 1950. They had come to Tollund Bog to cut peat, a form of rotted plant material that is used for fuel. The peat cutters wondered if they should call the police. As it turned out, the body in the bog was hardly a case for the Danish police. Instead, it was a lucky find for archaeologists. **Archaeology** is the recovery and study of artifacts, ruins, bones, and fossils remaining from the past.

In Denmark, archaeologists soon learned that Tollund Man hadn't been hanged and buried that day, that year, or even this century. The airtight peat bog had perfectly preserved Tollund Man's body for thousands of years. Using a technique called radiocarbon dating, archaeologists found out

that the man had died around 210 B.C. Using other scientific techniques, they even found out what Tollund Man ate for his last meal: cereal, made with seeds of plants that grew in Denmark more than 2,000 years ago. No one can say for sure why Tollund Man died. But evidence indicates he may have been killed in a religious ritual.

This cave painting from Lascaux, France, is 17,000 years old.

# Interpreting the Evidence

Techniques such as radiocarbon dating have given archaeologists valuable information about the past. Nevertheless, people can interpret the archaeological record in many ways. Archaeologists must interpret the evidence they collect just as historians do.

People tend to interpret past events in light of their own experiences. For example, imagine you are on an archaeological dig and you come upon a row of stones. You might assume the stones are part of a wall, because you are familiar with stone walls. However, the people of an ancient culture might have brought these stones together for other reasons. Perhaps they were trying to create an altar to their god or to keep track of lunar eclipses.

## Reconsidering the Past

As different archaeologists examine the archaeological record, they come to different conclusions about its meaning. For example, archaeologists disagree about the meaning of objects depicted in ancient cave art. These paintings were made by humans more than

◄ At left is a detail from the cave painting above. Some think the object shown is a spear; others identify it as a stalk of wheat. What do you think?

Learning About the Past

## How Do We Know?

**HISTORY** *Archaeologists conduct experiments to help them interpret the archaeological record. For example, they sometimes construct replicas of ancient buildings to observe how they decay. They even study garbage to find out what kinds of things people throw away.*

■ *Why do archaeologists reach different conclusions about the past?*

10,000 years ago. Some archaeologists believe the objects are weapons such as arrows, spears, and harpoons. If they are, it would indicate that early humans were hunters and warriors.

In recent years, however, some people have begun to challenge that interpretation. A scholar named Alexander Marshack, for example, used a microscope to examine these works of art closely. Marshack decided that the objects depicted in these early paintings might be plants, tree branches, and leaves instead of weapons. He believes the artwork may celebrate nature, not hunting. Perhaps our early ancestors were not as warlike as archaeologists have long believed.

### Interpreting the Past

Archaeologists must use all the evidence they can gather to interpret the archaeological record. The case of Tollund Man shows how archaeologists pull together information from many sources. Through radiocarbon dating, they were able to find out that the man in the peat bog died in about 210 B.C. But how and why did he die?

To find out, archaeologists had to do more research. From written records, they learned that the ancient Nordic people sometimes sacrificed people to their gods by hanging them. The archaeologists even learned that the food Tollund Man ate for his last meal might have been a part of the ritual of the sacrifice. Although archaeologists still cannot be sure, they think that Tollund Man was hanged, not as a punishment but as an offering to the gods.

Perhaps future generations of archaeologists will find additional information about Tollund Man. Future generations also might interpret the information that is already available differently. For archaeologists as well as for historians, interpreting the evidence is a never-ending process. ■

## REVIEW

1. **FOCUS** How do archaeologists investigate ancient cultures?
2. **CONNECT** How are grids used by cartographers similar to those used by archaeologists?
3. **ARCHAEOLOGY** Imagine you are an archaeologist working at a dig. You find a piece of wood used in building an ancient house. What are two techniques you might use to find out how old it is, and how would you apply them?
4. **CRITICAL THINKING** Imagine that 1,000 years from now a team of archaeologists discovers the remains of your home. What conclusions might they draw about life in the 20th century from the artifacts they find in your room?
5. **ACTIVITY** Pick four modern artifacts, for example, a coin, a tool, a wooden object, and a piece of pottery. Examine each artifact and then list the method you would use to determine its date.

# Examining Archaeology

*A t first I could see nothing, the hot air escaping from the
chamber causing the candle flame to flicker, but presently, as
my eyes grew accustomed to the light, details of the room
emerged slowly from the mist, strange animals, statues and gold—everywhere the glint of gold. For the moment—an eternity it must have
been to the others standing by—I was struck dumb with amazement,
and when Lord Carnarvon, unable to stand the suspense any longer,
inquired anxiously, "Can you see anything?" it was all I could do to
get out the words, "Yes, wonderful things."*

Howard Carter, *Tomb of Tut-Ankh-Amen*

**THINKING FOCUS**

*What can archaeologists
learn from an archaeo-
logical dig?*

### Key Terms

- sarcophagus
- kitchen midden

After five seasons of failure,
archaeologist Howard Carter
and his wealthy employer, Lord
Carnarvon, finally were successful on November 26,1922. They
had found the tomb of the young.
Egyptian pharaoh Tutankhamen
*(tut ahngk AH muhn)*.

The pharaoh's tomb had been
sealed since the time shortly after
his burial in 1352 B.C. It was
crowded full of beautiful carvings
and many objects made of gold
and precious stones. As a matter
of fact, Tutankhamen's tomb contained everything a wealthy king
would need for his afterlife. In the
most splendid of the tomb's four
rooms lay Tutankhamen's mummy.
It was buried in a solid gold **sarcophagus** *(sar KAHF uh guhs)*,
or coffin.

## A Classic Excavation

Tutankhamen is not remem-
bered for his political leadership or
his military ability. The boy-king
died before he was 20, after ruling
for only nine years. But his tomb
was an important find for archaeologists. Ancient tomb robbers had
taken the treasures from the other
tombs in Egypt's Valley of the
Kings. Robbers had apparently
even broken into one room of Tutankhamen's tomb, but for some
reason, had left much of it alone.
Until Howard Carter discovered it
in 1922, Tutankhamen's tomb remained well hidden underneath
the ancient foundations of workers' huts.

The excavation of Tutankhamen's  tomb is an example of
what is called classic archaeology.
Carter and his employer were
searching for spectacular artifacts
from a past culture.

71

Learning About the Past

# Tutankhamen's Treasure

*What did Howard Carter see when he looked inside the tomb? He saw four small rooms piled to the ceiling with gold jewelry, life-sized statues, furniture, games, chariots, and more.*

**Made of gold and** colored glass, this necklace represents a vulture goddess. It was one of 143 objects tucked into the cloth wrapped around Tutankhamen's body. Some were the king's favorite possessions. Others had a religious value.

**Fit to cool a king on a hot day**, this fan once had 30 ostrich feathers. The feathers were destroyed by insects over the centuries. The fan's golden surface still shows Tutankhamen hunting the ostriches whose feathers were used to make it.

**The head and** shoulders of the king's body were covered by this gold mask. Pictures of the king appear in many places in the tomb. This mask may be the best indication of what he looked like.

Calipers for measuring artifacts

Bamboo pick for prying dirt away from artifacts

Conveyor belt for carrying dirt out of the pit

Line level for measuring how far down an artifact was found

Paintbrush for cleaning artifacts

**Tiny seeds, bones,** and shells tell archaeologists what plants, animals, and fish ancient people ate.

**Diggers began at 7:00 A.M.** to avoid the worst heat of the day. Each student dug a tiny area, making sure nothing was missed. The most important work was writing detailed notes about what had been found.

Trowel for cutting through river valley clay

## R E V I E W

1. **FOCUS** What can archaeologists learn from an archaeological dig?

2. **CONNECT** Imagine you are a historian studying the artifacts found in Tutankhamen's tomb. What can you learn from these sources about daily life in ancient Egypt? What kinds of things cannot be learned from these sources?

3. **ECONOMICS** How have archaeologists like Howard Carter been able to get money to finance their many excavations?

4. **CRITICAL THINKING** Why are everyday objects as valuable as rare treasures to modern archaeologists?

5. **ACTIVITY** Observation skills are particularly important to archaeologists. Practice your observation skills by closely studying a location, such as your backyard, a garage, or a park. Look for artifacts on and even below the surface of the site, if possible. Record where you find each artifact. What conclusions can you make about the artifacts you find and the people who left them?

# The Henge

## Edward Rutherfurd

*Stonehenge is a huge stone temple built between 1800 and 1400 B.C. in England. The circle of large stones is still a mystery today—archaeologists aren't certain why or even how it was built. This story from the novel* Sarum *suggests some answers.*

In Lesson 4 of Chapter 3, you will read about Stonehenge.

Nooma was excited that the priests had chosen him to build the new henge: not only was this a great honour that made him stick out his chest with pride, but it was also a challenge to his craftsmanship; and he hurried towards the sacred grounds with eager anticipation.

But when he heard the priests' instructions, and when finally he comprehended the enormous scale of their plan, and the short time in which the work was to be completed, his solemn eyes grew larger. Despite the chill autumn day, he felt small beads of perspiration breaking out on his broad forehead.

"Such huge stones? Completed in ten years?" It was a wail of dismay.

The priests took no notice of his protests, and now the little mason began to tremble with fear. How could such a vast temple be completed so quickly? It would need an army of masons! But as he looked into the impassive faces of Dluc's priests, he had no doubt of his fate if he failed them.

"They will give me to the sun god," he thought. "They will sacrifice me at dawn."

When the priests next showed him the drawings that the High Priest had made and he bent his head to study them, his large oval face fell even further.

"Nothing like this has ever been done before," he muttered as he stared at the great arches. And jabbing his finger at one of the drawings he protested: "How am I to do that?"

For Dluc's designs made clear that each of the massive lintels of the ring of sarsens was to be slightly curved so that together they would form a perfect circle. How could such huge stones be transformed—thirty of them—into identical blocks each shaped with such precision?

"You must find a way," they told him.

**lintel** the horizontal stone that rests on top of two upright stones
**sarsen** an upright stone that supports the lintel

Nooma shook his head slowly. "I shall certainly be led to the altar stone," he thought sadly.

But there was nothing he could do. The priests could not be refused. Somehow, he must devise a way to build this huge new henge.

"I should need fifty masons to work under me," he said finally. "And as for labourers . . ." He tried to calculate the size of the army of men that would be needed to haul such enormous stones. For each sarsen would weigh up to thirty-five tons— the largest half as much again—and would have to be moved nearly twenty miles across the rolling high ground. "Why," he exclaimed, "it would take five hundred men at least, and teams of oxen too."

But the priests were unmoved by these astounding demands.

"You shall have all the men you need, and oxen," he was informed.

Nooma thought. The practical problems of organising such a force, of feeding and housing them would occupy much time. He could not do this and supervise the stone-working alone. "I shall need help to organise the men," he said.

"Choose whom you wish."

The little fellow considered.

"I should like Tark the riverman," he said.

It was a good choice. No one on the five rivers was cleverer than Tark, the best known and most highly regarded of all the riverfolk. The riverfolk at Sarum were an extensive tribe, somewhat apart from the farmers, and mostly descended in one way or another from the crafty fishermen and hunters who had first inhabited the place millennia before. It was not uncommon to see mean, hard little faces and long toes which bore a remarkable resemblance to those of Tep the hunter, along the riverbanks of any of the five rivers, as these people went about their business as trappers, fishermen and traders. Water rats they were often called by the Sarum people.

Tark was of this tribe, but a nobler specimen than most. Though he, too, had the long toes of the water rat, he was a tall, good-looking man with strong, rugged features, long black hair which he swept back, and a black beard which he kept meticulously trimmed and singed. His eyes, black as jet, could be hard when he was driving a bargain, but could also become gentle and luminous, especially when he sang, which he did in a fine, tuneful bass; and it was partly for this reason that he was well known from the trading post to the port to be popular with the women. Tark was an expert trader, with six boats and men of his own working under him. He was everywhere, even crossing the sea sometimes in search of slaves or special items that he knew would please Krona or the priests. Above all, he was wily in his dealing

*wily*  sly

with the priests, always making himself useful to them, while at the same time seeing to it that each transaction was to his benefit. He liked the little mason, whom he found slightly absurd, admired his craftsmanship and had formed a kind of friendship with him, often letting him have small items from his river-trading which the mason would never have been clever enough to bargain for himself.

Nooma was sure that he would know how to organise the provisioning and quartering of his men, and he was right.

"You have a month to prepare," the priests told the mason. "At the next moon, work must begin."

In the days that followed, Nooma found that his needs were more than supplied. The priests moved from house to house, picking young men whenever they were needed. Before the work was done, over a third of the adult male population would be engaged on the task at any one time. Under Tark's direction, grain stores were built near the site from which the sarsens would be brought, and the work of felling trees, which would be used as rollers over which the huge stones could be moved, was begun.

By the end of the month, despite the huge size of the task before him, Nooma felt the first dawning of a new confidence. Encouraged by Tark, who was delighted by such an opportunity to make himself useful to the priests, he began to go about his great work with a new optimism and before the end of the month confided to the trader: "Perhaps, after all, it can be done."

While the preparations were in hand, he also set his mind to the technical problems presented by the stones themselves: how were they to be handled, and above all, how were such cumbersome objects to be fitted together in so precise a design?

It was in this that Nooma showed a practical genius which amply justified the choice that the priests had made in putting the work under his hands.

For when he came to report to the priests at the end of the month, the little mason was brimming with suppressed excitement.

As he outlined his plans, jabbing the air with his stubby little fingers, he announced:

"We must cut the stones into their final shape before we move them."

The priests were surprised. It had been assumed that the rough-hewn rocks would be brought to the henge before they were shaped. But Nooma shook his head.

"First," he explained, "it is foolish to move the sarsens before they are almost shaped, because they will be heavier. And second, if we cut and dress the stones at the henge, the mess will be enormous: thousands of stone chippings to carry away."

"Then you mean to shape every stone of the temple a day's

*quartering* assigning lodgings to people

journey away, carry the finished stones to the sacred ground and assemble them there?" one of the priests asked in astonishment.

He nodded calmly. "Why not?"

Next he produced his own drawings.

To produce the identically curved lintels he proposed to make a wooden block, along which each stone could be cut, and in order to fix them in place he had devised an ingenious solution.

"See," he explained, "at the top of each upright we can make two tenons—these bumps—and on the underside of each lintel two matching sockets for the tenons to fit into."

He pointed them out to the priests.

"They will be fitted into each other just as we do blocks of wood," he explained. "And then," he continued, "I can make tongue and groove joints at the end of the lintels so that each one slots into the next."

"They will be solid," the priest who had spoken before remarked.

"Solid!" the quiet little fellow suddenly burst out. "Why each stone will be married to the next like husband to wife. The temple will be indestructible!" He was flushed with excitement.

It was from that moment that the priests knew the new temple of Stonehenge would be a masterpiece; and that night, when they gave Dluc an account of the mason's plans, the High Priest was pleased.

## Further Reading

*Canyons Beyond the Sky*. Lawrence Kettleman. An archaeological dig forms the backdrop for this story of time travel between modern and ancient cultures.

*Country of Broken Stone*. Nancy Bond. The excavation of a Roman fort provides a link to the past when hostile acts by some people opposed to the dig unleash supernatural forces.

*The Faraway Lurs*. Harry Behn. The love and friendship of a Bronze Age boy and girl is opposed by their families and tribes. This author based the story on an actual archaeological discovery.

*Pyramid*. David Macauley. How were the pyramids built? David Macauley's book offers a step-by-step illustrated description of the building of a pyramid.

L E S S O N    4

# Interpreting Sources

### Key Term

- megalith

▲ *This Roman amphora dates from about 700 B.C. The owner's name is shown on its surface.*

**D**uring the Roman Empire, nearly 2,000 years ago, people eagerly flocked to Roman ports to watch foreign ships empty their cargo. Nearly every day new items arrived from many lands abroad: fierce lions from central Africa, bolts of fine silk from China, and majestic horses from Spain. From India came the pepper and spices Romans needed for cooking, along with diamonds and pearls for the wealthy to wear. Pliny the Younger, author of the account of the eruption of Mount Vesuvius, wrote that the wealthy women of Rome even wore pearls on their shoes.

But a special treat for Romans was to watch a ship unload its cargo of fantastic beasts from India. Bengal tigers, elephants, apes, and peacocks would emerge from the holds of the ship. The noisy crowd would suddenly hush, gasping in amazement at the fantastic sight.

To obtain these luxuries, the Roman traders sailed to distant ports. The ships were loaded down with Roman goods such as gold, glass, silver coins, and amphorae *(AM fuh ree)*—pottery containers filled with wine and olive oil.

## Evidence of Cultural Contact

How do people today know about the ancient Roman markets and the goods traded there? In addition to the written records, such as Pliny's account, archaeologists have found Roman goods far beyond the empire's borders. For example, they have discovered amphorae in India, along with coins dating from before A.D. 100. These finds indicate that India and Rome once enjoyed a thriving trade.

The map on page 81 shows some of what archaeologists and historians have learned about the contacts between ancient cultures.

Notice the routes linking China and Rome. Archaeologists know about Chinese-Roman trade from many sources including accounts by Pliny who wrote, "Our imports from China and Arabia cost a hundred million sesterces per annum," the equivalent of 25 million silver Roman coins per year.

### Acquainted Cultures

Trade was one of several forms of contact between the cultures of the ancient world: China, Egypt, India, Mesopotamia, Greece, and Rome. Individuals traveled to foreign lands, even in ancient times.

Sometimes these travelers left behind evidence of their visits, such as the Romans who scratched their names on stone monuments in Greece and Egypt. Sometimes travelers and explorers left written accounts of their travels. For example, the Chinese monk Fa-xian *(FAH shee EHN)* traveled to India to study in the early A.D. 400s. He later wrote about his travels.

Different cultures came into contact not only through trade and travel, but also through war and migration. Clues about the different contacts between cultures are found in the archaeological record.

Archaeologists sometimes find signs that at a particular time, new types of food, pottery, or weavings appeared in a certain location. This might show that new people migrated to the area during the time period, bringing with them new ideas.

## Cultural Diffusion

Whenever different cultures come in contact, they exchange goods and ideas. This process is what is known as cultural diffusion, and it is one way that ideas have spread from one area of the world to another.

*Use the scale on the map to find the shortest route from China to Rome.*

81

Learning About the Past

Some historians believe developments in writing, art, architecture, and agriculture from a few areas spread throughout the world through cultural diffusion. Others argue that individual cultures developed similar ideas independently of one another. ■

## Evidence of Independent Invention

The archaeological record shows that some cultures borrowed ideas and technology from other cultures they were in contact with. Yet the record also shows that, in some cases, different cultures made similar developments without coming into contact with each other. Instead, these cultures each came up with their similar ideas independently.

### The Mystery of Stonehenge

A great example of independent development is found in the south of what is now Britain. More than 4,000 years ago, the people of this area built Stonehenge. It is a monument of huge stones, or **megaliths,** arranged in a circular pattern, as shown below.

Originally, this monument included 81 megaliths, each weighing about 50 tons. Archaeologists have determined that the stones were carted to their present location from a rock quarry 25 miles away. Scholars figure it must have taken 1,100 people seven weeks to move just one of the stones, using twisted hide ropes and wooden rollers. At that rate, it would have taken at least 10 years to get all 81 upright stones into place.

Imagine how hard it would be to stand one of these megaliths upright without the aid of modern machinery. Try to imagine hoisting the seven-ton horizontal stones found on top of each pair of upright stones. Builders began constructing Stonehenge around 2800 B.C. Later generations changed the arrangement of the huge stones and added new ones over a period of about 1,700 years.

Archaeologists and historians are still not sure why Stonehenge

▼ *To help them estimate the age of the megaliths, archaeologists used radiocarbon dating on charcoal found in underground pits at Stonehenge. The charcoal dates from around 1848 B.C.*

was built. The position of these megaliths could mean that the monument was built to help track the movements of the stars and planets. Whatever its purpose, Stonehenge has sparked debate among those who have studied it.

## Reinterpreting the Past

In the 1920s, many archaeologists and historians argued that the people who built Stonehenge could not have figured out by themselves how to build such a monument. They insisted that the builders of Stonehenge must have learned how from people of another culture. Most archaeologists believed that the pyramids of Egypt, which were built beginning in the 2600s B.C., were the oldest stone monuments in the world. The archaeologists argued that ideas about building large monuments were spread from Egypt by cultural diffusion to areas such as Britain.

However, the development of radiocarbon dating proved them wrong. In the 1960s, radiocarbon dating of the artifacts found inside the pyramids showed that stone monuments like Stonehenge were built in western Europe thousands of years before the pyramids. The builders of Stonehenge figured out how to do it on their own—not by cultural diffusion.

Most archaeologists now believe that people in different parts of the world struggled with similar problems and had similar needs. People searched for ways to feed themselves, to adapt to or change their environment, to record information, and to get along with their neighbors. In some cases, cultures adapted each other's ideas to meet their needs. In other cases, they independently came up with similar ideas on their own.

As archaeologists and historians debate the different ways in which ideas have spread throughout the world, they examine their sources again and again. They also reinterpret the information. As a result of this continuing study, the present-day view of the past is always changing. ■

▲ *Before 2800 B.C., the Egyptians made paper, similar to that shown at right, from the papyrus plant. In A.D. 105, a Chinese clerk independently invented rag paper, much like the paper shown at left. It was made from mulberry bark, old rags, and fishnet.*

■ *Why do archaeologists accept the idea of independent invention?*

## R E V I E W

1. **FOCUS** How have new historical sources and methods changed some interpretations of the past?
2. **CONNECT** What written source discussed on page 48 provides evidence of Phoenician trade?
3. **ARCHAEOLOGY** Why did radiocarbon dating force archaeologists to reconsider their assumptions about how ideas spread in the ancient world?
4. **CRITICAL THINKING** How do cultures today come into contact? What evidence of that contact might historians and archaeologists of the future find?
5. **ACTIVITY** What evidence is there of your presence in different places? Make a list of the evidence that exists of your presence at school, at a friend's home, or in a different town.

# Chapter Review

## Reviewing Key Terms

archaeology (p. 64)  oral tradition (p. 57)
artifact (p. 57)  prehistory (p. 57)
excavation (p. 65)  primary source (p. 60)
fossil (p. 57)  radiocarbon dating (p. 68)
kitchen midden (p. 73)  sarcophagus (p. 71)
megalith (p. 82)  secondary source (p. 60)

**A.** The following phrases could be headlines for newspaper articles. Pretend that you are a reporter. Write a paragraph for each headline. Use the key term in each headline at least once.

1. Artifacts from Pompeii Uncovered
2. Archaeologists Study Illinois Rubbish from 6500 B.C.
3. Lord Carnarvon Reveals 1352 B.C. Sarcophagus of King Tutankhamen
4. Archaeologists Debate the Mystery of Stonehenge Megaliths

**B.** The two words in each pair are related in some way. Write a sentence or two explaining how the words are related.

1. radiocarbon dating, fossil
2. primary source, secondary source
3. kitchen midden, excavation
4. oral tradition, prehistory
5. artifact, archaeology

## Exploring Concepts

**A.** Copy and complete the following outline to show the main ideas in the chapter.

I. Understanding history
  A. Historical evidence
    1. Nonwritten sources
    2.
  B. Evaluation of sources
    1. Primary sources
    2.
II. Examining sources
  A. Unlocking the archaeological record
    1.
    2. Study of the remains
  B. Dating the information
    1.
    2.
III. Examining archaeology
  A. Classic excavation
  B.
IV. Interpreting sources
  A. Evidence of cultural contact
  B.

**B.** Support each of the following statements with facts and details from the chapter.

1. Our understanding of history will always be changing.
2. Historians gather information about the past from many sources.
3. Historians should always evaluate the sources of their information.
4. The excavation of a site is an important part of putting together the archaeological record of an area.
5. There are many ways an archaeologist can find out the age of an artifact.
6. The goals of archaeology have changed over the years.
7. Radiocarbon dating changed people's ideas about the relationship between Stonehenge and the Great Pyramids.
8. Similar developments in writing, architecture, agriculture, and art have been found in different parts of the world. However, archaeologists do not always agree on how such similar developments took place in locations so far apart.

# Reviewing Skills

1. Some archaeologists think that Tollund Man was hanged as an offering to the gods. Is this statement a fact, an opinion, or a reasoned judgment? Explain your answer.
2. The ancient Romans traded with people from many other parts of the world. How do you know that this statement is a fact? Use examples to support your answer.
3. Archaeologists used evidence from the Koster dig to reconstruct what life was like for the settlement's inhabitants. Are their conclusions facts, opinions, or reasoned judgments? Why?
4. Look at the map on page 81 in your book. This map indicates known trade routes in A.D. 100. Notice the place names. Then compare this map with the map of Eurasia on page 508 of the Atlas. List two city or town names that appear on the map of the ancient world but do not appear on the modern map. Then list two city or town names that appear on both maps.
5. Imagine that you have discovered some artifacts in an Egyptian tomb. First you write an exact description of the artifacts. Then you write all the uses the artifacts probably had. Finally you write your feelings and ideas about the importance of the artifacts. What three types of information are you writing down?

# Using Critical Thinking

1. Historians often study popular songs of the past. Select a song from the 1940s, the 1950s, or the 1960s. What does the song tell you about Americans of that time period? Now select a modern song. What feelings or thoughts are being expressed? What does this song reveal about your generation?
2. "Those who cannot remember the past are condemned to repeat it." A great thinker made this statement about the past and its connection to the future. Think of a past mistake that you have repeated. How should you have learned a lesson? What problems in our society do we seem "condemned to repeat"?
3. We are creating written sources for archaeologists thousands of years from now. Which of these will be written sources: soup can labels, clay models, paintings, homework papers? Think of three more written sources.

# Preparing for Citizenship

1. **INTERVIEWING** A family's stories could be the beginning of an oral tradition. Interview an older family member to find out what his or her life was like at the age of 11 or 12. Prepare your questions before the interview. Some topics could be school, hobbies, games, friends, chores, or music. Write down or tape any stories from the interview. Think about your life. Has life changed? What have you learned about another time?
2. **GROUP ACTIVITY** Historians examine a variety of sources and evidence before forming an opinion. In small groups, select a major historical event to research. What sources could be used to find out what really happened? Have each member of the group bring in information about the event. Discuss your findings.
3. **COLLABORATIVE LEARNING** Archaeologists use many sources to study Mt. Vesuvius and Pompeii. With three classmates, give a presentation which compares information on a modern disaster with that on Pompeii. Two people can research Pompeii and two research the modern disaster. Together, decide how to present your comparison of ancient and modern sources.

# Unit 2
# The Earliest People

These people are preparing a feast fit for a king. The farmers are carrying grain. The herders are bringing livestock. This mosaic was made 4,500 years ago in Ur, a city in what is now Iraq. Our earliest ancestors lived by hunting and gathering whatever food they could find. After they learned to farm, small settlements, towns, and then cities such as Ur began to grow.

# 3,000,000 B.C.

The Standard of Ur. Sumerian mosaic, c. 2500 B.C. British Museum, London

2000 B.C.

# Chapter 4

## *The Depths of Time*

Pieces of bone, chipped stones, and the ashes of ancient campfires—these are the clues that have helped archaeologists uncover the story of our earliest ancestors. This story goes back to a time when simple discoveries, such as toolmaking or fire building, represented great achievements.

**3,000,000 B.C.** Early humans hunt wild animals and gather wild plants on the plains of what is now East Africa (above).

| 3,500,000 | 3,000,000 | 2,500,000 | 2,000,000 |
|---|---|---|---|

**2,500,000 B.C.** Early humans make the first stone tools, like the hand-axe above. With stone tools, people can hunt and gather foods more easily.

# 3,000,000 B.C.

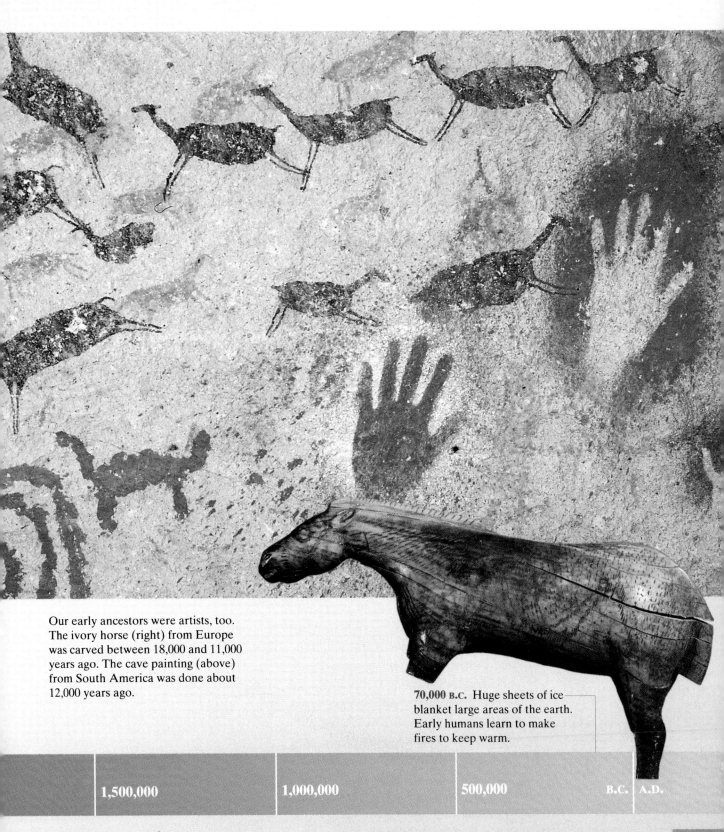

Our early ancestors were artists, too. The ivory horse (right) from Europe was carved between 18,000 and 11,000 years ago. The cave painting (above) from South America was done about 12,000 years ago.

**70,000 B.C.** Huge sheets of ice blanket large areas of the earth. Early humans learn to make fires to keep warm.

| 1,500,000 | 1,000,000 | 500,000 | B.C. | A.D. |
|---|---|---|---|---|

# 10,000 B.C.

3,500,000

3,000,000          10,000

L E S S O N   1

# Uncovering Clues to Our Past

**THINKING**
**F O C U S**

*What have scientists learned about our earliest ancestors?*

## Key Term

• glacier

O n the morning of November 30, 1974, I awoke, as I usually do on a field expedition, at daybreak. I was in Ethiopia, camped on the edge of a small muddy river, the Awash, at a place called Hadar. . . .

As a paleoanthropologist—one who studies the fossils of human ancestors—I am superstitious. Many of us are, because the work we do depends a great deal on luck. The fossils we study are extremely rare, and quite a few distinguished paleoanthropologists have gone a lifetime without finding a single one. I am one of the more fortunate. This was only my third year in the field at Hadar, and I had already found several. I know I am lucky, and I don't try to hide it. . . . When I got up that morning I felt it was one of those days when you should press your luck. One of those days when something terrific might happen.

Donald Johanson and Maitland Eddy,
*Lucy: The Beginnings of Humankind*, 1981

Something terrific did happen to Don Johanson, the archaeologist who wrote the above description. On that day, he and fellow scientist Tom Gray discovered the bones of an exceptionally complete skeleton of an early human ancestor. Johanson and his team named their skeleton Lucy.

Lucy is over 3 million years old and one of the oldest skeletons yet found. Her head was about the size of a baseball, so her brain must have been quite small. Nevertheless, she walked on two feet just as modern humans do. By studying Lucy, archaeologists have learned a lot about our earliest ancestors.

➤ *Don Johanson, shown here on a dig in Africa, made one of the most important discoveries in archaeology when he and his team found Lucy.*

90

## Clues from Archaeology

Archaeologists learn about ancient human cultures by studying the artifacts that those cultures left behind. Using this and other methods, archaeologists and historians have put together a good picture of the last few thousand years of human history. But the farther back in time we go, the more incomplete is the evidence available to archaeologists. To learn about our earliest ancestors, archaeologists rely on their analysis of fossil bones, tools, and other artifacts.

### Fossil Finds

Archaeologists rarely find complete fossil skeletons. Instead, they usually find bone fragments so small that few people would even notice them. They fit these bone fragments together like the pieces of a puzzle. All of the pieces together might form the back of a skull, a jawbone with a few teeth, or part of a leg bone and kneecap.

To the untrained eye, fossil bones are not much to look at. However, a trained scientist can learn a lot about our ancestors from these bones. Take a look at the Lucy skeleton on the right. By piecing together these bone fragments, Johanson and Gray found that Lucy was only about 3.5 feet tall, shorter than an average five-year-old today.

Scientists also gathered many other bits of information about Lucy by carefully analyzing the bones. From the shape of the pelvic bone, they could tell that she was female. From the size and shape of the leg bones, they determined that she walked upright and was

▼ *Lucy, shown below, is one of the most complete early skeletons ever found. Note how scientists have been able to piece the skeleton together even though many of the bones are still missing. Johanson and his team found Lucy near the site shown in the picture at left, at Hadar, Ethiopia, in eastern Africa.*

Scientists often provide a date for an important event, such as when a particular species appeared on earth. However, because no written records exist, scientists can only estimate the date. When estimating, they often use the Latin word circa, meaning "approximately." Circa is often abbreviated c.

about 25 years old when she died. And finally, the skull bones provided clues about the size of her brain—approximately one-third the size of the brain of modern humans.

Sometimes scientists find other artifacts along with fossil bones. In 1961, Louis and Mary Leakey, a husband-and-wife team working in eastern Africa, found fossil bones in the same layer of earth with simple stone tools. The Leakeys concluded that the fossils were the remains of early humans who had made and used these tools. They gave these early people the name *Homo habilis*, which means "handy human." Scientists use a two-word Latin name, such as *Homo habilis*, to distinguish one species, or type, of organism from another. The first word is the name of the genus—the large group to which the species belongs. The second word describes a characteristic of the individual species.

In addition to tools, archaeologists sometimes find the crushed bones of animals that were eaten by early human ancestors. They may also find ashes from prehistoric campfires. They combine the evidence they find with fossils and tools to put together a picture of how our ancestors changed over time.

## Earliest Ancestors

Lucy belongs to the oldest group of human ancestors, which are also known as australopithecines *(aw stray low PITH uh synz)*. Various groups of australopithecines lived between 3.75 million and 1 million years ago.

➤ Archaeologists make careful records of where they have found fossils, tools, and other artifacts. This information helps them piece together a picture of how our early ancestors may have lived.

Archaeologists have found australopithecine fossils throughout Africa. The first such fossil found, a child's skull, was discovered at Taung, in South Africa. Raymond Dart, the scientist who made this important discovery in 1924, was the first person to recognize the humanlike features of australopithecines. In the 1950s, Louis Leakey found more australopithecine fossils in the Olduvai *(OL duh vy)* Gorge in eastern Africa.

Although scientists disagree about the exact relationship

between the australopithecines and modern humans, they do agree that *Homo habilis* was one of our direct ancestors. *Homo habilis* lived from about 2.5 to 1.5 million years ago. These early ancestors had larger brains and more humanlike teeth and jaws than the australopithecines.

*Homo habilis* gave rise to another type of early human called *Homo erectus*. The oldest *Homo erectus* fossils have been found in Africa. They are about 1.5 million years old.

*Homo erectus* had a larger brain than *Homo habilis*. These early humans also made more complex tools than *Homo habilis* did. In addition, they were the first of our ancestors to leave Africa. Fossils of *Homo erectus* that date from 750,000 years ago have been found in Asia. Fossils of *Homo erectus* that date from 500,000 years ago have been found in Europe.

## Modern Humans

By about 200,000 years ago, *Homo erectus* had died out. At around the same time, modern humans arose. Scientists call modern humans *Homo sapiens*, which means "wise human." You are a member of the group called *Homo sapiens*.

The earliest *Homo sapiens* fossils are about 150,000 years old. These fossils are called Neanderthal after the Neander Valley in Germany, where fossils of this type were first found. Scientists distinguish Neanderthal fossils from those of *Homo erectus* by the size of the brain. The Neanderthals had a much larger brain than *Homo erectus*. Neanderthals also made more complex tools.

Although scientists classify the Neanderthals as modern humans, they did not look exactly like us. They had distinctive bony ridges above their eyes. Most Neanderthals had a protruding mouth and a very small chin.

The first completely modern-looking humans are called the Cro-Magnons. Fossils of these early humans were first found in the Cro-Magnon caves in southwestern France. These fossils date from about 40,000 years ago. Archaeologists have also discovered Cro-Magnon sites on other continents, including Africa and Asia. The locations of many of these sites are shown on the map on page 95.

Throughout early human history, the brain became larger. Thus, our human ancestors became more able toolmakers.

▲ *By fitting together pieces of fossil bone found in La Ferrasie, France, scientists reconstructed this Neanderthal skull.*

▼ *The map below shows where and when fossil remains of early human ancestors were found.*

**The Discovery of Fossil Sites**

Homo sapiens, 1856

Neander Valley

EUROPE

ASIA

*Mediterranean Sea*

AFRICA

Australopithecines, 1974-1975 — Hadar

*Nile R.*

Australopithecines, 1959; *Homo habilis*, 1960 — Olduvai

*INDIAN OCEAN*

Homo erectus, 1891 — Trinil

Australopithecines, 1924

ATLANTIC OCEAN — Taung

| 0 | 1500 | 3000 mi. |

| 0 | 1500 | 3000 km |

Robinson Projection

The Depths of Time

Toolmaking began with *Homo habilis* about 2.5 million years ago. This very important development marks the beginning of the Paleolithic *(pay lee oh LIHTH ihk)* Age, or Old Stone Age, which scientists believe ended about 10,000 B.C. in Europe and at varying times in other parts of the world.

The discovery of Stone Age tools has given us clues to the Paleolithic culture. You can find other clues to our past by studying geology. ■

## The Ice Age

Geologists—scientists who study the earth—have learned that at times in our planet's history, huge sheets of ice and snow called **glaciers** covered large areas of the earth. Today, in the Northern Hemisphere, glaciers cover parts of Alaska, Canada, Scandinavia, and the Soviet Union. However, thousands of years ago, glaciers extended from the North Pole southward into the middle latitudes of North America, Europe, and Asia. Glaciers also covered parts of South America, Africa, New Zealand, and Australia.

From about 2.5 million years ago until about 12,000 years ago, glaciers advanced and retreated

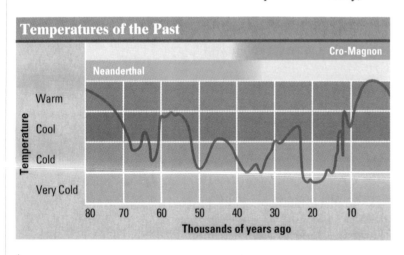

**Temperatures of the Past**

Cro-Magnon

Neanderthal

Warm
Cool
Cold
Very Cold

Temperature

80  70  60  50  40  30  20  10

**Thousands of years ago**

▲ *Note the wide variations in temperature shown on the graph above.*

➤ *Glaciers still exist in very cold parts of the world. Glaciers form when snow falls year after year but only partially melts. This melted snow then becomes ice. As more snow falls, the glacier gets larger and heavier, causing it to move.*

94

Map legend:
- ● Homo habilis
- ● Neanderthal
- → Migration route
- ● Homo erectus
- ● Cro-Magnon
- ▨ Ice sheet, 18,000 years ago

0    2000    4000 mi.
0    2000    4000 km
Robinson Projection

across the surface of the earth. This period was called the Ice Age. However, it included warmer periods as well as periods of intense cold. Each of these periods lasted thousands of years. During cold periods huge glaciers formed. During warmer periods the glaciers melted and retreated.

Adapting to the glacial periods was a challenge for our ancestors. Without a thick coat of fur, they had to find other ways to keep warm. *Homo erectus* learned to make fire. *Homo sapiens* sewed clothing from animal hides.

The glaciers also opened up new worlds for our ancestors. With much of the world's water frozen in these blankets of ice, the level of the oceans dropped dramatically. Land bridges, previously covered by water, emerged. One such land bridge connected Asia with the Americas across what is now the Bering Strait. Land bridges also linked the islands of Southeast Asia with Australia.

Look at the map on this page. Note how these land bridges made it possible for early humans to follow the animals they hunted into new lands. In this way, as the map above shows, our earliest ancestors colonized every continent except Antarctica. ■

▲ *Note how the presence of land bridges allowed early humans to migrate from southern Africa to Europe, Asia, Australia, and the Americas.*

■ *What can geologists tell us about conditions during the Ice Age?*

---

## R E V I E W

1. **FOCUS** What have scientists learned about our earliest ancestors?

2. **CONNECT** What method would archaeologists use to date the remains of early human ancestors?

3. **GEOGRAPHY** How did conditions during the Ice Age make it possible for human settlement to spread to new areas?

4. **CRITICAL THINKING** What evidence might scientists have used to discover that *Homo erectus* was able to make fires?

5. **ACTIVITY** Make a poster or a three-dimensional scene showing how people adapted to the cold temperatures of the Ice Age.

# Organizing Fossil Finds

## Here's Why

A table is one way to organize information so that it is clear and easy to read. Bus schedules, television listings, and team standings are usually presented in table form. Suppose you want to get a quick overall picture of where evidence of early humans has been found. Making a table can help you organize that information.

## Here's How

Look at the table below. Read the title. It tells you what kind of information the table contains. The table shows when and where some of the evidence of early humans has been found.

The information is arranged in rows and columns. Rows run across the table; columns run down the table. Look at the headings at the top of each column—Type, Location, Year, Discoverer. A heading tells what kind of facts is in each column.

Suppose you want to know where evidence of *Australopithecus* has been found. Look in the column headed "Type" to find *Australopithecus*. You will find two entries for *Australopithecus* because evidence of *Australopithecus* has been found in at least two locations. Then move across to the column headed "Location." Now you have the information: evidence of *Australopithecus* sites has been found in Taung, South Africa, and in Hadar, Ethiopia.

Continue across to the "Year" column. The two dates are 1924 and 1974. Where was evidence of *Australopithecus* found first?

Has all evidence of early humans been found in the same part of the world? By reading down the column headed "Location," you can quickly see that discoveries have been made in many different places.

## Try It

Make a table comparing *Homo habilis, Homo erectus,* and *Homo sapiens.* Use the following terms as column headings: Type, Time Period, Physical Development, and Lifestyle. Use the information presented in this chapter to help you fill in the table.

## Apply It

Make a table showing a week's homework assignments. What title will you use? What will the column headings be? How can you use the table?

### Evidence of Early Humans

| Type | Location | Year | Discoverer |
|------|----------|------|------------|
| *Australopithecus* | Taung, South Africa | 1924 | Raymond Dart |
| *Australopithecus* | Hadar, Ethiopia | 1974 | Donald Johanson |
| *Homo erectus* | Trinil (Java), Indonesia | 1891 | Eugène Dubois |
| *Homo erectus* | Terra Amata, France | 1965 | Henry de Lumley |
| *Homo sapiens* (Neanderthal) | Neander Valley, West Germany | 1856 | Johann Fuhlroyt and Herman Schaaffhausen |
| *Homo sapiens* (Neanderthal) | Le Moustier, France | 1908 | Marcellin Boule |
| *Homo sapiens* (Neanderthal) | Shanidar, Iraq | 1953 | Ralph Solecki |
| *Homo sapiens* (Cro-Magnon) | Altamira, Spain | 1879 | Marcelino de Sautuola |
| *Homo sapiens* (Cro-Magnon) | Lascaux Cave, France | 1940 | Henri Breuil |

Chapter 4

L E S S O N    2

# The Development of Culture

Imagine you could be moved back in time about two million years to the plains of eastern Africa. You find yourself settled on the shores of a large, quiet lake. Resting under the shade of a tree, you soak up the unfamiliar landscape.

Hours pass, and you begin to get hungry. At home, you might have gone to the kitchen for a snack. What will you do here on the plains of ancient Africa? You search along the lake shore for food but collect only a few sour berries. How will you survive?

Two naked persons walk down to the lake not far from you. Your only hope of survival is to make friends with them. You put on a friendly smile and walk towards them.

Their first reaction to you is to laugh. Giggling, they point at your clothes and shoes. You point to your open mouth to show them you are hungry. They nod, talk to each other in a strange language, and motion for you to wait.

One person walks off toward a field. The other person picks up two rocks and begins striking one

**THINKING FOCUS**

*Why were toolmaking and language important for the development of human culture?*

### Key Term

• technology

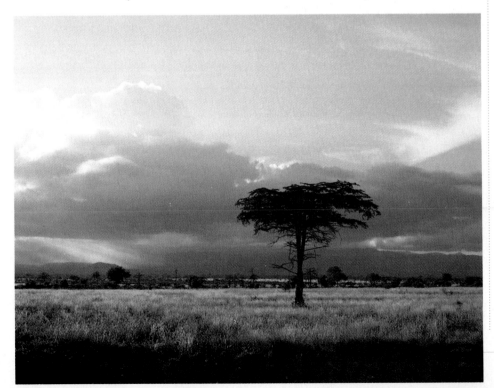

◄ *The lush lands of eastern Africa were a place where early humans lived.*

against the other, to make a sharp edge. Soon the first person returns with a bone. The people place it on the ground and pound it with the sharpened stone. They invite you to eat the marrow found inside the bone.

During your imaginary visit, you would come to appreciate the skill your friends possess at finding food. You might also be impressed with the way they are able to make simple tools from the materials at hand to meet their needs.

## Making Tools

The earliest flint tools were not complicated, but even these simple stone tools took skill and planning. First, the tool-maker had to choose the right kind of stone. The stone had to be hard enough not to crumble or shatter when struck. However it could not be so hard that it couldn't be chipped.

After finding a suitable stone, the toolmaker had to shape it into a tool. This task was usually done by striking that stone with another stone. By hitting the first stone at different angles, early toolmakers could make different kinds of tools. Even the small flakes that flew from the stone were useful. Their edges were almost as sharp as a razor.

Tools made life easier for early humans. Using tools, people could take advantage of a wider range of food sources. They were no longer limited to what they could kill or gather with their bare hands. With the sharp stone flakes, they could butcher larger animals, such as elephants, rhinos, and hippos. With sharpened pieces of antler, they could dig for underground roots.

### Early Tools

As far as we know, *Homo habilis* was the first of our early ancestors to make tools. The stone flakes found with *Homo habilis* fossils date back 2.5 million years.

▼ *Early humans used stones from landscapes similar to the one shown below. A variety of tools could be made from stones like the one at the far right.*

They were probably used for cutting meat.

As humans slowly developed and changed, so did their tools. The tools of *Homo erectus* were more sophisticated than the earlier tools. For example, *Homo erectus* made hand-axes with edges that could cut better than the tools of *Homo habilis.* Hand-axes were mainly used for butchering animals, but the patterns of wear show that they were also used for digging roots and cutting wood.

Early toolmaking marked the dawn of technology. **Technology** includes all the tools, methods, and materials that people use to control and improve their lives.

### Homo sapiens' Tools

*Homo erectus* used the same tool for a variety of purposes.

In contrast, early *Homo sapiens,* such as the Neanderthals, made tools that were used for specific purposes. They made spear points for hunting and thin scrapers for cleaning hides. They made piercing tools to poke holes in the hides so they could lace the hides together to make simple clothing. These tools helped the Neanderthals survive in the cold climate of Europe during the Ice Age.

Later *Homo sapiens*, such as the Cro-Magnons, made more sophisticated tools. They carved fishhooks, needles, and three-pronged fishing spears from pieces of bone or antler. They even made specific tools for creating other tools. Notice the type of tool the person in the Moment in Time on the following page has just made.

*The Neanderthal spear point, shown below, is an example of the careful workmanship of the period.*

## UNDERSTANDING TECHNOLOGY

Think back to your imaginary trip into the past. Your new found friends used a simple tool to obtain food from the inside of a bone.

### Hand-axe to Jackhammer

Toolmaking by early humans marked the beginning of technology, the knowledge that people use to fashion tools. Technology can be simple, such as modifying a stone into a hand-axe. Or it can be complex, such as shaping steel into a jackhammer.

### Importance of Technology

Think of a few ways technology has improved the quality of life throughout history. First, technology can make work easier. If you needed wood, would you rather search for a fallen tree or buzz through an upright tree with a saw?

Second, technology helps people produce more goods. Before the printing press was invented, people had to painstakingly copy books by hand. Books were thus extremely rare and expensive.

Finally, technology can improve people's lives. For instance, doctors can now help prevent blindness by using lasers to perform some types of eye surgery.

As our technology has changed, our way of life has changed. The earliest hand-axe was merely the beginning. Just as early technology allowed humans to hunt and cook in new ways, so too, modern technology has helped us to live and work in different ways.

# A Cro-Magnon Toolmaker

11:17 A.M., April 23, 12,011 B.C.
In a clearing near a cave in
La Madeleine, France

**Clean-shaven Face**
He could have used his sharp
carving tools to shave this morning.

**Teeth**
His teeth show no decay.
Perhaps that's because of
his healthy diet of roasted
meat, raspberries, nuts,
acorns, and grasses.

**Harpoon**
He has just completed this
fine piece. Perhaps he'll
give it to his oldest son.
The boy has been begging
to go hunting with the men.

**Flint Burin**
With this tool he carves other
tools—from simple needles to
harpoons and spear throwers.

**Necklace**
He traded one of his best spear
throwers for this bone and tooth
necklace. The tools he makes are
so good that even people from
other clans will trade valuable
objects to get one.

**Tunic**
His clothes keep him warm as
long as the sun is high overhead. When the clan moves to
its summer camp, he plans to
build his house facing the sun.

**Trousers**
His aunt sewed these pants
with an antler needle and fiber
thread six moons ago. She's the
fastest seamstress in their clan
of 29 people.

**Shoes**
They protect his feet from the
tiny, sharp pieces of antler that flew
off as he worked on his harpoon.

## Importance of Tools

With more than a hundred kinds of tools, the Cro-Magnons and other modern humans were able to take full advantage of their surroundings. They thrived in all different parts of the world, from the frozen arctic to the tropical jungles.

The ability to make tools was a key factor in the survival of early humans. Another key factor was the ability of early humans to create and use language. ■

■ *How did early humans make and use tools?*

# Using Language

Think back to your imaginary visit to ancient Africa. Remember that you managed to survive because you made friends with people who lived there. To show them you were hungry, you pointed to your open mouth. With gestures like this you could communicate.

People often communicate with one another without using language. For example, when you smile, cry, or shrug your shoulders, you are communicating. Indeed, all animals communicate in one way or another. Humans, however, are the only animals that can communicate through language. A bird may sing to communicate danger or attract a mate, but it has a limited number of songs for a limited number of purposes. When you use language, you can talk about the past or the future. You can discuss real things or imaginary things. You can even invent new words and put them together in new ways.

When did our early ancestors develop their ability to use language? No one knows for certain. However, scientists have learned that specific parts of the brain are involved in using language. Fossil skulls of *Homo habilis*, *Homo erectus*, and early *Homo sapiens* show that the parts of the human brain important for language became larger over time. Therefore, scientists conclude that humans have had an increasing ability to create and use language beginning around 2.5 million years ago.

Why was language important to early humans? Language allowed them to share information, to work together, and to pass on their knowledge and traditions. With language, early humans could discuss the advantages of different kinds of tools or plan hunting strategies. In other words, the ability to use language spurred the development of early human culture. ■

■ *Why was language important to early humans?*

## REVIEW

1. **FOCUS** Why were toolmaking and language important for the development of human culture?

2. **CONNECT** Discuss how tools changed over time, beginning with the tools developed by *Homo habilis* and ending with those used by the Cro-Magnons. How did this change in tools correspond to a change in brain size?

3. **HISTORY** How did tools help early humans survive?

4. **CULTURE** How is language more complex than other forms of animal communication?

5. **CRITICAL THINKING** How might an increasing ability to use language have affected the early humans' abilities to make tools?

6. **ACTIVITY** Invent a tool that will help you do something more easily. Make a drawing of the tool. Explain how the tool will be used and what it is made of.

The Depths of Time

# Attar

*Leonard Wibberley*

*Hunting for food was serious business for early humans. In this selection from* Attar of the Ice Valley, *a young boy finds an unexpected hunting partner. His discovery changes how he and his descendants hunt wild animals.*

This is one author's idea about how early hunter-gatherers developed a new approach to hunting.

*rua*    a deer

Attar began to see that the dungo had in fact been hunting with him rather than on his own. There was enough in the dungo's actions to suggest that it had deliberately driven the rua to where Attar had been hiding.

This was so great a wonder for Attar that he could scarcely believe it. Was it possible that there could be a lasting comradeship between a man and a dungo? Was it possible that they could help each other to get food, for the speed of the dungo would be of great aid in running down game? It often happened that a spear wounded an animal and then the man who had thrown the spear had to trail the animal, sometimes for days, before his prey was sufficiently exhausted for him to catch and kill it. But if he, Attar, could wound an animal and then the dungo could bring it down and kill it, the whole art of hunting would be changed.

These ideas came to him unbidden and greatly excited him. If this was so—if this new way of hunting was what the Great Bear had planned to bring about—there was one point that had to be made clear. The point was this: that the man was the master and director of the hunt and the dungo would be the assistant. The dungo must not get the idea that he was master and the man the assistant.

Watching the dungo gorging itself on the rua, Attar knew that he must assert his mastery. "Move," he cried. "That is my kill." And he took the butt end of his spear and brought it down sharply over the dungo's rump. The dungo howled, snarled, and backed away, but only an inch or two.

"Off," cried Attar. "Away. The rua is mine."

The dungo snarled and, made brave by the smell of the blood, crouched to leap at Attar despite its injured leg. Attar brought the shaft of the spear down sharply again on the animal's back. This time it yelped and moved away and, settling down on the snow, glared at Attar from yellow eyes full of anger.

"Farther," said Attar. "Move back more." He feinted as if to clout the dingo again, and without waiting for the blow, it slunk back in the snow.

"Good," said Attar. "Now you can eat. But it is I who feed you. You do not feed me." He took one of the snow rabbits he had killed and threw it at the dungo. The dungo disposed of the rabbit in three tearing gulps.

"That will do you," said Attar. "You will have more of the rua later. I myself have eaten nothing for two days." He was, in fact, so hungry that he trembled. With the edge of his spear, he cut a sliver of neck meat from the rua and ate it. It was delicious and immediately gave him strength. He cut another strip of the tender meat and that tasted just as good.

The dungo came bellying closer to him, its lips curled back a little, baring its teeth. Attar hit it on the nose, firmly but not savagely, with his spear shaft. The dungo moved back, yelping. Then Attar cut him a piece of meat and gave it to him. This time, having disposed of the meat with one gulp, the dungo moved its large tail slowly from side to side. Attar moved to place himself between the rua and the dungo and reached out a hand to pat the dungo on the head. The dungo not only accepted the pat but gave Attar's hand a brief lick.

"You and I, then, will hunt together, dungo," said Attar. "It is a wonder and something that has never been heard of before. But it is plain that by killing Black Ear I have become bound to you. This has been the plan of the Great Bear."

It was not Teth and Gurth who came to help Attar carry the carcass of the rua, but Odo, a young hunter not much older than Attar himself. He was especially skillful in catching birds and small animals and very good-natured. Everybody liked him because he was willing. Also, he could make very fine sounds by blowing through the hollow thighbone of a deer in which he had cut a hole in a special place.

The sounds he made were like the wind in all its differing moods—the morning wind and the night wind, which are quite different from each other, and also the wind of summer and that of winter; or to put it another way, which was the way Attar and his people put it, the wind of the flowers and the wind of the ice. All these varieties of sounds Odo could make on the thighbone of the deer. Although others could produce some sounds from it, none could do it with the accuracy and delicacy of Odo. For this, then, as well as his other qualities, he was very popular in his tribe, and nobody grumbled at him that he captured only small animals and birds when he went hunting.

As he approached Attar, however, he saw the dungo sitting in the snow beyond the rua and he stopped immediately. He surveyed the scene for a moment and then said softly to Attar, his

*feint*   to fake an attack

*carcass*   the dead body of an animal

103

eyes on the dungo, "I will move behind him, and when he turns his head to watch me, take him in the chest with your spear."

Attar laughed. "Welcome, Odo," he said. "Meet my new hunting mate. Mikdoo." He made up the name Mikdoo on the spur of the moment, and it was entirely suitable, for it meant Son of the Black One.

"If you run hunting with such as that," said Odo, "you will soon be in the miserable Cave of the Bear." He started to back away, frightened. "He has bitten you, Attar, and made you into a dungo like himself. That has happened before."

"No, Odo," said Attar. "He has not bitten me. See. We are friends." He reached down and touched the dungo's ears. The mane of thicker hair on the dungo's shoulders was bristling because of the presence of Odo, but it still permitted Attar to touch it. "I will tell you all about it," said Attar, and did so, without elaboration.

"You see, then, how it is," he concluded. "This is now my dungo. But let us get the rua up to the cave, where Huru will tell us if such a thing has ever happened before."

"First send the dungo away," said Odo.

"I cannot," said Attar. "His own people will not have him. I have touched him. He has my scent on him. They will tear him to pieces if he approaches them."

"Attar," said Odo. "You also have the scent of the dungo on you. I do not know if the others are going to agree with your pact with the dungo."

Attar shrugged. "We will see what will happen," he said. "This is not something I decided. It is something that was decided for me. Come, let us pick up the rua."

They slung the carcass on their spears and set off for the cave. The going was hard because the strange warm wind that had followed the storm had melted the snow, which was soft in many places where a few hours before it had been firm. Also, the weight of the rua made them sink even in the firmer places. They had not gone far before they were both sweating.

They sweated not only from the weight of the deer but from the warmth of the wind, which had started fitfully and was now blowing gently but evenly down from the ice cliffs. On the top of the cliffs themselves, three thousand feet above the floor of the valley, the air was colder than ever. But this mass of cold air, being heavy, tumbled down the cliff face and, in so doing, warmed up, so that the wind on the valley floor was like the south wind of summer. It first softened the snow and then melted it.

The two young hunters were two hours getting the rua back to the cave, and in that time a river of melted snow formed and was flowing over the still frozen surface of the true river down the center of the valley. High up on the cliffs, the terrible pendants

*pendant* something hanging from something else

of ice still draped the valley sides. Lower down, the black face of rocks began to show through the shroud of snow and ice.

A matting of drab brown grass and undergrowth appeared here and there, and from first one side of the valley and then the other came a rumbling growl, angry and deep. Masses of snow thundered downward to the valley in horrifying avalanches. It was, in fact, dangerous to be traveling along the valley, and Odo and Attar moved as fast as they could to get to the safety of the cave before they were cut off or trapped by a moving mass of snow.

All the while Mikdoo, the dungo, followed along, snarling at the avalanches, limping from his wound, and thoroughly uncomfortable because of the wetness of his coat, now drenched with melted snow. Mikdoo did not follow close. He kept some distance away and several times stopped as if debating whether to follow farther. But follow he did. Once, however, he stopped on a small knoll in the bottom of the valley and turned to where his home lay. Lifting his snout, he gave a long, mournful howl, either of pleading to be allowed to return or of farewell. Whatever the message, it was not answered, and Mikdoo started once again to follow Attar.

A decision had been made. Mikdoo would hunt with men in the future. He would lose his old freedom but gain security. For him and his descendants, there was no way back.

*knoll*   a small rounded hill or mound

### Further Reading

*The Ice Is Coming*. Patricia Wrightson. This fantasy takes place in present-day Australia, but the hero, an aborigine boy, must adopt the lifestyle of his prehistoric ancestors to prevent a second Ice Age.

*Light in the Mountain*. Margaret J. Anderson. Surviving in a harsh and cold climate is a challenge for the early Maori people of New Zealand.

*Prehistory*. Keith Branigan. Using evidence from early archaeological sites, the author recreates the food, technology, society, and religion of prehistoric peoples.

*The Way Home*. Joan Phipson. Three children, lost in the Australian Outback after an accident, travel between the present and the prehistoric time of early Aborigines while finding their way home.

LESSON 3

# Hunters and Gatherers

### THINKING FOCUS

*How did human culture develop from the time of* Homo erectus *to the time of the Cro-Magnons?*

### Key Terms

- hunter-gatherer
- band

▼ *Fire played an important role in the lives of* Homo erectus, *allowing them to live in cold climates, hunt large animals, and cook meat.*

A group of people sit in a circle around a large campfire. The leaping flames light up their faces, which shine with warmth and pleasure. A master storyteller has captured their attention with a fascinating tale. He is reciting a legend about a magic hunter who can transform himself into the animals he hunts. The storyteller's voice falls softly as he comes to the end of the story. The people sitting around the campfire are still and peaceful. The only other sounds are the crackle of the fire and the howl of a lone wolf baying in the distance.

The scene described in the paragraph above could have taken place at a present-day outing in northern Michigan. Or it could just as easily have taken place at a campsite along the shores of the Mediterranean Sea 400,000 years ago. Since prehistoric times, people have enjoyed gathering together around the light and the warmth of campfires. However, for early humans, fire was much more than a source of comfort—it was essential for survival.

## Early Fire Users

For hundreds of thousands of years during the glacial periods of the Ice Age, the climate in most of the Northern Hemisphere was much colder than it is today. Southern Europe, which now has a warm climate, was as cold as northern Alaska is today. To survive in this harsh world, people had to learn how to use fire. Archaeological evidence shows that groups of *Homo erectus* who lived in the colder parts of Europe and Asia were among the first humans to discover the advantages of building fires.

### Hunting and Gathering

Fire was important to *Homo erectus* for many reasons. It provided warmth and scared off dangerous animals. Early people also used fire to roast raw meat, making it tastier and easier to digest.

By studying these fire pits and other remains, archaeologists have learned a lot about how *Homo erectus* lived. Like all other Paleolithic peoples, these early humans were **hunter-gatherers.** That is, they hunted wild animals and gathered wild plants for food.

*Homo erectus* lived in **bands**—small, loosely organized groups of perhaps 20 to 30 individuals. During the year, they moved over a wide area, searching for ripe plants and following migrating animals. Evidence from sites in Spain indicates that groups of *Homo erectus* worked together to drive large animals, such as elephants, rhinos, and wild oxen, into traps. Coordinating such group hunting must have required some type of social organization and probably some type of language.

Let's visit a site called Terra Amata on the Mediterranean coast of southern France. Here *Homo erectus* set up a camp every spring for several years in a row.

### Terra Amata

Your first view of Terra Amata might give you a shock. All you would see are modern buildings, several stories high, surrounded by busy streets. Early humans camped on this spot, where the modern city of Nice, France, now stands. Before the apartment buildings went up, archaeologists studied this site in detail.

The first thing archaeologists found at Terra Amata was the foundation of a hut large enough to sleep about 20 people. The hut was most likely built of sturdy branches, with stones around the base of the hut for support.

At the center of the hut, archaeologists found the remains of a fire pit. Small stones on one side of the fire pit shielded the fire from the wind. The people of Terra Amata might have slept on animal hides near the pit, huddled close to the fire for warmth.

Near the fire pit was a flat stone. The people of Terra Amata probably used this hard surface for shaping their tools. Stone flakes were scattered all around the area. These flakes flew off as people chipped rocks into tools.

A second flat stone in another corner of the hut probably served as a cutting board for meat. The surface of this stone had many small scratches, and animal bones were strewn all around. From

*Plants were an important part of the diet of Homo erectus. Hunters would often learn which plants were edible by watching what animals ate.*

*Oval huts built at Terra Amata by visiting hunters probably looked something like this.*

Work space

Work space

Hearth

Work space

*Residents of Terra Amata ate a number of different kinds of foods, including almonds, plants, and oysters.*

■ *Based on evidence from Terra Amata, describe how Homo erectus lived.*

these bones archaeologists learned what kinds of meat the people of Terra Amata ate.

Deer was the most common meat, but they also ate many other types of animals, including elephants, oysters, and turtles.

By studying the layers of sand, archaeologists learned that Terra Amata was occupied for only a few days or a week at a time. If people had stayed there longer, the sand would have been more packed down. The layers also show that people came back and rebuilt their huts at Terra Amata year after year.

Because the area around Terra Amata was rich in resources, it was a good place to live. The land teemed with animals for hunting. People gathered dandelion leaves, wild wheat, almonds, figs, berries, and quail eggs. They could spear salmon in the rivers and harvest seafood from the Mediterranean Sea. Fresh water bubbled up from a nearby spring. It's no wonder that *Homo erectus* returned to Terra Amata again and again.

Human life changed little during the million years that *Homo erectus* roamed the earth. Then early *Homo sapiens*, the Neanderthals, appeared. Although the Neanderthal people still lived as hunter-gatherers, their culture became more complex. Community became more important to them. ■

## The Neanderthals: Community Builders

### How Do We Know?

**HISTORY** *How do scientists classify fossil remains? Archaeologists carefully study each fossil bone, tooth, and artifact discovered at one site. Then they compare the bones and artifacts with others already classified. Based on this comparison, they decide what species the fossil belongs to or whether it is evidence of a new species.*

In the summer of 1856, workers blasted open a cave in the cliffs bordering the Neander Valley in Germany. The cave was a quarry, rich in limestone. It was also rich in fossils. However, the workers weren't interested in old bones. They saved a few bones to show the quarry owner but chopped up most of the fossils as they dug out the limestone.

The quarry owner showed the bones to a local schoolteacher, who eventually showed them to an archaeologist. This fossil was named Neanderthal, after the valley where it was found. False conclusions based upon the Neanderthal fossil have led to many of the misconceptions people have had about early humans.

### Early Studies

Archaeologists who first studied the Neanderthal fossil concluded that these early humans were brutish people with little intelligence and bad posture. However, these archaeologists made some mistakes. Careful study of Neanderthal skulls has shown that, on average, the Neanderthal brain was at least as large as that of modern humans. In other words, Neanderthals probably were not stupid.

Reexamination of other bones has shown that, in general, Neanderthal posture was just as good as that of modern humans. However, some Neanderthals suffered from the crippling disease arthritis, just as some humans do today. The first archaeologists who studied the Neanderthal fossils failed to recognize the signs of this disease. That is why they incorrectly described all Neanderthals as stoop-shouldered people with bowed legs.

## Community Spirit

The camps Neanderthals built were generally larger than those *Homo erectus* built. This indicates that Neanderthals probably lived in larger groups—perhaps 20 to 50 people—and stayed in one place longer than *Homo erectus*.

The Neanderthals probably had a strong sense of community and took care of one another. The evidence for this is in the Neanderthals' bones. As you have read, fossils of aged Neanderthals show that some were crippled with arthritis. These people would not have survived unless other people helped them and gave them food.

Other examples of this community spirit are even more dramatic.

At Shanidar cave in present-day Iraq, archaeologists found the skeleton of a man with a birth defect that paralyzed the right side of his body. This handicapped man was probably one of the oldest people in his community when he died at age 40. All of his life, members of his community must have taken care of him. Perhaps he was valued for his wisdom, knowledge, or sense of humor, even though he could not have hunted or gathered food.

Shanidar cave also provides information about other aspects of Neanderthal culture, including burials. These Neanderthal burials are the earliest evidence we have of funeral ceremonies held to mourn the passing away of loved ones. For instance, at Shanidar, a man was buried on a bed of wildflowers gathered from nearby fields.

*Wildflowers like the trillium below were used in Neanderthal burials.*

◄ *These remains of a Neanderthal youth may be 50,000 years old. They were found in Kebara cave in modern Israel.*

The Depths of Time

At a grave in France, a teenage boy was found buried in a pit. He was lying on his right side with his head on his forearm and a pillow of flints. A stone axe and the bones of wild cattle were near his hand. The bones may be all that remain of an offering of meat placed in the pit at the time of burial. The axe and the meat suggest the Neanderthals had some belief in a life after death in which the boy would need the food and the trusted tool.

The burial sites at Shanidar show that some similarities exist between certain burial customs of the Neanderthals and the customs of some modern peoples. These similarities indicate that both early and modern humans probably have many of the same feelings about death. But however much we share with the Neanderthals, we have even more in common with our direct ancestors, the Cro-Magnons. ■

■ *What evidence do we have that the Neanderthals had a strong sense of community?*

## Cro-Magnons: Modern Humans

▼ *Cro-Magnons used spear throwers, like the one pictured here, to enable them to throw spears faster and further. A hunter would put the dull end of the spear in the hook on top of the spear thrower. Holding the thrower over his head, he would then snap his arm forward. Such a thrower would greatly improve his ability to hunt animals.*

About 35,000 years ago, the Neanderthals died out, and modern humans, the Cro-Magnons, arose. In terms of physical features, the Cro-Magnons looked like people today. In fact, if Cro-Magnons could come back to life dressed in modern clothes, you would not be able to pick them out in a crowd.

### Cro-Magnon Life

Cro-Magnons not only looked like modern people, they also had a lifestyle similar to that of modern hunter-gatherers. They used some of the same tools: nets for fishing, spear throwers for launching spears, and probably even bows and arrows. These tools were much more advanced than those of the Neanderthals. With these, the Cro-Magnons became better hunters.

### Cave Paintings

The clearest sign of the Cro-Magnons' advanced culture, however, was their art. As far as we know, the Cro-Magnons were the world's first artists. They carved

designs in their tools. They whittled small sculptures of female figures out of bone, ivory, and antlers. They painted graceful pictures of animals on cave walls. These cave paintings are so beautiful and look so much like modern paintings, that when the famous artist Pablo Picasso saw them for the first time he exclaimed, "We [modern artists] have invented nothing!"

As with many other important archaeological finds, the first cave paintings came to the attention of the modern world through a chance discovery. In 1879, a young Spanish girl and her father, Marcelino de Sautuola, were exploring a cave in northern Spain where Sautuola had found some stone tools. Sautuola had to crawl on his hands and knees to squeeze through some of the cave's narrow side chambers.

However, his daughter, Maria, was only five years old and short enough to walk through these tight passages. Maria wandered into one chamber, looked up, and saw a herd of life-sized bison painted on the ceiling. She called to her father to come see the lifelike paintings.

Sautuola was amazed by the ancient paintings. He showed them to an archaeologist, who was also very impressed. However, many other archaeologists did not believe that the cave paintings were real. One even accused Sautuola of paying an artist to paint the animals in the cave. Disgraced and disillusioned, Sautuola had the cave closed up and spoke no more about the paintings.

However, over the next 30 years, archaeologists discovered a number of caves in France with paintings similar to those found in Sautuola's cave. Research showed that these paintings, as well as those discovered by Sautuola, were authentic ancient art, painted between 12,000 and 35,000 years ago.

Some of the most stunning paintings were discovered in 1940 in a French cave called Lascaux. Four boys were playing in a forest when their dog disappeared down a hole. One of the boys lowered himself carefully down the hole to

## Across Time & Space

*The French government closed the Lascaux caves in 1963 because the visitors' breath was destroying the Paleolithic masterpieces. In 1983, the French opened a copy of the cave, called Lascaux II. In this artificial cave, artists copied the paintings using the same techniques the Cro-Magnon artists used.*

◄ *Cro-Magnon artists covered the ceiling of the entrance to the Lascaux caves, shown at left, with vivid paintings of animals. The drawing below shows the entrance to the cave.*

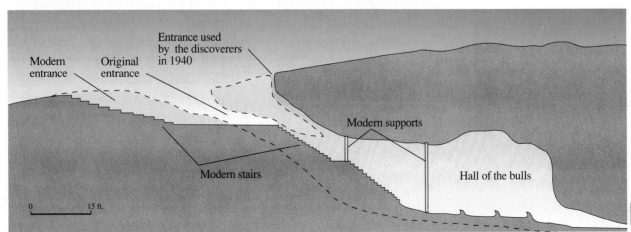

Modern entrance

Original entrance

Entrance used by the discoverers in 1940

Modern supports

Modern stairs

Hall of the bulls

0    15 ft.

▲ *The paintings in the hall of the bulls, shown above, vividly illustrate the animals hunted by Cro-Magnons. Note how the artists have used color to highlight the details of the animals' bodies.*

➤ *The overhead diagram of the Lascaux caves, shown at right, illustrates how large the caves are.*

Entrance

Hall of bulls

Passageway

N

0      30 ft.

Axial gallery

Chamber of felines

fetch the dog. When the boy returned, he was shaking. He thought he'd seen ghosts of wild animals. The next day the boys told their schoolmaster what they had found. The schoolmaster returned to the cave and crawled inside. He was astonished by what he saw. Huge, lifelike images of horses, deer, and bison covered the damp walls.

Examine these cave paintings. To see them as the Cro-Magnons did, you must imagine walking through the long, twisting passages of a dark cave. The air smells dank and moisture drips down the walls. A torch casts looming shadows in front of you, and the air is thick with smoke. You enter a large chamber, your footsteps echoing as you walk to the center of the room. Animated by the flickering light, bulls and deer seem to leap across the walls.

Perhaps these paintings played a part in hunting rituals of the Cro-Magnons. Modern hunting peoples sometimes draw pictures of animals and stab them as a way of bringing luck in the real hunt. The Cro-Magnons were probably trying to gain greater control of their unpredictable world by painting wild animals on cave walls. Magic rituals involving these paintings may have been an important part of Cro-Magnon life, because survival hinged on a successful hunt.

In time, as early people learned to tame animals and plant crops, their world became more predictable. They no longer had to rely on the magic of the paintings.

We will never know exactly what the cave paintings meant to the Cro-Magnons. Nevertheless, we can appreciate the artistic skill of the people who made these paintings. The paintings show us that the Cro-Magnons had a strong feeling for beauty and a sense of wonder like our own. Use the chart on page 114 to compare the achievements of Cro-Magnons to those of the other early humans you have learned about in this chapter. ■

■ *Why do we call the Cro-Magnons modern humans?*

## Achievements of Early Humans

| | Homo habilis, 2,500,000–1,500,000 years ago | Homo erectus, 1,500,000–200,000 years ago | Homo sapiens (Neanderthal), 200,000–35,000 years ago | Homo sapiens (Cro-Magnon), 40,000 years ago–present |
|---|---|---|---|---|
| **Tools** | Crude stone tools, 2,500,000 years ago | Hand-axe, 1,500,000 years ago | Side scraper, 100,000 years ago | Bone harpoon with barbs, 30,000 years ago |
| **Fire** | No evidence | Controlled fire, 400,000 years ago | Made fire, 70,000 years ago | Fired clay, 27,000 years ago |
| **Burial Rites** | No evidence | No evidence | Planned burial, 50,000 years ago | Bead blanket at burial, 23,000 years ago |
| **Art** | No evidence | No evidence | No evidence | Buffalo sculpture, 30,000 years ago |

## REVIEW

1. **FOCUS** How did human culture develop from the time of *Homo erectus* to the time of the Cro-Magnons?

2. **CONNECT** How has our picture of the Neanderthals changed with more careful study of early human remains?

3. **HISTORY** Which early humans first used fire, and why was fire such an important discovery?

4. **CULTURE** What evidence do we have of Cro-Magnons' advanced culture?

5. **CRITICAL THINKING** What are some stereotypes of "cavemen"? Based on what you have learned in this chapter, do you think these stereotypes are true? Explain your answer.

6. **WRITING ACTIVITY** Write a short story about a day at Terra Amata, Neander, or Lascaux. Set it in prehistoric times. Give your story a main character. Include a description of several events. Explain how your main character feels about the things that happen in his or her life.

# Recognizing Patterns

### Here's Why

Writers organize material in different patterns according to their purpose. To explain how to do something, writers may organize material in steps. To show how events relate to one another, they may use a cause-and-effect pattern. To make differences and similarities clear, a compare/contrast pattern is often used.

You will more easily understand the material you read if you can recognize the organizational pattern used.

You can then use the same pattern as you take notes.

### Here's How

The paragraphs below describe two methods that archaeologists use to date fossils and artifacts. The paragraphs are organized in a compare/contrast pattern.

Several clues tell you that these paragraphs follow a compare/contrast pattern. The first sentence tells you that you will be reading about two things—radiocarbon dating and potassium-argon dating. The second sentence provides a clue to the organizational pattern: the phrase *but how they are used differs* tells you that you will be reading about differences in the two methods.

Now read the remaining paragraphs. Each paragraph describes one of the dating methods. Look at the notebook page below. The notes show how you can use the compare/contrast pattern to organize these ideas in your notebook.

### Try It

Copy the sample notes from the notebook onto a sheet of paper. Then add information to each column about the time limit of each dating method.

### Apply It

Find an example of this same organizational pattern in another textbook. Take notes that show the compare/contrast pattern.

Radiocarbon and potassium-argon dating are two methods used by scientists to determine the age of fossils and artifacts. Both methods determine age based on the decay of radioactive elements, but how they are used differs.

Radiocarbon dating measures the breakdown of an organic material, carbon-14. Thus it is used to establish the age of once-living things—wood, bones, and shells. Using radiocarbon dating, scientists can determine the age of objects up to 60,000 years old.

Unlike radiocarbon dating, potassium-argon dating is used to determine the age of inorganic material, usually volcanic rocks. Fossil remains found in the rock are then dated according to the age of the rock. This method is not accurate for objects less than 500,000 years old. However, it can be used to determine the age of objects up to 10 million years old.

Radiocarbon Dating | Potassium-Argon Dating

Purpose: To determine age | To determine age

Method: measures breakdown of carbon-14 | Dates fossils by age of rock

Time limit:

# Chapter Review

## Reviewing Key Terms

**A.** Suppose you are an early human who has traveled forward in time to the present. You can speak English now. While talking to a person from the twentieth century, you want to explain what the following three words mean. On your own paper, write one or two sentences to describe each key term.

1. glacier
2. band
3. hunter-gatherer

**B.** Some of the following statements are true. The rest are false. Write *True* or *False* for each statement. Then rewrite the false statements to make them true.

1. Because the earth used to be warmer, glaciers covered nearly 30 percent of the earth's surface, more than today.
2. Trying to butcher an animal with a rock instead of a hand-axe showed progress.
3. *Homo erectus* may have organized themselves in bands to hunt better.
4. Hunter-gatherers would enjoy sitting around and listening to stories.

## Exploring Concepts

**A.** The diagram below should show three groups of early humans belonging to genus *Homo*. The names of two are filled in. Copy the diagram, and fill in the name of the third group. Then add to the diagram three traits, inventions, or other features of each group.

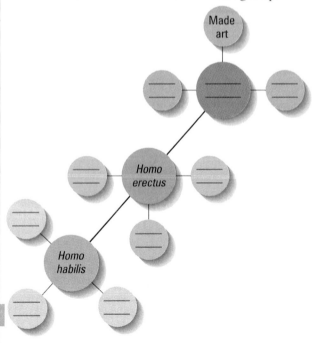

Made art

Homo erectus

Homo habilis

**B.** Support each statement with facts and details from the chapter.

1. If you look at fossil bones from early human ancestors, you will find clues about what they looked like and what their habits were.
2. You could easily tell apart the skulls of australopithecines, Cro-Magnons, and Neanderthals.
3. People have made and used tools from *Homo habilis* through *Homo sapiens*, but the tools and their uses have changed very much.
4. Because of glaciers, our ancestors could cross something we cannot.
5. Choosing the right stone was important to the early toolmakers.
6. Language is related to the development of culture.
7. *Homo erectus* was the first early human to leave Africa.
8. Although they were both *Homo sapiens*, there were many differences between Neanderthals and Cro-Magnons.

## Reviewing Skills

1. On a separate sheet of paper, copy the table Early Toolmakers. Then fill in the appropriate facts under each heading.
2. After completing the table, answer the following questions: Which tool was used for several different purposes? Which tools were made for specific purposes?
3. Review the section Modern Humans on pages 93 and 94. Then do the following:
   a. Tell what organizational pattern the author uses.
   b. Use that organizational pattern to take notes on the section.
4. Suppose you are preparing a bulletin board display that shows how much of the earth was covered by glaciers 20,000 years ago and how much is covered by glaciers today. Trace a map of the earth to make two copies and color in the appropriate areas. In what kind of book will you find the map?

| Early Toolmakers | | |
|---|---|---|
| **Type** | **Tools Used** | **Purpose** |
| *Homo habilis* | | |
| *Homo erectus* | | |
| Neanderthal | | |
| Cro-Magnon | | |

## Using Critical Thinking

1. To our ancestors, fire was more than a source of heat; it was essential for survival. Do we need fire to survive today, or have other energy sources replaced fire for our everyday needs? Explain your answer. Give specific examples of other methods or materials necessary for survival today.
2. Ancient hunter-gatherers lived very well in some areas, such as Terra Amata. There were plenty of fish, animals for hunting, leaves and berries, and fresh drinking water. How would they live in your area if all the modern conveniences and inventions were not there?
3. Scientists know that Cro-Magnons lived in huts lined with animal furs. Scientists also believe that they may have lived in caves sometimes. What evidence is reported in this chapter that supports scientists' ideas about Cro-Magnons?

## Preparing for Citizenship

1. WRITING ACTIVITY Imagine you are going back in time to observe a group of early humans. Choose the time period and one of these early human groups to observe: *Homo erectus,* Neanderthal, or Cro-Magnon. Now hide behind a rock, listen, and watch the early humans go about their daily lives. What kinds of tasks are they doing? Are the tasks helping to make their lives easier, more comfortable, or somehow better? How similar are their tasks to the jobs that we perform today? How are they different from jobs we perform today? Write down your observations and share them with the class.

2. COLLABORATIVE LEARNING Plan and create a display called "Tools of Yesterday and Today." Show early tools and the modern tools that grew out of them. Divide the class into groups of four. Then have each group choose two early tools and two modern tools to draw or make from clay. Choose early tools made from stone, shell, animal part, or wood. Then form two pairs within your group. The first pair will read about and make the early tools; the second pair will read about and make the modern tools. For each tool, write what it was made of, how it was used, who used it, and when it was used.

# Chapter 5

# *Development of Societies*

*A handful of seeds and a few captured animals helped start a quiet revolution. Instead of just harvesting wild grains and moving on, hunter-gatherers learned to save some seeds. Now they could plant crops in one place year after year. Instead of just hunting wild animals, they learned to tame them. Groups of hunter-gatherers settled down, becoming farmers and herders. Once they could control their food supply, they began to build villages and then cities.*

**c. 8500 B.C.** Groups of hunter-gatherers settle along the Tigris River in what is now the Middle East and begin farming.

| 12,500 | 10,000 | 7500 |
|---|---|---|

# 11,000 B.C.

**c. 8000–7000 B.C.** Settlers in Egypt and the Middle East begin planting crops including barley, shown above.

People learned to raise cattle and sheep to provide food and clothing. This sculpture, from about 2600 B.C., shows a milking scene. Today, shepherds like the man in Syria (below) still tend flocks of sheep.

Farmers used stone tools to tend their crops. This hoe found in Egypt dates to between 7000 and 4000 B.C.

**c. 3500 B.C.** The first cities, such as Ur in present-day Iraq, begin to develop.

| 5000 | 2500 | B.C. | A.D. |

**c. 6000 B.C.** Improved farming methods lead to larger settlements. One of the largest towns in the Middle East is Çatal Hüyük, with a population of about 5,000.

# 2000 B.C.

LESSON 1

# Learning to Farm

**THINKING**
**F O C U S**

*How did people's lifestyle change as they began to domesticate plants and animals?*

---

### Key Terms

* surplus
* environment
* domesticate
* agriculture

Imagine yourself standing on a hill overlooking a broad, rich valley. Several gazelles are grazing on tall grasses. A fish breaks the surface of a peaceful lake. Birds are nesting in the dense reeds along the shore. In the air is the spicy smell of evergreen shrubs. You reach down and pick a handful of ripe berries, popping them into your mouth one by one, enjoying their tart flavor.

For you, a hunter-gatherer living in 10,000 B.C., this valley is a wonderful spot. A spring provides fresh, cold water. Wildlife and plants to eat are everywhere. You and your family have camped here since spring when you gathered armful after armful of grain. Food is plentiful in this valley. Perhaps you should stay here all year.

The preceding description is based on the region around Ain Mallaha *(YN MAHL ah hah)*, an archaeological site in the Jordan River Valley. Of course, we can only guess at the thoughts of ancient hunter-gatherers. But the evidence from Ain Mallaha and other sites shows that between about 11,000 and 8,000 B.C., some people in this region began to settle down.

Find Ain Mallaha on the map on page 121. It is located in a green-colored area that's shaped like a crescent. Because this strip of land had particularly good soil, it was given the name Fertile Crescent.

## Living in Settled Communities

The trend toward settling down and living in one location also occurred in other places around the globe. But it happened at different times in different places. This change didn't happen overnight with people suddenly switching their lifestyle from wandering to staying put. It all came about gradually. In this chapter you'll learn about sites in the Middle East, one of the first areas where the hunter-gatherers started to settle in villages.

Hunter-gatherers searched for areas where they could hunt game, harvest wild grains, gather berries and nuts, and find tasty plants and roots. Surrounded by plenty of food, they were tempted to stay for months at a time. As they became more attached to one place, they built longer-lasting homes.

The structures at Ain Mallaha give clues to the changing lifestyle of the hunter-gatherers. The picture on the next page shows the remains of one structure. This home was a circular pit, dug well below ground level. Stones covered the dirt walls. The walls that extended above ground and the roof were made of reeds.

Artifacts found in this home show some of the activities that took place inside. Notice the fire pit in the center of the floor where meat and grain were roasted. Look near the fire pit for the mortar, a round object hollowed out in the center. Grain was placed in the mortar and pounded with a blunt tool called a pestle. Both mortar and pestle were made of stone.

Storage bins were kept along the wall. These bins were used for storing the **surplus**, or extra, grain. Surplus grain was important. It was needed for times when food wasn't as plentiful.

Both the mortars and storage bins provided good reasons for the hunter-gatherers to stay permanently in one place. The mortars were much too heavy to carry around. People also didn't want to wander far because intruders might steal their precious surplus from the storage bins. You'll see how these ancient people stored and processed their grain when you read A Closer Look on pages 122 and 123. ■

**Early Settlements in the Middle East, 11,000–8000 B.C.**

Fertile Crescent

∴ Early settlement

🌾 Agricultural settlement

---- Present-day boundary

0   150   300 mi.
0  150  300 km
Mercator Projection

▲ *The Fertile Crescent of ancient times extended through parts of today's Middle East. See the Time/Space Databank to learn what modern countries make up this particular area.*

■ *What conditions allowed some hunter-gatherers to start settling down?*

◀ *Ruins of a hunter-gatherer dwelling at Ain Mallaha in present-day Israel. Nearby are a burial pit and a spring.*

## Taming Animals and Sowing Seeds

### How Do We Know?

**HISTORY** *We learn about food gathering in ancient times from experiments today. Scientist Jack Harlan harvested wild grain in Turkey with a crude sickle like those used by hunter-gatherers 10,000 years ago. He gathered six pounds of wild wheat per hour.*

As the hunter-gatherers began to settle down, they learned more about their **environment**—all the living and nonliving things that made up their surroundings. They observed wild grains in different stages of growth. They noticed the conditions that allowed these grains to thrive. At harvest time, they didn't gather up all the grain. They left some of the plants so their seeds or kernels could drop to the ground and sprout next season, starting a new crop.

Hunter-gatherers also learned more about the habits of the animals they hunted: gazelle, wild sheep, and wild goats. Scientists believe that they might have protected these herds by driving away wolves and other enemies. Then the animals could breed and the herds would grow. In this way, people were learning to have an influence over the plants and animals in their environment.

As people gained greater knowledge, they did even more.

## A CLOSER LOOK

# Early Food Storage

*What can happen to grain that isn't stored properly? It can get smelly and moldy enough to make you sick. As people developed safe ways to harvest, store, and process grain, their inventions helped sprout civilization.*

**You can't just eat wheat.** Wheat and barley have to be changed into a form people can eat. Early farmers learned to cut the grain, separate the usable part from the chaff, and then grind the grain into flour for baking.

**Prehistoric people** set sharp flint stones in wooden handles and used them to cut grain. If they didn't work fast, wild birds would eat all the grain.

The hunter-gatherers searched the countryside, taking seeds from wild grain and other edible plants. Then they sowed these seeds and grew their own plants closer to home. They learned to save enough seeds so they could re-plant the same plants the next season. They also captured wild cattle, sheep, goats, and pigs and tamed them. Slowly, people learned how to control both the growth and the behavior of plants and animals. They **domesticated** plants and animals, making them more useful to humans.

The first evidence of domesticated plants—wheat, barley, and lentils—comes from archaeological sites in the Middle East dated around 8000 to 7000 B.C. Hunter-gatherers probably noticed that some plants were more produc-tive than others. By collecting and sowing the seeds of these plants, they could increase their harvest. Today's varieties of domesticated barley produce more than six times as many seeds as wild barley.

Sheep, goats, and dogs were among the first domesticated ani-mals. Sheep were domesticated

**Was this the first** kitchen pantry? Early villagers stored their extra grain in underground storage pits lined with rock, grass, and sometimes clay. The pits kept the grain dry and safe from rats.

Stored wheat

Grass lining

Stone lining

**Heavy, breakable pots** were impractical for nomads to carry around. But when people began to settle in one place, they needed a good way to store their food. In time, pottery became beautiful as well as useful.

Neolithic quern used to grind grain into flour for bread

123

Development of Societies

Wild sheep

Domesticated sheep

▲ *How many differences can you see between the domesticated sheep on the right and the wild one on the left?*

■ *How are domesticated plants and animals more useful to humans than wild ones?*

➤ *By excavating the remains of animals and plants, archaeologists learned the approximate dates of domestication shown on the chart.*

about 8500 B.C. Archaeologists know this because they can tell the difference between the bones of domesticated sheep and those of wild sheep. Over hundreds of years, animals living in a domesticated environment undergo physical changes. They tend to become smaller than wild animals of a related species. Their muzzles become shorter. Horns may disappear entirely or change their shape. Archaeologists can make out these differences in animal bones unearthed at sites.

Domestication causes another important change. When animals and plants are domesticated, they rely on humans for survival. For example, a wild dog knows how to find its own shelter, hunt its own food, and flee or fight when faced with an enemy. But once a dog is domesticated, its survival skills fade because the dog now looks to humans for its home, supper, and safety.

Examine the chart below to help you understand that plants and animals were domesticated at different times in different places. Which animal was the first to be domesticated? Which people first domesticated rice? Which plants were domesticated in the Middle East? Which plants were domesticated first in America, and when did this happen? ■

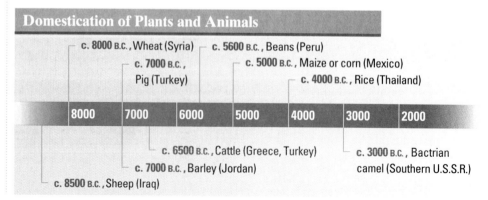

**Domestication of Plants and Animals**

c. 8000 B.C., Wheat (Syria) — c. 5600 B.C., Beans (Peru)

c. 7000 B.C., Pig (Turkey)

c. 5000 B.C., Maize or corn (Mexico)

c. 4000 B.C., Rice (Thailand)

| 8000 | 7000 | 6000 | 5000 | 4000 | 3000 | 2000 |

c. 6500 B.C., Cattle (Greece, Turkey)

c. 3000 B.C., Bactrian camel (Southern U.S.S.R.)

c. 7000 B.C., Barley (Jordan)

c. 8500 B.C., Sheep (Iraq)

124

# Farming as a Way of Life

Plant and animal domestication made possible the beginning of **agriculture**, or farming. Agriculture is the growing of plants and the raising of animals to supply food for humans. Evidence shows that by 7000 B.C. people in parts of the Middle East had learned to farm.

## The Advantages of Agriculture

The shift to farming and herding was a slow process, taking many hundreds of years. Even after agriculture had taken hold, many farmers continued to hunt, and many hunter-gatherers never adopted an agricultural lifestyle.

Why did some of the hunter-gatherers turn from food gathering to food producing? Agriculture offered some important advantages. Farmers and herders could raise much more food than hunter-gatherers could collect. They could support more people on small plots of land. And when the land was fairly fertile, they could move into regions where wild food and game were scarce. Perhaps most important of all, a farmer could grow more food than he needed to feed his family. The surplus could be traded or stored for winter months.

Certainly, farmers and herders faced problems, such as insects, bad weather, and plant and animal diseases. When such disasters struck, a farmer's food supply could be wiped out in a matter of days. But even with these drawbacks, agriculture seemed better than the gathering method for supplying food.

## Different Occupations

With the arrival of agriculture, not everyone was needed all day in the fields to raise food for the group. So, some people explored other activities. Gradually, they moved into other occupations, becoming tool makers, builders, fishers, craftspersons, priests, and leaders. The farming was eventually left to the farmers. Over time, agriculture had brought about a division of daily labors.

Farming also affected wild animals and open lands. Wild animals were often forced out of areas when farmers needed land for grazing domesticated flocks. Farmers also planted crops in areas once blanketed with wild plants and trees. Thus, through agriculture, people were changing their environment and their lifestyle in lasting ways.

*Ancient farmers learned to save some wheat kernels for future planting.*

*Some farmers in the Middle East still use the traditional farming methods of their ancestors.*

Development of

> The map shows areas where Neolithic people actually farmed. These cultures had advanced beyond the simple domestication of plants and animals to agriculture.

## A Major Change

Remember that humans had been on the earth for an extremely long time before they began to grow crops and herd animals. In all those thousands of years, they had lived by hunting and gathering. The beginning of agriculture was a new chapter in the human story.

Agriculture began during the Neolithic Era, a term that comes from two Greek words. *Neos* means "new" and *lithos* means "stone." The Neolithic Era, so named because people used stone tools, stretched from about 8000 to 5000 B.C. in the Middle East. In other parts of the world, the era covered different time periods. On the map above, locate the various areas showing Neolithic farming.

The Neolithic people also took steps in another new direction. They began to live in villages. They learned to make pottery for storing food and water. They mastered weaving, so that now they had cloth as well as animal hides for coverings. Basket weaving was another new skill. Toward the end of the Neolithic Era, villagers started to work with metal—first copper, then bronze.

In the next lessons, you'll discover how these advances were hints of things to come. These were the establishment of towns and the building of cities. ■

■ *What were the pros and cons of agriculture in ancient times?*

## R E V I E W

1. **FOCUS** How did people's lifestyle change as they began to domesticate plants and animals?
2. **CONNECT** Compare Neanderthals with early farmers. Include lifestyle, tools, and community spirit.
3. **GEOGRAPHY** Use the map on page 121 to name six modern countries that had early settlements.
4. **CRITICAL THINKING** Why do dogs and cats often live only a short time when abandoned in cities or woods by their owners?
5. **ACTIVITY** By using pantomime, show how the hunter-gatherers and early farmers and herders obtained their food.

12,500          10,000                          2500

8000                    5000

# Living in an Early Farming Town

I f someone were to give you the object in the picture below, what would you do with it? Before you read on, take out a piece of paper and jot down as many ideas as you can. The bowllike part of the object is made of solid stone and is very heavy. It might make a good doorstop. It has a dent in the center, so maybe you could use it for a salad bowl or candy dish. What ideas did you come up with?

It might be difficult to think of practical ways to use this object today. However, it was very useful about 8,000 years ago in the Neolithic Era when it was made. Take a closer look. The edges of the stone are bumpy, but other areas seem smooth. What do you think caused this?

Now look at the rounded object inside the stone. Archaeologists found this small object just as you see it, resting in the hollow of the large one. If you guessed that these two objects were used together, you're right. Maybe you also noticed that they're very similar to the mortar and pestle

found in the excavated ruins at Ain Mallaha. If so, you're right again.

The bowllike object is a mortar and the smaller object is a pestle. The pestle is used to grind food against the mortar. An ancient farmer would use this mortar and pestle, or quern *(kwurn)*, to grind grain into flour.

People ground so much grain that they wore the stone smooth in certain places. In this smoothing process, tiny pieces of grit chipped off the stone, mixing with the grain. Archaeological evidence shows that as people ate this gritty mixture over a long period of time, it gradually wore down their teeth. Querns similar to the one pictured below were used in many early settlements around the world where Neolithic farmers grew grains.

## THINKING FOCUS

*What would life be like in a Neolithic farming town?*

### Key Terms

- shrine
- self-sufficient

▼ *Querns varied in size but, generally, were as big as large bowls.*

127

Development of Societies

# A Large Neolithic Town

▼ *In a cutaway view, each layer of ruins represents a different time period when Çatal Hüyük was occupied. Only about three percent of the ruins have been excavated.*

Let's look at what life may have been like in one of those Neolithic towns. You've been transported back in time about 8,000 years. You're standing on the flat roof of a mud-brick building. Far off are the large twin cones of a volcano. You can see fields of wheat stretching out before you, making a golden carpet over the dry earth. A river winds lazily across the plain. A woman climbs out from a hole in the roof. With her broad smile she warmly welcomes you to her hometown, Çatal Hüyük *(chah TUHL hoo YUHK).*

Turn to the map on page 121. You will see that Çatal Hüyük was located on a plain in present-day Turkey. Around 6000 B.C., the town covered about 32 acres. That's roughly the size of 24 football fields put together. The town had about 1,000 houses, and the population numbered between 5,000 and 6,000. By today's standards, Çatal Hüyük wasn't large. But so far, it's the biggest Neolithic town discovered by archaeologists in the Middle East.

When dwellings in Çatal Hüyük collapsed from age or fire or other reasons, people simply built new homes on top of the old ones. That is the reason why these archaeological ruins are layered like a cake. The diagram below shows ruins with the most ancient remains on the bottom and the most recent on the top. These remains tell us much about the lifestyle, farming, and beliefs of the people of ancient Çatal Hüyük.

## Daily Life

Didn't you find it odd that your time travel took you to a Çatal Hüyük rooftop? Why didn't you land on a street corner or, at least, on someone's doorstep? That was not possible in Çatal Hüyük. This town had no streets, lanes, or alleys, and the doors of buildings opened onto roofs. To get from place to place, people walked across their neighbors' roofs. Notice, in the diagram on page 129, that the roofs were at different levels. You can see the ladders that allowed people to get from one level to the next. Ladders also led from the doors, at roof level, down into the houses. All that ladder climbing must have caused some nasty tumbles. It's no wonder that archaeologists have found many broken bones at the Çatal Hüyük site.

The houses of Çatal Hüyük were all about the same size. Most had two rooms—a small room for

**Excavations at Çatal Hüyük**

c. 5750 B.C. — c. 5720 B.C.

c. 5790 B.C.

c. 5830 B.C.

c. 5950 B.C. — c. 5880 B.C.

c. 6050 B.C.

c. 6200 B.C.

c. 6280 B.C. — c. 6380 B.C.

c. 6500 B.C.

unexcavated lower levels

storing food and a large room with a kitchen area and living quarters. By examining the storerooms, archaeologists have learned that wheat was Çatal Hüyük's main crop. Other evidence also shows that people raised cattle and

▲ *The drawing of Çatal Hüyük's mud dwellings shows how the different roof levels allowed sunlight to enter the rooms.*

hunted deer, bear, and wolves. For variety, they grew peas and gathered crab apples, juniper berries, and nuts such as acorns and almonds.

The kitchen area in each house featured both a hearth and a clay oven. Smoke escaped through the same hole in the roof that people used to climb in and out of the house. Basically, the furniture was built-in. Platforms that extended from the walls served as tables or benches during the day and as beds at night.

### Burial Practices

In some homes, simple graves were found under the platforms. Archaeologists think that people buried their relatives there. No one is sure why. Possibly, dead relatives were still considered part of the family so they were kept within the household.

Evidence suggests that a number of the buildings were **shrines,** or sacred places where people worship. Çatal Hüyük's shrines, however, may have been used for other activities, too. The shrines were no larger than the houses, but they were special inside. Bull horns decorated the benches, and plaster

Development of Societies

*This Çatal Hüyük ceremonial dagger has a blade of flint. The handle is shaped like a coiled snake.*

■ *What kind of lifestyle did people have in Çatal Hüyük, and how do we know?*

➤ *Shrines like this were mixed in among the houses at Çatal Hüyük. Find the sculpture of the bull head, a religious image that occurred often at Çatal Hüyük.*

sculptures of leopards, rams, and bulls adorned the walls.

The Çatal Hüyük people also painted in color on their shrines' white plastered walls. Subjects for the pictures ranged from colorful patterns to wild beasts to a village with volcanoes in the background. Archaeologists think that the paintings were connected with special events. These shrines with their paintings and sculptures may have attracted people from other areas of the plain. If so, Çatal Hüyük probably became the region's religious center.

### A Farming Economy

Fertile soil and a river helped to make Çatal Hüyük a large town. With good crops supplying plenty of food, people decided to stay in the town. As the population increased, the town grew. But sometimes groups of people left the town to start settlements nearby. They carried the Çatal Hüyük way of life with them.

The Çatal Hüyük people lived in their mud-brick homes and left town to tend their fields. Since the region was dry, farmers probably waited until the river flooded in late spring. After flood waters went down, they planted seeds in the moist earth.

The townspeople produced ample grain and cattle. They also had salt, reeds, a limited amount of wood, and plenty of mud for shaping bricks. These basic items made them **self-sufficient,** meaning they weren't dependent upon others for their survival.

### Çatal Hüyük Crafts

Since not everyone in Çatal Hüyük had to farm full time, the townspeople set up small industries. Archaeologists discovered the Neolithic talent for crafts.

The Çatal Hüyük craftspeople made tools by both grinding and chipping stone. From bone, they crafted needles, beads, hairpins, and fish hooks. They also wove woolen cloth, made baskets, and fashioned leather into pouches. From wood, they made bowls and boxes with lids. ■

◄ *In some areas of Iraq today, women still carry on the ancient tradition of making sun-dried bricks. Iraq also has large cities with modern buildings.*

# Trade in the Neolithic World

Çatal Hüyük was the hub of trade on the plain. Its people were excellent at crafts, making items that neighboring settlements wanted.

This town also had an item valued throughout the Neolithic Middle East—a black volcanic glass called obsidian. This shiny, dark glass is formed when hot lava from a volcano cools quickly. Obsidian is valued because it can be chipped to make fine, sharp-edged tools. Even today surgeons use obsidian blades for delicate operations.

The Çatal Hüyük people journeyed more than 120 miles to get obsidian at volcanic lava flows. Archaeologists believe they transported it on the backs of their domesticated cattle. At other times, Çatal Hüyük traders got their obsidian from neighboring towns. Then, they turned around and traded it to distant towns. Sometimes, they crafted the obsidian first, making arrowheads, tools, and mirrors.

Obsidian from Çatal Hüyük's area was unearthed about 620 miles away at the archaeological site of Jericho. Trade items from afar that were excavated at Çatal Hüyük include turquoise and copper from the Sinai Peninsula, also more than 600 miles away.

Çatal Hüyük was only one of a number of Neolithic towns in the Middle East that engaged in trade. One example was Umm Dabaghiyah *(OOM dah bah GEE ah)*, a small settlement that archaeologists

◄ *Learning to make clay pots like this one was a giant step forward for the Neolithic people.*

131

believe existed at the same time as Çatal Hüyük.

In about 6000 B.C., Umm Dabaghiyah was a village located on the dry northern plain between the Tigris *(TY gruhs)* and Euphrates *(yu FRAYT eez)* rivers. Find the site on the map on page 121. This town was tiny compared with Çatal Hüyük. It had fewer than ten houses.

But Umm Dabaghiyah had other buildings. These were long, narrow structures with rows of cell-like rooms. The walls were unplastered; the floors were dirt, and the roofs had trap doors. These rooms lacked the hearths, platforms, and tools needed for daily living.

What was the purpose of these cell-like rooms? In some rooms were large numbers of the same item. For example, one room held thousands of clay balls—ammunition for slingshots. This shows that

## UNDERSTANDING SURPLUS

When you have a surplus, you have an extra supply of something. It can be a surplus of just about anything imaginable—shoes or ships, timber, coal, or even baseball cards.

Through the ages, a surplus of food has kept people alive during lean years. It has also allowed them to change their lifestyles. For example, once the hunter-gatherers had a surplus of grain and wild game, they didn't have to roam to hunt food. If they chose, they could then become settlers instead of wanderers.

### Over and Above

The English word *surplus* comes from the Latin words *super*, meaning "over," and *plus*, meaning "more." Although ancient Romans coined this term, the idea of surplus goes much farther back. The first successful mammoth hunters, for example, certainly enjoyed a surplus of meat.

### Surplus and Trade

Think about surplus and how it affects us today. If oranges grow well in my state but not in yours, I'll have a surplus of oranges. You'll have the opposite of a surplus, which is a scarcity. However, if your state grows a surplus of apples and my state grows none, the answer seems easy. We can trade apples for oranges.

As a matter of fact, trade turned out to be the answer for people in early societies as well. In Çatal Hüyük, people traded their own surplus of obsidian for items they lacked, and soon trade became a vital part of their lifestyle.

Note, however, that each one involved in a trade must have something the other wants. One nation may have a surplus of something, such as coconuts, but unless another nation has a coconut scarcity, trade won't solve the problem.

### Surplus and Scarcity

In our day, too, the balance of surplus and scarcity has an effect on trade. The Middle Eastern countries, with their surplus oil, have become among the richest in the world. In recent years, the United States and many other countries throughout the world have had a scarcity of oil. How do you think our country's scarcity of oil might affect its trade with Middle Eastern countries?

hunting was important to these people. In fact, because of the number and types of animal bones found there, archaeologists concluded that this town was a hunting and trading outpost. These rooms must have been used for storage.

The people who lived in Umm Dabaghiyah hunted a wild, donkeylike animal called an onager *(AHN uh juhr)*. They skinned the onager and then traded the hides. During a 1974 dig, archaeologists discovered how this animal was hunted when they found a detailed wall painting. Hunters stampeded the onagers into an enclosed area built from stakes and nets.

The people of Umm Dabaghiyah did little farming because crops didn't grow well in their dry area. Thus, they weren't self-sufficient. However, they had a surplus of onager hides. This surplus allowed them to trade for necessities and luxuries they couldn't produce. By focusing on trade, this small town pioneered a new way of life. ■

▲ *An archaeologist at Umm Dabaghiyah sketched this floor plan of the storerooms.*

■ *What was the surplus item produced at Umm Dabaghiyah and how did the people make use of it?*

◄ *This artist's drawing, based on the floor plan above, shows how the storerooms at Umm Dabaghiyah might have looked. Entrance was through a trap door in the roof.*

## R E V I E W

1. **FOCUS** What was life like in a Neolithic farming town?
2. **CONNECT** In the area of industry, how did the Çatal Hüyük people differ from hunter-gatherers? What caused this difference?
3. **CULTURE** What is obsidian, and how is it formed?

What did the Çatal Hüyük people do with it?
4. **CRITICAL THINKING** Why do you think the Çatal Hüyük houses had only rooftop entries?
5. **ACTIVITY** Make a poster showing something about daily life in Çatal Hüyük or Umm Dabaghiyah.

# Making Inferences

## Here's Why

You know that when you read stories, not every detail is always explained. Sometimes you must look for clues and think about your own experiences to understand information the author did not state directly. This is called making inferences.

You can use the clues shown on a map and what you already know to make inferences. For example, suppose you wanted to know how obsidian was transported through Anatolia. If a map did not show the trade route, could you use clues along with what you already know to figure it out? Could you make an inference?

## Here's How

Look at the map below. The light green area shows Anatolia. Note the symbols for the sources of obsidian and for sites where obsidian objects, like those shown here, have been found. These are places where obsidian was used and traded. The locations of symbols are clues that will help you guess, or infer, how obsidian was transported.

Because the sources of obsidian are in the Taurus Mountains, you can infer that the trade route would begin there. You can also see that the route would go overland from the mountains to Çatal Hüyük. You already know that water routes were used. So you can infer that once the obsidian reached the Mediterranean Sea, it was probably loaded on boats and shipped to towns on or near the coast. By using clues and what you already knew, you were able to infer how obsidian was transported through Anatolia.

## Try It

Look at the pink area on the map. Where was the source of this region's obsidian? How do you think the obsidian was transported from place to place? Base your answers on map clues and what you already know.

## Apply It

Draw a map that shows the location of your school and home. Include streets and landmarks. Show your map to someone who lives in another area. Help that person infer the route you walk or ride to school each day. Give clues about landmarks you pass.

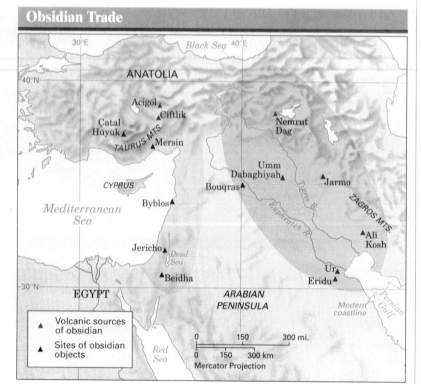

Obsidian Trade

Black Sea

ANATOLIA

Acigöl

Ciftlik

Çatal Hüyük

TAURUS MTS.

Mersin

Nemrut Dag

CYPRUS

Umm Dabaghiyah

Bouqras

Jarmo

Tigris R.

Euphrates R.

ZAGROS MTS.

Byblos

Mediterranean Sea

Jericho

Dead Sea

Ali Kosh

Beidha

Ur

Eridu

EGYPT

ARABIAN PENINSULA

Modern coastline

Persian Gulf

▲ Volcanic sources of obsidian

▲ Sites of obsidian objects

Red Sea

0    150    300 mi.

0   150   300 km

Mercator Projection

L E S S O N   3

# Starting Cities

In 1927, Sir Leonard Woolley dug into a cemetery at the ancient city of Ur, in what is now Iraq. The first shovelfuls of the British archaeologist yielded only dirt. However, over the next two years, Woolley dug up treasures beyond his wildest hopes. Buried in that cemetery were the kings and queens of the ancient city of Ur.

One of Woolley's priceless finds was the Standard of Ur. A standard is often carried before a king or queen in a procession. Usually, it's a flag. But the Standard of Ur is something quite different. It consists of two separate solid panels, one called War, and the other, Peace. Both panels are detailed mosaics—pictures made by putting together many small pieces of stones, shells, gems, or tiles.

The panels, each measuring 22 inches, were carried on a pole. Look at the War panel below. Woolley wrote this about it in his book, *Ur of The Chaldees:*

*In the second row, at the back, comes the phalanx of the royal army, heavy-armed infantry in close order with copper helmets exactly like those found by us in the king's grave, and long cloaks of some stiff material which I take to be felt, just such cloaks as are worn by the shepherds of Anatolia [part of Turkey] to-day, holding axes in their hands; in front of them are the light-armed infantry without cloaks, wielding axes or short spears.*

The king stands out because of his greater height and central location. His figure dominates the top

**THINKING FOCUS**

*What are the characteristics of a city?*

## Key Terms

- irrigation
- famine
- civilization

◄ *In a royal grave at the city of Ur, this War panel was found lying next to a man thought to be the king's standard-bearer.*

135

*These figures from the Peace panel show a harpist and a singer entertaining the king. The entire Peace panel appears on pages 86 and 87.*

row. Facing him stand prisoners of war, their hands bound behind their backs.

"The Standard is a remarkable work of art, but it has yet greater value as an historical document," said Woolley. He explained further that these panels make up the earliest known detailed picture of the army that fought throughout the Middle East.

Earlier in this chapter, a quern taught you about an important task carried out by Neolithic farm families. What does the Standard of Ur tell you about a warrior's duties in one of the world's first cities?

## A City on the Plain

*The land around the Tigris and Euphrates rivers is still a sun-baked plain.*

The city of Ur was located on the dry plain of the Tigris and Euphrates rivers. Find Ur on the map on page 121.

This city didn't just spring up on the plain. Ur and other cities in that river area arose because of advances in agriculture and changes in society. Here's how it happened at the city of Ur.

### The Sun-baked Land

Many farmers in the ancient world could count on rain to water their crops until harvest time. But this natural method didn't work in the land between the Tigris and Euphrates rivers. There, rain was scarce.

For most of the year, the land between the rivers is scorched by the sun. The clay soil bakes to a surface so hard you'd need a jackhammer to drill through it. When the rain finally arrives, it rolls right off. How could anyone farm such land? The people of Ur did it with irrigation. When people use **irrigation,** they bring needed water

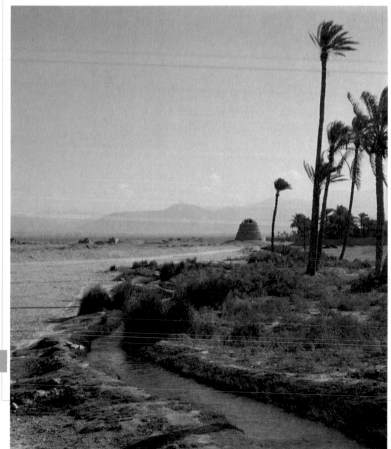

to their fields through canals, ditches, or pipes.

### An Irrigation System

People who settled by the Tigris and Euphrates rivers dug canals from the riverbeds to their fields. Their irrigation system made the dry, dusty plains bloom. In Chapter 6, you'll learn more about the workings of this irrigation system used by Ur and other cities on the plain.

Irrigation farming worked well because the times of watering and also the amounts of water could be controlled. Farmers produced surplus food, preventing famine and starvation. **Famine** is a terrible shortage of food that can cause starvation. Fields yielded bountiful harvests of barley, wheat, and vegetables. Date palms and grapevines also grew well on this land.

As you learned in Lesson 1, a food surplus enabled people to leave farming and take on specialized jobs, such as building or toolmaking. Where irrigation farming was practiced, the population grew rapidly. The boom in population around the Tigris and Euphrates rivers led to the growth of cities such as Ur. ■

*◄ This treasure from a royal tomb at Ur is called Ram-in-a-Thicket. When the statue was found, it was crushed and twisted. Only earth held the gems, shells, and gold in place.*

■ *How did irrigation make it possible for a city to grow in the land around the Tigris and Euphrates?*

## Features of a City

Ur, like every ancient or modern city, had a large number of people living close together. But it was more than just population that made Ur a city.

### Planning and Leadership

One characteristic or special feature of a city is that people work together. That is, they are organized. They have leaders who make rules so that life in the city will run smoothly. The early leaders of Ur were probably powerful priests. In time, the power shifted to government leaders—the kings.

Let's look at the evidence of organization that archaeologists have found. The region around the city of Ur was criss-crossed by a complicated network of irrigation canals. In Ur hundreds of people had to work together to build and to maintain the canals. A complex

Development of Societies

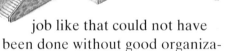

➤ *If you walked up this stairway, you'd find yourself on the first platform of the Ziggurat of Ur. The ruins are in good condition.*

▼ *This drawing shows you what the Ziggurat of Ur looked like in ancient times. A one-room shrine to the moon god crowns its top.*

### Across Time & Space

*When we use the words* city, town, *and* village *today, we are usually saying something about population. A city has more people than a town, and a village has fewer. A suburb may be small or large. It may be a town, a village, or a city. What makes a suburb?*

job like that could not have been done without good organization and strong, clear leadership.

Large public buildings also show how well Ur was organized. The structure in the above drawing is a ziggurat *(ZIHG uh raht)*, a type of temple tower with a one-room shrine at the top. The people who lived on this level land in effect had built themselves a mountain where they could worship their god. The ziggurat had many storerooms in addition to the temple. It also contained a large number of workrooms.

Constructing something as huge and grand as this ziggurat took a great deal of planning and organization. This meant that a large number of people had to work together to get the job done.

### Specialized Workers

Another characteristic of a city is that people are employed in all sorts of different jobs. Since irrigation gave Ur abundant crops, not everyone was needed to till the soil. People began to develop skills other than farming. These skills led them into a variety of jobs.

Sir Leonard Woolley excavated a tablet listing several of Ur's special workers. The chisel worker made sculptures; the gem cutter cut and polished gems, and the fuller stomped on woven wool to make it soft. The metalworker crafted everything from weapons to mirrors. Although Ur imported its wood from afar, the carpenter kept busy making boats and chariots. To the leatherworker went the job of making soldiers' tunics.

Ur also had judges and doctors and musicians who played harps, lyres, and drums. When different people in a society do different jobs, the arrangement is called specialization of labor.

## Richer and Poorer

Cities usually have different social groups, too. That is, some people are richer and more powerful than others.

Ur had three levels of society. At the top were the most powerful—government officials, priests, and soldiers. The society's second level was made up of merchants, teachers, laborers, farmers, and craftspeople. At the bottom of the social scale were the slaves, who often had been captured during battle.

Burials at Ur give insight into people's social standing. As you have seen, kings and queens had tombs filled with treasures. Other wealthy people were buried with cups of stone or metal, even gold. But the graves of common people held only a few simple items such as cups, axes, and fish hooks. Generally, the plainer the pottery in a grave, the poorer the person.

## Trade Near and Far

Long-distance trade is another sign of a city. For Ur, this trade was a lifeline to survival. Ur was located on a treeless, sun-baked plain, hundreds of miles from many valuable resources. The people of Ur traded grain and woven cloth for the items they needed. They traded for timber, for the stone used in making tools, and for the gems in their jewelry. They also traded for the gold, silver, tin, lead, copper, and bronze needed by their metalworkers.

As the population of Ur grew larger, trade expanded as never before. The priests kept records of goods that flowed in and out of the city. How did they do this? Ur had a unique system of writing. Fortunately, some records have survived to let us know that Ur was a key trading center.

Seagoing boats navigated along the Mediterranean coasts. Some also ventured to India. Crowding the river waterways were round basketlike boats made of reeds and covered with hides. ■

■ *What archaeological evidence tells us that Ur was a city?*

▼ *This bearded bull of gold decorates the sounding box of a lyre (a musical instrument) from a royal tomb. Lyres were frequently found in royal graves.*

# An Early Civilization

Cities like Ur often signal the rise of a **civilization.** Just what is a civilization? It's a complex society that usually has these five characteristics, or features:

1. Stable food supply
2. Specialization of labor
3. A system of government
4. Social levels
5. A highly developed culture that includes art, architecture, religion, music, and law. Frequently, civilizations also have a system of writing.

Would hunter-gatherer groups make up a civilization? No, they wouldn't because these people didn't always have a stable food supply, and they didn't develop much specialization of labor. They often had leaders but not organized government. Some had art, religion, and music, but not architecture. Although hunter-gatherers had a culture, they were not considered a civilization.

Ur, however, and other cities in the Fertile Crescent did have all the needed characteristics that make a civilization. In fact, these

➤ *This woman's fancy headdress of gold was unearthed in the Fertile Crescent.*

▼ *The chart shows how early farming with its surplus food often led to the rise of cities.*

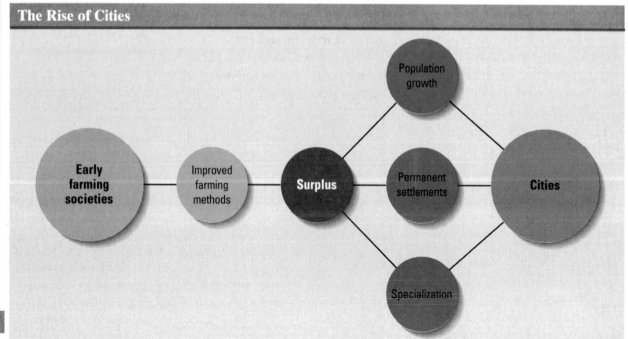

## The Rise of Cities

Early farming societies → Improved farming methods → **Surplus** → Permanent settlements → Cities

Population growth

Specialization

cities around the Tigris and Euphrates rivers formed one of the world's earliest civilizations.

You'll find that cities often speed up the growth of a civilization, but not always. For example, ancient Egyptian civilization reached an advanced level before cities were even built there. You'll read about this Egyptian civilization in Chapter 7.

Cities and civilizations often share the same features. So it's not surprising that both words come from the same Latin word, *civitas*, meaning "city."

ASIA

EUROPE

HUANG HE VALLEY
c. 1700 B.C.

MESOPOTAMIA
c. 3500 B.C.

NILE VALLEY
c. 3100 B.C.

INDUS VALLEY
c. 2500 B.C.

PACIFIC
OCEAN

AFRICA

Equator

ATLANTIC
OCEAN

INDIAN
OCEAN

AUSTRALIA

0        1500        3000 mi.

0    1500    3000 km
Robinson Projection

The Fertile Crescent and the Nile Valley were only two of the world's first civilizations. On the map above, find where other early civilizations began. Rivers often played a major role in their growth, as they did in the Fertile Crescent and Egypt.

More than 7,000 years have passed since hunter-gatherers began to settle down in villages of the Middle East. The very gradual change in their lives shows that it takes century upon century to mold a civilization. ■

▲ *On the map, notice the time periods associated with each of the early civilizations.*

◄ *These vessels of gold found in tombs indicate the advanced artistry of the Ur civilization.*

■ *What are five features of a civilization?*

## R E V I E W

1. **FOCUS** What are characteristics of a city?
2. **CONNECT** Hunter-gatherer groups were not civilizations. Give at least three elements that they lacked.
3. **GEOGRAPHY** How did the Euphrates River help Ur's development?
4. **ECONOMICS** Why was trade vital to the city of Ur?
5. **CRITICAL THINKING** An archaeologist unearthed a midden containing broken pottery, a dog bone, dried wheat, and a golden hairpin. What do these tell about the ancient people who once lived in that area?
6. **ACTIVITY** Make a picture chart showing the various elements of a city.

141

Development of Societies

# Surplus Grain: Store? Sell? Give It Away?

> I n 1988—perhaps for the first time ever—the U.S. produced less grain (196 metric tons) than it consumed (206 metric tons). . . . Another bad harvest in the next few years could trigger massive starvation in any of the more than 100 nations that buy U.S. grain.
>
> The Worldwatch Institute

> W orld food production is growing faster than population . . . if the food supply can be increased at the current pace (or even a slower one), there will be enough food for a stable world population of 10 billion in 100 years.
>
> Pierre R. Crosson and
> Norman J Rosenberg,
> *Scientific American*

## Background

Surpluses have always been important to human communities. In prehistoric times, they allowed people to survive hard winters or blazing summers when food was scarce. With surpluses, large groups of people could live together, because there was enough food for everyone. Surpluses also made it possible for people to specialize, since not everyone had to spend the day hunting or gathering food.

Finally, surpluses led to trade. When one group had extra meat or grain on hand, they would try to exchange it for something else they needed—tools, seeds, or animal skins.

From the beginning of civilization, people have had to decide what to do with surpluses. The United States is frequently faced with this decision today. This is a fertile and wealthy nation, and it often produces more than enough food for its own people. In the 1960s, new and more productive kinds of plants were introduced, along with new, more efficient farm machinery. With chemical fertilizers and insecticides, these advances made the land produce even more grain and added to our surpluses. Look at the graph on

**Total Grain Surplus, United States, 1974–1986**

Grain (in million metric tons) vs. Year

page 142. What should we do with the grain we have left each year? We have three alternatives: to keep our surplus grain, to sell it, or to give it away.

## Considering Alternatives

Maybe we'd be wise to keep our surpluses. In 1988, a drought made the U.S. harvest 10 percent smaller than it was in 1985. In 1970, a fungus cut the corn crop 15 percent. These natural events are unpredictable. We have to protect ourselves and be sure there is enough food. Why give away or sell our own insurance against hunger?

But with good weather, future harvests in the United States may bring us huge surpluses. Scientists are developing new varieties of plants and animals. Some experts predict that by the year 2000, annual U.S. corn production could reach almost 10 million bushels.

Then why not sell our surpluses? After all, we buy a great deal from other countries. The goods we buy are harvested or manufactured by workers in those countries, so they help to provide jobs. To assure work for our own people, we need to sell as much as possible to other nations. American farmers have had difficult years. Keeping our surpluses does not help them, but selling our surpluses does. It increases the demand for grain and keeps grain prices up.

We could give away our surplus grain to countries whose people are starving. In spite of advances in technology, starvation remains a fact of life in many parts of the world.

## Decision Point

1. What alternatives do we have in how we use our surplus grain?
2. What are the advantages of each alternative?
3. What disadvantages can you identify for each alternative?
4. Grain can also be used as feed for animals and in the production of certain fuels. Where would you look for more information about these uses?
5. What are some advantages and disadvantages of these other uses?

What should we do with our surplus grain?

- Store
  - Advantages
  - Disadvantages
- Sell
  - Advantages
  - Disadvantages
- Give Away
  - Advantages
  - Disadvantages

143

Development of Societies

# Chapter Review

## Reviewing Key Terms

agriculture (p. 125)    irrigation (p. 136)
civilization (p. 140)    self-sufficient (p. 130)
domesticate (p. 123)    shrine (p. 129)
environment (p. 122)    surplus (p. 121)
famine (p. 137)

**A.** Some of the following statements are true. The rest are false. Write *True* or *False* for each statement. Then rewrite the false statements to make them true.

1. When hunter-gatherers learned to control their environment, their lifestyle changed.
2. Agriculture could not have developed without the domestication of plants.
3. Famine would make people self-sufficient.

4. Surplus food helped the growth of trade.
5. The shrines of Çatal Hüyük, with their paintings and sculptures, were much like our art museums today.
6. Ur is considered a civilization because it learned to domesticate plants and animals.

**B.** If you were a farmer living 5,000 years ago, why would the following be important to you? Write an explanation of how each of these things would influence your farm life.

1. domesticated plants and animals
2. irrigation
3. surplus
4. environment

## Exploring Concepts

**A.** Ain Mallaha, Çatal Hüyük, Umm Dabaghiyah, and Ur were all very different types of communities. Copy the following chart on your paper. Then compare the size, occupation, and types of dwellings that these four historic areas had. Complete all the sections in your chart.

| Location and Date | Size | Lifestyle | Dwellings |
|---|---|---|---|
| Ain Mallaha | | | Round pits, dirt walls, reed roofs |
| Çatal Hüyük 6,000 B.C. | | | |
| Umm Dabaghiyah | | Hunters and traders | |
| Ur 3,000–2,000 B.C. | City | | |

**B.** You could draw the following conclusions from studying the ancient Middle East. Using facts and details from the chapter, give proof that these conclusions are correct.

1. Some hunter-gatherers began to settle down between 11,000 and 8000 B.C.
2. Early farmers domesticated plants and animals.
3. Neolithic farmers learned to make flour.
4. The people of Çatal Hüyük traded with distant communities.
5. Umm Dabaghiyah was a much different community than Çatal Hüyük and Ur.
6. The city of Ur was organized; it also had leadership.
7. The residents of Çatal Hüyük and Ur were self-sufficient, but the residents of Umm Dabaghiyah were not.
8. The early communities of Ain Mallaha, Çatal Hüyük, and Ur were formed because of their geography and environment.
9. Archaeologists' work is important.

## Reviewing Skills

1. The map on this page shows areas in the Middle East that receive at least 12 inches of rain each year. This is the minimum amount needed for growing wheat without irrigation. Suppose you were an archaeologist. Would you expect to find traces of ancient irrigation ditches at Eridu or Ali Kosh? Explain your answers.
2. Make a table that will show that Ur was a civilization. Across your paper write these column headings: Food Supply, Specialization, Government, Social Levels, and Cultural Development. Down the left-hand side of your paper, write Evidence of Ur's civilization. Use information on pages 135–139 to give examples of how Ur shows the characteristics of a civilized society.
3. The people of Ain Mallaha, Çatal Hüyük, Umm Dabaghiyah, and Ur all invented tools that helped them in their work. How could you show the tools used by these communities on a map?

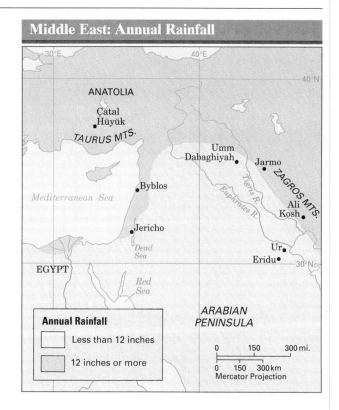

**Middle East: Annual Rainfall**

ANATOLIA
Çatal Hüyük
TAURUS MTS.
Umm Dabaghiyah
Jarmo
ZAGROS MTS.
Byblos
Mediterranean Sea
Ali Kosh
Jericho
Dead Sea
Ur
Eridu
EGYPT
Red Sea
ARABIAN PENINSULA

**Annual Rainfall**
Less than 12 inches
12 inches or more

0    150    300 mi.
0    150    300 km
Mercator Projection

## Using Critical Thinking

1. From earliest times, people have changed their environments. How have people changed their environment today? Discuss both good and bad changes.
2. Ancient peoples valued obsidian, copper, gazelle skins, and onager hides. Societies that had these resources developed a flourishing trade. Which resources do we prize in modern life? Why?
3. Communities develop differently. Use this list to compare Ur with your community. Geography—Why are Ur and your community located where they are? Government—Who makes the rules? Economy—How do people earn a living? Society—What social levels are there? Culture—Are art, architecture, religion, and music present?

## Preparing for Citizenship

1. **ARTS ACTIVITY** The drawings and symbols on the Standard of Ur tell us about the people of Ur and their beliefs. How would you design a standard for the United States? What symbols and words would tell about us and our beliefs? For ideas, look at the flag, coins, songs, the presidential seal, and monuments. When you show your standard, explain why you chose your design.
2. **COLLABORATIVE LEARNING** Ur was a successful city. It had planning and leadership. As a class, decide what problems need solving in your community. For each problem—such as litter or dangerous crosswalks—form a small group to decide what can be done about it. Each group should choose a leader and then plan tasks for its members. Present the group's plan to the class.

# Early Middle Eastern Civilizations

A nobleman and his wife, pleading for eternal life, make lavish offerings to a god. This beautifully painted scene, found in an Egyptian tomb, shows the richness of the Egyptian civilization 3,500 years ago. The people of ancient Egypt and Mesopotamia tamed the bleak land of the Middle East by controlling its rivers. Then they built two of the world's first great civilizations.

# 5300 B.C.

*From **The Book of the Dead of Khay,** painted on papyrus, c. 1400 B.C. Torino, Museo Egizio*

# Chapter 6

## *Mesopotamia*

*The blazing sun beat down, and the hot desert wind blew across the flat, dry land of Mesopotamia. This area in what we now call the Middle East would seem an unlikely place for a civilization to grow. Yet 7,000 years ago people used the waters of two nearby rivers to turn the land into fertile fields. They built the world's first cities along the riverbanks. Soon these cities became bustling centers of trade.*

Donkey caravans began carrying barley, wool, oil, and other goods from Sumer to faraway markets around 3000 B.C. Later caravans, like the one below, might have used camels.

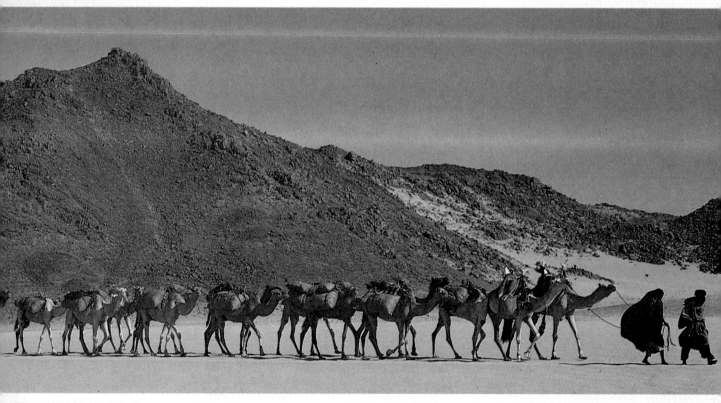

| 7000 | 6000 | 5000 | 4000 |
|------|------|------|------|

# 5300 B.C.

c. 3500 B.C. The Sumerians, who live in southern Mesopotamia, invent the wheel and the sailboat to help them transport goods.

The Sumerians traded farm products for copper, tin, and gold. They became skilled metalworkers. This helmet was made from a single sheet of gold around 2450 B.C.

c. 900–650 B.C. The Assyrians of northern Mesopotamia conquer distant lands and create one of the richest empires of ancient times. The stone carving above, from 640 B.C., shows an Assyrian warrior king.

| 3000 | 2000 | 1000 | B.C. | A.D. |
|------|------|------|------|------|

c. 3000 B.C. The Sumerians develop a system of writing so traders can keep track of what they buy and sell. The clay tablet above shows the wedge-shaped letters they began using around 2500 B.C.

539 B.C.

L E S S O N   1

# The Land Between Two Rivers

### Key Terms

- plateau
- plain
- city-state
- administrator
- artisan

Scrape and dig, scrape and dig. The young worker's bare feet sank into the soft mud of the canal. Water soaked the loose, skirtlike garment he wore around his waist. With a crew of fellow workers, he cleared the channel of the clay, sand, and gravel that blocked the water's flow.

The blazing sun scorched the young worker's bare back. The desert wind, blowing hot and dusty, only made his task more difficult. Slowly, he waded toward the bank. He threw down his stone hoe and sat, keeping his feet in the cool water.

Resting dreamily, he gazed over the unending flatness of his homeland. Only a few scrubby trees broke his view of the broad fields of wheat and barley. The walls of the great city of Kish rose in the distance.

Suddenly, the worn-out worker felt proud. Without these canals, he realized, none of this would be here—the trees, the fields of grain, the bustling city. The canals were part of an irrigation system that had turned a barren landscape into a rich, fertile plain. As you read on, you will see how irrigation became the key to developing one of the world's first civilizations.

## The Mesopotamian Plain

The young canal worker is imaginary, as you may have guessed, but his land and his city are not. The land is Mesopotamia *(mehs uh puh TAY mee uh),* and the city is Kish. Mesopotamia included all of present-day Iraq and parts of Syria and Turkey. The name *Mesopotamia* comes from the Greek language and means "the land between the rivers." Find ancient Mesopotamia on the map on the opposite page. You will note that the Tigris and Euphrates rivers wind their ways through Mesopotamia.

Using the map, find the city of Hit on the Euphrates River. Then trace an imaginary line northwest of Hit and around northern Mesopotamia between the rivers. The land in northern Mesopotamia is a **plateau,** a broad area of high, flat land.

Now begin again at Hit. This time trace a line downward along

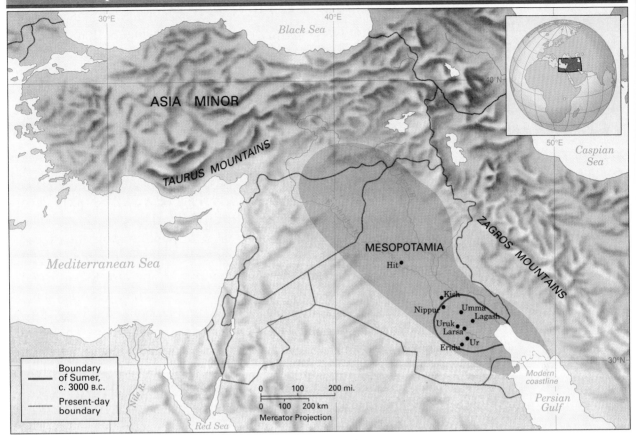

30°E
Black Sea
40°E
50°E
Caspian Sea
ASIA MINOR
TAURUS MOUNTAINS
40°N
MESOPOTAMIA
Hit•
ZAGROS MOUNTAINS
Kish
Nippur• •Umma
•Lagash
Uruk•
Larsa •Ur
Eridu
Mediterranean Sea
Modern coastline
30°N
Persian Gulf
Red Sea
Nile R.

Boundary of Sumer, c. 3000 B.C.
Present-day boundary

0        100        200 mi.
0    100    200 km
Mercator Projection

the Euphrates River to the Persian Gulf, then up the Tigris River and back to Hit. The area you have circled is a **plain**—a broad area of flat, open land, that is lower than the plateau. On the plain lay the region called Sumer *(SOO mur)*, making up much of the southern half of Mesopotamia.

Sumer spread over more than 10,000 square miles, an area about the size of Maryland. It was in Sumer that the world's first cities, including Ur and Kish, arose.

Scholars believe that the course of both rivers has changed a great deal in the last 5,000 years. The city of Kish was probably built just west of the ancient course of the Euphrates River.

Sumer was the homeland of the young canal worker we met earlier. Imagine him working on the irrigation canals in the 110-degree heat and the scorching, dusty wind. Historians believe that it was struggles with their harsh environment that caused the Sumerians,

▲ Use the map to locate Mesopotamia in relation to modern nations. Then describe the geography of northern and southern Mesopotamia.

◄ This modern Iraqi boat strongly resembles boats used 4,500 years ago in Mesopotamia.

151

Mesopotamia

the people who lived in Sumer, to develop many important new ways of life.

The Mesopotamian plain had a number of disadvantages—very hot summers, little rain, few resources, and parched, dry land. Heavy spring floods created spongy marshes and often killed young crops, and fall floods could destroy the harvest. Yet the Sumerians saw possibilities. The flooding, for example, spread rich soil, perfect for growing wheat and barley.

The ingenious Sumerians found a way to bring the land to life. They created an irrigation system with dams, gates, and canals. The Tigris and Euphrates rivers were slightly higher than the plain. The farmers dug canals from the rivers to the fields. Then, at the proper times in the growing cycle, they opened the gates and allowed gravity to pull the precious water down to the fields.

Because the times of flooding were unpredictable, the Sumerians also needed a method of flood control. For this they made artificial lakes or ponds to hold the excess water until it was needed. The Sumerians' irrigation system turned their dry land into a fertile plain.

But the Sumerians were not just successful farmers. They were also the builders of a great civilization. Let's take a closer look at what they achieved. ■

■ *Give evidence to support this statement: Irrigation was essential to the development of civilization in Mesopotamia.*

## The Remarkable Sumerians

The Sumerians were a creative and energetic people. In their land, archaeologists have discovered traces of farming villages and irrigation systems from as early as 5000 B.C. They have also found evidence of great cities and a complex civilization that developed around 3500 B.C.

### The Sumerian City-State

By 3000 B.C., 12 great Sumerian cities dotted the Mesopotamian plain. On the map on page 151, find Ur, Kish, and Lagash. Many thousands of Sumerians lived in these and other cities at this time. It is estimated that Lagash, for example, had as many as 20,000 people.

These centers of population were not just cities; they were city-states. Each **city-state** was made up of a city and the surrounding villages and farmland that it controlled. The farmers produced the food. City dwellers did other kinds of work. Some were brick makers,

▼ *Delicately carved stone cylinder seals like the one below illustrate the artistry of the Sumerians. The design on the seal impression at the right was made by rolling the seal in wet clay. The result was a raised picture that could be used to show ownership or record an agreement.*

152

canal builders, butchers, potters, and so forth. These workers exchanged their goods and services for food.

Mesopotamia is a region, not a country or nation. No central power controlled all the city-states, and there were no boundary lines. Each city-state was independent.

Priests ruled the early city-states, an indication of the primary role that religion played in Sumerian life. In fact, religion and government were combined. The priests ran the irrigation systems. They watched over the canals, planned new ones, gathered work crews, appointed inspectors, and settled arguments. They stored the surplus grain in the temples and distributed it during droughts and other hard times for farmers. In return, they collected taxes in the form of grain, animals, and other farm products. They also prayed and made sacrifices to please the Sumerian gods.

### A Typical City-State

Kish, like the other Sumerian city-states, was built of mud brick. Its streets were narrow and winding. Its houses were small, windowless, and closely packed. In the photo above, you can see the ruins

of houses on a typical Sumerian street. Try to imagine how these houses once looked. What do you think it would have been like to live in one?

Most houses were like those described above. But the cities also had larger houses, the homes of the wealthy. Some had two stories and were built around a courtyard, like the one in the drawing below.

Kish also had a number of large public buildings. No doubt the most impressive of these buildings was the temple. And, by about 2700 B.C., Kish also had a huge royal palace.

Finally, like the other Sumerian cities, Kish had a thriving marketplace. Farmers and merchants came to the market with their wares. Traders from far-off lands brought products that were not available in Mesopotamia. Like other Sumerian cities, Kish was a

◄ *The photo shows the ruins of typical Sumerian houses in the ancient town of Larsa.*

▼ *From excavations at Ur, an archaeologist created the drawing below to show what a large Sumerian house, perhaps the home of a wealthy family, might have looked like.*

153

The first wheel, invented sometime around 3500 B.C. by a Sumerian craftsman, was a solid wooden one, similar in design to this reconstruction. Lighter, spoked wheels came over a thousand years later.

This well-preserved game-board, about 4,500 years old, is a fine example of Sumerian craftsmanship. What other information does it give us about the Sumerians?

busy, exciting place, and trade was its lifeblood. This growing long-distance trade was an important part of the civilization that arose in the great cities of the Mesopotamian plain.

## Builders of Civilization

Why did the harsh land of Sumer give rise to the world's first civilization? Remember that irrigation was most likely the key.

Irrigation allowed farmers to produce a surplus of food. The surplus freed some people to live in cities and work at occupations other than farming.

To run the vast irrigation systems, the Sumerians had to work together. They needed **administrators,** or managers, to organize the building and upkeep of the canals. The first of these administrators were the priests.

To please the gods and to store the surplus, the people built great temples. These building projects required stone, wood, and metal. Sumer lacked these, so the Sumerians traded with merchants from places near and far, including the lands we know today as Iran and India. Farmers exchanged wheat, barley, dates, wool, and dairy products for the tools and other supplies they needed. These included large items, such as lumber for building projects, and smaller items, such as stone hoes and clay pots.

As trade became increasingly important, other workers made goods to exchange at the market. Some created glittering jewelry. Others crafted decorative pottery, musical instruments, and colorful fabrics. Some even invented fascinating board games like the one pictured at the bottom of page 154. A skilled worker who makes such goods by hand is called an **artisan.**

With the growth of trade, the Sumerians needed a way to keep track of business deals. For example, how much grain does this farmer owe for that stone plow? In order to help keep records, the Sumerians used small clay or stone tokens in various shapes. Each shape stood for a different item or product.

People put the tokens into a round or football-shaped clay container called a *bulla*. The bulla was sealed while the clay was still wet. With the bulla sealed in this way, no one could change or remove its contents. However, no one could tell what tokens were inside the bulla, either.

After a time, people began to press marks into the wet clay of the new bulla to stand for the tokens inside. Archaeologists believe that this simple system of keeping records with tokens and bullae may have led to the invention of writing. In the next lesson, you will discover how this great invention may have come about.

Another important achievement of the Sumerians was the development of new kinds of technology to meet their daily needs. To break through the hard clay soils of their farmlands, they invented the plow. To transport the goods they traded, they developed the wheel and the sailboat. The Sumerians traded for metal, and they became skilled at working with various metals. They made strong tools and weapons, mixing copper and tin to make bronze. All these advances were just the beginning of the wondrous civilization that the Sumerians formed in their harsh homeland. ■

▲ *The bulla and tokens shown here represent an early record-keeping system that may have led to the Sumerians' greatest invention, the world's first writing system.*

■ *What were some important advances that the Sumerians made in government, technology, and communication?*

R E V I E W

1. **FOCUS** What was the relationship between the geography of Mesopotamia and the civilization that developed there?

2. **CONNECT** How were the cities of Ur and Kish examples of civilization?

3. **GOVERNMENT** Kish was a city-state. How was it governed? What was its relationship to the other city-states?

4. **CRITICAL THINKING** The Sumerians traded grain, wool, and other products for the stone, metal, and wood they lacked. What can you conclude about surplus in the lands they traded with?

5. **ACTIVITY** Sumerian cylinder seals were something like a person's signature. Draw a seal you could use to mark property and sign agreements. Make its design show something distinctive about you.

L E S S O N 2

# The Contributions of the Sumerians

**THINKING**
**F O C U S**

*What were the Sumerian contributions in government, religion, and education?*

### Key Terms

- epic
- nomad
- polytheism
- pictograph
- cuneiform
- scribe

➤ *A Sumerian sculptor carved this stone relief of Gilgamesh about 2,000 years after the reign of the ancient king. By that time, Gilgamesh had long been a legendary hero in Mesopotamia.*

Through the tall cedar trees of the Forbidden Forest appeared the terrifying giant Huwawa. The towering creature had a head like a lion's and the teeth of a fierce dragon. His fiery breath struck fear into the hearts of all his enemies.

Facing the terrible monster were two men, both handsome, strong, and brave. One man, Gilgamesh, was king of the city of Uruk *(OO ruk)*. No one rivaled this great adventurer in strength and courage. Next to Gilgamesh stood Enkidu, his valiant friend and servant.

Gilgamesh approached the fearsome Huwawa. Seven huge trees blocked the king's way, but he ripped them from the ground. The angry monster stared at Gilgamesh with his "eye of death." Huwawa then let out a cry so frightening that even the brave Gilgamesh trembled and felt weak. The time was perfect for the giant to attack.

So begins one of the stories in *Gilgamesh*, which was probably the world's first **epic,** or long poem about a hero. The story goes on to tell how the two friends attacked the giant Huwawa. Later, aided by the sun god Utu, Gilgamesh and Enkidu defeated Huwawa.

The story of Gilgamesh was first written down sometime before 2000 B.C., but it had probably been a part of an oral tradition for hundreds of years before that.

The real Gilgamesh was the king of the Sumerian city of Uruk around 2700 B.C. The epic about him is myth, not history, but it teaches us a great deal about how the Sumerians viewed their kings and their gods.

Gilgamesh may have been the world's first super-hero. The epic introduces him this way:

*I* will proclaim to the world the deeds of Gilgamesh. This was the man to whom all things were known; this was the king who knew the countries of the world. He was wise, he saw mysteries and knew secret things.

N.K. Sanders, editor
from, *The Epic of Gilgamesh*

## The First Kings

The earliest Sumerian city-states were ruled by priests, not kings, and the largest structure in each city was the temple. By 3000 B.C., the ruling priests had begun to share power with kings. Soon most cities had a magnificent royal palace in addition to the temple. These changes came about because the Sumerians had enemies; their cities were no longer safe.

### The Rise of Kingship

Silently, under cover of night, they came. They swarmed through the streets, killing defenseless villagers and running off with precious grain and livestock. Who were these invaders? They were warriors from tribes that lived in the nearby mountains. No doubt they were attracted by the wealth of the thriving city-state.

An attack like this could have happened in any Sumerian city around 2900 B.C. Sometimes the raiders were **nomads,** people who moved with their flocks and herds. As the seasons changed, the nomads looked for water and pasture in new places, and they came into increasing conflict with their settled neighbors in the cities.

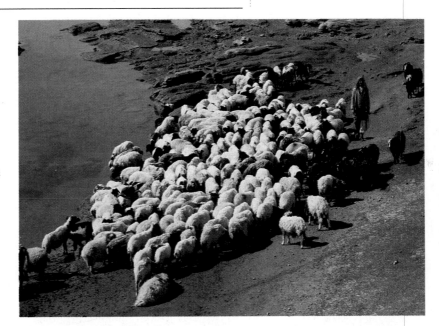

The population grew, and so did competition for land and water. Small skirmishes and great battles became common. The city-states even fought each other.

In the face of all these threats, the city-states looked for ways to protect themselves. Some cities built high walls to keep out invaders. But walls were not enough. The Sumerians needed strong military leaders. One by one, each city chose a temporary leader to rule during wars.

Each military leader eventually became a full-time ruler—a king,

▲ *In the Middle East, nomads and their flocks and herds still move with the changing seasons. Here a modern shepherd is watering his flock in the Euphrates River.*

157

who took over many of the priests' duties. He managed irrigation works, stored surplus grain, and became the chief judge.

### Kings and Gods

Over the years, the kings and priests took on separate tasks. The kings ruled the city-states, while the priests worked to please the gods. Yet kings remained closely tied to the Sumerian religion. Each city had its own god. The people believed that the city god gave the king his power and that their kings were appointed by the gods. They believed that kingship "came down from heaven." ■

■ *What circumstances in Mesopotamia led to the rise of kings?*

▼ *The Sumerians made these small statues of their gods and of themselves. They are wearing the typical Sumerian clothes, which were made of wool.*

## The Sumerian Religion

The religion of Sumer was a kind of **polytheism**—belief in many gods. The Sumerians believed that their gods controlled everything. Without the gods' help, cities could not be safe, and farmers could not grow crops. Drought, disease, floods, and invading armies—all of these evils came and went at the will of the gods. The Sumerians felt helpless against the forces of nature. Only by pleasing the gods, they believed, could they feel confident of good fortune.

### The Gods of Sumer

According to Sumerian legends, four all-powerful gods created the world and ruled over it. The father of all the gods was An, who ruled the sky. Later Enlil, the god of the air, replaced An as supreme god. Enki ruled the waters, and Ninhursag was the mother goddess. Other great gods were the moon god, the sun god, and the goddess of love and war.

Below these gods reigned about 3,000 lesser gods. The most important ones ruled the forces of nature. There was a lower god for each everyday object, such as the pickax or the mud brick.

The great Sumerian gods each ruled a city-state. Enki, for example, ruled the city of Eridu, and the moon god, Nanna, ruled Ur. Each city had a high priest, who worked to please all the gods.

Imagine a Sumerian priest explaining about the gods: "Our gods are hard to please. Like humans, they change their minds, get angry, feel love and hate. Sometimes they are happy. Other times they fall into a great sadness. Like us, they need to eat, and sleep. They even look like us.

"Yet they are not like us at all. They reign immortal and all powerful. They behave better than the best of us but can be more evil than the worst villain. At any time, a god's anger may strike as a flood, a disease, or a savage enemy raid.

"But remember," the priest might conclude, "they are the masters, and we are the servants. Our only purpose is to serve the gods."

## Service to the Gods

All Sumerians served the gods. Even the mightiest king was a servant of the city's god and of the god Enlil, who gave kings their power. One of the king's most important tasks was to oversee the building and repair of the temples. The priests spent their lives serving the gods. They left food in the temple for the city god, recited prayers, and presented offerings. The Sumerians believed that the work kept away misfortune, such as drought or illness.

Serving the gods was not only the task of kings and priests. All Sumerians sent food and animals to the temple. They prayed, attended religious ceremonies, and tried to live a good life. They believed that in return the gods would protect them and bring them good fortune.

Many Sumerians used their artistic skills to serve the gods. Stoneworkers created sculptures for the temple. They made small statues of the gods and of their worshippers. They carved the cylinder seals that were used to show ownership. Metalworkers created beautiful religious art. From gold and silver, they crafted good-luck charms, vases, and small statues of priests, kings, and heroes.

From these works of art, buried for centuries, archaeologists

▼ *This small copper chariot pulled by donkey-like animals was found in a Sumerian temple.*

have learned much about life in ancient Sumer. An even more important discovery—clay tablets covered with strange wedge-shaped marks—showed them something new and wonderful. The Sumerians, they discovered, had invented writing. ■

■ *Describe the Sumerians' religion and explain its important role in the lives of the people.*

## The Beginnings of Writing

Every day you read books, newspapers, and signs. You write school assignments and notes to friends. You may never consider the fact that for thousands of years people had no writing system. By inventing writing, the Sumerians brought us history, the written story of the human past.

Why did the Sumerians invent writing? The reasons were both simple and practical. Merchants and traders needed ways to keep track of what they bought and sold.

Earlier, they had kept records with clay tokens carried in the clay containers called bullae. These tokens had different shapes that stood for different goods and amounts. Eventually, traders put marks on the bullae to show what tokens were inside. The tokens began to seem unnecessary, since the marks on the bullae were enough of a record. Thus, the bullae may have become the first clay tablets, and the marks may have led to the idea of writing.

### Using Picture Writing

The Sumerians' first written symbols were pictures of items that were used in trade, such as a bull or a sack of grain. Such symbols are **pictographs,** or pictures that stand for words or ideas. The Sumerians used a sharpened reed, called a stylus, to draw the pictographs on moist clay.

Look at the chart on this page for typical Sumerian pictographs. As you can see, a pictograph might stand for an object or a related idea. For example, a picture of a sword might mean "power."

Next, the Sumerians extended the pictures to make them stand for syllables related only by sound, not meaning. For example, the Sumerian word for "fish" was *ha.* A picture of a fish could stand for the word *fish,* or it could stand for the syllable *ha* as a part of any word. Here is an example in English:

Now writers could string syllables together to form words. They could express abstract ideas like "belief."

### Simplifying the Pictures

Picture writing changed over time. By 2500 B.C., writers had simplified their symbols and made them wedge shaped. This type of writing is known as **cuneiform** *(KYOO nee uh fawrm),* meaning "wedge shaped." Cuneiform consisted of around 600 symbols, which range from a single wedge to complex patterns of about 30 wedges.

With cuneiform, there were few limits on the ideas that could be expressed. People could keep records about wars and treaties, or

*Sumerian scribes used a reed stylus to press the cuneiform letters onto moist clay tablets. Notice the wedge-shaped letters on the tablet. Then use the chart to trace the development of several cuneiform letters.*

| Origin of Cuneiform, c. 3100–2000 B.C. | | | | |
|---|---|---|---|---|
| **Meaning** | **Early Pictograph** | **Later Pictograph** | **Early Cuneiform** | **Later Cuneiform** |
| Bird | | | | |
| Fish | | | | |
| Foot | | | | |

| Meaning | Pictograph | Phoenician Letter | Greek Letter | Roman Letter |
|---|---|---|---|---|
| Ox | | | | |
| House | | | | |

*The shapes of our letters originated in Sumerian pictographs. The chart shows how we got the Roman alphabet we use today.*

they could write poems. They were also able to describe the gods or the planets. They could write down familiar legends like the story of Gilgamesh.

Few people could read or write in those days. Even kings could not do so. To read and write messages, people employed **scribes,** professional writers and record keepers. Future scribes studied cuneiform in school. The training was long and hard, and included hours of tedious copying and memorizing. But students knew that as scribes they would have a well-respected occupation—for example, secretary for the king or record keeper for the priest.

The cuneiform system was used in the Middle East for about 2,000 years. It spread to neighboring lands, and it became the writing system for several different languages.

Since about A.D. 1840, archaeologists have uncovered thousands of clay tablets filled with cuneiform. Many have not yet been translated. From those that have, we learn much about the people of ancient Mesopotamia.

## Using Symbols for Sounds

Much later, around 900 B.C., the Phoenicians (*fih NIHSH uhns*) devised a simpler way to keep records. The Phoenicians lived on the east coast of the Mediterranean Sea. They were seafaring merchants who traded throughout the area. Cuneiform, with its many symbols, was just too complicated to use in their growing trade. They invented a new writing system with only 22 symbols. Each symbol stood for one sound. If you think this system sounds familiar, you're right. The Phoenicians invented the alphabet. ■

**How Do We Know?**

HISTORY *For many years, historians studying Mesopotamia could not read cuneiform. Then, in 1835, linguists began to decipher a message carved in three languages on a giant rock formation in the Zagros Mountains. By 1857, all three languages had been translated. One was Sumerian. Deciphering cuneiform led to much of our knowledge of the ancient Middle East, including Sumer and the Sumerian people.*

■ *Describe the important steps in the invention of writing, including pictographs, cuneiform, and the alphabet.*

## R E V I E W

1. **FOCUS** What were the Sumerian contributions in government, religion, and education?
2. **CONNECT** Explain how Sumerian achievements in technology and communication helped to advance long-distance trade.
3. **HISTORY** What were the needs of the Sumerians that led to the establishment of kingships? To the invention of writing?
4. **CRITICAL THINKING** Religion had great importance for the Sumerians. What conditions of their lives might help to explain why?
5. **WRITING ACTIVITY** Examine the picture writing for *belief* on page 160. Try writing other words in the same way—*pantry* and *football,* for example. Combine letters and pictures as necessary—for example, in writing *catalog.*

# Writing Systems

*T*he Sumerians created written symbols to meet an everyday need—tracking the goods they traded. You, too, can develop symbols and use them to send secret messages. Like the Sumerians, you'll be limited only by your imagination—and your tools and materials.

### Get Ready

Find a clear, flat surface, such as a desk, table, or floor space. Use waxed paper, plastic, or oilcloth to protect the surface. Get a ball of pottery clay the size of an orange. Find a tool—a new, unsharpened pencil, a paper clip, or a popsicle stick.

### Find Out

Work the clay to soften it. Then flatten it into a sheet. Using the tool you've chosen, press symbols into the clay. Your symbols can stand for sounds, as our alphabet letters do. They can also stand for ideas, as in cuneiform or hieroglyphics (see the charts on the facing page), or for syllables. For instance, if you decide that / is the syllable *par,* and # is the syllable *tee,* how would you write *party?*

Work out a system of symbols. Use them to "write" each word below on your clay tablet:

flower flour  knee needle paddle friend ship friendship  am is are give take jump  true truth truly I you they

Write a few sentences using these words.

## Move Ahead

Find a place in the classroom to display the clay tablets. Can you tell which tool a person used, just by looking at his or her tablet? Do any of the written "languages" look alike? Can your classmates read the sentence you "wrote"?

Look at the examples of cuneiform and hieroglyphic writing on the charts. Which pictographs really look like the objects they represent?

Transfer your new language from clay to paper. Use a pen, pencil, crayon, or marker. Will the writing tool make a difference in the way your "words" look?

## Explore Some More

Make a "dictionary" of your new language. A friend can use it to read your messages. Also keep a list of symbols you notice in everyday life such as road signs and flags.

Create a special symbol to stand for your signature. That symbol on a note or drawing will show that it came from you.

▲ An Egyptian scribe keeps accounts for his master in this sculpture, inset against a detail of hieroglyphics from an Egyptian wall-hanging.

## Hieroglyphics Versus Alphabet

|  | Hieroglyphics | Greek Script |
|---|---|---|
| Soldier |  | στρατιώτης |
| Eye |  | μάτι |
| Beetle |  | χάνθαρος |
| Swallow |  | χελιδόνι |

## Development of Cuneiform Writing

|  | Early Pictograph | Later Pictograph | Early Cuneiform | Later Cuneiform |
|---|---|---|---|---|
| Donkey |  |  |  |  |
| Ox |  |  |  |  |
| Sun |  |  |  |  |
| Grain |  |  |  |  |
| Orchard |  |  |  |  |

▲ How do hieroglyphic writing and cuneiform differ from an alphabetic system?

Mesopotamia

# The Luring of Enkidu

### Bernarda Bryson

*Many myths have survived about the Mesopotamian King Gilgamesh. This selection from a book called* Gilgamesh *tells about the education of Enkidu, the wild man. Enkidu later becomes King Gilgamesh's friend and servant. Here, a shepherd's son describes Enkidu.*

*You learned about King Gilgamesh in Lesson 2. This is another myth involving the well-known king.*

*gazelle*   a hoofed, horned mammal of Africa and Asia

The hair springs out of his head like a field of grain, and he has the horns of a wild beast!"

"If he stole your catch of game, my son, why didn't you stop him?"

"He is taller and more powerful than Gilgamesh the King. I was numbed with fear!"

"If what you say is true, son, then we must report the matter to the King. But if you have lied, we will be in disgrace forever!"

The shepherd and his son went into the city of Uruk to make their complaint. But there the populace were already spreading rumors about the wild man. Some said, "He is covered with hair from head to foot," and others, "He is taller than a giant and eats grass with the gazelles!"

It was the eldest of the elders who led the hunter and his father before the King. "O Gilgamesh," said the elder, "there is a wild man that terrorizes the countryside. He robs the hunter of his game and disperses the herds of the shepherd. He turns all who see him numb with fear—indeed I've heard that he is taller and more powerful than Gilgamesh the King!"

Gilgamesh, who feared nothing, might have been expected to say, "Then it's I who will go out and subdue him and bring him captive to the city!" Not at all; he sent to the temple of Ishtar for a certain priestess, one called Harim, servant of the goddess.

He said to her, "Harim, I have a certain task for you; it is one that turns the boldest hunters numb with fear!"

"Then I am afraid," said Harim.

The eldest of the elders spoke angrily, "This is not a girl's task, O King; it is a task for a brave man—a hero!"

"Tut tut," said Gilgamesh. "It is a girl's task of smiles and charm. Go, Harim; soften the heart of the wild man and bring him back to the city!"

Harim was led by the hunter to the edge of the forest, and she noted that he began to tremble with fear. "Go back to the hut of your father," she commanded. "If I can tame the wild man, I will lead him into the city alone."

The hunter was shamed by the girl's bravery. "Do not enter the forest, O Harim; I myself will go." But the priestess laughed at him and sent him home.

She went among the dark cedars; she listened to the sounds of birds and of monkeys chattering. She noted the bits of sunlight that filtered through the branches and lit up the flowers, moss, and bracken on the forest floor. "How peaceful a place this is! How could any evil thing lurk here?" Harim found a fresh spring bubbling with cool water. She sat beside it on a stone, untied her sandals, and dipped her feet in the water.

Enkidu came to the place with the small wild horse and the gazelle. As they drew near, the two beasts became nervous, sniffed the air, and fled. But Enkidu stood still; he wondered what new danger was near, what unknown beast might have come to the water.

When he saw the girl sitting there his breath failed and he was overcome. He had not yet seen a human being, and this creature seemed to him the most admirable, the most enchanting being that he had ever seen. He stood quietly in order not to frighten her.

Harim gazed at this giant figure, his soaring horns, and his unkempt looks and would have run away, but she could not move. She opened her mouth to scream and could not make a sound. She was numb with terror. And Enkidu noting this remained quiet; he had made friends with many timid creatures and he knew their ways.

When the priestess saw the gentleness of his manner, her courage returned to her somewhat. She called out shyly, "Hello!"

Enkidu knew no words. He could babble somewhat as the monkeys did. He could bark quite like a fox, or trill like many birds. He had various calls of greeting for his wild friends, but this new animal made sounds that he could not understand.

He neither barked nor roared, but stood perplexed looking at the girl. Again she spoke, and now held out her hands to him in greeting.

Enkidu approached slowly and sat on the earth beside the white feet of Harim. She said all sorts of things to him and he understood nothing. She asked him many questions and he could not reply. But he felt ecstasy in his heart, and great contentment in merely sitting beside her.

How easy was her conquest of Enkidu! Harim smiled, but she now began to feel a new sort of fear. How could she lead this great fellow, so gentle and so innocent, back to the city of Uruk?

Would the people set on him and kill him? Would they jeer at him? Would the King have him put into a cage and carried through the streets on the backs of soldiers? She shuddered.

No, first she must teach him the ways of people, the conformity of life.

"Al-ka ti-ba i-na ga-ag-ga-ri!" said Harim. "Come, rise from the ground!" But the wild man did not understand. Thus, she taught him the word for standing, and then after that, the word for sitting. She taught him the words for walking, running, talking, laughing, eating, and he repeated each one, learning it. She taught him the words for trees and for stones and for water, for earth and for the trailing vines that grew beside the spring, and for the spring itself. She taught him the words for feet and hands and the names of all the fingers and all the myriad words of love.

Thus patiently, Harim taught Enkidu to be like ordinary men. She cut his hair and combed it in the way of people of the city. She made him bathe; she tore her long tunic into two parts, making of one-half a garment for Enkidu, keeping the other half for herself.

Again she spoke to him, and now he understood, "A-na-tal-ka En-ki-du ki-ma ili ta-ba-as-si!"—"I gaze upon you, Enkidu; you are like a god!"

He brought her gifts—all the things that he had come to know and love in the forest and from the open steppes; wild cucumbers and cassia melon, grapes and figs and caper buds from the dry rocks. He brought her blossoms of golden mimosa and fragrant branches of jasmine.

After some time had passed Harim said, "Now I will lead Enkidu out among the people and everyone will admire him!" But still she feared for his life so she took him first to the hut of the shepherd.

At the edge of the forest Enkidu stopped and turned back. He was overcome with regret; how could he leave forever his friends of the woods and wild places? Who would protect them? Who would release them from the traps? How could he leave behind his friend the little wild horse, or the gazelle, the rabbits, the monkeys that had taught him to play games?

But as he approached they leaped away startled. The rabbit hid trembling in the grass and the birds took off with a wild flutter of wings.

Enkidu threw himself to the ground weeping. "O Harim, what have I done? How have I made all my friends into strangers? Why do they run from me?"

"Enkidu is no longer a wild creature. He is no longer a beast of the forest and the open plain. Enkidu is now a man. He will live among men and be eminent among men!"

Enkidu followed regretfully as the priestess led him toward the hut of the shepherd. This man greeted him with awe and

**myriad** many; innumerable

**eminent** distinguished; outstanding

admiration, but his son fled from the place and hid in the sheepfold. After some time he returned, running. "Father, a lion has entered the fold! It is devouring the lambs!"

Enkidu went to the sheepfold where again he wrestled with the lion, his friend who no longer knew him. Again he overcame the beast, but he let it go free. He lifted the lambs gently, washing and tending the ones that bled. To his great joy they did not shun him or run away. Neither did the young calves nor the barnyard fowl. A dog followed him wagging its tail. A cat smoothed its fur against his legs, and again he was content.

In the hut of the shepherd Enkidu learned to sit on a chair and to wash his hands before eating. He learned how to care for animals, to make plants grow, and to build with mud and brick and reeds. He learned to play on a flute. He ate bread. There he drank the juice of the wild grape. His face shone, he rejoiced; he sang.

Harim smiled. "Now Enkidu has become like a man, we shall go into the city!"

## Further Reading

*Gilgamesh and Other Babylonian Tales*. Jennifer Westwood.

*He Who Saw Everything: The Epic of Gilgamesh*. Anita Feagles. This book and *Gilgamesh and Other Babylonian Tales* are other versions of the Gilgamesh epic.

*In the Land of Ur*. Hans Baumann. The author describes archaeological finds in Mesopotamia and tells what they reveal about the ancient civilizations of that area.

*The Three Brothers of Ur*. Jennifer G. Fyson. Here is an adventure story about three boys in the ancient city of Ur. The story also teaches about the boys' religion and customs.

L E S S O N   3

# The First Empires

THINKING
F O C U S

*How did three great rulers build and maintain empires in Mesopotamia?*

## Key Terms

- empire
- code

"I nvaders! We're under attack!" The words resounded through Uruk as a fearsome army thundered toward the great city. First came the chariots pulled by hardy, donkeylike animals. In each chariot stood a driver, and behind him a warrior, shooting deadly arrows. Next came the foot-soldiers, rushing forward as a solid block—metal helmets, a wall of metal shields, spears leveled to face their foes.

➤ *This bronze head is believed to be of Sargon of Akkad or his grandson, Naram-Sin, who extended Sargon's empire.*

The attack caught Uruk unprepared. Who were these invaders? Who would dare to rouse the anger of the great Lugal-zaggesi (*LOO guhl zuh GEE see*), king of Uruk and ruler of all Sumer? But Lugal-zaggesi was not in Uruk at the time, and the forces that he had left behind to protect the city could not stop the invaders.

The bold attackers battered down the city's gate. They ravaged the streets and avenues, burning and tearing down buildings. They killed some residents and terrorized the rest, seizing whatever riches they found. When Uruk lay in ruins, they used battering rams and ropes to tear down the city's wall.

A few days later, Lugal-zaggesi returned with his troops. The king saw his ruined city and savagely attacked the invaders. Again, arrows whizzed through the air. Metal clanked against metal as swords and shields met. After many hours, the battle ended. Now a captive, the great Lugal-zaggesi stood before his conquerors.

Who were those fierce warriors, and who was their general, who barked orders in a foreign tongue? He called himself Sargon, meaning "true king." Soon this warrior-king would be known throughout all Mesopotamia.

# Sargon of Akkad

Unlike most kings, Sargon did not begin his life in a palace. His parents were probably herders on the north edge of Sumer near the Euphrates River. They spoke a language called Akkadian.

When Sargon left home, he went to Kish and became a servant of its king. Historians believe he later killed the king and usurped his throne. Next, he gathered an army and founded a new capital— the city of Akkad *(AHK ahd),* on the Euphrates River.

Sargon's power grew. He led his strong army to the cities of Uruk, Ur, Lagash, and Umma, conquering each one. Finally, he reached the Persian Gulf. According to legend, he washed his weapons in the waters of the gulf as a sign that he had conquered all of Sumer's city-states.

Later, Sargon conquered northern Mesopotamia and lands as far east as modern Iran and as far west as the Mediterranean coast. His kingdom may have reached to Egypt.

Until Sargon's rule, the city-states were independent, each with its own king. They had walls to protect them from enemies, including other city-states. With each conquest, Sargon tore down the walls, showing that the city was part of his vast kingdom. He created the world's first **empire**—a nation and the city-states and nations it has conquered, under one ruler. Sargon ruled until 2279 B.C., about 55 years. For another 60 years, his sons and grandsons ruled.

As the years passed, problems developed, and the empire grew weaker. One problem was rebellion. The city-states never accepted the rule of a central government. They continued to struggle for independence. A second problem was frequent invasions. Enemies could easily invade the city-states on their flat, open plain. Around 2250 B.C., the Gutians, fierce warriors from the neighboring Zagros Mountains, invaded Akkad and left it in ruins. Sargon's empire had collapsed. ■

## How Do We Know?

**HISTORY** *As you read about the ancient world, do not be surprised if two sources give two different dates for the same event. Sargon of Akkad provides a good example, since historians do not agree about the exact years of his life and reign. To find out why this is true, review Chapter 3, Lesson 1. Remember that historians are constantly finding and interpreting new evidence.*

■ *What important change did Sargon make in the way Mesopotamia was governed?*

**Early Empires: Akkad, Assyria, Babylonia, 2350–1750 B.C.**

Akkad c. 2300 B.C.
Assyria c. 1800 B.C.
Babylonia c. 1750 B.C.

◄ *There were no official boundaries for Sargon's empire. The map shows the extent of the great king's influence.*

169

Mesopotamia

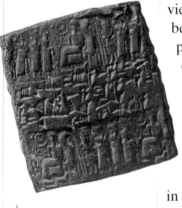

*Letters between the king of Mari and his sons were written on clay tablets like this one, shown with its clay envelope.*

# Rival Empires

During the next four centuries, the Sumerians recovered some of their lost power and made great achievements under the kings of Ur. But then power shifted to two new centers. Assyria, centered at the city-state of Assur in the north, and Babylonia, centered at the city-state of Babylon in the south, vied for power. In fact, the struggle between north and south, with power swinging from one to the other, became the pattern for much of Mesopotamia's history.

### A Strong Assyrian Ruler

Assyria reached its peak under the ruler Shamshi-Adad *(SHAM shee uh DAD),* in power from about 1813 to 1781 B.C. Like Sargon, Shamshi-Adad was a great conqueror. He led his army west and conquered what is now Lebanon, with its thick forests and mineral-rich mountains. Next he overthrew the King of Mari on the Euphrates, installing his son as the new king of the city.

Shamshi-Adad held his lands together by trade as well as force. Assyrian merchants exchanged Mesopotamian products such as fine cloth for valuable foreign goods including tin, copper, and silver. Their trade agreements were prepared by scribes like the one in A Moment in Time on page 171.

Shamshi-Adad appointed his two sons to help him rule his vast, rich kingdom. But he and his sons never felt safe. They feared attack by nomads who envied Assyria's riches. Even more, they worried about neighboring kingdoms. One neighbor, Babylonia, especially worried them.

### A Wise Babylonian Ruler

A young ruler named Hammurabi *(hah moo RAH bee)* came to power in Babylonia in 1792 B.C., during the last years of Shamshi-Adad's life. The Assyrians were right to fear him. One day, he would take over Assyrian lands and rule all of Mesopotamia.

In the fifth year of his rule, he set out with his strong army to gain control of the neighboring kingdoms. Over the next five years, he conquered lands east to the Zagros Mountains and south to Uruk.

Later, around 1760 B.C., the Assyrians joined some neighboring peoples and attacked Hammurabi's kingdom. The battles were fierce and bloody, but the great king defeated the invaders.

Hammurabi felt strong enough to begin extending his lands. He marched his victorious army north. He defeated other armies and added new lands, including Assyria, to his kingdom. Finally, Hammurabi ruled all of Mesopotamia. His kingdom included 24 great cities. Now Mesopotamia formed one enormous empire. Use the map on page 169 to find out the extent of Hammurabi's Babylonian Empire.

Hammurabi was a capable ruler. He sent governors to all his lands. He also sent out judges, tax collectors, and military commanders. He kept tight control over his far-flung cities and maintained a strong central government. Hammurabi was a wise king and a great military leader. Today, however, we remember him mainly for one of his achievements—the Code of Hammurabi.

# A Mesopotamian Scribe

*8:33 A.M., December 17, 1794 B.C.
On the bank of the Euphrates River,
in the port of the city of Mari*

**Seals**
Inside a purse under the scribe's robe are two seals. One prints her name. The other prints this important message: "May the gods curse anyone who changes what is here written!"

**Hands**
Her quick hands wrote as fast as the merchant dictated to her. Now she's making an envelope to protect the document.

**Pot**
Inside is a day's supply of wet clay and water. Her sister collected the clay at a special place near the Euphrates where it contains less sand.

**Envelope**
She pats it thin as a piecrust. Next she'll write on the envelope and wrap it around the tablet.

**Skirt**
A customer who expected to see her father was shocked to find a woman in the dead scribe's place. Since her father had no sons, he taught his elder daughter his trade. It took 11 years.

**Stylus**
She uses this sharpened reed to press words into the wet clay in the neat "handwriting" her father taught her.

**Tablet**
It lists the items being shipped—110 pounds of cedar wood, 10 pounds of silver, 60 lengths of cloth, 12 pounds of dyed wool, and 6 tanned cowhides. The tablet ends with a promise: "The boat captain will pay the merchant 100 pounds of silver in two years."

c. 2334–c. 2279 B.C.,
Sargon of Akkad

1813–1781 B.C.,
Shamshi-Adad of Assyria

2000

1500

1792–1750 B.C.,
Hammurabi of Babylonia

▲ On the timeline, locate the rulers of the three early empires presented in this lesson. In Lesson 4, you will read about the two later rulers.

### Hammurabi's Code

"I have brought justice to all my subjects." So boasted Hammurabi in words that were carved on an eight-foot slab of black stone. Below the king's words, the remarkable structure listed 282 laws of Babylonia. Most people couldn't read, but the laws were public now. Anyone could find out what they were, so no one could be punished at a ruler's whim.

Hammurabi chose carefully among the laws of his empire. He tried to cover all matters that were important to his people. He made sure that no laws disagreed with each other. Such a complete and organized set of laws is called a **code.** Hammurabi's Code was not the first or even the best of the early law lists. But we know more about it than about others, since it was preserved on a stone slab.

Some of Hammurabi's laws covered religion, irrigation, and military service. Others dealt with trade, property, slavery, and the duties of professional workers such as surgeons. Still others concerned marriage, family, and crime. Here are a few of them:

► The top of the stone slab that is inscribed with Hammurabi's Code is shown in this photo. Hammurabi is standing in front of the god, possibly the Babylonians' chief god Marduk, who is delivering the laws to him.

Items from Hammurabi's code:

*If a freeman has destroyed the eye of another freeman, they shall destroy his eye.*

*If he has broken another freeman's bone, they shall break his bone.*

*If he has destroyed the eye of a commoner or broken the bone of a commoner, he shall pay one mina [one to two pounds] of silver.*

*If a freeman hired an ox and has destroyed its eye, he shall give one-half its value in silver to the owner of the ox.*

744–727 B.C.,
Tiglath-Pileser III of the
New Assyrian Empire

| 1000 | 500 | B.C. | A.D. |

605–562 B.C.,
Nebuchadnezzar of the
New Babylonian Empire

Read the laws again. Which one suggests the importance of agriculture in Mesopotamian life? From our perspective today, we may see problems with these laws. Which one seems unfair? How do some laws vary according to a person's position in society?

Hammurabi's Code was an important advance. It helped to establish the kind of life that people should live, a responsible life framed by law and order. Some laws showed concern for the less powerful. For example, there were laws that protected wives from being beaten or neglected by their husbands.

Hammurabi's Code helped the king rule his empire. Yet even with a law code, with governers, and with armies, Hammurabi's kingdom began to crumble after the great king's death in 1750 B.C.

## The Next 750 Years

In this chapter you have seen that invasions by people from surrounding deserts and mountains were common throughout the history of Mesopotamia. Around 1600 B.C., the Hittites, a fierce mountain people from the northwest, invaded Mesopotamia and conquered the city of Babylon.

Other invaders included the Kassites from the Zagros Mountains to the northeast. The Kassites gained control of Babylonia and ruled the city for four centuries. They adopted the Babylonian language and culture. In addition, they brought peace and order to the land.

By now, several kingdoms outside of Mesopotamia were becoming increasingly prominent in the Middle East. Some of them made important contributions. For example, it was during this period that the Phoenicians invented the alphabet. The Jews developed their belief in one God. And by the 1200s B.C., in the north, a new Assyrian Empire was emerging that would become more powerful than ever. ■

■ *Support this statement: Although their empires did not survive long after they died, in many ways Shamshi-Adad and Hammurabi were capable rulers.*

R E V I E W

1. **FOCUS** How did three great rulers build and maintain empires in Mesopotamia?
2. **CONNECT** Besides land, what resources and achievements made the city-states desirable to conquerors?
3. **GEOGRAPHY** What features of the geography of Mesopotamia forced the Sumerians to develop trade?
4. **CRITICAL THINKING** Military leaders have often performed actions that serve as signs of power or conquest, such as Sargon's washing his weapons in the Persian Gulf. Why are such actions important?
5. **ACTIVITY** Plan a panel discussion about crime and punishment, focusing on what makes a punishment fair or unfair. In your discussion, refer to Hammurabi's Code and to present-day laws.

# Using Telescoping Timelines

## Here's Why

Some timelines give a broad view of events over many centuries. Other timelines, called telescoping timelines, give a more detailed view of a shorter period. Like a telephoto lens, a telescoping timeline allows you to "zoom in" on a certain period of time.

Suppose you wanted to use a timeline to present key events from one period in the history of Mesopotamia. A telescoping timeline is an effective way to do this.

## Here's How

The 2,000-year timeline at the bottom of the page shows major events in Mesopotamian history. The dates on the thick bar show you that the timeline covers the period from 2400 to 400 B.C.

Now look at the 150-year telescoping timeline above it. This timeline's subject is the rise and decline of Babylonian power. It covers the period from 650 to 500 B.C. The shaded triangle between the timelines helps you see where the telescoping timeline "fits" on the 2,000-year timeline.

On which timeline should an event from the chapter be plotted? That depends on when the event occurred. For example, Hammurabi's reign belongs on the 2,000-year timeline. His reign was over before 650 B.C. However, the burning of Jerusalem in 587 B.C. belongs on the 150-year timeline.

## Try It

Copy both of the timelines from the book onto your own paper. Decide on which timeline each of the following events belongs: the end of Nabonidus's rule, in 539 B.C.; Adad-Nirari's defeat of northern Mesopotamia, in 911 B.C.; the Hittite conquest of Babylon, in 1600 B.C. Plot each event in its proper place on the timeline.

## Apply It

Make your own timeline and telescoping timeline. Use the events of your own life, from birth until now, as your base timeline. Make a telescoping timeline of one year. Include any special events, such as a family trip, that happened during that year.

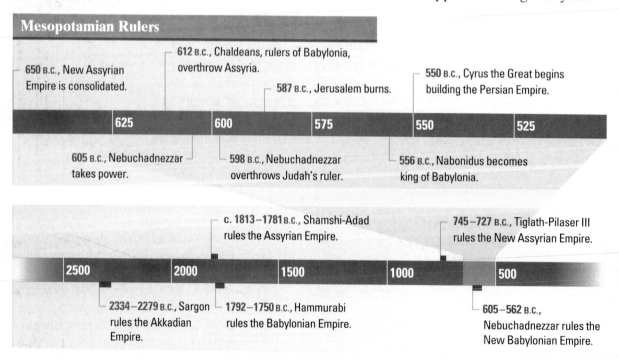

**Mesopotamian Rulers**

650 B.C., New Assyrian Empire is consolidated.

612 B.C., Chaldeans, rulers of Babylonia, overthrow Assyria.

587 B.C., Jerusalem burns.

550 B.C., Cyrus the Great begins building the Persian Empire.

625  600  575  550  525

605 B.C., Nebuchadnezzar takes power.

598 B.C., Nebuchadnezzar overthrows Judah's ruler.

556 B.C., Nabonidus becomes king of Babylonia.

c. 1813–1781 B.C., Shamshi-Adad rules the Assyrian Empire.

745–727 B.C., Tiglath-Pilaser III rules the New Assyrian Empire.

2500  2000  1500  1000  500

2334–2279 B.C., Sargon rules the Akkadian Empire.

1792–1750 B.C., Hammurabi rules the Babylonian Empire.

605–562 B.C., Nebuchadnezzar rules the New Babylonian Empire.

Chapter 6

L E S S O N   4

# New Empires

Three hundred feet above the city of Babylon towered the majestic ziggurat—seven stories high. Each story was smaller than the one below it, giving the whole structure a pyramid shape. In the shrine at the top, priests chanted prayers to Marduk, who was their chief god. The Babylonians believed that Marduk was the creator of the world, so they called the ziggurat E-temen-anki, "The House of the Foundation of Heaven and Earth."

Babylon had other marvels besides the grand ziggurat. Not far from the tower were the magnificent "hanging gardens." Sweetly scented plants and trees grew from high terraces, creating a lush, cool resting place, out of the blazing sun.

Beyond the gardens stood the city walls. These walls were so thick that a chariot drawn by four large horses could easily travel along on top of them. The great king of Babylon, Nebuchadnezzar *(neh buh kuhd NEHZ ur)*, had rebuilt the towering ziggurat, planted the gardens, and constructed the vast walls.

These glorious building projects tell us something important about the age that we are about to explore. In ancient Mesopotamia, the period after 1000 B.C. is recognized as the age of the great new empires of Assyria and Babylonia. The giant structures built at this time in Babylon and other cities were displays of the fabulous wealth and power of these empires and their rulers.

THINKING
F O C U S

*How were the New Assyrian and New Babylonian empires alike, and how were they different?*

## Key Terms

- exile
- astronomer

◄ *The ziggurat at Babylon was probably as old as the city itself. It had been destroyed and rebuilt more than once before Nebuchadnezzar's reign. This picture shows one artist's idea of what the ziggurat might have looked like.*

175

Mesopotamia

# A New Assyrian Empire

## How Do We Know?

**HISTORY** *In 1849 and 1852, archaeologists made an exciting find, 25,000 clay tablets written in cuneiform—the library of the Assyrian king Ashurbanipal. They contain writings of the Sumerians and Babylonians, whose cultures the king admired. Although remembered as cruel conquerors, the Assyrians were wise enough to collect and preserve these treasures from the ancient world.*

In the late 900s B.C., power again swung north to Assyria. But this New Assyrian Empire would reach far beyond Mesopotamia.

## A Path of Conquest

How did the Assyrians build such a vast empire, and how did they maintain it? The Assyrians had long been rugged warriors. Their tightly organized and well-equipped army stormed enemy cities like a mighty machine—on foot, in chariots, and on swift horses. Once Assyrian troops battered down a city's gates, they showed no mercy. They murdered, tortured, and enslaved their enemies. Those conquered by the Assyrians hated them forever.

The king of Assyria, Adad-Nirari (*uh DAD nih RAH ree*), set out to conquer new lands and gather riches around 911 B.C. The king secured the northern part of Mesopotamia for the Assyrians. Everywhere his army went, they looted and plundered, gathering gold, silver, jewels, and other wealth. The rulers who followed Adad-Nirari enlarged his path of conquest, moving west as far as the Mediterranean Sea.

Almost 200 years later, in 745 B.C., King Tiglath-Pileser III (*TIHG lath puh LEE zur*) came to the throne. He succeeded in extending the empire to the south by taking over Assyria's age-old rival, Babylonia.

Tiglath-Pileser III struggled to hold his far-flung empire together as many of the conquered peoples rebelled. Early in his reign, he developed a strategy to end rebellion. He forced many people to move from their homelands to faraway parts of the empire. For example, Assyrian soldiers took 30,000 Syrians on a scorching march across desert, valley, and highland into the Zagros Mountains. By doing this, he hoped to break the spirit of rebellion.

By 650 B.C., the New Assyrian Empire covered lands from the Persian Gulf to Egypt to present-day Turkey. Use the map below to

*Compare the extent of the New Assyrian and New Babylonian empires. Then compare them both with the early empires shown in the map on page 169.*

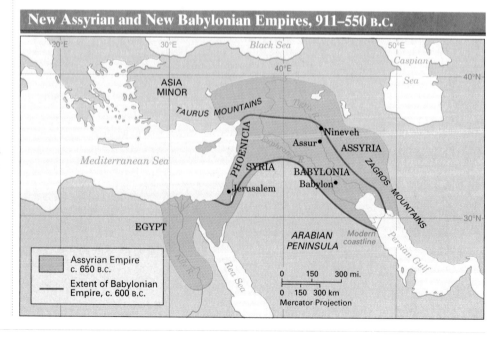

**New Assyrian and New Babylonian Empires, 911–550 B.C.**

Assyrian Empire c. 650 B.C.

Extent of Babylonian Empire, c. 600 B.C.

In the ruins of Assyrian temples and palaces, archaeologists have found remarkable examples of Assyrian artistry. Especially noteworthy are the reliefs—stone sculptures that project out from the walls, giving a three-dimensional effect. This example presents a vivid battle scene.

see the extent of the New Assyrian Empire at its peak.

### The Fall of Assyria

The Assyrians did little to win the favor of their subjects. They took much from them—slaves, silver, gold, iron, copper, crops, livestock. They used this wealth to build their own magnificent cities.

Their practice of relocating rebellious peoples made them even more despised, and the rebellions continued. The groups that had been displaced never gave their loyalty to Assyria. Neighboring armies built up their strength to defeat the empire. Finally, the Chaldeans (kal DEE uhns), who then ruled Babylonia, joined the Medes from the Zagros Mountains on the east to overthrow the Assyrians in 612 B.C. Once again, power had swung to the south. ■

■ What policies of the Assyrian rulers helped to cause the eventual downfall of their empire?

## A New Babylonian Empire

The Chaldeans of Babylonia ruled from their capital, the city of Babylon. Find this city on the map on page 176. Notice how large the New Babylonian Empire would become at its peak.

Like the Assyrians, the Babylonians were great conquerors. They were also great traders. Archaeologists have found thousands of cuneiform tablets telling of their complex trade networks. The Babylonians traded with Lebanon, Egypt, and Greece. To protect their trade routes, they sent their armies west.

### A Babylonian Emperor

Leading the Babylonian armies was the great king Nebuchadnezzar whose grand building projects you have read about. Nebuchadnezzar ruled from 605 to 562 B.C. He captured major cities such as Jerusalem and the Phoenician city of Tyre (tyr). He also drove

177

Mesopotamia

*The present-day city of Al Hillah, Iraq, is near the site of ancient Babylon. Little remains of the magnificent city. However, parts of it are now being restored by the Iraqi government, based on the discoveries of archaeologists. The restorations in process include the hanging gardens, the ziggurat, and Nebuchadnezzar's main palace.*

the Egyptians out of Syria and Phoenicia and thus was able to secure a rich trade gateway to the Mediterranean Sea.

The Phoenicians, the Philistines, and the Jews lived to the west of Babylonia, near the Mediterranean Sea. These conquered peoples were no better off than they had been under the Assyrians. They bitterly resented paying taxes to the Babylonians. Nebuchadnezzar was forced to work hard to maintain his empire. Every year he led his troops west to put down rebellions.

In 598 B.C., the Jews of the kingdom of Judah, the south part of Israel, refused to pay taxes to

Nebuchadnezzar. The Babylonian king overthrew Judah's ruler and forced 3,000 Jews on a torturous march to Mesopotamia. In 587 B.C., he put down another rebellion by burning the city of Jerusalem and destroying its great temple. This time, he sent thousands of Jews to Babylon as slaves.

The poem on page 179 expresses the sadness of the Jews in **exile**—forced absence from their country. The Babylonians had ordered the Jews to entertain them by playing stringed instruments, called lyres, and singing about their Lord, the God of the Jews. Zion is a Hebrew name for Israel, their homeland.

## UNDERSTANDING LIMITS OF AUTHORITY

When Sargon was king of Akkad, he had no authority over other city-states. Nor did other kings have authority over Akkad. Each king ruled within the territorial limits of his city-state.

### Real but Invisible

Territorial limits are not, of course, lines drawn on the earth, like the boundary lines drawn on maps. They are real, though, and they are recognized by people and governments everywhere in the world.

### War and Negotiation

Nations establish territorial limits either by war or negotiation. Sargon conquered neighboring city-states and combined them to make a single empire. He destroyed city walls to symbolize the end of the old limits. More recently, the United States and Great Britain signed a treaty in 1846 establishing the U.S. border with Canada at 49° north latitude.

### Kinds of Territorial Limits

Territorial limits are applied to states, provinces, and cities as well as to nations. What other examples can you think of?

Today, territorial limits often involve more than the boundaries we see on maps

and globes. For example, modern nations now claim air space within their territorial limits. Airplanes may not fly over a foreign country without permission. Countries with coastlines claim part of the ocean waters as their own. For the United States, this area extends 3 nautical miles, or 3.6 land miles, from shore.

In 1969, the American flag was planted on the moon. That event focused the world's attention on problems of territorial limits in space. As space exploration continues, the nations of the world will have to work at solving these new problems.

178

*The famous Ishtar Gate was the only structure still partially standing when archaeologists excavated Babylon. The gate, which stood at the city's entrance, was covered with a layer of glazed brickwork. The photo at left shows a detail of a dragon from the reconstruction in Iraq.*

By the waters of Babylon, there we sat down and wept, when we remembered Zion.
On the willows there we hung up our lyres.
For there our captors required of us songs,
And our tormentors, mirth, saying, "Sing us one of the songs of Zion!"
How shall we sing the Lord's song in a foreign land?

Psalms 137:1–4

## Babylonian Achievements

Nebuchadnezzar used much of the wealth from his conquests in grand building projects. He built walls and fortifications to protect Babylon and great temples to glorify the gods. He rebuilt the ziggurat. Travelers from Greece listed the "hanging gardens" as one of the seven wonders of the world. To learn more about the seven wonders, turn to the Minipedia in the back of this book.

Scientific studies flourished during Nebuchadnezzar's reign. Many priests became **astronomers,** scientists who observe and record the movements of stars and planets. For centuries, the Babylonians had excelled in astronomy and mathematics. Early astronomers developed calendars based on the phases of the moon. At first their calendars were not synchronized with the movements of the sun. Later, by adding a total of seven months every nineteen years, the astronomers created a more accurate calendar.

Another outstanding scientific achievement was the division of the hour into 60 minutes. Our current use of an hour that is 60 minutes long is a daily reminder of the Babylonians.

A third achievement was the introduction of place value into mathematics. Place value refers to the position of a numeral in relation to other numerals. For example, the numeral 6 has a different value in the numbers 6, 61, and

*Many artists have tried to portray the glorious "hanging gardens of Babylon," but no one knows what they really looked like.*

611. To find out how important place value is, try to multiply two numbers in Roman numeral form, such as XIV and XVIII.

### The Fall of Babylonia

The rulers of Babylonia made the same mistakes as the Assyrians. Like the Assyrians, they worked to maintain their empire but did little to make life better for the people they conquered. Instead, they drained the conquered lands of wealth through taxes and plunder. Like the Assyrians, they made many enemies. Babylonia was ready for a fall.

The story of that fall involves an odd Babylonian king. King Nabonidus *(na buh NY duhs)* ruled Babylon from 556 to 539 B.C.

*Why were the Babylonians finally unable to maintain their empire?*

Historians are baffled by his behavior. Nabonidus bragged of great victories he never won. He left Babylon for years at a time, perhaps to avoid civil war and a famine the city suffered during his reign. He tried to replace Babylon's god Marduk with another god named Sin. For all these reasons, Nabonidus had many enemies.

When a foreign invader came, he was welcomed by the people. The conqueror of Babylonia, Cyrus the Great, came from Persia, a region of mountains and plateaus to the east of Mesopotamia. Around 550 B.C., Cyrus began winning new lands and building an empire. His empire would grow to be the largest the world had known. ■

## R E V I E W

1. **FOCUS** How were the New Assyrian and New Babylonian empires alike, and how were they different?
2. **CONNECT** How do the geography and earlier history of Mesopotamia help to explain the importance of trade to both the Assyrians and the Babylonians?
3. **HISTORY** What were the policies of Tiglath-Pileser III and Nebuchadnezzar that led to the downfall of their empires?

4. **CRITICAL THINKING** Both the Assyrians and the Babylonians relocated conquered people, moving them from their homeland. What other way of dealing with conquered people might have helped the Assyrians and Babylonians maintain their empires?
5. **WRITING ACTIVITY** Imagine you've come from a Mesopotamian farm to the great city of Babylon. Write a letter home, describing what you've seen.

# Holding a Mesopotamian Fair

## Here's Why

Many accomplishments in sports, business, government, and other areas of activity are the result of group efforts. Working as a group to reach common goals is a complex task. It requires cooperation in setting goals, planning actions, and making decisions. For example, suppose your class decided to hold a Mesopotamian World's Fair. Like the students in the photograph, you would begin by organizing your project. How would you proceed?

## Here's How

Here are five steps for organizing your World's Fair:

1. Elect a moderator, or leader, to run meetings. This person should keep class meetings focused.
2. Decide, as a class, what to do and how to proceed. The class should develop a list of goals and ways of achieving them.
3. Divide up jobs, form committees, and select committee leaders. Each committee should have a list of specific tasks, and the leader should make sure the group stays on target.
4. Hold individual committee meetings to set goals and assign tasks. Each member should have specific jobs that lead to achieving the committee's goals.
5. Meet again as a class to review plans, report progress, and make recommendations. The class should consider what progress has been made, what problems have come up, and what changes should be made.

Following these steps, you should be able to plan a successful Mesopotamian World's Fair.

## Try It

Using the steps described in Here's How, plan a World's Fair at your school. Highlight Mesopotamian achievements in the following areas: public works, tools and inventions, literature, writing, and law.

## Apply It

Now you have seen how to effectively organize a group effort. How would you divide the jobs if you were planning a paper-recycling campaign for your school or a Saturday project to clean up your school's grounds?

181

# Chapter Review

## Reviewing Key Terms

administrator (p. 154)
artisan (p. 155)
astronomer (p. 179)
city-state (p. 152)
code (p. 172)
cuneiform (p. 160)
empire (p. 169)
epic (p. 156)
exile (p. 178)
nomad (p. 157)
pictograph (p. 160)
plain (p. 151)
plateau (p. 150)
polytheism (p. 158)
scribe (p. 161)

**A.** Compare the key terms in each pair.
1. plateau, plain
2. city-state, empire
3. nomad, exile
4. pictograph, cuneiform

**B.** The following sentences are false. Explain each key term correctly.
1. <u>Artisans</u> held high positions as <u>administrators</u> in the city-states.
2. <u>Epics</u> tell us about how the Sumerians kept track of business deals.
3. The Sumerians, who believed in <u>polytheism</u>, worshiped only one god.
4. Hammurabi's <u>code</u> of law allowed rulers to freely punish criminals.
5. <u>Astronomers</u> developed the first systems of writing and became <u>scribes</u> for their kings and priests.

## Exploring Concepts

**A.** Copy and complete this outline.

I. The land between two rivers
  A. The Mesopotamian plain
  B. The remarkable Sumerians
    1. The Sumerian city-state
    2.
II. The contributions of the Sumerians
  A. The first kings
  B.
    1. The gods of Sumer
    2. Service to the gods
  C. The beginnings of writing
    1.
    2. Simplifying the pictures
III. The first empires
  A. Sargon of Akkad
  B. Rival empires
    1.
    2. A wise Babylonian ruler
IV. New empires
  A. A new Assyrian empire
  B.

**B.** The history of Mesopotamia is marked by the rise and fall of many strong leaders. Support each of the following statements with facts and details from the chapter.
1. Sargon changed Mesopotamia's government by creating the world's first empire.
2. Shamshi-Adad was one of the most powerful rulers of the Assyrian Empire.
3. Hammurabi, like Sargon and Shamshi-Adad, was a fierce conqueror, but he also showed concern for his people.
4. Adad-Nirari's greatest interest was gaining wealth and power.
5. The policies of Tiglath-Pileser III were partly responsible for the fall of the New Assyrian Empire.
6. Nebuchadnezzar's reign was both cruel and magnificent.
7. The policies of Nebuchadnezzar resembled those of Tiglath-Pileser III and had similar results.
8. Nabonidus's kingdom was not secure because the people of Babylonia did not like his practices.

## Reviewing Skills

1. Look at the timeline on this page. Suppose you wanted to make a telescoping timeline of events during Hammurabi's rule. Would you make a 1,000-year timeline? A 150-year timeline? A 50-year timeline? Why?
2. Find a timeline and a map scale in your book. How are they alike? How are they different?
3. Suppose your class wanted to put on a Reader's Theater presentation of "The Luring of Enkidu" from *Gilgamesh*. Reader's Theater is a dramatic reading of a play or story without acting it out. To prepare for such a presentation, some class members might make posters for publicity. Others might print programs. How would you apply to your group preparation the five main steps for organizing a group project?
4. "I have brought justice to all my subjects," Hammurabi said. Was this a statement of fact or opinion? Use information from the chapter to support your view.
5. Suppose that you have taken many notes on the Babylonians and Sumerians. Now you have to give an oral report comparing the two societies. How could you help listeners to see both the likenesses and differences of Babylonians and Sumerians?

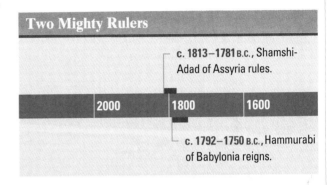

**Two Mighty Rulers**

c. 1813–1781 B.C., Shamshi-Adad of Assyria rules.

2000 | 1800 | 1600

c. 1792–1750 B.C., Hammurabi of Babylonia reigns.

## Using Critical Thinking

1. Ancient cultures had clearly defined roles for priests, kings, artisans, and scribes. What were the functions of these groups in Mesopotamian society? How are these groups of people and their roles different in American society today?
2. The first tools of written communication were a stylus and a piece of clay. The stylus, a sharpened reed, was used to draw pictographs on moist clay. Much later, paper replaced the clay tablets. What other tools of written communication have been invented since then?
3. The Sumerians' religion was extremely important to them. Their gods were involved in all aspects of their lives. Review the Sumerians' religious beliefs on pages 158 and 159. Then read in Lesson 3 about the war between King Lugal-zaggesi and Sargon. How do you think a Sumerian priest might have explained the invasion of Uruk to someone?

## Preparing for Citizenship

1. **WRITING ACTIVITY** Nebuchadnezzar built the towering ziggurat. He also built the Hanging Gardens, one of the seven wonders of the ancient world. What do these structures tell us about the values and beliefs of Babylonian society? Now choose two structures in American cities, and write an essay on the wonders of the modern world. What do these wonders reveal about the values and beliefs of our society?
2. **COLLABORATIVE LEARNING** The epic of *Gilgamesh* tells the story of a real king who became a legendary hero. Who are our American heroes today? Consider both the past and present. With two classmates, select an American hero. Have each person in your group research one part of your hero's life: childhood, public life, and private life. Together, decide how to present your hero to the class.

# Chapter 7

# *Ancient Egypt*

*Tombs filled with dazzling treasures tell us of the ancient Egyptians. Their civilization flourished in the valley along the Nile River in North Africa, a region rich in resources and protected from enemies by a vast desert. The valley seemed like heaven on earth to the Egyptians. In fact, life was so good that they hoped it would continue after death, in the afterlife.*

**4000 B.C.** People begin to settle along the Nile. In this tomb painting from a later period, an Egyptian couple happily plow their fields in the afterlife.

**4000**

**3000**

# 4000 B.C.

**c. 3100 B.C.** According to legend, the king of Upper Egypt conquers Lower Egypt and unites the two lands. This figure wears the crown of Upper Egypt.

Throughout this period, Egyptian kings built massive royal tombs. These pyramids date from the 2600s B.C. The giant figures (below) guard the temple built by King Ramses II about 1250 B.C.

c. 1570 –1070 B.C. Egyptian rulers conquer their neighbors and expand trade. This model boat, found in the tomb of King Tutankhamen, resembles the trading ships that sailed the Nile.

| | 1000 | | B.C. | A.D. | | 1000 |
|---|---|---|---|---|---|---|

1489 B.C. Queen Hatshepsut takes control. A skillful ruler, she promotes trade and brings peace. Like earlier rulers, she orders a grand temple built so she will be remembered forever.

A.D. 350

L E S S O N   1

# The Gift of the Nile

**Key Terms**

- cataract
- delta
- papyrus
- dynasty

Grain was scarce, and fruit was dried up. People robbed their neighbors. Babies were crying, and old men were sad as they sat on the ground with their legs bent and their arms folded.

So begins an ancient legend about the Nile River. The Egyptians depended on the flooding of the Nile to water their fields. Some years there were "high Niles," when crops grew well and people had plenty to eat. Other years there were "low Niles," when the fields became dry, baked by the sun, and few had enough food.

The legend tells of a time of low Niles, when Egypt had seven years of famine. This time fell during the reign of King Zoser in the 2600s B.C. The king watched the crops withering, and he saw his people starving. He turned to his chief advisor, Imhotep, for help. The answer was to learn the name of the god of the Nile so they could pray to him, said Imhotep. Later, he told the king that the Nile slept in two caverns below a temple near Egypt's southern border. The god Khnum *(kuh NOOM)* controlled the floodgates and let the Nile rush toward Egypt.

Later that night, Zoser dreamed that Khnum spoke to him: "I am Khnum. I know the Nile. When it covers the fields, it gives them life. Now the Nile will pour over the land without stopping. Plants will grow, bowing down with fruit. The years of starvation will be over."

When the king awoke, he told the people to honor Khnum by giving him a portion of each year's harvest. The "high Niles" returned, and the years of hunger ended.

➤ *In this scene at Aswan in south Egypt, the fertile riverbank contrasts sharply with the barren desert.*

# The Geography of the Nile

Egypt is on the northeastern coast of Africa. Look at the map below, and locate Egypt on the globe in the inset. Now find the Nile River on the large map.

The Nile is Egypt's lifeline. Without it, the land would be mostly desert. It is the longest river in the world, traveling over 4,000 miles from its source in the lakes and marshes of central Africa to its outlet in the Mediterranean Sea.

At six places along the Nile's winding course, stone cliffs and boulders force its waters through narrow channels. The rushing water forms waterfalls and rapids called **cataracts.** The first cataract marked the southern boundary of ancient Egypt. Find it on the map.

From the first cataract, the Nile flows north for about 600 miles. For most of this journey, it flows as a single river. But just south of what is today Cairo *(KY roh)*, it divides into many small channels and streams. This triangle of marshy wetlands is called the **delta.**

## Droughts and Floods

From the air much of the Nile looks like a brown snake wriggling north across a vast desert. Its narrow banks are green with crops and palms. Abruptly they turn into desert—red stones and hot sands. The people who lived there 4,000 years ago called their fertile, dark-soiled valley the Black Land. The desert was the Red Land.

Egypt gets almost no rain. The deserts on the east and west are parts of the Sahara, the desert that covers much of northern Africa. Desert on two sides, mountains on the south, and the Mediterranean Sea on the north—all of these natural barriers isolated ancient Egypt and thus protected it from invaders.

In this desert land, Egyptians depended on the Nile for water and for life. The amount of water the Nile carried on its journey to

*◄ The Egyptians used stone nilometers like this one to measure the yearly flood level of the Nile.*

*▼ Some have compared the shape of Egypt with that of a lotus flower. Can you see the flower's blossom and stem?*

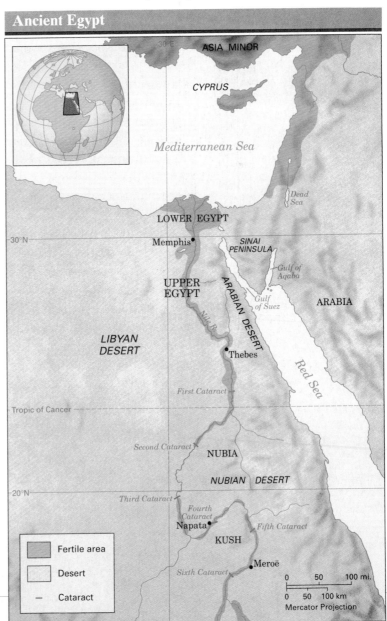

**Ancient Egypt**

- Fertile area
- Desert
- Cataract

ASIA MINOR
CYPRUS
Mediterranean Sea
Dead Sea
LOWER EGYPT
Memphis
SINAI PENINSULA
Gulf of Aqaba
UPPER EGYPT
ARABIAN DESERT
Gulf of Suez
ARABIA
LIBYAN DESERT
Nile R.
Thebes
Red Sea
First Cataract
Tropic of Cancer
Second Cataract
NUBIA
NUBIAN DESERT
Third Cataract
Fourth Cataract
Napata
Fifth Cataract
KUSH
Meroë
Sixth Cataract
0    50    100 mi.
0    50   100 km
Mercator Projection

187

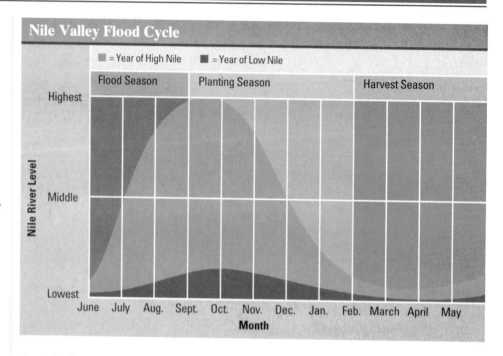

**Nile Valley Flood Cycle**

■ = Year of High Nile    ■ = Year of Low Nile

Flood Season    Planting Season    Harvest Season

Nile River Level

Highest

Middle

Lowest

June  July  Aug.  Sept.  Oct.  Nov.  Dec.  Jan.  Feb.  March  April  May

**Month**

➤ *Which months made up each of Egypt's three seasons? How did the years of "high Niles" differ from the years of "low Niles"? What might you be doing now if you were a farmer in ancient Egypt?*

➤ *Notice the fine carving and bright coloring in this small wooden statue of a woman who is carrying an offering.*

the Mediterranean varied from season to season. When rains fell in central Africa and snows began to melt in the mountains of east Africa, the water level of the river rose. As the river reached Egypt, it overflowed its banks. Farmers depended on the annual flooding to water their crops.

The floods of Egypt were more predictable than those of Mesopotamia. Farmers each year knew when the Nile would rise, and they planned ahead. The Egyptians measured time by the river, dividing the year into three seasons. Study the chart above. What was the season for planting? What was the season for harvesting? This seasonal cycle of flooding, planting, and harvesting gave a pattern to Egyptian life.

**The River's Gifts**

About 2,500 years ago, Herodotus *(hih RAHD uh tuhs)*, a Greek visitor to ancient

Egypt, called this land the "gift of the Nile." The Egyptians sang special hymns of praise to the river. The example below was first written down during the period known as the New Kingdom (from about 1570 to 1070 B.C.):

*H*ail to thee O Nile that issues from the earth and comes to keep Egypt alive! . . . He that waters the meadows which Ra created.

*Hymn to the Nile,* from papyrus documents, 1350-1100 B.C.

To take advantage of the annual flooding of the Nile, the people built irrigation channels to carry water into the fields. They also built dams to hold back the water for use during droughts. What they did may sound familiar to you. In some ways it was the same thing the Sumerians did. But the floods came at predictable times in Egypt, and farming was easier. The Egyptians needed less cooperation than the Sumerians to get the work done. As a result,

◄ *(1) Paper makers cut the stem of the papyrus and removed the inner pith. (2) They cut the pith into strips, (3) put one layer across another, and beat the layers into a single sheet. (4) They polished the sheet with a stone, and (5) finally, they trimmed the edges.*

they did not develop cities until much later.

Besides water, another gift of the Nile was the thick, black mud left behind in the flooding. This dark mud enriched the soil and made the farmland extremely productive.

The Nile gave other gifts as well. Fish, ducks, geese, and other edible water birds made their homes in the marshlands of the delta. **Papyrus** *(puh PY ruhs)*, a long, thin reed, grew wild along the riverbanks. The Egyptians harvested papyrus and made baskets, boats, sandals, and a lightweight writing material. Our word *paper* comes from the word *papyrus*.

The Egyptians used the gifts of the Nile wisely. Here in this land of contrasts—fertile riverbanks and barren deserts, floods and droughts, Black Land and Red Land—they managed to build a remarkable civilization. ■

■ *Explain how water, mud, plants, and animals were all "gifts of the Nile" to the Egyptians.*

## The Union of Two Lands

Ancient Egypt had two parts, Upper Egypt and Lower Egypt. Upper Egypt, the southern part, stretched for over 500 miles from the first cataract northward to the beginning of the Nile Delta. Lower Egypt, the northern part, was the Nile Delta. It was only 100 miles long but many times wider than Upper Egypt.

### Red and White Crowns

By about 3300 B.C., both Upper Egypt and Lower Egypt had kings. The king of Upper Egypt wore a tall, white, pear-shaped crown. The king of Lower Egypt wore a short, boxy, red crown with a tall spike at the back and a curlicue at the front.

Much of our knowledge of prehistoric Egypt is mixed with legend. One famous legend tells about Menes *(MEE neez)*, a king of Upper Egypt. Around 3100 B.C., Menes defeated the king of Lower Egypt, united the two lands, and named himself King of both Upper and Lower Egypt.

The legend goes on to tell how Menes designed a new crown to celebrate his victory. This double crown stood for the union of the two lands. Menes and his family

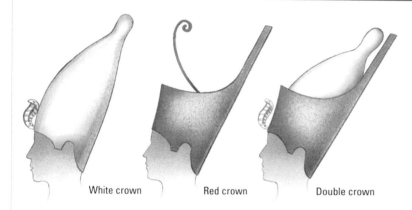

White crown     Red crown     Double crown

▲ *The white crown of the king of Upper Egypt was placed inside the red crown of the king of Lower Egypt, forming the double red and white crown that symbolized the union of the two lands.*

➤ *The slate palette of Narmer is from around 2950 B.C. King Narmer, who is wearing the white crown, is striking a kneeling prisoner.*

■ *What were some important early accomplishments of the Egyptians?*

formed the first Egyptian dynasty. A **dynasty** is a series of rulers from the same family. After Menes died, his son became king, and later his grandson. Throughout its history, 30 different dynasties ruled ancient Egypt.

Menes chose the city of Memphis as his capital. Find Memphis on the map on page 187. How do you think the city's location helped the king keep firm control of both parts of his newly united kingdom?

Historians believe that the "Menes" of this legend may have been a real king, possibly Narmer. They also believe it wasn't that king who first wore the red and white crown, but a later one.

### Three Kingdoms

History for ancient Egypt began around 3000 B.C., with the invention of hieroglyphic writing.

Within the history of ancient Egypt, historians have identified three periods when many important events took place.

In the Old Kingdom period, from 2750 to 2260 B.C., the Egyptians built the great pyramids. The Middle Kingdom lasted from 2061 to 1784 B.C. This was when Egypt became stronger, and the Egyptians achieved a great deal in literature, art, and architecture. In the New Kingdom period, from 1570 to 1070 B.C., Egypt became a world power by conquering other nations and building an empire.

Between periods of strength and discovery, weak kings ruled, or foreigners gained control of Egypt. These in-between periods were times of great confusion and disorder in Egyptian society.

In the 1,000 years before the Old Kingdom began, the Egyptian people accomplished many things. They learned to irrigate their fields. They learned to farm. They formed governments, with kings as rulers. They invented hieroglyphic writing. Finally, the Egyptians created the belief systems and customs that made Egyptian life unique. These early achievements formed the basis of ancient Egyptian society. ■

### R E V I E W

1. **FOCUS** What did the ancient Egyptians accomplish because of the "gifts of the Nile"?
2. **CONNECT** Compare and contrast the conditions for farmers in Mesopotamia and Egypt.
3. **GEOGRAPHY** Explain how the geography of Egypt affected its early development as a civilization.
4. **CRITICAL THINKING** The ancient Egyptians valued a

quiet, orderly life. They did not want things to change. How might these preferences help to explain why the story of Menes was important to them?

5. **WRITING ACTIVITY** Imagine you are a travel writer who has just visited ancient Egypt by time machine. Write an article called "Egypt: A Land of Contrasts."

L E S S O N   2

# Life in Ancient Egypt

The photo below might surprise you if you have seen pictures of Egyptian pyramids. This pyramid is different. It is called the Step Pyramid, and the name fits. To find out more about this unusual structure, we will revisit King Zoser.

Sometime in the middle of the 2600s B.C., the king began to plan for his burial. He called on Imhotep, his chief advisor and also a fine architect, to design his tomb. Until then, a royal tomb was a flat-topped, mud-brick structure built over a burial chamber that lay deep under the ground. Imhotep designed a grander, more permanent tomb for the king, and he did not build it of mud brick, but of stone.

No one knows whether Imhotep planned the design in advance or thought of it as the work went along. At any rate, his builders put one flat-topped structure on top of another. They made each level a few feet smaller than the one below it.

When Imhotep's pyramid was finished, a chamber for the king's body lay about 80 feet under the ground. A mile-long, 133-foot-high stone wall surrounded the tomb. The wall had 14 doors, only one of which actually opened.

Architects of later periods built on Imhotep's ideas to design and construct pyramids that were even grander. King Zoser had started an age of pyramid building that would last for more than a thousand years. Pyramid building reached its height during the Old Kingdom period. More than 80 pyramids have survived as reminders of that distant age.

**THINKING
FOCUS**

*Describe the religious ideas and the social structure of the ancient Egyptians.*

## Key Terms

- afterlife
- embalm
- mummy
- hieroglyphics

◄ *Zoser's Step Pyramid, the first large-scale stone structure in the world, was built in the mid-2600s B.C. on a plateau overlooking the ancient city of Memphis.*

191

Ancient Egypt

# The Egyptian Religion

➤ The Egyptians' love for animals can be seen in their portrayal of gods with animal heads, their animal sculptures, and animal mummies like this one of a cat.

King Zoser's pyramid was undoubtedly more than just a new idea in architecture. It showed the religious beliefs of the Egyptian people. Early Egyptian literature pictured the king climbing up to heaven on a stairway formed by the rays of the sun. People may have thought of that stairway when they looked at the Step Pyramid. The shape of the later pyramids might have seemed like the slope of the sun's rays. In that way, the later pyramids, too, might have pictured a king's passage to heaven.

## Preparing for the Afterlife

The Egyptians believed in an **afterlife,** a life that would continue after death. Their belief was so strong and important to the people that great preparation was made for death and burial. Pyramid building was just one part of this preparation.

Another part was the preparation of the body itself. Before an Egyptian's body could be placed in a pyramid or other tomb, it had to be prepared for the afterlife.

The Egyptians believed that without a body, a person's spirit couldn't eat, drink, dance, or enjoy the other pleasures that the afterlife would offer. If the body decayed, the spirit would die too. So the Egyptians developed a process called **embalming,** treating the body to protect it from decay. Embalming changed the body into a **mummy.** To learn more about this process, see A Closer Look on pages 194 and 195.

Once the mummy had been prepared, it was placed in the tomb along with items for use in the afterlife. These items ranged from food and drink to gold and jewelry. They included many objects that were useful in daily life, such as clothes, games, and hand mirrors. Some tombs even held mummies of cats, dogs, horses, and apes or contained small carved statues of servants. Tomb walls were painted with scenes from the everyday life of the dead person. See the example on pages 204 and 205.

Most of these objects and paintings were found in the tombs of royal or wealthy families. But even many of the less privileged were buried with some of their favorite possessions.

According to Egyptian belief, the objects and paintings in the tomb would help to ensure that the person would continue to enjoy the good things of this life. The Egyptians loved life in this world. Because they believed the afterlife would be much like this life, they wanted to be buried with the things they would need.

After a mummy was placed in its tomb, priests recited prayers or

▼ The sky god Horus, depicted with the head of a hawk, was closely connected with the king. In fact, the Egyptians saw their king as Horus on earth. Here Horus is shown standing in his sun boat. With him is an ibis, a sacred bird of ancient Egypt.

chanted magic spells. They called on the gods to help the person make the trip from this world to the next. The following words appear on the tomb of an Old Kingdom ruler named Pepi: "Gates of sky, open for Pepi, Gates of heaven, open for Pepi, Pepi comes to you, make him live!"

## The Book of the Dead

Hymns, prayers, and magic spells from the tombs are found in the Egyptian *Book of the Dead*. One part describes a trial in which the soul of a dead person argues its case before a jury of the gods. "In life, I fed the hungry," says the soul. "I respected my parents."

The soul also tells what it did not do. "I never stole." The gods then weigh the heart of the dead person against the feather of truth. The Egyptians believed the heart was the center of intelligence and memory. If the soul was too heavy with sin, they believed, it died a second death from which there was no returning. But the soul that passed the test would go on to a happy afterlife. Such a judgment scene is shown in the picture above.

## The Gods of the Egyptians

The religion of ancient Egypt, like that of Mesopotamia, was a form of polytheism, belief in a number of gods. Some of these gods were, of course, linked with death and the afterlife. Osiris *(oh SY ruhs)* was chief god of the underworld, or home of the dead. One helper of Osiris was Anubis *(uh NOO buhs)*, who had the body of a human and the head of a jackal. His job was to prepare the bodies of the dead for the afterlife.

Like the Mesopotamians, the Egyptians had great gods that they believed created and ruled the world. One of these was Ra *(rah)*, the sun god, who was later joined with another great god, Amon *(AH muhn)*, to become Amon-Ra.

Some Egyptian gods, like Anubis, had the body of a human and the head of an animal. Hathor *(HAH thawr)*, the goddess of love, had the head of a cow. Horus, the sky god, had the head of a hawk.

Each Egyptian village or city had its own local god. There were also gods of music and dancing, of love and beauty, and of healing and learning. Ordinary Egyptians built small shrines at home and dedicated them to their favorite gods. Especially popular was a dwarf like god named Bes, the god of the family. ■

▲ *This picture, painted on papyrus around 1250 B.C., shows the jackal-headed god Anubis weighing the heart of a dead person named Ani against the feather of truth.*

◄ *At one time Amon was a minor god, but he became the most powerful of all the Egyptian gods. This small gold statue shows Amon with a curved sword in his right hand and a key, the symbol of life, in his left hand.*

■ *What religious beliefs account for the pyramids and mummies of ancient Egypt?*

# Egyptian Burial

*Preparing for the afterlife was like packing
for a long trip. Every step in the process,
from preparing the body to protecting the tomb
against robbers, had to be done just right.*

**This huge boat was buried** near the Great Pyramid of Khufu, a king of the Old Kingdom. Was it used at his funeral, or was it for his use in his afterlife? No one knows for sure. Perhaps it symbolizes the soul's journey after death.

**To get the body ready,** embalmers removed all the internal organs except the heart and put them inside jars like this. Then they covered the body for about 40 days with natron, a kind of salt, which dried it out.

**Magic amulets** were tucked into the wrappings next to the body. A scarab over the heart, for instance, would make sure the heart could not speak against its owner during the trial in the afterworld.

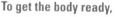

**Embalmers sealed** the dried corpse in a coat of hot, liquid tree sap. Then they washed and oiled the mummy. Finally, they wrapped it in up to 400 yards of linen strips.

**Once the body was placed** in the burial room of the pyramid, the workers needed to seal the tomb. As they left, the workers let huge stones crash into place and block the main passageway. To fool robbers, some Egyptian royal tombs had traps and false stairs that led nowhere.

*Air shafts allow workers to breathe and the king's soul to fly to heaven*

*The king's burial room*

*Stones seal the passageway*

*Workers' escape corridor*

**Craftsmen made coffins look like humans** and wrote spells and prayers of protection outside and inside. The face of the coffin was often a portrait of the dead person.

195

Ancient Egypt

## UNDERSTANDING THE IDEA OF AN AFTERLIFE

To us, the ancient Egyptians sometimes seem more interested in death than life. We marvel at the time, energy, and other resources they put into making pyramids and mummies. Yet we know that their love of life caused them to do these things. They thought an afterlife would be like this one, only better.

In every time and place, people have asked, "Is there life beyond this life?" and if so, "What kind of life is it?" These questions ask about the afterlife—life that continues after death.

### A Place of Darkness

The Mesopotamians painted a gloomy picture of the afterlife. For them, the world of the dead was under the earth. One of their stories called it a place "where they see no light and live in darkness." The hero-king Gilgamesh tried but failed to gain a happy afterlife. Eternal life was reserved for the gods.

### A Happy Afterlife

People's ideas about an afterlife are tied to their ideas about God or the gods. In our own twentieth-century Western society, many people are believers in Judaism, Christianity, or Islam. Followers of these faiths believe in one God. Most of them also believe in a human soul that will never die. They look forward to an afterlife in which they will live with God and with other human souls. Like the Egyptians, many believe in an afterlife that will be happier and better than this life. However, few cultures have placed more importance on the idea of an afterlife than the ancient Egyptians.

## A Writing System

▲ *The Rosetta Stone provided the key that unlocked hieroglyphics.*

The earliest Egyptian writing, also called **hieroglyphics** *(hy roh GLIH fihks),* used pictures to stand for objects, ideas, and sounds. Like cuneiform, the system was not easy to decipher. In fact, language specialists and archaeologists studied the symbols for years without success.

Then, in 1799, French soldiers near Rosetta, a village in the Nile Delta, unearthed a black stone slab. They found that on it the same passage was written in three ways: in Greek, in Egyptian hieroglyphs, and in a cursive form of Egyptian.

For 20 years, scholars tried in vain to decode the hieroglyphic writing on the Rosetta Stone. Then a brilliant Frenchman named Jean Champollion found the key. Champollion knew that part of the message was the same in all three cases. It praised the pharaoh Ptolemy V for gifts he had given the temples. One day in 1822, Champollion was comparing the hieroglyphs with the Greek words. He identified and compared the proper names *Ptolemy* and *Cleopatra.* He matched the sounds with the hieroglyphs as follows:

Now Champollion was able to decode the Rosetta Stone. Later, he went on to publish a dictionary of ancient Egyptian.

Fortunately, the Egyptians left us many written texts. Once scholars could decode hieroglyphic writing, they could read laws, songs, tales, jokes, magic spells, and business contracts. From these texts and others, scholars have learned about Egypt's past.

The hieroglyphic system was complex. It was made up of over 700 different signs that a person had to memorize in order to master it. Young people who wanted to be scribes spent years attending special schools. Their school day was long, sometimes lasting from just after sunrise until sunset. Teachers expected their students to pay attention, and punishments could be harsh. One father sent the following words of advice to his son, who was learning to be a scribe: "Learn to write, for this will be of greater advantage to you than all the trades. One day at school is useful to you and the work done there will last forever, like mountains."

Few Egyptian students, studying hard and copying the same lines over and over, would have found these words encouraging. However, those who completed the training would be well rewarded. Only a few people learned to read and write. As experts with special skills, they would have a good job and a respected place in society. ■

■ *Compare and contrast the writing systems of the Egyptians and the Mesopotamians.*

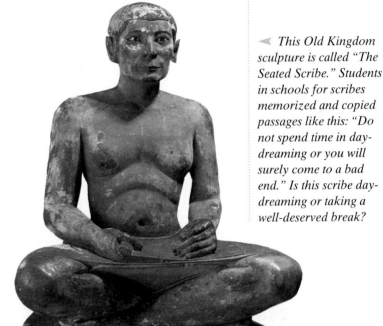

◄ *This Old Kingdom sculpture is called "The Seated Scribe." Students in schools for scribes memorized and copied passages like this: "Do not spend time in daydreaming or you will surely come to a bad end." Is this scribe daydreaming or taking a well-deserved break?*

## A Social Pyramid

Scribes and farmers, potters and brick makers—all Egyptians had a place in the social class system of ancient Egypt. A diagram of Egyptian society might look something like a pyramid.

### Kings and Priests

At the top of the social pyramid was the king. Remember that the Mesopotamians believed that their kings ruled on behalf of the gods. The Egyptians considered their kings even more powerful. They believed that their kings *were* gods.

The Egyptian king was extremely powerful. He owned all the land and had complete control over all of his people. Every worker, from farmer to artist, served the king, directly or through royal officials. The members of the royal family and the nobility ranked just below the king on the social pyramid.

They assisted the tax collectors in making careful records of what everyone owed and how they paid their taxes.

▲ *This fine painted woodcarving of a plowing scene was found in a Middle Kingdom tomb of around 2000 B.C. Why do you think it was put in the tomb? Where would these farmers have been on the social pyramid?*

The priests served the gods to which the temples were dedicated. Some people who worked at other occupations, such as law or medicine, also served in the temple on a rotating basis.

### Officials and Scribes

The king relied on government officials, who were also in the upper level of society. He counted on them to assist him in governing the country. Many were tax collectors. Some were responsible for the royal storehouses. When crops were poor, officials distributed grain to the people.

The scribes, another group of officials, held a privileged position. They were Egypt's writers and record keepers. Scribes might work at the king's palace, travel with high officials, or serve as public letter writers or record keepers.

■ *What were the occupations of people at the top, middle, and bottom of the Egyptian social pyramid?*

### Artisans and Farmers

Below scribes on the social pyramid were the artisans and other skilled workers. These included carpenters, painters, jewelers, brick makers, and stonemasons. Many of these skilled workers provided goods for the king and his family. For example, they might create furniture, make jewelry, weave fine cloth, and paint pictures inside the royal tombs. The king paid them in food, such as bread, beer, and milk.

Farmers formed the large base of the Egyptian social pyramid. Most Egyptians were farmers, and they spent their lives growing and marketing the products they raised on their farms. In this way, they supported all the other levels of Egyptian society.

But the farmers didn't provide food only. During the flood season, they could not work in the fields. They were required to work on royal building projects. These included the irrigation works, the pyramids, and later the temples. The great stone monuments that the farmers helped to build have outlasted both kings and commoners. ■

## R E V I E W

1. **FOCUS** Describe the religious ideas and the social structure of the ancient Egyptians.
2. **CONNECT** Compare and contrast the Egyptians' beliefs about their kings and their gods with the beliefs of the Mesopotamians.
3. **ECONOMICS** What was the importance of farming to the economy of ancient Egypt?
4. **CRITICAL THINKING** Give reasons for and against a young Egyptian's decision to become a scribe.
5. **ACTIVITY** Work with a group of three or four classmates, and make a pyramid diagram to illustrate the social structure of ancient Egypt. Draw pictures of people with different occupations and place them on your pyramid.

Chapter 7

L E S S O N   3

# The New Kingdom

The sculpture on the right shows a ruler of ancient Egypt wearing a false beard. False beards were not unusual in ancient Egypt. Sometimes, for a special occasion, a king would paste one on his chin as a symbol, or sign, of royal authority. Americans had the same kind of custom when Colonial judges wore long white wigs, also as symbols of authority.

Look again at the sculpture in the picture. What you see is something more unusual than just a false beard. It's a false beard pasted on the face of a woman. The woman is Hatshepsut *(hat SHEHP soot)*, a ruler of ancient Egypt. Hatshepsut was the daughter of one king and the wife of another, but she is best remembered as a ruler in her own right.

But it seems that some Egyptian scribes became confused. In telling the story of their woman ruler, they called her "his majesty herself."

**THINKING FOCUS**

*What were the achievements of the Egyptians during the New Kingdom period?*

## Key Terms

- pharaoh
- obelisk

◄ *Hatshepsut's beard, a sign of her kingship, does not hide the beauty of the pharaoh. In this sculpture from her temple, Hatshepsut is presenting an offering to the god Amon.*

## New Kingdom Rulers

The New Kingdom period lasted around 500 years, from about 1570 to 1070 B.C. During that time, Egyptians began to call their kings pharaohs. The term **pharaoh** meant "great house." Earlier, during the Old Kingdom, the term referred to the royal palace. However, the Egyptians later used it to refer to the king himself. The word was used as a sign of respect. Today Hatshepsut, too, is often called an Egyptian pharaoh.

She was the daughter of the pharaoh Thutmose I *(thoot MOH suh)*. After his death, his son, Thutmose II, became pharaoh. Hatshepsut, the new king's half-sister, became queen.

But Thutmose II lived only about seven more years. In ancient Egypt, the oldest male in line for the throne usually became the next ruler. Thutmose III, Hatshepsut's nephew, was next in line. But he was about 10 years old, too young

199

Ancient Egypt

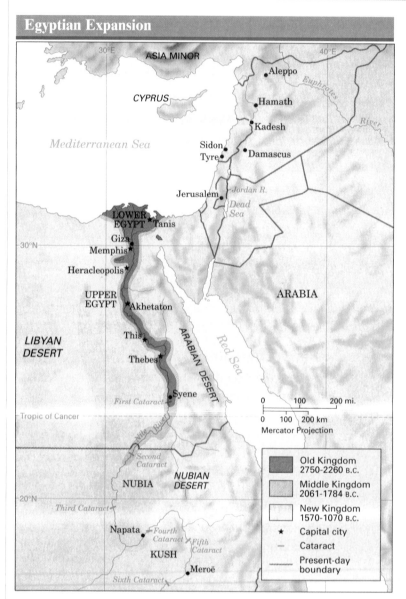

| | |
|---|---|
| ■ (dark) | Old Kingdom 2750-2260 B.C. |
| ☐ (medium) | Middle Kingdom 2061-1784 B.C. |
| ☐ (light) | New Kingdom 1570-1070 B.C. |
| ★ | Capital city |
| – | Cataract |
| ‒‒‒ | Present-day boundary |

▲ *Notice the extent of ancient Egypt during the three periods of its greatness.*

she would be remembered for all time. She ordered a great temple to be built along the banks of the Nile. She also had two enormous granite pillars called **obelisks** placed at the temple of the sun god Amon-Ra at Karnak. Stonecutters carved words on the four sides of each obelisk. They proclaimed the devotion of Hatshepsut to the sun god and asserted her right to rule.

Note that Hatshepsut built a great temple and erected obelisks, but she did not build a pyramid. By the time of the New Kingdom, pyramids were no longer built. Instead, rulers dug secret tombs in the cliffs west of their capital, Thebes. There they were buried in what we call today the Valley of the Kings.

### Hatshepsut's Achievements

As a ruler, Hatshepsut concerned herself with improving life at home rather than expanding Egypt's borders and building a great empire. One example is a trade expedition she sent to Punt, an African kingdom that may have been in present-day Somalia or Ethiopia. Its exact location is unknown. Relief pictures on the walls of her temple portray five large sailing ships carrying Egyptian products. The artist also portrayed the people and houses of Punt, providing us with the oldest pictures we have of tribal life in Africa. The expedition returned to Egypt with many items, including gold, ivory, leopard skins, ostrich feathers, incense, rare woods, greyhounds, and monkeys.

Hatshepsut was responsible for a number of public projects. She restored old temples that had been destroyed during foreign invasions

to govern Egypt. Hatshepsut took over the government in his place. The Egyptian people probably expected her to rule only until young Thutmose III was old enough to take over his royal duties.

### Hatshepsut's Reign

But Hatshepsut had other ideas. This bold queen seized power for herself and became the new pharaoh. She ruled Egypt for about 20 years, and she turned out to be a shrewd and skillful ruler.

Like earlier Egyptian rulers, Hatshepsut wanted to make sure

2750–2260, Old Kingdom

c. 2650, The Step Pyramid is built for King Zoser.

1570–1070, New Kingdom

c. 1502, Pharaoh Hatshepsut expands trade.

c. 1482, Pharaoh Thutmose III builds a great empire.

3000    2500    2000    1500    1000

c. 3100, The legendary King Menes unites Upper and Lower Egypt.

c. 1991, King Amenemhet I and his successors increase Egypt's power.

2061–1784, Middle Kingdom

of an earlier era, the time between the Middle and New Kingdoms. She also sent workers to mine the deserts for ores, a practice that those earlier invasions had interrupted. Under Hatshepsut's rule, Egypt enjoyed a time of renewed peace and prosperity.

## Later Pharaohs

After Hatshepsut died, her nephew Thutmose III took the power she had denied him. Now at last he had the chance to govern, and he became a successful military leader, one of Egypt's mightiest pharaohs.

In a period of 20 years, Thutmose led 16 military raids into the Middle East, conquering Syria and Palestine. Fear of him, and of the Egyptian army, maintained Egypt's southern border at the fourth cataract of the Nile. Find the fourth cataract on the map on page 200. Notice the extent of Thutmose's empire, stretching from

modern Sudan to the Euphrates River.

Scribes recorded Thutmose's campaigns in detail. In his fifth campaign, for example, a list of items taken from two ships that were seized includes slaves, copper, lead, wheat, and "every good thing." The scribe adds, "Afterwards his majesty proceeded southward to Egypt . . . with joy of heart."

Victories like the fifth campaign brought great wealth to Egypt. Conquered nations were forced to send yearly gifts to prove their loyalty to Egypt's rulers. Gold, ivory, and ebony, a beautiful dark wood, poured into Egypt's treasuries. Even rulers of unconquered states such as Babylonia and Assyria sent gifts to show their friendship with one of the Mediterranean's most powerful kingdoms.

Later rulers continued to enlarge Egypt's empire abroad and build

▲ During the Old, Middle, and New Kingdom periods, a number of strong and effective rulers were in power. Later, as you read more about ancient Egypt, you can add other great rulers to this timeline.

◄ The obelisk of Hatshepsut, erected in the temple of the god Amon-Ra, was carved from Aswan granite. The shaft is 97 feet tall. Its pyramid-shaped top was once covered with precious metal to reflect the sun's rays.

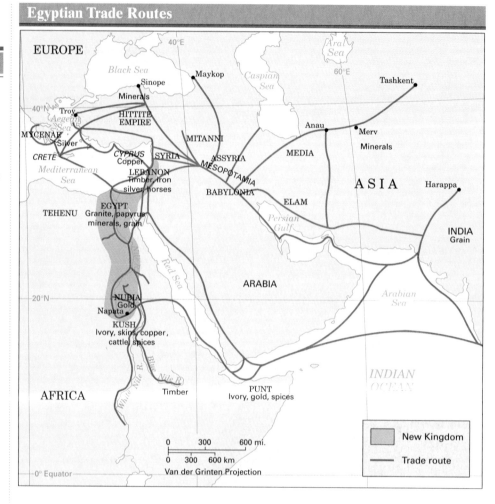

*In 1960, planners of Egypt's Aswan High Dam realized that the lake it created would cover the two temples built by Ramses II at Abu Simbel. Saving them required cutting them into huge blocks and hoisting them by machine to higher ground. There they were rebuilt to look as much as possible as they had before.*

➤ *How far did Egypt's trade routes extend during the New Kingdom? What products did Egypt give and receive in trade with other nations?*

■ *Compare and contrast the two strong rulers Hatshepsut and Thutmose III.*

impressive monuments at home. Ramses II, who ruled in the 1200s B.C., ordered four enormous stone statues of himself placed in front of the temple he had workmen build in his honor. Each statue was 67 feet tall, about the height of a modern four-story building. Ramses' temple can be seen today at Abu Simbel. Read Across Time and Space on this page to find out more about it. ■

## Achievements of the Egyptians

The Egyptian rulers of the New Kingdom built great temples that are lasting reminders of their skills as architects, sculptors, and engineers. The Egyptians excelled in other areas as well.

### A Better Calendar

Remember that the Babylonians created a lunar calendar, one that was based on the moon. The Egyptians also invented a lunar calendar, but it was based on both the moon and a star. The Egyptians had observed the annual appearance of Sirius, the brightest star in the sky. They noticed that it was invisible for several months, but then it appeared each year just at the time of the flooding. Their calendar was more accurate than the Babylonian one, corresponding almost exactly to the seasons.

## Medicine

An unknown Egyptian doctor wrote the world's oldest known scientific document in the first part of the 1500s B.C. Scholars think it may have been a handbook for army surgeons. He described 48 injuries and illnesses, their symptoms, and their treatments. Although no modern doctor would use his cures, his attention to detail and the accuracy of his observations of the human body were remarkable for that time.

In one case the writer described the treatment of "a man having a wound in his head" but not "a perforation [hole], a split, or a smash." He advised doctors to treat this type of injury by wrapping it "with fresh meat the first day and treat afterward with grease, honey, and lint every day until he recovers."

## The Arts

Some of the best information we have about the daily lives of the Egyptian people comes from the paintings on the inner walls of their tombs. Remember that these paintings were not meant to be interior decoration but were to provide for the afterlife of the deceased.

Unlike most modern artists, the painters and sculptors of ancient Egypt did not seek to make a name for themselves. Instead, their works were done to serve the king, his officials, the community, and the gods. Nevertheless, the works of these artists reveal great ability and probably represent long years of apprenticeship. For us today, tomb paintings are among the finest achievements of ancient Egypt. ■

■ *What were some important achievements of the Egyptians during the New Kingdom period?*

▼ *These statues of Ramses II are part of the temple to the sun god Ra at Abu Simbel.*

---

**R E V I E W**

1. **FOCUS** What were the achievements of the Egyptians during the New Kingdom period?
2. **CONNECT** Which Egyptian ruler was more like Sargon of Akkad in goals and achievements, Hatshepsut or Thutmose III? How?
3. **HISTORY** After the death of an Egyptian ruler, who usually ruled next? How does this custom explain why some texts call Hatshepsut a king?
4. **CRITICAL THINKING** Scholars have concluded that the Egyptians feared change and disorder. Both Hatshepsut and Thutmose III brought changes to Egypt. What changes might have worried the Egyptians?
5. **WRITING ACTIVITY** Imagine that you are Hatshepsut, and your first Egyptian trading ship has just returned from Punt. Write a diary entry describing the event and your feelings about it.

Ancient Egypt

# Interpreting Egyptian Art

### Here's Why

One way to learn about the daily lives and beliefs of people of the past is to study their art. Suppose you wanted to learn more about what life was like in Thebes, the capital of Egypt at the time of the New Kingdom. Art from that time period is rich in information about daily life. But first you must know how to interpret art from the past.

### Here's How

When you look at art from the past, ask yourself these questions:

1. What was its purpose?
2. What is its main subject?
3. What does it tell you about the past?

The illustration on these pages is from a wall painting found in a tomb at Thebes. The tomb, which dates from about 1380 B.C., belonged to Nebamun *(NEHB uh muhn)* and Ipuky *(ee POO kee).* Both were important artists who worked for the king.

Now ask: What was the painting's purpose? Why was the painting created? The chapter tells you that a tomb painting's purpose was to help ensure a happy afterlife for the person buried in the tomb.

Next, what is the main subject of the painting? To answer this question, you need to figure out who is shown in the painting and what each person is doing.

Notice that horizontal lines divide the painting into sections, called registers. Look at the large, seated figure to the left of the registers. In Egyptian paintings, people of high rank are often shown as being larger than others. In this case, the large figure is a supervisor.

Look at the man on the far left of the upper register. He is weighing gold rings against a counterweight shaped like a bull's head.

The four seated men in the upper register are all carving symbols. To the right, two craftsmen are fitting the symbols into a framework. They are building a catafalque *(KAT uh fawlk),* an ornamental structure used in funerals.

Now look at the bottom register. Here you see six artisans at work. To their left, two men show finished objects to the supervisor.

Now do you know what the painting is about? If you guessed that it shows a royal workshop of artisans, you are right. Both Nebamun and

Ipuky were supervisors in the royal workshop. The items being made were for the king's tomb.

Next, consider the third question. What does the painting tell you about the past? Most important, it shows how deeply the Egyptians believed in the afterlife. As you can see, much effort went into the crafting of items for the next life.

The painting also tells you about Egyptian customs. For example, think about how the people in the painting are dressed. Notice that the supervisor wears a large ornamental collar and a thin, full-length garment. The workers dress in simple cloths wrapped at the waist.

## Try It

Look closely at the bottom register. Try interpreting the rest of the painting by answering the following questions. What are the six seated men in the bottom register making? What kinds of tools are they using? What does this tell you about ancient Egyptian technology? What are the workers wearing? What does this say about Egypt's climate?

## Apply It

Now that you have learned some skills for interpreting wall paintings, try your hand at making a painting of your own. Working alone or in a small group, create a mural that shows some scene from your daily life. For example, you might paint a scene from the lunchroom. Or you could paint a scene of your classroom or a special area such as the library. Be sure to show a number of different activities in detail. Display your murals. Then study and interpret each other's paintings.

Ancient Egypt

# Isis and Osiris

*Charles Mozley*

*This 5,000-year-old Egyptian myth tells the story of Isis, who became a goddess but lived as a mortal on earth, and her husband Osiris, who became a god and left earth to rule the underworld. In this excerpt from* The First Book of Ancient Egypt, *read how Isis and Osiris win over evil.*

**Osiris** (oh SY rihs)

*In Lesson 3 you read about some of the Egyptian gods. Now read a myth about two of the most popular gods.*

Under the rule [of Osiris and Isis] Egypt prospered and all men loved them. All, that is, but a few who were under the influence of the jealous brother of Osiris, Set. Being a goddess, Isis could see the wickedness in Set's heart and she warned her husband against him. But Osiris could not believe that there was evil in his own brother.

One day, Set invited Osiris to his palace on the River Nile. That night there was a huge banquet for the King. There was much feasting and drinking and merrymaking.

Suddenly eight huge Ethiopian slaves marched into the great hall, bearing upon their shoulders a large chest. This they set upon the floor and Set said,

"My brother! See this magnificent chest. It is made of the most precious wood I could find. It is bound with gold and silver bands, and as you see, I have had gems set into the lid. I shall give this chest to one of my guests—and you, dear brother, shall help me decide which one it shall be."

"How can I do that?" Osiris asked.

"Well," said the evil brother. "It will really be simple. The chest shall belong to that one of my guests who best fits into it. He must, however, fit into it exactly. Therefore he must not be too tall or too short, too fat or too thin. And, you, my brother, shall be the judge of all, as befits your rank."

"An unusual game," Osiris commented smiling. "Proceed."

Now the guests at this banquet had been carefully selected for two reasons: one, because they hated the good Osiris and wished to make the evil Set Pharaoh in his place; two, because not one of them could comfortably fit into the chest.

After all had tried and this became evident, Osiris said, "Now what do you suggest, dear brother?"

Set had the answer ready. "Since obviously I am too short for the chest, you are the only one left to try it—but first, let me hold your crown."

"Of course," replied the unsuspecting Osiris, and handing the crown over to his brother, he stepped into the chest and lay down full length. "Why," he exclaimed, "it is a perfect fit! As if it were made for me!"

"And so it was!" shouted the traitor, Set, and with a mighty heave slammed the lid shut upon Osiris.

The Ethiopian slaves were then ordered to lock the clasps and take the chest up on their shoulders. Thus they marched out of the palace, straight to a deep part of the river, and heaved the chest into the rushing water.

So the good Osiris perished, and the chest bearing his body floated down the River Nile. Seeing it pass, the birds ceased their singing, the fish sank to the bottom of the river, and the wind, like a great sigh of sorrow, swept over the land.

Isis, playing in the royal palace with her little son, Horus, lifted up her face and listened to the wind. With a broken-hearted cry she buried her face in her hands. "Set has slain Osiris!" she wailed. "My beloved husband is dead."

She had lived as a mortal woman for so long that in her sorrow she did not remember she was a goddess who knew the secret of life and death. All at once, however, power and knowledge came to her and she leaped to her feet. If she could but find the body of Osiris she might yet bring him back to life! But first she must put her little son, Horus, into a safe place.

Taking the child, she hastened to a distant part of the kingdom and gave him into the care of a dear friend. Then she cast a spell over the area, so none could find the boy and harm him. Having done this, Isis set out on her sad search along the River Nile.

Many people had seen the mysterious chest float down the river, but none knew where it had gone. At long last some children told Isis that they had found the chest, cast up by the waves into a bush near the shore.

"And then," the children cried, "the bush grew into a great tree, all around the chest!"

"Yes, yes!" Isis cried. "Where is this tree? Show it to me!"

"We can't," said a little boy. "The tree was so tall and so straight, our King had it made into a pillar for his palace."

Within that pillar was the body of her beloved husband, Isis knew, and hastened to the palace. But she did not go inside. Instead she sat weeping beside the fountain. Presently the Queen's maidens came out and seeing the sad stranger, spoke kindly to her.

Isis smiled at the maidens. "You are so kind to me, a lonely wanderer," she said, "that I wish to do something for you. I am skilled in beauty arts. Let me braid your hair more becomingly."

*raven tresses* long,
black and shiny hair


*Astarte* (a STAHR tee)




*pined for* missed




*treacherous* not to be
trusted; dangerous

And this she did, and as she arranged the maiden's hair, each one seemed to become more beautiful. As Isis worked with the raven tresses of the girls, she breathed upon their hair and it instantly took on a wonderful fragrance.

When the maidens returned to the palace they ran to their Queen, Astarte, and told her of the stranger at the fountain.

"Remarkable," said the Queen, "and the scent which she has given you is exquisite. Bring this woman to me."

And so Isis came into the palace, looking like a humble servant, for all that she was a far greater Queen than Astarte. But though she served the Queen well, she spent every moment possible playing with one of the young princes, who was rather sickly. Whenever Isis was with the child, Astarte noticed that the little prince appeared stronger and rosier, and whenever she left him, he pined for her. Before long, Isis was made chief nurse for the child and the prince thrived under her care.

There were some in the palace who were jealous of the preference shown to the stranger, and they spied upon her. One night, after Isis had put the little prince to bed, these jealous ones peeked through a crack in the door and what they saw sent them racing to Astarte. They related so horrifying a tale, that the mother forgot all her queenly dignity. Picking up her fine linen skirts she ran down the palace halls and burst into the room where Isis had the young prince.

Imagine the mother's feelings when she saw her child lying in a pile of burning sticks and a swallow flying around the flames and twittering mournfully.

With a loud cry Astarte rushed forward and plucked her child from the flames.

In that instant Isis returned to her human form—and to all her queenly dignity. "You have deprived the prince of immortality!" she said. "Another few moments and all would have been accomplished." Then she told the frightened mother who she was, and Astarte fell on her knees and begged forgiveness.

"I forgive you," Isis said sadly. "But you must give me the central pillar from this palace, for it contains the body of my slain husband, Osiris."

"You shall have it," Astarte promised, and commanded slaves to take the pillar down at once. "Why did you not tell me your story in the beginning?" she then asked gently.

Isis shook her head. "After the treacherous murder of my husband, I dared trust no-one," she said.

When the slaves had taken the pillar down, Isis caused it to be split open, and there was the casket. A magic boat of papyrus reeds was built for Isis, and having had the casket put in it, she guided the boat into the marshes of the Nile.

# Egypt Dominates Kush

Find Kush on the map below. Note that it is south of Egypt in what is now known as the Sudan. In ancient times, it was part of the area known as Nubia. Like Egypt, Kush lies on both banks of the Nile River.

Beginning around 2000 B.C., Egypt's pharaohs sent ships south to buy or seize gold and cattle from Kush. Egyptian stonecutters carved huge granite blocks from the cliffs in Kush and floated them on barges back to Egypt. The pharaohs used the granite for their temples, tombs, and obelisks.

Egyptian rulers realized the riches that Kush offered. During the Middle Kingdom, they had their soldiers build forts and trading posts in Kush. In this way, they protected their trade routes and made sure they had **access** to, or the ability to reach, Kush's gold and ivory. Egyptian rulers came to depend on Kush for police and soldiers as well.

In the period between the Middle and New Kingdoms, the Hyksos *(HIHK sahs)* invaded Egypt from the north. Hyksos pharaohs actually ruled Egypt for more than 100 years. Eventually, Kushite soldiers aided the Egyptians in driving the Hyksos out of Egypt.

The Egyptians had long considered Kush to be a part of their empire. However, Egyptian rulers had to "reconquer" Kush from time to time in order to maintain their control. In the 1400s B.C., Thutmose III invaded Kush again. Egypt demanded that Kush pay an annual **tribute**, or gift—ebony, ivory, ostrich feathers, perfumes, oils, and grains. Sometimes the tribute included exotic animals, such as giraffes and monkeys. Tribute scenes—pictures of Kushites carrying and presenting their tribute to Egyptian rulers—became popular during the New Kingdom.

*What did Kush have that Egypt wanted?*

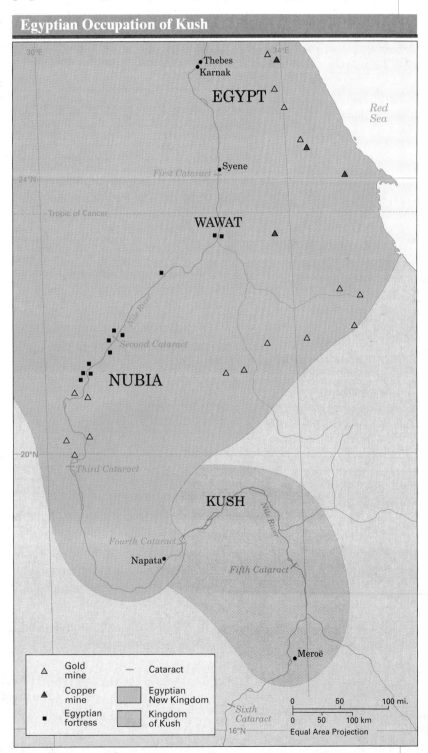

**Egyptian Occupation of Kush**

Legend:
- △ Gold mine
- ▲ Copper mine
- ■ Egyptian fortress
- — Cataract
- Egyptian New Kingdom
- Kingdom of Kush

0  50  100 mi.
0  50  100 km
Equal Area Projection

➤ *This painting was found in a c. 1420 B.C. Egyptian tomb. Kushites are carrying tribute to their Egyptian rulers.*

■ *How did Kushite society and Egyptian society influence each other?*

Not surprisingly, Egyptian culture had a strong influence on the Kushites. For example, Egyptian priests built temples in Kush where the Kushites worshiped Egyptian gods. The Kushites also adopted the Egyptian belief in the afterlife. Kushites learned Egyptian crafts. Some learned Egyptian hieroglyphic writing, too. Some Kushite leaders even studied at the Egyptian court. ■

## Kush Conquers Egypt

Kush remained a part of Egypt until the end of the New Kingdom period. Then, around 1070 B.C., Egypt fell into a period of decline. The all-powerful New Kingdom pharaohs were dead, and later rulers lacked their military skills. Priests and nobles fought with kings for control of the government, further weakening Egypt. Other countries in the empire no longer feared the pharaoh's authority and stopped paying tribute. Riches no longer poured into Egypt's treasury.

In addition to these problems, the Egyptian rulers were so busy struggling to stay in power that they did not have the energy and resources to make the rulers of Kush obey them. The Kushite ruler Kashta (*KAHSH tuh*) recognized Egypt's weakness. He saw the chance to break away from Egyptian control and extend the boundaries of his own kingdom. By 750 B.C., Kashta had conquered Upper Egypt and its capital city, Thebes.

Next, Kashta's son Piankhy (*pee AHNG kee*), known to the Kushites as Piye (*PEE ay*), defeated the warring princes who controlled the Nile Delta. Later, Piankhy put up a granite tablet on which he described the attack on the city of Memphis. It began:

> When day broke, at early morning, his majesty reached Memphis. . . . Then his majesty saw that it was strong, and that the wall was raised by a new rampart, and battlements manned with mighty men. There was found no way of attacking it.
>
> . . .
>
> But his majesty was enraged against it like a panther. He said, "I swear, as Ra loves me . . . this shall befall it [the city]. . . . I will take it like a flood of water."
>
> Piankhy, from a granite tablet near Napata, 700s B.C.

The city of Memphis fell to the Kushite army. Piankhy then went on to complete his conquest of Egypt by taking the rest of Lower Egypt. His successor, Shabaka, became the first Kushite pharaoh of Egypt. Shabaka's kingdom extended from the shores of the Mediterranean Sea to the borders of what is today the country of Ethiopia in Africa. ■

### How Do We Know?

**HISTORY** *Much of what scholars know about Kush is skillful guesswork. For example, scholars think some Indian beliefs influenced Kush. One clue is a three-headed lion god, Apedemak, which the Kushites worshiped. Wall paintings and statues show Apedemak with two sets of arms. Many-armed gods were common in India.*

■ *How did the Kushite leaders become Egyptian pharaohs when Egypt was weak?*

# Kush's Last Thousand Years

The dynasty that began with Kashta did not last long. Kush controlled Egypt for less than a hundred years. By 671 B.C., Assyria, which was by now the strongest power in the Middle East, attacked Egypt and attempted to overthrow the Kushite ruler King Taharqa *(tuh HAHR kuh)*. Assyrian soldiers, armed with iron weapons, easily defeated the Kushites, whose weapons were made of bronze and stone. King Taharqa's troops fled south. By 654 B.C., Assyrian troops had expelled the Kushites from Egypt.

Kushite kings continued to rule their former kingdom from their capital at Napata *(nuh PAH tuh)*. No longer the rulers of Egypt, they still wore the double crown of the Egyptian pharaoh. Their court ceremonies and religious practices remained Egyptian, and scribes still used the Egyptian language for official documents.

### Meroë, a New Capital

In 591 B.C., an Egyptian army defeated Kushite forces. For reasons still unexplained, the kings of Kush soon after moved their capital city from Napata to Meroë, a city about 150 miles south on the banks of the Nile River. Meroë became a great city, the center of Kushite culture.

Meroë was a good choice for the new capital of Kush. The area was rich in the natural resources necessary for iron production—iron ore and a good supply of wood. Iron was in great demand. Iron tools and weapons were much stronger than those of bronze. Kushite kings had learned iron making from the Assyrians, who had once used iron weapons to drive them out of Egypt.

Meroë became an important center of iron making. It also became a meeting place for traders from the Middle East, the Far East, and many parts of Africa. Camel caravans from the south brought leopard skins and ostrich eggs to Meroë's markets. Merchants from Syria and Palestine came to Meroë seeking gold and ivory. In ports on the Red Sea, Kushite merchants exchanged iron tools and spearheads for glass, fine cloth, and other luxury goods from China and India.

Arts and crafts flourished at Meroë. Workers made delicate vases and bowls, decorated with

*No one knows how this small gold sheath was used. Its intricate design illustrates the fine work done by the Nubians.*

*Leopard skins, ostrich feathers, granite, and ivory were some of the products Kush traded with Egypt and other nations.*

213

Ancient Egypt

sketches of hunters, animals, and flowers. Jewelers cast bracelets and earrings of silver and gold.

Some Egyptian practices continued. As in Egypt, the Kushite kings built great palaces along the Nile. They built temples to honor the gods and pyramids in which royal families were buried.

But over time, Egyptian influence on Kushite life lessened. The Kushites developed their own hieroglyphic writing. Later they worshiped an African lion god called Apedemak, their god of war.

■ *What happened to the Egyptian influence in Kush in the centuries after the Assyrian conquest?*

➤ *This elaborate royal crown made of silver was found in an excavation of ancient Nubia. Archaeologists date the crown in the A.D. 200s or 300s.*

### The Fall of Kush

Meroë remained an important cultural and trade center for more than 600 years. In A.D. 350, King Ezana, the ruler of a neighboring African kingdom called Axum, invaded and conquered Meroë. Ezana left a record of the defeat:

*I made war on them. . . . They fled without making a stand, and I pursued them . . . killing some and capturing others . . . I burnt their towns, both those built of bricks and those built of reeds, and my army carried off their food and copper and iron . . . and destroyed the statues in their temples, their granaries, and cotton trees and cast them into the [Nile].*

*Ezana, ruler of Axum, A.D. 300*

For many centuries after this brutal conquest, Meroë was forgotten. Modern archaeologists have explored the city and other ruins of ancient Kush. They have learned much about them, but much more is still unknown. Meroitic hieroglyphic writing remains a mystery.

Almost everything we know about the kingdom of Kush today comes from two sources. One source is the writings of other ancient peoples whose languages have been deciphered. The other source is writings from the time when Egyptian writing was still used in Kush. Someday, when scholars learn to read the Meroitic language, we will learn much more about the kings, queens, and commoners of one of Africa's first great civilizations. ■

---

R E V I E W

1. **FOCUS** Why does Kush deserve to be called one of the great civilizations of ancient Africa?

2. **CONNECT** What was the meaning of the double crown of Egypt? What achievement of King Piankhy made it an appropriate crown for Kushite kings?

3. **HISTORY** What benefits did Egypt receive from Kush, and what benefits did Kush receive from Egypt?

4. **CRITICAL THINKING** Why did Meroë become an important center of culture and trade?

5. **ACTIVITY** Imagine that you live during the time of Kush's greatness. Using information from this lesson, draw or paint a travel poster urging people to visit your country.

# Reading a Cross Section

## Here's Why

A cross section is a special kind of diagram. It shows how the inside of an object looks, how it is made, what it is made of, or how it works. Cross sections are often used to show how things such as toys and machines are put together.

Cross sections can be especially helpful for understanding how something works. For example, cross sections can help you understand how smelting furnaces, such as those used during the iron age, worked.

## Here's How

Look at the diagrams on this page. Get the "big picture" first—read the titles and look over the diagrams to see what they show in general. Then read the labels and refer to the glossary as you study each diagram closely.

Look at the cross section on the left. The labels tell you what each part of the diagram is. For example, the labels explain that the furnace walls were made of clay bricks covered by a layer of mud. The labels also identify hollow clay pipes and bellows. The bellows were used to pump air through the pipes. Find the arrows that indicate the movement of the bellows.

Now look at the contents of the furnace. The labels tell you there are alternating layers of charcoal and iron ore in the upper part of the furnace. What is in the bottom part of the furnace?

## Try It

The diagram on the right shows the same furnace after it was fired. Compare this diagram to the one on the left. What is the same in the two diagrams? What is different? What happened to the charcoal? What happened to the iron ore?

## Apply It

Find a cross-sectional diagram in your science textbook or another source. Explain the diagram by answering these questions: What does the diagram show? What parts are labeled? Why is the cross section useful?

### Glossary

**bellows** (běl´ōz)  A pump device used to produce a current of air

**bloom** (bloom)  Purified iron that is the result of the smelting process

**slag** (slăg)  Impurities and waste from the smelting process

**smelting** (smělt´ĭng)  The use of heat to remove pure metal from ore

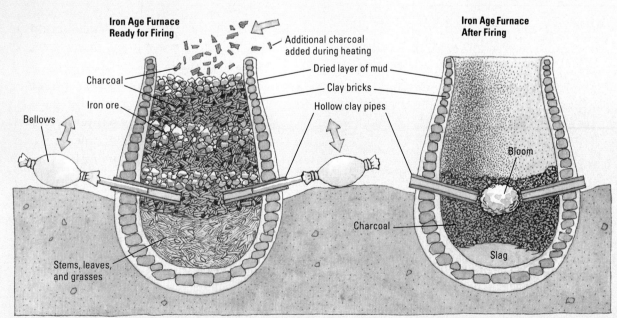

**Iron Age Furnace Ready for Firing**

Additional charcoal added during heating

Dried layer of mud

Charcoal

Clay bricks

Iron ore

Hollow clay pipes

Bellows

**Iron Age Furnace After Firing**

Bloom

Charcoal

Slag

Stems, leaves, and grasses

215

# Chapter Review

## Reviewing Key Terms

access (p. 211)    hieroglyphics (p. 196)
afterlife (p. 192)    mummy (p. 192)
cataract (p. 187)    obelisk (p. 200)
delta (p. 187)    papyrus (p. 189)
dynasty (p. 190)    pharaoh (p. 199)
embalm (p. 192)    tribute (p. 211)

**A.** The two words in each pair are related in some way. On your own paper, write a sentence explaining how the words are related.

1. cataract, delta
2. papyrus, hieroglyphics
3. pharaoh, tribute
4. dynasty, pharaoh
5. mummy, afterlife
6. hieroglyphics, obelisk

**B.** Some of the following statements are true. The rest are false. Write *True* or *False* for each statement. Then rewrite the false statements to make them true.

1. A dynasty was made up of several rulers from different families.
2. Cataracts are the plants from which papyrus is made.
3. Hatshepsut placed pillars called obelisks across the river from her temple.
4. The Egyptians built forts in Kush to protect their access to Kush's gold and ivory.
5. Embalming turned the body into a mummy.
6. The part of the Nile called the delta is found in southern Egypt.

## Exploring Concepts

**A.** The following cause-and-effect chart about ancient Egypt lists facts about the Nile, an important discovery, a new ruler, and a power struggle. Copy the chart on your own paper. Then, fill in a sentence to the right of each cause that tells the effect. The first one has been done for you.

| Cause | Effect |
|---|---|
| 1. The Nile flooded its banks each year, depositing rich mud in farmers' fields. | Ancient Egypt could grow crops in the desert and feed its people. |
| 2. In 1799, soldiers found a stone with three kinds of ancient writing. | |
| 3. Thutmose III was next in line for the throne, but he was only 10 years old. | |
| 4. The rulers of Egypt could no longer make the rulers of Kush obey. | |

**B.** Support each statement with facts and details from the chapter.

1. Natural borders isolated ancient Egypt and protected it from invaders.
2. The seasons in Egypt were based on the flooding of the Nile.
3. A famous Egyptian legend tells the story of King Menes.
4. Historians have identified three periods in Egypt's history when many important events took place.
5. Imhotep, advisor to King Zoser, brought about an important change in Egypt.
6. The Egyptians left many written texts.
7. As a ruler, Hatshepsut concerned herself with improving life at home rather than building an empire.
8. The Babylonians and the Egyptians each created a lunar calendar.
9. Kush's riches were important to the Egyptians.
10. King Kashta's dynasty did not last long.

# Reviewing Skills

1. Look again at the picture of the god Anubis on page 193. You can see that the figure representing Anubis is larger than the figures to his left. Do you think that the difference in the size of these figures is significant? Use what you have learned about interpreting Egyptian paintings to help you expalin your answer.

2. Turn to the cross-section diagram on page 422. The ancient Romans built many roads, some of which are still in use today. This diagram shows how the Romans built roads. You can see that rubble forms the road's bottom layer. This means that the rubble was the first layer that workers laid down. What were the next two layers? What material makes up the road's surface? Look at the diagram again. Notice that the Roman road is higher in the middle than it is near the curbs. Why might the Romans have constructed roads this way?

3. Imagine that your class plans to present a short play about ancient Egypt. Explain how to prepare this project by using the five steps for organizing a class project described on page 181.

4. Imagine that you are an ancient Egyptian sailor measuring the depth of the Nile River at different times of the year. What is the best way to organize the measurements you have recorded?

# Using Critical Thinking

1. One way scientists learn about early people is by studying the objects they left behind. Which Egyptian artifacts are the most helpful for learning about ancient Egypt? Why?

2. Having paper allowed the Egyptians to leave many written records. From such records and the objects the people left behind, we learned the information you read in this chapter. Do you think this information gives us a full picture of Egyptian society? If not, tell what you think is missing.

3. The ancient Egyptians accomplished many things. They formed governments, became a world power, and built an empire. They invented a writing system and developed a belief system and customs. The ancient Egyptians also created outstanding literature, art, and architecture. If you had lived in ancient Egypt, which achievement would you have wanted to be a part of? How might a person do something similar today?

4. To become a scribe, a student copied the same lines over and over. What kinds of schoolwork do you think best prepare students for life in our society today?

# Preparing for Citizenship

1. **ARTS ACTIVITY** Make a diorama of a pharaoh's burial chamber. The illustrations in A Closer Look on pages 194 and 195 will help you. Include a model of a mummy and objects buried with the pharaoh. Decorate part of the wall with a mural. On the other part, write a message about the afterlife using hieroglyphic symbols from page 506 of the Minipedia. Explain why we display objects from Egyptian tombs in museums today.

2. **COLLABORATIVE LEARNING** Form groups, one for each Egyptian achievement mentioned in Using Critical Thinking (3) on this page. In your group, decide what modern achievement can be compared to the ancient one. Have one group member describe the Egyptian achievement. Have another describe a modern achievement that can be compared to it. Have two students illustrate the achievements. Combine the work of all the groups into a class presentation.

# Unit 4

## Early Asian Civilizations

*Horse-drawn chariots carried the wealthy people of China 1,800 years ago. By then, the civilizations in the Near East had fallen, but Asian civilizations continued to flourish. China, cut off from the rest of the world by mountains and deserts, grew with little outside influence. India accepted people and ideas from many places. Both civilizations developed traditions that live on into the present.*

# 2500 B.C.

*Bronze horse and chariot from a tomb at Wuwui, c. A.D. 100*

A.D. 467

# Chapter 8

# *Ancient India*

*Like the brightly colored cotton cloth woven in India for thousands of years, the culture of India has been fashioned from many strands. The earliest Indian civilization arose about 4,500 years ago. Gradually, other ancient peoples moved to India. Over the centuries, the people blended old and new customs and beliefs, just as weavers blend the multicolored threads of their fabrics. The unique mixture of religious and social traditions continues in India today.*

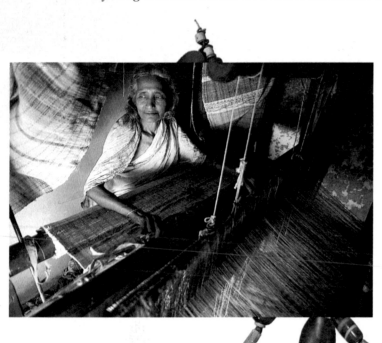

More than 4,000 years ago people in the Indus Valley were weaving cotton cloth. Hand looms like this are used today in some parts of India.

**c. 2500–1500 B.C.** The Indus Valley civilization flourishes along the Indus River. This bead necklace is from the ancient city of Harappa.

| 3000 | 2500 | 2000 | 1500 |
|------|------|------|------|

# 2500 B.C.

**c. 1500 B.C.** The nomadic Aryans settle in the Indus Valley. They compose sacred hymns called the Vedas, still recited today.

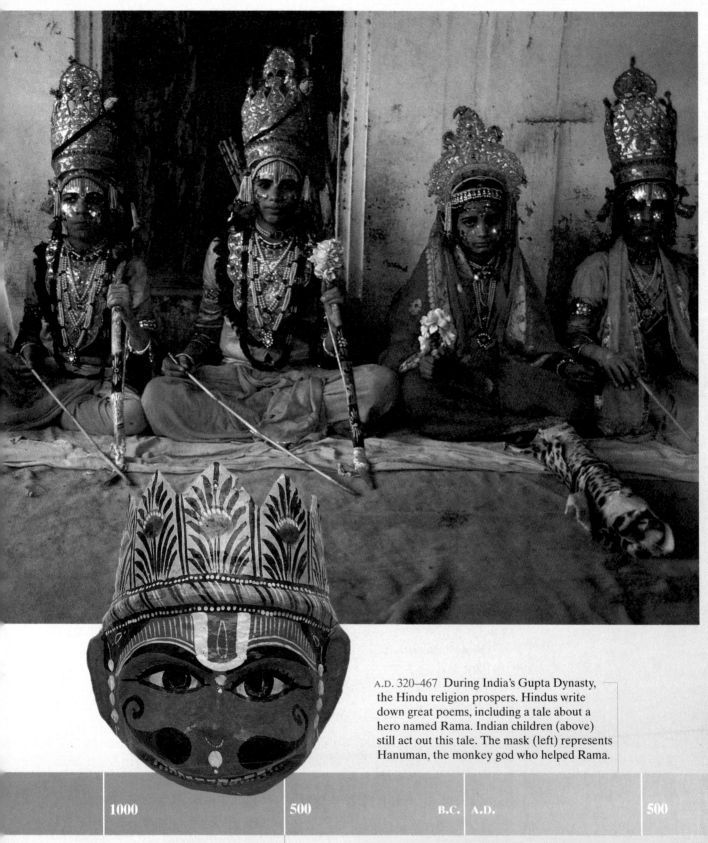

A.D. 320–467 During India's Gupta Dynasty, the Hindu religion prospers. Hindus write down great poems, including a tale about a hero named Rama. Indian children (above) still act out this tale. The mask (left) represents Hanuman, the monkey god who helped Rama.

| 1000 | | 500 | | B.C. | A.D. | | 500 |

c. 500 B.C. A new religion, Buddhism, arises from the teachings of Siddhartha Gautama.

A.D. 467

L E S S O N  1

# The Indus Valley Civilization

### Key Terms

- subcontinent
- silt

*The seal is a smooth black stone without polish. On it is engraved very deeply a bull . . . Above the bull there is an inscription in six characters, which are quite unknown to me . . .*

Archaeological Survey
of India, 1872–1873

Those are the words used by archaeologist Alexander Cunningham in 1873 to describe a curious, cracker-sized object much like the one shown on this page. He identified it as a seal, an object commonly used to imprint pictures, writing, or numbers. Cunningham had found the seal in Harappa, a mysterious, ruined city in what is now northern Pakistan.

The seal and the strange writing captured Cunningham's attention, but he could not solve the riddle of their origin. Though we now know more about the history of the seal, the script on its surface still remains a mystery.

The trail that led Cunningham to the seal began in the early 1800s

*The strange symbols on this water buffalo seal still puzzle decoders.*

with travelers' accounts of Harappa. Partly buried beneath mounds of earth, Harappa had long been deserted. Yet the ruins that remained above ground showed that this was a highly developed civilization. Who were the builders? No one knew.

The reports of Harappa eventually reached Cunningham, who was a leading British archaeologist working in India. He decided to visit the ruins. It was on his third trip that Cunningham came upon the puzzling seal.

In the years that followed Cunningham's find, other archaeologists explored Harappa and Mohenjo-Daro, a ruined city 400 miles southwest of Harappa. What they found was astonishing: traces of a civilization thousands of years older than anything ever before discovered in India. This civilization became known as the Indus Valley civilization. It thrived for approximately 1,000 years from about 2500 to 1500 B.C.

The Indus Valley was once a well-watered plain that may have provided homes for the animals shown on the carved seals. Although these animals are no longer found in the valley, it must have once been their home.

Blessed with fertile fields and water, the people of the Indus Valley raised wheat and barley year after year. This stable food supply encouraged others to settle in the area. Eventually, these people began to build cities. ■

■ *How did the geographical location of the Indus Valley make possible the growth of a civilization there?*

## The Great River Civilization

Besides Mohenjo-Daro and Harappa, more than 70 other sites have been discovered in the Indus Valley. Even though no written records have been found, archaeologists have learned much about this civilization.

*◄ This rhinoceros seal uncovered by archaeologists helps to confirm that this animal once lived in the Indus River Valley.*

### Central Planning

The Indus sites are scattered across the river plain, an area three times larger than California. Archaeological digs reveal that most of these towns were neatly laid out according to similar plans. Workers constructed the buildings, streets, and sewer systems with skill and care. Even their bricks were equal in size and shape.

This matching suggests a strong central government for the entire area with information flowing freely between towns. To achieve such order, a central group must have planned the projects and overseen the work in the various towns.

### Widespread Trade

Besides being in contact with their neighbors along the river, the people of the Indus Valley traded with communities many miles away. We have learned this from Mesopotamian writings that refer to trade between the Indus Valley and Sumer. In addition, stone beads, bone inlays, and seals from the Indus Valley have been discovered in Mesopotamia. Traces of Indus products also were found near the Persian Gulf.

Cube-shaped stone weights for use by merchants give further evidence of trade. These finely crafted and apparently accurate weights were unearthed throughout the Indus Valley. Some were tiny enough to balance small amounts of gold, while others were so large they had to be hoisted with ropes.

Historians also believe that merchants had their own trademarks that were carved on stone seals. An example is pictured on this page. Merchants used these seals to stamp their identification on their belongings. In A Closer Look, on pages 226 and 227, you'll learn more about archaeological discoveries made at the Mohenjo-Daro site in the Indus Valley. ■

▲ *Can you imagine an ancient merchant using these weights to measure out grain and gold?*

■ *What products did the Indus Valley cities export, and how do we know?*

225

# Mohenjo-Daro

*This was once a busy city of 35,000 people, filled with footsteps, shouts, laughter, and the smells of food cooking. What was it like to live here? What skills and ideas did people have? The clues found at Mohenjo-Daro can help tell us.*

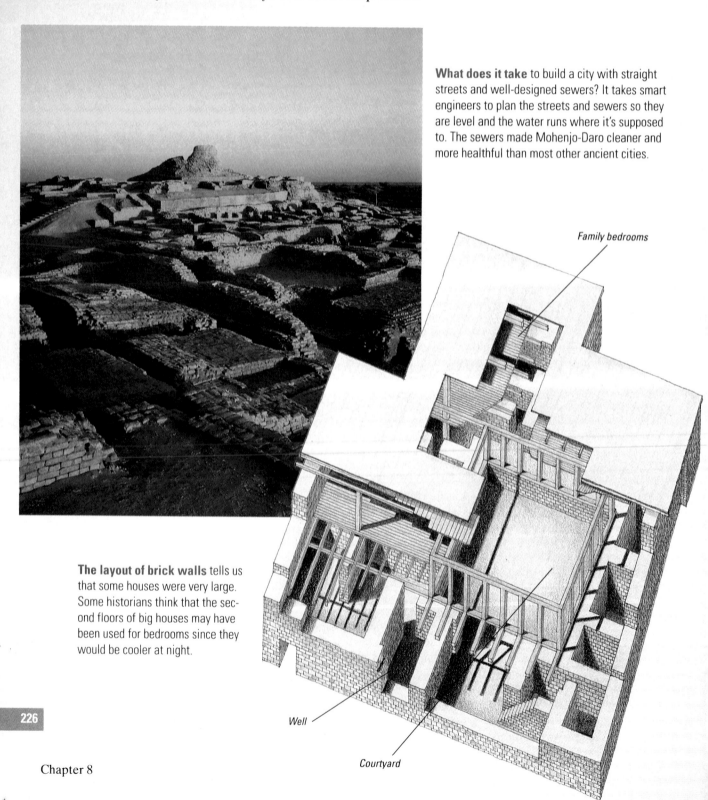

**What does it take** to build a city with straight streets and well-designed sewers? It takes smart engineers to plan the streets and sewers so they are level and the water runs where it's supposed to. The sewers made Mohenjo-Daro cleaner and more healthful than most other ancient cities.

Family bedrooms

**The layout of brick walls** tells us that some houses were very large. Some historians think that the second floors of big houses may have been used for bedrooms since they would be cooler at night.

Well

Courtyard

**Look at the clothing** carved on this statue, which may represent a priest or a king. Based on carvings like this and scraps of cotton cloth archaeologists think that both women and men dressed in colorful robes.

**This pool with steps leading into it** is known as the Great Bath. Why did the ancient citizens put this pool in the most important part of town? Since ritual bathing is still an important part of some present-day Indian religions, perhaps the Great Bath was a part of Mohenjo-Daro's religious life.

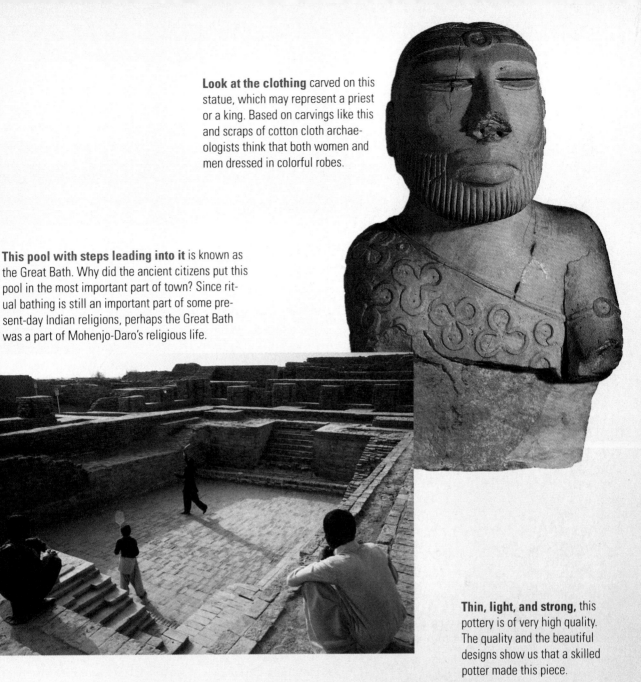

**Thin, light, and strong,** this pottery is of very high quality. The quality and the beautiful designs show us that a skilled potter made this piece.

**What's for dinner?** Archaeologists found tiny bits of food in huge grain storage rooms in the center of the city. These clues suggest that dinner in Mohenjo-Daro could have been warm, tasty wheat bread served with barley or rice.

Ancient India

# Echoes from Abandoned Cities

▲ *Today, you can still see traditionally styled carts with two wheels on India's rural roads.*

➤ *This miniature cart of terra cotta pulled by two bulls was discovered in the Mohenjo-Daro ruins*

■ *What evidence of the Indus Valley civilization is found in modern India?*

After lasting for 1,000 years, the Indus Valley civilization finally declined and vanished around the year 1500 B.C. No one knows exactly why. Perhaps an earthquake caused great floods. Human skeletons have been found huddled together in the digs at Mohenjo-Daro, as if they may have been trapped in such a disaster. Some historians believe that invaders simply finished off a civilization that had already grown weak.

Though the Indus Valley civilization is long gone, faint echoes of its culture remain. Among treasures found at Mohenjo-Daro was a statue of a woman wearing bracelets. In India today, many women wear similar jewelry.

The people of the Indus Valley were the first to raise chickens for food. Today, chicken appears on menus worldwide.

By 2000 B.C., the Indus people had begun to spin and weave cotton cloth. Today, the making of cotton cloth is one of India's most important industries.

Archaeologists still have much to learn about the Indus Valley civilization. But they're faced with a major problem. The river that gave its wonderful living waters so that the Indus civilization could flourish now hinders the work of archaeologists. Because the cities were built so close to the Indus River, archaeologists can't dig deep trenches and pits to explore the remains of this ancient civilization. If they do, these sites might flood, destroying valuable evidence. ■

## R E V I E W

1. **FOCUS** What evidence have archaeologists found of a highly developed civilization in the Indus River Valley?

2. **CONNECT** Compare the rise of civilization in the Nile River Valley and the Indus River Valley.

3. **CULTURE** What do the large, well-constructed houses at Mohenjo-Daro tell us about the people who lived there 4,500 years ago?

4. **CRITICAL THINKING** Archaeologists discovered 10 cities at Mohenjo-Daro, built one on top of the other, each less carefully built than the one before. What conclusions can you draw from this?

5. **ACTIVITY** List five imaginary finds from an archaeological site. Exchange lists. Tell what these finds reveal about the early inhabitants.

LESSON 2

# Arrival of the Aryans

L et's travel back in time about 3,500 years to a large wheat field in the Indus Valley. Imagine you are standing in that field, helping your family cut wheat with short, stone knives. It's a hot day, and the sweet smell of wheat rises from the ground.

Suddenly, you hear a rumble, a kind of quiet thunder in the distance. As the sound grows louder, strange figures come into view, speeding toward you. Everyone in the wheat field stops working. They seem to have frozen where they stand.

The fast-moving figures are now close enough for you to see clearly. Large, powerful animals, unlike any you've ever seen before, are galloping across the plain, pulling two-wheeled carts behind them. Tall men stand upright in the onrushing carts, their swords flashing bronze in the sunlight. Terrified, you hide in the uncut wheat as the carts clatter by you.

As you soon learn, those large animals are horses, and the two-wheeled carts are called chariots. Both of these were unknown in the Indus Valley before this time.

More important, the men aboard the chariots are called **Aryans.** The arrival of the Aryans in the Indus Valley will change the course of Indian history.

**THINKING FOCUS**

*What did the Aryans contribute to Indian culture?*

### Key Terms

- Aryan
- migration
- caste

## Who Were the Aryans?

To the people of the Indus Valley, the Aryans must have seemed strange, indeed. They looked different. They were generally taller than the people who lived in the valley, and they had lighter skin. They spoke a strange language and worshiped unfamiliar gods. Also, their lifestyle was centered on herding rather than farming.

But the Indus Valley people had time to become used to these new arrivals because the Aryans didn't make a mass invasion. Rather, they moved into the Indus Valley, little by little, over a long period of time.

### Indo-European Migrations

Long before they reached India, the Aryans lived in the grasslands of eastern Europe north of the Black and Caspian seas. They were part of a larger group we now call the Indo-Europeans.

The Indo-Europeans were a seminomadic people who herded cattle, goats, and sheep. They generally traveled from place to place in tribes, groups made up of

229

Ancient India

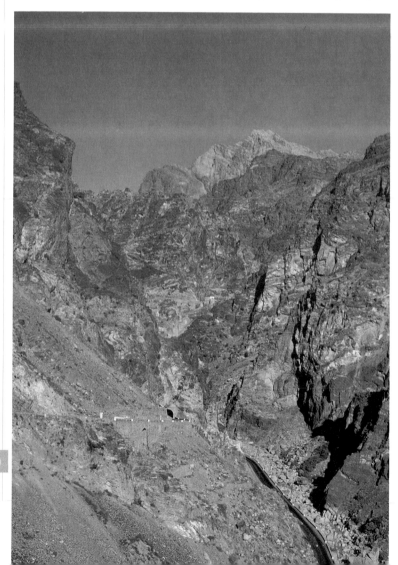

The adz side (left) of this Aryan tool shaped wood; the ax chopped it.

■ *What advantages enabled the Aryans to successfully take over the Indus Valley?*

▼ *Aryans pushed their way through passes in the Hindu Kush mountain range, like this one near Kabul, Afghanistan.*

related families. Because the Indo-Europeans were on the move much of the time, they didn't build cities. But they did tame the horse and develop a sturdy wheel with spokes for their two-wheeled chariots. These speedy chariots allowed them to move freely over large areas and to wage war more effectively than warriors on foot.

About 2000 B.C., conditions in the Indo-European homeland changed. Historians aren't exactly sure what happened. Perhaps the Indo-Europeans ran out of good grazing pasture for their herds. Perhaps their population had simply grown so much that they needed more space. Or they may have suffered an outbreak of disease or an attack by invaders.

Whatever the reason, sometime around 2000 B.C., huge groups of Indo-Europeans left their homes and began moving to new regions. This movement of people to new surroundings is called **migration.** As the map on page 231 shows, some groups of Indo-Europeans moved west and south. Others, the Aryans, moved east toward the Indian subcontinent.

### Through the Mountain Passes

By around 1500 B.C., the first Aryans found their way through the difficult, high passes in the Hindu Kush, the mountains along the northwestern edge of the Indian subcontinent. One route was through the Khyber Pass. These passes would serve as highways for other migrating and invading peoples for the next 3,000 years.

### Aryan Hymns: The Vedas

Although we have little archaeological evidence of the early Aryans, we do have other sources of information. Aryan beliefs and daily life are described in the Vedas (*VAY duhs*), a collection of sacred hymns and poems. They were composed by the Aryans sometime around 1500 B.C.

The early Aryans had no written language, yet they passed down the Vedas for centuries. Aryan priests memorized the Vedas and taught younger priests. Imagine memorizing long school books, word for word, by having them read aloud to you. That gives you some idea of what the Aryan priests did. Passing knowledge from generation to generation by oral tradition wasn't an easy task. ■

The Aryans who rode into India were not the only people at that time who were on the move. Similar migrations of people took place east, south, and west of the Indo-European homelands in eastern Europe.

What is a migration? What causes people to leave their homes and move thousands of miles to places they may never have seen? What happens when migrating people meet the people already there?

## A Trip Isn't Migration

A migration is a permanent move, not a short-term one. About 200 years ago, Indians such as the Pawnee were often on the move. They hunted the many buffalo that roamed the midwestern plains. Once or twice a year they went on trips to hunt buffalo. The Pawnee carried everything they needed with them, and set up temporary wood-and-skin homes called tepees. But the Pawnee were not migrating. They always returned to their permanent villages.

## Why People Migrate

People migrate to leave where they are, as well as to arrive at a new place. Natural disasters such as floods or earthquakes may push people out of their homes. Or, invaders may force them out. The attraction of more food or better jobs may pull people to a new place. Historians call this the "push-pull" of migration.

## Some Major Migrations

Major migrations have taken place throughout history. Thousands of years ago people settled North and South America by crossing the Bering Strait from Asia. Bantu migrations took place in Africa around A.D. 700, in 1200, and again in 1800. In the 1980s, many people from Central America migrated to the United States.

## Results of Migration

People who migrate are influenced by the culture of their new land. But they also cause changes in that culture. The map below shows how the Indo-Europeans fanned out in different directions on their migrations. With them, they took their flocks, their horses, chariots, clothes, and weapons. But they also took along something more lasting: their language.

As they settled in their new homelands, their Indo-European language was taken into the cultures already there. Language experts have discovered that many of the languages spoken in Europe and India today have the same root: the language spoken by Indo-Europeans. In this way, those early migrations made a lasting imprint on history.

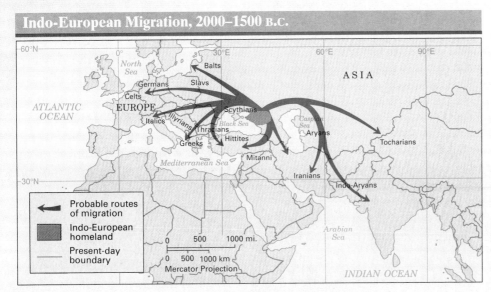

**Indo-European Migration, 2000–1500 B.C.**

Probable routes of migration

Indo-European homeland

Present-day boundary

0     500     1000 mi.

0   500  1000 km
Mercator Projection

60°N · North Sea · Balts · Germans · Slavs · Celts · EUROPE · ATLANTIC OCEAN · Italics · Illyrians · Thracians · Greeks · Hittites · Scythians · Black Sea · Mitanni · Mediterranean Sea · ASIA · Caspian Sea · Aryans · Iranians · Indo-Aryans · Tocharians · Arabian Sea · INDIAN OCEAN · 30°N · 0° · 30°E · 60°E · 90°E

231

Ancient India

# What Do the Vedas Reveal?

**How Do We Know?**

**HISTORY** *Most information about the Aryans comes from the Vedas. All other evidence is scarce. When the Aryans first arrived in the Indus Valley, they were still seminomadic. They probably built their houses with the materials at hand—mud, wood, and reeds. Unlike brick, mud crumbles easily; wood and reeds quickly decay. Thus, little physical evidence of these early settlements remains.*

The Vedas are the main source of information about the Aryan people and their way of life. For this reason, historians call the period from about 1500 to 600 B.C. the Vedic Period.

The Aryans first settled in northwestern India in an area now known as the Punjab. From the native people, they learned to grow wheat and barley. They also continued to raise livestock. In fact, cows were so highly prized by the Aryans that these animals were used as a kind of money. According to the Vedas, Aryan priests were paid in cows for performing religious services.

## Social Classes

When the Aryans first came to India, their social system had three classes—the ruler, or raja *(RAH jah),* and his warriors; the priests; and the commoners.

Eventually, a new four-class system emerged, probably as a result of intermarriage between the Aryans and the Indus Valley people. In this system, priests, or brahmans, were the most powerful class. They were followed by rajas and warriors. Merchants and peasants were the third class. At the bottom were the servants. The diagram on page 233 shows the relationships between the four classes, or *varnas.*

Little by little, as people learned new skills, another set of divisions came about within the classes. These subgroups were named **castes.** Castes were ranked one above the other like steps on a ladder. Yet you couldn't climb that ladder. You were born within a caste, and you stayed there all your lifetime. You both worked and married within the caste.

Classes and castes aren't the same. Over time, castes can gain or lose importance. New ones can be added; old ones can fade. But the four classes have remained the same for centuries. Even though classes and castes are different, people often use the word "caste" to include both groupings.

## A Nature-Based Religion

Natural forces were very important in the lives of the Aryans. Without the right balance of sun and rain, for example, crops would fail and people would starve. It is not surprising, then, that the Aryans worshiped a number of nature gods. One of the most powerful gods was Indra. Indra was the god of war and a thrower of thunderbolts. Each morning, Indra defeated a dragon of darkness. Indra's victory allowed the sun to rise and the dawn goddess to

➤ *Indra, the mighty storm god, rides across the sky on his white elephant in this Indian painting from the 1600s. Indra has answered the call of the priests who are tending the sacred fire.*

Diagram labels:

**1 Priests**

**2 Rajas and Warriors**

**3 Merchants and Peasants**

**4 Servants**

Gave gifts; protected and ruled the kingdom

Made offerings to the gods; taught the Vedas

Served others

Supplied food, clothing, other goods

Made offerings to the gods; taught the Vedas

Protected and ruled the kingdom

Supplied food, clothing, other goods

Made offerings to the gods

Served others

Protected and ruled the kingdom

Served others

Supplied food, clothing, other goods

*As the diagram shows, Aryan society was a complex system in which each class gave something to the others, and received something in return.*

arrive. The power of Indra is shown in the *Rig Veda:*

*I*ndra, who wields the thunderbolt in his hand, is the king of that which moves and that which rests, of the tame and of the horned. He rules the people as their king, encircling all this as a rim encircles spokes.

In order to keep the earth's natural forces in balance, Aryan priests called to the gods by singing and chanting Vedic hymns. In the later Vedic Period, animals were sacrificed to the gods. According to the priests, it was hard to keep nature in balance. The hymns had to be recited in just the right way or the outcome might be a disaster. Because rituals played an important role in religion, priests became very powerful in Aryan society.

## Music, Dance, and Races

The Vedas tell us, too, that music and dance were valued by the early Aryans. Stringed instruments, flutes, and drums are all mentioned in the Vedas. The Aryans also were fond of chariot racing and gambling. ■

■ *What do the Vedas reveal about Aryan society and religion?*

233

Ancient India

# What Remains Today of Aryan Ways?

■ *What evidence of the Aryan tradition is found in modern India?*

▼ *A Vedic fire is still used at Hindu weddings.*

As the centuries passed, the growing Aryan population continued to spread over the region. By 1000 B.C., these one-time nomads had reached as far east as the fertile banks of the Ganges River.

They still raised livestock, but gradually, they began to settle down. They had learned how to work with iron to make stronger axes and plows. With these two tools, they could cut down forests to create new farmlands. They grew a variety of crops, including rice.

Crafts and trades had also increased. The Aryans now had skilled weavers, dyers, jewelers, and potters. This new settled life brought about another change, too. Slowly, over time, the Aryan people began to establish small kingdoms.

The Aryans first migrated to India more than 3,500 years ago. Remarkably, the effects of that migration are still seen in India today. Sanskrit, the language spoken by the Aryans, is the root of Hindi, one of the most common languages in modern India.

Castes, too, are reminders of the ancient Aryans. Many people in India still live, marry, and choose jobs strictly within their family's caste. But today, the constitution of India makes it unlawful to be unjust to anyone because of his or her lower caste. Yet, the caste system continues to be important in some ways in modern India. ■

## REVIEW

1. **FOCUS** What did the Aryans contribute to Indian culture?
2. **CONNECT** Contrast the Aryans with the Indus Valley people. Be sure to include way of life, power structure, tools, and equipment.
3. **HISTORY** Who were the Indo-Europeans, and how is their influence felt in the world today?
4. **CRITICAL THINKING** Since the Vedas were composed by Aryans, the information is presented from an Aryan point of view. Why is this important?
5. **ACTIVITY** Draw a map of present-day India and Pakistan. Label the Aryans' route through the Khyber Pass. Also show how they later spread eastward to the Ganges River.

Chapter 8

L E S S O N   3

# Beginning of Buddhism

An old man, a sick man, a dead man, and a holy man. These four sights led to the start of a new religion in India. To understand how, you must go back over 2,500 years to a small kingdom in northern India.

The king of this region had a son named Siddhartha Gautama *(sihd DAHR tah GAW tah mah)*. Religious men predicted the boy would become a great ruler.

But one lone wise man foretold that the boy would become a spiritual ruler, not a worldly king. Somehow, somewhere, Siddhartha would see signs of suffering. These signs would so grieve the prince that he would give up his worldly kingdom. He would then turn to spiritual ways to help people overcome their sufferings and sorrow.

The king despaired. He wanted his son to inherit the throne, not follow spiritual callings. So, the king decided to direct the boy's future. He swore to protect Siddhartha from all signs of suffering. According to legend, the king ordered that everyone with an illness or injury be kept off the royal roads when Siddhartha traveled about in his chariot. Thus, the prince lived a sheltered life of luxury. More than that, he saw no sorrow during his early years.

But in the end, the king's efforts failed. One day while traveling beyond the palace, Siddhartha saw a man, old and frail. The years had bent his body and traced lines upon his face. This sight grieved the prince. He had never seen old age before. On a second ride, he saw a sick man, shivering with fever. Again, the

prince was troubled. On his third ride, he watched while mourners carried a dead man to his funeral. The prince now knew about death.

Old age, sickness, and death. Why must people suffer? The prince knew that he, too, would one day grow old and die. Was

**THINKING FOCUS**

*What are the main teachings of Buddhism?*

## Key Terms

- Buddhism
- moderation
- reincarnation

◄ *The young Siddhartha (center) is pictured in the royal palace in this copy of an Ajanta cave painting. Near Ajanta, India, cave walls are covered with paintings dating back to about 200 B.C.*

235

Ancient India

there no way to escape? Then Siddhartha saw a wandering holy man. The wanderer had no possessions but a simple bowl. Despite his age and poverty, the holy man seemed calm and content. Siddhartha wondered if this way of living would help him find his own peace. He decided to put aside his riches and to leave his comfortable home and family.

In the black of night while all slept, Siddhartha left the palace. He set out to search for a truth that would help erase suffering and sorrow from the world.

*In this modern-day comic strip, Siddhartha and his charioteer, Channa, see a holy man. This scene prompted the young prince to begin his search.*

## Life of the Buddha

The story about Siddhartha's birth and childhood is legend. However, a man named Siddhartha Gautama actually did live on the Indian subcontinent from about 563 to 483 B.C. This same man wandered over the countryside, seeking new ideas to live by. Eventually, he established **Buddhism,** one of the world's major religions.

### Siddhartha's Search

Siddhartha's search for truth took place at a time of religious unrest on the subcontinent. He wasn't the only one seeking answers to spiritual questions. Others were looking, too. Some people had begun to doubt the need for the priests' Vedic rituals and animal sacrifices. Seekers of truth were a common sight on Indian roads in those days.

What we know about Siddhartha's search comes mainly from Buddhist writings and from oral tradition. On his journeys he wore a simple yellow robe and owned nothing but a small bowl. To stay alive he accepted rice that people offered. He wandered. He questioned. Sitting at the feet of the great religious teachers of the day, Siddhartha sought his answers. But he found none. He then decided to look within himself for wisdom. Sitting in the shade of a fig tree, he vowed not to leave until he had found his answers.

For days, he sat in meditation, thought so deep that no passerby, no bird's song disturbed him.

the next life. However, a person's personality does not make this journey. If you have a bad karma, you have much to overcome in your next life. But a good karma takes you closer to enlightenment.

The chain of birth, suffering, death, and rebirth goes on and on until enlightenment is gained. Once enlightened, a person is finally free from further rebirth with all its earthly suffering.

### The Three Jewels

The Buddhist tradition is made up of three parts called The Three Jewels. The first jewel is the Buddha himself. The second jewel is the dharma, the law the Buddha passed on to his followers.

The third jewel is Buddhism's religious community, called the *sangha*. In the sangha are monks and nuns, as well as everyday followers. As time went on, devoted monks built centers of learning, which are called monasteries. Here, they practiced the Buddha's way of life.

▲ *A Buddhist monk studies today in a monastery in northern India.*

Gradually, Buddhism extended beyond the subcontinent. Missionaries first traveled to the island of Ceylon, southeast of India, now called Sri Lanka. By about A.D. 650, Buddhism extended to China, Korea, Japan, Tibet, Burma, and other areas of Southeast Asia.

Although Buddhism became less popular in India over the years, it gained followers in other countries. Today more than 250 million people throughout the world practice Buddhism. ■

■ *What is the Eightfold Path, and where does it lead?*

# A Great Buddhist Ruler

Buddhism found a faithful follower in the emperor, Asoka *(Ah SOH kah)*. He was the first ruler to send missionaries beyond Indian borders. Thus, he started Buddhism on its worldwide path.

Asoka belonged to a line of conquering kings known as the Mauryas, who ruled from about 324 to 183 B.C. The Mauryas built the first great Indian empire. It was the largest empire on the subcontinent until the British claimed India in 1876. Note on the map the empire's boundaries during Asoka's rule.

**Asoka's Empire, 269–232 B.C.**

Extent of Mauryan Empire, c. 250 B.C.

30°N
Taxila
Indus R.
Mathura
Ganges R.
Pataliputra
Tamralipti
20°N
Bay of Bengal
Arabian Sea
INDIAN OCEAN
0  300  600 mi.
0  300  600 km
Equidistant Projection
80°E          90°E

◄ *Within his Mauryan empire, Asoka built public wells and baths, free clinics for the sick, rest houses for travelers, and watering places for cattle.*

239

Ancient India

## Asoka's Conversion

Not long after Asoka came to power in 269 B.C., he went to war. He set out to conquer Kalinga, an independent area in eastern India.

Asoka won that war. But the campaign was extremely cruel. The battles were horribly bloody. A short while after that experience, Asoka converted to Buddhism.

During the rest of his rule, he spread the dharma by sending Buddhist missionaries to many places around the subcontinent. In addition, he sent missionaries to Ceylon, Burma, and the high Himalayan regions.

## Asoka's Edicts

The Buddhist beliefs of the emperor were spelled out for the people in his public announcements, or edicts. Asoka had these edicts carved into rocks and pillars around the empire. Beautiful carvings often decorated the tops, or capitals, of the pillars.

Rock Edict I explains Asoka's support of ahimsa (*uh HIHM sah*), which is the Buddhist belief in nonviolence. It forbids harming humans or animals.

*N*o living creature shall be slaughtered here . . . Many hundreds of thousand living creatures were formerly slaughtered every day for curries in the kitchens of His Majesty. At present, when this edict on Dharma is inscribed, only three living creatures are killed daily, two peacocks and a deer . . . In the future, not even these three animals shall be slaughtered.

The Kalinga Edict II in eastern India shows how Asoka felt toward his people:

*A*ll men are my children. Just as I seek the welfare and happiness of my own children in this world and the next, I seek the same things for all men.

## Breakup of the Mauryan Empire

After the emperor Asoka's death in 232 B.C., the rulers that followed him couldn't hold the Mauryan empire together. Gradually, it broke down into many little warring kingdoms.

Within 50 years, the last Mauryan ruler was killed by his own army commander. This violent deed contrasted sharply with Asoka's hopes for an Indian empire of nonviolence. ■

▲ *This lion capital sits atop an Asokan pillar. India's national emblem is patterned from it.*

■ *How did Asoka's Buddhist beliefs influence his rule?*

## REVIEW

1. **FOCUS** What are the main teachings of Buddhism?
2. **CONNECT** How did Buddhism differ from the Vedic religion?
3. **GEOGRAPHY** Trace a map of Asia. Color in areas where Buddhism had spread by A.D. 650.
4. **CRITICAL THINKING** Why might the merchant class have been particularly attracted to Buddhism?
5. **WRITING ACTIVITY** In 50 words or less, write a column edict as Asoka might have done. In your edict, instruct people how to act toward other human beings and toward animals. Draw your pillar. Design a carving for its capital.

# Recognizing the Buddha

### Here's Why

Suppose you visited a museum. How would you be able to recognize a statue of the Buddha?

You identify individuals through visual features such as curly hair or brown eyes. In the same way, you can use identifying features to help you recognize symbols such as the Buddha.

### Here's How

Some 600 to 700 years after the Buddha's death, his followers wanted a painting or statue of him to worship. However, no one who was alive then knew exactly what the Buddha had looked like.

You will remember that at Gautama's birth, a wise man predicted that the child would become a great man. This was because he had 32 or more identifying marks, or features, on his body. Some of them are shown on the diagram below. These identifying features, when they come together, create a symbol of the Buddha. The Buddha symbol represents both the great man and his teachings. Artists still use such features to represent the Buddha.

Not all these features are clearly visible on all images of the Buddha. But when you see three or four of these features together, you'll know that you are looking at the Buddha.

### Try It

Look at the sculpture of the Buddha on page 237. Compare it to the diagram below. Which identifying features do you see? In what other ways are the two images alike?

### Apply It

Uncle Sam is a figure often used to symbolize the United States. Look in books, newspapers, and weekly news magazines for pictures of Uncle Sam. What identifying features help you to recognize him?

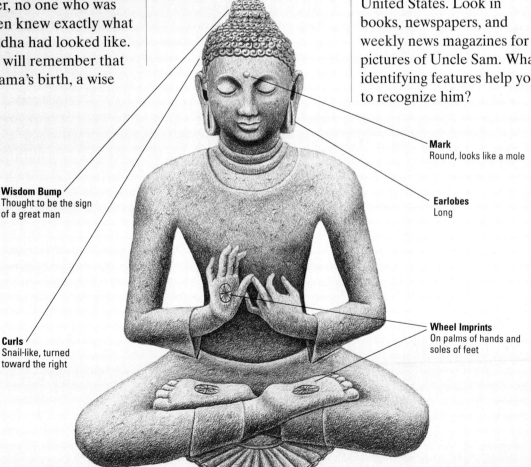

**Wisdom Bump**
Thought to be the sign of a great man

**Curls**
Snail-like, turned toward the right

**Mark**
Round, looks like a mole

**Earlobes**
Long

**Wheel Imprints**
On palms of hands and soles of feet

241

Ancient India

# Popularity

*A Jataka Tale*

*The Buddha told as many as 500 stories that taught about human behavior. Today these stories are known as* Jataka *tales. This modern version of one of the stories appears in the book* Jataka Tales, *edited by Nancy DeRoin.*

*As you learned in the last lesson, the Buddha taught that greed is wrong. Here is one of his teachings on a certain kind of greed.*

***Jataka*** (JAH duh kuh)
***Dhananajaya***
(duhn uhn JY uh)
***Potthapada***
(puht duh PAH duh)

Once upon a time when Dhananjaya was king of Benares, two parrots lived in the nearby forest. One was named Radha, the other Potthapada. Both were big and perfectly formed. Their feathers were beautiful to see.

A hunter, seeking the king's favor, trapped these two birds and gave them to the king as a present.

Pleased with the beautiful birds, the king put the pair in a golden cage. They were given honey and parched corn to eat from a golden dish and sugar water to drink. The king spent a lot of time talking to them, and the parrots became the favorites of the whole court.

Then one day a forester, also seeking the favor of the king, brought a big black monkey named Kalabahu as a present.

Quickly, all the attention was turned to the big monkey. He was so comical! His funny faces made the lords and ladies laugh, and the king himself was very much amused when the monkey played the clown. No one payed any attention to the parrots anymore, although they were still fed and cared for.

The older parrot, Radha, said nothing. But the younger bird, Potthapada, complained. "Brother, in this royal house we used to get much praise. Now we get none. Lords and ladies used to give us treats to eat. Now we get our daily food. The king used to visit us and talk to us daily. Now he passes our cage without looking. And," he wept, "that monkey has all the attention that belongs to us!"

Radha said to his brother parrot, "By what right does it belong to us?"

Potthapada replied, "Because we were so good, so true, so loyal. We never bit, we never squawked. We were well-behaved birds!"

"And why not?" Radha asked. "If you were being yourself, brother, you have no cause to complain. Perhaps you were just putting on an act to please the king."

Potthapada hung his head in shame.

Things continued as they were for a long while. But, at last, the monkey (who was only a foolish fellow) grew bored with his pleasant life. He even grew tired of all the good things he had to eat and drink. He became devilish and began to steal. When caught, he would put on a long face and everyone could not help but laugh.

Then, not knowing what to do next, the monkey began to amuse himself by frightening the king's children. When they came near, he would shake his ears and show his teeth. The children cried and ran away. Soon they would not enter the room for fear of the monkey. The king asked them one day why they were so afraid of Kalabahu, and the children told him how the monkey had been scaring them.

The king became angry and ordered his men to drive the monkey out of the palace and back into the forest. The parrots once again became the favorites. Potthapada sang for joy, but his brother, Radha, warned him to remember:

Gain and loss, and praise and blame,
Pleasure, pain, dishonor, fame,
All come and go like wind and rain!

## Further Reading

*The Five Sons of King Pandu.* Elizabeth Seeger. The author retells the story of the *Mahabharata*, a 2,500-year-old epic poem of India.

*Jataka Tales.* Nancy DeRoin, editor. This is a collection of 30 of the Buddha's stories, including *Popularity*.

*Seasons of Splendour: Tales, Myths and Legends of India.* Madhur Jaffrey. This book retells many of the myths about the Hindu gods.

L E S S O N   4

# The Golden Age

### Key Terms

- Hinduism
- guild
- epic

► *This miniature painting from the* Maha-bharata *shows Arjuna and Krishna in battle. You can usually find Krishna because his face is painted blue. Krishna means "the dark one."*

Drumbeats thunder across the plain. Cymbals clash while horns blare. Warriors and chariots stand ready, their horses stomping nervously. Then the trumpeting of elephants pierces the air.

Arjuna prepares for battle. He's a skilled archer and a mighty warrior. He has proved his bravery many times before. Looking across the battlefield, he searches the faces of the foe. Suddenly, Arjuna throws down his bow. In the enemy lines, he can see his uncles, his cousins, and friends. How can he kill them?

This civil war has set family members against each other. Arjuna cries, "I see no good in killing my kinsmen in battle. . . . I do not want to kill them even if I am killed."

Troubled, he turns to his charioteer, Krishna, for advice. Krishna is no ordinary man. He is a Hindu god in human form. In strict terms, Krishna tells Arjuna how a Hindu should carry out his duty. Arjuna must fight. He was born into the warrior class. Fighting is his duty.

"If you fail to wage this war of sacred duty, you will abandon your own duty and fame only to gain evil," says Krishna. "Rise to the fight, Arjuna!" In obedience, Arjuna aims his arrows.

# Beliefs of Hinduism

This scene between Arjuna and Krishna shows how important class and duty are to the followers of **Hinduism,** the major religion of India today. The tale comes from the *Bhagavad Gita,* which means "Song of the Blessed One." The *Bhagavad Gita,* in turn, is part of Hinduism's well-known poetic work, *Mahabharata.*

For centuries, Hindu parents have handed down this story about Hindu duty to their children. Actually, Krishna parades through many Hindu stories, guiding the faithful away from evil and reminding them of their duties.

## A Way of Life

The many duties required by Hinduism make it more than a religion. It's also a way of life, setting the rhythms of daily routine. Over the centuries, Hinduism has been shaped into a faith that touches every corner of its followers' lives.

Hinduism has no central figure such as Jesus in Christianity or the Buddha in Buddhism. Instead, Hinduism combines the religious thinking of peoples from various time periods. Hinduism had its beginnings before Buddhism. Its roots are in the Vedic religion of the Aryan people (1500–600 B.C.). Over the years, these Vedic teachings blended with the religious beliefs and practices of early Indian villagers. By A.D. 400, Hinduism's main teachings were set.

## Caste and Duty

Hinduism has always been linked to the class and caste system. The four classes of the Vedic period, as well as various castes, continued into Hindu times. In ancient days, castes gave Hindus a sense of security. Each caste cared for its members.

People within a caste also knew what their occupation would be. If you belonged to the ivory carvers' caste, you didn't sell spices. That wasn't your duty. Your job was to carve ivory. Your duties and rules for behavior were set forth in the sacred Hindu law, or dharma. As the *Bhagavad Gita* explains, "There is more joy in doing one's own duty badly than in doing another man's duty well."

◄ *The god Shiva reveals his divine identity to the bowing goddess, Parvati. Brahma, Krishna, and other gods also bow while heavenly musicians play. This painting, created about 1770 in the Punjab Hills, illustrates a work by the famous Indian poet, Kalidasa, of the Gupta period.*

Ancient India

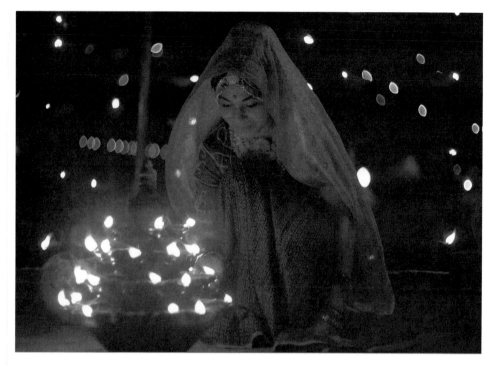

*Lamps burn brightly when Hindus mark their New Year. The celebration, which comes in either October or November, honors the goddess of plenty.*

### Reincarnation and Karma

Reincarnation is a major belief of Hinduism. And your karma determines where your soul will go in the next life—up or down on the caste ladder. Stepping up to a higher caste isn't easy. For the soul to advance, you must be a good citizen and family member during your lifetime. But even more is required. You also must carry out your caste duties to the fullest. Your performance of these duties makes up a big part of your karma.

### Life's Four Stages

Only Hindu males of the three upper classes are allowed to read the Vedas. Once they undertake this sacred study, they're called "twice born." For these males, life is divided into four stages.

In the first stage, a young boy studies the Vedas with a guru, or spiritual teacher. You'll learn more about gurus in A Moment in Time on page 247.

In the second stage of life, a young man marries and becomes a householder. In stage three, many householders choose to put aside their possessions and live in a forest. Here, they meditate and draw closer to their god. Women also can take part in this stage. Until this time, they've been busy caring for the home and children. During the fourth stage, a man or woman gives up everything, including caste membership, to become a wandering holy person.

What if you had been a boy of the warrior class in ancient India? How would you have entered stage one? Let's look back.

You're 11 years old. You've waited impatiently for this special day because you're about to be "twice born." You'll go through the sacred ceremony that permits you to begin your religious studies.

Your head has been shaved except for a topknot. You wear new ceremonial clothes, too. Your parents, relatives, and friends cluster around the sacred fire, waiting and watching. With dignity, you stand before your guru.

# Guru and Pupil

*9:13 A.M., November 17, A.D. 406*
*Forest School near Kashi, India*

## Earlobes

The guru's earlobes held heavy gold earrings for 20 years. On the day his first grandson was born, the guru took the earrings off, gave up everything he owned, and became a teacher in the forest.

## Topknot

The guru won't shave off this tuft of hair until he enters the next stage of life and becomes a wandering holy man.

## Lines

The ash marks on their foreheads and shoulders show that the guru and pupil worship Shiva above all other Hindu gods.

## Fingers

For the very first time, the pupil recites one whole book of the *Rig Veda*—1,080 verses. His fingers help him keep the rhythm of the lines.

## Crossed Legs

His legs would usually be tired after sitting cross-legged for three hours. But today he feels only excitement about doing so well with the poem he's memorized.

## Sacred Thread

Guru and pupil both wear this cotton cord. The guru will break the thread when he leaves his forest home to wander alone.

During the ceremony, your guru places a sacred cord over your shoulder. You will wear such a cord always, a sign that you've been "twice born." Now, for the first time, you announce in public the secret name given to you at birth. The guru then hands you an antelope skin, symbol of strength and bravery. You will sometimes sit on it when you meditate. This ceremony marks a new beginning for you, the start of your studies.

### Two Popular Gods

In Hinduism, people often choose the god worshiped by their families over the years. Shiva and Vishnu are popular gods today.

■ *In what ways is Hinduism a way of life?*

Shiva is often known as "death" or "time," both of which destroy. Sometimes in paintings and sculpture, this god is shown seated in deep meditation or in his role as lord of the dance.

According to Hinduism, a god can appear on earth in various forms called incarnations. Hindus believe that Vishnu has appeared on earth in nine of his 10 incarnations. These earthly forms included a fish, a tortoise, and a dwarf. One of Vishnu's most important incarnations was Prince Rama, who represented the ideal human. Another important incarnation was Krishna, the charioteer from the story of Arjuna. ■

## The Gupta Empire

Between A.D. 320 and 467, Hinduism reached new heights. The rulers during this time were the Guptas. Although they ruled less than 200 years, they brought a Golden Age to ancient India. Not only did Hinduism flower, but borders expanded and trade boomed.

By conquering neighboring areas, the Guptas created an In-dian empire. Compare the Gupta boundaries on this map with the Mauryan empire on page 239.

### Ships and Caravans

Gupta trade routes hummed with activity. Elephants and ox-drawn carts loaded with goods bumped along the overland trails. Carts' wooden wheels creaked through desert, forest, and jungle. Cargo ships also sailed the seas. Huge eyes sometimes decorated a ship's prow. They were put at the front of a ship to scare the imagined monsters of the deep.

Westward, Gupta trade routes led to Rome and the rest of the Mediterranean, as well as to Africa. Eastward, trade was carried on with China, Southeast Asia, and Indonesia. The Guptas offered luxury exports—gems; pearls; perfumes; pepper, ginger, cinnamon, and other spices; finely woven cotton cloth; red dye; and

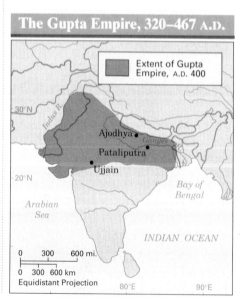

**The Gupta Empire, 320–467 A.D.**

Extent of Gupta Empire, A.D. 400

Indus R.
30°N
Ajodhya
Ganges
Pataliputra
Ujjain
20°N
Bay of Bengal
Arabian Sea
INDIAN OCEAN
0   300   600 mi.
0   300  600 km
Equidistant Projection
80°E          90°E

➤ *The Gupta Empire brought splendor to the northern portion of the subcontinent.*

timber such as teak and ebony. Goods flowing into the Gupta empire included gold from Rome, silk from China, and horses from Saudi Arabia and Central Asia.

## Town Trade and Guilds

Trade in towns bustled, too. Crowds jammed the cobblestone streets. Some shoppers walked while the wealthy were carried in curtained litters, or chairs. Peddlers balanced baskets on their heads, offering their fruits and flowers. Edging each side of the street were covered stalls. Here, tradesmen sat cross-legged all day, selling their wares.

Along with Gupta's increased trade came the growth of **guilds,** groups of craftspeople and merchants who did the same type of work. Each guild occupied its own section of town. For example, the weavers worked and lived together; so did the potters, the ivory carvers, and the carpenters. The guilds set prices and wages, checked the quality of work, and looked after the needs and interests of their members.

Guilds and castes aren't the same. Yet, they sometimes overlap. Guilds are organized according to crafts and trades, castes according to social levels. ■

■ *Where did trade routes lead during Gupta times, and what was traded?*

# Achievements of Ancient India

Ancient India's scholars in the arts, sciences, and technology gave golden gifts to future generations. In Gupta days, both rulers and merchants helped to pay for these great achievements.

## Famous Poetic Tales

Hindus learned much about their gods, myths, and religious duties from two glorious **epics**—long poems in fine language. An epic usually tells of heroic deeds. For years, these epics had made their way from generation to generation through oral tradition. But in Gupta times, they were written down in a regular form.

The first epic, known as the *Mahabharata,* tells of a great civil war between two branches of a ruling family. It's probably the world's longest poem. One section of this poetic work is the *Bhagavad Gita.* A much shorter epic, the *Ramayana,* tells the story of Rama, the princely incarnation of the god

Vishnu. This tale tells of Rama's rescue of his wife, who was stolen by a terrible demon.

## Other Advances

Scholars excelled in science, too. In astronomy, Aryabhata determined that the world was a sphere, rotating around the sun. Some Europeans still hadn't accepted this fact 1,000 years later when Columbus sailed for the Indies in 1492. Aryabhata also figured out that the solar year had 365.358 days. Today's figures say 365.242. Aryabhata missed by about three hours.

The mathematicians of ancient India also made advances that were astounding.

▼ *This 11th century sculpture of the god Ganesha shows the continuing influence of the Gupta period.*

249

> *A kathakali dancer from South India puts finishing touches to his costume. He'll take part in a dance drama performed in the ancient tradition. The sacred epics are among the performances these dancers give.*

> *Gold came to ancient India from Rome. Metalworkers then crafted it into golden coins showing Gupta scenes.*

■ *Explain some of the achievements of the Gupta Period.*

They gave you the number system that you use in your math classes today. This system features nine digits, the zero, and the decimal.

Metalwork also stands high on the Guptas' list of accomplishments. Proof of the great skill of ironworkers is the one-piece pillar that stands 23 feet high at Mehrauli, near the city of Delhi. Modern ironworkers had been unable to duplicate this feat until the 1800s. Because of the iron's purity, the pillar shows few signs of rust even though it has been battered by more than 1,500 monsoon rains.

## Gupta Days and Decline

An eyewitness account of Gupta's golden days comes to us from Faxian *(fah shee AHN)*, a Buddhist monk from China. He took notes in his diary while traveling through India in A.D. 399. He wrote that "the people are prosperous and happy." His diary tells, too, that there was little crime, and in certain areas, hospitals gave free care to the poor and helpless.

Fifty years after Faxian's travels, the Gupta empire began to decline. Invaders called White Huns swooped down from Central Asia. The attacks weakened the empire, causing it to break up into small kingdoms. By A.D. 467, India's Golden Age was almost over. ■

## R E V I E W

1. **FOCUS** What are some of the main features of Hinduism?
2. **CONNECT** How did the Mauryan and Gupta empires differ in boundaries?
3. **ECONOMICS** Why do you think Gupta guilds were important?
4. **CRITICAL THINKING** In earlier times, Hindus were required to marry within their caste. How did this duty help to strengthen the caste system?
5. **ACTIVITY** Draw a "Moment in Time" picture of you and one of your teachers. Write short paragraphs that point out significant details about each of you.

# Computing Travel Time

### Here's Why

Suppose you want to figure out how long it took the Buddhist monk Faxian to walk from his home in Changan, China, to a shrine in Kara-shahr, China. If you know how to calculate the real distance between points on a map, you can compute his travel time.

### Here's How

Look at the map of Faxian's travels. The scale shows that ⁵/₈ inch on the map stands for 600 miles on the earth.

To measure the distance between two points on a map along a straight route, use a ruler or a piece of paper. If the route you are measuring is not straight, use a piece of string.

To measure the distance between Changan and Kara-shahr, lay a small piece of string on the map so it follows Faxian's route. Put a mark on the string next to each city.

To find the number of miles, compare the distance marked on the string to the map scale. The distance between marks on the string is about 2¹/₂ times the length of the scale, or about 1,500 miles. So, Faxian traveled 1,500 miles from Changan to Kara-shahr.

Historical records show that Faxian may have walked about 25 miles a day. Divide the total number of miles (1,500) by the number of miles he could walk in a day (25). The answer will tell you how long it took Faxian to complete the walk—60 days.

### Try It

Measure the sea route between Tamluk, India, and Trincomalee, Ceylon (now Sri Lanka). What is the distance in miles? Traveling by water, Faxian could cover 21 miles per day. How long would the trip from Tamluk to Trincomalee take him?

### Apply It

Look at the map of North America shown on page 512 of the Atlas. If you traveled at 55 miles per hour, how long would it take to go from Los Angeles, California, to Seattle, Washington?

**Travels of Faxian, A.D. 399–414**

Faxian's route by boat

Faxian's route by foot

GOBI (DESERT)

Kara-shahr

Kashgar

PAMIR MTS.

TAKLIMAKAN (DESERT)

Zhangye

Changguang

Peshawar

Changan (Xi'an)

Huang He

Nanjing

East China Sea

TIBET

Brahmaputra R.

Chang Jiang

CHINA

HIMALAYAS

Indus R.

Kapilavastu

Pataliputra (Patna)

Ganges R.

Guangzhou

FORMOSA

Narmada R.

INDIA

Tamluk

BURMA

Xi Jiang

PACIFIC OCEAN

Bay of Bengal

SIAM

Mekong R.

South China Sea

Trincomalee

Kandy

CEYLON

INDIAN OCEAN

SUMATRA

BORNEO

Equator

JAVA

0    300    600 mi.

0    300   600 km

Lambert Azimuthal Equal-Area Projection

100°E    120°E    140°E

40°N

20°N

Ancient India

# Chapter Review

## Reviewing Key Terms

Aryan (p. 229)
Buddhism (p. 236)
caste (p. 232)
epic (p. 249)
guild (p. 249)
Hinduism (p. 245)

migration (p. 230)
moderation (p. 238)
reincarnation (p. 238)
silt (p. 224)
subcontinent (p. 223)

**A.** In each statement below, a key term has been used incorrectly. Rewrite each sentence using the correct key term.

1. The busy trade and commerce of the Gupta period encouraged the growth of *castes*— groups of craftspeople and merchants.
2. History has seen many periods of *reincarnation*, in which whole populations move from one area to another.
3. *Buddhists* who migrated to northern India introduced a new religion.
4. *Moderation* helped the Indus Valley farmers to grow their crops.
5. The *guild* system has been an important part of Hinduism.

**B.** Use a dictionary to find the origins of the following words. Then explain how the meaning of the word applies to India.

1. subcontinent
2. Buddhism
3. moderation
4. reincarnation
5. Hinduism

## Exploring Concepts

**A.** Reminders of India's ancient civilizations can still be found in today's world. Copy and complete the following chart on your own paper. List at least two examples of the past that still exist today.

| Civilization | Modern Reminders |
|---|---|
| Indus Valley Civilization | |
| Aryans | |
| Mauryan Empire | spread of Buddhism<br>India's national emblem |
| Gupta Empire | |

**B.** Answer each question with information from the chapter.

1. Why were archaeologists excited about the discovery of the Harappa and Mohenjo-Daro sites in India?
2. What helped the people of the Indus Valley to be successful in their farming?
3. What kinds of evidence still exist of the Indus River civilization?
4. How was the Aryan society different from the society of the Indus Valley?
5. Why were the Vedas important to the Aryans and to archaeologists?
6. How did the migration of Indo-Europeans influence life in India?
7. What are the advantages and disadvantages of the caste system?
8. How are Buddhism and Hinduism similar? How are they different?
9. How did the religious beliefs of Emperor Asoka influence his rule?
10. Why is the Gupta period often called a Golden Age?
11. How are guilds different from castes? How are they similar?
12. What do the *Mahabharata* and the *Ramayana* have in common with the Vedas?

# Reviewing Skills

1. Look at the sculpture of the Buddha receiving his enlightenment on page 237. What identifying marks help you know that this is the Buddha?
2. Look at the map on this page. Imagine that you are an archaeologist in Karachi, Pakistan. Using the map scale, figure out how far it is to travel to Harappa. At 20 mph, how long would it take?
3. Look at the map on this page. Using the grid, estimate Mohenjo-Daro's location. Your answer should give the latitude first, then the longitude.
4. Imagine that you are writing an archaeological report on artifacts you have discovered. The report has two parts: first, a description of the artifacts; second, your ideas about their importance. How is the first part of your report different from the second part?

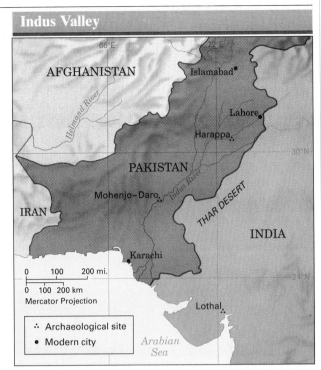

Indus Valley

# Using Critical Thinking

1. The success of crops and trade depended on the regular monsoons. What might have happened if the monsoon was early or late?
2. About 2,500 years ago, the Buddha stated that suffering and sorrow are caused by the greedy desire for power, pleasure, and possessions. Do you think this is true today? Explain your answer.
3. In the Buddha's time, priests, rulers, and warriors were in the upper class. How might they have felt about Buddhism? Why?
4. Under the Guptas, art and science prospered along with trade and commerce. Do you think there is a connection? Explain.

# Preparing for Citizenship

1. **COLLECTING INFORMATION** Archaeologists find, record, and interpret traces of past life. Your community has a past. Discover any traces left from its past inhabitants. You could interview older residents; research photographs, maps, and books; or study the buildings and land. Share your research with the class.
2. **GROUP ACTIVITY** The Buddhist teachings focus on how people should think and act. In small groups, make a set of laws for your school. What do you think is good school behavior? Display your laws on a poster.
3. **COLLABORATIVE LEARNING** The Indus Valley and the United States both received migrating peoples. In small groups, give a presentation on a migrant culture in America. Have one person discover the reasons why the migration took place. Have another find photographs or articles from that time period. A third person can interview someone from the migrant culture, and a fourth could research the native culture to discover how it differs from ours. Everyone should then decide on how to present your findings to the class.

Ancient India

# Chapter 9
# *Ancient China*

*For many centuries, China remained a well-guarded secret. Towering mountains, vast deserts, and the Pacific Ocean limited contact between the ancient Chinese and other civilizations. Cut off from the outside, the Chinese developed a unique civilization—one of the oldest to live on into the present.*

**c. 1100 B.C.** The Chinese develop a new way of writing, in which pictures stand for whole words. Some of the earliest Chinese writing appears on bones or bamboo strips (above).

| 2500 | 2000 | 1500 | 1000 |
|------|------|------|------|

# 2200 B.C.

**c. 1600 B.C.** During the Shang dynasty, metalworkers learn to make bronze from copper and tin. Soon craftspersons create works of art like the giant cooking pot above.

good can come of this."

Children fidgeted and cried, while the restlessness of the by-standers increased as their anxiety mounted.

"Silence!" shouted the official. "I bring an order from the emperor." The murmuring ceased. "Wild horsemen are attacking from the north. These barbarians are looting and killing, burning whole villages to the ground. The emperor has issued a call for all able-bodied men to build a great wall, the highest and thickest wall ever built by men. The enemy will never be able to break through its impenetrable defense, and our people will be able to live in peace. It is the duty of every man to obey the emperor's summons. Anyone who refuses does so on pain of death."

*impenetrable* can't be entered or crossed

"Forward!" he commanded. Lined up three abreast, the men were marched off. Soldiers carrying spears walked along the sides of the column. Escape was impossible.

Tearful parents, wives, and children were left behind to fend for themselves. An old farmer leaning on a cane shook his head sadly.

"Heaven alone knows if I shall ever see my son before my life is over," he said in a hoarse whisper.

Only a few months had passed since that terrifying day, but for Meng-Jiang Nyu it seemed like ages. Without her husband at her side, time dragged interminably. In her fervent prayers she asked that he be kept from hunger and thirst. The winter would bring its bitter winds that blow unceasingly from the mountains. How was Chi-liang going to survive in so hostile a climate without a warm jacket and cotton quilted shoes?

*interminably* without end; tiresomely long

The last days of autumn were drawing to an end. It was the time of year when the dusk came early, but Meng-Jiang Nyu would not stop until darkness forced her to lay aside her sewing. Her needle flew ever faster as she layered fabric with cotton padding, fashioning a comfortable outer garment. She took particular care to design thick-soled shoes, sewing them with extra strong thread. Time was her enemy as she worked to finish the task she had set for herself.

Meng-Jiang Nyu swore a solemn oath. Chi-liang would not do without winter clothes. This she vowed. No matter how perilous the journey, she would take them to him herself. A woman traveling alone might encounter unexpected dangers, and she wondered if she would endure the long trek on foot. But she banished the troubling thoughts from her mind.

The evening before her departure, she prepared a small bag of rice and another of millet, only the barest necessities to sustain her along the way. On a large cloth square she placed Chi-liang's jacket and shoes. By tying the opposite corners of the square together, she made a bundle to carry over her arm.

Before daybreak she left her home. No one was yet awake,

and the narrow streets of the village were deserted. It was still quite dark. In the east, Meng-Jiang Nyu saw a rosy glow that announced the beginning of a new day. "A good omen," she mused.

Word had come back to the village that the section of the wall where Chi-liang was working lay at a great distance. If the snows came early, there was no telling how long it would take to get there. Meng-Jiang Nyu had learned that she must travel in a northwesterly direction, but beyond that she did not even know for certain where she would find her husband.

Never having traveled more than a few miles from her village, she could not imagine the vastness that lay beyond it. Nor could she conceive, in her wildest flight of fancy, the size and length of the wall that the emperor had planned. Neither could she picture a wall three thousand miles long that would climb over high mountains, descend into deep valleys, and cross forbidding deserts. But the grandeur of the emperor's ambitious undertaking meant nothing to her. She only knew she must plod ahead for as long as it would take her to join Chi-liang.

As the days wore on, Meng-Jiang Nyu found she had to rest more and more frequently. Often, as she passed through little villages, she begged for food. She had finished her rice and millet long ago. People who spoke to her and learned where she was bound praised her devotion but shook their heads in disbelief.

Once she heard a woman lamenting loudly to a friend, "Our sons are gone, our daughters widowed, and the pile of dead grows ever larger at the foot of the emperor's great wall." Meng-Jiang Nyu shuddered.

*doggedly* stubbornly

From sunrise to sunset she doggedly trudged on. When darkness fell, she looked for a place to lay her head. Many a night her bed was just a pile of scratchy straw.

The day Meng-Jiang Nyu reached the Yellow River, her strength was beginning to fail. At the point where she stood, the river was wide and the current of its silt-laden water, swift. For the peasants who lived along its banks it was life-sustaining, but for Meng-Jiang Nyu it was yet another obstacle that had to be overcome. Except for a lone shepherd grazing his flock of sheep, there was not a soul in sight.

"I have not come this far in vain," she thought. "I will not turn back!"

With determination born of despair, she walked into the water holding Chi-liang's clothes over her head to keep them dry. A few yards out from the shore her feet could no longer touch bottom, and she tried to swim. The effort to keep afloat was beyond her endurance. Finally she gave up the struggle and let the river claim her. The cold water dragged her toward the murky bottom— down, down into an inky blackness.

Meng-Jiang Nyu's distress did not go unnoticed. A river god

came to her rescue, plucking her from the deep and carrying her to the opposite shore.

When Meng-Jiang Nyu opened her eyes, a shadowy specter was hovering over her.

"My brave child, do not abandon hope," it soothed. "All the spirits along the way will help you to the end of your journey." The shadow drifted away and melted into the air. Meng-Jiang Nyu was alone. She had no recollection of how she had reached the other side of the river. Nor was she sure she had heard the encouraging promise of help.

Wearily, she picked up her bundle. Everything was wet through. Before moving on she would have to wait for the clothes to dry. She wrung out Chi-liang's jacket and spread it on the ground. When she reached for his shoes, a miracle occurred. Spellbound, she saw the shoes turn into two blackbirds. From then on, never ceasing their shrill chatter, the blackbirds led her day after day in a northerly direction. Whenever she tired, they alighted on the ground near her and waited until she had regained her strength. At night they roosted in a nearby tree while she slept. One morning, Meng-Jiang Nyu awoke, trembling with cold. Her fingers and toes were numb and she ached all over. Reaching to pick up her bundle, she was surprised to see Chi-liang's shoes standing neatly, side by side. The blackbirds, her guides and constant companions, were gone. They had fulfilled their mission, for they had led Meng-Jiang Nyu close to her destination.

Meng-Jiang Nyu dragged her swollen, painful feet along a dusty road. At first the road was flat; then it began to climb steeply. When she reached high ground, her eyes took in an incredible scene. The figures she saw moving about resembled a scurrying swarm of ants. She quickened her pace. Now she could see more clearly. Files of men, backs bent under the weight of heavy stones, were struggling to the top of the unfinished wall. Others were lugging buckets of mortar to fill the spaces between the rocks. Covered from head to foot by the dry, brown sand, they were indistinguishable, one from the other. How could she ever find Chi-liang among that multitude?

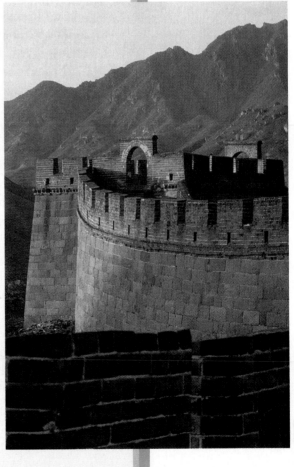

With unaccustomed boldness, she approached a small group of men who were attempting to warm their hands over a smoldering fire. Timidly she explained, "I am looking for my husband. He is called Chi-liang." She told them the name of their village and the day on which he was conscripted, but they only looked at her with pity.

"I am sorry I cannot help you," said one of the men. "This wall has no beginning and no end. The wind batters us, the white snow blinds us, we have little food and no warm clothing. There is only toil without rest. Every day we see good comrades fall, and many more will die of exhaustion. Hundreds are already buried inside the wall. We admire your loyalty to your husband, but you should not endanger your own life trying to do the impossible. Better that you return home. You will never find him."

But Meng-Jiang Nyu could not be discouraged. Bravely she continued to search. Wherever she went she asked for Chi-liang. The relentless wind tore at her clothing, her face and hands became rough and red from exposure. She ate very little and slept hardly a wink. At last, fatigue conquered her, and Meng-Jiang Nyu fell asleep on the frozen ground. She did not know how much time had passed before she became aware of someone prodding her. "You must not lie here or you will freeze to death," a man warned.

Shaking uncontrollably, she managed to say, "I am looking for my husband. He bears the name Chi-liang." Once again, she recited the name of their village and the date on which he was taken.

"Yes, I knew your husband," the stranger responded. "I remember him well. We were assigned the task of making bricks and he was the best worker in the section. It pains me to tell you that we found him one morning covered by newly fallen snow, lifeless. With many others he lies buried within the wall."

Meng-Jiang Nyu could not hold back the flood of salty tears that stung her cold cheeks. She blamed herself for Chi-liang's death. She had come too late to save him.

"How can it be that so gentle a husband has perished so young? The Great Wall takes more lives than the plundering enemy."

A wife's devotion can sometimes move mountains. Wailing bitterly, Meng-Jiang Nyu cried out to heaven. The sun vanished behind threatening clouds. A violent tempest churned up the powdery sand, and rain fell in icy sheets. Bolts of lightning streaked through the sky. With a deafening clap of thunder, a section of the wall collapsed, bricks and stones spilling out together with human bones and skulls.

"Do not be alarmed, brave wife of Chi-liang. Heaven has witnessed your sorrow. You will seek out your husband's bones from among all the others." The words were sharp and clear, but there was not a soul in sight. Meng-Jiang Nyu stood transfixed amid the pile of rubble.

"But how will I know which among the many are his?"

"Have no fear. You will succeed, for when love is sincere and true, two people become as one. They share thoughts, hopes,

*plundering* stealing; taking by force

feelings. Their blood, their bones, their very tissues mingle. Do not despair, you will find a way."

"Alas," moaned Meng-Jiang Nyu. "In this jumble lying here, strewn this way and that, are the bones of Chi-liang. Oh mountains, hills, desert of yellow sands," she pleaded, "favor me, and give me a sign that I may recognize those that belong to him. I cannot choose for I cannot tell one from another." Unaware of what she was doing, she bit down on her thumb until she drew blood. She watched a drop fall upon a bone, slide off the surface, and reach the ground. Suddenly the words she had just heard took on meaning.

"If the bones are Chi-liang's, my blood will mingle with his and sink into them. If the bones belong to others, the blood will remain apart."

This time, with determination, she bit down harder and then shook her hand, spattering the blood about. What she hoped for did not happen. Again, and still again, she tried. Each time her blood slid quickly off the bones. "One last time," she told herself. Though the pain brought tears to her eyes, she bit down with all her might. The blood flowed freely and she flung it as far and as wide as she could. One quivering red dot landed on a bone lying apart from the others. At once the blood sank into its chalky whiteness. This bone must belong to Chi-liang. Of this she was certain. Feverishly she continued to search, and soon she recovered the rest. Chi-liang's bones would receive a proper burial, and his soul would not have to wander aimlessly in search of peace.

Laden with the heavy blow fate had dealt her, Meng-Jiang Nyu turned to the south and began her sad journey homeward.

## Further Reading

*China Homecoming*. Jean Fritz. In this book Jean Fritz returns to the country where she spent her childhood.

*Heaven's Reward: Fairy Tales from China*. Catherine Edwards. These six fairy tales present Confucian and Taoist philosophies.

*Homesick: My Own Story*. Jean Fritz. The author describes her experiences as the child of American missionary parents in China.

*Young Fu of the Upper Yangtze*. Elizabeth Lewis. A teenage country boy travels to the city of Chongqing to become a coppersmith's apprentice in the 1930s.

L E S S O N   1

# China's Early History

*What advances were made by these ancient cultures—the Yangshao, the Lungshan, the Xia, the Shang, and the Zhou?*

## Key Terms

- ancestor
- oracle
- feudalism
- dialect

➤ *High peaks, fertile valleys, desert wastes— these are some of the varied land forms of China.*

> The towering heights of
>   the Southern Mountains
> Soar dizzily like a stack of
>   cooking pots,
> Precipitous and sheer.
> Their sides are furrowed with
>   ravines and valleys. . . .
> While from their folds the
>   mountain streams leap
>   and tumble,
> Spilling out upon the level
>   plains.
> There they flow a thousand
>   miles along smooth beds,
> Their banks lined with dikes
> Blanketed with green orchids.
>
> From "The Shanglin Park"

More than 2,000 years ago, the Chinese poet Sima Xiangru *(suh mah shahng roo)* wrote these lines about his native land. He described a rugged land of towering mountains, powerful rivers, and vast plains. Look at the physical map of China on the next page. What major land forms can you identify?

On the southwest, China is bounded by huge mountains. On the north and west lie more mountains and deserts. And on the east, the ocean stretches to the horizon. These land forms act as natural barriers. They set China apart from the rest of the world. They help to preserve one of the oldest continuous civilizations in the world, dating back almost 4,000 years.

# China's Geography

The geography of China has helped to create numerous regions within this vast land. Regions developed separately from each other. Thus China became a patchwork of different customs, cultures, and languages. The task of unifying this varied land has never been an easy one.

To understand why, look at the map below. Mountain ranges ripple across the land, making travel and communication difficult. Find the Himalayas (hihm uh LAY uhz) in the southwestern part of China. These are the world's highest mountains. Many peaks rise more than 24,000 feet above sea level. Mount Everest, the highest mountain in the world, soars to 29,028 feet. Other great mountain ranges are the Kunlun Shan, the Tian Shan, and the Altai in the west and the Da Hinggan Ling in the north.

Deserts also create barriers within China. Across the north and northwest regions lie dry wastelands. The greatest of China's deserts is the massive Gobi. Find it on the map.

Though mountains and deserts have served to divide the Chinese, rivers have helped to link them. Trace China's major rivers on the map. The Huang He (hwahng hay) begins within the Plateau of Tibet and runs across the farmlands of

▼ As the map shows, nature built a wall around China with mountains, plateaus, seas, and deserts.

**China**

northeastern China. Rich in minerals, it gets its name—meaning "Yellow River"—from the rich yellow dirt that it leaves behind when it overflows its banks.

Along with the minerals that enrich the soil, these floods often bring disaster. The Huang He is nicknamed "China's Sorrow." It has destroyed property and claimed the lives of thousands who have been swept away in its swirling waters.

Another river, the Chang Jiang *(chahng jyahng)*—also known as the Yangtze *(YANG see)*—winds across the farmlands of central and southern China. Trace the Chang Jiang on the map. Farmers use the river's many tributaries to send their crops easily and cheaply to Pacific ports. ■

■ *How did geography isolate ancient China from the rest of the world?*

## Prehistoric Cultures

Like the other great ancient civilizations—Mesopotamia, Egypt, and India—the earliest known Chinese civilization started along a river. By about 10,000 B.C., a group of Neolithic people called the Yangshao *(yahng show)* had settled near the Huang He in north central China.

### Two Neolithic Cultures

On the map, trace the Huang He from its source in the Tibetan Highlands. Follow its course as it flows north, east, and then south. At the place where it meets the Wei *(way)*, the Huang He bends like an elbow and heads northeast. It's not surprising that the Yangshao settled there. First, the two rivers provided plenty of water for people, animals, and crops. Second, the rich, sandy soil was easy to farm with the simple tools that were used by Neolithic farmers.

Archaeologists have uncovered many Yangshao villages in northern China. In one village, Banpo, they have found the remains of farmhouses, many of which were built partly underground. The houses had plastered floors, and their roofs were held up by wooden posts.

By about 3000 B.C., another Neolithic culture, the Lungshan, had developed in northeast China. The Lungshan people were farmers too. They raised cattle, sheep, pigs, and dogs. They grew wheat and millet, two grain crops that grow well in the dry climate of northern China. They also hunted, fished, and gathered wild foods. Over time, Lungshan farmers also settled in the south of China. It rained more there, and they were able to grow rice.

The Lungshan people were advanced for their time. For example, they harvested silk from silkworms and used it to weave fine fabrics. They used a potter's wheel, and they baked strong, durable pottery in kilns, or ovens. The Lungshan even used simple written symbols and numbers.

In order to survive and farm the land along the river, the Lungshan needed to work together on flood control and irrigation projects. Gradually, leaders arose to organize these projects. One of the leaders was a man named Yu, the "Great Engineer." According to early Chinese legends, Yu founded the first great Chinese dynasty, the Xia *(SHEE uh)*, around 2000 B.C.

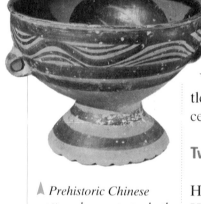

▲ *Prehistoric Chinese pottery demonstrates both skill and artistry. This painted ceramic cup was found during the excavation of a Yangshao village.*

**Across Time & Space**

*Don't get confused if you see China's capital city of Beijing written as* Peking *or* Peiping *on older maps.* Beijing *is spelled according to the Pinyin system for writing Chinese in our Roman alphabet. In 1958, the Chinese officially adopted Pinyin, replacing earlier systems.*

### A Legendary Dynasty

Knowledge of the Xia dynasty comes mostly from legend. There are no written records. Legend tells us the Xia ruled for nearly 300 years. The last Xia ruler, Chieh *(CHEE uh)*, was an evil king.

Chang Tang *(chahng tahng)*, or Tang the Successful, defeated Chieh in 1766 B.C. Tang's victory marked the beginning of a new dynasty called the Shang *(shahng)*. The Shang dynasty ruled China for over 700 years, from 1766 to 1122 B.C. ■

■ *What were some achievements of China's Neolithic river cultures, the Yangshao and the Lungshan?*

## The Shang Dynasty

Trace the boundaries of the Shang dynasty on the map below. Notice that Shang China included much of the Huang He plain.

During the Shang dynasty, most people were still peasants, or poor farmers. They lived in villages and spent their lives working in the fields and struggling to control the flooding rivers. They farmed small plots of land and lived in simple houses.

### Walled Cities

Archaeologists have discovered that most Shang people lived in farming villages. Some, however, lived in large walled cities. For example, one Shang city was surrounded by an earth wall 30 feet high, 65 feet thick, and four and a half miles long. With simple hand tools, it would probably have taken 10,000 workers 18 years to build such a wall. To complete it, Shang rulers must have developed complex ways of organizing people. They must also have become skillful in engineering.

Within the walls lived rulers, priests, and warriors. Their huge temples and palaces were built on raised earth terraces. Skilled craftworkers lived outside the walls in neighborhoods made up of people who practiced the same craft. Farmers lived in nearby villages.

In the Shang capital of Anyang, archaeologists have found thousands of cowrie shells like those shown on this page. Cowrie shells served as an early form of money to buy small items like tools and weapons. They were used in the 1000s B.C., before the Bronze Age brought the use of metal coins.

### The Bronze Age

Around 1600 B.C., Shang craftworkers in the city of Yenshih *(yen shee)* made an important discovery. They learned to mix tin and copper to produce a hard and beautiful metal called bronze. This new metal was quite valuable because bronze was much stronger than tin or copper. In Anyang, archaeologists have found bronze pots, plates, ceremonial vessels,

▲ *Cowries are snails found in the coastal waters of the Pacific and Indian oceans. The shells shown here are life-sized.*

▼ *Find the Huang He on this map. Shang farmers learned to tame the wild water buffalo that roamed the river's flood plain.*

**Shang Dynasty**

0   250   500 mi.
0   250 500 km
Mercator Projection

75°E
90°E   105°E   120°E   135°E
45°N
TIAN SHAN
GOBI (DESERT)
DA HINGGAN LING
Huang He
KUNLUN SHAN
Sea of Japan
Wei He
Anyang
Zhengzhou
Yellow Sea
East China Sea
30°N
HIMALAYAS
Chang Jiang

Extent of Shang Dynasty, 1122 B.C.

Present-day boundary of China

TAIWAN
Xi Jiang
South China Sea
HAINAN
PACIFIC OCEAN

*Shang craftworkers created this 14-inch-high bronze vessel in the shape of a man within a tiger's open jaws. No one knows whether the tiger is protecting the man or eating him. What do you think?*

### Across Time & Space

*Westerners wear black as the color of mourning when someone dies. The Chinese wear white. These seem the opposite until you realize that both cultures are really doing the same thing—avoiding colorful clothing.*

■ *How did the Shang people live, and how did their religious beliefs affect their lives?*

spears, and even chariots. These Shang pieces are skillfully decorated with complex patterns and animal faces.

### Religion

The early Chinese believed in many gods. They worshiped individual gods that they believed controlled the sun, moon, stars, rivers, and mountains. They also worshiped a supreme god, Shang Di *(shahng dee),* who took a personal interest in the world and its people. They believed their priests could communicate directly with Shang Di.

### Ancestor Worship

As important to the Shang as their gods were their **ancestors**—relatives who had lived before them. The Chinese believed that the wise spirits of their ancestors controlled every part of their lives. Chinese fathers, as the heads of their households, made frequent offerings to their ancestors. Even the king would make offerings to his ancestors at special religious ceremonies.

### Burials

Shang leaders believed that when they died, they joined their ancestors. They were buried in deep pits dug in the shape of a cross. Like the Egyptian pharaohs, Shang kings were buried with the things they might need in the next life. These included pottery jars, bronze weapons, jade ornaments, and even war chariots.

In one royal tomb at Anyang, archaeologists found the remains of nine guards and nine dogs that had been killed and placed around the prince's coffin. They also found the prince's chariot with its four horses and three armed warriors buried alongside.

### Oracle Bones

To guide them in this world, Shang kings consulted their ancestors by means of oracle bones. An **oracle** is a prediction about the future. First, the priest would carve the king's question on an animal bone or a turtle shell. Then he would drill holes in one side of the bone and heat it. When the heated bone cracked, the priest looked at the pattern of cracks to find the oracle and answer the king's question.

Kings often asked questions about daily life—for example, whether the day's hunt would be successful. Like us, they also wanted predictions about the weather. The question on one oracle bone reads, "Will the weather be fine tomorrow?" The priest's forecast was, "This evening it will rain; tomorrow, it will be fine." Some of the bones have notes telling whether the oracle was correct. This priest was apparently a good weather forecaster. The bone notes, "In the night rain was granted; the next day it was fine."

Archaeologists have found more than 100,000 of these oracle bones. They contain the earliest known examples of Chinese writing. Readers today can recognize many of the more than 2,000 characters engraved on the 3,600-year-old bones. Read A Closer Look on page 267 to discover more about the development of Chinese writing. ■

# Chinese Writing

*The brush races across the paper as your Chinese friend draws the word you see below. Can you guess what it means? It's the word for horse! Chinese writing has a long history. Look how the word for horse developed step by step.*

**Turtle shells** were sometimes used to write on in ancient China. The writing on this shell was done around 1200 B.C. Notice that the writing uses mostly straight lines, which are easy to draw.

**c. 2000 B.C.**
The earliest writers scratched small pictures like this onto bones and shells.

**c. 600 B.C.**
In this period, writing started to look less like a picture.

**c. A.D. 300**
When writers began to use brushes, their lines got longer. Where are the horse's feet?

**Present**
Today the Chinese are trying to simplify their writing by using characters like this one.

*Jade brush rest*

*Signature seal*

**Take this stick of ink** and grind it slowly back and forth on this ink stone. Add water until the ink is just the shade you want it, from the deepest black to the palest gray. Now you are ready to dip your brush and paint the word *horse*.

**Is this writing** or painting? Chinese people began to write with brushes over 2,000 years ago. For centuries writers in China have worked to make their words look as beautiful as possible. So, making a Chinese letter or poem is actually both writing and painting.

**Ancient China**

# The Zhou Dynasty

In the Wei Valley, west of the bend in the Huang He, lived a group of people called the Zhou *(joh)*. The Zhou were farmers. They also helped their Shang rulers by patrolling the country's borders, guarding them against raiders from the west.

One Zhou leader, King Wen, tried to overthrow the Shang. Eventually King Wen's son, Wu the Martial, became the leader of the Zhou. True to his name, Wu the Martial carried out his father's wishes and conquered the Shang. In 1122 B.C., Wu's forces attacked the Shang king. They burned the royal palace and set up their own dynasty. The Zhou dynasty would be the longest in China's history.

## The Mandate of Heaven

The Zhou worshiped an impersonal power called *tian,* or heaven. Unlike the Shang, the Zhou did not believe their priests could communicate with *tian*. Instead, they believed *tian* was simply a power that demanded right behavior and good government. They believed that *tian* required this especially of the king, whom they called the "son of heaven." If a king ruled well, he earned heaven's support, called the "mandate of heaven." If he ruled poorly or was evil, he lost the mandate of heaven and was overthrown. The Zhou used this idea to justify their overthrow of the last Shang ruler.

## Feudalism

Zhou kings spread their rule over China through a system called **feudalism** *(FYOOD uh lihz uhm)*. Under a feudal system, nobles own the farmland, which is worked by peasants, or serfs. In feudal China, the Zhou put their relatives and even some Shang nobles in charge of the land. The serfs paid the nobles for the use of the land. In turn, the nobles paid the king a portion of what their peasants produced. The nobles also promised to send the king soldiers in times of war.

The king granted each noble complete control of his own land. The noble was like a king on his land. A noble's land consisted of a walled town and the farms around it. By about 700 B.C., there were 200 of these feudal states, each with its own government.

*▲ This bronze ceremonial vessel in the shape of a rhinoceros suggests the playful side of the artisan who designed it. The vessel dates from the late Shang or early Zhou period.*

*➤ To the ancient Chinese, the imaginary dragon was king of all animals. Dragons with five claws on each foot symbolized an emperor. Nonroyal dragons had four claws.*

As methods of farming improved, the nobles' stores of surplus grain grew. Since grain was valuable, the nobles became richer and more powerful. They grew greedy and waged wars against each other to gain even more land .

To run their powerful states and do business with neighbors, the nobles needed skilled and educated people. They needed engineers to plan and build flood control projects. They needed tax collectors to gather payments from their serfs. And because few people could read or write, they needed scholars to keep records and to advise them. In fact, men who could read and write wandered through China, offering their services to the nobles. For a fee, these wandering scholars also taught common people to read and write. The earliest surviving Chinese books were written during the Zhou period.

## A Unifying Language

During the Zhou dynasty, as today, people in China's many regions spoke a variety of languages and dialects. **Dialects** are different forms of the same language. Thus, communication from region to region was often a problem.

To solve this problem, the Zhou took a new approach to

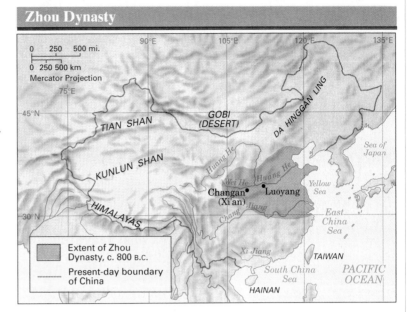

**Zhou Dynasty**

Extent of Zhou Dynasty, c. 800 B.C.

Present-day boundary of China

writing. They used pictures, or characters, to stand for whole words. That way, no matter how a word was pronounced in different parts of China, its written form could be understood everywhere.

In the time of the Zhou, the Chinese language had more than 3,000 written characters. At last, people from feudal states hundreds of miles apart, speaking different dialects, could communicate with each other.

Writing helped to bridge the barriers created by China's geography. Writing helped to unify the Chinese people. Finally, writing made possible the growth and spread of China's unique culture and civilization. ■

*China under the Zhou dynasty was made up of feudal states ruled by powerful nobles.*

■ *In what ways were the Zhou walled cities like small countries?*

**R E V I E W**

1. **FOCUS** What advances were made by these ancient cultures—the Yangshao, the Lungshan, the Xia, the Shang, and the Zhou?

2. **CONNECT** How did China's Neolithic cultures resemble those of Mesopotamia and Egypt?

3. **GEOGRAPHY** How did China's geography affect its early history? Consider both the regions within China, and China's relationship to the rest of the world.

4. **CRITICAL THINKING** How did the Shang and Zhou religions differ? How did each religion give a special role to the king?

5. **ACTIVITY** Imagine that you are a feudal noble. Make a chart comparing the advantages and disadvantages of your position. List the benefits on one side and the risks and responsibilities on the other side.

Ancient China

L E S S O N   2

# The Age of Confucius

**THINKING**
**F O C U S**

*How did the teachings of Confucius compare with those of the Moists, the Legalists, and the Daoists?*

### Key Terms

- nobility
- Confucianism

➤ *The portrait of Confucius on this page was made from an ancient marble relief. Today, nearly six million people follow the teachings of Confucius.*

T he gentleman first practices what he preaches and then preaches what he practices."

"Do not do to others what you would not want others to do to you."

China's greatest teacher, Confucius *(kuhn FYOO shuhs)*, taught such rules for living about 2,500 years ago. Some of his ideas may even sound familiar to you. Wise people throughout history have taught us the same lessons. Indeed, Confucius's advice on how to treat others has echoed down through the ages.

About 20 B.C., the great Jewish teacher Hillel said, "What is hateful to yourself, do not do to your neighbor." And in the Christian New Testament, the same message is written in the following way: "Treat others as you would like them to treat you."

At the root of Confucius's teachings lay a basic idea—that people could get along peacefully if only they followed the rules of good behavior. In a time of chaos and change, this great thinker longed for order and mutual respect among people. Little did he know that his simple lessons for living would instruct and inspire millions for centuries to come.

## An Age of Change

Confucius lived during the last years of the Zhou dynasty. Gradually, the Zhou had lost more and more power. By the time of Confucius, they were rulers in name only. And as the rule of the Zhou weakened, China tumbled into chaos.

How did the Zhou fall from power? They needed help ruling China's vast lands, and so they sent military leaders to control faraway outposts. These leaders, or lords, ruled walled cities and maintained powerful armies. Soon, independent lords governed their own lands. Finally, in 771 B.C., powerful lords invaded the Zhou capital and drove out the rulers.

### A Follower of Confucius

About 100 years after Confucius died, his disciple Mencius (*MEHN shee uhs*) began spreading the ideas of Confucianism. Mencius had his own ideas too. He felt people should extend the love and respect they felt for family members to people outside their families.

Mencius also had strong beliefs about rulers. He thought that a bad king should be driven from the throne. Of the evil Xia and Shang kings, he said: "Losing the throne arose from . . . losing the people, and to lose the people means to lose their hearts. There is a way to get the kingdom: get the people and the kingdom is got." ■

■ *What were some basic teachings of Confucius?*

## Opponents of Confucianism

In the last days of the Zhou dynasty, China's marketplaces bustled with merchants, who sold everything from fine silk to chopsticks. Farmers lugged grain to market, and people and animals crowded the busy streets.

Clusters of scholars gathered and held lively street-corner debates. They argued over how people should behave and how rulers should govern.

Not all these scholars supported the teachings of Confucius. For example, Moists (*MOH ihsts*), people who followed the teachings of Mo-Tzu (*MOHD zuh*), believed in universal love, equal love for all people—not just rulers and family members. Universal love, they believed, would bring benefits such as peace.

Another group, the Legalists, held a different view. They thought that people were bad by nature. Only a strong government, with strict laws and harsh punishments, would keep evil under control.

A third group, the Daoists (*DOW ihsts*), insisted that human nature was neither good nor bad. They believed that people should live a simple and thoughtful life, in harmony with nature. They cared little for politics.

Imagine you are on a busy street corner in a Chinese city around 250 B.C. You listen as three men engage in a heated debate.

A thin man, a Moist, seated on a box, waves his arms excitedly as he speaks: "Confucius believed that men of learning should guide rulers, but why shouldn't men of learning *be* rulers?"

"That's an easy one," replies the fat man they call a Legalist. "Rulers must make strict laws because people are evil. The ruler must be an all-powerful king. Now here's a question

◄ *This wooden carving shows a Daoist wise man. The 12-inch carving dates from the Southern Song dynasty, A.D. 1127–1279.*

273

## Two Schools of Chinese Thought

|  | Confucianism | Legalism |
| --- | --- | --- |
| Goal | Virtuous conduct, peaceful society | All power in the hands of the ruler |
| Government | Rule by good example | Rule by law, including rewards and punishments |
| Emphasis | The past | The present |

for you," he goes on. "Confucius said rulers should govern by virtue, not by power. But when powerful states fight with one another, who wins?"

"The most powerful leader wins," admits the Moist. "But going to war is the biggest waste of time and money."

The third man, who is a Daoist, smiles at the others. "Arguing about these things is silly," he says. "And working in government is pointless. After all, the world is neither good nor evil. It certainly can't be changed by anything that people do."

The thin Moist answers, "You seem to be saying that there's nothing to be done at all. But we should love everyone as much as we love ourselves. What could be a better way of showing love than feeding the hungry and housing the poor? Whatever enriches the country and brings order to society is good."

The Legalist shifts his bulky weight to his other leg. "You have a good point," he says. "If we keep trying to rule by looking back to the past, as Confucius did, we're just like the man of Song. Then the Legalist goes on to tell this story:

"Once there was a man of Song who plowed his field around a tree stump that stood in the center. One day, a hare, running at full speed, bumped into the stump, broke its neck, and died. So the farmer left his plow and kept watch at the stump. He always hoped to catch another hare, but he never did. Those who try to rule today the way the early kings ruled are doing the same thing as that foolish man of Song!"

The stories and arguments went on and on as the day drew to an end. Soon the merchants would be counting their money and packing up their wares. The horse-drawn carts would be plowing their way through the muddy streets. And finally the three arguing scholars would go home to their beds, each one dreaming his own vision of China's future. ■

## R E V I E W

1. **FOCUS** How did the teachings of Confucius compare with those of the Moists, the Legalists, and the Daoists?
2. **CONNECT** What might Confucius say about evil kings such as the last ruler of the Xia dynasty?
3. **POLITICAL SYSTEMS** What were Confucius's ideas about how a government should be run?
4. **CRITICAL THINKING** What might Confucius say about the relationships between family members in U.S. society today?
5. **ACTIVITY** Form groups of four and discuss the ideas presented in the imaginary debate. Then let each member take one of the four roles. Act out a debate in which Confucius answers the arguments of the other three.

# Evaluating Arguments

## Here's Why

People often disagree about things. In any debate, you need to be able to understand the arguments on both sides of a question to figure out which one makes the most sense.

You have learned that philosophers of the Hundred Schools debated many subjects. Often the cause of their disagreements was a basic difference in how they saw the world. For example, Confucius believed that humans are good by nature; others disagreed. Who was right?

To respond to such questions, you must be able to evaluate ideas or arguments as they are presented. You must ask which ideas fit the point.

## Here's How

Read the paragraph below. It was written by Han Fei Tzu, a Legalist. To evaluate his argument, first identify its main point: Love spoils people, but punishment makes them obedient. Then identify his supporting arguments. Decide whether the arguments are consistent —do they agree with other ideas presented? Also ask whether the arguments are relevant—do they fit the point he is making? For example, if you take out the sentence "His friends may like him," does it change the argument? No, because the statement is irrelevant to the argument. Statements of this type weaken the debater's position.

## Try It

What would you identify as the main point of the argument if it ended with the following sentence? "With a boy who is a good character, however, love of parents, conduct of neighbors, and wisdom of teachers have a positive and lasting effect." Which sentence in the paragraph would be inconsistent with this ending?

## Apply It

Prepare a written argument for or against this idea: "Every citizen should vote." Be sure to use supporting arguments. Then trade papers with a classmate. Evaluate each other's work, looking for inconsistencies and irrelevant statements.

---

**Irrelevant.** This says nothing about how or what a person learns of morality.

**Consistent.** This summarizes the argument.

Take a boy who is a bad character. His parents may get angry with him; he does not change. His teachers may teach him moral conduct; he does not conform. His friends may like him. Parents' love and teachers' wisdom have no effect on him. Not a hair on his shins changes. But when the police come around looking for wicked characters, he becomes afraid, changes his principles, and reforms his conduct. The love of parents is not enough to teach a boy morality; the severe punishments of the law are needed. People become naturally spoiled by love but obedient to severity.

**Inconsistent.** Showing anger is not necessarily love; it may really be punishment.

**Relevant.** This emphasizes the major point of the argument.

Ancient China

LESSON 3

# A Unified China

**THINKING FOCUS**

*How did Qin Shihuangdi unify China, and what did he do to maintain his empire?*

## Key Terms

- province
- bureaucracy
- censorship

▼ *This striking photo shows a small part of Qin's amazing clay army.*

I magine facing an army of fearsome warriors from more than 2,000 years in the past. That's what journalist Audrey Topping saw in 1974 near the ancient Chinese city of Xian *(shee YAHN)*. The troops were, in fact, life-sized pottery figures. Yet Topping still felt a sense of awe as she looked upon the legions of warriors.

L *ooking into the pit . . . was like looking back more than two thousand years at an ancient battlefield. . . . Some figures were almost completely unearthed and stood as if poised to attack; others were half buried, or smashed and scattered. . . . Proud heads, fallen from broken bodies, looked up from their centuries-old grave, their fierce eyes fixed on us.*

Audrey Topping, "Clay Soldiers:
The Army of Emperor Ch'in"

Peasants had made the discovery while drilling a well. Topping was the first Western reporter to visit the site. The huge clay army consisted of more than 6,000 life-sized warriors, plus horses and chariots. Armed with swords, spears, and crossbows, the clay warriors appeared ready for battle. Nearby in his ancient grave lay the once-powerful ruler—Qin Shihuangdi *(chihn shee hwahng dee)*. The statues had been crafted to guard the emperor Qin in his afterlife.

# The Qin Dynasty

In the last years of the Zhou dynasty, the feudal state of Qin became very powerful. In 256 B.C., Qin forces defeated the last Zhou ruler. They spread their control over more and more of China.

In 246 B.C., Cheng, who later was the emperor Qin Shihuangdi, became king of the state of Qin. Twenty-five years later, he led his mighty state to victory over its final rival. Now he ruled all of China. Note the extent of the Qin dynasty on the map below.

The new ruler wanted a new title. For 1,500 years, Shang and Zhou rulers had been called *wang*, meaning "king." But this wasn't good enough. Believing his family's rule over China would last 10,000 generations, the king added *shi*, meaning "first," to *huangdi*, meaning "emperor," and called himself Qin Shihuangdi. The Qin dynasty lasted only 15 years, but Chinese emperors were called *huangdi* until 1912.

No matter how fine his title, an emperor cannot rule without power. Qin Shihuangdi knew this well. He set out to run the empire as he had run the state of Qin. He worked to unify the many warring states. To do so, he divided the empire into 36 **provinces,** or territories. He divided each of the provinces into districts. Over each province were two officials, a governor and a defender. Thus, the emperor kept firm control over his entire empire.

Qin Shihuangdi also set up a system of rewards and punishments. He urged people to spy on neighbors and turn in lawbreakers. This system strengthened his control and gave him power to make great changes in his empire. ■

◄ *This life-sized clay soldier appears ready to defend his emperor Qin Shihuangdi from any foe.*

■ *What did Qin Shihuangdi hope to accomplish by appointing governors to rule the provinces?*

◄ *Compare the extent of the Qin dynasty with the Shang and Zhou dynasties shown on pages 265 and 269.*

## Qin Dynasty

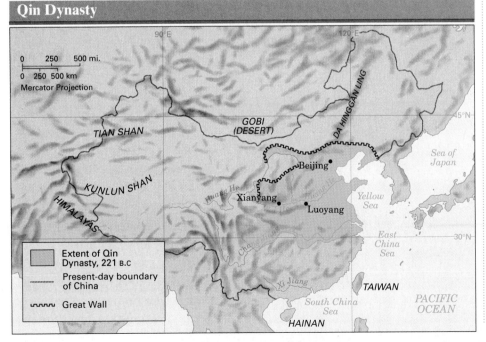

0   250   500 mi.

0   250  500 km
Mercator Projection

TIAN SHAN

GOBI (DESERT)

DA HINGGAN LING

Huang He

Beijing

Xianyang

Luoyang

Yellow Sea

KUNLUN SHAN

HIMALAYAS

Sea of Japan

45°N

East China Sea

30°N

Chang Jiang

Xi Jiang

TAIWAN

South China Sea

PACIFIC OCEAN

HAINAN

90°E

120°E

Extent of Qin Dynasty, 221 B.C

Present-day boundary of China

Great Wall

277

Ancient China

# The Legacy of Qin

Could Qin rule all China from his palace? Even with governors and defenders, he needed more help. Qin set up a new system that would be used in China for centuries to come.

## Qin's New System

Before Qin, officials passed their jobs on to their sons. Qin changed all that. He set up a **bureaucracy** *(byoo RAHK ruh see)*, a system in which each worker is appointed to a job and is trained for that job. Each worker gets a salary, follows strict rules, and answers to a superior. People at each level supervise those below them.

Heading the bureaucracy was the emperor Qin Shihuangdi. Eleven chamberlains managed the emperor's household. Three high officials, sometimes called the "Three Dukes," held the highest government and military posts. Find their titles on the chart below. The chart shows only the top levels of the Qin bureaucracy. Beneath all the officials on the chart labored a host of minor officials.

## New Standards

Qin made other changes to help unify his empire. People in different parts of China had developed their own systems of measurement and money. Over time, different regions had even come to use different characters for writing.

Qin set new standards for all of China. All measurements had to be the same, and only one kind of money was legal. Qin also decreed standard written characters. Now people all over China could communicate in writing. To this day, Chinese writing remains much the same as in Qin's time.

## Land Ownership

Qin also changed the rules about ownership of land. He feared the nobles as a threat to his power, so he took land away from thousands of noble families. Thus Qin ended the Chinese feudal system. Now any man, rich or poor, could own land, as long as he paid the land tax. And now Qin's government, not the lords, controlled the peasants.

## Book Burnings

The emperor's advisor, Lisi *(lee suh)*, saw still another way for Qin's government to strengthen its control. Like other Legalists, Lisi hated the works of Confucius and others

*The most powerful persons in a bureaucracy are usually those with the most people working beneath them. Use this chart to compare the positions of the "Three Dukes." Which one seems to have had the most power? You're right if you said the Counselor-in-chief. What officials were beneath him?*

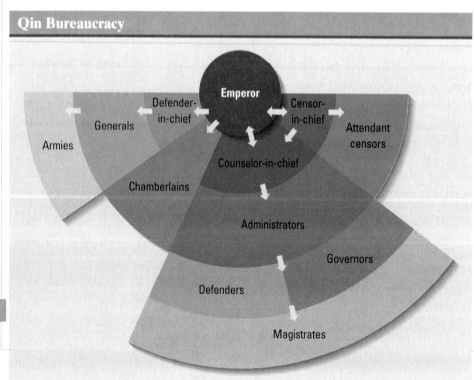

### Qin Bureaucracy

Emperor

Defender-in-chief — Censor-in-chief

Generals — Attendant censors

Armies

Counselor-in-chief

Chamberlains

Administrators

Governors

Defenders

Magistrates

who disagreed with Legalism. In 213 B.C., he ordered the burning of "useless" books. According to Lisi, all books were useless unless they were about medicine, agriculture, or prophecy.

The Qin government attacked writers and readers as well as their books. "Anyone referring to the past to criticize the present . . . should be put to death," Lisi told the emperor. Several hundred scholars who refused to turn in their books were buried alive or punished in other ways.

Qin's book burning was an early example of **censorship**—control of what people read or write, hear or see. Look again at the bureaucracy chart on page 278. How does it show that censorship was important in Qin's government?

## UNDERSTANDING CENSORSHIP

The idea for burning books came from Qin's advisor, Lisi: "Your servant suggests that all books in the imperial archives, except Qin's memoirs, be burned." Lisi was telling the emperor to stop people from reading, writing, saying, or even hearing words that might challenge the government. Efforts such as these to prohibit free expression are called censorship.

### A Matter of Policy

Your local bookstore can choose not to sell a certain book or magazine. That isn't censorship. Censorship is an official policy of stopping the spread of works and ideas that the government or some other group does not like.

### A Long History

Censorship has been practiced throughout history. Around 500 B.C., leaders of the Greek city-state of Sparta banned poems and music that they felt made people behave badly. About 2,000 years later, King Henry VIII of England ordered his officials to read every piece of writing before it was printed.

In June 1989, Chinese college students staged a peaceful demonstration in Beijing. They demanded rights such as freedom of speech. But the Chinese government sent troops into the crowd, killing hundreds. Officials insisted there had been no killings—despite photographs and videotapes of the massacre. They did not allow Chinese television or newspapers to report what really happened.

### An Ancient Debate

Throughout history, the debate over censorship has raged. On one side are those who believe that people should have free access to all ideas. On the other side are those who fear the consequences of freedom. They fear that knowledge might make people dissatisfied. It might lead to criticism of the government or even rebellion.

### A Reason for Alertness

Citizens of a democracy cherish their freedom of expression. That freedom can be threatened, even in a democracy. We need to be alert when people tell us what Lisi told the emperor—that certain books or other kinds of expression are "dangerous" and ought to be censored.

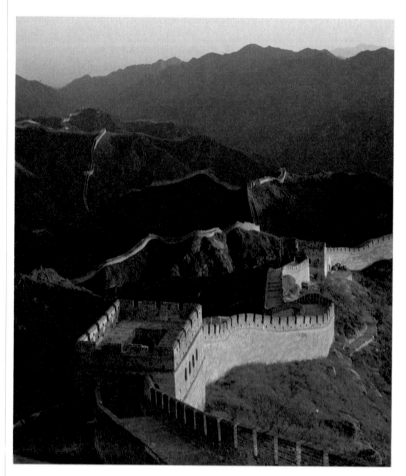

*This picture shows part of the Great Wall of China as it is today. Some emperors after Qin Shihuangdi extended and strengthened the Wall.*

■ *What are three things that Qin Shihuangdi standardized, and how did each change affect China?*

nomads. Second, it was built to keep out enemy invaders. Guards on its watchtowers kept a lookout for enemy forces. They signaled invasions with flags or fires, holding off the enemy until help came.

To complete this massive structure, Qin used a forced-labor crew of 300,000 men. These workers connected several existing walls to form one single, massive wall. The Great Wall is nearly 30 feet high. At most points, it is wide enough to allow five horses to run atop it side by side. If it were in the United States, the Great Wall would stretch from Washington, D.C., to Denver, Colorado.

The Wall was not a complete success. First, it never really kept out invaders. They swarmed over and around it. Second, thousands of workers died on the long journey to the Wall. Thousands more died while building it. The folktale "Meng-Jiang Nyu," on pages 256 to 261, shows how some lives were changed by the Great Wall.

## The Great Wall

Some of the scholars punished under Lisi were sent to work on the emperor's huge building project. That project would later be known as the Great Wall of China.

The Great Wall still stands. It snakes through the mountains of northern China for more than 1,500 miles. The Wall was built for two reasons. First, it was meant to keep in peasants who might otherwise leave their farms to become

## A Unified Empire

In a sense, Qin, a brilliant and sometimes cruel emperor, gained the immortality he wanted. In his lifetime, he unified states that had been fighting for centuries. And even today outsiders call the land "China" from *Qin* (or *Ch'in*), the name of its first emperor. ■

## R E V I E W

1. **FOCUS** How did Qin Shihuangdi unify China, and what did he do to maintain his empire?

2. **CONNECT** Qin Shihuangdi unified China. Who were the rulers that unified Mesopotamia and Egypt? How did each ruler create a unified empire?

3. **GOVERNMENT** How was Qin's rule different from the rule of the Shang and the Zhou?

4. **CRITICAL THINKING** What would you have liked about living under Qin's rule? What would you have disliked? Explain.

5. **WRITING ACTIVITY** If you lived in Qin's China, what occupation would you choose? Scholar? Bureaucrat? Peasant? Write a day's entry in your diary discussing your job, your problems, and your life in general.

Chapter 9

LESSON 4

# The Han Dynasty

O n one occasion one of the dragons let fall a ball from its mouth though no perceptible shock could be felt. All the scholars at the capital were astonished at this strange effect occurring without any evidence of an earthquake to cause it. But several days later a messenger arrived bringing news of an earthquake in Longxi [Kansu, about 400 miles away to the northwest].

Han court historian, A.D. 132

What is this mysterious instrument that tells of a faraway earthquake? The carved bronze dragons and the toads below them are fine works of art. But this amazing device is much more than art. Today we call it a **seismograph** (*SYZ muh graf*), a machine that detects earthquakes.

Here's how the Han dragon-and-toad seismograph worked. In the center of the huge jar stood a pendulum. With the slightest shaking from a far-off earthquake, the pendulum would fall into one of the slots, hitting a rod. The rod would slip into the dragon's mouth, hitting a ball. The ball would fall into the mouth of a toad. The loud crack of bronze against bronze signaled that an earthquake had happened. But it told even more. It told what part of the country had suffered the quake. The ball fell into the mouth of the toad that stood in that direction.

THINKING
FOCUS

*What kind of government did Han rulers create, and how did it affect people's lives?*

## Key Terms

- seismograph
- middleman

◄ *This seismograph is a copy of the Han dynasty model. The drawing shows its inner workings.*

0          6 ft.

281

Ancient China

Han rulers needed to know when earthquakes happened. Frequent quakes destroyed farms, roads, and cities, causing food shortages. Starving peasants often revolted. Informed by the dragon-and-toad seismograph, the rulers could rush food supplies and soldiers to the earthquake area.

Indeed, this brilliant invention seems to symbolize the explosion of scientific advances that were made during the Han dynasty. The Han rulers were in power from 206 B.C. to A.D. 220. During this time, China seemed centuries ahead of the rest of the world in science, art, and culture.

# Revival of Confucianism

During this period of creativity, Han scholars, like Zhou scholars before them, searched for new ideas. They looked for new ways to organize China's political life. Legalist teachings had helped Qin to unite China's states under a single government. But as a Legalist, Qin ruled harshly. He ignored moral principles such as kindness and respect. As a result, only a few people supported his rule. Finally, soldiers and peasants rebelled, overthrowing the Qin dynasty a few years after Qin Shihuangdi's death. One leader of the rebellion became the first emperor of the Han dynasty.

## Legalism and Confucianism

The Han leaders saw that China's government could not be based on Legalism alone. Confucianism—the belief in moral behavior and rule by good example—became popular again.

The first Han emperor, Han Gaozu *(hahn kow dzuh)*, was uneducated. He appointed learned people to help him run the government. Some were Confucian scholars. Gaozu even lifted the Qin ban on books in 191 B.C. and permitted scholars to rewrite some old Confucian texts from memory.

Government officials no longer destroyed books on Confucianism.

➤ *Compare the Han empire in this map with the Shang dynasty shown on page 265.*

**Han Dynasty**

0   250   500 mi.
0   250  500 km
Mercator Projection

TIAN SHAN
KUNLUN SHAN
HIMALAYAS
GOBI (DESERT)
DA HINGGAN LING
Beijing
Huang He
Wei He
Huang He
Changan (Xi'an)
Luoyang
Chang Jiang
Changsha
Guangzhou
Xi Jiang
HAINAN
TAIWAN
Sea of Japan
Yellow Sea
East China Sea
South China Sea
PACIFIC OCEAN
90°E   120°E   45°N   30°N

Extent of Han Dynasty, 87 B.C
Present-day boundary of China
Great Wall

Instead, they began to study them. Later, in 136 B.C., emperor Wudi *(woo tee)* made Confucianism part of the law of the empire. Students even read Confucian books in school.

Yet Confucianism alone was not enough to guide the government. In fact, the Han rulers combined Confucianism with Legalism. They kept the Legalist ideas of a strong ruler and a strict set of laws. But they added the Confucian view that the emperor was a "good father" to his people. He ruled by setting a good example, not by threats of punishment.

Confucianism and Legalism may seem like opposites. In some ways they are. But the Chinese understood how such opposites could work together through the idea of Yin and Yang.

### Yin and Yang

During the late Zhou dynasty, some thinkers had explained life as a blend of two opposing forces—Yin and Yang. *Yin* means "the dark side of the hill." Yin has the qualities of darkness, calm, and weakness. Earth, winter, sorrow, and death are examples of Yin. *Yang* means "the bright side of the hill." Yang is active and strong. Examples include heaven, summer, joy, and life.

The Chinese knew that opposites depend on each other. There can be no light without darkness, or life without death. And opposites, they knew, often take turns, as day gives way to night. Thus, a combination of opposites such as Confucianism and Legalism seemed reasonable. ■

▲ *The Yin and Yang symbol is the center of this design, which is part of a carved door ornament.*

■ *How did the Han and Qin governments differ?*

## Daily Life in the Empire

Written records tell us little about how the Han Chinese lived their daily lives. Han tombs, however, contain a wealth of information. For example, the Han people buried their dead in underground tombs decorated with paintings of scenes from daily life. They also buried small pottery models like those you see below. These models tell much about the furniture, houses, and villages of China 2,000 years ago.

### Life in the Country

Then, as now, most of China's people were farmers. Han farmers lived in mud houses that stood on earthen platforms. Tile or thatched roofs topped these one-story or two-story houses. Rough hemp curtains covered the farmhouse windows. Barns and other buildings surrounded the houses. Often several farm families lived together

▼ *These clay figures, found in a Han tomb, show an ordinary farm scene. Like the ancient Egyptians, the Han believed such images might be useful in the afterlife.*

283

in small villages. In this way, they could work the fields together.

A wealthy farmer could afford strong oxen to pull his carts and iron tips to strengthen the ends of his plows. He used simple machines to carry water to his fields.

His poorer neighbor worked with wooden hand tools. To water his fields, the poorer farmer hauled heavy buckets of water on his shoulders. He lugged the buckets on a yoke across his back, carrying two buckets at a time.

These Chinese farmers dressed in simple, rough clothes. They wore shirts and pants made of scratchy cloth. They wore sandals made of straw. In cold weather, they wore clothing that was padded, stuffed like a quilt to keep them warm.

Farmers cooked their simple meals in boxlike stoves. They steamed much of their food over boiling water, as Chinese people still do. Those living in the north ate wheat or a grain called millet. Those living in the south ate rice. Farmers enjoyed steamed dumplings, small portions of fish, and even smaller portions of meat. Many families planted garden plots and grew ginger, garlic, and onions. These crops added flavor to their meals and could even be sold at the market to bring them a few coins.

*This funeral suit, made of a green stone called jade, covered the body of the princess Tou Wan, who lived before 100 B.C. Some people believed jade would prevent the body from decaying, and small pieces of jade were sometimes buried with the bodies. This princess went further. Her suit has 2,160 jade pieces.*

■ *How were the lives of China's wealthy farmers different from the lives of poor farmers?*

### Life in the City

By the time of the Han dynasty, perhaps one in 10 Chinese people lived in a city. The cities were laid out neatly according to compass directions. They had earthen and stone walls so strong that some are still standing today. The cities were centers of government, education, and trade. There, in busy marketplaces, merchants traded everything from coarse cloth to fine silk, from the heaviest ox cart to the most elegant horse-drawn carriage.

Then, as now, rich and poor shared city life. According to one writer of the time, the poor lived in houses packed together as tightly as the teeth of a comb. And then, as now, some youngsters joined street gangs. These gangs roamed the city, terrorizing its people. Gang members also wore special clothes and armor.

Rich city people lived in huge houses built so that they opened onto courtyards. They decorated their houses with woolen rugs and fine draperies. They wore belted robes with long sleeves. In winter, the rich wrapped themselves in squirrel or fox furs. They slipped their feet into leather slippers lined with silk.

City life also included lively entertainment. Musicians played bells, drums, and wind and string instruments. Jugglers and acrobats delighted audiences with their tricks and stunts. ■

## Achievements of the Han Dynasty

Early Han rulers ended many of the harsh Qin laws and heavy taxes. Thus, the Han gained their subjects' loyalty as Qin Shihuangdi never could. With peace and prosperity, the Han dynasty marked the beginning of an age of creativity at home and expansion abroad.

## Expansion of the Empire

Emperor Wudi, who ruled from 141 to 87 B.C., sent out armies to expand the empire. His soldiers captured lands in southern China and started colonies in what are now North Korea and North Vietnam. Wudi's troops also crossed the Great Wall. They subdued the raiding tribes of the Gobi Desert and brought these northern people under Chinese rule.

In 139 B.C., Wudi sent out Zhang Qian (*jahng chyee YAHN*), a military officer and explorer. He journeyed west into what is now Afghanistan. When he returned to China 10 years later, he described the fabulous riches and wonders of the West. He brought back tales of new plants—alfalfa and grapes. He told of splendid, swift horses that "sweat blood when they perspire." His stories stirred the emperor's curiosity.

Zhang Qian added, "There are cities with mansions and houses, as in China." He gave the first hint that a civilized world lay beyond China.

Zhang Qian's explorations and Wudi's new interest in the West resulted in the growth of a major trade route—the Silk Road. Along the Silk Road, traders exchanged China's fine silk for Western goods such as glassware from Syria and gold from Rome.

## Advances and Inventions

Since prehistoric times, only the Chinese knew how to make silk. Skilled Chinese silk makers unwound the long threads from the silkworm's cocoon. Then they wove the thread into strong, beautiful cloth. For hundreds of years, China guarded the secret of how to make silk. Rulers even threatened a horrible death to anyone who told an outsider the secret, or gave away a silk moth.

Chinese workers used foot-pedaled looms to weave complex patterns into the silk. Silk became even more precious to the world beyond China.

People of the West knew little about the land that produced silk. Han rulers kept their lands closed

*In this painting from a vase of the Ming dynasty, A.D. 1368–1644, two women are spinning silk cloth. What else do you see in the painting?*

Ancient China

➤ *These bronze leopards illustrate the fine work of Han artisans. Less than one and a half inches high, they are inlaid with silver and precious stones called garnets. Four of them were found in the princess Tou Wan's tomb, dating from about 100 B.C.*

▼ *In Afghanistan, the explorer Zhang Qian saw horses that were larger and finer than any the Chinese had known. In 101 B.C., the Chinese brought some of these horses home. This 26-inch pottery figure, made in the first century B.C., shows one of those early horses.*

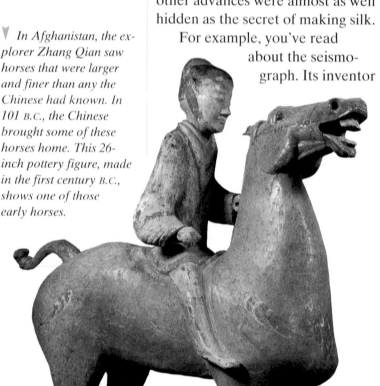

to outsiders. They used **middlemen**—agents who go between the buyer and seller. These middlemen from neighboring lands—now known as India, Pakistan, and Afghanistan—carried on most of the Silk Road trade. Thus, China's other advances were almost as well hidden as the secret of making silk.

For example, you've read about the seismograph. Its inventor was Zhang Heng. He and other Chinese astronomers learned how to predict eclipses and how to calculate the length of a year.

Han doctors understood many kinds of medicine. They studied the healing powers of herbs and plants. They invented the unique Chinese medical practice with needles called acupuncture.

Chinese engineers of the Han period were the first to use iron-tipped bamboo poles for deep drilling. They drilled salt water out of mines thousands of feet underground. They heated the water with piped-in natural gas until it evaporated, leaving salt.

The Han Chinese invented paper, too. Paper makers beat mulberry bark fibers into tiny particles. They mixed these and other fibers with water and poured the mixture out on a flat mold. There it dried, forming a sheet of paper.

Han artists also produced exceptional art and writing. Han artisans crafted bronze and gold belt hooks, glazed pottery dishes, and jade jewelry. Han writers wrote dozens of great books. Historian Sima Jian *(soo muh chih yehn)* completed the first full history of China during Wudi's reign. He set a high standard for later historians.

Han writers also wrote brilliant works in the fields of mathematics, medicine, and poetry. They

## Dynasties of Ancient China

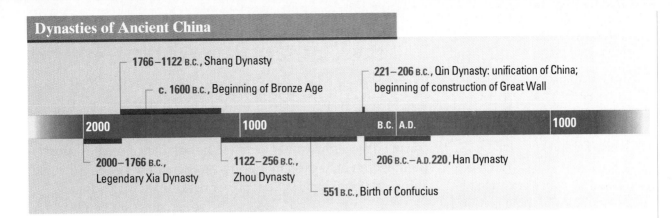

1766–1122 B.C., Shang Dynasty

c. 1600 B.C., Beginning of Bronze Age

221–206 B.C., Qin Dynasty: unification of China; beginning of construction of Great Wall

| 2000 | 1000 | B.C. | A.D. | 1000 |

2000–1766 B.C., Legendary Xia Dynasty

1122–256 B.C., Zhou Dynasty

206 B.C.–A.D. 220, Han Dynasty

551 B.C., Birth of Confucius

enriched the written language itself, increasing the number of characters from 3,000 to 9,000 by about A.D. 100. At that time, scholars completed the first Chinese dictionary.

Considering the many Han accomplishments, it's not surprising that the Chinese still refer to themselves as Han people. Yet the Han empire fell in A.D. 220, and another period of warfare between the states followed. Not until A.D. 589 would the empire again become united. ■

How long did each ancient Chinese dynasty last? What was one major achievement of each dynasty?

◀ Han doctors used medicinal herbs to reduce fevers, soothe sore throats, and increase energy. The Chinese still use herbs for these purposes.

■ What were some of China's greatest achievements under the Han dynasty?

## REVIEW

1. **FOCUS** What kind of government did Han rulers create, and how did it affect people's lives?

2. **CONNECT** Compare the burial practices of the Han with those of the Egyptians. How do their burial practices tell us about the daily lives of people in those cultures?

3. **HISTORY** Why did the Han rulers need the ideas of both Confucianism and Legalism?

4. **CRITICAL THINKING** What feelings about the outside world might have led the Chinese to use middlemen for trade?

5. **ACTIVITY** Draw or paint a picture showing one important aspect of Han life. For example, you might draw a scene from daily farm life, or one showing some people using a Chinese invention.

287

Ancient China

# Learning How Silk Is Made

**Here's Why**

In many cases the most effective way to explain or describe something is to use a picture of it. One special kind of picture that can help make an explanation clearer to you is a process diagram.

You are probably familiar with some process diagrams already. Manufacturers often provide process diagrams with products that you must put together. For example, instructions for building a model airplane are likely to include a process diagram; so are instructions for assembling a bicycle. Manufacturers know that it is often easier for people to understand how something is done or made by seeing pictures of the process than by reading a description with no pictures.

Suppose you want to understand the steps involved in the making of silk. The drawings on this page and the facing page show you how diagrams can help explain the process of making silk.

**Here's How**

The fine fiber used to produce beautiful silk fabric is made by silkworms. Like other caterpillars, the silkworm wraps itself in a cocoon. There, the silkworm spends several weeks before it emerges as an adult moth, as shown in the photo on page 289.

The silkworm makes its cocoon by spinning a fine silken fiber around itself. To produce this fiber, the silkworm forces a gummy substance out from two openings beneath its mouth. This sticky material dries into a delicate strand of silk as soon as it is exposed to the air. The silkworm spins one continuous thread to make its cocoon.

Workers gather the cocoons and carefully unwind the silk threads. They must be extremely skillful to avoid breaking the threads.

The diagram below shows how the delicate strands of silk are unwound from several cocoons and twisted together to form a single, stronger silk thread. The thread can then be combined with other silk threads and woven into silk fabric.

Notice that labels identify each part of the process. Arrows show the direction of movement. In this case, the arrows show you that the crank moves clockwise, turning the reel toward you. Diagrams that describe longer processes often use numbers or letters to show the order of steps.

**Try It**

The diagram on page 289 shows another part of the silk-making process—preparing skeins of silk thread for

**Unwinding Silk from Cocoons**

Dry cocoons    Seven strands    Crank handle

Reel

Chapter 9

dyeing. Twisting the silk into skeins keeps the threads from becoming tangled while they are being dyed. Study the diagram below. See how well you understand the process based on looking at the diagram by answering the following questions:

1. What parts of the diagram show movement?
2. Which way are the silk threads moving, up or down?
3. As the silk threads are pulled from the reels at the bottom onto the take-up reel, what do they pass through?
4. What makes the threads move?
5. Which way does the crank handle turn, clockwise or counterclockwise?
6. Does the take-up reel turn in the same direction as the crank handle, or does it turn in the opposite direction?
7. What is the final product of this process?
8. Does the diagram tell you what a skein is? Where can you go to find this information?

**Apply It**

Now that you know how to read a process diagram, try making one of your own. Think of some process you perform in your daily life. It can be something as simple as making a sandwich for lunch or as complex as operating a video game. Make sure that you clearly label all important parts of your diagram. Also be sure that you use arrows to show the proper direction of all movements. If necessary, number the steps in your diagram so that someone else can follow them.

When you complete your diagram, exchange diagrams with a classmate. Read each other's diagrams to see whether you can each describe the process the other is explaining.

**Preparing Silk Thread for Dyeing**

Take-up reel

Skeins of silk thread

Crank handle

Crossboard with holes

Reels of silk thread

Ancient China

# The Silk Road

**F**or hundreds of years, people, animals, and goods streamed along the Silk Road. This famous route linked China with the Middle East and Europe. East met West in gorgeous fabrics, precious metals, food, and wine.

*This pottery figure of a Middle Eastern wine merchant was made in China. It serves as evidence of trade between East and West.*

### Get Ready

Take a notebook and a pen to your school or local library. You'll need reference books and magazines to help you imagine a journey on the Silk Road.

### Find Out

First, decide whether you are a merchant, a caravan leader, or an adventurer. A merchant will be interested in products to buy and sell. A caravan leader will concentrate on the weather and terrain.

He will also see that the camels and horses have enough food and water and time to rest. An adventurer will focus on new experiences, unfamiliar sights, unusual sounds, and new people and customs.

Next, choose a place along the Silk Road (use the map to help you). The books and magazines will give you some ideas about what you would see and do there. In your diary, write about a day spent in this place.

You may draw pictures to go along with your diary entry. If you prefer, you may substitute pictures of your day on the Silk Road for the written diary entry.

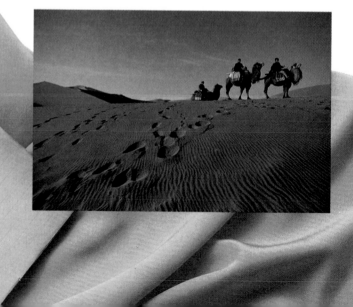

## Move Ahead

Separate into groups based on the place you wrote about or drew. Read your diary entry or show your pictures to a classmate who chose the same character you did. How does your information compare? How does it contrast?

Display your group's pictures on the bulletin board. What items are included in most of the pictures? Camels? Silk?

Find two classmates who chose to be the other two characters. Use your diaries to write a short skit. The characters can talk and interact as they visit a stopping-place along the Silk Road.

## Explore Some More

Visit a shopping area and look at silk products. You'll find them in sporting goods stores as well as in clothing stores. Check labels to see what countries silk comes from now. Then look at other types of products, such as shoes, watches, or radios. Make a list of the countries that produce them. Which countries appear most often on your list? Find these countries on a world map or globe.

▲ *These Chinese pottery figures show a merchant and his camel loaded with trade goods.*

◄ *Traders on the Silk Road crossed the mountains of Afghanistan, shown at the left, and the vast Gobi, pictured below.*

### The Silk Road

ROMAN EMPIRE
Rome
Sardis
Antioch
Palmyra
Tyre
Charax
Hamadan
PARTHIA
Barbaricon
Samarkand
TIAN SHAN
Mirv
HINDU KUSH
HIMALAYAS
INDIA
Kashgar
Miran
Dunhuang
Jade Gate Pass
GOBI (DESERT)
Changan (Xi'an)
Luoyang
CHINA
Hanoi
Guangzhou

Silk Road
Other trade route
• Trade center

0    500    1000 mi.

N

# Chapter Review

## Reviewing Key Terms

ancestor (p. 266)
bureaucracy (p. 278)
censorship (p. 279)
Confucianism (p. 271)
dialect (p. 269)
feudalism (p. 268)

middleman (p. 286)
nobility (p. 271)
oracle (p. 266)
province (p. 277)
seismograph (p. 281)

Be sure you understand the meanings of the key terms. Then answer each question by writing one or more sentences.

1. How might your dialect tell people where you have lived?
2. If an ancient Chinese farmer had used oracle bones, what might he have asked?
3. If you lived in a feudal society, would you rather be a serf or a noble? Why?
4. Why would a bureaucracy not work in a one-person business?
5. Why do people value a seismograph?
6. If you followed Confucianism, how would you behave toward your parents?
7. Why would a newspaper reporter dislike censorship?
8. What are some ways of finding out about your ancestors?
9. How is a middleman used if two people have something to sell to each other?
10. Why would an emperor decide to form 36 provinces?
11. Why would you expect a military commander to be a member of the nobility?

## Exploring Concepts

**A.** Five dynasties of China appear on the timeline below. Copy the timeline. Fill in the items associated with each dynasty from this list: the Great Wall of China, the Mandate of Heaven, the dragon-and-toad seismograph, the Bronze Age, bureaucracy, Confucius the teacher, oracle bones, feudalism, the invention of acupuncture, the Silk Road. Choose two related items and discuss the relationship between them.

**B.** The Chinese people were responsible for many inventions and ideas. Complete the following statements by telling why each invention or idea came about.

1. Irrigation of fields began when . . .
2. A new metal called bronze resulted . . .
3. A picture language developed because . . .
4. Feudalism was the outgrowth of . . .
5. A bureaucracy was formed to . . .
6. The seismograph was necessary because . . .
7. Emperor Wudi governed through Legalism and Confucianism because . . .
8. The concept of using a middleman developed because the emperors . . .
9. Iron-tipped drilling poles were invented because of a need to . . .
10. Lisi advised Qin to censor writers, scholars, and books because . . .

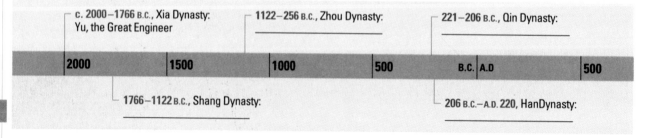

c. 2000–1766 B.C., Xia Dynasty: Yu, the Great Engineer

1122–256 B.C., Zhou Dynasty: _____

221–206 B.C., Qin Dynasty: _____

2000   1500   1000   500   B.C. | A.D   500

1766–1122 B.C., Shang Dynasty: _____

206 B.C.–A.D. 220, HanDynasty: _____

## Reviewing Skills

1. In the heated debate recorded on pages 273 and 274, the Moist asks the question "why shouldn't men of learning be rulers?" The Legalist's response contains some points that are irrelevant. Identify those points.
2. What point does the Moist make that is also irrelevant?
3. List four pieces of equipment shown in the paper-making process diagram on the right.
4. Using the diagram, write a brief description of the paper-making process.
5. Look at the map on page 265 of the Shang Dynasty in 1122 B.C. and the map on page 282 of the Han Dynasty in 87 B.C. What hypothesis can you make based on a comparison of the two maps?
6. The Yin-Yang stands for the blend of life's two opposing forces: the dark side and the bright side. What do you call something that stands for an idea?

**Paper-making Process**

Vat contains fibers in water solution

Mold is immersed, fibers distributed evenly, then drained

Molds dry on rack

Stirring pole

Mold with mesh screen

Paper is peeled off molds and stacked

## Using Critical Thinking

1. The thinkers of the Zhou dynasty explained life as a blend of two opposing forces—Yin, "the dark side of the hill," and Yang, "the bright side of the hill." How would you apply this idea to present-day events in the world or the nation? Which events are Yin, and which are Yang?
2. Ancestor worship and respect for the past were important ideas in ancient China. How do these ideas compare to present-day attitudes in America toward elderly people and toward the past?
3. During the Qin dynasty, an advisor named Lisi decreed that all books were useless unless they were about agriculture, medicine, or prophecy. What would you say to convince Lisi that other kinds of books are valuable too?

## Preparing for Citizenship

1. **WRITING ACTIVITY** If you could ask Confucius which qualities he thinks a candidate for president of the United States should have, what do you think he might reply? Base your answer on information concerning his teachings and beliefs that you read in this chapter or in other sources.
2. **COLLABORATIVE ACTIVITY** Reread the description of Qin's bureaucracy on pages 278–280. Think about the needs and responsibilities you have in working together as a class. Then set up a bureaucratic form of government in your class for a specified time. In class discussions, decide how many levels you will have and what they will be. Team up with two other people and choose a level. Each person on the team is responsible for one of the following decisions:
   (1) what the jobs will be at your level,
   (2) how you will determine who will do each job, and
   (3) what written rules you will need.
   Share your decisions with the other teams. Implement all decisions. At the end of the time allowed, each team should decide how well this system of government worked.

# Unit 5

# The Foundation of Western Ideas

*Just as these graceful columns support this Greek temple, the contributions of the Greeks and Israelites support our civilization today. The Greeks gave us basic ideas about government, arts, and thought. The Israelites contributed religious ideas that led to present-day Judaism and Christianity. The world we live in has its roots in all the peoples of the past. Yet our civilization—Western civilization—owes a special debt to the ancient Greeks and Israelites.*

# 2500 B.C.

**The Erechtheum, located on the Acropolis at Athens, Greece, built 421–405 B.C.**

323 B.C.

# Chapter 10

# *The Ancient Israelites*

Time after time, conquerors invaded Jerusalem, a city in present-day Israel. They destroyed its holy temple and drove its people away. But each time, the faith of the people drew them back. Jerusalem holds an important place in the history of three religions—Judaism, Christianity, and Islam. The shared traditions of the first two religions helped shape Western civilization.

The story of the Israelites, told in the Jewish Bible, is also part of the Old Testament of the Christian Bible (below).

| 2000 | 1500 | 1000 |
|------|------|------|

# 1900 B.C.

c. 1000 B.C. David, shown playing a harp in the painting above, becomes king of the Israelites. Under his leadership, they make Jerusalem their capital.

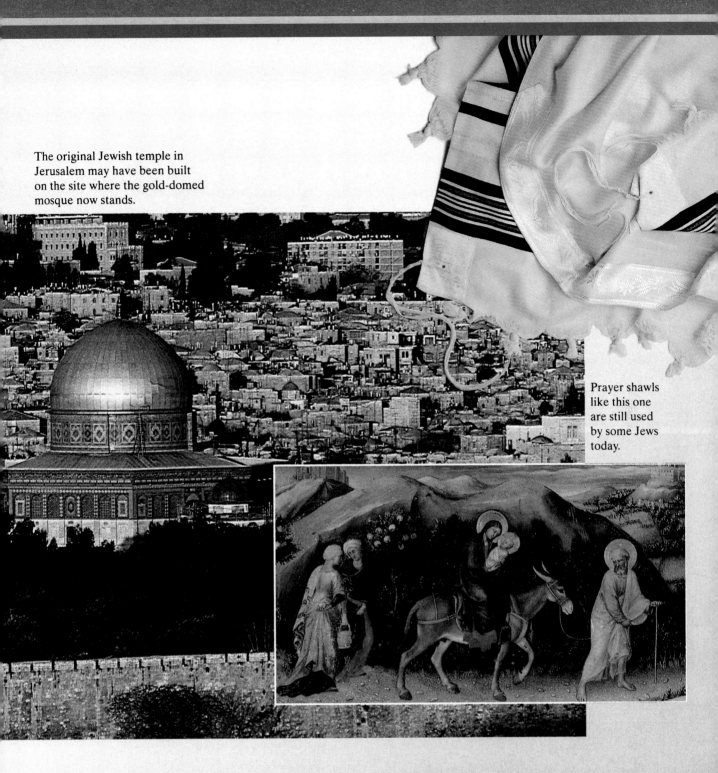

The original Jewish temple in Jerusalem may have been built on the site where the gold-domed mosque now stands.

Prayer shawls like this one are still used by some Jews today.

**587 B.C.** The Babylonians destroy Jerusalem and force the Jews into exile.

**c. 4 B.C.** The Christian story begins with the birth of Jesus. The painting above, from the A.D. 1400s, shows Mary, Joseph, and the baby Jesus.

| 500 | B.C. | A.D. | 500 |

**A.D. 132** After a Jewish revolt, Romans keep Jews from living in Jerusalem. Yet the Jewish religion endures.

A.D. 135

L E S S O N   1

# Early Biblical History

**THINKING**
**F O C U S**

*What role did the Israelites' relationship with their god play in the formation of their nation?*

### Key Terms

- monotheism
- Judaism
- Exodus
- covenant

"**W**as it for want of graves in Egypt that you brought us to die in the wilderness?" That is the question the Israelites asked their leader, Moses, as thousands of Egyptian soldiers chased them toward the sea in about 1250 B.C.

The Israelites were the early settlers of what is now the country of Israel. According to the Torah, the sacred book of the Jewish people, they were fleeing from slavery in Egypt. But they were trapped. They had no way to get across the water. The Torah tells the story of what happened next:

*T*hen Moses held out his arms over the sea and the Lord drove back the sea with a strong east wind all that night, and turned the sea into dry ground. The waters were split, and the Israelites went into the sea on dry ground, the waters forming a wall for them on their right and on their left.

Exodus 14: 21–22

Egyptian soldiers followed Moses and the Israelites, but the Torah teaches that Moses held out his arms, and the waters crashed down on the Egyptians. The entire army drowned.

➤ *Biblical stories have inspired many artists. This version of Moses and the Israelites escaping from the Egyptians, painted in the A.D. 1400s, shows how Europeans interpreted biblical events.*

# The Belief of the Israelites

The Israelites believed their god made their escape from Egypt possible. In fact, the Israelites saw themselves as the chosen people of their god.

### The God of the Israelites

The Israelites came to believe that there was only one true God. This idea was new to the ancient world. Other peoples prayed to different gods for different purposes. For example, the people of Mesopotamia had more than 3,000 gods. The Egyptians worshiped nature gods, the sun and spirits, and their own kings. In contrast, the god of the Israelites' was all-powerful, all-knowing, and present everywhere. **Monotheism** is the belief that there is only one god. This idea has had a lasting impact on Western civilization.

Many of our present-day beliefs about how people should treat each other can be traced to the people, events, and ideas you will study in this chapter. And like the ancient Israelites, many people today find meaning in history by viewing it as directed by one all-powerful god.

### The History of Biblical Times

The story of how the Israelites developed as a people is found in the first five books of the Bible. In **Judaism,** or the religion of the Jewish people, these books are called the Torah. The Torah contains the basic laws of Judaism and traces the history of the Israelites through the 1200s B.C. In the Christian Bible, these books are the first five books of the Old Testament.

Historians rely on the stories told in the Bible to understand the history of the Israelites and the development of their belief in one god. But it is important to remember that the Israelites wrote their stories to explain their faith in God. These stories celebrate the power of God over nature and history.

Although many people believe that the scriptures are a factual record of biblical times, most historians combine them with other kinds of evidence. Historians use the Bible, archaeological artifacts, and other written records of the time period to interpret the events and ideas of biblical times. ■

*The ancestors of the Israelites worshipped many gods, including Baal, shown in this goldplated bronze statuette from about 1300 B.C. However, the Israelites came to believe that there was only one true God.*

■ *What is monotheism?*

# The Origins of the Israelites

According to Genesis, the first book of the Torah, God created the heavens and earth. But God became upset with humankind and finally decided to create a new nation within the human family. God commanded a shepherd named Abraham from the city of Ur in Mesopotamia to move to Canaan in about 1900 B.C. According to Genesis, God told him, "Go forth from your native land and from

The Ancient Israelites

your father's house to the land that I will show you. I will make of you a great nation." (Genesis 12: 1–2) Genesis tells how God brought that nation into being, beginning with the descendants of Abraham.

### The Land of the Israelites

Canaan was a small area, but it held an important place in the ancient world because of its location. Find Canaan on the map below. Why do you think the location was so important to the neighboring nations?

Canaan was an important trading route, market, and battlefield. It lay in the path of expansion for both Egypt and Assyria, two of the larger and more powerful nations of the ancient world. The land of Canaan was quite varied. It included fertile plains, grassy slopes, rocky hills, and arid deserts.

Many different people lived together in Canaan. Most were herders rather than farmers. These nomads lived in tents and traveled from place to place seeking pasture for their sheep, goats, or cattle. Gradually, they came together as a people and were called the Hebrews.

Canaan became the homeland of the Hebrews, but the area was not always a good place to live. As a result of several famines, some Hebrews migrated into Egypt. According to the Torah, the Hebrews became slaves of the Egyptians

▼ *Where was Canaan in relation to Babylonia and Egypt?*

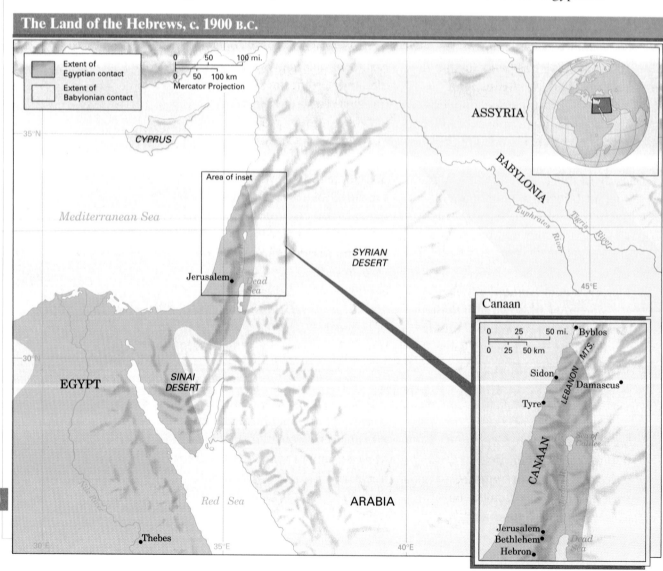

**The Land of the Hebrews, c. 1900 B.C.**

Extent of Egyptian contact
Extent of Babylonian contact

0  50  100 mi.
0  50  100 km
Mercator Projection

ASSYRIA
CYPRUS
35°N
BABYLONIA
Area of inset
Mediterranean Sea
Euphrates River
Tigris River
SYRIAN DESERT
45°E
Jerusalem
Dead Sea

Canaan
0  25  50 mi.
0  25  50 km
Byblos
Sidon
LEBANON MTS.
Damascus
Tyre
CANAAN
Sea of Galilee
30°N
EGYPT
SINAI DESERT
Jerusalem
Bethlehem
Hebron
Dead Sea

Red Sea
ARABIA
Nile River
Thebes
30°E
35°E
40°E

◄ Imagine what it would have been like for the Israelites to travel through the barren, rocky landscape around Mount Sinai.

## How Do We Know?

**HISTORY** *Unlike other religious scriptures you have encountered so far in learning about ancient cultures, the Bible is an important source of historical information. In addition to explaining the faith of the Israelites, the Bible describes events of biblical times. It also provides a record of the thoughts, ideas, and laws of the people in the land of the Israelites.*

about 1700 B.C. and remained slaves for 430 years.

The Hebrews became known as Israelites because of Abraham's grandson Jacob. The book of Genesis states that God appeared to Jacob one day and said, "You shall be called Jacob no more, but Israel shall be your name." (Genesis 35: 10) Jacob's children, and the generations of believers in this god that followed, came to be known as Israelites.

### The Leadership of Moses

The Torah teaches that the Israelites bitterly resented their slavery in Egypt, but they did not revolt because they lacked a strong leader. Finally, in the early 1200s B.C., the Israelites found a strong leader in Moses. According to the Torah, God armed Moses with miraculous powers to persuade the Egyptian ruler to free the Israelites. Terrifying plagues, or outbreaks of disease and destruction, rained down on the Egyptians. Water turned into blood. Frogs, lice, and insects swarmed over Egyptian cities and fields. Hail, thunder, locusts, and darkness

also covered the land. After each plague, the frightened pharaoh agreed to free the Israelites. But time and again he changed his mind.

The tenth plague was the most terrible. According to the Torah, God killed the first-born child in every family in Egypt. When the Egyptian ruler saw so many of his people dead, he let the Israelites go. Moses led them across the sea.

The escape was the beginning of a long and difficult journey back to their homeland. This journey is called the **Exodus,** or departure. Great stretches of desert wilderness separated the Israelites from their homeland. As the map on page 303 shows, the Israelites took a roundabout route to reach their homeland. The Torah states that the trek lasted 40 years. The Exodus is celebrated in the Jewish festival of Passover. Refer to A Closer Look on page 302. What parts of the Seder ceremony relate to Exodus experiences? ■

▲ *According to the Torah, a plague of locusts descended on Egypt, ruining crops.*

■ *Trace the origins of the Israelites.*

The Ancient Israelites

# A Meal That Tells a Story

*The Seder is a meal Jews eat during the springtime holiday of Passover. Every item on the table symbolizes part of the Passover story.*

**A roasted egg** stands for spring as well as ancient holiday offerings.

**Flat matza bread** reminds Jews how quickly their ancestors left Egypt: they had no time to let bread dough rise.

**A special bowl** and pitcher are often part of the opening ceremonies of the Seder. The pitcher holds water used for a ritual washing of the hands.

**Four cups of wine** remind the drinker of the four promises God made to the Israelites.

**When the temple stood** in Jerusalem, priests sacrificed a lamb at Passover. The roasted bone symbolizes that ancient rite.

**Like salty tears of slavery,** a green vegetable dipped in salt water symbolizes the captivity and renewal of the Jewish people.

**The sharp taste** of bitter herbs (horseradish) recalls the bitterness of slavery.

**A mixture of apples,** honey, nuts, wine, and spices, Charoset stands for the mortar binding the bricks that the enslaved Jews baked for the Egyptians.

## An Agreement with God

The Torah teaches that during the Exodus Moses climbed to the top of Mount Sinai, where God spoke to him and gave him a message to pass on to his people. This message was about a **covenant,** or special agreement, that would bind the Israelites to God. According to the covenant, God promised to love and protect the Israelites. In return, the Israelites agreed to love God and follow God's laws: "And now, O Israel, what does the Lord your God demand of you? Only this: to revere the Lord your God, to walk only in His paths, to love Him, and to serve the Lord your God with all your heart and soul." (Deuteronomy 10:12)

The Torah explains that the first of these laws were written down on two great stone tablets that Moses carried down with him from Mount Sinai. These written laws are also known as the Ten Commandments:

I the Lord am your God who brought you out of the land of Egypt, the house of bondage: You shall have no other gods besides Me.

You shall not make for yourself a sculptured image. . . .

You shall not swear falsely by the name of the Lord your God . . .

Remember the sabbath day and keep it holy. . . .

Honor your father and your mother, that you may long endure on the land that the Lord your God is assigning to you.

You shall not murder.

You shall not commit adultery.

You shall not steal.

You shall not bear false witness against your neighbor.

You shall not covet [desire] . . . anything that is your neighbor's.

Exodus 20: 3–14

By accepting the covenant, the Israelites accepted God as their king. They accepted the commandments as laws of God's kingdom.

**The Exodus of the Israelites from Egypt**

*Find Mount Sinai on the map.*

In the centuries that followed, this religious idea of a covenant between a single god and a people would become the basis for both Judaism and Christianity. The Jewish and Christian belief that people serve God by acting responsibly toward each other can be traced directly to the special covenant made by the Israelites. In addition, the Ten Commandments form the basis of much of the Western world's ideas about law and justice. ■

■ *Why did the Israelites agree to obey the Ten Commandments?*

## R E V I E W

1. **FOCUS** What role did the Israelites' relationship with their god play in the formation of their nation?
2. **CONNECT** The Ten Commandments contained rules of conduct for the Israelites to follow. What teachings of Buddhism contained rules of conduct for Buddhists to follow?
3. **BELIEF SYSTEMS** Explain the covenant the Israelites made with their god.
4. **CRITICAL THINKING** The Israelites wrote the stories contained in the Torah to explain why they believed in their god. Why would this fact be important to historians?
5. **ACTIVITY** The land of the ancient Israelites is now divided into several nations. Use the map on page 300 and the maps of the Time/Space Databank to find out what nations now occupy the land.

303

The Ancient Israelites

# Esther

## Miriam Chaikin

*The ancient Israelites believed that God would protect them from persecution. But they often were involved in fighting persecution themselves. This story is about Esther, Queen of Persia, who risks her life to save her people.*

*One of the heroines of the Hebrew Bible is Esther. Here is a retelling of her story.*

*Mordecai* (MAWR dih ky)

*Ahasuerus* (ay haz yoo EE ruhs)

S hushan was a large and busy city. Persians, Medes, Indians, Jews, and others lived there. One of the Jews was Mordecai, the scribe. In those days, most people could not read or write. Mordecai wrote letters and documents for them from his seat inside the palace gate.

The king's ministers arrived in the street where Mordecai lived. Esther, his orphan niece, lived with him. She was very beautiful. Mordecai told her, "If the ministers choose to bring you before the king, do not tell them that you are a Jew. There are those who would do us harm."

The ministers *did* choose Esther.

And when King Ahasuerus saw her, he fell in love with her and made her his queen.

Mordecai and Esther kept secret the fact that they were related. But each day, Mordecai stopped at the queen's gate to ask the guards how Esther was.

In the spring, in the Hebrew month of Nisan, Mordecai heard two guards plotting to poison the king. Mordecai told Esther, and Esther told the king. The king ordered the guards hanged. His secretary, who recorded all important events, recorded this event also in the royal diary.

In the same month the king promoted Haman, a palace noble, to chief minister. Haman thought of himself as a god to be worshiped. The people of Shushan bowed down to Haman because of his high position. But Mordecai would not bow to him.

Each time Mordecai refused to bow, Haman's anger grew. One day, he decided to kill not only Mordecai, but all the Jews. And he went to a fortuneteller to pick a lucky date for his scheme.

The fortuneteller took up his *pur*, a stone marked "yes" on one side and "no" on the other. "Is the first month Haman's lucky month?" he asked, and tossed the *pur*.

The *pur* answered,"No." The fortuneteller kept tossing the *pur* until Haman received as a lucky date the thirteenth day of the month of Adar.

Needing the king's permission for his scheme, Haman went to the palace. "There are people in your kingdom who are different from us," he said. "They obey strange laws. They are a menace and a danger. With the king's permission, I will have them killed."

The king removed his ring. He gave it to Haman and said, "The ring is yours—the people also. Do as you see fit."

The ring was the royal seal, the king's own signature. With it Haman could pass laws. He passed this law and sent copies throughout the kingdom:

To all governors in Persia and in the 127 provinces, Attention! Kill all Jews, young and old, on the thirteenth of Adar, and seize their possessions.

A copy of the law was posted in Shushan. And when Mordecai and the Jews read it, they wept and cried aloud.

Esther, in the palace, heard their cries. She sent a servant to find out what had happened. Mordecai gave the servant a copy of the law for Esther. He also sent her this message: "Go to the king. Speak to him. Save your people."

To this Esther answered, "I am not allowed to go before the king unless he sends for me."

"You must," replied Mordecai. "Don't think you will escape harm on the thirteenth of Adar. Besides, it is possible that you became queen so that you could save your people."

Esther agreed. She asked Mordecai and all the Jews to pray for her safety and to fast for three days. She planned to do the same. "Then I will go in to the king," she said. "And if I perish, I perish."

After the fast, Esther put on a royal gown and went to see the king. She was frightened. The king had not sent for her. He might order the guards to seize her, or have her beheaded for coming without permission. Instead, he received her kindly. He raised his scepter to her and invited her in.

"What is your wish, my queen?" Ahasuerus asked. "I am prepared to give you up to half my kingdom."

"If it please the king," Esther said, "let him come with his chief minister to a wine banquet that I have prepared."

The king sent his servants to fetch Haman. And he and the chief minister went in to Esther's banquet.

"What is your wish, my queen?" the king asked again as Esther's servant poured wine. "I am prepared to give you up to half my kingdom."

Esther still did not tell Ahasuerus the real reason for her banquet. "Let the king and his chief minister come here again tomorrow," she said. "I will speak of it then."

gallows   two upright
beams and a cross
beam supporting a
noose used for hanging

Haman left the palace feeling mighty. What an honor he
had received. He had been the only guest of the king and queen!
Everyone moved aside to make way for him—everyone but
Mordecai, who remained standing where he was.

Haman spoke of his fury to his wife and ten sons. "The queen
honored me today," he said. "She will honor me again tomorrow.
But it all means nothing to me when I see the Jew, Mordecai. Why
must I wait to see him dead?"

"Why wait?" asked his wife. "Order a gallows made, and in
the morning go to the king and ask for permission to hang
Mordecai."

Haman did as his wife suggested—he ordered a gallows.

Meanwhile, in the palace the king could not sleep. To pass the
time, his secretary read aloud to him from the royal diary. The
secretary read how Mordecai had saved the king's life. "What
honor did I bestow upon Mordecai?" the king asked.

"None," said the secretary.

Outside, Haman arrived in the courtyard to ask the king for
permission to hang Mordecai.

"Haman wishes to see the king," the guard announced.

"Let him enter," the king said.

"There is a man I wish to honor," the king told Haman. What
shall I do for him?"

Haman was sure the honor was for himself. "Let the man be
seen riding the king's horse, on whose head a royal crown has
been set," he said. "And let a palace noble lead him through the
streets crying, 'Here is the man the king wishes to honor!'"

"Do as you suggest," said the king. "You are the palace noble.
Mordecai is the man I wish to honor."

Bitter and ashamed, Haman led Mordecai through the streets
crying, "Here is the man the king wishes to honor!"

Later, when Haman sat reclining beside the king at Esther's
banquet, he tried to hide his feelings behind a smile.

"You promised to speak of your wish today, my queen," Ahasuerus said to Esther.

Now, at last, Esther told the king what was in her heart. "A
law has been passed in your name saying that my people and I
are to be killed."

The king leaped from his couch. "Who would dare do such a
thing?" he asked.

"This evil man," Esther said as she pointed to Haman.

Harbonah, a guard, said, "What's more, your Majesty, Haman
has built a gallows. He plans to hang Mordecai this very night."

"Hang Haman on it instead!" the king cried.

Esther now told the king that Mordecai was her uncle. And
when Mordecai came before the king, the king gave Mordecai the

ring he had taken from Haman. And he named Mordecai the new chief minister.

All would have been well but for Haman's law. Esther threw herself at the king's feet. "Please cancel Haman's evil decree. Let my people live," she pleaded.

The king lifted her up. "Not even the king can cancel a royal decree in the Persian empire," he said. "But Mordecai now wears my ring. He can pass whatever law he wishes concerning the Jews."

This was the law that Mordecai passed and sent throughout the kingdom:

To all governors in Persia and in the 127 provinces.

Attention! Let the Jews organize to defend them-selves on the thirteenth of Adar. Let them slay their attackers.

Mordecai was now a great man in Persia.  How proud the Jews were to see him in his robes of royal blue and wearing a crown upon his head. Nevertheless, on the thirteenth of Adar the evildoers rose up to slay the Jews. But the opposite happened. The Jews slew their attackers instead, including the ten sons of Haman.

Upon Esther's request, the king ordered Haman's ten sons hung in the public square as a warning to any who would harm the Jews.

The Jews celebrated their rescue with great rejoicing and a feast. And Esther and Mordecai wrote a letter to all Jews throughout the kingdom telling them to celebrate the rescue for-ever. They called the holiday Purim because of the *pur*.

From that day more than two thousand years ago, Jews all over the world celebrate Purim each year on the fourteenth and fifteenth of Adar. They read aloud Esther's story, send presents to one another, and make merry.

**Further Reading**

*Brothers, A Hebrew Legend*. Florence B. Freedman. Dan and Joel are brothers who look out for each other in this ancient Hebrew legend.

*Digging Up Bible Lands*. Ronald Harker. Historians study archaeological finds to learn about history. This book examines eight archaeological digs in the Middle East for information about Biblical history.

*Exodus*. Miriam Chaikin. This is the story of how Moses led the Israelites out of Egypt over 3,000 years ago.

*I Am Joseph*. Barbara Cohen. A young boy named Joseph is sold into slavery and taken to Egypt. By helping the pharaoh, he wins his freedom and is able to reunite with his family.

L E S S O N   2

# Kings, Prophets, and Priests

*How did Israel develop as an independent Jewish nation?*

---

## Key Terms

* prophet
* messiah

**D**ay and night for 40 days, the giant Goliath shouted his challenge to the soldiers of Israel. "Choose one of your men and let him come down against me. If he bests me in combat and kills me, we will become your slaves; but if I best him and kill him, you shall be our slaves and serve us." (I Samuel 17: 8–9)

According to the story told in the Bible, Goliath was the great warrior of the Philistines, a people who were fighting the Israelites for control of Canaan during the 1000s B.C. No one in the Israelite camp would accept Goliath's challenge. No one, that is, until a boy named David came into the camp.

David went to a nearby brook,

gathered five smooth stones, and put them in his leather bag. Then he went out to face Goliath. According to the Bible,

*D**avid put his hand into the bag; he took out a stone and slung it. It struck the Philistine in the forehead; the stone sank into his forehead, and he fell face down on the ground. Thus David bested the Philistine with sling and stone; he struck him down and killed him.*

I Samuel 17: 49–50

When the Philistines saw their warrior was dead, they ran. The Israelites treated David as a hero. This young boy grew up to become the king of the Israelites.

➤ *In the time of David, slings and stones were common weapons. This stone carving illustrates the Bible story of David slaying Goliath.*

## The Monarchy

The battle with the Philistines was one of many the Israelites fought with other peoples living in Canaan between the 1200s and the 1000s B.C. During this time, the Israelites formed a loose association of tribes in the central hill country of Canaan. However, the battles between the Israelites and other peoples for the control of Canaan convinced the Israelites that they needed a king to unite them and lead them.

In 1020 B.C., the Israelites chose a man named Saul as their first king. Saul led the Israelites in the fight against the Philistines, but he was unable to defeat them. That job fell to David, who became the second king of the Israelites.

### The Reign of David

David was 30 years old when he became king, and he governed Israel for 40 years. David brought together all the tribes of Israel. Under his leadership, the Israelites were finally able to defeat the Philistines. They also captured the city of Jerusalem and made it the capital of the Israelite nation. The Israelite empire grew to include land from the Sinai Peninsula as far east as Damascus.

David began a dynasty that lasted for more than 400 years. According to the Bible, the dynasty fulfilled a pledge God made to David: "I will establish a home for My people Israel and will plant them firm, so that they shall dwell secure and shall tremble no more." (II Samuel 7: 10–11)

When David died in 961 B.C., his son Solomon came to power. During Solomon's rule the kingdom was at peace. Solomon showed his skill as a diplomat by making treaties with the pharaoh of Egypt and other rulers. These treaties assured Israel's safety.

Solomon also found new trading partners so that the Israelites could increase the country's wealth. Finally, he began a royal building program, constructing many palaces, forts, and temples throughout the land.

### A Temple for Jerusalem

Solomon's most famous building project was the main temple in Jerusalem. The temple became the center of religious life for the

309

The Ancient Israelites

Israelites and a symbol of their faith. The Bible tells of the great beauty of the temple. Cedar beams specially brought from Lebanon held up the roof. Ivory covered the outer doors. Gold decorated the walls of the holiest rooms.

When Solomon died in 922 B.C., Israel was a much stronger nation. But its growth had put a burden of heavy taxes on the people. These taxes were needed to pay for the building projects. King Solomon also required the men of Israel to work on the buildings without pay.

### Two Kingdoms

People began to resent the burden the king placed upon them. After Solomon's death, this resentment turned into revolt. The tribes in the northern part of Israel decided to choose their own king and move their capital to Samaria. Solomon's son Rehoboam, who had been chosen to succeed, was not strong enough to stop them.

The land of the Israelites was divided into two kingdoms. The northern kingdom continued to be known as Israel. The southern kingdom, with its capital city Jerusalem, was renamed Judah. (The word "Jew" comes from the name Judah.)

Because the temple was there, Jerusalem remained an important city for both northerners and southerners. The two kingdoms were divided politically, but they remained united by their religion.

The two kingdoms existed side by side for about 200 years. Then both fell to foreign powers. The Assyrians conquered Israel in 721 B.C. In 587 B.C., Judah fell to the Babylonians. ■

■ *What caused Israel to be divided into two kingdoms?*

## The Message of the Prophets

The Babylonians not only took control of Judah but destroyed the entire city of Jerusalem and the temple. About 15,000 Jews were taken to Babylonia as prisoners.

At this point, the future of the Israelites looked very bleak. Had the god of the Israelites abandoned the chosen people? According to a remarkable group of men known as the prophets, the answer to this question was no.

The **prophets,** who interpreted the will of God, told the Jews that they had only themselves to blame. The Jews had failed to obey God's teachings—they had broken their covenant with God. Now they were being punished.

The prophets were not fortune tellers who predicted the future.

*The French artist Jean Fouquet painted this version of the detruction of Jerusalem by the Babylonians in the A.D. 1400s.*

Instead, they preached a message about how the people should act in the present.

The prophets warned that God would punish greed, unfairness to others, and the worship of other gods. Punishment would fall not only on the individual wrongdoer but on the nation as a whole.

The Jews believed the message meant that God would use other nations to punish the Jews. In other words, the prophets taught that God had power over all peoples, not just the Jews. As a result, the Jews came to believe that their god alone controlled all nations and directed the course of history.

Jeremiah, one of the better-known prophets, preached during the time that the Babylonians conquered Judah. The Bible records his speech at the gates of the temple in Jerusalem. Jeremiah urges the Jews to change their ways, telling them that God declares:

> I f you do not oppress the stranger, the orphan, and the widow; if you do not shed the blood of the innocent in this place; if you do not follow other gods, to your own hurt—then only will I let you dwell in this place, in the land that I gave to your fathers for all time.
>
> Jeremiah 7: 6–7

According to the prophets, the people did not heed the warning. As a result, the Jews were exiled from the promised land when the Babylonians conquered them.

However, by accepting the prophets' explanation for the disaster, the Jews could keep their faith in God and survive exile. In this way, the prophets offered hope for the future. They preached that if the Jews obeyed the laws of God, they would someday be able to return to their homeland. ■

■ *According to the prophets, why was Judah captured by Babylonia?*

## A People Governed by Priests

The exile of the Jews in Babylon lasted about 50 years. Then in 540 B.C., the Persian ruler Cyrus the Great took control of Babylon.

Cyrus allowed the Jews in Babylon to return to Judah. However, the Jews were not allowed to rule their homeland. Jerusalem and the surrounding territory remained a province of the Persian empire.

Without a king of their own, the leadership of the Jewish people fell to their priests. They saw to it that the great temple of Jerusalem was rebuilt. They also guided the people in celebrating religious holidays and in following Jewish law. The Jews used their religious beliefs to govern themselves.

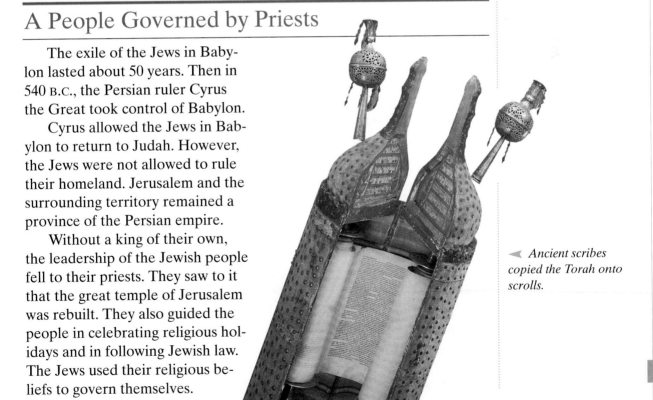

◄ *Ancient scribes copied the Torah onto scrolls.*

The Ancient Israelites

### The Laws of the Torah

The laws of the Jews were contained in the writings that made up what are now the first five books of the Bible. However, at that time there were many different versions of these holy writings. No one version was accepted as law by Jews in all parts of the ancient world.

Then in the 400s B.C., a priest and scribe named Ezra returned from exile in Babylon. He brought with him a collection of the many versions of holy writings that had been put together by Jewish scribes in Babylon.

This document was the Torah, the sacred history and laws of the Israelite people. The Torah contains the books of Genesis, Exodus, Leviticus, Numbers, and Deuteronomy, which then became

## UNDERSTANDING LAW

When Ezra, the priest and scribe, returned to Jerusalem from exile in Babylon in the 400s B.C., he carried with him a letter from the King of Persia. The letter told Ezra's duty: "For you are commissioned by the king and his seven advisers to regulate Judah and Jerusalem according to the law of your God, which is in your care." (Ezra 7: 14)

All societies establish laws to govern themselves. The authority may come from a supreme leader or from the people. In most societies, an important part of law is a sense of justice, or fairness.

### What Is Law?

Every society or group of people needs to establish customs, rules, and patterns of accepted behavior. Law is the set of guidelines a group of people or society uses to govern itself.

However, law is more than just individual rules. Law is a code of conduct for a group of people. The law of the Torah established the religious and social rules by which the Jews governed themselves. The law code of a nation establishes the rules governing both the rights and obligations of its people.

### Who Makes Laws?

In early societies, laws often came from the authority of the king or ruler. One of the early written codes was Hammurabi's code. This was a set of rules of behavior and punishments established by the Babylonian king Hammurabi in the 1700s B.C. The Jews believed that the law of the Torah came from the authority of God, whom the Jews accepted as their king.

In the United States today, federal, state, and local officials elected by the people have the power to make laws. The courts have the power to review laws and even change them to make sure they are just. The courts also decide the punishments for breaking laws.

### What Is Justice?

Today, most people agree that laws should be just—they should be applied in a way that treats people fairly. The law of the Torah played an important role in establishing the ideal of justice. In the book of Leviticus, judges are told that they "must not make an unfair decision. Do not favor the poor or show deference to the rich. Judge your neighbor fairly." (Leviticus 19: 15) what is today the first part of the Jewish Bible.

The Torah brought back by Ezra became the accepted version of Judaism's holiest writings. With the backing of the Persian authorities, Ezra demanded that the Jews obey the Torah and separate themselves from people who did not. From the 400s B.C. forward, Judaism was defined by obeying the laws set down in the Torah.

### The Hope for a Messiah

In the 400s B.C., the Jews had both the Torah and a rebuilt temple to help them guide their faith. However, they did not have their independence. Many Jews hoped that one day Israel would again be an independent nation, as it had been during the time of King David.

They searched for a leader who would free them from foreign rule.

The name they gave this hoped-for leader was **messiah** *(muh SY uh)*, which means "anointed one." They believed the Messiah would bring peace and justice. The idea that a messiah would someday come and free the people became a part of the Jewish belief. ■

*Jews examine a Torah scroll in Jerusalem, near the site of the original temple.*

■ *How was the Torah of central importance to the Jews?*

## The Revolt of the Maccabees

The Jews continued to govern themselves by the laws of the Torah with little outside interference until about 200 B.C. Then the reign of the Torah was challenged by new rulers from Syria. These new rulers brought with them ideas from the Greek culture that had flourished for centuries across the Mediterranean Sea.

Some Jews also admired Greek culture. They learned to speak Greek, gave themselves Greek names, and dressed in Greek robes. Some even accepted Greek religious ideas.

Many other Jews, especially highly religious Jews, rejected Greek religious beliefs. Religious Jews did not object to Syrian rule,

but they did not want Syrian rulers to interfere in Jewish religious practices. They feared that the Syrians would try to make them worship Greek gods.

Their fears came true in 175 B.C., when a new ruler, Antiochus *(ahn TEE uh kuhs)*, came to power in Syria. Antiochus forced Jews to adopt Greek customs. His officials even placed a statue of the Greek god Zeus on the temple gate. Officers of the Syrian king went throughout the land ordering Jewish priests to make offerings to Greek gods.

However, a Jewish priest named Mattathias refused. He and his five sons fled into the hills of Judah to organize a revolt. Many

The Ancient Israelites

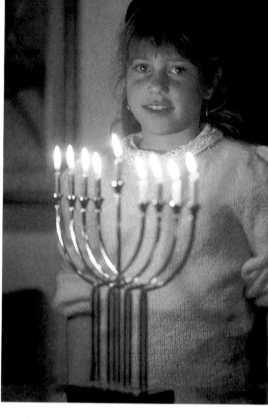

➤ *When the Jews rededicated the temple after defeating the Syrians, they only had enough oil to light their holy lamps for one day. Yet according to tradition, the lamps burned for eight days. Today, during the festival of Chanukah, Jews light the candles of the menorah to celebrate this event.*

Jews joined the fight, hoping for a chance to free their land from foreign rule and gain independence. Led by Mattathias's son Judah Maccabee, the rebels fought a two-year war against the Syrian soldiers.

The word *Maccabee* means "hammer." Like hammers, Judah Maccabee and his followers were hard-hitting fighters. They were known as the Maccabees. They used hit-and-run tactics against the Syrians. The Maccabees attacked in the dark and set fire to Syrian camps. They hid themselves behind rocks and jumped down on the Syrians as they came through narrow paths in the hills.

In 164 B.C., the Maccabees drove the Syrians out of the area around Jerusalem. The reign of the Torah was restored. For the next 80 years, Judah was an independent nation once again.

The temple in Jerusalem was rededicated with a special service in December of 164 B.C. Since that time Jews everywhere have celebrated the victory of Maccabean rebels on the festival known as Chanukah *(HAH nuh kuh)*. ■

■ *What was the result of the revolt of the Maccabees?*

## R E V I E W

1. **FOCUS** How did Israel develop as an independent Jewish nation?
2. **CONNECT** Why did King Nebuchadnezzar of Babylonia conquer Judah in 587 B.C. and force the Jews into exile?
3. **GEOGRAPHY** Why did the location of the Israelites' homeland make them particularly subject to invasion?
4. **BELIEF SYSTEMS** The prophets said that the Jews had broken their covenant with God. Summarize the things the Jews needed to do to "mend their ways."
5. **CRITICAL THINKING** The land of the Jews was conquered by several foreign powers. Why was Judaism able to survive and prosper?
6. **WRITING ACTIVITY** Imagine you were with the Jews when they were conquered by the Babylonians and forced into exile. Write a journal entry describing what it is like to be forced to live away from your homeland.

314

Chapter 10

L E S S O N   3

# Religious Developments

A man was going down from Jerusalem to Jericho, and he fell among robbers, who stripped him and beat him, and departed leaving him half dead." So begins the parable of the good Samaritan. **Parables** are stories that teach moral lessons. In the first century A.D., a popular Jewish teacher named Jesus told this para-ble to answer the question, "Who is my neighbor?"

According to this parable, told in the New Testament of the Christian Bible, a priest came upon the beaten man, who was a Jew, but did not stop to help him. Instead, he passed by on the other side of the road. So did an assistant to a priest, also called a Levite. Finally, a Samaritan came upon the man.

THINKING
FOCUS

*How are Judaism and Christianity related?*

## Key Terms

- parable
- Diaspora
- disciple
- Resurrection
- Christianity
- rabbi
- synagogue

◄ *The teacher called Jesus is shown spreading his message in this Italian painting from the A.D. 1400s.*

315

The Ancient Israelites

➤ *Many artists have represented what Jesus may have looked like. This mosaic, from A.D. 1148, is inside the dome of the cathedral in Cefalu in northern Sicily.*

**Across Time & Space**

*In A.D. 532, a Christian monk named Dionysius Exiguus introduced the system used today to count years. He numbered years beginning with the year he believed Jesus was born. The initials A.D. mean* anno Domini, *"in the year of the Lord." The initials B.C. mean before Christ. Some people often prefer to use the initials C.E., meaning common era, and B.C.E, for before common era.*

He bandaged the man's wounds, brought him to an inn, and took care of him.

Samaritans, the people who lived in the city of Samaria, did not share all Jewish beliefs and practices. In fact, the Jews and Samaritans had little to do with each other, and were not expected to go out of their way for each other. Yet the Samaritan had sympathy for the injured man.

"Which of these three, do you think, proved neighbor to the man who fell among the robbers?" Jesus asked (Luke 10: 36). The answer, of course, was the Samaritan. Even though he might be expected to dislike Jews, the Samaritan showed compassion.

Jesus taught people to respect and love other people, no matter who they were. He stressed that the Kingdom of God was at hand and that people needed to come into a right relationship with God. In time, his ideas would grow into a new religion.

## The Teachings of Jesus

By the time Jesus started teaching, the Jewish community had changed a great deal. Jews had been settling in small groups all over the Mediterranean ever since their release from exile in Babylonia in the 500s B.C.

This scattering of Jewish settlements was called the **Diaspora** *(dy AS pur uh)*. The Jews of the Diaspora kept strong religious ties to their homeland. At the same time, they were also influenced by other cultures.

The Jews who returned to Judah after their exile began to disagree among themselves about how they should practice their religion. One major group, the Sadducees *(SAJ uh sees),* were in favor of following the traditional rituals in the temple. The other major group, called the Pharisees *(FAIR ih sees),* called on Jews to strictly follow the laws of the Torah in their daily lives, too.

Other, more radical groups existed as well. One was made up of the followers of Jesus. They believed that Jesus was the messiah promised in the Bible.

## The Life of Jesus

The story of the life of Jesus is told in the New Testament of the Bible. According to the New Testament, an angel appeared to a woman named Mary in the city of Nazareth about 2,000 years ago. The angel told her that she would have a child. The angel told Mary to name the child Jesus.

Mary and her husband Joseph were Jews, and when Jesus was born they raised him as a Jew. Jesus learned the laws and customs of Judaism and studied the Torah. As he grew older, Jesus became a religious teacher.

He based his teachings on traditional Jewish beliefs. For example, he stressed that people should obey the Ten Commandments and the teachings of the prophets. According to the New Testament, he told his followers, "Think not that I have come to abolish the law and the prophets; I have come not to abolish them but to fulfil them." (Matthew 5: 17)

According to the New Testament account, Jesus called for a new covenant. In the Sermon on the Mount, Jesus told people that they should act with kindness and love toward others, even their enemies. This teaching is best understood in the light of Jesus' preaching about the coming of God's kingdom.

You have heard that it was said, "An eye for an eye and a tooth for a tooth." But I say to you, Do not resist one who is evil. But if any one strikes you on the right cheek, turn to him the other also; and if any one would sue you and take your coat, let him have your cloak as well; and if any one forces you to go one mile, go with him two miles. Give to him who begs from you, and do not refuse him who would borrow from you.

Matthew 4: 38–42

*According to the New Testament, Jesus healed the sick and performed other miracles to demonstrate the power of God.*

Jesus taught that the day of judgment by God was nearing. He

317

The Ancient Israelites

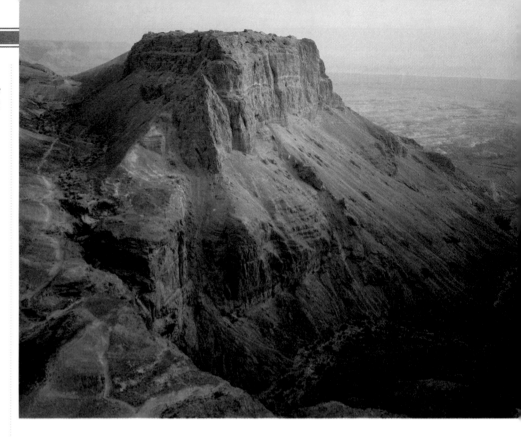

> *To attack Masada, the Romans built a ramp and placed it against the left side of the rock.*

sides of the rock. Instead, they decided to build a ramp of wood and earth.

They intended to place it against the side of the rock. Then they would roll their battering ram up the ramp and break down the wall of the fort.

After seven months of hard work, the ramp was ready. The Romans made their attack. Throughout one night, Roman soldiers battered the wall of the fort again and again with their battering ram.

Early in the morning, the wall came crashing down. However, the crash was followed by an eerie silence. The astonished soldiers heard no cries or screams. They saw no Jews ready to fight back.

What they saw instead was a horrifying sight: the bodies of 960 men, women, and children inside the fort. As a final act of resistance, they had killed themselves. They had not wanted to be taken prisoners by the Romans.

The Great Revolt had ended. Jerusalem was in ruins, and the temple was destroyed. Many Jews were taken by the Romans to other parts of the empire to work as slaves. The Jews revolted once again in A.D. 132, but the power of the Roman Empire was too strong.

After three years, the Romans crushed the Jewish resistance. After this last revolt, the Romans prohibited Jews from living in Jerusalem. ■

*■ Why did the Jews revolt against the Romans?*

## The Jewish Legacy

The battles with the Romans left the Jews without their temple, their priests, and their homeland. Yet the Jewish people did not disappear from history as some other ancient peoples had. The Jews adapted to their new situation.

Wherever Jews settled, they held on to their religion by relying on the Torah. Their temple had

Chapter 10

been destroyed, but the Torah was their portable temple. They viewed the Torah as the presence of God wherever they found themselves.

They also had **rabbis** to teach them the Torah. *Rabbi* is the Hebrew word for master or teacher. Beginning about the first century A.D., this title was given to teachers of the Torah. Over time a rabbi came to mean someone who could decide questions of Jewish law.

As Jews settled in other lands, rabbis helped them continue to learn about and practice Jewish traditions. Rabbis were leaders of the community as well. They settled arguments and taught people how to treat each other fairly according to the laws of the Torah.

In addition to relying on the Torah and the rabbis, the Jews built **synagogues**, the Jewish houses of worship. The temple in Jerusalem had been the center of sacrificial Jewish worship, but long before the Roman invasion, the Pharisees had built synagogues throughout the Roman empire. They were places for Jews to pray and study the Torah.

After the destruction of the temple by the Romans, the synagogue became the center of Jewish religious and community life. Wherever groups of Jews settled, they built synagogues. In their new homelands, Jews made the synagogue a place for social gatherings as well as religious worship.

Even though the Jewish people did not have a homeland after the Romans defeated them, their religion did not die out. By relying on the Torah and the teachings of the rabbis, the Jews developed ways of practicing their religion and ideas of social justice that are still ongoing today. ■

## Across Time & Space

*Because of the central role played by rabbis, the form of Judaism that began to emerge in the first century is called rabbinic Judaism. Through the centuries to come rabbis interpreted the law to cover new situations as they arose. Their interpretations drew not only on the written Torah but also on oral tradition believed to have been passed down from the time of Moses. Around the year 200, rabbis compiled this oral tradition in written form as the Mishnah. The Mishnah plus commentaries on it form the Talmud, which along with the Torah has guided traditional Jewish belief and practice up to the present.*

■ *How did the Jewish religion survive after the Roman attacks?*

▼ *Trace the early history of the Jewish people.*

## The History of Biblical Times

c. 1900 B.C., Abraham settles in Canaan.

c. 1250 B.C., Moses leads the Exodus from Egypt.

c. 721 B.C., Assyria conquers Israel.

c. 164 B.C., The Maccabees revolt.

C. A.D. 73, Masada falls to the Romans.

| 2000 | 1500 | 1000 | 500 | B.C. | A.D. | 500 |

c. 1000 B.C., David becomes king.

c. 587 B.C., Babylonia conquers Judah.

4 B.C.– A.D. 33, The life of Jesus.

## REVIEW

1. **FOCUS** How are Judaism and Christianity related?
2. **CONNECT** How were the teachings of Jesus similar to those of other Jews? How were they different?
3. **BELIEF SYSTEMS** The Jewish people did not disappear from history after the Romans put down the Jewish revolts. Summarize the ways the Jews kept their religion alive.
4. **CRITICAL THINKING** Why were Roman leaders more concerned with Jesus' power as a leader than with his religious teachings?
5. **ACTIVITY** Imagine you are a television reporter covering the Roman assault on Masada. Prepare a news report on this event. Be sure to answer the questions who, what, when, where, why, and how.

# Using Analogies

### Here's Why

Sometimes the best way of explaining something is to compare it to something else, more familiar. When you compare two things that have something in common but are otherwise quite different, you are using an analogy.

Jesus, like many other wise teachers before and since, often used analogies to make a point. His parables were more easily understood when he compared the unfamiliar with the familiar. By learning about analogies you will more quickly uncover their messages. You will also be able to use analogies yourself, to make your points more effectively.

### Here's How

Jesus sometimes told people who came to hear him that if they wanted to become one of his followers they would have to sell all that they owned. On one occasion, he said:

> Truly I say to you, it will be hard for a rich man to enter the kingdom of heaven. Again I tell you, it is easier for a camel to go through the eye of a needle than for a rich man to enter the kingdom of God.
>
> Matthew 19:23-24

The "eye of a needle" to which Jesus referred was actually a land formation in Israel. This was a pass between two rocks that was so narrow that camels had to be unloaded before they could squeeze through. Jesus was not saying that rich men and camels were alike. But a rich man, like the camel, had to be willing to give up some things in order to enter heaven.

### Try It

If you wanted to make a similar point now, how would you express it? What analogy could you use instead of a camel? How would you replace the "eye of the needle"?

Here is another analogy, this time from Hebrew scriptures:

> Like a loose tooth and an unsteady leg,
> Is a treacherous support in time of trouble.
>
> Proverbs 25:19

What is the analogy used here? What things are being compared? How would you make the same point if you were talking to one of your friends today?

### Apply It

Write some analogies of your own, and be prepared to read them to the class. In each case use for your comparison something that your classmates will understand. Begin with these:
1. Getting a good grade when you've cheated on an exam is like _____ .
2. An unfaithful friend is like _____ .
3. A kind word on a sad day is like _____ .
4. Not doing the best you can is like _____ .
5. Missing the school bus is like _____ .

# Reviewing Skills

1. Explain this analogy from a speech by Jesus called the "Sermon on the Mount":

> Enter by the narrow gate; for the gate is wide and the way is easy, that leads to destruction, and those who enter by it are many. For the gate is narrow and the way is hard, that leads to life, and those who find it are few.
>
> Matthew 7:13–14

2. Your best friend asks you to look at her science project on frogs. The presentation is good but very messy. What do you say?

3. Look at the map of Jerusalem on pages 492 and 493 of the Minipedia. Find the fortress and the road leading away from the fortress. What does that suggest to you about the enemies of Jerusalem? Were they more likely to be from Gaza, Jericho, or Bethlehem? Why do you think so?

4. Now look at the walls on the map. Where do you think the earliest city of Jerusalem was located? Compare the houses on either side of the Theater and its wall. What hypothesis might you make about the people who lived in each area?

5. Suppose you wanted to present a comparison of the religious views of the Sadducees and the Pharisees. In your presentation, you would like to show their differences very clearly. What would be the best way to do it?

# Using Critical Thinking

1. In most major religions, there are groups of people who share the same basic beliefs but differ as to how scriptures and laws should be interpreted. Sadducees, Pharisees, and the early followers of Jesus were examples of three such groups of Jews. Why do you think such groups arise?

2. Passover is a Jewish tradition not commonly observed by Christians today. Yet the events celebrated at Passover, as well as the celebration itself, are part of Christian tradition. Explain why both the story and the observance of Passover are important in the Christian tradition.

# Preparing for Citizenship

1. **WRITING ACTIVITY** When the word *exodus* is not capitalized, it refers to large numbers of people leaving an area. Examples of exoduses include the migrations of southern black people to northern cities, of Vietnamese "boat people" to the United States, and of eastern Europeans to the West in the 1980s. Learn all you can about an exodus. Then write a paragraph about it.

2. **WRITING ACTIVITY** Write an imaginary diary entry for a boy or girl who might have lived in Canaan, Israel, or Judah during the time period covered by the chapter. The entry should cover one day. It can be about an important event as seen through that boy or girl's eyes, or it can be about daily life. Give the entry a specific date.

3. **COLLABORATIVE LEARNING** Make a class bulletin board on the history and culture of the Jews from their beginnings around 1900 B.C. up to A.D. 400. To do this, form four to seven groups. Each group should then decide what to contribute to the bulletin board. For example, your group might work on the Hebrew calendar, language and writing, the Temple, King David, King Solomon, or dates and events. After each group has decided what to contribute, work as a whole class to plan the entire bulletin board. Then each group should complete its part of the bulletin board. For a look at Jerusalem see pages 492 and 493 in the Minipedia, and for important dates refer to the chapter.

# Chapter 11

## *The Ancient Greeks*

The blue waters of the Aegean Sea and the rugged mountains rising from its shores helped shape the civilization of the ancient Greeks. The mountains and the sea divided Greece into separate city-states. Shared customs and backgrounds drew these communities together. But at times bitter rivalries tore them apart.

**c. 2000–1450 B.C.** The Minoan civilization prospers on the island of Crete. The Minoans used golden axes like this one in religious ceremonies.

| 2500 | 2000 | 1500 |
|---|---|---|

# 2500 B.C.

**c. 1450–1100 B.C.** The Mycenaeans, the first mainland Greek civilization, conquer the Minoans and rule the Aegean region.

Spartan warriors march into battle on this vase, painted about 640 B.C.

Steep mountains limited travel on land, as this map from a later period shows. The Greeks turned to the sea instead.

c. 500 B.C. The city-state Athens, named after the Greek goddess Athena, develops the world's first democracy. Athena, shown above, was the goddess of warfare and wisdom.

| 1000 | 500 | B.C. | A.D. |

c. 700 B.C. Sparta becomes one of the most powerful city-states in Greece.

479 B.C.

LESSON 1

# The Early Greeks

### THINKING FOCUS

*What were some of the forces that influenced the rise of civilization in ancient Greece?*

### Key Term

• city-state

*B*ut come now, put it for me clearly, tell me the sea ways that you wandered, and the shores you touched; the cities, and the men therein, uncivilized, if such there were, and hostile, and those god-fearing who had kindly manners.

Homer, the *Odyssey*, c. 700 B.C.

An ancient king made this request of a great Greek hero named Odysseus (*oh DIHS yoos*), according to the *Odyssey*, an early masterpiece of Greek literature. The *Odyssey* retells the legends of the travels and adventures of Odysseus 3,000 years ago.

For 10 years, Odysseus wandered among the islands and coastal regions of what is now Greece, according to the tale. He endured shipwrecks, escaped from strange creatures such as a one-eyed giant called a cyclops, and met a variety of strange and wonderful people. Finally, he found his way back to his home.

These tales are just part of the rich heritage of the Greeks, a people who have had a lasting impact on Western civilization. Many present-day concepts of government, art, literature, science, and ideas can be traced to the ancient Greeks.

➤ *The ancient Greeks sailed in warships like the one shown on this vase painting. Note the soldiers' shields displayed above the oars.*

# The Land Around the Sea

According to the *Odyssey*, Odysseus wandered throughout the region known today as the Aegean *(ih JEE uhn)* Sea. He was seeking to return to his home in Ithaca after fighting in the Trojan War. Find the Aegean Sea and Ithaca on the map below. What do you notice about the geography of the region?

## The Geography of Greece

The area in which the ancient Greeks lived was centered on the Aegean. Between the 2000s B.C. and 100 B.C., these people developed a civilization there that grew to control the ancient world. Although many people settled on the peninsula called the Peloponnesus *(pehl oh puh NEE suhs)*, others settled on the numerous islands sprinkled throughout the Aegean.

The rugged mountains and the bays and inlets of the seas divided Greece into many small, isolated regions. The people who settled in each region formed closely knit communities. Sometimes neighboring groups became bitter enemies. At various times in Greek

▲ *The blue water of the Aegean Sea along the coast of Samos is shown above. Find Samos on the map below.*

## Ancient Greece, c. 1500 B.C.

The main crops grown in ancient Greece were grapes, grain, and olives (above). The vases below were used in the 500s B.C. to store crops. What crops were stored in each jar?

■ How did sea trade influence the growth of civilization in Greece?

history, these fierce rivalries erupted into wars.

The sea connected the peoples who became known as the Greeks. In fact, no point on the mainland is more than 40 miles from the sea. As a result, the sea became the Greeks' link to other peoples, products, and ideas.

## Farming in Ancient Greece

The geography of Greece helped to shape its economy as well as its history. As was the case with other ancient civilizations, such as those in Sumer and Egypt, most people in ancient Greece were farmers.

Greece had a climate similar to that of southern California—mild winters and hot, sunny summers. As a result, farmers could raise crops all year round.

In spring and summer, Greek farmers tended vineyards and olive groves. In fall they harvested grapes and olives, and they also planted wheat and barley. They harvested these crops in the spring.

The hilly terrain was ideal for growing grapes and olives, so the Greeks could produce plenty of these crops. However, less than one-fourth of Greece's land was level enough for planting grains, so at times grains were scarce. To supplement their stores of wheat and barley, the Greeks sailed west to Sicily and east to the Black Sea region to trade for grains. They may also have sailed south to trade with the Egyptians.

Greece was ideally located for sea trade. The Greeks made extensive contacts with people from advanced cultures—Egyptians, Phoenicians, Persians, and others. These contacts led to the spread of ideas that spurred the development of Greek civilization. ■

# Early Civilizations

The roots of Greek civilization can be traced to two nearby cultures that flourished and declined between 3000 B.C. and 1100 B.C. Find Crete on the map on page 329. On this island the first major civilization of the region arose. According to legend, its leader was a conqueror and lawgiver named King Minos. The period from about 2000 B.C. to 1400 B.C. is called the Minoan Age.

## Minoan Civilization

The Minoans developed a system of writing, and they created fine artwork, including carved statuettes, pottery, metal bowls, jewelry, and weavings. The Minoans also were great sailors. They carried on a rich trade with the people of Egypt, Phoenicia, and Mesopotamia.

The Minoans were master builders as well. At Crete's main city, Knossos *(NAHS uhs)*, and in other cities they built huge palaces. These palaces had a mazelike series of rooms surrounding a central courtyard.

Although they were built nearly 4,000 years ago, the palaces were quite advanced . The Minoans equipped them with underground plumbing and piped running water to luxurious bathing rooms. The walls of the palaces

▼ *An acrobat leaps over a charging bull in this Minoan bronze sculpture from about 1600 B.C. (shown full size). The sport, called bull dancing, was popular in ancient Crete.*

▼ *Trace the early history of the ancient Greeks.*

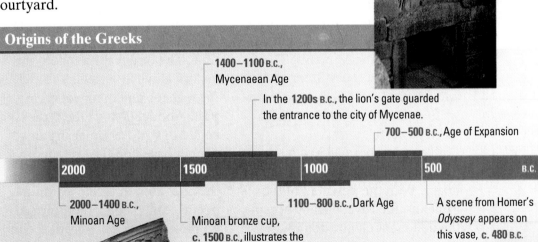

## Origins of the Greeks

**1400–1100 B.C., Mycenaean Age**

In the **1200s B.C.**, the lion's gate guarded the entrance to the city of Mycenae.

**700–500 B.C.,** Age of Expansion

| 2000 | 1500 | 1000 | 500 | B.C. | A.D. |

**2000–1400 B.C.,** Minoan Age

Minoan bronze cup, **c. 1500 B.C.,** illustrates the legend of the bull of King Minos.

**1100–800 B.C.,** Dark Age

A scene from Homer's *Odyssey* appears on this vase, **c. 480 B.C.**

▲ *Much of the palace of Knossos was restored in the early 1900s. Colorful paintings like the one shown at right once decorated palace walls.*

were decorated with colorful murals of daily life in ancient Crete.

## Mycenaean Civilization

While the Minoan civilization was thriving on the island of Crete, people began settling on the Greek mainland as well. About 1900 B.C., they began building cities high on hilltops, overlooking the surrounding countryside and the sea. The largest of these cities was Mycenae (*my SEE nee*). Find Mycenae on the map on page 329.

Like the Minoans, the Mycenaeans (*my suh NEE uhnz*) built a large fleet of ships. They set out to capture rich trade routes and establish colonies. The Mycenaeans learned from the Minoans. They built palaces in the Minoan style and adopted the Minoan system of writing. Gradually, they became more powerful.

Then, in about 1450 B.C., the Mycenaeans conquered the Minoans. With the downfall of the Minoans, the Mycenaeans became the dominant civilization in the Aegean region. The period between 1400 B.C. and 1100 B.C. is called the Mycenaean Age.

## The Dark Age

In the 1100s B.C., the Mycenaean culture began to decline. No one knows for sure why, but by about 1150 B.C. Mycenae fell to invaders. Soon afterwards, the Dorians, who were groups of related peoples from the northern part of Greece, moved into the area. Many Mycenaeans fled. Greece was entering a period of decline called the Dark Age.

During the Dark Age, which lasted from about 1100 B.C. to 800 B.C., trade came to a standstill. The written language disappeared. People lived in isolated villages.

However, the early history of Greece was not lost during this time. The oral tradition kept the history alive. Storytellers retold the legends and myths of their past. About 800 B.C., the Greeks began to write again, using an alphabet based on the system of the Phoenicians. During the 700s B.C., the poet Homer wrote down long poems, called epic poems, based on these oral tales. His epic poem the *Odyssey* was one of the most important literary achievements of the early Greeks. ■

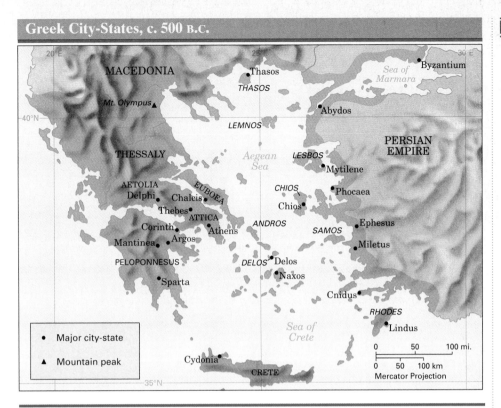

◄ *Which city-states were located on the Peloponnesus? Which ones were in Attica?*

# The Rise of the City-States

Around 750 B.C., Greece's Dark Age came to an end. The population of Greece had increased during the Dark Age, and the isolated villages began to develop into cities. As the cities grew, trade increased. People in each city traded among themselves. They also traded with people living in neighboring cities. Leaders arose among the people in each city.

The isolated cities of the Dark Ages developed into **city-states**—independent, self-governing units. Each city-state included a city and the territory surrounding the city. As the city-states grew, however, they sometimes did not have enough farmland to support their people. They began to fight with one another over boundaries and other matters. Many Greek colonists left their city-states and founded new ones. Look at the map above. How far west did the city-states extend? How far north did they extend?

In the 600s and 500s B.C. the Greek city-states flourished. This period is called the Age of Expansion. In the next lessons, you will read about the great achievements of the city-states in government, art, literature, and science. ■

■ *What was the Age of Expansion?*

1. **FOCUS** What were some of the forces that influenced the rise of civilization in ancient Greece?

2. **CONNECT** In what ways were the Greek city-states described above similar to the cities of ancient Mesopotamia?

3. **CULTURE** How did the Greeks keep their history alive during the Dark Age?

4. **GEOGRAPHY** Why did Greece develop as a group of individual city-states rather than a unified state?

5. **CRITICAL THINKING** Why are epic poems such as the *Odyssey* important sources of information about the Greek civilization?

6. **WRITING ACTIVITY** Imagine that you had traveled with Odysseus. Write an account of what you saw.

# The Cyclops's Cave

### Bernard Evslin

*Odysseus, known as* Ulysses *to the Romans, encountered many troubles on his way home after the Trojan War. In this excerpt from* Greeks Bearing Gifts, *Ulysses and his crew land on the island of the Cyclopes, one-eyed giants. They enter a cave where they are trapped by one of the giants.*

A s Ulysses and his horrified men watched, the great hand bore the struggling little men to the giant's mouth. He ate them, still wriggling, the way a cat eats a grasshopper; he ate them clothes and all, growling over their raw bones.

The men had fallen to their knees and were whimpering like terrified children, but Ulysses stood there, sword in hand, his agile brain working more swiftly than it ever had before.

"Greetings," he called. "May I know to whom we are indebted for such hospitality?"

*Polyphemus* (pahl uh FEE muhs)

The giant belched and spat buttons. "I am Polyphemus," he growled. "This is my cave, my mountain, and everything that comes here is mine. I do hope you can all stay to dinner. There are just enough of you to make a meal. Ho, ho. . . ." And he laughed a great, choking phlegmy laugh, swiftly lunged, and caught another sailor, whom he lifted into the air and held before his face.

*phlegmy* full of mucus

"Wait!" cried Ulysses.

"What for?"

"You won't enjoy him that way. He is from Attica, where the olives grow. He was raised on olives and has a very delicate oily flavor. But to appreciate it, you must taste the wine of the country."

"Wine? What is wine?"

"It is a drink. Made from pressed grapes. Have you never drunk it?"

"We drink nothing but ox blood and buttermilk here."

"Ah, you do not know what you have missed, gentle Polyphemus. Meat-eaters, in particular, love wine. Here, try it for yourself."

Ulysses unslung from his belt a full flask of unwatered wine. He gave it to the giant, who put it to his lips and gulped. He coughed violently, and stuck the sailor in a little niche high up in the cave wall, then leaned his great slab of a face toward Ulysses and said:

"What did you say this drink was?"

"Wine. A gift of the gods to man, to make women look better and food taste better. And now it is my gift to you."

"It's good, very good." He put the bottle to his lips and swallowed again. "You are very polite. What's your name?"

"My name? Why I am—nobody."

"Nobody. . . . Well, Nobody, I like you. You're a good fellow. And do you know what I'm going to do? I'm going to save you till last. Yes, I'll eat all your friends first, and give you extra time, that's what I'm going to do."

Ulysses looked up into the great eye and saw that it was redder than ever. It was all a swimming redness. He had given the monster, who had never drunk spirits before, undiluted wine. Surely it must make him sleepy. But was a gallon enough for that great gullet? Enough to put him to sleep—or would he want to eat again first?

"Eat 'em all up, Nobody—save you till later. Sleep a little first. Shall I? Won't try to run away, will you? No—you can't, can't open the door—too heavy, ha, ha. . . .You take a nap too, Nobody. I'll wake you for breakfast. Breakfast. . . ."

The great body crashed full-length on the cave floor, making the very walls of the mountain shake. Polyphemus lay on his back, snoring like a powersaw. The sailors were still on the floor, almost dead from fear.

"Up!" cried Ulysses. "Stand up like men! Do what must be done! Or you will be devoured like chickens."

He got them to their feet and drew them about him as he explained his plan.

"Listen now, and listen well, for we have no time. I made him drunk, but we cannot tell how long it will last."

Ulysses thrust his sword into the fire; they saw it glow white-hot.

"There are ten of us," he said. "Two of us have been eaten, and one of our friends is still unconscious up there on his shelf of rock. You four get on one side of his head, and the rest on the other side. When I give the word, lay hold of the ear on your side, each of you. And hang on, no matter how he thrashes, for I am going to put out his eye. And if I am to be sure of my stroke you must hold his head still. One stroke is all I will be allowed."

Then Ulysses rolled a boulder next to the giant's head and climbed on it, so that he was looking down into the eye. It was lidless and misted with sleep—big as a furnace door and glowing softly like a banked fire. Ulysses looked at his men. They had done what he said, broken into two parties, one group at each ear. He lifted his white-hot sword.

"Now!" he cried.

Driving down with both hands, and all the strength of his back and shoulders, and all his rage and all his fear, Ulysses stabbed the glowing spike into the giant's eye.

His sword jerked out of his hand as the head flailed upward, men pelted to the ground as they lost their hold. A huge screeching curdling bellow split the air.

"This way!" shouted Ulysses.

He motioned to his men, and they crawled on their bellies toward the far end of the cave where the herd of goats were tethered. They slipped into the herd and lay among the goats as the giant stomped about the cave, slapping the walls with great blows of his hands, picking up boulders and cracking them together in agony, splitting them to flinders, clutching his eye, a scorched hole now from which the brown blood jelled. He moaned and gibbered and bellowed in frightful pain; his groping hand found the sailor in the wall, and he tore him to pieces between his fingers. Ulysses could not even hear the man scream because the giant was bellowing so.

Now Ulysses saw that the Cyclops's wild stampeding was giving place to a plan. For now he was stamping the floor in a regular pattern, trying to find and crush them beneath his feet. He stopped moaning and listened. The sudden silence dazed the men with fear. They held their breath and tried to muffle the sound of their beating hearts; all the giant heard was the breathing of the goats. Then Ulysses saw him go to the mouth of the cave, and swing the great slab aside, and stand there. He realized just in time that the goats would rush outside, which is what the giant wanted, for then he could search the whole cave.

Ulysses whispered, "Quickly, swing under the bellies of the rams. Hurry, hurry!"

Luckily, they were giant goats and thus able to carry the men who had swung themselves under their bellies and were clinging to the wiry wool. Ulysses himself chose the largest ram. They moved toward the mouth of the cave, and crowded through. The Cyclops's hands came down and brushed across the goats' backs feeling for the men, but the animals were huddled too closely together for him to reach between and search under their bellies, so he let them pass through.

Now, the Cyclops rushed to the corner where the goats had been tethered, and stamped, searched, and roared through the whole cave again, bellowing with fury when he did not find them. The herd grazed on the slope of the hill beneath the cave. There was a full moon; it was almost as bright as day.

"Stay where you are," Ulysses whispered.

He heard a crashing, peered out, and saw great shadowy figures converging on the cave. He knew that the other Cyclopes of the island must have heard the noise and come to see. He heard the giant bellow.

The others called to him: "Who has done it? Who has blinded you?"

"Nobody. Nobody did it. Nobody blinded me."

"Ah, you have done it yourself. What a tragic accident."

And they went back to their own caves.

"Now! said Ulysses. "Follow me!"

He swung himself out from under the belly of the ram, and raced down the hill. The others raced after him. They were halfway across the valley when they heard great footsteps rushing after them, and Polyphemus bellowing nearer and nearer.

"He's coming!" cried Ulysses. "Run for your lives!"

They ran as they had never run before, but the giant could cover fifty yards at a stride. It was only because he could not see and kept bumping into trees and rocks that they were able to reach the skiff and push out on the silver water before Polyphemus burst out of the grove of trees and rushed onto the beach. They bent to the oars, and the boat scudded toward the fleet.

*skiff* a flat-bottomed open boat

*scudded* skimmed swiftly

Polyphemus heard the dip of the oars and the groaning of the oarlocks, and, aiming at the sound, hurled huge boulders after them. They fell around the ship, but did not hit. The skiff reached Ulysses' ship, and the sailors climbed aboard.

"Haul anchor, and away!" cried Ulysses. And then called to the Cyclops, "Poor fool! Poor blinded drunken gluttonous fool—if anyone else asks you, it is not Nobody, but Ulysses who has done this to you."

But he was to regret this final taunt. The gods honor courage, but punish pride.

Polyphemus, wild with rage, waded out chest-deep and hurled a last boulder, which hit mid-deck, almost sunk the ship, and killed most of the crew—among them seven of the nine men who had just escaped.

And Polyphemus prayed to Poseidon, "God of the Sea, I beg you, punish Ulysses for this. Visit him with storm and shipwreck and sorceries. Let him wander many years before he reaches home, and when he gets there let him find himself forgotten, unwanted, a stranger."

*Poseidon* (poh SYD n)

*sorceries* acts of evil supernatural power

Poseidon heard this prayer, and made it all happen just that way.

## Further Reading

*Ancient Greece*. Susan Purdy. Step-by-step directions show how to make models of ancient Greek columns, statues, and catapults.

*The God Beneath the Sea*. Leon Garfield and Edward Blishen. This book retells Greek myths about the gods and goddesses on Olympia.

LESSON 2

# Athens: A City-State

THINKING
FOCUS

*How did democracy develop and work in Athens?*

### Key Terms

- democracy
- monarchy
- oligarchy
- tyrant
- barter

▼ *The ancient Greeks used these tokens to cast their votes.*

The trial promised to be one of the most important the citizens of Athens would hear all year. In 406 B.C., six navy generals were accused of abandoning hundreds of shipwrecked soldiers and leaving them to drown. Were the generals guilty of causing the deaths of these men? A jury of 2,000 Athenian citizens would decide the fate of the generals.

Early in the morning, the trial began. First the six generals took the stand. They testified that they had done all they could to save the men. The deaths were just an unfortunate turn of fate.

Next, witnesses testified, including a survivor who had floated to shore in a flour barrel. He claimed that the spirits of his drowned comrades urged him to testify against the generals.

Professional mourners, dressed in black, made their way through the crowd. They hoped to convince the jurors to convict the generals.

Xenophon (*ZEHN uh fuhn*), a Greek historian, told of a public crier who announced how the jury would decide:

> *Let every one who finds the generals guilty of not rescuing the heroes of the late sea-fight deposit his vote in one urn. Let him who is of the contrary opinion deposit his vote in the other urn. Further, in the event of the aforesaid generals being found guilty, let death be the penalty.*
>
> Xenophon, *Hellenica*, Book I
> c. 400 B.C.

The jurors' tokens were counted. The generals were found guilty and sentenced to death.

# The Evolution of Democracy

Trials such as the one of the navy generals were an important part of the government developed by the citizens of Athens. Between the 700s and 400s B.C., the Athenians developed a new form of government that put the power to make decisions into the hands of the people. This form of government is called a **democracy,** which means government by the people.

## The Origins of Democracy

The idea of democracy was developed over several centuries. Before the Dark Age, the people in the Greek city-states were ruled by kings. A system of government in which a king rules over a group of people is called a **monarchy.** In ancient Greece, the king of a city-state was also usually the head of the most powerful family.

When the king died, he usually passed on his power to govern to his eldest son.

During the Dark Age, Greek kings began to rely on wealthy landowners, or nobles, to help them defend their land from invaders. Not surprisingly, the nobles began to demand some of the king's powers. By the end of the Dark Age, a small group of nobles shared power equally with the king in many city-states. This system of government in which a few people hold power over a larger group is called an **oligarchy.** This system was a step toward democracy, since a group of men, rather than just one man, held power.

The leaders of the oligarchies improved the government of the city-states, but during the 500s B.C., some city-states had problems of a different kind.

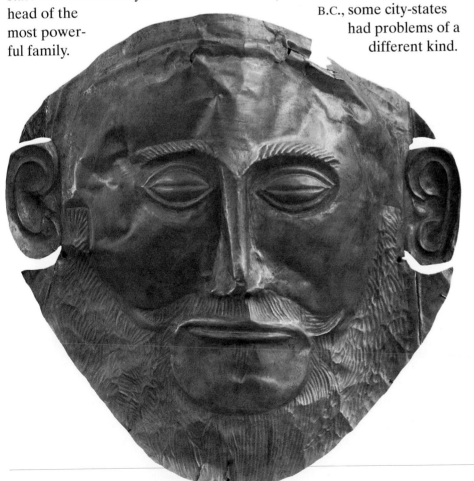

◄ *The earliest governments of Greece were monarchies. This mask shows the face of a king who ruled about 1500 B.C.*

The Ancient Greeks

Some grew to be so large that their farmers could not provide enough food. Food shortages caused unrest and discontent. During this period, poorer farmers suffered greatly. Many lost their land to the wealthy and were forced to sell themselves into slavery. The discontent with the leaders of the oligarchies led to the rise of new leaders called tyrants.

## The Rule of Tyrants

Greeks called a leader who seized power by force and ruled the city-state single-handedly a **tyrant.** Many people supported tyrants because these leaders promised to reform the laws and to aid the poor. The tyrants of Athens, for example, accomplished their aims by canceling all debt, redistributing land, and allowing

## UNDERSTANDING DEMOCRACY

When the tyrant Hippias was driven out of Athens in 510 B.C., the people of Athens established a form of government that was new to the ancient world. This government—a democracy— has had a lasting impact on Western civilization.

A democracy is a form of government that places the power in the hands of the citizens. Some democracies are governed directly by the citizens, and some are governed by elected representatives.

### Rule of the People

The word *democracy* comes from two Greek words, *demos*, meaning people, and *kratos*, meaning "rule." Thus democracy means "rule of the people."

Unlike an oligarchy, in which only a few rule, all citizens take part in the government of a democracy.

However, democracies can take different forms.

### Forms of Democracy

In ancient Greece, the citizens met regularly in an assembly to vote on important issues. This type of democracy is known as direct democracy because all citizens take part directly. For smaller communities, such as the early Greek city-states, direct democracy worked because it was possible to bring together all citizens to make decisions.

Many democracies today are representative democracies. In a representative democracy, the citizens elect representatives to make decisions for them.

The United States today has a representative democracy, which is more practical for large communities and nations. Can you imagine trying to get all the people

of the United States together at one time to make decisions?

Even in ancient Greece, the people gave some decision-making power to representatives of the people. One feature of Greek democracy was a council of 500 citizens. They were chosen each year to propose new laws for the assembly of all citizens to consider.

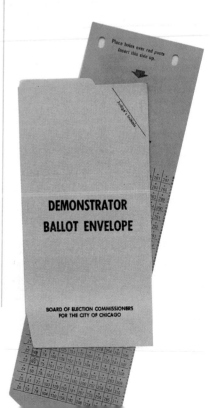

DEMONSTRATOR
BALLOT ENVELOPE

BOARD OF ELECTION COMMISSIONERS
FOR THE CITY OF CHICAGO

other people besides the nobles to have a say in government.

The tyrants played an important role in the development of democracy. They taught citizens that by uniting behind a leader, they could gain the power to make changes. However, some tyrants were harsh and greedy. The people of a city-state sometimes threw out one tyrant and replaced him with another.

## The Democracy of Athens

About 510 B.C., the citizens of Athens became upset with the harsh rule of a tyrant named Hippias. With the help of soldiers from the city-state of Sparta, Hippias was driven out of Athens. But he was not replaced by a new tyrant. Instead, the citizens of Athens chose to share the decision-making power among themselves. This was the beginning of the world's first democracy.

Several institutions assured citizens of Athens a voice in their government. A council of 500 citizens, chosen at random every year, proposed new laws. An assembly of all the citizens of Athens met about every nine days to vote on the laws. In the law courts, citizens served as jurors. They interpreted the laws and decided guilt or innocence in cases such as that of the navy generals.

All of these institutions had existed before 500 B.C. However, now they were open to more people and they were administered more fairly. For example, the government of Athens paid council members and jurors for their ser-

*A tyrant is put to death in this vase painting.*

vices. Thus, poorer citizens, as well as rich ones, could afford to take time off from their work to take part in the government of their city-state.

Not all citizens of Athens liked this new form of government. Some wealthy citizens believed the democracy gave too much power to poor citizens. Nevertheless, most Athenians appreciated their form of government.

The development of democracy has greatly influenced Western civilization. It also was an important step for the Athenians.

### Across Time & Space

*Today the word* tyrant *means "dictator" or "a ruler who governs in a harsh or cruel way." However, in ancient Greece the word did not have those negative meanings. Although the Greek tyrants took power by force, often they ruled well and fairly.*

*Athenians voted to banish people from a city. They wrote the name of the person they wanted to banish on pieces of clay pottery.*

341

The Ancient Greeks

The Greek historian Herodotus (*hih RAHD uh tuhs*) wrote that when the Athenians were ruled by tyrants, they "were not a whit more valiant than any of their neighbors." But when they established their democracy,

T hey became decidedly the first of all. These things show that, while undergoing oppression, they let themselves be beaten, since then they worked for a master; but so soon as they got their freedom, each man was eager to do the best he could for himself.

Herodotus, *The Persian Wars,*
c. 430 B.C.

Athens was not the only city-state with a democratic government. Several other ancient Greek city-states developed democracies. However the democracy that developed in Athens was the most successful. ■

■ *Trace the development of democracy from the monarchy.*

## Citizenship in Athens

The democracy of Athens opened participation in government to all citizens. However, citizenship was a privilege reserved for relatively few people. Only men over the age of 18 could become citizens. And except under special circumstances, a man became a citizen only if his father had been a citizen. After 451 B.C., the rules regarding citizenship became stricter. A man became a citizen only if both his father and his mother's father were citizens.

Of the 300,000 inhabitants of Athens, only about 45,000 of them were citizens. Their wives and children, who were not citizens, accounted for about 145,000 inhabitants. Note that women, whether they were married or unmarried, had no political rights and they could not own land.

About 35,000 residents of Athens were metics, or foreigners. They came from other Greek city-states or from other parts of the Mediterranean region. Many were traders, shopkeepers, craftsmen, or moneylenders. Metics could not vote or hold public office, but they were protected by Athenian law.

Slaves made up the rest of Athens's population. Many had been captured during foreign wars. Slaves could not vote, and they could not choose their jobs. They were not even allowed to have a family without the permission of their master. They had to do the jobs their owners assigned them. Many worked as farmhands. Others did household chores. Some learned crafts such as metalwork or pottery. These slaves were paid for their work. A few of them earned enough money to buy their freedom from their owners. ■

➤ *What group of people made up the largest part of Athenian society?*

■ *Find evidence in the lesson to disprove this statement: In Athens everyone took part in the government.*

**Population of Athens**

- Adult male citizens 15%
- Citizens' wives and children 48%
- Metics 12%
- Slaves 25%

# The Economy of Athens

Farming was the main economic activity in Athenian society. Most citizens owned just enough land to support their families. However, some wealthy Athenians owned large estates on which slaves did most of the work. On other estates, tenant farmers worked the land. These farmers leased plots from the owner and paid rent by giving the owner part of their crops.

## Trade and Coinage

Until the 500s B.C., Athenians did most of their trading through **barter.** Using this system people exchanged one type of product, such as grain, directly for another, such as olives. As Athens became an international trading center around 600 B.C., barter became an inconvenient way to trade.

Trade in Athens became easier around 570 B.C., when the government began to make gold and silver coins. People were willing to exchange their goods for coins. In contrast to the barter system, the system of trade using coins allowed the purchase of any product.

## Redistributing Wealth

The use of coins spurred the Athenian economy, and Athens became a very wealthy city. The active trade drew many foreigners, who came to Athens to make their fortunes.

However, wealthy people in Athens usually did not hold on to their wealth for many generations. Foreigners who became wealthy usually went back to their own city-states. Wealthy citizens were expected to contribute large amounts of money to government projects. For example, they might have been asked to give money to outfit one of the navy's ships or sponsor a religious festival.

The cost of the Athenian government was high. As a result, few families managed to stay rich for more than three generations. By then the family had used up its wealth on projects that benefited all Athenians. This system kept money flowing to citizens throughout the city-state. It also gave work to merchants and craftsmen. ■

▼ Greeks traded with these coins during the 500s and 400s B.C.

■ Why did wealthy families in Athens have difficulty staying rich?

## REVIEW

1. **FOCUS** How did democracy develop and work in Athens?

2. **CONNECT** How was the democracy of Athens different from the governments led by the pharaohs of Egypt and the kings of Mesopotamia?

3. **ECONOMICS** What were the advantages for Athens' of coined money?

4. **CRITICAL THINKING** How was the democracy in Athens similar to the democracy in the United States today? How was it different?

5. **WRITING ACTIVITY** Write a journal entry on what it would be like to be a noncitizen in Athens. You can choose to write from the point of view of a slave, metic, woman, or child.

343

The Ancient Greeks

# Comparing Graphs

## Here's Why

Graphs can help you organize information. They can help you see patterns and make comparisons. Certain kinds of graphs are best used to present particular kinds of information.

The graphs on this page are based on estimates of the population in ancient Greece. They show information in different ways. One is a line graph; the other is a pie graph.

By comparing the two graphs, you can get more information than you can from a single graph. Also, by understanding what each graph does best, you will learn which type of graph to choose to present your own information.

## Here's How

A line graph shows change over time. The line graph at the lower left shows that 30,000 male citizens lived in Athens in 500 B.C. The upward slope of the line to the right of 500 B.C. shows that the male population increased to about 45,000 during the 50 years between 500 B.C. and 450 B.C. The downward slope of the line from about 450 B.C. to about 325 B.C. shows a decrease in the male population during that time.

A pie graph shows how something is divided into parts. For example, if you created a pie graph of your class, you might show how the class is divided into boys and girls.

The pie graph at the lower right shows the five groups that made up the estimated 300,000 people living in Athens in 451 B.C. Each section of the pie shows how the number of people in that group relates to the total population. For example, 75,000 slaves equals 25 percent of the total pie.

## Try It

Suppose that by 200 B.C. the population of Athens had fallen to 100,000. Suppose that of that 100,000, there were about 20,000 male citizens, 20,000 wives of citizens, 35,000 children of citizens, 15,000 metics, and 10,000 slaves.

Use this information to make two graphs—Male Citizens of Athens, 500–200 B.C., and Population of Athens, 200 B.C.

## Apply It

Find out your school's total enrollment each year for the past 10 years and the number of students who participated in various sports. For each set of data, decide whether a line graph or a pie graph is more appropriate. Then create the graphs.

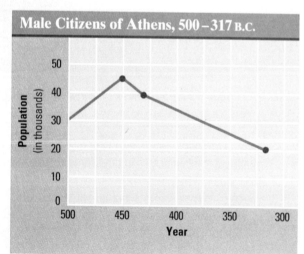

Male Citizens of Athens, 500–317 B.C.

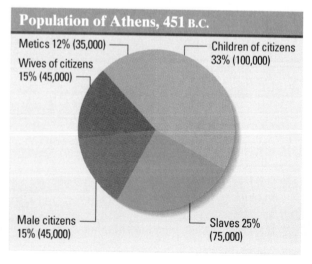

Population of Athens, 451 B.C.

Chapter 11

LESSON 3

# Ancient Greek Culture

A crowd of 45,000 gathered on the grassy slopes of the stadium at Olympia one summer afternoon in 776 B.C. Below them, the runners prepared for the foot-race. The race began, and the crowd rose and cheered as one runner burst ahead of the others. He was Coroebus, a cook from the nearby city of Elis. When he crossed the finish line, Coroebus became the first recorded winner at the Olympic games.

Sports events were important in ancient Greece, just as they are in the United States today. Every four years, beginning in 776 B.C., the Greeks held an athletic competition called the Olympics, which was open to all Greek men. At first this competition consisted of one event, a foot-race of about 200 yards. Later the Olympics were expanded to include longer races, wrestling, boxing, discus throwing, horse races, and chariot races. The modern-day Olympics are modeled after these Greek games.

The Greeks considered the

Olympics so important that nothing, not even war, was allowed to interfere with them. However, the function of these competitions was not simply to entertain. The main purpose of the Olympics and other public events and festivals was to honor the gods.

*What religious beliefs and customs did all Greeks share?*

## Key Terms

- sanctuary
- tragedy
- comedy

◄ *An Olympic athlete throwing the discus is shown in this Roman copy of a Greek sculpture from about 450 B.C.*

345

# The Family of Greek Gods

The Olympic Games honored Zeus, the father of the Greek gods. The games were named after Mount Olympus, the highest peak in Greece. The Greeks believed that Zeus sat on a golden throne atop Mount Olympus and ruled all other gods and all of the Greeks. In fact, they thought of Zeus as master of the entire world.

All Greeks, no matter what city-state they lived in, worshiped Zeus and his family of gods. The Greeks thought these gods controlled both the world of nature and the human world.

The myths and legends of the Greeks celebrated their gods. These traditional stories explained the roles of the gods in creating the world and causing natural events.

The stories also told of the great power of their gods. For example, Zeus was portrayed as powerful, stern, and commanding. In Homer's poem the *Iliad*, Zeus boasts about how he could control the world with a cord of gold dropped from the sky.

*The image painted on an Athenian cup about 550 B.C. shows the birth of Athena. According to Greek myth, Athena sprang full grown from the head of Zeus, which was split open by an ax.*

*Yet whenever I might strongly be minded to pull you, I could drag you up, earth and all and sea and all with you, then fetch the golden rope about the horn of Olympus and make it fast, so that all once more should dangle in mid air. So much stronger am I than the gods, and stronger than mortals.*

## The Roles of the Gods

The gods of Greek myths formed a family, and each member had a specific role with particular duties and powers. Zeus, as head of the family, set standards of justice and made sure that humans and gods followed them. He also controlled the weather and punished wrongdoing with bolts of thunder and raging storms.

Poseidon, Zeus's brother, was the god of the sea. Hera, Zeus's wife, was the goddess of marriage. Zeus's son Ares was the god of war. Another of his sons, Dionysus (*dy uh NY suhs*), was the god of wine. His son Apollo was the god of light, who drove the sun across the sky each day in his golden carriage. Apollo also was the god of health, herding, and prophecy.

## Worshiping the Gods

The Greeks prayed to specific gods for things they wanted. For example, a sick person might pray to Apollo for a speedy recovery. The Greeks thanked the gods by making animal sacrifices when their prayers were granted. They also made sacrifices to the gods before competing in sports, going off to war, or setting sail on a long voyage.

The Greeks also built sacred places called **sanctuaries** to honor their gods. People from the entire Aegean world traveled to these sanctuaries to worship their many gods. ■

■ *Describe some of the Greek gods and their powers.*

## Sanctuaries to the Gods

The sanctuaries were built in areas of great natural beauty. Each sacred site had its own unique traditions that had been established over hundreds of years. Find the four sanctuaries on the map on page 348.

### Olympia

Olympia, where the Olympic games were held, was a sanctuary to Zeus. A winding river ran through the site, and a thickly wooded area made it a place of peace and serenity. Olympia was a perfect site for sports competition, because the land in the broad river valley was flat. On this level plain, the Greeks easily laid out large courses on which the foot races, horse races, and chariot races could be run during the Olympics. The Greeks believed that Zeus and the other gods took special delight in watching great athletes display their skill and strength in open competition.

### Delphi

The Greeks honored Apollo at Delphi *(DEHL fy)*. Each city-state sent gifts to the sanctuary. Because the site was considered sacred, no thief would think of robbing it. Therefore, many people left their gold and silver in the shrines at Delphi for safekeeping.

Located halfway up a mountain overlooking a lush river valley, Delphi was a most impressive site. The sanctuary was most famous for its oracle to the god Apollo. Like the ancient Chinese, the Greeks believed oracles were predictions. The Greeks believed gods and goddesses revealed hidden knowledge through these oracles. The Greeks also called the shrines where these messages were revealed oracles.

At these oracles, priests or priestesses interpreted the messages of the gods. The messages were often hard to understand. For example, the Athenian generals appealed to the Delphic oracle for advice during the Persian Wars in the late 400s B.C. The generals wanted to know how they could turn back the Persian invaders. The message they received from the oracle was that "wooden walls" would save Athens. After much debate, the generals decided that wooden walls meant new wooden ships. The generals built a new fleet of ships, and the fleet played

▼ *To please the gods, Greeks sacrificed animals in the temples of the sanctuaries. This wall mosaic shows a sheep being led to a sacrificial altar.*

The Ancient Greeks

a crucial role in defeating Persia. Therefore, the Greeks believed the oracle was right.

The oracle at Delphi was considered the most powerful of the Greek oracles. People from all over the Aegean world came to Delphi seeking advice.

### Delos and Eleusis

According to Greek myth, the island of Delos *(DEE lohs)* was Apollo's birthplace. Like Delphi, the Delos sanctuary had an oracle to Apollo. Every five years the Greeks held a sports competition there to honor Apollo.

Eleusis *(ih LOO suhs)*, on the coast of mainland Greece near Athens, was the site of a sanctuary to Demeter *(dih MEET ur)*, the goddess of grain. Athenians made pilgrimages each year to Eleusis during the planting and harvest seasons. They also made sacrifices to Demeter and offered prayers for an abundant harvest. These religious rituals highlighted the importance of agriculture in ancient Greece.

### Religious Festivals

The Greeks also honored their gods and goddesses by holding religious festivals. Many of these festivals, such as the Olympic games, centered on sports. Other ceremonies featured religious rituals and animal sacrifices.

One group of festivals has had a lasting influence on Western civilization. These were the drama festivals honoring Dionysus, the god of wine. ■

■ *How did the Greek people use sanctuaries?*

➤ *The ruins at Delphi of the Temple of the Treasury of the Athenians are shown at the right. Find the treasuries at Delphi on the map below.*

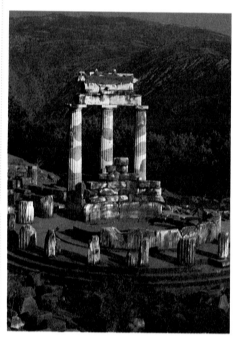

## Major Sanctuaries of Ancient Greece

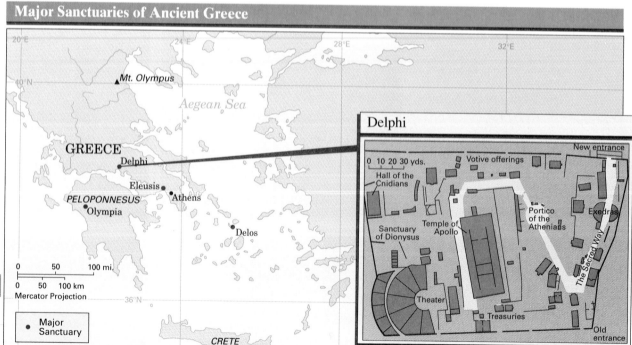

Delphi

# A Greek Actor

*10:00 A.M., March 24, 441 B.C.
Theater of Dionysus, Athens*

## Mouth Hole

The opening allows the actor's fine voice to project the words of Sophocles' play *Antigone* all the way to the last row. Our actor is just about to step back out onto the stage.

## Mask

Newly made of linen and smelling of fresh paint, the mask is much better than the ones at last year's festival. The citizen who is paying for this year's plays has spent a lot more money on costumes.

## Padding

A band around the actor's head holds his mask in place. He hopes to exchange the band for the wreath of ivy leaves given to the festival's best actor.

## Goose Bumps

He's not only chilled by the cold morning air. He's also nervous about remembering his lines, which are very important.

## Sash

His belt is smaller than the one he wore at the festival last year because he has been fasting to improve his voice.

## Long Sleeves

Earlier in the play, these sleeves hid the actor's manly arms when he acted the part of a young woman. Today he will play eight different parts in three brand-new tragedies by Sophocles.

## Cape

Purple, the color of kings, tells the audience that the actor is playing the role of King Creon. Our actor is happy because Creon is a very important part with many good lines.

# Greek Drama

Twice a year, writers throughout Greece composed plays that were presented at festivals in Athens to honor Dionysus. The plays produced on the Athenian stages are one of the lasting contributions of the Greeks.

Most of the plays told stories about Greek gods or heroes. They combined religion and history with entertainment. Most popular were the **tragedies,** sad stories in which the hero was brought to ruin by a flaw in his character.

Look at the Moment in Time on page 349. The actor is preparing to appear in the tragedy *Antigone (an TIHG uh nee)* by Sophocles. The actor will be playing a king who ordered the death of the woman his son loved. The son, stricken with grief, then killed himself as well. Here are the sad lines the king will speak as he gazes at his son's body.

*By wearing different masks, actors in Athenian plays could play more than one part.*

*How was the festival of Dionysus different from the festivals to other gods?*

> Sirs, ye behold the slayer
>   and the slain.
> Such is the end my schemes
>   unblessed have won,
>   By a boy's blow
>   Undone, undone!
> For you have died, have willed
>   to go,
> And I was all to blame, not
>   you, my son, my son.

Sophocles, *Antigone,* 441 B.C.

During a festival for Dionysus, plays were presented from dawn until dark for four days. Three days were devoted to tragic plays. **Comedies**—funny plays—were presented for only one day during the festival. Like comedies today, the Greek comedies made fun of a wide range of topics, from politics to everyday life.

All businesses in Athens closed during the festivals to Dionysus. Thousands of people headed to the open-air amphitheater to watch the plays. The city even released prisoners from jail so that they could go to the festival.

A jury of Athenian citizens judged the plays and awarded ivy crowns to the writers of the winning plays. Many of the prize-winning plays are still performed today. ■

## REVIEW

1. **FOCUS** What religious beliefs and customs did all Greeks share?

2. **CONNECT** Compare the Greek gods to the Egyptian gods and the Mesopotamian gods.

3. **CULTURE** What is a tragedy?

4. **CRITICAL THINKING** Why were plays and sports competitions considered important religious events by the ancient Greeks?

5. **WRITING ACTIVITY** Make up a story about the Greek god Zeus and one of his children mentioned in the chapter. You might use your story to explain an event in Greek history, an aspect of Greek culture, or a natural phenomenon such as a thunderstorm, earthquake, or flood.

Chapter 11

L E S S O N  4

# A Tale of Two City-States

I n 490 B.C., Persia's fleet of 600 ships loomed off the Greek shores not far from Athens. According to legend, the general of the Athenian troops sent his fastest runner, Phidippides *(fy DIHP uh deez),* to ask for help from Sparta. Phidippides ran for two days and two nights to reach Sparta, about 140 miles away. He gave the message to the Spartans. They agreed to send troops—but not for nine days, when their religious festival would be completed.

Phidippides ran back to Athens with the Spartans' reply. The Athenian general decided he could not wait that long. He ordered his troops to advance and meet the Persians before the invaders could move inland toward Athens. The two armies clashed at a town called Marathon. The lightly armed Persian soldiers were no match for the well-disciplined Greek forces. About 6,400 Persian soldiers were killed, while the Athenians lost only 192 men.

According to the legend of the battle of Marathon, the Athenian general ordered Phidippides to run back to Athens and spread the good news. The distance between Marathon and Athens was about 25 miles, a short distance for a professional runner such as Phidippides. But he was still exhausted from his long run to Sparta. Nevertheless, he set out for Athens, running as fast as he could. When he reached Athens, he managed to gasp, "Rejoice! We won." Then he fell to the ground and died.

THINKING
FOCUS

*How were the cultures of Athens and Sparta similar? How were they different?*

## Key Terms

- ephor
- helot

## Sparta and Athens

At the time of the battle of Marathon, Sparta and Athens were the two largest city-states in Greece. Size, however, was about all the two cities had in common. Events that took place over the preceding centuries had pointed Sparta and Athens in different directions.

Unlike Athens, which held on to its Mycenaean culture during the Greek Dark Age, Sparta was invaded and conquered by the Dorians around 1100 B.C. During the next few hundred years, the Dorians took over the region surrounding the city-state of Sparta. They enslaved the former inhabitants of

351

The Ancient Greeks

## Spartan Government

■ = Kings ■ = Senate
■ = Ephors ▨ = Citizens' Assembly

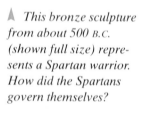

*This bronze sculpture from about 500 B.C. (shown full size) represents a Spartan warrior. How did the Spartans govern themselves?*

## The Government of Sparta

Like the government of Athens, Sparta's government began as a monarchy. However, Sparta had two kings who ruled together. This custom probably began because the original Dorian invaders of Sparta included two tribes, each with its own leader. As in Athens, the Spartan monarchy developed into an oligarchy. The two kings became part of a 30-man senate. The members of the senate were elected by the citizens, who included all male landholders over age 30. However, a person could not become a senator until he reached 60 years of age.

All Spartan citizens belonged to an assembly similar to the one held in Athens. However, Spartan citizens could not propose laws. They could only vote yes or no on laws proposed by the senate or by the **ephors** *(EHF awrz)*, five government leaders elected by the assembly. Even if the assembly voted down a law, the senate and ephors often ignored this vote.

Although the Spartans had an assembly and held elections for government offices, power was really in the hands of a few families. These families dominated the senate and could control the ephors. A truly democratic government never developed in Sparta. This city-state remained an oligarchy throughout its history.

## The Economy of Sparta

Sparta's emphasis on maintaining a strong army shaped the economy. By law, the only occupation a Spartan man could hold was that of a soldier. The people living in the communities around Sparta provided trade and craft items for

Sparta. Although people in towns near Sparta remained free, they were forced to serve in the Spartan army.

The slave population of Sparta was much larger than the population of Spartan citizens. When Sparta was at the height of its power, its population consisted of 25,000 citizens and 250,000 slaves. The Spartans were concerned about the possibility of uprisings by their slaves. Because of this fear, they built a strong army. In fact, Spartan men spent almost their entire adult lives in military service. The Spartans bragged that they needed no walls to protect their city; their soldiers were the only walls they needed.

the city-state. During much of Sparta's history, the government forbade Spartans to have luxury goods. Thus, Spartans led very simple lives. Today we refer to a simple lifestyle without luxuries as "spartan."

Each Spartan citizen received a plot of land from the government. **Helots** *(HEHL uhts)*–state slaves assigned to a particular plot—farmed the land. They received some of the crops as wages and turned over the rest to the owner. The owner gave a portion of his crops to the government, which provided him with daily meals. If, for some reason, a Spartan could not pay for these meals, he lost his rights as a citizen. ■

■ *Why did the economy of Sparta center on a strong army?*

## Education in Sparta and Athens

The differences between the two city-states were also reflected in the ways children were treated. Look at the chart on page 354. How did growing up differ in Sparta and Athens?

The Spartan government had a huge influence on the daily lives of its citizens. In fact, when a Spartan baby was born, a government inspector came to look it over. If the baby did not seem healthy, the inspector took the baby to a distant cave on a mountainside and left it there to die. The Spartans wanted only babies who they thought would grow into strong adults.

### Training Spartan Children

All Spartan children lived at home until they were seven years old. Then the boys had to leave their families to live in barracks with other boys their own age. From that moment on, the government took over their education and controlled their lives.

Although the boys were taught to read and write, their training emphasized physical skills, including running, jumping, boxing, and wrestling. Conditions in the Spartan schools were harsh, and discipline was strict. The boys slept on the floor. Even when the weather was cold, they wore only light clothes. The Spartans thought that such hardships made the boys stronger. Anyone who disobeyed orders received severe punishment. Even obedient children were whipped from time to time. According to the Spartans, such beatings were good training for soldiers.

Beginning at age 18, young men devoted all their time to the army. By age 30, a Spartan man

▼ *Many Spartan girls excelled at sports. This bronze sculpture from about 520 B.C. shows a girl running.*

353

## Growing Up in Sparta and Athens

| Citizens | Ages 0–7 | Ages 7–18 | Ages 18–? |
|---|---|---|---|
| Spartan | A government inspector decides whether the new-born baby is healthy; if not, the baby is taken to a cave and left to die. Children remain in the home, learning traditional discipline. | Boys leave their homes and live in barracks with other boys as they begin their education. Physical education and military training are stressed. Girls receive training in physical education. Girls often marry at age 15. | Men enter the army and continue military training. At age 30, men complete their military training and gain full citizenship. Women take care of the home and raise children. |
| Athenian | Baby boys are more prized than girls. Some girls are left at the gates of the city, where people passing by might find them and raise them. Children in wealthy families may begin their education with a private tutor. | Wealthy Athenian boys attend school, receiving training in reading, writing, arithmetic, fine arts, and athletics. Girls remain at home, learning crafts and poetry from their mothers. Girls often marry at age 15. | Men enter the army for two years. Then they enter the army reserve force. Men manage farms or estates and participate in the government. Women take care of the home and raise children. |

▲ *Compare and contrast the lives of girls and boys in Sparta and Athens.*

completed his military training and gained full citizenship. However, even if he married, he continued to eat his meals in the mess hall with other soldiers. He also continued to devote much of his time to taking part in military exercises.

Although the training Spartan girls received was not as extensive as that of boys, the girls did get a strong physical education. They practiced running, wrestling, and discus throwing. The Spartans believed that girls had to be strong in order to bear healthy children.

Although the Spartans emphasized military training, they also enjoyed several forms of entertainment. At religious festivals they participated in chorus contests, with boys and girls singing traditional songs. Dance contests were also popular.

### Training Athenian Children

The Athenians valued cultural education as well as physical education. However, only boys in wealthy families received formal education. Upon reaching seven years of age, wealthy Athenian boys began school. Unlike Spartan boys, however, Athenian boys did

not have to live in barracks with other boys. They lived at home with their families.

Athenian schoolboys learned reading, writing, arithmetic, poetry, music, and dance. They also devoted much time to athletics. When they reached 18 years of age, they joined the army for two years of military training. Upon graduation, these young men received a shield and spear and joined a reserve force. The reserve force was called to duty in times of war.

Unlike the Spartan government, which trained girls in athletics, the Athenian government basically ignored the training of women. Girls learned crafts and poetry from their mothers.

Because of the rich culture of Athens, an Athenian's education continued throughout his or her adult life. Athenians often discussed the myths about the gods and the poetry of Homer. They looked forward to seeing new plays at the yearly festival to Dionysus. In addition, during the late 300s B.C., Athens developed academies where wealthy adults could continue their schooling.

## Comparing Cultures

The differing values of Sparta and Athens produced different cultures. Ancient Greek thinkers admired the Spartans because their military background made for a stable society. Although Athens is admired today for its democracy and its personal freedoms, many ancient Greeks thought Athenian freedom made its citizens restless and unpredictable. ◼

◀ Athenians continued their education as adults by discussing myths. This vase painting from the 500s B.C. illustrates the myth of the twin gods Kastor and Pollux.

◼ How did education differ in Sparta and in Athens?

# Allies Against Persia

Although Sparta and Athens were quite different, their leaders occasionally put their differences aside and joined together to fight a common enemy. The greatest foreign challenge to the Greek city-states came from the Persian empire in the 490s B.C.

During the 500s B.C., Persia built a vast empire in what is today called the Middle East. Stretching from Egypt in the west to the Indus River in the east, the Persian empire brought the entire region under one ruler. The Persians began to extend their control into the city-states along the eastern edge of the Aegean Sea.

In 499 B.C., Athens sent soldiers to help these city-states fight off the Persians. After five years of fighting, Persia crushed the revolt. However, Persia's king Darius wanted to punish Athens for aiding the rebellion.

In 490, the Persians sailed toward Athens, landing at the Bay of Marathon. As you have read, the Athenian forces defeated the invaders. The Persians fled, leaving thousands of dead soldiers on the battlefield. However, the Persians did not give up their desire to punish Athens. They also hoped to one day conquer all of Greece.

## Fighting Xerxes' Army

Ten years later, in 480 B.C., the Persian army returned under Darius's son Xerxes (ZURK seez). Historians estimate that as many as 200,000 soldiers set sail from Persia. When the Greek city-states learned of this huge army about to attack them, they banded together under the military leadership of the Spartans.

The first battle between the combined Greek forces and the Persians took place at Thermopylae (thur MAHP uh lee), a mountain pass on the Greek mainland. The Greeks sent about 7,000 soldiers to guard the pass. For two days, the Greek soldiers held off the Persians. On the second night, however, a Greek traitor led a group of Persians over a secret mountain path so that they could attack the Greek forces from the rear. Most of the Greek army retreated to avoid being surrounded. However, 300 Spartan soldiers remained at the pass, fighting to the death. Although the Greeks lost the battle at Thermopylae, the

### Across Time & Space

The long-distance race called the marathon is named after Phidippides' run from Marathon to Athens. The modern marathon covers a distance of 26 miles 385 yards. Marathons are held in many cities throughout the world. The marathon also is an event in the Olympic games.

**1**
In the Battle of Salamis, the Greek ships (in red) were clustered at the island of Salamis. The Persians divided their fleet (in yellow), sending some ships around the island to cut off the Greeks. However, those ships did not arrive in time to fight in the battle.

**2**
As the Greek ships left the island, the remaining Persian ships sailed into the narrow passage between the island and the Greek mainland.

*Three rows of oarsmen, one located atop another, powered the Greek and Persian ships.*

How did the Greeks finally win the Persian Wars?

brave stand of the Spartans allowed the rest of the Greek army to withdraw.

After the battle of Thermopylae, the Persian army overran mainland Greece and burned Athens to the ground. However, most Athenians had escaped by ship to the island of Salamis. Thus, "wooden walls" did indeed save the Athenians as the oracle at Delphi had predicted.

**The Final Battles**

The next major battle in the Persian Wars took place off the coast of Salamis about a month after the battle of Thermopylae. Look at the illustrations above. How did the Greeks trick the Persians and defeat them?

The Greeks sank about half the Persian fleet. Xerxes led his remaining troops back to Persia. The following summer, in 479 B.C., the Persians tried one more time to invade Greece. At the battle of Plataea *(pluh TEE uh)*, Greek forces led by the Spartans overwhelmed the Persians. By banding together, the Greek city-states defeated the immense Persian army. This victory showed the amazing things Athens and Sparta could achieve when they united. In the next chapter, you will read about the terrible destruction that resulted when they fought. ■

▲ *Both the Persians and the Greeks sailed in ships called triremes. The ships had strong bronze bows that were used as battering rams.*

**3**
The Greeks tricked the Persians into believing the Greek ships were retreating. The Persian fleet bunched together as it prepared to attack.

**4**
The Greeks reversed their course and attacked first. They surrounded the Persian ships and rammed them. About 200 Persian ships were sunk. The Greeks lost only 40 ships.

## R E V I E W

1. **FOCUS** How were the cultures of Athens and Sparta similar? How were they different?

2. **CONNECT** How was the economy of Sparta different from the economy of Athens?

3. **SOCIAL SYSTEMS** Why did some ancient Greek thinkers admire Sparta more than Athens?

4. **CRITICAL THINKING** If you had a choice, would you rather be an Athenian or a Spartan? Why?

5. **WRITING ACTIVITY** Write a newspaper account describing the battle between the Greek and Persian fleets off the coast of Salamis.

The Ancient Greeks

# Chapter Review

## Reviewing Key Terms

barter (p. 343)
city-state (p. 333)
comedy (p. 350)
democracy (p. 339)
ephor (p. 352)
helot (p. 353)
monarchy (p. 339)
oligarchy (p. 339)
sanctuary (p. 347)
tragedy (p. 350)
tyrant (p. 340)

**A.** On your own paper, use each word below in a sentence that shows what the word means. Write your sentence as if it were the beginning of a story.

1. monarchy
2. tyrant
3. barter
4. sanctuary
5. city-state

**B.** Answer the following questions about the key terms.

1. Which three key terms are words for people? If you could be one of these people, which would you be? Why?
2. Which two words describe a play? If you could see one of these plays, which would you see? Why?
3. Which three words name forms of government? If you could live under one of these governments, which would you choose? Why?
4. Which word names a method of trading? If you use this method, what problems might occur?

## Exploring Concepts

**A.** Copy the timeline below. After each date, write the importance of the date in the history of ancient Greece. The first entry is done for you. Choose two entries and write a paragraph for each one that explains the historical event more fully. Use information from the chapter.

**B.** Answer each question with information from the chapter.

1. How did living within 40 miles of the sea affect the unity of the Greeks?
2. How did geography help Greek civilization advance?
3. Describe the first Aegean civilization.
4. How did the first Aegean civilization influence the Mycenaeans?
5. Describe the four different forms of government used in ancient Greece.
6. Using facts in the chapter, tell how the ancient Olympics differed from today's.
7. How did the Greeks individually worship their gods?
8. How did the governments of Athens and Sparta develop differently?
9. How were Spartan boys trained for the military?
10. How did the Spartans help lead the Greeks to victory over the Persians?

2000 B.C., Minoan Age begins in Crete.

1100 B.C., ___

776 B.C., ___

570 B.C., ___

2000 | 1750 | 1500 | 1250 | 1000 | 750 | 500

1400 B.C., ___

600 B.C., ___

479 B.C., ___

# Reviewing Skills

1. The table at the right gives information about the discus throw event in the Olympics. What kind of graph would be the best one to use to show this information? Explain why this is the best graph to use.

2. On your own paper, create a graph using the information from the table at the right. Make the kind of graph you chose as your answer to question 1.

3. Decide which kind of graph would best show the following information about Spartan life. Then create the graph on your own paper.

| Age | Living Quarters /Activity |
|-----|---------------------------|
| 0–7 | Home/early training |
| 7–18 | Barracks/physical training |
| 18–20 | Barracks/army training |

4. Look at the detailed map of Delphi on page 348. Based on the information on this map, what could you say about the people who lived there?

**Olympic Discus Records**

| Year | Distance (in nearest feet) |
|------|----------------------------|
| 1896 | 96 |
| 1912 | 148 |
| 1932 | 162 |
| 1956 | 185 |
| 1972 | 211 |
| 1988 | 226 |

5. It is 400 B.C. You are a metalworker who makes coins. You have decided that you want to record the coinmaking process for future generations. How would you choose to show it? Name the type of drawing you might make.

# Using Critical Thinking

1. One reason Spartan men spent most of their adult lives in the military service was that Spartans were concerned about uprisings by their slaves. Do you think the history of ancient Greece might have been different if Sparta had had fewer slaves? Explain why you think as you do.

2. Because a young girl in Athens was not educated, she could not take part in the political life of her community. Do you think this strengthens or weakens a society? Explain your answer, thinking about what life in your community would be like if only boys went to school.

3. The Olympic Games were an important part of Greek life. Do sports play an important role in your school or community? Do you think good athletes should concentrate on athletics instead of school subjects? Why or why not?

# Preparing for Citizenship

1. **COLLECTING INFORMATION** Look in a dictionary for words with Greek origins. Write the definitions of five words you find.

2. **WRITING ACTIVITY** Long ago, myths were used to explain natural events. Sometimes mythic characters acted out qualities that a society admired or disliked. Find a Greek myth to read. Does any character act out a quality that we admire or dislike? Explain.

3. **COLLABORATIVE LEARNING** In small groups, plan brief Athenian-style trials to present to the class. One group member is accused of a crime. A witness supports the innocence of the accused. A second witness denies the innocence of the accused. A public crier announces the decision facing the jurors. The class (the jury) decides each case.

# Chapter 12

# *Classical Greece*

*"Our city is an education to Greece," boasted Pericles, the leader of Athens, in 430 B.C. This was Greece's Golden Age, when Athens blossomed as a center of democratic government and achievements in the arts and sciences. Although Athens and the other Greek city-states eventually fell to foreign invaders, their accomplishments have been passed down through the ages.*

| 550 | 500 | 450 |
|---|---|---|

# 500 B.C.

**447–405 B.C.** The Athenians build beautiful temples on a rocky hill called the Acropolis. The Parthenon (above) is a marble temple dedicated to the goddess Athena.

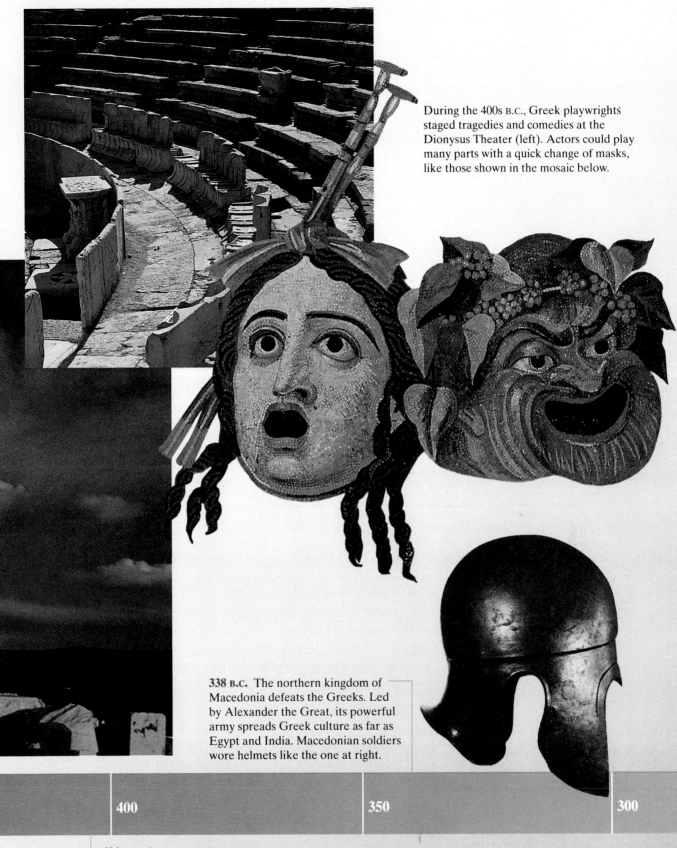

During the 400s B.C., Greek playwrights staged tragedies and comedies at the Dionysus Theater (left). Actors could play many parts with a quick change of masks, like those shown in the mosaic below.

**338 B.C.** The northern kingdom of Macedonia defeats the Greeks. Led by Alexander the Great, its powerful army spreads Greek culture as far as Egypt and India. Macedonian soldiers wore helmets like the one at right.

400

350

300

**404 B.C.** Sparta conquers Athens, bringing an end to the Peloponnesian War.

# 323 B.C.

# The Golden Age of Athens

## THINKING
## FOCUS

*Why were the years of Pericles' leadership called the Golden Age of Athens?*

### Key Term

• agora

➤ *Pericles led Athens during much of its Golden Age. This bust portrays him as a general with his helmet on.*

The messengers sent to Athens in 480 B.C. urgently sounded an alert: The Persians are going to invade. Everyone leave the city immediately!

A 15-year-old boy named Pericles *(PEHR ih kleez)* heard the warning, and he fled from Athens with the other citizens. They escaped to an island off the southern coast of Greece. Soon, terrifying news reached them: the Persians had burned their great city. Athens had been destroyed.

Was it at that moment that young Pericles vowed to build up Athens again and make it the greatest city of its time? No one can know for sure. But Pericles did return to Athens, and he became its most outstanding leader. From 460 to 429 B.C., Pericles led Athens through an age so glorious that it became known as the Golden Age of Athens.

## The Age of Pericles

The Greeks defeated the Persians in 479 B.C., just one year after the invasion of Athens. Pericles then returned home. As a young man, he became well known in the law courts, where he won many cases because of his intelligence and his excellent speaking ability. The Greek historian Plutarch wrote the following about Pericles' ability: "Like Zeus, he was said to speak with thundering and lightning, and to wield a dreadful thunderbolt in his tongue."

Because he was a persuasive speaker, Pericles was able to convince the citizens that his ideas were important. As a result, in 460 B.C. they elected him as one of the 10 generals, the main elected officers in the Athenian democracy. The term for generals lasted just one year, but Pericles was elected over and over again.

Pericles set three major goals for Athens. His military goal was to protect Athens. His artistic goal was to make Athens beautiful. His political goal was to strengthen democracy.

## Protection

Pericles' first goal was to protect Athens from its enemies. He was determined to prevent another disaster such as the burning of the city by the Persians just 20 years earlier.

The Athenians had already built a strong stone wall around Athens after the war with Persia. But enemies could still surround the city and block Athens from Piraeus, its harbor five miles away. If that happened, the city would be cut off from necessary food supplies that came into the city by ship. So the Athenians extended the wall to the sea. The new barricaded corridor became known as the Long Walls.

To protect their city further, the Athenians also built up a very powerful navy. In the years to come, Athens's navy would be the key to its defense.

## Beautification

Pericles' second goal was to make Athens the most beautiful city in the world. To do that, the Athenians built new public buildings and temples. Plutarch wrote that the buildings "gave most pleasure and ornament to the city of Athens, and the greatest admiration and even astonishment to all strangers."

The most magnificent of these buildings were built on the Acropolis *(uh KRAHP ah lihs)*. The Acropolis was a flat-topped, fortified hill in the middle of Athens. It stood about 200 feet above the rest

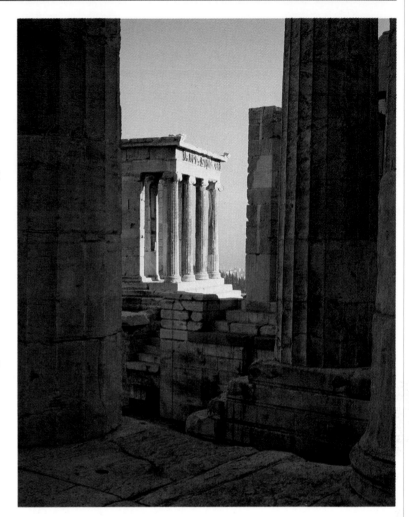

of the city and covered a little more than 10 acres. Temples had adorned the Acropolis for many years. But the Persian troops had destroyed all of them when they invaded the city.

The most beautiful new temple, called the Parthenon, was dedicated to Athena, the city's patron goddess. The Parthenon was 60 feet high, built from marble, and surrounded by 46 tall, graceful columns. Inside the Parthenon stood a 40-foot-tall gold and ivory statue of the goddess Athena. The Parthenon was a tribute to the outstanding artistry of the Athenians during the Golden Age. Many historians consider it to be the most beautiful building in ancient Greece.

*During the Golden Age of Athens, the Athenians beautified their city greatly. One of the most beautiful buildings from that age was the Temple of Nike, the goddess of victory.*

363

As many as 20,000 citizens were on the public payroll during the Golden Age of Athens. Everyone in the government received a salary. As a result, even poor citizens could afford to hold office and have their voices heard.

## Athens's Golden Age

During the Golden Age, Athens was called the "school of Greece," because it was a center for art, literature, and ideas. In the same speech in which he praised the Athenian democracy, Pericles stated some of the basic beliefs of the Athenians:

*Our love of what is beautiful does not lead to extravagance; our love of things of the mind does not make us soft. We regard wealth as something to be properly used, rather than as something to boast about. As for poverty, no one need be ashamed to admit it: the real shame is in not taking practical measure to escape from it. Here each individual is interested not only in his own affairs but in the affairs of the state as well.*

Note how these beliefs differ from those of Athens's rival, Sparta. ◼

*▲ The Parthenon can still be seen today. It has been badly damaged by pollution and by an explosion that occurred in 1687 when Turkish troops were storing gunpowder in the Parthenon.*

### How Do We Know?

**HISTORY** *Pericles gave his speech to the citizens of Athens in 430 B.C., after the first year of fighting in a war with Sparta. The speech was recorded by Thucydides, one of the first great historians. Thucydides spent 27 years writing a history of the war with Sparta.*

◼ *What were Pericles' three major goals for Athens?*

## Democracy

Pericles wanted to make Athenian democracy even stronger by spreading power more evenly between rich and poor. He said to the citizens of Athens:

*It is true that we are called a democracy, for the administration is in the hands of the many and not of the few. When it is a question of settling private disputes, everyone is equal before the law; when it is a question of putting one person before another in positions of public responsibility, what counts is not membership of a particular class, but the actual ability which the man possesses.*

## Life in a Citizen Family

The citizens of Athens generally enjoyed a pleasant life during the Golden Age. Here is an account of how a family in Athens might have spent a typical day. As the first few rays of sunlight shimmered into the center court-yard of a citizen's house, the family would begin to prepare for their day. A typical household included a mother, father, two or three children, and one or two slaves or hired servants.

## Men at the Marketplace

Everyone in the family ate a light breakfast of pieces of bread soaked in wine mixed with water. Afterward, the father headed down the narrow, crooked streets toward the **agora,** or marketplace. The agora was a large, open square located near the Acropolis. Beautiful public buildings and temples lined two sides of the square. On the other sides of the square, men debated the issues of the day. In the huge open center, vendors sold items ranging from food and pottery to goats and sheep. Athenian merchants hawked their wares or argued with customers over prices.

Each man walking in the agora was dressed in the usual Greek fashion—a woolen tunic that fell either to his knees or ankles. Only the richest men could afford cotton or linen tunics.

Men also might go to the Assembly or serve as jurors at the law courts. At the Assembly, citizens debated current political issues. Some of these debates were so important that citizens walked into the city from 10 to 20 miles away to hear them. At the law courts, jurors listened to speeches for and against an accused person. Then the jury members cast votes of guilty or innocent. Juries in Athens consisted of between 201 and 2,501 citizens.

In the afternoons, Athenian men went to

*Athenian men spent much of their day at the gymnasium. Here they took part in sports such as boxing, discus and javelin throwing, and wrestling. The gymnasium was also a popular place for conversation.*

Athenian women did many of the household tasks. This vase shows women collecting water. Athenian homes did not have indoor plumbing, and so women had to carry water from wells to their homes.

Athenian women spent most of their time in the house. There they might work in the looming room upstairs, making clothing, and the kitchen downstairs, making bread.

one of the outdoor gymnasiums and exercised. In the evenings, the men socialized together as well.

## Women and Children at Home

While men were in the agora, women were at home. Women were not allowed to vote or hold office. Instead, a woman spent much of her time in a double room called the looming room. There she made the family clothes. First she spun sheep's wool into threads on a spinning wheel. Then she dyed the threads red, yellow, black, blue, or green. Finally, she wove the threads into fabrics.

Next to the looming room was a small kitchen. There women ground grain for bread and baked the bread in small clay ovens. Preparing bread was an important task, because bread was a staple of the family's diet.

Women did all of the other cooking over a small portable hearth. During a festival, however, a family often hired a cook to roast an animal.

Women also cared for their young children. Once sons reached the age of seven, they attended school during the day. Daughters stayed home and learned how to do household tasks.

Most girls married around the age of 15. Generally their fathers chose the girls' future husbands. Sometimes a father might arrange a marriage years before the marriage was to occur. Such an arrangement made sure that the girl would marry into a good family.

The houses where women spent much of their time generally looked alike. They were made out of mud bricks that had been dried in the sun. Roofs were made from baked tiles. A door from the street opened onto a courtyard that had an altar to Zeus at its center. The rooms surrounding the courtyard were dark because they had no windows. These rooms stayed cool in the summer and warm in the winter.

Many rich citizens could have lived in more luxury. However, they believed that their wealth should be used for the good of the whole community. The famous Greek speaker Demosthenes (dih MAHS thuh neez) noted that the Athenians made public buildings that "their successors can never surpass; but in private life, they practiced so great a moderation" that an observer would not be able to tell the homes of the rich from the homes of the poor.

### Evenings in the Home

As the sun started to set, the men returned home for dinner. A husband and his wife ate together only if he had not invited guests. Often, however, a husband would bring home several friends. The men ate in a separate room called the men's dining room. This room was bare except for some couches against the walls where the men reclined as they ate.

Wives joined their husbands publicly for only two events. They might attend a play together or a religious parade or festival. ■

■ *How did citizens of Athens spend their days?*

## Life for Noncitizens

One reason wealthy citizens enjoyed a pleasant lifestyle was that noncitizens did much of the work. Two groups of noncitizens, metics and slaves, lived in Athens.

### Metics and Slaves

In order to live and work in Athens, metics were required to register with the government and to pay a monthly tax. They could not own property in Athens. Metics were allowed to attend the theater and religious festivals, and they had the right to use the law courts.

Citizens looked down on metics as inferior or second-class people. However, many metics became wealthy in Athens and returned to their own city-states, where they enjoyed both wealth and all the benefits of citizenship.

In contrast to metics, slaves had no legal rights. Most Athenian citizens owned at least one slave. Wealthy landowners often kept several slaves to farm their land, including one slave to oversee the others. Even an ordinary farmer kept one slave so the farmer could be free on certain days to go into Athens and attend the Assembly.

Slaves often did the same jobs as other Athenians, sometimes

◄ *Athenians and their slaves dressed similarly. This vase shows a slave handing a pot to her mistress. Notice the similarity of their dress.*

367

Classical Greece

▲ *Some Athenian slaves were skilled craftsmen. Here a pottery maker finishes a pot while his completed work lies around him.*

working alongside them. One Greek historian wrote that foreigners could not tell slaves apart from citizens because "they [citizens] are no better dressed and no better in appearance."

The better-off slaves held jobs that required great skill, such as goldsmithing or pottery making. Their owners often paid these slaves for their services. Slaves who saved enough of their earnings could buy their freedom. Once freed, however, slaves did not become citizens. They could only move into the ranks of metics.

One talented slave named Pasion did become a citizen as a result of his skill. Because Pasion was very smart, his master put him in charge of his bank. Pasion made so much money that his owner not only set him free, but also gave Pasion the bank. Over the years, Pasion multiplied his wealth and used his money to acquire a shield factory. He probably had many slaves of his own working there. A generous man, Pasion donated large sums of money for government projects in Athens. Before his death in 370 B.C., the grateful Athenians made him a citizen.

**The Mining Slaves**

In sharp contrast to Pasion's pleasant life were the terrible lives of the slaves who worked in the silver mines. As many as 40,000 slaves at a time worked in the mines. These slaves, who were owned by the state, had perhaps the worst lives in all of Athens. Forced to work 10-hour shifts while chained to rocks, the slaves had to crawl in tunnels that were only three feet high. They worked all day in near-darkness, chipping at stone with small picks. Many mining slaves died from overwork or disease.

Except for the miners, slaves in Athens were generally treated well, especially compared to other Greek city-states. All ancient societies had slaves. And Athens—as advanced as it was in politics and the arts—was no exception. ■

■ *How was a metic's life different from a slave's?*

---

### R E V I E W

1. **FOCUS** Why were the years of Pericles' leadership called the Golden Age of Athens?
2. **CONNECT** How was life in Athens during the Golden Age different from life in Greece during the earlier Dark Age?
3. **CITIZENSHIP** What were the roles of men and women in a citizen family?
4. **CRITICAL THINKING** Do you think life for citizens would have been different if Athens had not allowed slavery? Explain your answer.
5. **WRITING ACTIVITY** Divide a paper into two columns marked Citizens and Noncitizens. Compare and contrast the lives of these two groups in Athens during the Golden Age.

Chapter 12

Meanwhile, the war against Sparta and her allies went on relentlessly. For many years, neither side seemed to be winning. Sparta had the more powerful army, and Athens had the more powerful navy. Therefore, the war was often at a deadlock.

A turning point in the war came in 413 B.C., when the Athenian troops suffered a serious defeat at Sicily. Many of the small cities of the Delian League that had been ruled by Athens decided to take advantage of the weakened condition of the Athenians. To free themselves from Athens's control, these cities joined forces with Sparta.

The fighting continued in Greece for another 10 years. Athens's final defeat became nearly certain when Persia agreed to give Sparta funds to build a bigger and better fleet. Although Persia was still an enemy of all of Greece, the Persians gave Sparta funds because they hoped that the Greek city-states would destroy each other.

### End of the War

Meanwhile, in one last effort to defend themselves, the Athenians melted down the gold and silver ornaments in the temples to pay for building new ships. However, in 405 B.C., the Athenians made a mistake so crucial that it led to their final defeat.

The battlefront had moved to the coastal cities of the Hellespont. In the summer of 405 B.C., the Athenians sailed their fleet to a port called Aegospotami *(EE guh SPAHT uh mee)*. For five days, the Spartans did not begin a battle. Believing that the harbor was safe, the Athenians went ashore to obtain badly needed food and supplies. While they were gone, the Spartan forces captured almost the entire Athenian fleet—without a single fight.

When news of the defeat at Aegospotami reached Athens, the citizens reacted with despair. In his description of that dreadful time, the Greek historian Xenophon wrote,

> On that night no man slept. There was mourning and sorrow for those that were lost, but the lamentation [expression of grief] was merged in even greater sorrow for themselves, as they pictured the evils they were about to suffer.
>
> Xenophon, *Hellenica*, c. 400 B.C.

The Athenians refused to surrender immediately. Instead, they barricaded themselves inside the city walls for several months. In the meantime, the Spartans cut off their grain supply by both land and sea. Starvation at last set in and forced the Athenians to surrender in 404 B.C. ■

### Across Time & Space

Outbreaks of the plague have devastated many other societies. In A.D. 262, about 5,000 people a day died in Rome. From 1334 to 1351, plague swept through China, India, Persia, Russia, Italy, France, England, Germany, and Norway. Between 1894 and 1914, more than 10 million people in India died of the plague.

◄ Athens suffered greatly as a result of the Peloponnesian War. This funeral sculpture honors a dead soldier. Thousands of Greeks died as a result of the wars.

■ What caused the Peloponnesian War, and what were its consequences?

371

# End of the Golden Age

The Peloponnesian War had raged for 27 years. Xenophon recorded the bleak terms of the Athenian surrender.

> That the Long Walls . . . should be destroyed; that the Athenian fleet, with the exception of twelve vessels, should be surrendered; that the exiles should be restored; and lastly, that the Athenians should acknowledge the [leadership] of Sparta in peace and war.
>
> Xenophon, *Hellenica*

Many Spartans wanted to burn Athens to the ground and sell its citizens into slavery. However, Spartan leaders decided to spare Athens. They recognized that Athens had saved all of Greece from the Persians at the battles of Marathon and Salamis.

## Decline of the Democracy

At first, the Spartans destroyed the Athenian democracy and set up rule by tyrants. These tyrants ruled arbitrarily and harshly. By 403 B.C., the Athenians had forced out the tyrants. The Spartan king allowed them to restore their democracy. However, the democracy no longer united Athenians as it had during the Golden Age.

A great number of citizens—especially the younger citizens—refused to take any role in public affairs after the war. Other citizens became suspicious of anyone who seemed the least bit antidemocratic. One of the great tragedies of this stormy time was the death of one of Greece's greatest teachers, Socrates.

## The Trial of Socrates

Socrates was a **philosopher,** a person who searches for the truth and the meaning of life. He asked the following questions: What is justice? What is wisdom? What is goodness?

Socrates became a well-known teacher in Athens. His primary method of teaching was to ask questions that made his pupils examine their own beliefs. However, his method upset many Athenian leaders. They thought that by teaching the young to question every aspect of life, Socrates was challenging the authority of the government.

In the period of suspicion following the war, Socrates was arrested. He was charged with neglecting the worship of the gods and "corrupting the youth."

Socrates stood trial in 399 B.C. In those times, most men on trial tried to gain the sympathy of the jury by bringing their weeping wife and children to court or by dressing in poor or dirty clothes. Socrates refused

➤ *Socrates was one of the greatest of the Greek philosophers.*

to use any such tactic. Instead, he stood with dignity before a jury of 700 Athenian citizens and pleaded his own case. However, the jury convicted Socrates by a narrow margin. His penalty was death by drinking hemlock, the juice from a poisonous plant.

During the month between the famous trial and his death, Socrates could have escaped several times. Seventy years old by that time, Socrates explained to his friends that he had obeyed the law throughout his long life and would not break it then. Later, a student of Socrates' named Plato (*PLAY toh*), wrote the following about his teacher's last moments:

*He raised the cup to his lips and very cheerfully and quietly drained it. Up to that time most of us had been able to restrain our tears fairly well, but when we watched him drinking and saw that he had drunk the poison, we could do so no longer, but in spite of myself my tears rolled down in floods, so that I wrapped my face in my cloak and wept for myself.*

Plato honored his teacher when he said, "It was not for him [Socrates] that I wept, but for my own misfortune in being deprived of such a friend." ∎

▲ *Socrates' death is illustrated in this French painting from the 1700s by Jacques Louis David. What attitude toward his death does Socrates seem to have in this painting?*

■ *Why did the teachings of Socrates upset Athenian leaders?*

---

## R E V I E W

1. **FOCUS**  Why did the Golden Age come to an end?
2. **CONNECT**  Was Athens justified in forming the Delian League? Why?
3. **HISTORY**  How might the plague have affected the outcome of the Peloponnesian War?
4. **CRITICAL THINKING**  How did democracy in Athens differ before and after the Golden Age?
5. **ACTIVITY**  Socrates taught his pupils to question every aspect of life. Athenian leaders thought his questioning threatened the democracy. Who do you think was right? Prepare and give a speech defending either Socrates or the Athenian leaders.

L E S S O N   3

# Alexander the Great and His Influence

**THINKING FOCUS**

*How did Alexander the Great spread Greek culture throughout the ancient world?*

### Key Terms

- conquest
- Hellenistic

Alexander rode his horse Bucephalus on most of his military campaigns. Bucephalus fell in battle on the Hydaspes River in 326 B.C.

King Philip of Macedonia and many of his subjects looked on one day in 342 B.C. as men attempted to tame a horse. The huge horse kept rearing up, kicking its legs wildly and throwing its head back and forth. The king wanted to buy the horse, but he decided it was too mean and wild. Then his 14-year-old son Alexander spoke up. "What a horse they are losing, and all because they don't know how to handle him, or dare not try!" According to the historian Plutarch:

Philip kept quiet at first, but when he heard Alexander repeat these words several times and saw that he was upset, he asked him, "Are you finding fault with your elders because you think you know more than they do, or can manage a horse better?" "At least I could manage this one better," explained Alexander.

Alexander bet his father that he could ride the horse. Alexander approached the horse and stroked it to calm it down. Then Alexander mounted it and galloped around the field. Plutarch wrote:

Thereupon the rest of the company broke into loud applause, while his father, we are told, actually wept for joy. And when Alexander had dismounted he kissed him and said, "My boy, you must find a kingdom big enough for your ambitions. Macedonia is too small for you."

Alexander would indeed follow his father's advice. Riding this horse, he would venture far beyond Macedonia to create the largest kingdom the ancient western world had yet known.

# The Rise of Macedonia

From 399 B.C. to 338 B.C., individual Greek city-states fought each other for power. However, no city-state could establish the kind of power Athens had enjoyed during the Golden Age.

## The Rise of Macedonia

Macedonia was a large state just north of Greece. It had little power because it was far less organized than the smaller Greek city-states. However, when King Philip, Alexander's father, took the throne in 359 B.C., he turned Macedonia into a military power.

Most ancient armies were made up of soldiers who served for a limited time and then returned home. Philip, however, established a professional army of full-time, well-paid, highly skilled soldiers.

A military genius, Philip developed new battle formations and a large number of weapons for his army. These new weapons included catapults, machines that could hurl burning spears or 50-pound rocks over walls, and battering rams on wheels that could smash through locked doors and closed gates.

## Greece Falls to Macedonia

Philip used his powerful army to build an empire. Soon after coming to rule in 359 B.C., he defeated large tribes to the north and west of Macedonia. Then he turned south to Greece. The Greek armies were no match for the Macedonian military and fell at the Battle of Chaeronea (*KEHR uh NEE uh*). In 338 B.C., Philip became ruler of Greece.

Philip might have ended Greece's independence after his victory. Yet he did not. After he had defeated the Greeks, Philip ordered that Athens not be destroyed because he admired its culture. Philip had gained respect for Greek ways during his youth when he spent three years in Thebes as a hostage.

When Philip defeated the Greeks, he reorganized their armies and combined them with Macedonia's troops. Philip then set out to conquer the great Persian empire with his powerful army. However, shortly before his first expedition to Persia, Philip was murdered. Philip's son Alexander would have to fulfill Philip's dreams of empire. ■

*This gilded sheeting for a bow-and-arrow case is believed to have been Philip's. It gives an idea of the wealth and power of Philip and his son.*

■ *How did Macedonia become a powerful state?*

# Alexander's Conquests

Alexander was only 20 when his father was murdered in 336 B.C. But he firmly took charge of his father's kingdom. He put down the revolts that sprang up. Then he turned his ambitions toward winning new lands.

With his troops, Alexander began a 20,000-mile journey of **conquest,** or victory by force over other peoples. Look at the map in A Closer Look on pages 376 and 377. How far south did Alexander extend his empire? How far east? ■

■ *How did Alexander build an empire?*

# Alexander's Conquests

*Alexander the Great was a brilliant general. By outwitting his enemies, he defeated armies much larger than his own. Alexander was only 16 when he joined his father's army. For the rest of his life, he marched from battle to battle.*

**1 Pella**
**April 334 B.C.**
At the age of 21 Alexander left the Macedonian capital with an army of 35,000 men. He never returned.

**2 Tyre**
**January–July 332 B.C.**
Before invading Egypt, Alexander had to conquer Tyre, the last base the Persian navy controlled. Alexander's soldiers took seven months to build a bridge to the walled island, while Tyrian soldiers hurled molten lead at them from catapults.

**ALEXANDER'S CONQUESTS**

—————— Alexander's Route

∙∙∙∙∙∙∙∙∙ Extent of Empire

N

MACEDONIA
THRACE
Black Sea
Pella
Aegean Sea
Thebes
Troy
ASIA MINOR
Magnesia
Corinth
Gordium
Athens
Miletus
CRETE
Issus
Mediterranean Sea
Ga
LIBYA
Arbela
CYPRUS
Tyre
Opis
Alexandria
Jerusalem
Babylon
Memphis
Siwa
EGYPT
ARABIA
Red Sea
AFRICA

**Spearpoints** like this one have been found wherever Alexander fought. His infantry carried 14-foot spears, while most armies at the time carried much shorter ones.

**3 Alexandria**
**November 332 B.C.**
The Persian rulers of Egypt gave their land and money to Alexander without a fight. In Egypt, Alexander founded Alexandria, the first of many cities he would name after himself.

**King Darius III of Persia** stood between Alexander and the rest of Asia. Their armies fought at the Gulf of Issus in 333 B.C. and at Guagamela two years later. Each time Darius had more soldiers. But Alexander's clever planning won the battles, forcing Darius to flee for his life.

*Roman mural from the first century A.D. shows Alexander (left) and Darius (right)*

CHINA

ASIA

Alexandria Eschate

Caspian Sea

SYRIA

HIMALAYAS

Maracanda

HINDU KUSH

Taxila

Bactra Zariaspa

Alexandropolis (Meshed)

Alexandria (Kabul)

MEDIA

Hecatompylus (Damghan)

Alexandria (Herat)

Ecbatana

Alexandria (Kandahar)

Susa

PERSIA

Persepolis (capital of Persian Empire)

Pura

Patala

INDIA

Persian Gulf

Arabian Sea

**6** **Hyphasis River**
**Summer 326 B.C.**
After months of heat and rain, the army reached the Hyphasis River and refused to go any farther. To punish the army, Alexander led them on a harsh homeward route through the desert. Three years later, at the age of 33, Alexander became ill and died in Babylon.

**4** **Persepolis**
**330 B.C.**
After marching 400 miles through mountains and fighting battles in sub-zero cold, Alexander's army looted and destroyed Persepolis.

**5** **Khyber Pass**
**Summer 327 B.C.**
Alexander's army began to move more and more slowly. The treasure they had captured made mountain travel difficult. Alexander finally burned his share of the loot and ordered his men to do the same.

Classical Greece

# The Spread of Greek Culture

**Across Time & Space**

Today Alexandria is the chief port of Egypt. It also is the second largest city in Egypt, after Cairo, the nation's capital.

▼ The legend of Alexander lived on. This Persian painting from the 1500s shows Alexander as a horseman dressed in Persian clothing.

Like his father, Alexander had both a military genius and an appreciation for Greek culture. Alexander had learned to appreciate the accomplishments of Greek culture as a child. In fact, his father, Philip, had hired Aristotle (AR ih staht l), one of Greece's greatest philosophers, to teach Alexander about literature, philosophy, and science. Years later, Alexander would tell people that from his father, he had received life, but from Aristotle he had learned how to lead a good life.

During Alexander's lifetime, he became known as Alexander the Great. His greatness is remembered not only because he created a vast empire, but also because he spread Greek culture throughout his empire. The influence of Greek culture remained long after Alexander's empire fell apart. The legend of Alexander remained even longer. Alexander's life and conquests continued to be a popular topic for stories and paintings for more than a thousand years in India, Persia, and Egypt.

## New Greek Colonies

As Alexander conquered lands, he established colonies and built cities modeled after Greek cities in the conquered lands. Alexander realized that he could not maintain control over these conquered lands with force alone. So when he and his armies moved on, Alexander left behind Greeks to rule these lands.

In addition, he adopted some features of the conquered cultures. For instance, Alexander began to wear Persian clothing and urged his men to worship him as a god, as Persian kings had been. It was Alexander's hope that by doing these things the Persians would not see Greek rule as alien. Thus they would not rebel against the Greeks. Not only did they not rebel, many people in these countries actually learned the Greek language, worshiped the Greek gods, and read the Greek literature.

Eventually, the Greek influence became so widespread that the period from Alexander's rule to 146 B.C. became known as the Hellenistic Age. **Hellenistic** means "Greek-like." The art and culture of the Hellenistic period was a mixture of Greek and Eastern art and culture. During the Hellenistic Age, Greece became the teacher of the western world in the areas of science, art, literature, and philosophy.

Most of the lands that Alexander had conquered, such as Egypt and Persia, did not give up their own cultures altogether. Instead, these countries adopted two systems of life. One system was Greek for the people who lived in the cities. The other system was a native system for the people who lived in the country and therefore were not in close contact with the Greeks.

## The Museum at Alexandria

During the Hellenistic Age, the center of Greek culture shifted from Athens to the new city of Alexandria—named after Alexander the Great. Located in Egypt, Alexandria was founded by Alexander in 332 B.C.

A magnificent museum, which was the intellectual center of the world during the Hellenistic Age,

*The Alexander legend also continued in India. This Indian painting from the 1500s supposedly illustrates an event from Alexander's life. According to the legend, Alexander had asked to be lowered into the sea in a glass barrel. Alexander hoped to study marine life while under water.*

was built at Alexandria. At the museum, mathematicians, poets, philosophers, and astronomers gathered to explore the mysteries of numbers, words, ideas, and the heavens.

To help the scholars do their research, the museum opened a library. This library, which grew into the largest library in the ancient world, had a collection of both Greek and non-Greek scrolls. Scholars at the library translated these non-Greek scrolls into

Greek. In fact, some scientists believe that the oldest manuscript of the Old Testament—still in existence today—was first translated into Greek at the great museum in Alexandria.

Besides having a huge impact on the ancient world, the museum at Alexandria influenced future generations. It remained an important intellectual center for about seven centuries, until it was destroyed in the A.D. 200s. Thus, Alexander's conquests continued to affect the world for years after his death. ■

■ *What is Hellenistic culture?*

## UNDERSTANDING CONQUEST

Alexander the Great's many conquests built the greatest empire that the world had known up to that time. What is conquest? Why do leaders and nations set out on conquests? What are the results of conquest?

### Victory Is Not Conquest

A conquest begins when one power overcomes another power in a war. However, conquest is more than just the defeat of one army by another. During a conquest, the conquerors remain in the lands that they have won and control the defeated people by establishing a new system of government. In addition, the conquerors use the resources of the defeated country as they see fit.

### Leaders Make Conquests

Leaders and nations generally make conquests to increase their power and wealth. For example, 100 years after Alexander's death, Rome, a powerful city-state in Italy, began making conquests. The Romans hoped to increase their power by controlling trade in the lands around the Mediterranean.

Sometimes a rival nation may have great wealth but may at the same time lack the power to defend itself. The potential conqueror then attempts to conquer the rival nation to gain that wealth. For example, in the early 1500s, Spain began making conquests in the Americas. Spain wanted to acquire silver and gold from mines in America and to build Spain into a world power.

### Conquest Brings Change

The results of conquest are similar in some ways to the results of migration. Defeated peoples adopt elements of their conquerors' cultures, and conquerors borrow from the cultures of the defeated. For example, in Latin America today,

the majority of the people speak Spanish. However, the people of Spanish descent in Latin America eat many foods that were adopted from the native population, including corn and beans.

In much the same way, Alexander's armies spread Greek language and culture throughout the vast empire. But Greeks eventually began to build enormous monuments and palaces that looked more Persian than Greek. The merging of Greek and eastern cultures through conquest was to change both cultures forever.

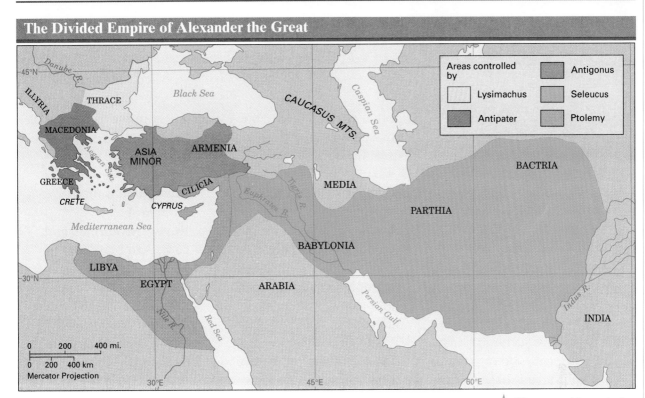

Areas controlled by

| | |
| --- | --- |
| Lysimachus | Antigonus |
| Antipater | Seleucus |
| | Ptolemy |

▲ *How was Alexander's empire divided after his death?*

# After Alexander

In 323 B.C., Alexander suddenly died of a fever. He was 33 years old. During the 13 years of his rule, he had created the largest empire in the western world.

After Alexander's death in 323 B.C., Greek culture still united the empire. But politically the empire broke apart because no single leader had enough power to take Alexander's place.

When Alexander the Great died, his generals split his empire among themselves. The giant empire was cut up into as many as 34 kingdoms. In bloody fighting, five generals took control of different parts of the empire, as shown on the map above. Which three generals controlled the largest areas? Eventually, the regions led by Antigonus *(an TIHG uh nuhs)*, Seleucus *(sih LOO kuhs)*, and Ptolemy *(TAHL uh mee)* became stronger than the rest. Yet even these had only a fraction of the power and size of the former empire of Alexander the Great. ■

■ *Why did Alexander's empire decline after his death?*

## R E V I E W

1. **FOCUS** How did Alexander the Great spread Greek culture throughout the ancient world?

2. **CONNECT** What methods did Alexander use to rule his empire? How did these methods differ from the methods the Athenians used to rule the Delian League?

3. **GEOGRAPHY** What were the major regions included in Alexander's vast empire?

4. **CRITICAL THINKING** What qualities do you think made Alexander a great leader?

5. **WRITING ACTIVITY** Imagine you are a soldier traveling with Alexander on his great march of conquests. Write a letter home telling about some of your adventures.

# Presenting Information

## Here's Why

Writing a report is a good way to add to your knowledge and to share information with others. Suppose you were asked to write a report about the outcome of the Peloponnesian War. Would you know what to do? Where would you begin?

## Here's How

Here are six basic steps for writing a good report.

1. **Explore your topic.** Make a list of five things you want to know about your topic. Consider narrowing your topic to one of the five questions.

2. **Do research.** You can find a lot of information about the Peloponnesian War in this chapter, but you should use other sources (encyclopedias, books, and magazines) also.

3. **Take notes.** As you read, record information on note cards like those below. Write each different idea on a separate note card. When you finish taking notes, group the cards according to the main ideas.

4. **Write an outline.** Look at the outline below. Notice how the important ideas from the note cards become the main points shown by Roman numerals in the outline. After you identify the main parts, go back and fill in the details. Notice how the details from the note cards become the subheads listed on the outline.

5. **Write a first draft.** Use the items with Roman numerals in your outline as paragraph topic sentences in your report. Use the subheads as supporting details. Write in complete sentences and paragraphs.

6. **Revise, proofread, and copy.** After completing your first draft, read it over to see how you can improve it and to correct any mistakes you may find. Then prepare the final copy.

## Try It

Follow the first four steps of writing a report. Use the following topic: Some people say Sparta won the Peloponnesian War; others say Athens lost it.

## Apply It

Use the first three steps of writing a report to learn more about a hobby. Then make an outline.

The Peloponnesian War
I. Sparta invades athenian countryside
   A. Farmhouses burned
   B. Crops destroyed
   C. Athenian citizens forced into the walled city
II. Plague hits athens
   A. Spreads in overcrowded city
      1. One in four die
      2. Pericles dies

A  Spartan Invasion
Spartans burn athenian farmhouses

B  Spartan Invasion
Spartans destroy crops of athenians

C  Spartan Invasion
citizens of athens forced into walled city of athens

LESSON 4

# Contributions of the Greeks

High on a hill, a Greek temple overlooks the riverfront. Along the banks of the river, the reflection of graceful Greek columns and simple Greek shapes shimmer in the water. Could this scene, pictured below, be a photograph of a well-preserved section of Greece?

Actually, it's a photograph of present-day Philadelphia. The Philadelphia Museum of Art, the temple on the hill, was modeled after the temples built by the Greeks 2,500 years ago. It was even painted with the bright colors favored by the ancient Greeks. Likewise, the buildings along the banks of the river were built in the classic Greek style. Even the name Philadelphia comes from the Greek word for "brotherly love."

The influence of the ancient Greeks can be seen throughout the United States. Many of our houses, churches, government buildings, and schools have been built in the style that can be traced to the ancient Greeks. And the influence is not only found in architecture. It's also in artwork, literature, history, philosophy, science, and mathematics.

**THINKING FOCUS**

*How does the culture of ancient Greece still influence our lives today?*

### Key Term

- lyric poetry

◀ *The riverfront of Philadelphia shows the strong influence of Greek architecture today.*

Classical Greece

383

The theater at Epidaurus, shown at right, was built over 2,300 years ago. Even today, because the theater was so well designed, anyone sitting in one of the theater's 14,000 seats can hear the faintest whisper.

## Greek Arts

You have probably seen many buildings that look Greek. Greek styles have influenced architecture in many countries during the past 2,000 years. Look at the Minipedia on pages 490 and 491 to see the features of Greek architecture.

The most noticeable feature of Greek architecture is the use of columns to support the roof. Look at the Explore feature on pages 388 and 389 for a discussion of the three types of Greek columns.

### Literature

Many of the forms of literature that have been popular throughout history can be traced to the Greeks. Although the Greeks did not invent these literary forms, they did perfect them. One popular Greek literary form was epic poetry, long poems celebrating heroic deeds. You have read about the epic poems of Homer, the *Odyssey* and the *Iliad*. The Greeks also wrote a shorter form of poetry called **lyric poetry.** Lyric poetry deals with personal feelings rather than great events. One of the greatest Greek lyric poets was Sappho *(SAF oh)*. She wrote poems celebrating friendship and love in the 600s B.C.

Perhaps the greatest contribution of Greek literature was Greek theater. Greek tragic plays are still admired today because they deal

Because Greek theaters were so large, actors wore masks so everyone in the audience could see them. Note the two masks sitting next to two of the actors in the mosaic below.

with timeless issues about how people behave.

The Greeks also introduced styles of comedy that we still see today. For example, in the 400s B.C., Greeks enjoyed biting comedies that made fun of politics, public figures, and social issues. One of the most popular Greek writers of such comedy was Aristophanes *(ar ih STAHF uh neez)*, who often made fun of important people in his plays.

## Art and Sculpture

Painters and sculptors throughout history have learned from the Greeks. Look at the sculpture pictured here. Notice the natural and lifelike form. The body looks almost real. The Greeks showed the human body in a way that is both beautiful and without flaws. As with Greek architecture, other cultures greatly admired and copied Greek art and then passed it on to future generations.

## History

The Greeks were the first people to examine the past critically and write down their findings. In the 400s B.C., two Greeks wrote accounts of wars that changed the way history was written.

The historian Herodotus *(hih RAHD uh tuhs)* is called the "father of history." His history of the Persian Wars was one of the

first factual accounts of a past event. The word *history* actually comes from the Greek word that Herodotus uses in his first line, *historia,* meaning researches or inquiries. In the opening sentence of his book, he wrote:

> These are the researches of Herodotus of Halicarnassus, which he publishes with a view to preserving from oblivion [from being forgotten] the remembrance of what men have done. Thus, the great and wonderful deeds of the Greeks and foreign peoples will not lose the acclaim that is due them. At the same time, the reasons for their hostility will be put on record.

The other great historian of the 400s B.C., Thucydides, took history a step further when he wrote an account of the Peloponnesian War. In his history, Herodotus had traced many events to the will of the gods. Thucydides, on the other hand, tried to understand events from people's actions. He also used sources and documents and interviewed eyewitnesses. His method of sifting through evidence set a new standard for future historians. ■

■ *What are three forms of literature that the Greeks are famous for?*

◄ *This statue, believed to be Zeus preparing to throw a thunderbolt, illustrates the ancient Greek style of sculpture. Note how real the figure looks.*

385

Classical Greece

➤ *The Socratic method of questioning students rather than lecturing to them is used today in most law schools in the United States. Note also the auditorium style of the room, similar to the seating at a Greek theater.*

# Greek Ideas

Just as Thucydides looked beyond the will of the gods to explain history, Greek philosophers and scientists looked beyond the gods for answers to other questions about the world. The Greeks thought people themselves could answer these questions.

continued this search for explanations. These philosophers developed ways of seeking knowledge that are still used today. In particular, many American universities use Socrates' method of repeatedly questioning students rather than lecturing to them.

## Philosophy

The search for answers, however, was not always successful. For example, Greeks at the time of Homer had believed that Poseidon, the god of the waters, caused earthquakes. In the 500s B.C., the first Greek philosopher, Thales, challenged that belief. Thales claimed that the world rested on water. Therefore, he concluded, earthquakes resulted from wind making waves in the water. Thales' explanation was wrong, but he had taken a first step in searching for explanations rather than blaming the gods.

Later philosophers, such as Socrates, Plato, and Aristotle,

## Science

The Greeks also asked basic questions about the natural world. These questions led them to make early discoveries in such diverse areas as astronomy, medicine, and mathematics.

The Greek astronomer Aristarchus *(ar ih STAHR kuhs)* was one of these early discoverers. He expressed a theory in the 200s B.C. that the earth revolved around the sun. Until Aristarchus was proven correct a thousand years later, many Europeans continued to believe that the sun revolved around the earth.

A mathematician named Pythagoras *(pih THAG ur uhs)*

386

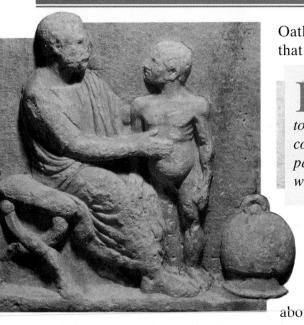

Oath. Medical doctors still take that oath today. Part of it reads,

> I will follow that method of treatment which, according to my ability and judgment, I consider for the benefit of my patients, and abstain from whatever is [harmful].

*◄ The Greeks became famous for their medicine. This relief shows an ancient doctor treating a patient.*

### The Legacy of Greece

In addition to their great achievements in the arts and sciences, the Greeks' ideas about democracy and government have been passed down through the centuries. In fact, the Greek civilization is sometimes called the starting point of Western civilization. ■

*▼ The drawing illustrates a famous theorem of Pythagoras. Adding together the squares of the lengths of two sides of a right triangle you get the square of the length of the third side. Try writing an equation that describes the triangle below.*

made important discoveries in a field of mathematics called geometry. Today, students still learn about some of Pythagoras's discoveries. Another great Greek mathematician, Euclid, is sometimes called the father of geometry. He wrote a book explaining geometry that was used as a textbook until about 1900.

In medicine, Hippocrates *(hih PAHK ruh teez)* was one of the first doctors who looked for natural causes for diseases. Previously, people had believed that acts of the gods caused diseases. In the 400s B.C., Hippocrates also wrote a pledge about the duty of doctors, called the Hippocratic

*■ How did Greek philosophers and scientists react to and try to understand the natural world?*

R E V I E W

1. **FOCUS** How does the culture of ancient Greece still influence our lives today?
2. **CONNECT** Think about the philosophers and scientists from the other cultures you have learned about. Choose one, such as Confucius or Asoka. How did their works differ from the works of Greek philosophers and scientists?
3. **CULTURE** Why is the Greek civilization considered the starting point of Western civilization?
4. **CRITICAL THINKING** Many American government buildings are designed in the Greek style. In addition to the beauty of the Greek style, what do you think are the reasons why government officials choose to use the Greek style?
5. **ACTIVITY** How does ancient Greece influence your daily life? For one week, keep track of the things you see and do that have been influenced by the Greeks. Make a chart listing the items you discover under headings such as math and science, art, literature, and government.

387

Classical Greece

# Greek Architecture in Your Community

▲ *The three classical types of Greek capitals are Doric (top), Ionic (middle), and Corinthian (bottom).*

*Y*ou don't have to travel to Greece to see what the ancient Greeks left to the modern world. Their influence reached far beyond their own borders. For instance, you can explore the Greek contribution to architecture right here at home.

## Get Ready

Pack up a sketch book and a pencil. Take along a camera if you have one. You are searching for examples of ancient Greek building styles in your own city or neighborhood.

## Find Out

Look for columns—tall pillars that support a roof or ceiling. When you find some, sketch or photograph the capitals. Are they simple Doric, graceful Ionic, or elegant Corinthian? Note the pediments—the triangular segments between the capital and the roof.

Record the location of the building and its name, if it has one. Write down what it is used for: Is it a house? A store? A government building? A bank?

## Move Ahead

Back in your classroom, compare your sketches or photographs to the drawings of the capitals on these pages and in the Architecture

PEDIMENT
CORNICE
FRIEZE
ARCHITRAVE
CAPITAL
SHAFT
COLUMN
BASE
STYLOBATE
CREPIDOMA

*This scale model of Buckingham Palace is entirely made up of interlocking plastic bricks. What elements of Greek architecture can you identify?*

entry of the Minipedia on pages 490 and 491. Correct your sketches or labels, if necessary.

Make a list of all the buildings you and your classmates saw. How many are there? What were the buildings used for?

Your class can draw a large mural showing the classical Greek architecture you found in your exploration. You can also combine many of the drawings and photographs in a collage.

### Explore Some More

Use the architectural terms on pages 490 and 491 to identify features of other buildings you find in your city or neighborhood. Some of the buildings you see may have a round dome.

The ancient Romans were the first people to borrow the Greek style. Since then, it has been copied often and in many places. In the late 1700s, architects in the United States imitated Greek architecture. Historians call this time the Federalist period of American arts.

Since Greece was the world's first democracy, Greek building styles symbolized the ideals of the new nation. The buildings were statements in stone, reminders of the people's right to govern themselves.

*Early Greek temples were painted in many bright colors. As you explore your neighborhood, do you find colors used together with elements of Greek architecture?*

Classical Greece

# Chapter Review

## Reviewing Key Terms

agora (p. 365)     lyric poetry (p. 384)
alliance (p. 369)    philosopher (p. 372)
conquest (p. 380)    plague (p. 369)
Hellenistic (p. 379)

**A.** Be sure you understand the meanings of the key terms. Then answer each question by writing one or more sentences.

1. How were the daily activities in the agora in ancient Greece similar to and different from those in the downtown part of a large city today?
2. What benefits and problems did belonging to an alliance present to a city-state?
3. What was the effect of plague on Athens?
4. Why is Alexander the Great sometimes called Alexander the Conqueror?
5. Find the origin of the word lyric in the dictionary. What does the origin of the word tell you about the meaning of the term lyric poetry?

**B.** Use each of the words below in a sentence that gives a specific fact about ancient Greece.
1. agora        3. philosopher
2. plague       4. Hellenistic

## Exploring Concepts

**A.** The timeline below covers the span of time roughly from the birth of Pericles to the death of Alexander. Copy the timeline on your own paper. For each event, fill in the date on your timeline. For each date, fill in the event. Then color the span of Pericles' lifetime in one color and the span of Alexander's lifetime in another.

**B.** Answer each question with information from the chapter.
1. In what years did the Golden Age of Athens begin and end? What important event took place in each of those two years?
2. How did the lives of male and female citizens differ during the Golden Age?
3. What rights and privileges did metics have that slaves did not have?

4. What other extremely important event took place about the same time Athens suffered an outbreak of plague?
5. Why didn't the Spartans destroy Athens after the Athenian defeat?
6. Why did the part of the world around the eastern Mediterranean Sea become Hellenized under Alexander?
7. Why was Alexander's life remarkable?
8. Compare the outcome of the Peloponnesian Wars with that of Alexander's conquests. Think of the span of time in each.
9. Describe the contributions of ancient Greece to each of the following:
   a. architecture
   b. the study of history
   c. drama and literature

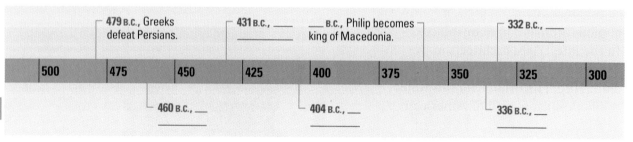

479 B.C., Greeks defeat Persians.

431 B.C., ____

____ B.C., Philip becomes king of Macedonia.

332 B.C., ____

| 500 | 475 | 450 | 425 | 400 | 375 | 350 | 325 | 300 |

460 B.C., ____

404 B.C., ____

336 B.C., ____

# Reviewing Skills

1. Reread the section The Trial of Socrates on pages 372 and 373, and make a list of five questions you might want to explore in research if you were writing a report about Socrates.
2. Make a list of resources you would use to find information to answer your questions about Socrates.
3. Place the following six steps for writing a report in the proper order:
   Do research.
   Write an outline.
   Explore your topic.
   Take notes.
   Write a first draft.
   Revise, proofread, and copy.
4. Choose two sports with which you are familiar. Compare and contrast them by finding at least two similarities and two differences.
5. You know that Greek culture spread far and wide during the time of Alexander the Great, but you want to know just how far. What kind of resource would best help you determine the distance from one end of Alexander's empire to the other? Describe how you would use that resource to find out how far Alexander spread Greek culture.

# Using Critical Thinking

1. During its Golden Age, Athens forced many other city-states to remain in the Delian League. Athens's navy attacked and captured cities along the Aegean Sea. The Parthenon was paid for with money taken from Athens's allies. Write one argument that supports Athens's policies and one argument against those policies.
2. In ancient Athens there were three social classes: slaves, metics, and citizens. Only male citizens had political power. Women were not allowed to participate in government. And yet the Athenian form of government was called a "democracy"—a political system in which the people rule. In what way was Athens a democracy? Would you be satisfied with that kind of a democracy today? Write a paragraph in which you explain why or why not.

# Preparing for Citizenship

1. **ARTS ACTIVITY** Design a building in the ancient Greek style of architecture. For ideas, use pictures and information about Greek architecture from the chapter and the Explore feature. Also use information in the Minipedia article on Architecture on pages 490–491. Carefully draw three different views of your building. Show the building's proportions and the design of its columns. Indicate how large the building would be. Either give measurements on your drawing or draw objects such as trees for comparison.
2. **COLLABORATIVE LEARNING** In groups of four, discuss the question of why there could or could not be an Alexander the Great today. Assignments should be made as follows. One person in each group should learn in detail what Alexander did. Another should learn about "balance of power," especially as that term is used today. Each should report to the group what they have learned. Based on that information, the third group member should write an explanation of what it would mean to be an Alexander the Great today. The group then should come up with a written statement of its position, with reasons for taking that position. This statement should be revised until all group members agree to it. The fourth group member then will speak for the group in a class debate with the other groups' spokespeople.

# Rome: A World Power

A row of soldiers, strong and proud, stands as a symbol of Rome at the peak of its power. Rome began as a humble village in what is now Italy. The Romans used their military strength to build a vast empire. They developed ideas of government and law to unite this empire. Over a 1,000-year period, Rome grew to rule the Mediterranean world.

# 753 B.C.

*Marble relief of a cavalry parade from the base of the column of Emperor Antoninus Pius in Rome. A.D. 161*

A.D. 476

# Chapter 13

# *The Rise of Rome*

*At a time when Greece was home to powerful city-states, Rome was just a village of straw-roofed huts. But the Romans learned quickly from their contacts with other civilizations. Within 600 years, Rome had conquered Greece and much of the rest of the Mediterranean world.*

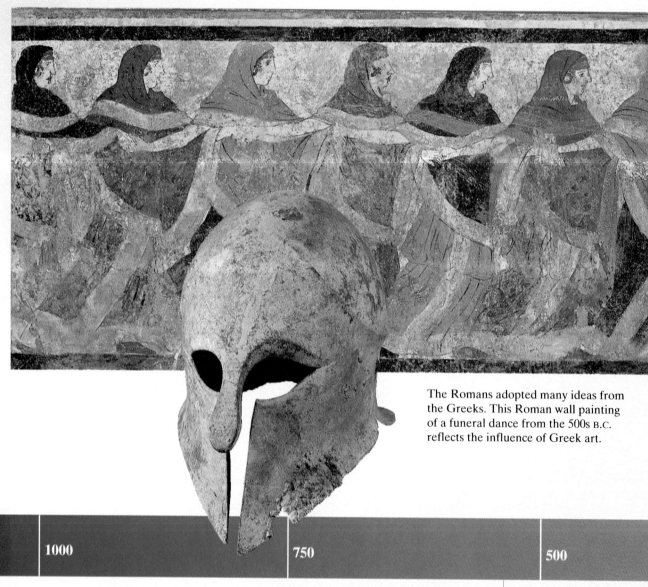

The Romans adopted many ideas from the Greeks. This Roman wall painting of a funeral dance from the 500s B.C. reflects the influence of Greek art.

1000

750

500

**753 B.C.**

c. 575 B.C. The Etruscans of northern Italy conquer Rome and spread their culture among the Romans. The helmet (above) is from the tomb of an Etruscan warrior.

The wolf symbolizes the legend of Rome's founding.

**146 B.C.** With its victory over Greece, Rome now rules the Mediterranean world. The center of Roman government is the Forum, a great open-air market and meeting place (above).

250

B.C. | A.D.

250

**264 B.C.** The First Punic War marks the beginning of Rome's overseas expansion.

49 B.C.

LESSON 1

# The Birth of Rome

### THINKING
### FOCUS

*How was Rome founded, and how did it grow?*

### Key Terms

- omen
- Senate

Down the river floated a tiny reed basket carrying two babies, left to die. The basket came ashore at the foot of a hill. There a wolf found the crying orphans and cared for them. Later, a shepherd came upon the children and took them home to raise as his own. They were twin boys, and he named them Romulus and Remus.

Years later, the two brothers decided to build a city. This would be a city where others who were homeless, as they once were, could come to live. But the brothers argued over where to build the city.

One night Romulus and Remus agreed to watch for an **omen,** a sign from the gods, to settle their argument. At dawn, Remus saw six vultures flying overhead. However, as the sun rose higher in the sky, Romulus saw 12 vultures.

The brothers quarreled over the meaning of the omens, and in a rage, Romulus killed Remus. He then began to build his city on the spot he had chosen—the hill where the tiny basket containing the two babies had come to rest years before. He named his new city after himself—Rome.

➤ *According to legend, Romulus and Remus floated down the Tiber River. At the right is the Tiber as it looks today.*

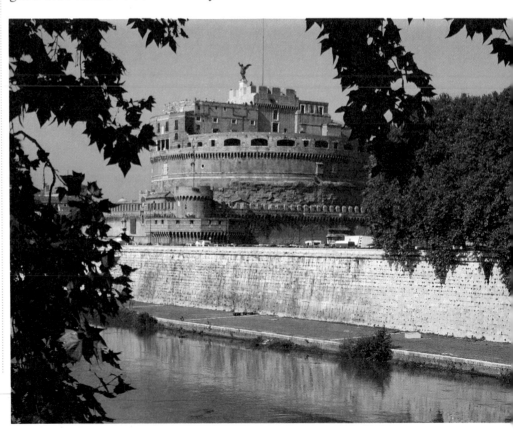

396

Chapter 13

# Seven Kings

Much of the early history of Rome comes to us in the form of legends, like the story of Romulus and Remus. Though they are not historically accurate, legends are useful. They tell us what qualities people admired and the values they wished to pass on to future generations.

## Rome's Early Kings

According to legend, Rome was founded in 753 B.C., and Romulus was the first of seven kings. He was believed to be a great warrior-king and is credited with starting Rome's first army and its first government.

Rome's second king was Numa Pompilius. He brought peace to Rome and, according to legend, founded the Roman religion.

The early kings were advised by a **Senate** (from the Latin word for "old men"), a council of elders from Rome's leading families. A citizens' assembly voted on decisions made by the king and the Senate.

At the time of the early kings, government and religion were closely linked. The king was also the chief priest. He chose other priests from members of the Senate. In addition, the king and his priests performed religious duties and interpreted omens.

## The Etruscans

During the rule of the early Roman kings, Rome's powerful neighbors to the north, the Etruscans, were expanding their territory, Etruria. The Etruscans traded in the western Mediterranean and had established many wealthy city-states in northern Italy. About 575 B.C., the Etruscans moved into Rome. Etruscan kings ruled Rome for the next 66 years.

The Etruscans had an older, more advanced civilization. Rome made rapid progress under their influence. The Etruscans introduced their alphabet and taught the Romans new building techniques, including the use of the arch.

Under the Etruscan kings, Rome grew from a village of straw-roofed huts into a walled city with paved streets. During this time, the Romans began a tradition of great building that eventually far

*This Etruscan fresco, or wall painting, shows the advanced art of the Etruscans.*

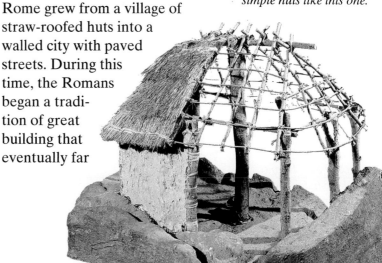

*Prehistoric villagers of central Italy lived in simple huts like this one.*

surpassed that of their teachers. The Romans built the Circus Maximus, an arena that seated thousands, and the Temple of Jupiter in honor of their highest god. They also built the Cloaca Maxima *(kloh AY kuh MAX suh muh)*, a sewer that is still in use today. The sewer drained a marshy valley that became the Forum.

Rome flourished under the Etruscans, until Tarquin the Proud, the seventh and last Roman king, came to power. He was a cruel ruler who ignored the Senate and terrorized the people. In 509 B.C., the people rebelled against him and finally sent him into exile. Never again would Romans be ruled by a king. ■

▲ *The inkwell above is inscribed with the Etruscan alphabet.*

■ *How did the Etruscans influence the Romans?*

## Midpoint of the Mediterranean

At the time of the early kings, Rome was just one of many city-states in Italy, a peninsula centrally located in the Mediterranean Sea. Rome lay near the center of that peninsula on a broad plain known as Latium. Archaeologists have found evidence of settlements dating to the 1100s B.C. throughout the region.

### The Latium Plain

The area once known as Latium has a typical Mediterranean climate. Summers are hot and dry, and winters are wet and

➤ *In 509 B.C., Rome shared the Italian peninsula with the Etruscans to the north and Greek settlers to the south.*

### Settlement of Italy, c. 509 B.C.

Mantua
Po R.
45°N
Felsina
A P E N N I N E  M O U N T A I N S
Volaterrae
Cortona
Rusellae
Perusia
Clusium
Vetulonia
Volsinii
CORSICA
Volci
Tarquinii
Veii
Caere
Rome
LATIUM
Adriatic Sea
Cumae
Neapolis
Tyrrhenian Sea
SARDINIA
40°N
Elea
Laus
Croton
Mediterranean Sea
Panormos
Locri
Rhegium
SICILY
Agrigentum
Syracuse

Etruscans
Greeks

0      50      100 mi.
0   50   100 km
Mercator Projection

mild. The people of Latium were called Latins, and they spoke the same language, Latin. Like other Mediterranean peoples, the early Latins were herders and farmers who harvested wheat, grapes, and olives.

To the north of Rome lay the Etruscan city-states, and to the south lay Greek colonies. The Etruscans and the Greeks carried on much trade in the Mediterranean. Look at the map on page 398. Which power controlled the greater portion of the Italian peninsula?

### The Advantages of Latium

Rome's location offered many advantages. As the Roman historian Livy described it, "Not without good reason did gods and men choose this spot as the site of a city."

Livy, who lived from 59 B.C. to A.D. 17, noted that Rome was built on several hills, which made the city a difficult place for enemies to attack. He also pointed out the advantages of being on the Tiber River, "by means of which the produce of inland countries may be brought down and inland supplies obtained." The Tiber flows into the Mediterranean Sea 15 miles away, which means Rome is "near enough [to the sea] for all useful purposes, but not so near as to be exposed to danger from foreign

fleets." Livy wrote that Rome was "in the very center of Italy, in a word, a position singularly adapted by nature for the growth of a city."

From its location in the center of the Italian peninsula and

Rome's Strategic Location, c. 300-200 B.C.

▲ A network of roads connected the city of Rome to the countryside.

◄ Rich farmland near Rome was one advantage of the city's location. Farming is still important here.

the center of the Mediterranean, Rome was within easy reach of Greece to the east, Spain to the west, and the northern coast of Africa to the south. In the centuries that followed, Rome expanded to all of these areas. Eventually, the Romans would rename the Mediterranean *Mare Nostrum*— "our sea." ■

■ What part did geography play in the development of Rome?

---

## REVIEW

1. **FOCUS** How was Rome founded, and how did it grow?
2. **CONNECT** Compare the early government of Rome with the early government of Greece.
3. **CULTURE** What contributions did the Etruscans make to Roman society?
4. **CRITICAL THINKING** What does the legend of Romulus

and Remus tell you about early Roman life? What kind of people do you think the early Romans were?

5. **WRITING ACTIVITY** Write a news story that describes how Romulus and Remus tried to found the city of Rome. Be sure to tell who, what, when, where, and how.

The Rise of Rome

# The War over Latium

### Alfred J. Church

*After Troy was destroyed by the Greeks, the hero Aeneas and the other Trojan survivors left to find a new home in Italy. In this story from* The Aeneid for Boys and Girls, *the goddess Juno, who hates Aeneas, is determined to keep the Trojans from settling in the Latium Plain. She decides to seek help from the underworld.*

*The Roman poet Virgil wrote the* Aeneid (ih NEE uhd), *an epic poem about the beginnings of Rome. Here is a retelling of parts of the* Aeneid.

*Aeneas* (ih NEE uhs )

*treachery* betrayal

*J*uno went down into the lower parts of the earth, and called to her Alecto, who was one of the Furies, who loved anger and war and treachery, and all evil and hateful things. Even her own sisters, the Furies, could not bear to look on her, so dreadful was she to behold. Juno said to her: "Daughter of Night, I have suffered a great wrong and disgrace, and I want you to help me. A man whom I hate, Aeneas by name, desires to have a kingdom in Italy; keep him from it. He wishes to have Lavinia, the daughter of King Latinus, to wife: see that he does not. You can set brother against brother; you can bring strife into kingdoms and into homes. Break this peace that the Latins and the Trojans are making. Bring about some occasion of war."

Alecto first went to the palace of Latinus. There she found the queen, Amata by name, in great anger and trouble. She was much displeased by the doings of the king, her husband. She did not wish to have Aeneas for her son-in-law, and she loved the prince Turnus with all her heart. Then the Fury thought to herself: "The queen hates Aeneas already; I will turn her hatred into madness." So she took a snake out of her hair and thrust it into the bosom of the queen. The evil beast crept about her so that the poison got into her heart; then it changed itself into a collar, as of twisted gold, round her neck, and poisoned her very breath.

At the first, before the evil altogether overpowered her, she spoke gently to her husband, weeping as a mother might weep when she is afraid that she may lose her daughter. She said: "Are you not afraid, my husband, to give Lavinia to this exile from Troy? Have you no pity for her or me or yourself? Well I know that so soon as the north wind begins to blow, he will fly from this land and carry her away with him. Do you not care for the promise that you made to Turnus—yes, made with an oath—that he should have Lavinia for his wife? You say that she must marry a stranger. Is he not a stranger? Are not all who are not subjects of your kingdom strangers? This, and this only, is what the gods command. Further, if you look into the matter, you will see that he is a stranger also in race, for he is of the family of Inachus, and is by race a Greek."

But when she saw that her husband was not moved at all by her words, the madness altogether overcame her. She rushed out of the palace, and through the streets of the city, taking her daughter with her. And, as she went, she called to the other women to follow her, so that a whole multitude went after her. Like so many wild creatures, they ran through the woods, the queen leading them, holding a burning torch in her hand, and singing the marriage song of her daughter and Turnus.

The next thing that the Fury did was that she went to the city where Turnus lived. He was asleep, and the Fury went in and stood by his bedside. She had taken the shape of an old woman, the priestess of the Temple of Juno, and she said: "Turnus, are you content that you should lose that which is your right, and that your kingdom should be taken from you? King Latinus takes from you the wife that he had promised, and is about to hand over his kingdom to a stranger from over the sea. Juno bade me come and tell you this. Arm your people; drive these strangers out of the land, and burn their ships with fire. And if the king will not keep his promise, let him learn for himself that Turnus is not one who will suffer wrong."

So the old woman spoke, and Turnus answered—for so it seemed to him in his dream—"Old woman, I know that the ships of the strangers have come to the Tiber. But these are idle tales that you tell me. I know that Queen Juno cares for me; therefore, I am not afraid. But you, mother, are old, and wander somewhat in your wits, and trouble yourself for nothing, and are afraid when there is nothing to fear. Keep, I pray you, to your own business; serve the temples of the gods, but leave war and the things of war to men, for such matters belong to them."

And then it seemed to Turnus in his dream that the old woman grew very angry, yea, that she changed into the shape of a Fury, and that a thousand snakes hissed round her. And when he tried to speak again, the words would not come, and when he would have risen from his bed, she thrust him back, and caught two snakes from her hair and lashed him with them, crying: "I am old, forsooth! and I wander from my wits! and I am afraid when I have nothing to fear! Nay, but I am the greatest of the Furies, and war and death are in my hands." And it seemed to him, still in his dream, that she threw a lighted torch at him, and that it fixed itself in his heart. Then he woke with a great start. He did not know whether the things which he had seen and heard in his sleep were true or not, but his heart was full of anger. He called for his arms, and commanded all the young men to make themselves ready for war. "I will drive these Trojans," he cried, "out of Italy, and if Latinus and his people stand by them, then they shall go also."

And now there was one thing left for the Fury to do, and this was to make a cause of quarrel. King Latinus had a man to keep his cattle, and this man's daughter, Silvia by name, had a tame stag which her brothers had found when it was a fawn, and had brought to her. The girl was very fond of the creature, and would put garlands of flowers about its neck, and comb its hair, and give it a bath. All day long the stag would wander about the woods, and at night it came back to the house. Now it so happened that Ascanius, with other Trojan lads, was hunting that day, and his dogs caught the scent of the stag and followed it. And Ascanius, riding after them, saw the beast, and shot an arrow at it, and hit it, for the Fury took care that the arrow should not miss its aim. Then the stag, being wounded to death, ran back to the herdsman's house, and filled it with most lamentable cries. Silvia heard it, and was greatly grieved to see her dear pet in such a case, and cried out for help. And here again the Fury—for she was hiding in the woods—did all she could to increase the trouble. From all sides the country folk came together, each picking up for a weapon anything that came to hand. One had a brand that had been half burned in the fire, and another a great stick with knots in it. The herdsman himself carried an ax in his hand. On the other hand, the Trojans ran together to help Ascanius, and soon there was a regular battle. Some were slain both on the one side and on the other.

*Now the scene is set for war. Driven to anger by the Fury, Turnus gathers an army of Latin soldiers to try to force the Trojans to leave. One of the greatest Latin soldiers is Camilla.*

Now the story of Camilla is this. She was the daughter of a certain king, Metabus by name, who was driven out of his kingdom by his subjects on account of his cruelty. He fled for his life, taking with him his little daughter, whom he carried in his arms. He came in his flight to a certain river, and the river was swollen with rain, so that it ran high and strong. The man could not swim with the child in his arms, and his enemies were close behind, so he took the spear that he carried on his back, and bound the child to it, with strips of bark, and made ready to throw it. As he balanced it in his hand, he prayed to Diana, saying: "O Goddess! I give thee this child to be thy servant forever, if thou wilt save her now." Then he cast the spear across the river with all his might, and, Diana giving strength to his arm, it fell on the other side. Then he himself leaped into the water, and, swimming across, so escaped from his enemies. After this he never lived in house or town, but with the shepherds on the hills, and the child he fed with mare's milk and the like things. As soon as she could walk he gave her a little javelin to carry, and when she was a little stronger, a bow and arrows. She wore no gold or jewels, nor had she long skirts like a girl. From a child she could sling a stone in a wonderful way, hitting the cranes and the wild swans as they flew high in the air. Tall and strong and beautiful was she when she grew up, and many Tuscan mothers desired to have her for a daughter-in-law, but she had no thought of marriage, only of hunting and fighting.

The goddess Diana, as she sat in heaven, said to Opis, who was chief of the nymphs who waited on her: "Opis, Camilla goes to fight in this war. Would that she had not thought of it! There is not a girl in Italy that I love more, and have loved her ever since she was a child. But her fate is on her, and she must die. Now I give you this charge. Go down to the Latin land, where they are beginning just now this evil war; take with you your bow and your arrows, and see that any man who harms her shall himself be slain. And when she is dead no man shall spoil her of her arms; but I will carry back her body to her native land."

And now Aeneas and the Trojans came towards the city, the horsemen being in front. One of these, a Tuscan, was the first to kill his man. He charged against a Latin chief, and drove him from his horse, making him fly through the air, as a stone flies from an engine. When the Latins saw him, they turned and fled. And the Trojans and Tuscans followed them. But when they came near the city, then those that stood upon the walls, the old men and the boys and the women, threw sticks and stones at them, and the soldiers took courage and faced about. Then the Trojans, in their turn, fled, and the Latins pursued them. So it happened twice. But when they met for the third time, then neither would the one side nor the other give way. Both of them stood firm, and there was a great slaughter. Many died valiantly, but none was equal to Camilla. Sometimes she would fight with a battle-ax and sometimes with her bows and arrows. Never did she strike a man with her battle-ax but she laid him low upon the earth; never did she aim an arrow at a man, but she killed him. One of these was the hunter Ornytus, who was the tallest of the Tuscans. He had a wolf's head with great white teeth for a helmet, and in his hand he carried a hunting spear. But strong as he was, Camilla overcame him, and as he lay dying on the ground she mocked him: "Did you think, O Tuscan, that you were hunting wild beasts today? Lo! a woman's arms have brought all your boasts to nothing." So she raged through the field, slaying Trojans and Tuscans

*nymphs* in Greek and Roman mythology, one of the female spirits representing nature

*Ornytus* (AWR nih tuhs)

alike. One of the Ligurians, the son of Aunus, thought to escape in this way. He said to her: "Let us fight on foot; you have so swift a horse that no one can fight with you on equal terms." Camilla answered: "Be it so; we will fight on foot." And she leaped from her horse, and gave it to one of her companions to hold. But the other turned his horse to flee, foolish man, not knowing that Camilla could run faster than any horse in the world. But so it was, she outran the horse, and stood in front of it, catching the reins in her hand, and so killed him.

Then Tarchon the Tuscan shouted out to his horsemen: "What is this, you cowards? Shall a woman drive you before her? You are ready for the dance and feast, and you lag behind in battle. Follow me." And he rode at Venulus, prince of Tibur, and caught him in his arms, dragging him from his horse. So an eagle catches up a snake in his claws and carries him off, and the snake winds himself round the bird, and hisses. Thus did Tarchon carry off his enemy, looking for a place where to strike him, for he was covered with armor, and the man tried to keep the sword from his throat. When the Trojans and the Tuscans saw this, they took courage again.

All this time a certain Arruns, a great archer, was watching Camilla, looking for a chance to kill her. There was a certain priest who was riding in the midst of the battle very splendidly adorned. There were clasps of gold on his armor and the armor of his horse. He wore a purple robe which had come from Tyre; he had a Lycian bow, adorned with gold; his helmet also shone with gold; and his scarf had a ring of gold, and his tunic was rich with the finest needle-work. Never was there such a sight to see.

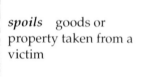

And Camilla, having a woman's love of beautiful things, followed him, caring for nothing, and thinking of nothing, but how she might take these splendid spoils. Now Arruns lay in ambush, and when he saw Camilla, how she followed the priest, and thought of nothing else, he said to himself, "Now is the time." And he prayed to Apollo: "Lord of the bow, help me now, if ever I and my people have done honor to you. I ask no glory for myself. Only let me slay this fury, though I go back to my country without honor." Part of this prayer the god heard and answered, but part was scattered by the winds. For he drew his bow to the full, and let fly the arrow. And when the people heard the twang of the bow, for they could not see the man, they all turned. But

*spoils* goods or property taken from a victim

Camilla took no heed; she had no thought of the arrow till it struck her under the left breast. She reeled upon her horse, and her companions closed round her and caught her as she fell. Once she laid her hand on the arrow and would have drawn it out, but it had gone too deep. Then her eyes swam in death, and the color that was as the color of a rose faded from her cheek. Only as she died, she said, for her thoughts were still with the battle, so keen a fighter was she: "Acca, my sister, tell Turnus to come forth from his ambush, and join in the battle, if he would keep the Trojans from the walls of the city." So she died.

Now Arruns, at the first, lay in hiding, for he was afraid, so great a deed had he done. After a while, he came out from his place, and began to boast. Then Opis drew her bow with all her strength, till the ends came almost together. With her right hand she held the bow-string, and with her left the arrowhead. So she let the shaft fly. Arruns heard the twang, and even while he heard it, he fell dead upon the plain. And now the companions of Camilla flew, as did also the Latins and the allies. The dust of the battle came nearer and nearer to the walls, and a great cry went up to the heaven. Great was the fear and the confusion. Some were trodden down by their own people, so that they died even in sight of their own homes. And the keepers of the gates shut them close, so that their own friends were left outside.

And now Acca had carried to Turnus, as he lay in ambush, the news of how her sister was dead, and how the battle went against his people. Immediately he rose up from his place, and made all haste to the city. And it chanced that at the very same time Aeneas had come through the valley and passed over the ridge. The two saw each other; but the night was now falling, so that they could not meet in battle.

### Further Reading

*City*. David Macaulay. Detailed illustrations of a Roman city explain the Roman approach to construction and planning.

*They Marched with Spartacus*. Eric Houghton. During the time of the rebellion of Spartacus, a young slave confronts his Roman captors.

*The White Wall*. Eric Houghton. In this story a young boy joins Hannibal's army after his village is destroyed by a warlike tribe.

# The Rise of the Republic

## THINKING
## FOCUS

*What internal and external struggles occurred during the rise of the Roman Republic?*

### Key Terms

- republic
- consul
- patrician
- plebeian
- debt bondage

T*here was great panic in the city, and through mutual fear, all was suspense. The people left in the city dreaded [feared] the violence of the senators; the senators dreaded the people remaining in the city, uncertain whether they should prefer to stay or to depart; but how long would the multitude [crowd] which had seceded [left] remain quiet? What were to be the consequences then, if, in the meantime, any foreign war should break out?*

Livy wrote that description, telling of the crisis in Rome in 494 B.C. The common people of Rome had seceded, or moved out of the city. They were very angry over their treatment by the rich and powerful leaders of Rome. The leaders knew that their city was in serious danger unless the common people returned. So they agreed to give the people more rights. This crisis between the Roman leaders and the people marked the beginning of a 200-year struggle by the common people of Rome to gain equal rights.

## Patricians and Plebeians

With the overthrow of the last Etruscan king in 509 B.C., Roman leaders adopted a very new form of government—a republic. In a **republic,** citizens elect leaders to run their government. The leaders the citizens elected to replace the king were called consuls. These **consuls** were leaders elected by a citizen assembly and advised by a Senate. Although the citizens elected their representatives, the early Roman Republic was not a democracy because not every citizen had the same economic power.

Citizens were divided into two classes, patricians and plebeians. **Patricians** *(puh TRISH uhns)* were members of the small number of wealthy Roman families. **Plebeians** *(plih BEE uhns)* were the bulk of the population—artisans, shopkeepers, and peasants. Class was determined by birth.

As citizens, both patricians and plebeians had the right to vote. However, only patricians could hold political, military, or religious offices. All power was in the hands of the patricians.

During the 300s B.C., the plebeians gained more and more of the rights already held by the patricians. The priesthood was opened to plebeians. Debt bondage was outlawed. Eventually, plebeians even won the right to become members of the Senate.

Though the plebeians had made many gains, the plebeians and patricians still had separate political bodies. The laws passed

The ruins of the Forum shown at the far left stand on the Palatine hill. Below is a reconstruction of the Forum, looking towards Capitoline Hill. You can find more information about architecture like this in the Minipedia.

As you have read, the patricians were desperate. They knew that Rome could not survive without plebeians. Who would do the work? Who would protect the Republic from enemy attacks?

The patricians had no choice but to let the plebeians keep their assembly and their tribunes. Tribunes were to protect plebeian rights. The plebeians could vote against any unjust law passed by the Senate.

Next, the plebeians demanded a reform of the laws. Rome's laws had never been written down. The plebeians believed that patrician judges took advantage of this fact to rule unfairly against plebeians.

### The Twelve Tables

Finally in 450 B.C., the laws were engraved on 12 bronze tablets called the Twelve Tables. The tablets were then displayed in the Forum, so all citizens could appeal to them, though few could actually read them.

by the patrician Senate applied to everyone. However, the laws passed by the plebeian assembly applied only to plebeians.

### Equality for Plebeians

The plebeians demanded that the laws passed by their assembly apply to all citizens, plebeian and patrician alike. Once again, the plebeians forced the issue by withdrawing from Rome. This time, the patricians gave in and, in 287 B.C., agreed to meet the demands of the plebeians. After more than 200 years of struggle, plebeians and patricians were finally equal under Roman law. ■

■ What were the major steps in the plebeians' struggle for greater rights?

# Roman Government

### Across Time & Space

*The U.S. Constitution owes one of its very basic concepts to the Romans. Neither the President, nor the Congress, nor the courts can dominate the government. Each branch of government has ways to check the actions of the others, and the actions of each branch balance the others. This idea of checks and balances was first developed in the government of the Roman Republic.*

■ *How was the government of the Roman Republic organized?*

As the plebeians gained power, the Republic became more democratic. Since 509 B.C., the Roman government had been headed by two consuls. By 367 B.C., one of these consuls had to be a plebeian. The consuls had the same powers as the early kings, but with two important limitations. To avoid one-person rule, consuls were elected to serve only one year, and each consul could veto the other's actions. Our word *veto* is from the Latin word meaning "I forbid."

The consuls carried on the daily business of the government and of the army. They were also advised by a Senate made up of 300 citizens. The Senate controlled the Roman treasury and foreign policy. Most of the senators were members of wealthy Roman families. Though the consuls changed each year, senators were chosen for life. The Senate was the most powerful group in the government of the Roman Republic.

Laws proposed by the Senate could be approved or disapproved by citizen assemblies. Candidates for consul were also elected by these assemblies. The government of the Republic spread its power among many groups. ■

➤ *The chart of Roman government structure shows how the power of each level was balanced by the power of the other levels.*

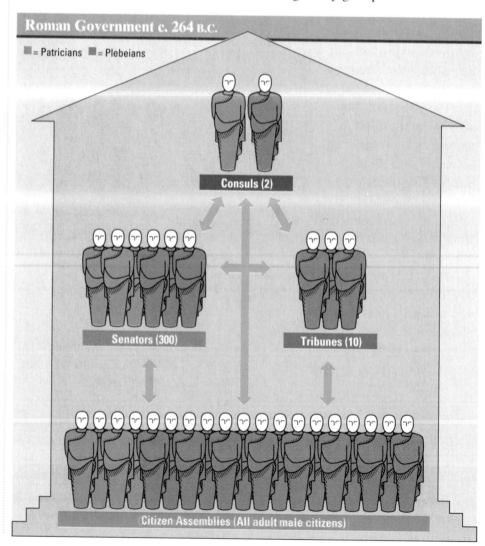

**Roman Government c. 264 B.C.**

■ = Patricians  ■ = Plebeians

Consuls (2)

Senators (300)

Tribunes (10)

Citizen Assemblies (All adult male citizens)

# Early Expansion

While the patricians and plebeians struggled for power within the city's walls, other battles raged on the outside. Year after year, the Roman army marched off to wage war against its neighbors and to expand the area under Roman control. The army was not always victorious, however. In fact, in 390 B.C., Rome itself was attacked and destroyed by the Gauls, a warlike people from the north.

Nevertheless, Rome rebuilt and continued to grow. By 338 B.C., Rome had conquered Latium and Etruria. By 275 B.C., Rome ruled the whole Italian peninsula.

Rome was so successful, in part, because instead of punishing the people it conquered, Rome made them allies. As allies, they had to fight for Rome in any future wars. In return, Rome promised them protection and a share in the profits from future victories. In some cases, Rome even granted citizenship to conquered peoples.

By 270 B.C., Rome had more citizens and well-trained soldiers than any other Mediterranean power. During the next century, Rome used those resources to conquer the Mediterranean world. ◼

◄ *Roman legionaries like this one were stationed in the various provinces of Rome, but never in Rome itself.*

## How Do We Know?

**HISTORY** *The history of Rome written by Livy contained 142 books. Only 35 of these have survived. From these books we learn much about the Roman republic.*

◼ *What made the Romans successful conquerors?*

## REVIEW

1. **FOCUS** What internal and external struggles occurred during the rise of the Roman Republic?
2. **CONNECT** Compare the Roman government of the Republic with that of the Athenians in the 400s B.C.
3. **HISTORY** How did the Roman Republic expand its territory beyond Italy?
4. **LEGAL SYSTEMS** What was important about the Twelve Tables, and how did they help the plebeians?
5. **CRITICAL THINKING** How was the government of the Roman Republic like that of the United States today? How was it different?
6. **ACTIVITY** Make a chart that compares the rights of the plebeians and the patricians. You might compare their political rights, their social rights, and their economic rights.

411

The Rise of Rome

1000    750    500

270         49

250

L E S S O N    3

# Overseas Expansion

**Key Term**

• dictator

L et's leave Rome for a moment and travel across the Mediterranean to the coast of North Africa. The time is 238 B.C. The place is the Phoenician city of Carthage. The great Carthaginian (*kahr thuh JIHN ee uhn*) general, Hamilcar, is preparing to leave for Phoenician outposts in Spain where he hopes to raise a new army. Carthage has just been defeated in a long and bitter war with Rome for the island of Sicily, and the general is angry and humiliated at the loss.

Hamilcar is making sacrifices to the gods, so that they will bring him good luck in Spain. His young son, Hannibal, looks on. Livy describes the scene:

H annibal, then about nine years old, was childishly teasing his father to take him too. His father, still angry at the loss [to the Romans] led him to the altar and made him swear to be the enemy of Rome as soon as he was able.

Hamilcar took the young boy to Spain with him and taught him to be a soldier. Twenty years later, Hannibal fulfilled his oath to his father. He became a brilliant general, one of the greatest foes Rome ever faced.

## The Punic Wars

In the 200s B.C., Rome was conquering Italy. Another power, Carthage, existed on the opposite side of the Mediterranean. It was a prosperous Phoenician city with trading posts all around the Mediterranean. Carthage and Rome became fierce rivals and fought three long and bloody wars over which power would control the Mediterranean.

### The First Punic War

Find Rome and Carthage on the map on the next page. What large island lies between them at the tip of the Italian peninsula? By the 200s B.C., Carthage had settlements on Sicily. Rome feared it would gain complete control of the island. In 264 B.C., the two powers went

▼ *Notice the plank at the front of the Roman boat. What advantage did it give the Romans in sea battles?*

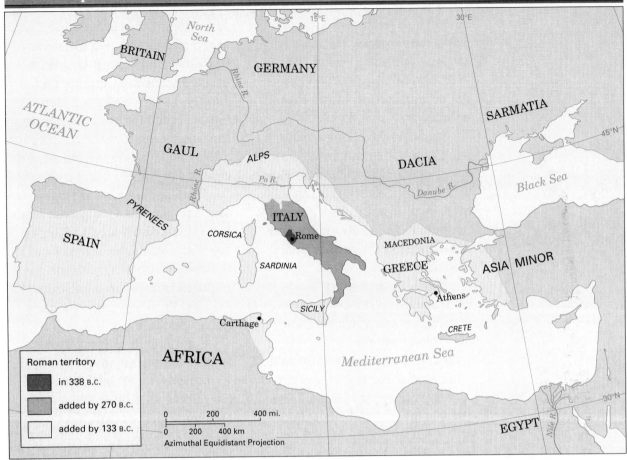

Notice how Rome increased its influence in the Mediterranean area between 338 and 133 B.C.

was about to admit defeat, Hannibal returned from Italy. Scipio fought Hannibal at Zama, a town near Carthage. With the help of the Numidians, Scipio won. He was given the name "Africanus" in honor of this victory in northern Africa.

This defeat marked the end of Carthage's empire. Carthage was forced to give up its territories and its ships, and to pay Rome vast sums of money.

In 149 B.C., Carthage rebelled against Rome, thus beginning the Third Punic War. Rome once again defeated Carthage. And as punishment, Rome sold all of the surviving Carthaginians into slavery and leveled the city. ■

■ *What were the Punic Wars?*

## Conquest of the Eastern Mediterranean

With the defeat of Carthage, Rome became the most important power in the western Mediterranean. Next, Rome turned eastward, conquering Greece and Macedonia, the country to the north of Greece, by 146 B.C.

By 50 B.C., Rome controlled the entire area around the Mediterranean. Find these Roman provinces on the map above: Greece, Spain, Gaul, Asia Minor, and North Africa.

How was it possible for Rome to conquer so much so quickly? Historians give several reasons. First, the Romans took great pride in their Republic and fiercely defended it. The Greek historian Polybius, who lived among the Romans in the 100s B.C., wrote that the power of the Roman people under their balanced government was stronger than the power of any one opposing leader. Not even Hannibal could overcome the determination of the Roman people.

Second, by treating conquered peoples as allies and, in several cases, making them citizens, Rome was able to raise a large army. Moreover, Rome's allies generally remained loyal to Rome because they shared in the profits from Roman wars.

Third, Rome's army was highly disciplined and seasoned by years of war. Few other armies could match its strength.

Fourth, Romans greatly valued military success. In fact, military success was needed for political advancement. The highest honor

■ *How could Rome conquer so much of the Mediterranean so quickly?*

for a general was a "triumph," a grand parade through the streets of Rome. The victorious general, dressed up as the supreme god Jupiter, rode in a chariot. Behind him marched the soldiers, carrying the many valuables seized from the enemy and leading the unfortunate captives of war.

Finally, wars were a great source of wealth. Conquered lands were often distributed to Roman colonists. Valuables seized from the enemy enriched both the government treasury and individual leaders. Prisoners from the conquered lands became slaves.

For all these reasons, Roman leaders were ready to go to war year after year. From 338 to 50 B.C., Rome steadily extended the area under its control. ■

## Trouble at Home

By 50 B.C., Rome ruled the Mediterranean world, but it had serious problems at home. Before the Punic Wars, Italy was a land of small family farms and farmer-soldiers. Wars were fought nearby between planting and harvest. In 458 B.C., Cincinnatus, a citizen farmer, laid down his plow to lead the Roman army. At the request of his fellow citizens, he was made dictator. According to legend, within 16 days he had defeated the neighboring tribe, resigned his dictatorship, and gone back to his farm.

However, as Rome expanded, wars were fought farther away, and farmers were gone for longer periods of time. Many of them were killed in battle.

The Second Punic War had destroyed Roman farms. Returning from war, farmers often did not have the money needed to begin farming again. Wealthy Romans bought up the land and created plantations run by slave labor, thus putting more farmers off the land.

Many landless farmers moved to the city, but few found jobs. Slaves, captured in Rome's many wars, provided cheap labor, putting poor Romans out of work. As the numbers of poor and unemployed people grew, the Roman leaders feared that violent mobs would demand a solution to their troubles. Some Roman leaders wanted to help the poor, but their efforts were blocked by wealthy senators. In fact, two tribunes who tried to help the poor were killed for their efforts.

▼ *The message on this slave tag promised a reward for the return of the runaway slave.*

Rome's large population of slaves caused other problems. Most slaves, who had been free in their homelands, were treated brutally by their Roman masters. Desperate for freedom, the slaves rebelled. In 73 B.C., the slave Spartacus gathered an army of more than 100,000. They fought the Roman army for two years. In 71 B.C., the Romans killed Spartacus and crucified 6,000 slaves. ■

■ *What problems did Rome have at home?*

## Fall of the Roman Republic

By 50 B.C., Rome ruled an area about the size of the United States. Rapid expansion brought about change in the Republic. The small farm society had changed, the gap between rich and poor had grown, and the slave population had greatly increased. And wealth from the wars had made Roman leaders greedy.

Dishonest leaders had huge incomes and ignored the poor. The poor, in turn, felt no loyalty to a government that was keeping them poor. Conflicts broke out between rich and poor.

Also, by 50 B.C., the army was made up of professional soldiers, mostly poor citizens who couldn't find work elsewhere. They were fighting for money, not for Rome. And money depended on victory in battle. Thus, these soldiers were loyal only to the generals, who hired them and paid them with land and money. Power-hungry generals fought one another for control of the government.

One of those generals was Julius Caesar. Caesar came from an old patrician family, and he was very ambitious. In 59 B.C., Caesar

**Across Time & Space**

*One of Julius Caesar's accomplishments was the development of a new calendar. By 46 B.C., the Roman calendar was three months behind the sun. Caesar added the three months and then changed the way the calendar was arranged. For his efforts, the Senate named the month of July in his honor, a name still in use today.*

◄ *Andrea Mantegna painted* Triumph of Caesar *in the late 1400s. Notice the banner with the letters SPQR. These are the initials for the Latin words "The Senate and the people of Rome."*

417

The Rise of Rome

**146 B.C.**, Rome conquers Greece.

**753 B.C.**, According to legend, Romulus founds Rome.

**450 B.C.**, Roman laws are recorded on the Twelve Tables.

**46 B.C.**, Julius Caesar d♦ himself dictator for life, ♦ the Republic to an end.

| 800 | 700 | 600 | 500 | 400 | 300 | 200 | 100 |

**509 B.C.**, The era of the Roman Republic begins.

**201 B.C.**, Rome defeats Carthage in the Second Punic War.

▲ *Trace the events of early Roman history on the timeline above.*

➤ *Julius Caesar's great popularity among his troops enabled him to become dictator.*

■ *Who was Julius Caesar?*

was elected consul, but he knew he must win military glory to fulfill his ambitions. He took command of Roman troops and left to tame the Gauls, who still threatened Italy. Nine years later, he had succeeded.

Caesar's successes in Gaul worried his rivals in Rome. They feared that Caesar was becoming too powerful. They persuaded the Senate to declare Caesar a public enemy.

The Senate ordered Caesar to return to Rome without his troops. But Caesar feared that if he did, his life would be in great danger. Instead, he decided to lead his troops to Rome.

On January 11, 49 B.C., Caesar and his army crossed the Rubicon River, which divided Gaul and Italy. Since it was treason for a general to leave his assigned province and bring his army to Rome, this was a serious action. Caesar

knew he must win or die.

Civil war broke out and lasted for three years. Eventually, Caesar defeated his rival, Pompey, and in 46 B.C. declared himself dictator. A **dictator** is a ruler who has absolute power.

Earlier Roman dictators had been chosen by the city officials only for emergencies. The citizen farmer, Lucius Cincinnatus, you recall, resigned 16 days after saving the city. When Caesar made himself dictator for life, he ended the Republican system. ■

## R E V I E W

1. **FOCUS** How was Rome able to control the Mediterranean world?

2. **CONNECT** Compare Hannibal as a leader with Pericles of Athens. How successful was each in battle? Why is Hannibal considered a great general?

3. **ECONOMICS** In what ways did wars make Rome strong economically? How did wars weaken Rome?

4. **HISTORY** Why didn't Rome's allies in Italy defect to join Hannibal?

5. **CRITICAL THINKING** Caesar crossed the Rubicon River during his return to Rome. Today, we use the expression "crossing the Rubicon" as a figure of speech. What does it mean? Have you ever crossed a Rubicon?

6. **ACTIVITY** One of the "weapons" used by Hannibal's army was the elephant. Use your imagination to draw a war elephant. You might show it wearing armor and carrying soldiers.

Chapter 13

# Evaluating Sources

## Here's Why

To learn about the past, we rely on the eyewitness accounts of events and records left behind. As you know, sources produced at the time of the event are *primary sources.* Sources produced after the event and that use primary sources for information are *secondary sources.*

You learned in Lesson 3 about some of Hannibal's remarkable deeds in the Punic Wars. Suppose you wanted to learn more about Hannibal. You might look for primary or secondary sources about him and then evaluate them.

## Here's How

In order to evaluate a primary or secondary source, you can apply the questions used by historians. See the box at the bottom of this page.

First find out whether the source is primary or secondary. Try answering the first question. The passage on the right was written sometime between 27 and 25 B.C. The Punic Wars took place between 264 and 149 B.C. Obviously, this passage is a secondary source, because it was not produced at the same time as the event it tells about.

Look at the second question. Since this is a secondary source, it is not an eyewitness account.

Next find out who the writer was. The writer of this source, Titus Livius, or Livy, was a well-known Roman historian.

Next determine the type of source you are reading. The passage on this page is from a history book, Livy's history of Rome.

Finally, it is important to know why the source was written. A campaign poster about a person will have a different slant than will a historical account of the same person. The passage on this page was written by Livy to give an idea of how forceful a leader Hannibal was.

> . . . It was under Hannibal that the soldiers displayed greatest confidence and daring. He was fearless in undertaking dangerous enterprises, he was prudent in discharging them. Toil could not weary his body or subdue his spirit. Heat and cold he endured alike.

## Try It

Apply the five questions for evaluating sources to all of Lesson 3 in this chapter. Use what you know about primary and secondary sources, and about the parts of a book. Then tell whether Lesson 3 is a primary source or a secondary source.

## Apply It

Newspapers and books of today will be sources that people of the future will use to learn about our times. Find two articles about the U.S. President. Apply the five questions for evaluating sources. Then decide how reliable each source is.

1. When was the source produced? (Was it at the time of the event—primary source; or some time after the event—secondary source?)
2. Where was the source produced? (Was it an eyewitness account or a secondhand account?)
3. Who was the writer? (How might the writer's background affect the account?)
4. What kind of source is it? (Is it a letter, speech, or book?)
5. Why was the source produced? (To describe, to prove a point, or to comment?)

419

The Rise of Rome

L E S S O N 4

# Greece and Rome

**THINKING**
**F O C U S**

*How strong was Greece's influence on Rome?*

---

### Key Term

• aqueduct

---

➤ *Romans admired and imitated many Greek sculptures like the famous* Nike of Samothrace, *c. 200-190 B.C. This statue is often called* Winged Victory.

"A lthough we conquered Greece, she conquered us: She brought Art to rustic Rome," wrote Horace, the great Roman poet, in about 35 B.C. Many Roman citizens agreed with him. The Romans may have triumphed militarily over Greece in 146 B.C. However, the resulting close contact with Greek culture dramatically changed many parts of Roman life. Greek ideas, art, and customs all were to become an important part of the Roman heritage.

## Greek Influence on Rome

The Greek roots of Roman culture run deep. As early as the 600s B.C., Greece had established powerful colonies in southern Italy and Sicily. Greek culture spread quickly as Greek merchants traded Greek goods, such as fine pottery and metalwork, with neighboring peoples. By the 200s B.C., the Greek epic poem the *Odyssey* had been translated into Latin.

Greek influence grew even more when the two cultures came into greater contact after Rome's conquest of Greece. Victorious Roman troops brought Greek statues and paintings back to Rome, where they were admired and copied. Greek scholars were brought to Rome as slaves to teach wealthy Roman children.

In fact, Greek culture influenced Roman culture so much that the result is called Greco-Roman culture. With the growth of the Roman Republic, Greco-Roman culture spread throughout the Mediterranean world.

The Romans borrowed heavily from the Greeks. They worshiped Greek gods and gave them Roman names. The Greek god Zeus, ruler of the gods, became the Roman god Jupiter; Aphrodite, goddess of love, became Venus; Ares, the god of war, became Mars.

Roman writers often turned to the Greeks for inspiration. The Roman poet Virgil began to write the *Aeneid (ih NEE uhd),* his epic poem, as the Trojan War was ending. This is where the Greek epic closes.

In the *Aeneid,* a Trojan hero known as Aeneas *(ih NEE uhs)* escapes from the Greeks and sails to Italy. It is then Aeneas's descendant, Romulus, who founds the city of Rome. In this way, Virgil links one of the central myths of Greek culture with the birth of Rome.

In architecture, the Romans adopted basic Greek forms. A number of Roman temples, for example, have columns surrounding the main structure, just as most Greek temples do.

Many Romans, including Horace, were not pleased that Greek culture was so widely admired and imitated in Rome. One of the most vocal critics was a well-known Roman senator of the 100s B.C., Cato the Elder.

Cato, who had a great love for Rome, feared that Greek ideas would make the Romans weak. The Romans did borrow very heavily from Greek culture. However, they also created many original works of their own. ■

■ *What is Greco-Roman culture?*

## Roman Genius

The Greeks were inventive, bringing out new ideas and new art forms. The Romans were practical, using and adapting whatever ideas and forms suited their needs. The early Romans were bent on expansion, and they mastered the skills necessary for building and governing an empire. Among these skills were military organization, legal administration, and special engineering ability.

### Military Organization

The Roman army was one of the greatest military forces the world has ever seen. Before the Romans, most armies triumphed over their enemies simply by outnumbering them. The Roman army, however, won its victories mainly because of its determination and discipline.

Although the early Republic relied on citizen-farmers, after about 100 B.C., Rome began to build a full-time army. Roman soldiers enlisted for periods of up to

▼ *The Romans took care to protect themselves from attack. How many lines of defense are in the sketch of Roman siegeworks below?*

Stimulus pit
"Lily" pits
"Lily"
Staked trench
Stimulus
Flooded trench
Trench
Wooden tower
**The Siegeworks at Alesia**

20 years. They became hardened by years of fighting.

The Roman army was well organized with a strict chain of command. The army was divided into legions of 6,000 men each. Each legion was a self-contained unit with all the workers necessary to supply the army during long campaigns. Arrow makers, nurses, and engineers traveled with the soldiers. Thus the army could wage long battles without returning to Rome for supplies.

The Roman army was also unusually good at adapting to changing conditions. Specially trained troops of skilled archers, spear throwers, or horse riders could be called into battle.

In contrast, most Greek city-states (except for Sparta) had small armies of citizens, not professional soldiers. These armies served only when needed.

### Engineering Skill

To unify and control their huge Republic, the Romans built more than 50,000 miles of roads—many of them paved with stone. With the paved roads, both messengers and troops could race to remote Roman provinces in case of enemy attack. The network of roads was also a great help to trade and communication.

Roman roads were built so well that some are still in use. In the city of Rome, honking cars and buses filled with commuters and sightseers clatter over the Appian Way, one of the very first Roman roads, built in 312 B.C.

In contrast, the mountainous countryside of Greece made road-building difficult. Since no part of their country was very far from the sea, the Greeks turned to it instead. Sea lanes became Greek highways.

Romans also used their engineering skills to perfect the arch they had inherited from the Etruscans. In addition, they invented a new building material—concrete. Concrete is long-lasting, but compared to stone, lightweight. With arches and concrete, the Romans were able to build huge public works—bridges, aqueducts, and stadiums.

Among the engineering skills developed by Roman builders was surveying. In A Moment in Time on page 423, you see a Roman surveyor at work.

▲ *The Appian Way, which leads through the countryside to the city of Rome, is still used today.*

➤ *In this cross section of a Roman road, you can see that the Romans built their roads to last.*

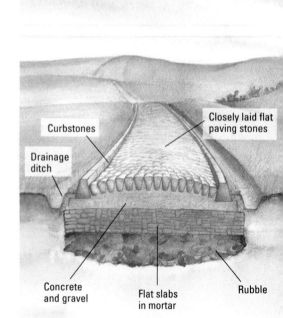

Curbstones

Drainage ditch

Concrete and gravel

Closely laid flat paving stones

Flat slabs in mortar

Rubble

# Comparing Greece and Rome

## Here's Why

It is hard to remember everything you read. Identifying the main ideas can help. The conclusion of a section of text is often also its main idea.

A conclusion is a reasoned judgment based on evidence. The lesson that compared Rome and Greece presented a great deal of evidence about both of these powers.

## Here's How

Use the summary below of Military Organization from Lesson 4 to draw a conclusion about the strength of Roman army legions compared to Greek armies. Follow these steps:

1. **Study the evidence.** As you read, look for facts. Facts in the paragraph on military organization include these important points:
   a. Roman soldiers were professionals.
   b. Greek soldiers were citizen-soldiers.
2. **Draw a conclusion.** Use the facts from step 1 along with anything else you know about the subject. Here, it is reasonable to conclude that the Roman legions were stronger than the Greek armies, because professional soldiers are probably better than part-time soldiers.
3. **Think about the evidence again.** Does it support the conclusion? Be ready to change your conclusion if necessary. The evidence is this: Roman troops spent 20 years as professional soldiers. The legions were well supplied and organized, and they had specially trained troops to adapt to changing battle conditions. The conclusion is supported.

## Try It

Read the summary of Engineering Skill below. What facts are given about Roman and Greek achievements? What conclusion can you draw?

## Apply It

Find an article in a local newspaper or magazine. Use the three-step strategy to draw a conclusion from it.

### Military Organization

The Roman army was a powerful military force. Unlike other armies, it defeated enemies with its determination and discipline. Whereas most Greek city-states relied on small armies of citizen-soldiers, Roman soldiers were professionals who remained in the army for 20 years. The Roman legions traveled with workers to supply them with arms and medical help, so they seldom needed to return to Rome. Moreover, they adapted to changing battle conditions by using specially trained troops, something less organized armies could not do.

### Engineering Skill

The Romans owed much to Greek culture but made many important practical achievements of their own. Engineering skill enabled the Romans to build long-lasting roads throughout the empire. Greeks, by contrast, used the sea for most transportation, because Greek mountains made road building difficult. The Roman invention of concrete helped not only with road building but also with huge public works—bridges, aqueducts, and stadiums. The most impressive of these projects are the Appian Way and the 50-mile aqueduct to Carthage.

# Chapter Review

## Reviewing Key Terms

**A.** Some of the following statements are true. The rest are false. Write *True* or *False* for each statement. Then rewrite the false statements to make them true.

1. Ancient Romans often waited for omens from Senators before making decisions.
2. Young patricians made up the Senate.
3. In the Roman republic, a series of kings passed down leadership.
4. People had more to say about who became consuls than who became kings.

5. If a plebeian borrowed money from a patrician, he was forced into debt bondage and treated almost as a slave.
6. Julius Caesar became dictator of Rome because the Romans knew he would seek wise advice from his advisors.
7. Romans in the cities were able to get fresh water from an aqueduct.

**B.** Write a sentence to answer each question. Use at least one key term in each sentence.

1. Which terms listed above are related to government even today? Explain.
2. Which ones are related to social class? Explain.
3. Which one describes something outlawed by the Romans? Explain.

## Exploring Concepts

**A.** In this chapter, you learned about the history of the city of Rome. Write a four-paragraph summary of the chapter based on the following information.

I. The birth of Rome
  A. Seven kings
  B. Midpoint of the Mediterranean
II. The rise of the republic
  A. Patricians and plebeians
  B. Struggle for rights
  C. Roman government
  D. Early expansion
III. Overseas expansion
  A. The Punic wars
  B. Control of eastern Mediterranean
  C. Trouble at home
  D. Fall of the Roman republic
IV. Greece and Rome

**B.** Support each statement with facts and details from the chapter.

1. The Etruscans were more advanced than the early Romans in some areas.
2. With effort and time, the plebeians gained legal rights that made them equal to the patricians.
3. The Roman government set an example for modern balance of power.
4. Romans treated people in areas they conquered in a special way.
5. The First Punic War lasted 23 years because both sides had strengths in certain areas.
6. Scipio Africanus was given his last name as an honor.
7. Spartacus was an important leader.
8. Crossing the Rubicon River was extremely risky for Julius Caesar.
9. Roman culture borrowed heavily from Greek culture.

# Establishing Peace and Order

Caesar had seized control of the government of the Roman world in 49 B.C., making himself dictator for life. As dictator, Caesar seemed to have little respect for the constitution. According to the constitution, a Roman leader was supposed to share power with the senators. But many senators thought Caesar acted as if he were above the law. They thought he treated them as servants. They saw his behavior as haughty and insulting. Many began to think of him as both a personal enemy and an enemy of the Roman Republic.

Senators and other Roman citizens whispered among themselves that Caesar intended to make himself king. If he did so, he could establish a dynasty. His family line would rule the Roman world even after his death, and the Senate would then have no role in choosing the next leader. Outraged, more than 60 senators met secretly. They planned how they would **assassinate** Caesar—murder him for political reasons. One leader of the group was Brutus, the so-called friend of Caesar.

When Brutus and his men killed Caesar on the ides of March, they thought they had saved the Republic. But by the end of that day, the assassins had to hide from angry mobs of Roman citizens. Many were outraged by Caesar's murder. Caesar was well liked because he made many reforms that improved people's lives. For example, he reorganized the government and lowered taxes. He founded new colonies and gave people land to farm. He hired people to build temples and public buildings. He made citizens of many people in the colonies.

A power struggle followed Caesar's death. Caesar's adopted son Octavian *(ahk TAY vee uhn)* was the leader of one group that was fighting to control Rome. He defeated his rivals in 31 B.C. and led Rome into a new era.

## The Empire of Augustus

Octavian brought peace to the Roman Empire and became a popular leader. In 27 B.C., the Senate voted to give him the title Augustus *(aw GUHS tuhs)*, meaning "respected one." He ruled the empire until A.D. 14.

Augustus learned from his father's mistakes. He continued many of the reforms that had been started by Caesar. He knew that the people wanted a republic, so he always claimed to be restoring the government of the Roman Republic.

But Augustus held the real power. He controlled almost all of the military troops. He appointed the most important officials of the government—those who governed the provinces. He carefully avoided using the title of king. Instead, he called himself "first citizen" to show that he was one of the people.

Augustus ruled an empire. He is considered to be the

▼ *This detail from a tomb relief, carved in the A.D. 100s, shows work in progress on a building project in Rome. Notice that the machine moving the building materials looks something like a modern crane.*

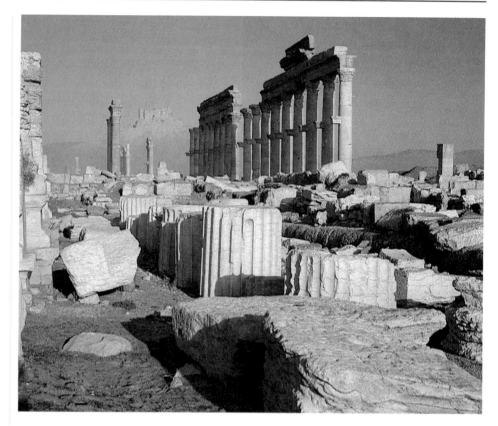

▶ *In modern Morocco, these ruins, once part of the Roman city of Volubilis, are reminders of how vast the Roman Empire was.*

first Roman emperor. The people welcomed him because they craved a strong leader. They desperately wanted peace and order after the time of turmoil that followed Caesar's death.

### Order in the City

Augustus once boasted, "I found Rome built of sun-dried bricks. I leave her covered in marble." During the 41 years of his rule, Augustus built or restored 82 temples. Most of them were dressed in the smooth marble from the quarries that were just opening north of Rome.

Augustus also worked to improve life in the city of Rome. With a population of nearly one million people, Rome had no city services. Some of the worst problems were hunger and poverty. Violence and disorder increased, and Rome had a major crime problem. In addition, fires regularly swept

through the city. Augustus created a police force and a fire brigade. He set up a department to supply food to the city's citizens.

### Growth in the Provinces

The Roman Empire beyond Italy was divided into about 40 **provinces,** or territories. Each province had a governor, who was appointed by the emperor or named by the Senate. The governors' work included keeping order and collecting taxes.

Augustus and the emperors who followed him expanded the empire by conquering new territories. Look at the map on page 433 to see how the Roman Empire grew in the 200 years after Augustus came to power. At its peak in A.D. 117, the Roman Empire had a population of about 60 million. This was more than one-fifth of the total population of the world at that time.

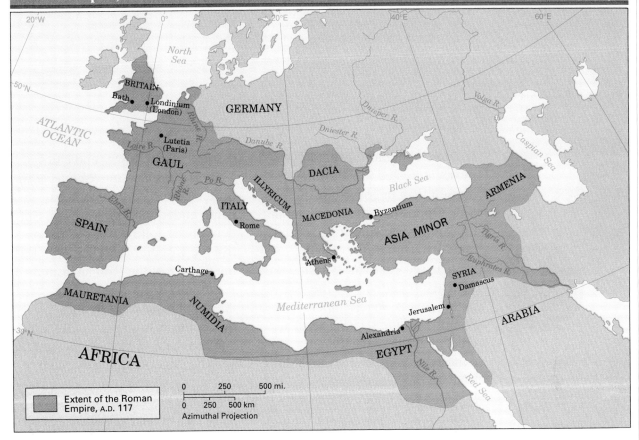

Roman Empire, A.D. 117

Extent of the Roman
Empire, A.D. 117

0    250    500 mi.
0    250   500 km
Azimuthal Projection

## The *Pax Romana*

Augustus's reign marked the beginning of a remarkable period in Rome's history. For more than 200 years, the vast Roman Empire was united and, for the most part, peaceful. This period from 27 B.C. to A.D. 180 is called the *Pax Romana (paks roh MAH nuh),* or "Peace of Rome." ◼

*Notice that Roman rule extended as far north as Britain. Where were the western and eastern borders? How far south did the empire extend?*

# Ruling the Empire

Remember the problems that arose after Caesar's death over who would be the next emperor. Augustus hoped to avoid the same problems. He wanted his stepson Tiberius *(ty BIHR ee uhs)* to be the next emperor. To make sure it would happen, Augustus began to share his power with Tiberius. When Augustus died in A.D. 14, Tiberius stepped into his stepfather's position. In that way, Augustus established a new way of choosing emperors. Each emperor chose his successor from his family or adopted someone he thought would make a good emperor.

During the 200 years after Augustus's death, four family lines, or dynasties, ruled the Roman Empire. Some emperors in each dynasty ruled wisely. Others were cruel or foolish. Each of the four dynasties ended with the violent overthrow of an unpopular or unfit emperor.

### The Dynasties

Augustus's family line ended in disgrace in A.D. 68 with Emperor Nero *(NEE roh).* Nero came to power when he was just a boy of 17. He did not gain the respect of the senators or the army. Many

◼ *What did Augustus do for the city of Rome and for the provinces?*

A.D. 98–117, Trajan expands the Roman empire to its greatest size.

A.D. 117–138, Hadrian constructs walls to protect the empire's borders.

| 50 | | B.C. | A.D. | | 50 | | 100 | | 150 | | 200 |
|----|--|------|------|--|----|--|-----|--|-----|--|-----|

27 B.C.–A.D. 14, The *Pax Romana* begins with the rule of Caesar Augustus.

A.D. 161–180, The *Pax Romana* ends with the rule of Marcus Aurelius.

*Examine the timeline to see which emperor had the longest reign. The Roman coins, which picture Trajan and Marcus Aurelius, were used during their reigns.*

■ *How did the reigns of the "good emperors" contrast with the reigns of Nero and Domitian?*

### Across Time & Space

*In Britain, Emperor Hadrian ordered his soldiers to build a stone wall 73 miles long to keep invaders out of the empire. Parts of Hadrian's Wall are still standing today.*

Romans complained that he was more interested in entertaining himself than in governing the empire. Opposition to his rule mounted. A bloody civil war broke out, and Nero committed suicide.

The second dynasty lasted only 26 years. It ended with the assassination in A.D. 96 of Emperor Domitian *(duh MIHSH uhn)*, a cruel and ruthless leader. The third dynasty became known as the dynasty of the "good emperors." It included five talented emperors. Trajan *(TRAY juhn)*, for example, pushed the boundaries of the empire beyond the Danube and into Armenia and Mesopotamia. He also gave low-cost loans to farmers and helped support poor children and orphans.

Hadrian *(HAY dree uhn)* was the first emperor to settle on fixed borders marked by physical defenses—walls. Under Hadrian, small settlements around forts and castles became towns and cities. Marcus Aurelius *(aw REE lee uhs)* protected the borders, but his death ended the *Pax Romana*. Emperors who followed failed to control the vast empire. They even lost the respect of the Roman army.

Finally, Emperor Severus Alexander was assassinated by his own soldiers in A.D. 235. His death marked the end of the dynasties and the start of 50 years of civil war within the empire.

### Rebellion in the Provinces

Most of the Roman provinces lived in peace during the *Pax Romana*. However, a few areas resisted Roman rule. The Roman army had to put down rebellions in Gaul and Britain. The greatest resistance, however, came from the Jews in Judea. The Jews rebelled in A.D. 66 and again in A.D. 132. Each time, the Roman army crushed the Jewish resistance. ■

## Unifying the Empire

Despite resistance to Roman rule in some provinces, the empire remained unified during the *Pax Romana*. However, maintaining unity was a large task. Over the centuries, the Romans conquered vast areas and diverse peoples. These millions of people spoke many different languages, had different customs, and worshiped different gods. The Roman emperors, though, managed to unify them.

They did so in several ways. They encouraged the conquered people to build cities. They made these people Roman citizens. And they involved them in the government of Rome.

### Policies for the Provinces

These new cities that the people in the provinces built followed the model of Rome. The city center surrounded a main square called the forum, like the one in Rome. The new cities also had temples for Roman gods, an amphitheater for games, and public baths. These and other public buildings were patterned after the ones in the city of Rome. The ideas of the Romans, their customs, and their Latin language gradually spread from the cities into the surrounding areas.

As a second way of unifying the empire, Rome gradually granted citizenship to people in the provinces. In A.D. 212, Emperor Caracalla granted citizenship to the entire free population of the empire. As citizens, the people gained some important new rights. For example, citizens were protected by Roman law. They could do business and own property in Rome. They could also pass their property and citizenship on to their children.

As a third means of unifying the empire, Rome allowed officials in the provinces to govern their own cities. They collected taxes and kept order on Rome's behalf.

Rome allowed some of these officials from the provinces to participate in the central government in Rome. By A.D. 200, more than half of the 600 senators came from the provinces. Some of these senators even became emperors. Emperor Trajan, for example, came from Spain. Septimius Severus, who ruled from A.D. 193 to 211, came from North Africa.

These policies of Rome made the people who lived in the provinces feel that they were a part of the empire. Therefore, most of them did not have any reason to rebel.

## Rome at Its Peak

One of Rome's greatest poets described the purpose of the empire in this way:

*The city of Bath, England, is a health resort noted for its warm springs. This photo shows the public baths that were built there under the Romans.*

> Remember, Roman, that it is for you to rule the nations. This shall be your task: to impose the ways of peace, to spare the vanquished and to tame the proud by war.
>
> Virgil, *Aeneid,* c. 19 B.C.

For 200 years, Rome did just that. The *Pax Romana* is remembered as the period during which Rome reached the peak of its political and cultural achievement. ■

■ *What policies did the Roman emperors follow in order to unify the empire?*

---

## REVIEW

1. **FOCUS** How did the Romans build a peaceful and prosperous empire?

2. **CONNECT** Caesar's assassins thought the assassination had saved the Republic. Why do you think they might have expected the Roman people to approve?

3. **GOVERNMENT** Why did the Roman people welcome Augustus's rule?

4. **HISTORY** In what ways was the *Pax Romana* a remarkable period in Rome's history?

5. **CRITICAL THINKING** The Roman people did not want a king or dictator. Do you think Augustus and the emperors that followed him were different from kings or dictators? Explain your answer.

6. **ACTIVITY** Imagine that you live in the Roman province of Gaul, and you have heard rumors of a rebellion against Rome. Discuss the rumors with a partner, taking opposite sides about whether you ought to join the rebels.

LESSON 2

# Social Rank in the Empire

**THINKING
F O C U S**

*What role did social rank
play in Roman life?*

### Key Term

- elite

It's a beautiful day in A.D. 150. The people of ancient Rome are heading eagerly to the Colosseum. They are going to watch an afternoon of games in which professional fighters called gladiators will fight lions, bears, other wild beasts—and each other. "Such a throng flocked to all these shows," wrote Suetonius, "that many strangers had to lodge in tents pitched . . . along the roads, and the press was often such that many were crushed to death."

Now the people are pushing and shoving as they scramble toward the entrances to the giant outdoor stadium. Like sports fans today, the Romans pass through the gates and head for their seats.

Where they sit, however, depends on their social status. The emperor and his guests are seated nearest the field on a magnificent platform. In the first rows are senators and other wealthy Romans. They wear flowing white robes called togas. The togas are trimmed with purple borders—the mark of the **elite,** the upper class.

Sitting in the rows above the elite are ordinary citizens, also dressed in togas. Their togas are plain white. Only the elite are allowed to wear the purple border.

Crowded near the top of the stadium, above the ordinary citizens, are poor people and slaves in drab, grey clothes. They have no seats and must stand for hours waiting for the games to begin.

➤ *Gladiators like these, pictured in a detail from a Roman mosaic, often faced each other in the Colosseum and in other arenas.*

# Three Social Classes

Roman social status determined what people could wear, where they could sit—even what their job could be. Roman society was divided into three major classes—the elite, the "more humble," and the slaves. Birth and wealth determined social class.

### The Elite Class

The best seats at the Colosseum were saved for the elite. This group included senators and other government officials and wealthy citizens. The elite made up less than 2 per cent of the people, but they were the most powerful. They even had special legal rights. If they were guilty of a crime, they could not be punished as severely as ordinary citizens or slaves.

Only a few jobs were acceptable for a man of the elite class. The emperor appointed members of the elite class to serve as government officials. Also acceptable for the elite were jobs in law and ownership of farms. Jobs in business were not acceptable. If a man of the elite class wanted to make money in business, he would hire someone of the "more humble" class to do it for him.

### The "More Humble" Class

The people seated above the elite in the Colosseum were the ordinary citizens, who belonged to the "more humble" class. The more humble class included most of the free men and women in the empire. Farmers, laborers, shopkeepers, soldiers, and other working people were in the more humble class. Some of the more humble were fairly wealthy. Others just scraped by.

### The Slaves

Crammed together with the poorest people at the top of the Colosseum were the slaves—

*The Colosseum was completed in A.D. 80. It had four stories and covered over seven and one-half acres. Its 80 entrances allowed 50,000 spectators to find seats in 10 minutes. The emperor's family came in through a special gate. Wild animals were kept in cages under the floor.*

Slaves

Ordinary citizens

Elite

human property that could be bought and sold. Slaves could not own property. By some estimates, slaves made up as much as a third of the people of Roman Italy during the empire.

Besides working in households and on farms, trained slaves worked in mining, shipping, road building, and construction. Slaves also might hold office jobs in the provinces. Conditions for slaves varied widely. Slaves on the farms worked long hours in the fields. Sometimes they were chained together.

■ How did life differ for people in the three Roman social classes?

Slaves in cities usually worked as servants in the homes of wealthy masters. They had an easier life than the slaves on farms. Some city slaves even gained important positions as heads of household staffs. But all slaves were at the mercy of their masters, who could beat or torture them.

Some Romans complained about the mistreatment of slaves. However, no one in the ancient world thought seriously about the end of slavery. Apparently, people saw slavery as a necessary part of the social system. ■

## The Importance of Social Level

Social level was important to all Romans. Let's visit the home of an elite Roman to see the role it played at a dinner party.

### A Roman Dinner Party

As the guests arrive, they are led to the special dining room. Painted on the walls are sayings like this: "Let the slave wash and dry the feet of the guests, and let him be mindful to spread a linen cloth on the cushions of the couches."

Couches rather than chairs surround the tables because Romans prefer to lean back as they eat. Eating in a reclining position is considered a mark of elegance. Only children and slaves sit upright as they eat. On holidays, the slaves in this house are allowed to recline like their masters.

Soon an usher announces the guests and shows them to their places at the tables. Elite Romans follow a complex formula for seating people according to their social status. The most honored guests may even be served better food than the other guests. Pliny the Younger once complained about the favoritism shown by a host: ". . . very elegant dishes were served up to himself and a few more of the company; while those placed before the rest were cheap and paltry." Pliny said that the host even served his guests wines of three different qualities, depending on each guest's social status.

▼ *This painting found at Pompeii shows some elite Romans being entertained at a dinner party.*

The host at this dinner party has invited a man who belongs to the "more humble" class. The invitation is a reward for services performed. Unfortunately, the other guests treat this man as an inferior. They joke about his clothes, his table manners, and his vocabulary.

Slaves serve the dinner. The Roman writer Seneca described such slaves: "The unfortunate slaves are not allowed to move their lips, let alone talk. . . . A cough, a sneeze, a hiccup is rewarded by a flogging, with no exceptions."

## Changes in Social Level

As this dinner party shows, social divisions were clearly defined in ancient Rome. However, people were occasionally able to improve their social position. The key was gaining wealth, and for most, becoming wealthy was impossible. According to Juvenal, the Romans decided the importance of a man in this way:

> The first question to be asked will be about his wealth, the last about his character. How many slaves does he maintain? How much land does he possess? How many courses does he have served at table and how much does he provide for his guests?

Romans could improve their social position if they became wealthy. If they lost wealth, however, they could lose their social status. Raising one's social level was not easy. The great majority of people in the "more humble" class worked on farms, and they were usually lucky just to get by each year. They had little chance of becoming rich. Soldiers had a better chance. Some earned promotions and wealth during long military careers. When they retired, they were rich and respected enough to join the elite class.

Even slaves had a chance to better themselves. Through a master's kindness, an urban slave might be set free as a young adult. His master might even set him up in business, and then he might join the "more humble" class. Rural slaves had harder lives and fewer opportunities. They had little chance of gaining freedom or improving their lot in life. ■

▼ Wealthy Roman families used beautiful dishes like this plate and pitcher.

■ How could Romans improve their social position?

## R E V I E W

1. **FOCUS** What role did social rank play in Roman life?
2. **CONNECT** Compare the Roman social class system with the caste system of ancient India.
3. **SOCIAL SCIENCE** How did the ancient Romans feel about slavery? How would you compare their attitude with ours today?
4. **CRITICAL THINKING** Compare the Roman system for seating people in the Colosseum with the way people are seated at sporting events today. Who gets the best seats, and why?
5. **ACTIVITY** According to the U.S. Declaration of Independence, all people are created equal. Plan a debate about equality. Have one side, the Romans, argue that people are unequal and should be treated as such. Have the other side, the Americans, explain what the Declaration means by equality.

439

The Roman Empire

L E S S O N   3

# Daily Life in Ancient Rome

### Key Terms

- rhetoric
- ritual

B efore it is light I wake up, and, sitting on the edge of my bed, I put
on my shoes and leg-wraps because it is cold. . . . Taking off my
nightshirt I put on my tunic and belt; I put oil on my hair, comb
it, wrap a scarf around my neck and put on my white cloak. Followed by
my school attendant and my nurse I go to say good morning to daddy
and mummy and I kiss them both. I find my writing things and exercise
book and give them to a slave. I set off to school followed by my school attendant. . . .

I go into the schoolroom and say "Good morning master." He kisses
me and returns my greeting. The slave gives me my wax tablets, my writing things and ruler. . . . When I finish learning my lesson I ask the master to let me go home to lunch. . . . Reaching home I change, take some
white bread, olives, cheese, dried figs, and nuts and drink some cold water.
After lunch I go back to school where the master is beginning to read. He
says, "Let's begin work."

At the end of the afternoon I'm off to the Baths with some towels with
my slave. I run up to meet the people going to the Baths and we all say to
each other "Have a good bathe and a good supper."

A Roman schoolboy, quoted by F. R. Cowell,
*Everyday Life in Ancient Rome*

A boy from a wealthy Roman family wrote the above description of a typical day in about A.D. 300.

Accounts like this are one source of information about daily life in ancient Rome.

## Rich and Poor

The boy who wrote this account belonged to an elite family in Rome. Only the rich could send their children to school and have slaves wait on them. His home may have looked like the Roman house shown in A Closer Look on page 442. What parts of the house were open to let in light, air, and rain? Where would you spend the most time if you lived in this house?

A rich family in one of these homes might own 500 slaves. Some very wealthy Roman families might own 4,000 slaves. An emperor might command a personal slave population of 20,000. Household slaves did just about every job imaginable. They cooked, served meals, cleaned, and took care of the children. Each slave might have only one job—folding the master's clothes or fixing the mistress's hair, for example.

In contrast, the vast majority of those who lived in the city had tiny apartments in five-story apartment buildings called *insulae (IHN suh ly)*. In some cases, an entire family would crowd into a single room.

For every wealthy home in Rome, there were 26 blocks of *insulae*. Most *insulae* were dark and dirty and had no heat or running water. The poor got water from public fountains outside.

The Roman writer Juvenal described the poorer neighborhoods of Rome in the A.D. 100s:

> Most of the city [is] propped up with planks to stop it collapsing. Your landlord stands in front of cracks that have been there for years and says, "Sleep well!" although he knows that the house itself may not last the night. I wish I lived where there were no fires, no midnight panics.

In these crowded conditions, fires and crime were serious problems. Lack of sanitation also contributed to the spread of disease. The problem was so severe that about one-fourth of the babies born in Rome did not live through their first year. Half of all Roman children did not live to be 10 years old. ■

*The Roman father and son in this marble relief are shown at different stages of the son's life. In the last scene, the boy may be answering the age-old question, "What did you learn in school today?"*

*This make-up box and the hairpin shown with it once belonged to a wealthy Roman woman.*

■ *How did the housing of the rich Romans compare with the housing of the poor?*

441

The Roman Empire

# A Roman House

*Imagine living in a home that was also your parents' work place. Relatives, friends, servants, and clients would always be coming and going. There might be a vegetable garden and a couple of stores under your roof, too.*

**If you put** out this dog-shaped oil lamp, your bedroom would be totally dark—even during the day! That's because bedrooms rarely had windows.

**Would you walk** on your artwork? The Romans did. Romans decorated their floors with mosaics like this one.

**The father of the family** sits here, where he can see all the action.

Back yard

Garden

Kitchen

Statue of great-grandfather

Stores

Door, open all day

Bedroom

Reading room

**Can you eat lying down?** Romans held dinner parties in a room called the *triclinium*, which means "three-couch place." The room had three couches, and dinner guests ate while lying on their sides.

**Like a living room today,** the *atrium* was the place where Roman families entertained their guests. But the Roman living room had a hole in its roof. Rainwater poured into a pool where it was stored for drinking and washing.

**Only the rich** could afford glass pitchers and bowls like these.

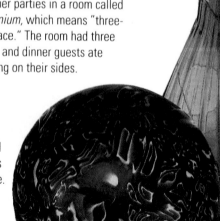

the years A.D. 106 to 114, 23,000 gladiators fought to entertain the citizens. The Romans were so fond of bloody events that during the intermissions, Roman officials executed condemned criminals for the entertainment of the audience.

However, the benefits of life in Rome such as free food and spectacular entertainment did not appeal to all Romans. Some claimed that the citizens took too much interest in those things and not enough interest in their government. Even members of the elite class, who benefited the most, saw problems. The Roman historian

Tacitus said that the empire made slaves of free men. The Roman writer Juvenal also complained that the public "longs for just two things—bread and circuses." ■

*Circuses were a major form of entertainment in the Roman Empire. This "Mosaic of the Circus Games" was found in Roman Gaul. It dates from about A.D. 175.*

## Religious Practices

Many Romans believed that they had been able to build their empire and find peace because they had kept their gods happy. Like many other ancient peoples, the Romans had gods for every act and event in their lives.

### The Many Gods of the Romans

The great gods of the Roman state were Jupiter, Juno, and Minerva. Jupiter was the supreme god. He controlled the thunder and lightning and was the special guardian of Rome. Juno was his wife. She was the queen of the gods and the protector of women. Minerva was the goddess of wisdom and guardian of craftworkers. The Romans joined together on specific days to worship these gods. In this way they showed their unity and their loyalty to the state.

At home, the Romans worshiped household gods, such as Vesta, Lares (*LAIR eez*), and Penates (*puh NAY teez*). Vesta guarded the fireside, where people

cooked and kept warm. Lares guarded the land, and Penates watched over the stored food. Family members made daily offerings to these gods and asked for protection in exchange.

Many of these Roman gods had been borrowed from the Greeks at an earlier time. For example, Jupiter was the Greek god Zeus, and Juno was the Greek goddess Hera. Diana, the Roman goddess of the hunt, was the Greek goddess Artemis. Mars, the Roman god of war, was the Greek god Ares.

In A.D. 126, the Romans erected a magnificent temple called the Pantheon (*PAN thee uhn*) to honor all the Roman gods and goddesses. They built it in the shape of a drum, with a dome rising 14 stories above the ground. They covered the dome with gleaming brass so that people could see it

■ *How did the emperors provide "bread and circuses" for the people of Rome?*

*Found in the ruins of Pompeii, this household shrine contains small statues that include one of Lares, the guardian of houses.*

shining all over the city. The Pantheon is still standing today.

During the empire, the Romans also began to worship their emperors. The emperor was not a god like Jupiter, but he was so powerful that people believed he was divine.

➤ *This statue of Jupiter, the supreme god of the Romans, was found with a statue of his wife Juno. It is made of terra cotta, a hard ceramic clay.*

### Religious Ceremonies

The Roman religion was based on **rituals,** or ceremonies, rather than a written creed or right behavior. If a priest carried out the rituals properly, the Romans thought that the gods would be happy and would reward them with protection and wealth.

In one of the most important rituals, priests sacrificed animals to please the gods. The priests also made sacrifices in order to find signs, or omens, in the organs of the sacrificed animals. These signs, the people believed, would tell the will of the gods and would help them make decisions. How were the beliefs of the Romans similar to certain ideas of the ancient Greeks and Chinese?

■ *What was the Roman state religion like, and why were some people dissatisfied with it?*

### Other Religions

By the A.D. 100s, many Romans were becoming dissatisfied with the state religion. Since their religion did not teach about how people ought to act, some Romans started looking for other religions. Some gods and religious beliefs from Greece, Asia, Persia, and Egypt began to gain popularity during the first two centuries A.D. People in many parts of the empire were becoming Christians. Like the Jews, the Christians believed in just one god. They honored their God above the gods of the empire or the orders of the emperor.

For the most part, the Romans were tolerant of other religions within the empire. However, when the fortunes of the empire began to decline, emperors tried to force people to follow the state religion. A struggle lay ahead over what religious beliefs should guide the Roman people. ■

R E V I E W

1. **FOCUS** How was daily life different for rich and poor Romans?

2. **CONNECT** How does the class system help to explain why the only Romans who studied rhetoric were wealthy men?

3. **BELIEF SYSTEMS** How did their religion make the Romans feel they had some control over the unknown?

4. **CRITICAL THINKING** Why did the emperors of Rome go to so much effort and expense to entertain the poor people? What might have happened if they had ignored the poor?

5. **ACTIVITY** Make a chart listing the pros and cons of having as many holidays as the Romans had. Consider both Roman society and our own.

446

L E S S O N    4

# The Roman Economy

In 1957, a 16-year-old boy who was skin-diving near the Italian island of Sardinia made an important discovery. He saw a group of large jars on the floor of the sea, about 65 feet below the surface. These jars turned out to be amphorae from a Roman ship that had sunk more than 2,000 years ago.

A team of underwater archaeologists was called in to investigate. To search the floor of the sea, they used techniques similar to those used in excavations on land. They took underwater photographs of the area. They placed a grid of tape over the area so that they could make records about where they found evidence. Then they brought the amphorae up to the surface.

From what the archaeologists found, they determined that the ship had probably set sail from a port in Italy. It had run aground near the little island of Sparghi off the coast of Sardinia.

The Sparghi ship, as it is now called, was part of the vast fleet of ships that carried goods between ports on the Mediterranean Sea beginning in the 200s B.C. By the time of the Roman Empire, the Romans sent ships to the far corners of the ancient world as they knew it. The olive oil and wine found on the Sparghi ship were probably on their way from Italian farms to people in Spain or Gaul.

**THINKING FOCUS**

*What were some important products of the Roman economy, and why were they important?*

**Key Term**

- market

◄ *This marble relief shows a Roman ship from about A.D. 200. The sails were probably of cloth, reinforced with leather at the corners. The relief, which was found in Carthage, was probably made in the country that is present-day Tunisia.*

447

# An Agricultural Economy

Agriculture was the backbone of the Roman economy. In Italy itself, farmers grew grain and planted olive groves and vineyards. Olive oil and wine were shipped to cities throughout the empire. As the empire expanded, olive oil and wine were also produced in Gaul, Spain, and North Africa as well as Italy.

But on the whole, Roman farming methods were not very advanced. As a result, crops were small, and many people were needed to work the land. Four out of five people in the Roman Empire worked on farms. Compare that with about one in forty-five people who farm in America today. What does the comparison

## UNDERSTANDING EMPIRE

Rome began as a village, a dot on the map of Italy. Yet by A.D. 117, Rome controlled the Mediterranean world. The Roman Empire spread out in all directions from its capital of Rome.

### A Nation Is Not an Empire

Remember that an empire is made up of a nation and the nations it has conquered, under one ruler. The Roman Empire under Augustus is an example. An empire usually covers a large territory, but size alone doesn't make an empire. Both Canada and the United States are large, yet neither is an empire.

### Building an Empire

A nation may conquer new territories for a number of reasons. For one, it may be seeking natural resources. The Romans needed grain to feed their people. When Egypt became part of the Roman Empire, it had to give Rome grain as payment of taxes.

A nation might expand, too, as it seeks borders it can defend. Mountain ranges and bodies of water make good natural borders. The Roman Empire at some points extended north to the Danube River.

Often the native people in the new territories, or colonies, have cultures and languages different from those of the ruling power. These colonies may even be located thousands of miles away. Portugal, for example, set up colonies in Africa and Brazil during the 1500s.

The conquered peoples in an empire often resent foreign rule and rebel against it. Beginning some 300 years ago, the British built the largest empire ever known. The eastern United States was once part of it. Most colonial Americans shared British culture, but they rebelled against British rule in 1776.

### Results of Empire Building

As it works to unify its empire, the ruling power spreads its culture—sometimes by force. In that way it leaves its mark on its colonies, sometimes long after the empire breaks up.

The Roman Empire is a good example. Its language, Latin, spread throughout the empire. French, Spanish, and Italian are called "Romance languages" because of their roots in Latin.

tell you about Roman agriculture?

Another reason for the poor performance of Roman agriculture was taxation. The emperors required farmers to give most of their surplus grain to the government in taxes. Farmers could not make money by selling surplus grain at a profit, and so they had little to spend.

## The Market for Roman Industry

One result was a limited demand for manufactured items. Modern industry employs so many people and produces so many items because there is a large **market,** or demand, for its products. In ancient Rome, most people could afford only simple clothes and inexpensive pottery. Only the wealthy could afford decorated pottery and fine jewelry. As a result, the market for such items was small.

Most manufacturing plants in ancient Rome were small. An example is the pottery shop in Arretium *(uh REE shuhm),* one of the empire's best-known manufacturing operations. It employed only about 50 slaves. In contrast, a modern manufacturing plant might employ thousands of workers.

For all its accomplishments, the Roman Empire never developed a complex economy. It did not create large banks and other financial institutions. Instead, the Roman economy was mainly concerned with the basic task of feeding the empire's soldiers and city dwellers. This same basic task made Rome the hub of an extensive network of trade routes. ■

*This branch was part of an olive tree, a plant that had great importance to the ancient Romans. Even today, Italy leads the world in production of olives.*

■ *Why was Roman farming so poor?*

*This olive crusher was a useful tool for a Roman farmer. The wheels and basin are made of lava from Vesuvius. The crosspiece is wooden. The wheels rotate against an iron pin inside the basin, separating the pulp from the seeds.*

## Trade in the Empire

Here's how the Greek writer Aelius Aristides *(air ih STY deez)* described Roman shipping in the A.D. 100s:

So many merchant ships arrive in Rome with cargoes from everywhere, at all times of the year, and after each harvest, that the city seems like the world's warehouse. The arrival and departure of ships never stops—it's amazing that the sea, not to mention the harbor, is big enough for these merchant ships.

Ships hauled goods, such as wine, grain, and exotic animals, to and from ports in every part of the Roman Empire. On land, carts pulled by oxen or mules and even caravans of camels carried such items as lumber, clothing, and household goods over the empire's extensive system of roads. A side benefit was that trade brought news of other cultures and foreign places.

### Feeding the Empire

The most important item that the Romans traded for was grain. Wheat and barley were used in making the bread

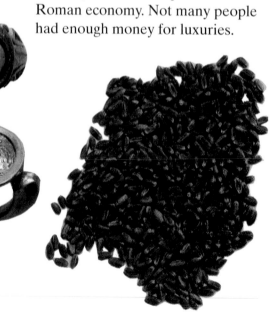

## Across Time & Space

*Just as ancient Rome could not produce enough grain for its people, many modern nations must seek grain from other sources. The United States supplies grain to such countries as the Soviet Union, China, Argentina, and Australia.*

▼ *The Romans traded for wheat, barley, and other foods they needed for survival. They also imported luxury items like marble, gold, and ostrich eggs.*

and other foods that formed most of the Roman diet. Grain was needed for the people of the cities as well as the army legions throughout the empire. Providing enough was a constant challenge.

Rome itself had become a city with about one million people by the A.D. 100s. The farmland around Rome could not grow enough grain to feed everyone. Therefore, the city depended heavily on products imported from North Africa, Egypt, and Sicily. Look at the map on page 451 to see the main regions that sent grain to the city.

An added problem was that as many as 300,000 people in the city of Rome were so poor that they could not buy grain. The government had to give it to them. Free handouts became important to the peace of the city. An emperor might face riots if he did not provide enough grain for the people.

Another 300,000 men in the army stationed in the empire's provinces also had to be fed. Food was generally supplied by the provinces where the men were stationed. Sometimes, though, the provinces could not produce enough for themselves and the army too. Then the government had to send more grain from other parts of the empire.

### Manufacturing and Mining

The largest industry in the empire was mining. Marble and other materials for the empire's great building projects were mined in Greece and northern Italy. Gold and silver came from mines in Spain. Lead and tin came from Britain. The metals were needed to manufacture weapons and other items, including coins for trade within the empire. Metals were also exchanged for luxury goods from foreign lands.

Italian communities manufactured pottery, glassware, weapons, tools, and textiles for use in Rome and for trade throughout the empire. In contrast to farm products, however, trade in manufactured goods was limited.

### Luxury Trade

The trade in luxury goods made up the smallest part of the Roman economy. Not many people had enough money for luxuries.

## Major Grain-Producing Areas of the Empire

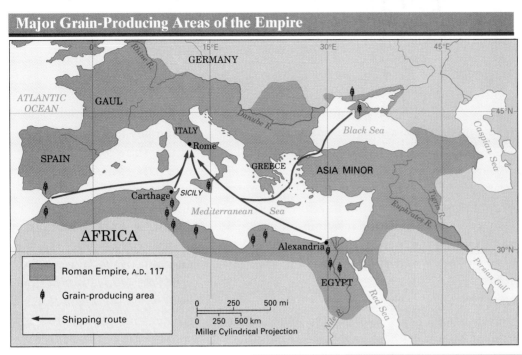

Roman Empire, A.D. 117

Grain-producing area

Shipping route

◄ What seas and rivers watered the major grain-producing regions of the empire?

▼ Roman trade in the Mediterranean Sea increased as the empire expanded and decreased as the empire declined. How does the number of shipwrecks reflect the rise, the peak, and the decline of the Roman Empire?

However, traders traveled far beyond the borders of the empire to bring back unusual items for wealthy Romans.

Traders went south into the Sahara and brought back ostrich eggs and ivory, which were strange and wonderful to the Romans. They went north and brought back blond slaves from the land that is now Germany. These blond slaves were so intriguing to the dark-haired Romans that some rich Romans even began wearing blond wigs. The traders also went into the Far East, bringing back silks from China, and spices and gems from India.

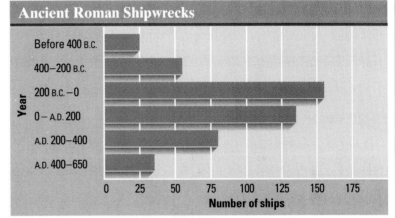

### Ancient Roman Shipwrecks

Such items, of course, were always far less important than grain. Remember that both trade and agriculture had the same primary purpose. They provided food for the vast numbers of people in the Roman Empire. ■

■ *Why did the Romans need to import grain?*

---

## R E V I E W

1. **FOCUS** What were some important products of the Roman economy, and why were they important?
2. **CONNECT** How was Rome's economy similar to that of other ancient civilizations?
3. **ECONOMICS** People are productive when they expect to be rewarded for their efforts. Relate this idea to the poor productivity of Roman farmers.
4. **CRITICAL THINKING** The Roman culture was not an

innovative culture—one that tried new ways of doing things. Is our culture innovative? Explain.

5. **WRITING ACTIVITY** Imagine that you are a farmer in a province of the Roman Empire. You have just found out that you have to give one-third of your wheat crop in taxes. Your grain is needed to feed the poor people of Rome. Write a newspaper editorial explaining your opinion of the tax.

The Roman Empire

# Reading Cartograms

### Here's Why

Maps can show statistical information, such as population, rainfall, or yearly income, in many ways. For example, cartographers may choose to use a standard map base and then add thematic information. Or they might use a cartogram.

Cartograms are chart maps that present statistical information. On a cartogram, the sizes of geographic areas are changed, or distorted, in order to help show the statistical information. Thus, cartograms allow you to see facts at a glance and to make comparisons quickly.

Approximately 60 million people lived in the Roman Empire at its height. Suppose you want to know about population distribution in that part of the world today. A cartogram can help you.

### Here's How

Look at the maps on these pages. Read the titles; then find out how each map shows information.

The map on the left is a thematic map. It shows the extent of the Roman Empire at its height, around A.D. 117. As the key indicates, color is used to show which areas were part of the Empire.

The map also includes modern political boundaries to show you which modern nations contain land that was once part of the Roman Empire. The scale tells you how distance on the map relates to distance on the earth.

Now look at the cartogram on page 453. Each shape represents a country. Notice that the cartogram has no scale of miles. The sentence in the lower left

**Roman Empire, A.D. 117**

Extent of the Roman Empire, A.D. 117

Present-day boundary

0    250    500 mi.
0  250  500 km
Azimuthal Equidistant Projection

# Reviewing Skills

1. Look at the map and cartogram on pages 452 and 453. On the standard map on the left, Libya is larger than Italy. Why is Italy larger than Libya on the cartogram?
2. Turn to the World Nutrition cartogram on page 43. In this cartogram, why is India shown larger than the Soviet Union? Why is Australia shown as one of the smallest nations? What does the cartogram's color coding tell you about nutrition in Bangladesh?
3. Prepare an opening or closing statement for a debate on the following: "The system of rule by emperors improved people's lives during the time period called the *Pax Romana*." Evaluate your work. Make sure your written statement is clear and forceful.
4. Suppose you are a close friend of Nero. He asks you to tell him how highly the people think of him. How could you answer him truthfully without making the emperor angry?

# Using Critical Thinking

1. Look at the map on page 499 of the Minipedia. Find the Roman Empire, the Han Dynasty, and the Gupta Empire. Which empire spans the greatest distance? Would you expect communication within the empire you chose to be easier or more difficult than in the other two empires? Explain your answer.
2. One Roman writer said that Romans wanted only "bread and circuses." What did this writer mean? Do you think people in the United States today want only "bread and circuses"? Use examples to explain your answer.
3. In ancient Rome, birth and wealth determined everyone's social class. Social class determined what people's legal rights were, where they sat in the Colosseum, what clothes they wore, and what kinds of jobs they held. Think about the social system in the United States today. How do you think it compares to the social system of ancient Rome?

# Preparing for Citizenship

1. **COLLECTING INFORMATION** By the terms of the Roman constitution, a leader was expected to share power with the senate. Think about Caesar's attitude toward the senate. Then study the United States Constitution. Write down two powers the president shares with Congress. Do you think that sharing power in government is a good idea? Why or why not?
2. **WRITING ACTIVITY** A 13-year struggle for power followed Caesar's assassination. Look up *presidential succession* in an encyclopedia. Find out what would happen if both the president and vice president were unable to complete their terms of office. Imagine that someone is proposing to change the existing laws about presidential succession. Write a letter to your senator or Congressional representative. Tell why you are for or against the proposed change.
3. **COLLABORATIVE LEARNING** The ancient Romans respected both Caesar and Augustus because of what they did to improve people's lives. Divide the class into two groups, one researching improvements under Augustus and the other researching improvements under Caesar. Then form small groups, each with representatives of both rulers. Plan how you will present the contributions of both rulers to the class. After the class presentations, discuss some improvements that modern leaders have brought into people's lives.

# Chapter 15

# *Christianity and the Fall of Rome*

By the A.D. 200s, Rome's great era of peace and prosperity was just a memory. Military leaders fought each other for power. Invaders from beyond the borders defeated the mighty Roman army. The economy crumbled. As Rome declined, another power rose—the Christian Church.

**A.D. 200–300** Barbarian invasions weaken the empire. This relief from a stone coffin shows a bitter battle between the Romans and invaders from the north.

| B.C. | A.D. | | 100 | | 200 |
|------|------|--|-----|--|-----|

## A.D. 36

**A.D. 64** A great fire sweeps through Rome. Emperor Nero blames Christians for the fire and orders them killed.

During the A.D. 300s Christianity became the main religion and a power in the empire. An eastern emperor gave this cross to the Pope around A.D. 570.

A.D. 476 The Western Roman Empire falls, but the eastern empire remains strong. The mosaic above shows Empress Theodora, a ruler of the eastern empire during the A.D. 500s.

300

400

500

A.D. 330 Emperor Constantine builds the capital of Constantinople for the eastern empire.

457

A.D. 476

LESSON 1

# The Early Christians

### Key Terms

- persecute
- conversion
- sect
- Gentile

➤ *In the A.D. 1400s, the French artist Jean Fouquet painted this version of Saul's conversion to Christianity.*

One day in about A.D. 36, a Jew named Saul was on the road to Damascus, a city in ancient Syria. He was tracking down Christians, the followers of the Jewish teacher Jesus. Saul was one of many Jews who believed these Christians should be **persecuted,** or punished, for their failure to obey all the Jewish laws.

The New Testament of the Christian Bible describes what Christians believe happened next:

*N ow as he journeyed he approached Damascus, and suddenly a light from heaven flashed about him. And he fell to* the ground and heard a voice saying to him, "Saul, Saul, why do you persecute me?" And he said, "Who are you, Lord?" And he said, "I am Jesus, whom you are persecuting; but rise and enter the city, and you will be told what you are to do."*

Acts 9: 3–6

According to the New Testament, Saul was blinded by the light from heaven. He did not regain his sight until a follower of Jesus touched him. At that moment, Saul's life changed forever. Once a persecutor of Christians, Saul now became one of the most devoted followers of the new faith.

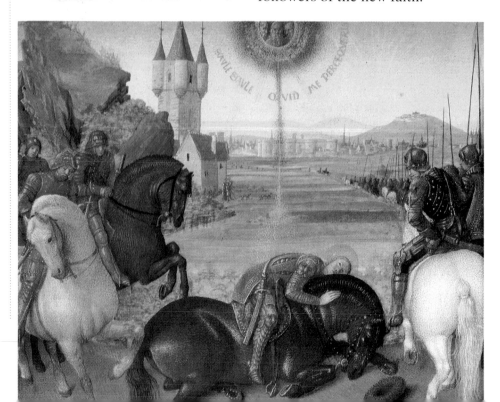

# The New Faith

Saul's **conversion,** or change from one belief to another, came a few years after the death of Jesus, which you read about in Chapter 10. At the time of Saul's conversion, Christianity was not a separate religion. The Christians were a **sect,** or group, among Jews.

## Religions in the Roman Empire

Judaism was one of many religions practiced in the Roman Empire. The Romans themselves followed a number of religions. Romans were even willing to accept the gods of other people alongside their own. They also allowed a great deal of freedom to different religious groups, so long as the groups respected the gods of the Roman state.

Nevertheless, the beliefs of the Jews (and of the Christians) clashed with those of the Romans. The Jews believed in one god, and they were unwilling to worship the many Roman gods. The Jews also lived by the laws of their god, as set forth in the Torah, and the teaching of their prophets. The Romans believed in serving their gods by following certain rituals, such as sacrificing animals. They believed that keeping their gods happy would keep the empire strong.

Even so, Judaism was a legal religion in the Roman empire. Jews and Romans disagreed mainly on political grounds. However, Jews and Christians began to disagree on religious grounds. As a result, Christianity slowly became a separate religion. The growth of Christianity had a lasting impact on Western civilization.

## New Testament

At first, however, few people in the Roman Empire took much notice of this small band of believers, the Christians. This is why there are few written accounts of the history of early Christians. Much of what we know comes from the part of the Christian Bible called the New Testament, a collection of books that tells the story of Jesus and his followers.

Besides telling stories about Jesus, the New Testament tells about the birth and early development of Christianity. It also includes the story of Saul and his conversion to Christianity.

The New Testament books were collected between A.D. 100 and 200 to teach and to inspire Christians. As a result, the New Testament tells the story of Christianity from the point of view of the Christians only—not the Romans or the Jews. ■

▲ *The Romans adopted gods and goddesses from other religions. This wall painting from around A.D. 60 shows the Roman goddess Diana, who is based on the Greek goddess Artemis.*

■ *How did the Jewish and Christian religious beliefs differ from those of the Romans?*

◄ *The fish was one of the earliest Christian symbols. The Greek word for fish contains the first initials of the words,* Jesus Christ, Son of God, Savior.

# Jews and Christians

The Christians felt that their faith was the fulfillment of Judaism. The Jews and early Christians shared the same basic beliefs. But their ideas differed on the messiah, or savior. The Jews believed that the messiah had not yet come. They expected the messiah to overthrow the Roman governors and reunite the Jews. The Christians believed that Jesus was the messiah. Instead of bringing freedom from Rome, Christians believed he would bring eternal life.

## Jews and Gentiles

Nevertheless, the Jewish roots of Christianity ran deep. In addition to sharing many beliefs, Jews and Christians lived in the same communities. Since the Diaspora, the scattering of Jewish settlements throughout the Mediterranean that began in the 500s B.C., Jews had been gathering together in communities within the cities of the Roman Empire.

Jews saw themselves as the chosen people of their god. Jews, including sects such as the Christians, saw the world as divided into two groups—Jews and **Gentiles,** or non-Jews.

▼ *The Psalms, shown on this fragment from a Greek manuscript, are scriptures that are studied by both Christians and Jews.*

The Jews and Gentiles did not always get along. In fact, at times violent hatred led to open conflict between them.

## Preaching to Gentiles

The early Christians concentrated on trying to convert other Jews. However, Jewish leaders opposed their efforts. They charged that Christians were not obeying Jewish law. The Christians insisted that belief in Jesus and in Jesus' love was more important than strict obedience to Jewish law. As Christians spread their message, tensions grew between Christians and Jews.

The friction led to a serious debate within the early church: Should Christians reach out to all people, or just to other Jews? According to the New Testament, the turning point came in about A.D. 48. That was when Peter, a disciple who had been chosen by Jesus to spread his teachings, was instructed in a vision from God to break some of the Jewish rules. Jewish law prohibited Jews from eating food that was not prepared according to their rules.

According to the book of Acts, Peter went to the house of a Roman soldier and visited with a group of Gentiles. Peter said to the Gentiles:

> Y*ou yourselves know how unlawful it is for a Jew to associate with or to visit anyone of another nation; but God has shown me that I should not call any man common or unclean.*

Acts 10:28

From that point on, Peter and other Christians decided to preach Christianity to all people. One of the first to set off on this mission was Saul, the former persecutor of Christians. Saul, who came to be known by the Roman name Paul, traveled throughout the Roman Empire spreading the word about Christianity. ■

■ *Why did tension grow between Jews and Christians?*

## The Work of Paul

Paul played an important role in early Christianity. Because he was a devout Jew, he could speak to fellow Jews and be heard. He was also a Roman citizen. Not only could he claim all the benefits of citizenship, but he could be seen by the Romans as one of their own. Finally, he was a passionate supporter of the new faith, and he devoted his life to this cause.

From about A.D. 47 until his death in about A.D. 64, Paul made three long journeys during which he spread Christian teachings. He also established Christian communities. As the map on this page shows, Paul's second journey began in Asia Minor and took him through much of the eastern Mediterranean region. How far west did Paul travel during this second journey?

Paul's journeys were not easy. His preaching angered many Jews. After all, he was challenging the very foundations of Jewish belief. For centuries, Jews had lived by the commandments of God as given to them in the Jewish scriptures. Now Paul was telling them that simply obeying God's laws was not enough. Paul said that people needed to accept Jesus as their savior.

Many Jews rejected the ideas that Paul preached, and some Jews even attacked him. They believed that Paul was trying to spread ideas that went against Jewish beliefs.

▼ *On his second journey, Paul visited many important cities in Asia Minor and Greece.*

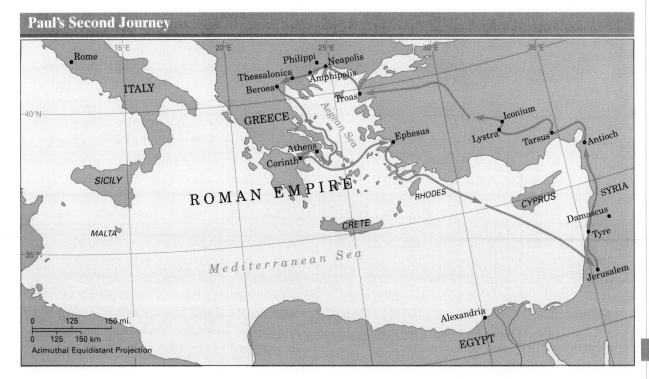

**Paul's Second Journey**

Rome · ITALY · GREECE · Philippi · Neapolis · Thessalonica · Amphipolis · Beroea · Troas · Aegean Sea · Iconium · Lystra · Tarsus · Antioch · Ephesus · Athens · Corinth · SICILY · ROMAN EMPIRE · RHODES · CYPRUS · SYRIA · Damascus · MALTA · CRETE · Tyre · Mediterranean Sea · Jerusalem · Alexandria · EGYPT

0  125  150 mi.
0  125  150 km
Azimuthal Equidistant Projection

461

Christianity and the Fall of Rome

*The ruins of Corinth, one of the cities Paul visited on his second journey, are pictured at the right. Find Corinth on the map on page 461.*

Here is how Paul described the sufferings his preaching caused him:

Five times I have received at the hands of the Jews the forty lashes less one. Three times I have been beaten with rods; once I was stoned. Three times I have been shipwrecked; a night and a day I have been adrift at sea; on frequent journeys, in danger from rivers, danger from robbers, danger from my own people, danger from Gentiles, danger in the city, danger in the wilderness, danger at sea, danger from false brethren.

2 Corinthians 11: 24–26

■ *How did Paul help spread Christianity?*

Paul also insisted that Gentile converts to Christianity did not have to observe all the Jewish laws. This angered the Jews, and it also angered some Christian leaders whose backgrounds were Jewish.

Paul was becoming a troublemaker in the eyes of the Roman authorities. He was eventually arrested in Jerusalem and sent to Rome to stand trial. For two years, he remained there, continuing to preach and teach. According to Christian tradition, Paul was executed in about A.D. 64.

By this time, Christianity had become a religion that was separate and distinct from Judaism. In the centuries to come, the gulf between the two faiths would continue to widen. ■

## R E V I E W

1. **FOCUS** How were Judaism and early Christianity alike, and how were they different?
2. **CONNECT** In Chapter 10 you read about the life of Jesus. How did Roman leaders react to the teachings of Jesus?
3. **BELIEF SYSTEMS** Why did Jews oppose the preaching of Paul?
4. **CRITICAL THINKING** The Christians decided to preach to Gentiles as well as to Jews. Why do you think that decision was important to the development of Christianity?
5. **ACTIVITY** Look at the map of the Middle East today on page 510 of the Atlas, and compare it with the map on page 461. Then trace Paul's second journey through the modern world. List the countries he passed through.

LESSON 2

# Rome and the Christians

In A.D. 64, a great fire swept through Rome. It burned for six days, and it destroyed much of the city. Here is how the Roman historian Tacitus described the scene:

*First, the fire swept violently over the level spaces. Then it climbed the hills—but returned to ravage the lower ground again. When people looked back, menacing flames sprang up before them or outflanked them. When they escaped to a neighboring quarter, the fire followed. . . . Some who had lost everything—even their food for the day—could have escaped, but preferred to die.*

Tacitus, *Annals*, c. A.D. 120

Look at the map at the right. What parts of Rome suffered the greatest damage in the fire? What important buildings were destroyed?

At the time of the fire, Nero was the emperor. He was a young man who was known for his ruthless hunger for power, not for his leadership. In fact, Nero's poor leadership made many Romans turn against him.

Some people even accused him of setting the fire, although no proof of his guilt exists. Nero was crafty, though. He knew that he needed to blame someone for starting the fire. He chose the Christians. They were already unpopular with most people in Rome because they refused to worship the Roman gods.

Emperor Nero gave orders that the Christians be killed for starting the fire. Tacitus described the cruel way in which they were put to death:

*Mockery of every sort was added to their deaths. Covered with the skins of beasts, they were torn by dogs and perished, or were nailed to crosses, or were doomed to the flames and burnt.*

## THINKING
## FOCUS

*How did Christianity grow between A.D. 64 and A.D. 400?*

## Key Terms

- martyr
- excommunication
- pagan

▼ *The great fire destroyed central Rome.*

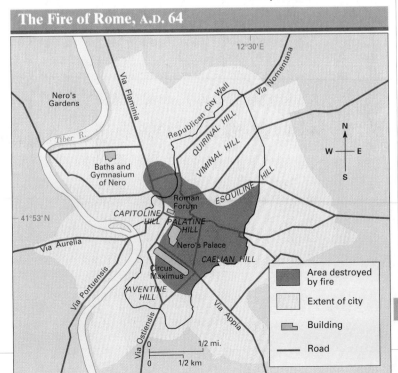

### The Fire of Rome, A.D. 64

Nero's Gardens

Via Flaminia

Republican City Wall

Via Nomentana

QUIRINAL HILL

VIMINAL HILL

Tiber R.

Baths and Gymnasium of Nero

ESQUILINE HILL

Roman Forum

CAPITOLINE HILL

PALATINE HILL

Nero's Palace

Via Aurelia

CAELIAN HILL

Circus Maximus

Via Portuensis

AVENTINE HILL

Via Appia

Via Ostiensis

12°30'E

41°53'N

N W E S

| | |
| --- | --- |
| ■ | Area destroyed by fire |
| □ | Extent of city |
| ⌂ | Building |
| — | Road |

0 1/2 mi.
0 1/2 km

# Rome's Early Response

▼ *This painting illustrates two New Testament accounts of persecution. On the left, Paul defends himself in front of a Roman governor. On the right, he is lowered from the walls of Damascus to escape persecution.*

Tacitus, like many Romans, did not really believe that the Christians had set Rome on fire. Yet he shared the view of many Romans that Christians should be convicted, "not so much of the crime of firing the city, as of hatred against mankind."

The Christians did not act like other Romans, and this made some Romans suspicious. Christians kept to themselves—almost like a secret club. Since they did not worship Roman gods, Christians no longer went to public festivals or took part in the life of their communities.

Jews also refused to worship the Roman gods. Yet Romans generally excused them because Judaism was an old, established religion. Christianity was a new invention, so Romans saw Christians as troublemakers.

Some Christian ideas, too, seemed shocking. Wealth and private property, for example, were very important measures of status in the Roman social hierarchy. Yet the Christians taught that money and earthly pleasures were not important at all, and that property should be shared.

The Romans considered their government and their religion to be closely linked, while the Christians saw religion and government as separate. Also, Romans believed that their gods protected them and their empire. Romans feared the failure of Christians to honor Roman gods would harm the empire.

## The Roots of Persecution

Nevertheless, Nero's treatment of the Christians was unusually harsh. For the most part, the Roman state ignored the early Christians.

Before A.D. 64, most of the persecution suffered by the Christians came at the hands of other Jews. The Roman government would not get involved in these conflicts. For example, the New Testament describes the reaction of a Roman governor when a group of Jews brought Paul before him. The governor said:

> I f it were a matter of wrongdoing or vicious crime, I should have reason to bear with you, O Jews; but since it is a matter of questions about words and names and your own law, see to it yourselves.

Acts 18:14-15

By A.D. 200, Christian settlements had spread throughout the empire. In these settlements, Christians gathered to practice their religion. The unleavened bread and wine of the Jewish Passover celebration became symbols for Christians of the Last Supper.

The Romans generally did not try to change the differing religious beliefs of the people in the empire. And Christian leaders such as Paul taught Christians to obey Roman laws. "Let every person be subject to the governing authorities," Paul wrote in his letter to the Romans. "Pay all of them their dues, taxes to whom taxes are due, revenue to whom revenue is due, respect to whom respect is due, honor to whom honor is due." (Romans 13:7)

## Roman Law and Early Christians

By A.D. 100, Roman law stated that anyone who admitted to being a Christian must be killed. However, this policy was seldom enforced. In general, the Roman emperor let officials in the provinces decide how Christians should be treated. But these officials were often unsure as to what to do. In fact, written records indicate that many Roman officials had little experience in dealing with Christians.

The governor of Asia Minor, Pliny the Younger, wrote to Emperor Trajan in about A.D. 110:

So far, this is how I have dealt with people who were brought to me for being Christians. I ask them if they are Christians: if they admit it, I ask them twice more, and warn them what the punishment is: if they persist I order them to be executed.

But the Christians were not a real danger to Pliny. "If we give these Christians a chance to repent, a large number of people could be brought back on to the right path," he said.

Trajan agreed with Pliny's actions. His response indicates

465

Christianity and the Fall of Rome

that the Romans did not actively seek to persecute Christians.

> I t is not possible to lay down strict rules to deal with every case, but certainly the Christians must not be hunted down. But if they are brought to you and found guilty, then they must be punished, with this exception: if anyone denies he is a Christian, and makes this fact quite clear by praying to the Roman gods, he must be pardoned, whatever his previous record.
>
> Pliny, *Epistles*, c. A.D. 112

■ *What was the attitude of Romans towards the early Christians?*

As the above exchange shows, Romans did not generally seek out Christians for punishment. In fact, Christian settlements existed in North Africa for 100 years before the first Christian was executed.

Still, Christians were at times treated cruelly. Some Christians were even put into an arena to fight lions as entertainment for Romans. Later Christian writers attached great importance to these events. They used the events to reinforce the suffering endured by Christians who remained faithful to their beliefs.

However, historians do not believe that many Christians were actually sent to the lions. Overall, most Christians lived in peace until the A.D. 200s. ■

# The Roman Catacombs

*You enter a small chapel outside the city of Rome and walk down a stone staircase. You are in the catacombs, underground cemeteries built and used by the early Christians.*

*Side view of a Roman catacomb*

Via della Sette Chiese

Basilica of Nereus and Achilleus

Domitilla Catacombs

Road

0  10 m
0  33 ft
Scale approximate

**This map** shows one series of Roman catacombs called the Domitilla Catacombs. Catacomb cemeteries of Christians were located outside the walls of Rome, because burials were forbidden inside the city.

who opposed his views. Constantine feared that conflicts about worship would displease God and bring misfortune to the empire. Just as earlier emperors persecuted Christians for fear of displeasing Roman gods, Constantine now persecuted Romans for fear of displeasing the Christian god.

Constantine's interest in Christianity helped to strengthen the religion. At the same time, the relationship between Constantine and the church brought up an issue that is still the subject of debate today—how much the church should be separated from the state.

## The Power Shift

By the end of the A.D. 300s, church leaders felt powerful enough to give orders to emperors—or even to punish them. For example, in A.D. 390, Christian leaders punished Emperor Theodosius for ordering the massacre of a rebellious village. Bishop Ambrose of Milan threatened Theodosius with **excommunication,** or banning from the church, until he repented of his actions.

The fact that a Roman emperor would consider excommunication a punishment shows how powerful the church had become. Only a hundred years earlier, an emperor would have considered the church's opinions to be unimportant.

Just as Roman leaders had persecuted Christians when they were in power, now some fanatical Christians persecuted **pagans,** people who were neither Christians nor Jews. These Christians burned pagan temples. Then, in A.D. 391, Theodosius outlawed all pagan religions.

The tables were turned. Now Christians forced their views on the pagans. In response, the pagans begged the Christians not to punish them for their beliefs. This was the same plea that the early Christians had once made to the pagans. This pattern—the majority forcing its views on the minority—has been repeated throughout history.

By the end of the A.D. 300s, the new faith had become a well-organized and powerful community with churches, priests, and bishops throughout the empire. In fact, Christianity was gaining power and members as the Roman Empire was declining. ■

*The chi-rho combines the Greek letters chi (X) and rho (P), the first two letters of* Christos, *the Greek word for Christ.*

■ *How did Constantine help Christianity become the main religion in the empire?*

---

## REVIEW

1. **FOCUS** How did Christianity grow between A.D. 64 and A.D. 400?

2. **CONNECT** In Chapter 10 you studied how the Romans treated the Jews. How was Roman treatment of Jews similar to Roman treatment of Christians? How was it different?

3. **BELIEF SYSTEMS** How did the persecution of the Christians hurt the growth of Christianity? How did it help?

4. **CRITICAL THINKING** Is our culture today more like the Roman culture or the Christian culture in its attitudes toward money and property?

5. **WRITING ACTIVITY** Imagine you could explore the catacombs described in A Closer Look on pages 466 and 467. Write a journal entry about the experience. Describe what you would see and how you would feel exploring underground.

# Comparing Art Forms

### Here's Why

A work of art not only shows its subject. It also tells about the beliefs and culture of the artist's times. Choice of tools and materials, and the artist's personal style will also affect the work. While many works of art may present the same subject, each will reflect its artist's vision.

Below are two works of art that probably depict Jesus of Nazareth. No one knows what he really looked like. Artists show Jesus as they understand him. Comparing different artists' visions of a subject provides a broader view of the subject through different times and cultures.

### Here's How

The sculpture shows a shepherd carrying a lamb on his shoulders. Many scholars believe the statue by an unknown Roman artist depicts Jesus. What qualities of Jesus do you think the artist was attempting to convey?

Note that the sculptor shows Jesus with short, curly hair and wearing a Roman tunic. Why, do you suppose, did the artist depict Jesus in Roman dress and hairstyle?

On the right is a 12th-century mosaic from the Cathedral of Torcello, an island in a lagoon north of Venice, Italy. Mosaics are formed by placing small bits of colored glass or stone in mortar. This mosaic shows Jesus as a mature man with a beard and a serious face.

Note the halo and the rich use of gold. Christians believe that Jesus, as the son of God, was both human and divine. Which aspect of Jesus do you think the mosaic artist was emphasizing?

### Try It

The painting of Jesus healing on page 317 is by Sebastiano Ricci, who lived from 1659 to 1734. How is the background in the painting different from the sculpture or the mosaic? What does this painting tell about how the artist and the people of his time viewed Jesus?

### Apply It

Draw a picture of the President of the United States. Compare it to pictures drawn by your classmates. How do differences in the pictures reflect each person's views?

LESSON 3

# The Decline of Rome

In A.D. 192, the signs for the future of Rome were not good. The Roman historian Dio Cassius wrote that, "many eagles of ill omen soared about the Capitol and moreover uttered screams that boded nothing peaceful, and an owl hooted there." Then a fire swept through some of Rome's government buildings, destroying many of the empire's records. Dio Cassius warned,

*This, in particular, made it clear that the evil would not be confined to the City, but would extend over the entire civilized world under its sway.*

Dio Cassius, *History*, c. A.D. 192

Dio Cassius, who was a senator at the time, believed bad times were ahead for the empire. Indeed, the Roman Empire was beginning a century of decline.

**THINKING FOCUS**

*Why did the Roman Empire begin to decline?*

**Key Term**

• edict

## The End of the *Pax Romana*

The *Pax Romana* had been a 200-year period of peace and great achievements for Rome. But the *Pax Romana* ended in A.D. 180 when Emperor Marcus Aurelius died. He was succeeded by his 19-year-old son Commodus, who proved to be an unpopular and wicked ruler. He was finally killed in A.D. 193. This was the beginning of a period when military leaders fought for power and the empire began to decline.

Commodus was followed by Emperor Septimius Severus, a strong ruler who held the empire together by his tough military leadership. When he died in A.D. 211, the dynasty of Severus continued to rule Rome. Yet conditions in the empire got worse. The last emperor of this dynasty, Severus Alexander, was finally killed by his own men in A.D. 235.

Even worse times were ahead. In the next 50 years, 25 different emperors ruled Rome. Some ruled only a few months. All but one were killed.

Political upset was only one of the many problems troubling the empire. The

◄ *Commodus was only 19 when he became emperor.*

471

Christianity and the Fall of Rome

## Roman Empire, A.D. 235–284

**238,** Four emperors die in one year.

**244,** Emperor Gordian III is murdered.

**250,** Emperor Decius orders first large-scale persecution of Christians.

**268,** Emperor Gallienus is assassinated.

**240** | **250** | **260** | **270** | **280**

**238,** Emperor Maximinus is declared a public enemy.

**249,** Emperor Philip is killed in battle with foreign invaders.

**257,** Emperor Valerian orders second wave of persecution.

**150** | **200** | **250** | **300** | **350**

**193–235,** Severan Dynasty

**235–284,** Period of Unrest

**284–205,** Reign of Diocletian

**312–337,** Reign of Constantine

---

■ *What problems did the Empire face after the Pax Romana?*

▼ *Diocletian divided the empire. He ruled the Eastern empire and Maximian, the Western empire. They are shown below.*

economy was a disaster. Prices were out of control. In Egypt, 30 liters of wheat had cost 12 to 20 drachmas, an ancient coin, in the early A.D. 200s. By the 280s, the same amount of wheat cost 120,000 drachmas.

At the same time, the empire was under attack from outside forces. Tribes from northern Europe overran the borders.

To pay for the empire's defense, the government raised taxes. Many people left their farms and jobs because they could no longer pay the high taxes that Rome demanded.

Warfare left much of the empire in ruins. There wasn't enough food to go around. Trade was disrupted. Poverty and unemployment increased. Some Romans believed the empire stretched across too many lands to be well managed. With unrest inside and threats from outside, the empire badly needed strong leadership. ■

## The Reign of Diocletian

Finally, in A.D. 284, the army declared Diocletian emperor. Diocletian then ordered the persecution of Christians in the hope of making the gods look with favor upon the empire once again. However, he also used more direct means to restore order.

### The "New Empire"

Diocletian introduced a number of major reforms. That is why his reign is called the "New Empire."

In order to improve the economy, Diocletian issued the Edict on Prices. This **edict,** or command, told farmers and merchants how much they could charge for various items. If a seller tried to charge higher prices, the penalty was death. But the edict failed to control the economy, and prices continued to rise.

To fight off foreign threats, Diocletian increased the size of the army from about 300,000 to 450,000 soldiers. He also increased government systems, including elected assemblies, and their own cultural values.

## Battles with the Barbarians

In the A.D. 200s, the Romans' internal troubles allowed barbarian invasions to reach the heart of the empire. Diocletian and the emperors who followed him fought the invaders to make the frontiers of the empire secure.

As the invasions continued, the empire needed more soldiers to defend itself. Look at the chart on the right. How did the army grow from A.D. 117 to A.D. 425?

To relieve the pressure of barbarian attacks, some Roman emperors tried to "buy off" the invaders. These emperors gave the tribes land to live on, and they hired barbarians to serve in the army. By the A.D. 200s, the frontier of the empire was no longer a clear-cut boundary between the barbarians and the Roman world. The barbarians were gradually becoming part of the empire.

In the late A.D. 300s, pressure from the barbarians was growing. In A.D. 378, the Visigoths, who had settled in the eastern part of the empire, revolted against the Romans. They killed the leader of the eastern part of the empire, Emperor Valens, and defeated his army. Then, encouraged by their victory, the Visigoths marched into Rome in A.D. 410.

## The Fall of the Empire

The success of the invasions showed the weakness of the Roman army. Gradually, the emperors were losing control of their territories. In the early A.D. 400s, the barbarians overran and looted Britain, Gaul, Spain, and North Africa.

In fact, barbarian chiefs took control of much of the western part of the empire during the A.D. 400s.

### The Army of the Roman Empire

| | |
|---|---|
| A.D. 117 | |
| A.D. 284 | |
| A.D. 425 | |

Graph shows number of soldiers per 1,000 inhabitants of empire.

▲ *How many soldiers did Rome have for every 1,000 people in A.D. 425?*

◄ *Hadrian's wall in Britain, built in the A.D. 120s, marked the northern boundary of the empire. From the A.D. 200s on, barbarians repeatedly overran that border.*

477

Historians use the year A.D. 476 to mark the fall of Rome. In that year, the Germanic chief Odoacer *(oh doh AY suhr)* forced the last emperor out of the western part of the empire. Unlike Rome, Constantinople withstood barbarian attacks. The eastern part of the Roman Empire remained intact for another thousand years. ■

## Growth of the Church

As the Roman empire grew weaker under the pressure of barbarian attacks, Christianity grew stronger. During the A.D. 300s and 400s, even barbarian tribes such as the Goths, Vandals, and Franks had converted to Christianity.

### UNDERSTANDING BARBARIANS

The Roman historian Tacitus said of the barbarians, "they love idleness yet hate peace." As his description shows, Romans thought barbarians were uncivilized and warlike people.

*Barbarian* is a term that shows a point of view. It expresses the attitudes of one group of people toward another. It indicates the fears groups have about people they do not understand.

**The Roman Point of View**

The word *barbarian* comes from a Greek word. It means a person from another country. The Romans used the word to refer to the people beyond the frontier. However, a barbarian was not just a foreigner. A barbarian was someone the Romans believed was less refined or had lower social and cultural standards.

**A Lack of Respect**

Although many barbarians entered the empire peacefully, they were still outsiders. They had different beliefs and values. Throughout history, groups have tended to look down on others who were different from themselves.

For example, the European settlers who came to America in the 1700s and 1800s called American Indians "savages and barbarians." The settlers did not respect the American Indians and felt justified in driving these people from their lands.

**An Outside Threat**

Groups also tend to feel threatened by people who are different from themselves. The Romans felt threatened because they didn't understand the culture of the barbarians. As the barbarians continued to move into the empire, the barbarians became a more direct threat. They invaded Roman cities and drove out Roman leaders.

As a result, the Romans looked upon barbarians as fierce, brutal, and cruel invaders. That viewpoint has shaped the way barbarians are remembered today.

One of the barbarian tribes is remembered in an even more negative way. Today, *vandal* means someone who destroys things without reason. At the time of the fall of Rome, the Vandals were one of the many barbarian tribes that destroyed cities of the Roman Empire.

As you learn about why Rome fell, you can see the challenge of studying history. You cannot understand the past just by collecting facts and dates. History is also explaining the facts and dates.

Historians have studied for centuries the causes that led to the fall of Rome. Yet they have come to many different conclusions about which causes were the most important. The more you learn, the more skilled you will be at understanding the puzzles of history. ■

■ *What are the major causes that led to the fall of Rome?*

## The Roman Legacy

After the great Roman Empire fell to the German barbarians, Europe entered 500 years of decline. This period is known to historians as the Early Middle Ages.

European cities that had just begun to blossom declined as increased warfare disrupted trade. The education system broke down. In many communities the priests were the only people who knew how to read and write.

Day-to-day survival became the main concern for most people. Under these conditions, the learning of the Greeks and Romans could easily have been lost to the world. Fortunately, several factors kept that from happening.

In Europe, the church began to develop religious communities known as monasteries. These **monasteries** were centers of learning containing schools and libraries. They preserved Rome's heritage in book form.

Centers of learning were also found in the Eastern Roman Empire, which did not fall with Rome. In Constantinople, the capital, scholars copied the many important works of the Greeks and Romans for study.

Through the efforts of scholars at these centers of learning and others like them, the ideas of Greco-Roman civilization were saved for future generations. The achievements of the ancient Greeks and Romans have made lasting impressions on Western civilization. ■

◄ *The Eastern Roman Empire continued to flourish after the fall of Rome. This mosaic from the A.D. 500s shows Theodora, the wife of Emperor Justinian. She is considered the most powerful woman in the history of the Eastern empire.*

■ *What were the Early Middle Ages?*

R E V I E W

1. **FOCUS** Why did the Roman Empire fall?
2. **CONNECT** How was the fall of Greece to the Macedonians similar to the fall of Rome to the barbarians? How was it different?
3. **HISTORY** Who were the barbarians that invaded the Roman Empire? What drew them to the empire?
4. **CITIZENSHIP** How can studying the reasons for the fall of Rome help you understand events of today?

5. **CRITICAL THINKING** Not all historians agree on the reasons for the fall of Rome. What do you think were the most important reasons? Why?
6. **WRITING ACTIVITY** You have read Tacitus's description of the barbarians. Now imagine that you are a Visigoth and write a short description of your encounters with the people of the Roman Empire.

481

Christianity and the Fall of Rome

# Public Policy: Spend Less? Raise Taxes?

U ncontrolled prices are widespread in the sales taking place in the markets and in the daily life of the cities. . . we have decided that maximum prices of articles for sale must be established. . . Thus, when the pressure of high prices appears anywhere . . . [greed] will be checked by the limits. . . of the law.

Emperor Diocletian, *Edict on Prices*, A.D. 301

W hen . . . he brought about enormously high prices, he attempted to legislate the prices of [goods]. Then much blood was spilled. . . nothing appeared on the market because of fear, and prices soared much higher. In the end, after many people had lost their lives, it became absolutely necessary to repeal the law.

Lactantius, Christian writer living in Rome, A.D. 245-325

▼ *Diocletian and his co-emperor Maximian ruled the empire together.*

## Background

When Diocletian became emperor of Rome in A.D. 284, he faced an empire in crisis. Enemies along the empire's borders were constantly waging war against Rome. The once-powerful Roman army was no longer strong enough to fight off their attacks. Warfare left the cities and countryside in ruins.

In addition, the empire had grown so large that the government in Rome wasn't able to rule it efficiently. Lawsuits in distant provinces were often left unsettled because there were no government officials to hear them.

Closer to home, arguments and civil wars broke out each time an emperor died or retired: Who would follow him to the throne? Prices were also rising rapidly, making it harder for people to survive.

Finally, the treasury—the money used to pay for the government and army—was running out. The empire was falling apart. What could Diocletian do to save it?

Diocletian began by making a number of decisions. First he re-organized the government. He appointed a co-emperor and two junior emperors. Each of these men ruled a portion of the empire. In this way a local problem could be quickly brought to the attention of one of the rulers. This same system would help ensure a peaceful transfer of power at the end of an emperor's reign.

The four regions of the empire were further divided into more than a hundred provinces—double the number that had existed before. Each province was run by a governor and hundreds of government officials.

To safeguard the borders, Diocletian increased the size of the army. In addition to the troops stationed along the empire's frontiers, he created specially trained troops stationed in cities nearby. These troops stood ready to move quickly to any point along the border in case of enemy attack.

To fight rising prices, Diocletian issued his Edict on Prices, setting the top price to be charged or paid for any item. He also introduced a new system of coins.

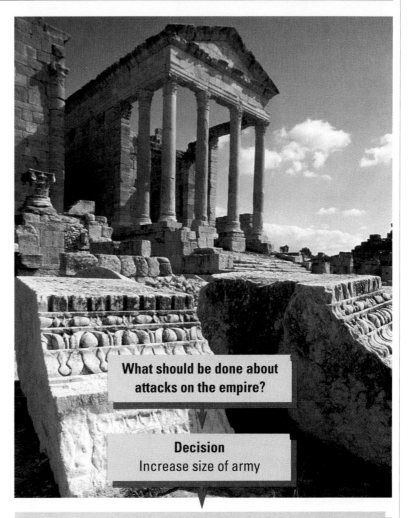

**What should be done about attacks on the empire?**

**Decision**
Increase size of army

| Outcomes | |
|---|---|
| • More soldiers | • Fewer workers |
| • Borders defended | • More money spent on army |
| • Cities, countryside safe | • Increased taxes |
| • Empire strong, unified | • Unhappy taxpayers |

## The Cost of Decisions

What did Diocletian hope to achieve with these changes? He wanted to bring peace and make the empire secure. He also wanted to make government more effective and efficient and to keep the economy stable.

Though many Romans agreed that these were worthy goals, some of the decisions Diocletian made based on these goals were not so popular. All of these changes cost money, and that meant higher taxes. Now there were four royal courts to pay for, not just one. There were nearly three times the number of government workers as before, and all of these workers had to be paid. As the army increased in size, more money had to be spent on soldiers' salaries, training, and supplies.

*What were the goals behind Diocletian's decision to increase the size of the army? Did the outcome of that decision support his goals?*

Christianity and the Fall of Rome

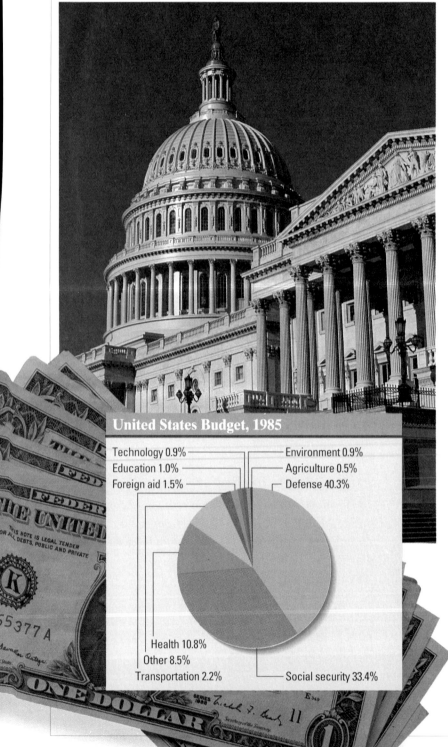

The U.S. Congress meets in the Capitol building in Washington, D.C. The pie chart represents the total amount of money that the federal government had to work with and how it was spent in 1985.

Enforcing new laws, like the Edict on Prices, meant more money for officials, lawyers, and courts.

Many Romans suffered under the huge tax burden. Lactantius complained that, "The number of those receiving [pay from the state] was so much larger than the number of those paying [taxes] that . . . the resources of the tenant farmers were exhausted [and] fields were abandoned."

As emperor, Diocletian had no need to ask for support from the public or even from the Senate. He could simply raise taxes to pay for his reforms.

Like Diocletian, our representatives at the local, state, and national levels must pass laws and provide services that people need. They must also find ways to pay for them. In our democratic system, however, government leaders must consider the goals and values of the people they represent as well as their own.

## Decision Point

1. What were the goals and values that led to each of Diocletian's decisions? What were some of the outcomes of each decision? Did the outcomes support the goals?
2. Look in a newspaper or magazine for information about a federal government program whose goals you support. How much will the program cost?
3. Look at the pie chart on this page. Where does your program fit?
4. Suppose you are a U.S. representative. What arguments would you present to persuade other representatives to spend money on your program?
5. Whenever Congress adds a new government program, it must pay for it by raising taxes, reducing spending on some other programs, or borrowing the money. What are the advantages and disadvantages of each of these alternatives?

### United States Budget, 1985

Technology 0.9%
Education 1.0%
Foreign aid 1.5%
Environment 0.9%
Agriculture 0.5%
Defense 40.3%
Health 10.8%
Other 8.5%
Transportation 2.2%
Social security 33.4%

# Chapter Review

## Reviewing Key Terms

barbarian (p. 476)
conversion (p. 459)
edict (p. 472)
excommunication (p. 469)
Gentile (p. 460)

martyr (p. 467)
monastery (p. 481)
pagan (p. 469)
persecute (p. 458)
sect (p. 459)

**A.** Write a sentence to answer each question. Each sentence you write should include the key term in parentheses following the question.
1. Why did Saul of Tarsus, a hunter of Christians, suddenly begin risking his life to spread the Christian message? (conversion)
2. In what way did the Bishop of Milan's threat to Emperor Theodosius in A.D. 390 show how powerful the church had become? (excommunication)
3. Who took control of much of the western part of the Roman Empire during the A.D. 400s? (barbarian)
4. How did Diocletian set the prices that farmers and merchants could charge for goods? (edict)
5. Where did most learning take place during the Early Middle Ages? (monastery)

**B.** For each pair of words, write one sentence that includes both words and that gives information from the chapter.
1. conversion, Gentiles
2. persecute, pagan
3. sect, martyr

## Exploring Concepts

**A.** On your own paper, copy and complete the following summary of events.

The first ___?___ years A.D. saw the rise of the ___?___ religion and the ___?___ of the Roman Empire. The Romans ___?___ Christians on and off for the first 300 years A.D. Rome blamed many of its problems on Christians' refusal to worship Roman ___?___. Two problems facing the empire were ___?___ and ___?___. To solve these problems, Emperor ___?___ started policies that greatly limited individual freedom. Soon after ___?___ became emperor in A.D. 312, ___?___ became the main religion of the empire. After Constantine's death, the empire split into two parts, the ___?___ and the ___?___ Roman Empires. In A.D. 410, the ___?___ invaded the city of Rome. The Roman Empire ended when Odoacer, a ___?___, forced out the last emperor of the ___?___ in A.D. 476.

**B.** Support each statement with facts and details from the chapter.
1. Some Christian values seemed to conflict with Roman values.
2. Early Christians suffered persecution by different groups for different reasons.
3. By A.D. 280, the economy of Rome was a disaster.
4. By A.D. 280, Rome's government had become very unstable.
5. Many individual freedoms vanished under the emperor Diocletian.
6. Although not himself a Christian until late in his life, Constantine promoted Christianity throughout the Roman Empire.
7. The Roman Empire had encountered barbarians long before Rome was invaded in A.D. 410.
8. Although the rise of Christianity and the fall of the Roman Empire took place in the same time span, Christianity itself did not cause the empire to fall.

# Reviewing Skills

1. Look at the bust of Socrates on page 372 and at the painting of the death of Socrates on page 373. Describe your impressions of Socrates from each of these. What was the main idea or feeling that each artist was trying to convey?

2. a. Make a timeline showing the dates of these important events in Roman history from 0 to 476 A.D.

   | | |
   |---|---|
   | 0—200 | *Pax Romana* |
   | 303 | Diocletian persecutes Christians |
   | 410 | City of Rome falls to Visigoths |
   | 313 | Emperor Constantine gives religious freedom |
   | 100 | Roman courts execute Christians |
   | 64 | Rome burns during Nero's reign |
   | 250 | Emperor Decius orders Roman gods worshiped |
   | 395 | Roman Empire splits |
   | 476 | Roman Empire falls |

   b. Find the dates of the following events in the chapter. Show these dates on a telescoping timeline based on the timeline you made in *a*.

   > Saul converts to Christianity
   > Christians begin preaching to Gentiles
   > Paul executed
   > New Testament books collected

   c. Find the dates of the following events in the chapter. Show these dates on a telescoping timeline based on the timeline you made in *a*.

   > Emperor Constantine gives religious freedom
   > Constantine becomes a Christian
   > Julian tries to restore pre-Christian religions

3. Suppose you are a historian. You are interested in adding to our factual knowledge of the early Christian church. What kinds of written sources might contain the information you are looking for?

# Using Critical Thinking

1. The fall of the Roman Empire had many causes. Think of an example of a problem today that has many causes. Pollution is one example. In a paragraph, describe the problem and some of its causes. Then explain the danger of finding only one cause and acting on that information.

2. The emperors Decius and Diocletian adopted some very harsh policies. Write a paragraph explaining what those policies were intended to accomplish. Then suggest some solutions to the problems of the Roman Empire during the A.D. 200s. Why might your solutions have worked?

# Preparing for Citizenship

1. COLLECTING INFORMATION During the first 400 years A.D., the Roman Empire suffered an economic collapse. Clip newspaper articles about economic problems around the world today. Look for words in headlines such as economy, shortages, prices, and supply. List causes of economic problems and their effects on the people of a country. Use the library to find more information.

2. COLLABORATIVE LEARNING Constantinople, once Byzantium, is now Istanbul, Turkey. In groups of three, find an interesting way to present the city's three historical periods. Your group might produce an illustrated timeline, an oral report, or written descriptions. Each group member should research one historical period. The group should work together on the final presentation.

# Time/Space Databank

## Alphabet

**Alphabet** is the series of letters used in writing a language. The name means exactly what the term ABC's means as a name for the 26 letters of our alphabet. The word comes from *alpha* and *beta,* the first two letters of the Greek alphabet.

Most books, magazines, and newspapers are printed in the 26-letter alphabet called *Roman.* But the Romans did not invent it. They put finishing touches on a system that had been growing for thousands of years.

### The earliest writing

In early times, people could communicate with one another only by speaking or by making gestures. They had no way to keep records of important events, unless they memorized the story of a great battle or important happening. They had no way to send messages over long distances unless they passed them from one person to the next by word of mouth, or had one person memorize the message and then deliver it.

The first stage in writing came when people learned to draw pictures to express their ideas. In *ideography,* each picture conveyed an idea. Ideography enabled even people who did not speak the same language to communicate with each other. Then people learned *logography,* expressing ideas indirectly by using signs to stand for the words of the idea. Instead of drawing pictures of five sheep to show a herd of five animals, a person could draw one sign for the numeral "five" and one for "sheep." Gradually people learned to use a *syllabic* system, in which a sign that stood for one word could be used not only for that word but also for any phonetic combination that sounded like that word. This is what we call *rebus writing.* If we used rebus writing in English, we could draw a sign for the word "bee" followed by a sign for the word "leaf" to stand for the word "belief." Finally, people developed alphabets in which indi-

**Development of the English alphabet**

The English alphabet developed from a number of early writing systems, beginning with the sign writing of Ancient Egypt. The Romans had given most capital letters their modern form by A.D. 114. But the letters *J, U,* and *W* were not added to the alphabet until the Middle Ages.

| Egyptian About 3000 B.C. | Semitic About 1500 B.C. | Phoenician About 1000 B.C. | Greek About 600 B.C. | Roman A.D. 114 | Modern |
|---|---|---|---|---|---|
| | | | A | A | A |
| | | | B | B | B |
| | | | Γ | C | C |
| | | | Δ | D | D |
| | | | E | E | E |
| | | | F | F | F |
| | | | Γ | G | G |
| | | | H | H | H |
| | | | I | I | I |
| | | | I | I | J |
| | | | K | K | K |
| | | | Λ | L | L |
| | | | M | M | M |

| Egyptian About 3000 B.C. | Semitic About 1500 B.C. | Phoenician About 1000 B.C. | Greek About 600 B.C. | Roman A.D. 114 | Modern |
|---|---|---|---|---|---|
| | | | N | N | N |
| | | | O | O | O |
| | | | Γ | P | P |
| | | | G | Q | Q |
| | | | P | R | R |
| | | | Σ | S | S |
| | | | T | T | T |
| | | | Υ | V | U |
| | | | Υ | V | V |
| | | | Υ | V | W |
| | | | X | X | X |
| | | | Υ | Y | Y |
| | | | I | Z | Z |

**Some important alphabets** The alphabets of five important languages are shown below. Hindi is India's most widely spoken language. People throughout the Middle East and northern Africa use Arabic, which is read from right to left. Gaelic, along with English, is the official language of Ireland.

**Greek**   Α Β Γ Δ Ε Ζ Η Θ Ι Κ Λ Μ Ν Ξ Ο Π Ρ Σ Τ Υ Φ Χ Ψ Ω

**Russian**   АБВГДЕЁЖЗИЙКЛМНОПРСТУФХЦЧШЩЪЫЬЭЮЯ

**Hindi**   अ आ इ ई उ ऊ ऋ ए ऐ ओ औ क ख ग घ ङ च छ ज झ ञ ट ठ ड ढ ण त थ द ध न प फ ब भ म य र ल व श ष स ह

**Arabic**   ا ب ت ث ج ح خ د ذ ر ز س ش ص ض ط ظ ع غ ف ق ك ل م ن ه و ي

**Gaelic**   ᴀ ʙ ᴄ ᴅ ᴇ ꜰ ɢ ʜ ɪ ʟ ᴍ ɴ ᴏ ᴘ ᴘ ᴛ ᴜ

vidual signs stood for particular sounds. Today, most written languages in the world use alphabetic writing systems.

### The earliest alphabets

**The Egyptians** used a system of several hundred signs that stood for full words or for syllables. They could write the word *nefer,* or *good,* with a single sign for the whole word, or with three signs, for the sounds *n, f,* and *r.* These signs specified the consonants in syllables, but not the vowels. Egyptian writing, which developed around 3000 B.C., was formally a picture writing, and structurally a word and syllabic writing.

**The Semites,** who lived in Syria and Palestine, knew something of the Egyptian writing system. They worked out an alphabetic writing about 1500 B.C. They used signs to show the consonants of syllables, just as the Egyptians did. The Semites seem to have adapted some of the pictures from Egyptian hieroglyphics, but they used these symbols for sounds in their own language. The oldest Semitic alphabet comes from the Sinai Peninsula.

**The Phoenicians,** who lived along the coast of the Mediterranean Sea, developed a system of 22 signs about 1000 B.C. Their alphabet was structurally related to Semitic and Egyptian, with signs for consonant sounds, not vowel sounds. Early Phoenician writing consists partly of pictographic forms, which they may have borrowed from older pictographic systems, and partly of geometric or diagrammatic signs that they invented. Historians find it difficult to trace the formal relations between Semitic and Phoenician signs, because Phoenician has both pictographic and diagrammatic signs, and because so little is known of the ancient systems used in Syria and Palestine.

**The Cypriots,** the people of the island of Cyprus, developed an alphabet of their own. Starting with an unknown word-syllable system, they worked out an alphabet of 56 signs, each standing for an initial consonant and a different vowel. The next step was to create separate signs for vowels and consonants.

**The Greeks** came in contact with Phoenician traders, and learned from them the idea of writing individual sounds of the language. Sometime during the period before 800 B.C., they borrowed Phoenician symbols and modified them to form the Greek alphabet. The Phoeni-

cian alphabet included more consonants than the Greeks needed for their language, so they used the extra signs for vowel sounds. In this way, the Greeks improved on both Phoenician and Cypriot ideas, because they could combine individual letters for both consonants and vowels to spell any word they wanted.

The Greeks took over the Phoenician names for their signs, and in most cases the signs themselves. The first letter of the Phoenician alphabet, ✝, and its name, *aleph,* meaning *ox,* became ∆, or *alpha* in Greek. The second letter, ⅃, or *beth,* meaning *house,* became Β, or *beta* in Greek. The Greeks later modified the shapes of these letters, adding and dropping some letters, to form the 24-letter Greek alphabet of today.

### The Roman alphabet

**The Etruscans** moved to central Italy from somewhere in the eastern Mediterranean region sometime after 1000 B.C. They carried the Greek alphabet with them. The Romans learned the alphabet from the Etruscans, and gave it much the same form we use today. The early Roman alphabet had about 20 letters, and gradually gained 3 more.

**Capital letters** were the only forms used for hundreds of years. Many people consider the Roman alphabet to have been perfected by A.D. 114. That year, sculptors carved the inscriptions on a memorial column built to honor the emperor Trajan. The style of lettering they used is considered one of the most beautiful in the world.

Carving letters in stone is not an easy job, and Roman stonecutters rounded or squared, simplified, and polished their letters. They developed the beautiful thick-and-thin strokes we use today. They also added *serifs* (little finishing strokes) at the tops and bottoms of many letters. The practical reason for serifs was that the carvers found it difficult to end wide strokes without ugly blunt lines. And if a chisel slipped while squaring off an end, they could not erase the mistake. But serifs also added a touch of strength and grace to Roman lettering, and are still used today.

**Small letters** gradually developed from capitals. Scribes who copied books often used *uncials* (rounded letters) that were easier to form than some capitals. True lower-case letters developed later, when scribes saved space in books by using the smaller letters.

Excerpted from the Alphabet article in *World Book.*
Copyright © 1990 by World Book, Inc.

# Architecture

## Architectural terms

**Ambulatory** is a continuous aisle in a circular building. In a church, the ambulatory serves as a semicircular aisle that encloses the apse.

**Apse** is a semicircular area. In most churches, the apse is at one end of the building and contains the main altar.

**Arcade** refers to a series of arches supported by columns or piers. A passageway formed by the arches is also called an arcade.

**Arch** is a curved structure used to support the weight of the material above it. A stone at the top of an arch, called the *keystone,* holds the other parts in place.

**Architrave** makes up the lowest part of an entablature. It rests on the capital of a column. For a drawing of an architrave, see Entablature on the opposite page.

**Buttress** is a support built against an outside wall of a building. A *flying buttress* is an arched support that extends from a column or pier to the wall.

Buttress                    Flying Buttress

**Cantilever** is a horizontal projection, such as a balcony or a beam, which is supported only at one end.

**Capital,** in an order, forms the upper part of a column. It separates the shaft from the entablature.

Doric          Ionic          Corinthian

**Colonnade** means a row of columns, each set an equal distance apart.

**Column** is a vertical support. In an order, it consists of a shaft and a capital and often rests on a base.

**Composite order** is a Roman order. It resembles the Corinthian order but has a capital that combines the Corinthian acanthus leaf decoration with volutes from the Ionic order.

**Corinthian order** became the last of the three Greek orders. It resembles the Ionic order but has an elaborate capital that is decorated with carvings of leaves of the acanthus plant.

Composite          Corinthian
Order              Order

**Cornice** forms the upper part of an entablature and extends beyond the frieze.

Raking Cornice

Cornice

**Doric order** was the first and simplest of the three Greek orders. The Doric is the only order that normally has no base.

Doric Order

**Entablature** refers to the upper horizontal part of an order between a capital and the roof. It consists of three major parts—the architrave, frieze, and cornice.

**Facade** is the front of a building. Most facades contain an entrance.

**Frieze** forms the middle part of an entablature and is often decorated with a horizontal band of relief sculpture.

**Ionic order** was the second of the three Greek orders. It has a capital decorated with carved spiral scrolls called *volutes.*

**Module** is a measurement, such as the diameter of a column, which architects use to establish the proportions of an entire structure.

**Nave** is the chief area within a church. It extends from the main entrance to the transept.

Entablature:
Cornice
Frieze
Architrave

Ionic Order

Nave

Transept

**Order,** in classical architecture, consisted of a column and an entablature. Orders served as the basic elements of Greek and Roman architecture and influenced many later styles.

**Pediment** is a triangular segment between the horizontal entablature and the sloping roof at the front of a classical-style building.

Pediment

**Pendentive** is a curved support shaped like an inverted triangle. Pendentives hold up a dome.

**Pier** refers to a large pillar used to support a roof.

Dome

Pendentive

**Post and lintel** is a method of construction in which vertical beams (posts) support a horizontal beam (lintel).

Lintel

Post

**Shaft** is the main part of a column below the capital. Many shafts have shallow vertical grooves called *fluting.*

**Transept** forms the arms in a T- or cross-shaped church.

**Tuscan order,** a Roman order, resembles the Doric order, but the shaft has no fluting.

**Vault** is an arched brick or stone ceiling or roof. A *barrel vault,* the simplest form of vault, is a single continuous arch. A *groined vault* is formed by joining two barrel vaults at right angles. A *ribbed vault* has diagonal arches that project from the surface.

Tuscan Order

Barrel Vault     Groined Vault     Ribbed Vault

WORLD BOOK illustrations by Robert Keys

# Jerusalem at the time of Jesus Christ

No one knows exactly what Jerusalem looked like during the lifetime of Jesus Christ. This exclusive *World Book* illustration is based on research by a scholar dealing with how the city may have appeared at that time. The index at the right identifies the points of interest numbered on the illustration. The Temple (13), which was the largest building in the city, stood on a hill in eastern Jerusalem. West and north of the Temple lay a small area of shops, stores, and houses. The First Wall (24) almost encircled southern Jerusalem. A shorter, jagged wall cut across this area and separated sections called the Lower City and the Upper City. The crowded Lower City, east of the jagged wall, was the commercial and industrial center of Jerusalem and the chief residential area of its poor. Most of Jerusalem's wealthy people lived in the Upper City, west of the jagged wall. There, King Herod's Palace (35) and many large homes had spacious courtyards with gardens and pools.

1. Road to Galilee
2. Wood Market and Stores
3. North Gate
4. Second Wall
5. Hill of Calvary (Golgotha)
6. Stores
7. Barracks
8. Market Halls
9. Fortress of Antonia
10. Jannaeus Monument
11. Sheep Pool and Market

The distance from the North Gate (3) to the Gate of Essenes (28) was about 1¼ miles (2 kilometers).

North

This illustration is based on a model of the ancient Holy City that was built by the Holyland Hotel in Jerusalem. Plans for the model were developed by Michael Avi-Yonah, Professor of Archaeology at the Hebrew University of Jerusalem, from the best archaeological, Biblical, and historical information available. The model was built from architectural drawings by his wife, Eva Avi-Yonah. The illustration was created by George Suyeoka, and it was critically reviewed by Professor Avi-Yonah.

**Jerusalem**

12. Tyropoeon Valley
13. Temple
14. Mount of Olives
15. Garden of Gethsemane
16. Road to Jericho
17. Absalom's Tomb†
18. Bene Hezir Tomb
19. Zechariah's Tomb†
20. Herod's Basilica
21. Huldah Gates
22. Huldah Monument

23. Kidron Valley
24. First Wall
25. Synagogue of Freedmen
26. Pool of Siloam
27. Rose Gardens
28. Gate of Essenes
29. Road to Judean Desert
30. Valley of Hinnom
31. King David's Tomb†
32. Dyers' Quarter
33. Palace of Caiaphas

34. Serpents' Pool
35. Herod's Palace
36. Upper Market
37. Theater
38. Hippodrome
39. Robinson's Arch*
40. Site of Wailing Wall
    (Western Wall)
41. Wilson's Arch*
42. Town Hall
43. Hasmonean Palace

44. Hananiah's Palace
45. Hippicus Tower
46. Mariamme Tower
47. Barracks
48. Phasael Tower
49. Towers Pool
50. Hyrcanus Monument
51. Road to Gaza
52. Road to Bethlehem
53. Herod's Family Tomb

*Discovered and named in the 1800's.
†So-called.

Copyright © 1990 by World Book, Inc.

# Seven Wonders of the Ancient World

**Ancient Greeks and Romans** made up many lists of notable objects. These illustrations show the objects that have been most commonly listed as the Seven Wonders of the Ancient World. The map, *below right,* shows the location of the Seven Wonders of the Ancient World in red.

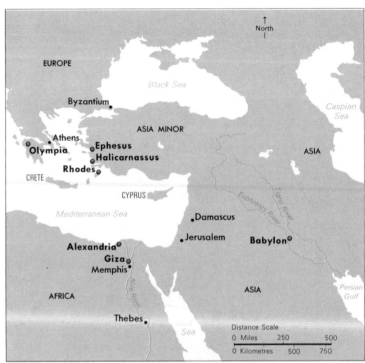

WORLD BOOK map

**The Temple of Artemis** at Ephesus was one of the largest temples built by the Greeks. It was famous for its decoration and extensive use of marble.

**The statue of Zeus** at Olympia, Greece, was probably the most famous statue made by the Greeks. People who came to watch the Olympic Games admired this gold and ivory figure.

**The pyramids of Egypt** at Giza are the best preserved of the Seven Wonders of the Ancient World. They still attract many visitors to Giza, just outside the present-day city of Cairo.

## Seven Wonders of the Ancient World

**The Mausoleum at Halicarnassus** was a great marble tomb. It was built for Mausolus, a local ruler, by some of the most famous Greek sculptors and architects.

**The Lighthouse of Alexandria,** Egypt, was the world's first important lighthouse. It guided ships into the city's harbor for about 1,500 years before being toppled by an earthquake.

WORLD BOOK illustrations by Birney Lettick

**The Hanging Gardens of Babylon** probably were built by King Nebuchadnezzar II after he married a mountain princess. He apparently hoped the gardens would make her feel at home.

**The Colossus of Rhodes** was built in honor of the sun god Helios. It was constructed after the people of Rhodes survived a yearlong siege by a large force of Macedonians.

# World

## Independent countries of the world*

| Name | Area In sq. mi. | Area In km² | Rank in area | Population† | Rank in population | Capital |
|---|---|---|---|---|---|---|
| Afghanistan | 251,773 | 652,090 | 38 | 15,885,000 | 50 | Kabul |
| Albania | 11,100 | 28,748 | 122 | 3,248,000 | 107 | Tiranë |
| Algeria | 919,595 | 2,381,741 | 10 | 25,174,000 | 33 | Algiers |
| Andorra | 180 | 465 | 156 | 49,000 | 163 | Andorra |
| Angola | 481,354 | 1,246,700 | 21 | 10,000,000 | 65 | Luanda |
| Antigua and Barbuda | 171 | 442 | 158 | 86,000 | 160 | St. John's |
| Argentina | 1,073,400 | 2,780,092 | 8 | 32,361,000 | 29 | Buenos Aires |
| Australia | 2,966,150 | 7,682,300 | 6 | 16,365,000 | 49 | Canberra |
| Austria | 32,377 | 83,855 | 105 | 7,493,000 | 78 | Vienna |
| Bahamas | 5,385 | 13,878 | 135 | 251,000 | 148 | Nassau |
| Bahrain | 265 | 688 | 153 | 516,000 | 137 | Manama |
| Bangladesh | 55,598 | 143,998 | 87 | 116,000,000 | 8 | Dhaka |
| Barbados | 166 | 430 | 159 | 260,000 | 147 | Bridgetown |
| Belgium | 11,783 | 30,519 | 120 | 9,895,000 | 67 | Brussels |
| Belize | 8,867 | 22,965 | 129 | 182,000 | 151 | Belmopan |
| Benin | 43,484 | 112,622 | 93 | 4,737,000 | 95 | Porto-Novo |
| Bhutan | 17,950 | 46,500 | 114 | 1,513,000 | 124 | Thimphu |
| Bolivia | 424,165 | 1,098,581 | 26 | 7,311,000 | 80 | La Paz; Sucre |
| Botswana | 224,607 | 581,730 | 42 | 1,283,000 | 126 | Gaborone |
| Brazil | 3,286,488 | 8,511,965 | 5 | 150,557,000 | 6 | Brasília |
| Brunei | 2,226 | 5,765 | 142 | 277,000 | 146 | Bandar Seri Begawan |
| Bulgaria | 42,823 | 110,912 | 96 | 8,985,000 | 71 | Sofia |
| Burkina Faso | 105,869 | 274,200 | 66 | 8,996,000 | 70 | Ouagadougou |
| Burma | 261,218 | 676,552 | 37 | 41,279,000 | 24 | Rangoon |
| Burundi | 10,747 | 27,834 | 124 | 5,450,000 | 91 | Bujumbura |
| Cameroon | 183,569 | 475,442 | 47 | 11,236,000 | 60 | Yaoundé |
| Canada | 3,849,674 | 9,970,610 | 2 | 26,279,000 | 31 | Ottawa |
| Cape Verde | 1,557 | 4,033 | 144 | 378,000 | 140 | Praia |
| Central African Republic | 240,535 | 622,984 | 40 | 2,911,000 | 112 | Bangui |
| Chad | 495,755 | 1,284,000 | 19 | 5,674,000 | 89 | N'Djamena |
| Chile | 292,258 | 756,945 | 35 | 13,185,000 | 55 | Santiago |
| China | 3,696,032 | 9,572,678 | 3 | 1,100,258,000 | 1 | Beijing |
| Colombia | 440,831 | 1,141,748 | 25 | 31,863,000 | 30 | Bogota |
| Comoros | 863 | 2,235 | 147 | 518,000 | 136 | Moroni |
| Congo | 132,047 | 342,000 | 56 | 2,183,000 | 119 | Brazzaville |
| Costa Rica | 19,730 | 51,100 | 112 | 3,017,000 | 110 | San José |
| Cuba | 42,804 | 110,861 | 97 | 10,279,000 | 63 | Havana |
| Cyprus | 3,572 | 9,251 | 141 | 701,000 | 135 | Nicosia |
| Czechoslovakia | 49,373 | 127,876 | 90 | 15,659,000 | 51 | Prague |
| Denmark | 16,632 | 43,077 | 115 | 5,119,000 | 93 | Copenhagen |
| Djibouti | 8,958 | 23,200 | 128 | 552,000 | 111 | Djibouti |
| Dominica | 290 | 751 | 150 | 98,000 | 158 | Roseau |
| Dominican Republic | 18,816 | 48,734 | 113 | 7,172,000 | 82 | Santo Domingo |
| Ecuador | 109,484 | 283,561 | 65 | 10,782,000 | 61 | Quito |
| Egypt | 386,662 | 1,001,449 | 28 | 53,522,000 | 21 | Cairo |
| El Salvador | 8,124 | 21,041 | 130 | 5,655,000 | 90 | San Salvador |
| Equatorial Guinea | 10,831 | 28,051 | 123 | 411,000 | 138 | Malabo |
| Ethiopia | 471,778 | 1,221,900 | 23 | 48,630,000 | 22 | Addis Ababa |
| Fiji | 7,056 | 18,274 | 132 | 772,000 | 133 | Suva |
| Finland | 130,559 | 338,145 | 57 | 4,981,000 | 94 | Helsinki |
| France | 210,026 | 543,965 | 44 | 56,236,000 | 19 | Paris |
| Gabon | 103,347 | 267,667 | 68 | 1,172,000 | 128 | Libreville |
| Gambia | 4,361 | 11,295 | 148 | 820,000 | 132 | Banjul |
| Germany, East | 41,828 | 108,333 | 99 | 16,645,000 | 48 | East Berlin |
| Germany, West | 96,005 | 248,651 | 70 | 60,471,000 | 14 | Bonn |
| Ghana | 92,100 | 238,537 | 73 | 15,020,000 | 53 | Accra |
| Great Britain | 94,248 | 244,100 | 72 | 57,293,000 | 16 | London |
| Greece | 50,962 | 131,990 | 88 | 10,053,000 | 64 | Athens |
| Grenada | 133 | 344 | 161 | 96,000 | 159 | St. George's |
| Guatemala | 42,042 | 108,889 | 98 | 9,117,000 | 69 | Guatemala City |
| Guinea | 94,926 | 245,857 | 71 | 6,871,000 | 86 | Conakry |
| Guinea-Bissau | 13,948 | 36,125 | 118 | 985,000 | 130 | Bissau |
| Guyana | 83,000 | 214,969 | 77 | 868,000 | 131 | Georgetown |
| Haiti | 10,714 | 27,750 | 125 | 5,777,000 | 88 | Port-au-Prince |
| Honduras | 43,277 | 112,088 | 94 | 5,144,000 | 92 | Tegucigalpa |
| Hungary | 35,920 | 93,032 | 102 | 10,545,000 | 62 | Budapest |
| Iceland | 39,800 | 103,000 | 100 | 250,000 | 149 | Reykjavik |
| India | 1,269,219 | 3,287,263 | 7 | 853,532,000 | 2 | New Delhi |
| Indonesia | 741,101 | 1,919,443 | 14 | 180,594,000 | 5 | Jakarta |
| Iran | 636,300 | 1,648,000 | 16 | 56,800,000 | 17 | Teheran |
| Iraq | 169,235 | 438,317 | 51 | 18,048,000 | 44 | Baghdad |
| Ireland | 27,136 | 70,283 | 109 | 3,637,000 | 103 | Dublin |
| Israel | 8,019 | 20,770 | 131 | 4,585,000 | 96 | Jerusalem |
| Italy | 116,320 | 301,268 | 63 | 57,380,000 | 15 | Rome |
| Ivory Coast | 124,504 | 322,463 | 61 | 12,053,000 | 58 | Abidjan |
| Jamaica | 4,244 | 10,991 | 139 | 2,520,000 | 115 | Kingston |
| Japan | 145,870 | 377,801 | 55 | 123,749,000 | 7 | Tokyo |
| Jordan | 35,475 | 91,880 | 103 | 3,065,000 | 109 | Amman |
| Kampuchea | 69,898 | 181,035 | 82 | 6,993,000 | 85 | Phnom Penh |
| Kenya | 224,081 | 580,367 | 43 | 25,081,000 | 35 | Nairobi |
| Kiribati | 277 | 717 | 152 | 69,000 | 162 | Tarawa |
| Korea, North | 46,540 | 120,538 | 91 | 22,965,000 | 39 | Pyongyang |
| Korea, South | 38,625 | 99,106 | 101 | 43,650,000 | 23 | Seoul |
| Kuwait | 6,880 | 17,818 | 133 | 2,096,000 | 120 | Kuwait |
| Laos | 91,430 | 236,800 | 75 | 4,070,000 | 101 | Vientiane |
| Lebanon | 4,015 | 10,400 | 140 | 2,947,000 | 111 | Beirut |
| Lesotho | 11,720 | 30,355 | 121 | 1,757,000 | 122 | Maseru |
| Liberia | 43,000 | 111,370 | 95 | 2,552,000 | 114 | Monrovia |

MINIPEDIA

| Name | Area | | Rank in area | Population† | Rank in population | Capital |
|---|---|---|---|---|---|---|
| | In sq. mi. | In km² | | | | |
| Libya | 679,362 | 1,759,540 | 15 | 4,356,000 | 97 | Tripoli |
| Liechtenstein | 62 | 160 | 165 | 28,000 | 166 | Vaduz |
| Luxembourg | 998 | 2,586 | 146 | 367,000 | 142 | Luxembourg |
| Madagascar | 226,658 | 587,041 | 41 | 11,969,000 | 59 | Antananarivo |
| Malawi | 45,747 | 118,484 | 92 | 8,198,000 | 75 | Lilongwe |
| Malaysia | 127,317 | 329,749 | 59 | 17,344,000 | 46 | Kuala Lumpur |
| Maldives | 115 | 298 | 163 | 215,000 | 150 | Male |
| Mali | 478,841 | 1,240,192 | 22 | 8,278,000 | 74 | Bamako |
| Malta | 122 | 316 | 162 | 350,000 | 143 | Valletta |
| Mauritania | 397,956 | 1,030,700 | 27 | 2,021,000 | 121 | Nouakchott |
| Mauritius | 788 | 2,040 | 148 | 1,105,000 | 129 | Port Louis |
| Mexico | 756,067 | 1,958,201 | 13 | 88,560,000 | 11 | Mexico City |
| Monaco | 0.73 | 1.9 | 169 | 29,000 | 165 | Monaco |
| Mongolia | 604,250 | 1,565,000 | 17 | 2,185,000 | 118 | Ulan Bator |
| Morocco | 177,117 | 458,730 | 49 | 25,169,000 | 34 | Rabat |
| Mozambique | 308,642 | 799,380 | 32 | 15,627,000 | 52 | Maputo |
| Nauru | 8 | 21 | 168 | 9,000 | 168 | — |
| Nepal | 56,827 | 147,181 | 86 | 19,157,000 | 43 | Kathmandu |
| Netherlands | 14,405 | 37,310 | 117 | 14,765,000 | 54 | Amsterdam |
| New Zealand | 103,883 | 269,057 | 67 | 3,402,000 | 106 | Wellington |
| Nicaragua | 50,200 | 130,000 | 89 | 3,606,000 | 104 | Managua |
| Niger | 489,200 | 1,267,000 | 20 | 7,905,000 | 84 | Niamey |
| Nigeria | 356,669 | 923,768 | 30 | 112,765,000 | 10 | Lagos |
| Norway | 149,405 | 386,958 | 54 | 4,213,000 | 99 | Oslo |
| Oman | 82,030 | 212,457 | 78 | 1,469,000 | 125 | Muscat |
| Pakistan | 307,374 | 796,095 | 33 | 113,163,000 | 9 | Islamabad |
| Panama | 30,193 | 78,200 | 107 | 2,421,000 | 117 | Panama City |
| Papua New Guinea | 178,704 | 462,840 | 48 | 3,824,000 | 102 | Port Moresby |
| Paraguay | 157,048 | 406,752 | 52 | 4,278,000 | 98 | Asunción |
| Peru | 496,225 | 1,285,216 | 18 | 22,330,000 | 40 | Lima |
| Philippines | 116,000 | 300,000 | 64 | 62,446,000 | 13 | Manila |
| Poland | 120,728 | 312,683 | 62 | 38,441,000 | 26 | Warsaw |
| Portugal | 34,340 | 88,941 | 104 | 9,903,000 | 66 | Lisbon |
| Qatar | 4,416 | 11,437 | 137 | 369,000 | 141 | Doha |
| Romania | 91,700 | 237,500 | 74 | 23,279,000 | 38 | Bucharest |
| Rwanda | 10,169 | 26,338 | 127 | 7,222,000 | 81 | Kigali |
| St. Christopher and Nevis | 101 | 261 | 164 | 48,000 | 164 | Basseterre |
| St. Lucia | 238 | 616 | 155 | 143,000 | 154 | Castries |
| St. Vincent and the Grenadines | 150 | 388 | 160 | 117,000 | 156 | Kingstown |
| San Marino | 24 | 61 | 166 | 23,000 | 167 | San Marino |
| São Tomé and Principe | 372 | 964 | 149 | 123,000 | 155 | São Tomé |
| Saudi Arabia | 830,000 | 2,149,690 | 12 | 12,939,000 | 56 | Riyadh |
| Senegal | 75,750 | 196,192 | 79 | 7,360,000 | 79 | Dakar |
| Seychelles | 175 | 453 | 157 | 71,000 | 161 | Victoria |
| Sierra Leone | 27,699 | 71,740 | 108 | 4,146,000 | 100 | Freetown |
| Singapore | 239 | 618 | 154 | 2,704,000 | 113 | Singapore |
| Solomon Islands | 10,639 | 27,556 | 126 | 329,000 | 145 | Honiara |
| Somalia | 246,201 | 637,657 | 39 | 7,106,000 | 83 | Mogadishu |
| South Africa | 471,445 | 1,221,037 | 24 | 36,696,000 | 27 | Cape Town; Pretoria; Bloemfontein |
| Spain | 194,897 | 504,750 | 46 | 39,623,000 | 25 | Madrid |
| Sri Lanka | 25,333 | 65,610 | 110 | 16,779,000 | 47 | Colombo |
| Sudan | 967,500 | 2,505,813 | 9 | 23,797,000 | 37 | Khartoum |
| Suriname | 63,037 | 163,265 | 85 | 408,000 | 139 | Paramaribo |
| Swaziland | 6,704 | 17,364 | 134 | 779,000 | 134 | Mbabane |
| Sweden | 170,250 | 440,945 | 50 | 8,346,000 | 73 | Stockholm |
| Switzerland | 15,943 | 41,293 | 116 | 6,509,000 | 87 | Bern |
| Syria | 71,498 | 185,180 | 81 | 12,471,000 | 57 | Damascus |
| Taiwan | 13,900 | 36,000 | 119 | 20,454,000 | 41 | Taipei |
| Tanzania | 364,900 | 945,087 | 29 | 25,955,000 | 32 | Dar es Salaam |
| Thailand | 198,115 | 513,115 | 45 | 55,760,000 | 20 | Bangkok |
| Togo | 21,925 | 56,785 | 111 | 3,451,000 | 105 | Lomé |
| Tonga | 289 | 748 | 151 | 101,000 | 157 | Nukualofa |
| Trinidad and Tobago | 1,980 | 5,128 | 143 | 1,283,000 | 127 | Port-of-Spain |
| Tunisia | 63,170 | 163,610 | 84 | 8,095,000 | 76 | Tunis |
| Turkey | 300,948 | 779,452 | 34 | 56,549,000 | 18 | Ankara |
| Tuvalu | 10 | 26 | 167 | 8,000 | 169 | Funafuti |
| Uganda | 91,074 | 235,880 | 76 | 17,593,000 | 45 | Kampala |
| Union of Soviet Socialist Republics | 8,649,500 | 22,402,000 | 1 | 288,239,000 | 3 | Moscow |
| United Arab Emirates | 32,278 | 83,600 | 106 | 1,731,000 | 123 | Abu Dhabi |
| United States | 3,618,770 | 9,372,571 | 4 | 250,372,000 | 4 | Washington, D.C. |
| Uruguay | 68,500 | 177,414 | 83 | 3,130,000 | 108 | Montevideo |
| Vanuatu | 4,706 | 12,189 | 136 | 164,000 | 153 | Port-Vila |
| Vatican City | 0.17 | 0.44 | 170 | 1,000 | 170 | |
| Venezuela | 352,145 | 912,050 | 31 | 19,744,000 | 42 | Caracas |
| Vietnam | 127,242 | 329,556 | 60 | 67,084,000 | 12 | Hanoi |
| Western Samoa | 1,093 | 2,831 | 145 | 170,000 | 152 | Apia |
| Yemen (Aden) | 128,587 | 333,038 | 58 | 2,486,000 | 116 | Aden |
| Yemen (Sana) | 75,300 | 195,000 | 80 | 7,993,000 | 77 | Sana |
| Yugoslavia | 98,766 | 255,804 | 69 | 23,853,000 | 36 | Belgrade |
| Zaire | 905,365 | 2,344,885 | 11 | 35,330,000 | 28 | Kinshasa |
| Zambia | 290,586 | 752,614 | 36 | 8,459,000 | 72 | Lusaka |
| Zimbabwe | 150,804 | 390,580 | 53 | 9,700,000 | 68 | Harare |

*Each country listed has a separate article in *World Book*.
†Populations are 1990 estimates based on the latest figures from official government and United Nations sources.

## World, History of the

### Major developments in early centers of civilization

WORLD BOOK illustrations by Tak Murakami

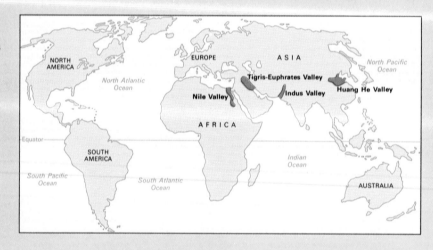

The *Epic of Gilgamesh* and the *Epic of Creation*, the oldest epic poems in world literature, were written in Mesopotamia about 2500 B.C.

The Pyramids and Great Sphinx were built in Giza, Egypt, about 2500 B.C.

The making of iron began about 1400 B.C.

The Code of Hammurabi, one of the first law codes, was drawn up in the 1700's B.C.

**Huang He Valley Civilization** (1700's-1122 B.C.)

The Sumerians developed cuneiform writing about 3000 B.C.

**Indus Valley Civilization** (c. 2500-1700 B.C.)

Judaism was founded in the 1700's B.C.

**Nile Valley Civilization** (c. 3100-1070 B.C.)

**Tigris-Euphrates Valley Civilization** (c. 3500-2000 B.C.)

| 3100 B.C. | 2550 B.C. | 2100 B.C. | 1650 B.C. | 1200 B.C. |

**The earliest civilizations** arose in four river valleys in Asia and Africa between about 3500 B.C. and the 1700's B.C. The fertile soil of the valleys supported flourishing farming villages. Civilization began when such villages developed into cities.

WORLD BOOK map

### Important dates

**c. 9000 B.C.** The development of agriculture began with the growing of crops and the domestication of animals in the Middle East.

**c. 3500 B.C.** A number of small cities, centers of the world's first civilization, appeared in Sumer, the lower part of the Tigris-Euphrates Valley.

**c. 3500 B.C.** The Sumerians invented the first form of writing. It was later simplified to produce wedge-shaped *cuneiform* writing, which spread throughout the Middle East.

**c. 3100 B.C.** King Menes of Upper Egypt united Lower and Upper Egypt.

**c. 2500 B.C.** The Indus Valley civilization began to flourish in the cities of Moen-jo-Daro and Harappa in what is now Pakistan.

**c. 2500-1100 B.C.** The Minoan civilization on the island of Crete rose and fell.

**2300's B.C.** Sargon of Akkad conquered the Sumerians and united all Mesopotamia under his rule, creating the world's first empire.

**1700's B.C.** The Shang dynasty began its rule in the Huang He Valley of China.

**c. 1792-1750 B.C.** Babylonia flourished under King Hammurabi.

**1500's-c. 1100 B.C.** The city of Mycenae was the leading political and cultural center on the Greek mainland.

**c. 1595 B.C.** The Hittites, a warlike people from what is now central Turkey, conquered the Babylonians.

**c. 1500 B.C.** The Aryans of central Asia began migrating to India.

## Major developments from about 1200 B.C. to A.D. 500

WORLD BOOK illustrations by Tak Murakami

The Greek epic poems the *Iliad* and the *Odyssey* were composed in the 700's B.C.

Buddha was born about 563 B.C.

In the 400's B.C., Hippocrates showed that diseases have natural causes.

**Gupta Empire** (A.D. 320-c. 500)

The Hanging Gardens of Babylon were built in the 500's B.C.

**Roman Empire** (27 B.C.-A.D. 476)

**Han Dynasty** (202 B.C.-A.D. 220)

The first recorded Olympic Games were held in Greece in 776 B.C.

**Maurya Dynasty** (321-185 B.C.)

**Hellenistic Age** (323-30 B.C.)

**Persian Empire** (c. 550-331 B.C.)

**New Babylonian Empire** (626-539 B.C.)

**Greek Civilization** (c. 800-338 B.C.)

**Assyrian Empire** (800's-612 B.C.)

The Romans crucified Jesus Christ about A.D. 30.

The Chinese invented paper in A.D. 105.

**Zhou Dynasty** (1122-256 B.C.)

| 1200 B.C. | 775 B.C. | 425 B.C. | A.D. 75 | A.D. 500 |

**Powerful empires** emerged as civilization advanced and spread between 1200 B.C. and A.D. 500. The Roman Empire covered much of Europe and the Middle East, and the north coast of Africa. The Han dynasty of China and the Gupta dynasty of India also ruled huge empires.

WORLD BOOK map

## Important dates

**1020 B.C.** The Hebrews founded a kingdom in what is now Palestine.

**800's B.C.** The Etruscans settled in west-central Italy.

**750-338 B.C.** Athens, Corinth, Sparta, and Thebes were the chief city-states of Greece.

**c. 550 B.C.** Cyrus the Great established the Persian Empire.

**509 B.C.** The people of Rome revolted against their Etruscan rulers and established a republic.

**338 B.C.** Philip II of Macedonia conquered the Greeks.

**331 B.C.** Alexander the Great defeated the Persians at Arbela, opening the way to his conquest of northern India.

**221-206 B.C.** The Qin dynasty established China's first strong central government.

**202 B.C.** The Han dynasty began its 400-year rule of China.

**146 B.C.** The Romans conquered Greece.

**55-54 B.C.** Julius Caesar led the Roman invasion of Britain.

**27 B.C.** Augustus became the first Roman emperor.

**c. A.D. 250** The Maya Indians developed an advanced civilization in Central America and Mexico.

**313** Constantine issued the Edict of Milan, which granted freedom of worship to Christians of the Roman Empire.

**320** India began its golden age under the Gupta dynasty.

**395** The Roman Empire split into the East Roman, or Byzantine, Empire and the West Roman Empire.

**476** The Germanic chieftain Odoacer overthrew Romulus Augustulus, the last emperor of the West Roman Empire.

# World, History of the

## Major developments from A.D. 500 to about 1500

Muhammad, the founder of Islam, began preaching about 610.

Under Justinian I, Byzantine scholars organized a great code of Roman law during the 500's.

The Chinese invented the magnetic compass about 1100.

Notre Dame Cathedral was completed in Paris in 1250.

The first books printed in Europe with movable type appeared in the mid-1400's.

**Yuan Dynasty** (1279-1368)

**Song Dynasty** (960-1279)

Christopher Columbus reached America in 1492.

**Toltec and Aztec Empires** (900-1521)

**Abbasid Caliphate** (750-1258)

The Italian poet Dante Alighieri wrote the *Divine Comedy* in the early 1300's.

**Tang Dynasty** (618-907)

**Byzantine Empire** (395-1453)

| 500 | 750 | 1000 | 1250 | 1500 |

**Between 500 and 1500,** new civilizations appeared in Africa and the Americas. In the Middle East, the Muslim Arabs rose to power and conquered a huge empire by the mid-700's. In the 1200's, Mongol warriors swept through Asia, creating one of the largest empires in history.

NORTH AMERICA
EUROPE
ASIA
North Pacific Ocean
North Atlantic Ocean
Mongol Empire 1300
Islamic Empire 750
Maya 800
Aztec 1500
Mali 1337
AFRICA
Equator
SOUTH AMERICA
Inca 1500
Mwanamutapa 1400's
Indian Ocean
South Pacific Ocean
South Atlantic Ocean
AUSTRALIA

## Important dates

**527-565**  The Byzantine Empire reached its greatest extent under Emperor Justinian I.

**622**  Muhammad, founder of Islam, fled from Mecca to Medina. His flight, called the Hegira, marks the beginning of the Islamic calendar.

**700's-mid-1000's**  The Ghana Empire, the first great black empire in western Africa, flourished as a trading state.

**732**  Charles Martel and the Franks defeated invading Muslims in fighting in west-central France. The victory prevented the Muslims from overrunning Europe.

**750**  The Abbasids became the caliphs of the Islamic world.

**800**  Pope Leo III crowned Charlemagne, ruler of the Franks, emperor of the Romans.

**c. 988**  Vladimir I converted the Russians to Christianity.

**1054**  Rivalries between the church in Rome and the church in Constantinople resulted in their separation as the Roman Catholic Church and Eastern Orthodox Churches, respectively.

**1192**  Yoritomo became the first shogun to rule Japan.

**1215**  English barons forced King John to grant a charter of liberties called Magna Carta.

**1279**  The Mongols gained control of all China.

**1300's**  The Renaissance began in Italy.

**1368**  The Ming dynasty began its nearly 300-year rule of China.

**1453**  The Ottoman Turks captured Constantinople (Istanbul) and overthrew the Byzantine Empire.

## Major developments from A.D. 1500 to about 1900

WORLD BOOK illustrations by Tak Murakami

Nicolaus Copernicus proposed in 1543 that the sun is the center of the universe.

Michelangelo completed painting the ceiling of the Sistine Chapel in the Vatican in 1512.

William Shakespeare wrote many of the world's greatest dramas between 1590 and 1616.

Charles Darwin published his theory of evolution in 1859 in *The Origin of Species.*

**European Colonial Expansion in Africa and Asia** (1870-1914)

**Latin-American Wars of Independence** (1791-1824)

**French Revolution** (1789-1799)

**Revolutionary War in America** (1775-1783)

**Industrial Revolution** (1700-mid-1800's)

**Manchu Rule of China** (1644-1912)

**Tokugawa Shogunate in Japan** (1603-1867)

**Mogul Empire** (1526-1707)

**Voyages of Discovery** (1400's-1500's)

**Ottoman Empire** (1326-1922)

**Renaissance** (1300-1600)

Ludwig van Beethoven composed many of his greatest symphonies between 1800 and 1815.

Alexander Graham Bell invented the telephone in 1876.

1500    1600    1700    1800    1900

**European colonial empires** had spread over much of the world by the late 1800's. The largest empires of the period belonged to Great Britain, France, and Germany.

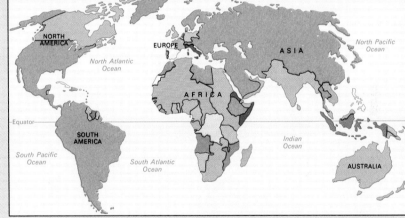

- Belgium
- France
- Germany
- Great Britain
- Italy
- Netherlands
- Portugal
- Spain

WORLD BOOK map

## Important dates

**1500's** The Reformation led to the birth of Protestantism.

**1519-1521** Ferdinand Magellan commanded the first globe-circling voyage, completed in 1522 after his death.

**1521** The Spanish conquistador Hernando Cortés defeated the Aztec Indians of Mexico.

**1526** Babar, a Muslim prince, invaded India and founded the Mogul Empire.

**1588** The Royal Navy of England defeated the Spanish Armada, establishing England as a great naval power.

**1644-1912** The Manchus ruled China as the Qing dynasty.

**1776** The 13 American Colonies adopted the Declaration of Independence, establishing the United States of America.

**1789** The French Revolution began.

**1815** Napoleon Bonaparte was defeated in the Battle of Waterloo, ending his attempt to rule Europe.

**1853-1854** Commodore Matthew Perry visited Japan and opened two ports to U.S. trade, ending Japan's isolation.

**1858** Great Britain took over the rule of India from the East India Company after the Sepoy Rebellion.

**1865** Union forces defeated the Confederates in the American Civil War after four years of fighting.

**1869** The Suez Canal opened.

**1871** Germany became united under the Prussian king, who ruled the new empire as Kaiser Wilhelm I.

**1898** The United States took control of Guam, Puerto Rico, and the Philippines following the Spanish-American War.

## WORLD: *Political*

### ABBREVIATIONS

| | |
|---|---|
| **CEN. AFR. REP.** | Central African Republic |
| **DEN.** | Denmark |
| **FR.** | France |
| **GR.** | Greece |
| **IT.** | Italy |
| **N.** | North, Northern |
| **NETH.** | Netherlands |
| **P.D.R. YEMEN** | People's Democratic Republic of Yemen |
| **PORT.** | Portugal |
| **S.** | South |
| **SP.** | Spain |
| **TERR.** | Territory |
| **U.A.E.** | United Arab Emirates |
| **U.K.** | United Kingdom |
| **U.S.** | United States |
| **W.** | Western |

— National boundary

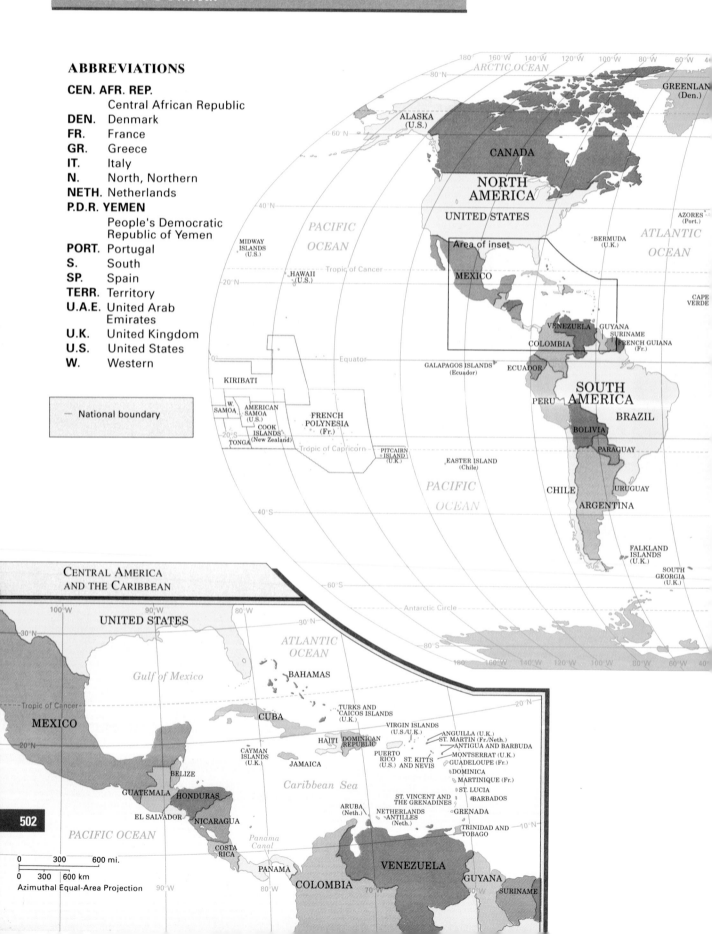

CENTRAL AMERICA AND THE CARIBBEAN

0    300    600 mi.

0    300    600 km

Azimuthal Equal-Area Projection

**Land Elevation**

| Feet | Meters |
|---|---|
| 9,840 | 3,000 |
| 6,580 | 2,000 |
| 3,280 | 1,000 |
| 656 | 200 |
| 0 | 0 |
| Below sea level | Below sea level |

Ice-covered land

▲ Mountain Peak

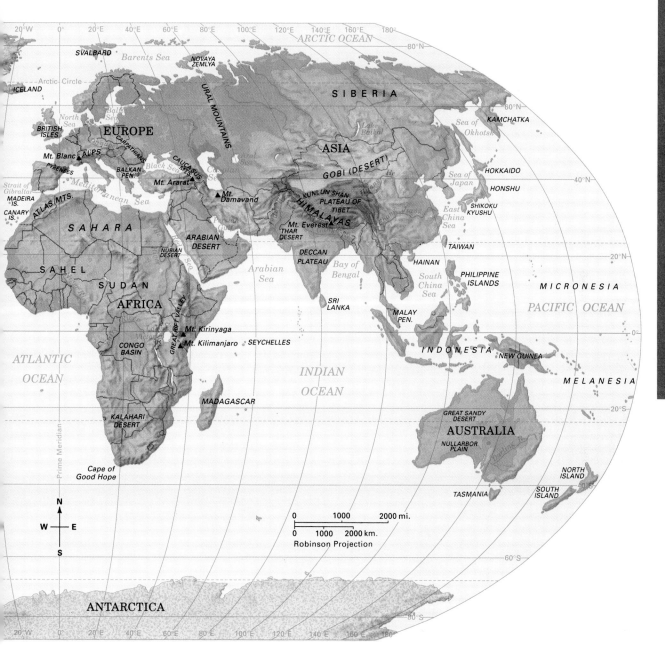

20°W  0°  20°E  40°E  60°E  80°E  100°E  120°E  140°E  160°E  180°

ARCTIC OCEAN

SVALBARD  80°N

Barents Sea  NOVAYA
ZEMLYA

ICELAND  Arctic Circle

SIBERIA  60°N

North
Sea  Baltic
Sea  URAL MOUNTAINS  KAMCHATKA

BRITISH
ISLES  EUROPE  Sea of
Okhotsk

Mt. Blanc ▲ ALPS  CARPATHIANS  ASIA

PYRENEES  CAUCASUS MTS.  Black Sea  Sea of
Japan  HOKKAIDO

Strait of
Gibraltar  Mt. Ararat ▲  Caspian Sea  GOBI (DESERT)  HONSHU  40°N

MADEIRA
IS.  ATLAS MTS.  Mediterranean Sea  ▲ Mt.
Damavand  KUNLUN SHAN
PLATEAU OF
TIBET  SHIKOKU
KYUSHU

CANARY
IS.  HIMALAYAS  East
China
Sea

SAHARA  ARABIAN
DESERT  Mt. Everest ▲  TAIWAN  20°N

NUBIAN
DESERT  Red Sea  THAR
DESERT  DECCAN
PLATEAU  HAINAN

SAHEL  Arabian
Sea  Bay of
Bengal  South
China
Sea  PHILIPPINE
ISLANDS  MICRONESIA

SUDAN  PACIFIC OCEAN

AFRICA  GREAT RIFT VALLEY  SRI
LANKA  MALAY
PEN.

CONGO
BASIN  Mt. Kirinyaga ▲  0°

Mt. Kilimanjaro ▲  SEYCHELLES  INDONESIA  NEW GUINEA

ATLANTIC
OCEAN  INDIAN
OCEAN  MELANESIA

MADAGASCAR  20°S

KALAHARI
DESERT  GREAT SANDY
DESERT

AUSTRALIA

NULLARBOR
PLAIN  NORTH
ISLAND

Cape of
Good Hope  TASMANIA  SOUTH
ISLAND

N
W E
S  0  1000  2000 mi.

0  1000  2000 km.
Robinson Projection  60°S

80°S

ANTARCTICA

20°W  0°  20°E  40°E  60°E  80°E  100°E  120°E  140°E  160°E  180°

# THE WORLD: *250 B.C.*

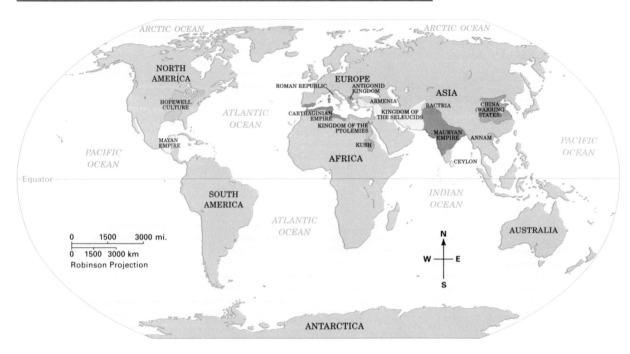

NORTH AMERICA
HOPEWELL CULTURE
ATLANTIC OCEAN
PACIFIC OCEAN
MAYAN EMPIRE
ROMAN REPUBLIC
EUROPE
ANTIGONID KINGDOM
CARTHAGINIAN EMPIRE
KINGDOM OF THE PTOLEMIES
ARMENIA
BACTRIA
KINGDOM OF THE SELEUCIDS
ASIA
CHINA (WARRING STATES)
KUSH
MAURYAN EMPIRE
ANNAM
PACIFIC OCEAN
CEYLON
AFRICA
Equator
SOUTH AMERICA
ATLANTIC OCEAN
INDIAN OCEAN
AUSTRALIA
ANTARCTICA
ARCTIC OCEAN

0  1500  3000 mi.
0  1500  3000 km
Robinson Projection

N W E S

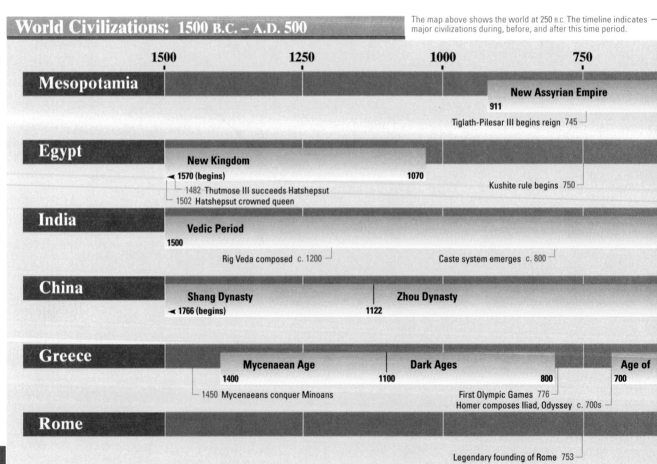

## World Civilizations: 1500 B.C. – A.D. 500

The map above shows the world at 250 B.C. The timeline indicates major civilizations during, before, and after this time period.

| | 1500 | 1250 | 1000 | 750 |
|---|---|---|---|---|

**Mesopotamia**

New Assyrian Empire
911
Tiglath-Pilesar III begins reign  745

**Egypt**

New Kingdom
◄ 1570 (begins)          1070
1482 Thutmose III succeeds Hatshepsut
1502 Hatshepsut crowned queen
Kushite rule begins  750

**India**

Vedic Period
1500
Rig Veda composed  c. 1200
Caste system emerges  c. 800

**China**

Shang Dynasty
◄ 1766 (begins)
Zhou Dynasty
1122

**Greece**

Mycenaean Age
1400
1450 Mycenaeans conquer Minoans
Dark Ages
1100
First Olympic Games  776
Homer composes Iliad, Odyssey  c. 700s
800
Age of
700

**Rome**

Legendary founding of Rome  753

90°E    105°E    120°E    135°E    150°E    165°E    180°    165°W    150°W    135°W    120°W

ARCTIC    OCEAN

75°N

SIBERIA

NORTH
AMERICA

60°N

Bering Sea

...OCIALIST REPUBLICS

Lena River

STANOVOI RANGE

Sea of
Okhotsk

SAKHALIN
(U.S.S.R.)

Amur River

180°

Irkutsk

Lake
Baikal

DA HINGGAN LING

ALTAI MTS.

Ulan Bator

MONGOLIA

Harbin

KURIL ISLANDS

45°N

Vladivostok

Sapporo

GOBI (DESERT)

Beijing

N. KOREA
Pyongyang

Sea of
Japan

JAPAN

...HAN

Seoul
S. KOREA

Tokyo

PLATEAU
OF
TIBET

Huang He

PEOPLE'S REPUBLIC
OF CHINA

Yellow
Sea

Osaka

Shanghai

East
China
Sea

30°N

Thimbu
BHUTAN

PACIFIC

BANGLADESH
Dacca

Taipei
TAIWAN

OCEAN

Calcutta

Yangtze

Guangzhou

MYANMAR
(BURMA)

LAOS

MACAO
(Port.)

HONG
KONG
(U.K.)

Hanoi

Gulf
of
Tonkin

HAINAN

Philippine

15°N

Bay of
Bengal

Vientiane

Rangoon
THAILAND

Da Nang

Sea

ANDAMAN
ISLANDS
(India)

Bangkok

CAMBODIA

VIETNAM

Manila

PHILIPPINES

NICOBAR
ISLANDS
(India)

Phnom
Penh

Ho Chi Minh City
(Saigon)

South China
Sea

Bandar Seri
Begawan
BRUNEI

MALAYSIA

Kuala Lumpur

MALAYSIA

Singapore
SINGAPORE

BORNEO

0°

SUMATRA

INDONESIA

CELEBES

NEW GUINEA

Java Sea

Jakarta

JAVA

Arafura Sea

15°S

Timor
Sea

AUSTRALIA

90°E    105°E    120°E    135°E    150°E    165°E

# MIDDLE EAST: *Political/Physical*

EUROPE

*Black Sea*

ASIA

*Caspian Sea*

Istanbul
*Bosporus*
*Sea of Marmara*
*Dardanelles*
PONTIC MOUNTAINS

Izmir

*Aegean Sea*

TURKEY

Ankara

ARMENIA

ELBURZ MTS.
Teheran
*Lake Urmia*

KURDISTAN

DASHT-E-KAVIR
(DESERT)

TAURUS MTS.

Aleppo

*Mediterranean Sea*

Nicosia
CYPRUS

SYRIA

Damascus

SYRIAN DESERT

*Euphrates River*

Baghdad

*Tigris River*

ZAGROS MOUNTAINS

PLATEAU OF IRAN

IRAN

DASHT-E-LUT
(DESERT)

LEBANON
Beirut

*Jordan River*

ISRAEL
Tel Aviv
Jerusalem
Port Said
Gaza
WEST BANK
Amman
*Dead Sea*
NEGEV DESERT
JORDAN

IRAQ

Alexandria

QATTARA DEPRESSION

Cairo

*Suez Canal*

SINAI PEN.

*Gulf of Suez*
*Gulf of Aqaba*

AN NAFUD
(DESERT)

KUWAIT

Kuwait

NEUTRAL ZONE

*Persian Gulf*

*Strait of Hormuz*

*Gulf of Oman*

EGYPT

SAHARA

ARABIAN DESERT

LIBYAN DESERT

*Tropic of Capricorn*

*Nile River*

*Lake Nasser*

Medina

Manama
BAHRAIN
Doha
QATAR

Riyadh

UNITED ARAB EMIRATES

Abu Dhabi

Muscat

OMAN

SAUDI ARABIA

*Red Sea*

Jidda
Mecca

RUB AL KHALI
(DESERT)

AFRICA

N
W    E
S

HADRAMAUT

PEOPLE'S
DEMOCRATIC
REPUBLIC OF
YEMEN

*Arabian Sea*

Sana

YEMEN

SOCOTRA
(P.D.R. Yemen)

Aden

*Bab el Mandeb*

*Gulf of Aden*

INDIAN OCEAN

⊛ National capital

• Major city

-- National boundary

510

0    200    400 mi.
0    200    400 km
Lambert Conformal Conic Projection

48°N    24°E    32°E    40°E    48°E    56°E    64°E

40°N

32°N

24°N

16°N

8°N

32°E    40°E    48°E    56°E

# AFRICA: *Political/Physical*

**ATLAS**

EUROPE

ASIA

*Strait of Gibraltar*

★ Algiers
★ Tunis
Casablanca ●
Rabat ★
MADEIRA ISLANDS (Port.)
TUNISIA
Tripoli ●
*Mediterranean Sea*
*Suez Canal*

Marrakech ●
ATLAS MOUNTAINS
MOROCCO

CANARY ISLANDS (Sp.)

WESTERN SAHARA (Morocco)

Alexandria ●
*QATTARA DEPRESSION*
Cairo ★

ALGERIA
LIBYA
EGYPT

S A H A R A

*Tropic of Cancer*

MAURITANIA
Nouakchott ★
*AHAGGAR MOUNTAINS*
MALI
*TIBESTI MOUNTAINS*
NIGER
CHAD
*NUBIAN DESERT*
*Red Sea*

Cape Verde
Timbuktu ●
S A H E L
*Nile River*
*NILE BASIN*

Dakar ★
SENEGAL
Niamey ★
Khartoum ★
ERITREA
*Gulf of Aden*
*Bab el Mandeb*

Banjul ★
GAMBIA
Bamako ★
BURKINA FASO
*Lake Chad*
S U D A N
*Blue Nile R.*
DJIBOUTI
Djibouti ★

Bissau ★
GUINEA-BISSAU
Ouagadougou ★
● Kano
N'Djamena ★
SUDAN
*White Nile R.*
AMHARA
Addis Ababa ★

GUINEA
BENIN
NIGERIA
PLATEAU
ETHIOPIA

Conakry ★
TOGO
*L. Volta*
CENTRAL AFRICAN REPUBLIC
SOMALIA

Freetown ★
SIERRA LEONE
IVORY COAST
GHANA
Porto Novo ★
Lagos ●
UGANDA
KENYA
Mogadishu ★

Monrovia ★
LIBERIA
Abidjan ●
Accra ★
Lomé ★
CAMEROON
Bangui ★
*Lake Albert*
Kampala ★
Nairobi ★

Malabo ★
Yaounde ★
CONGO BASIN
Kigali ★
*Lake Victoria*

*Gulf of Guinea*
EQUATORIAL GUINEA
*Zaire River*
RWANDA
*SERENGETI PLAIN*

SÃO TOMÉ AND PRINCIPE
Libreville ★
CONGO
Bujumbura ★
BURUNDI

São Tomé ★
GABON
*Kasai R.*
*L. Tanganyika*
TANZANIA
ZANZIBAR
*INDIAN OCEAN*

*Equator*
ANNOBÓN (Equatorial Guinea)
Brazzaville ★
Kinshasa ★
*GREAT RIFT VALLEY*
Dar es Salaam ●
Victoria ★
SEYCHELLES

*ATLANTIC OCEAN*
CABINDA (Angola)
ZAIRE
*MITUMBA MTS.*

ASCENSION (U.K.)
Luanda ★
*Quanza R.*
KATANGA PLATEAU
Lubumbashi ●
MALAWI
Lilongwe ★
Moroni ★
COMOROS

ANGOLA
ZAMBIA
*Lake Malawi*
MAYOTTE (Fr.)

ST. HELENA (U.K.)
Lusaka ★
Harare ★
MOZAMBIQUE
Antananarivo ★

*Tropic of Capricorn*
NAMIB DESERT
*OKAVANGO BASIN*
Windhoek ★
BOTSWANA
ZIMBABWE
*Victoria Falls*
*Limpopo River*
MADAGASCAR
Port Louis ★
MAURITIUS ★
RÉUNION (Fr.)

WALVIS BAY (S. Africa)
NAMIBIA
*KALAHARI DESERT*
Gaborone ★
Pretoria ★
Maputo ★
Mbabane ★
SWAZILAND

*Orange River*
Johannesburg ●
*Vaal R.*
LESOTHO
Maseru ★
Durban ●
*DRAKENSBERG MTS.*

*GREAT KAROO*
SOUTH AFRICA

Cape Town ★
*Cape of Good Hope*
*Cape Agulhas*

N
W E
S

★ National capital
● Major city
— National boundary

0 400 800 mi.
0 400 800 km
Azimuthal Equal-Area Projection

511

EUROP

ASIA

ARCTIC OCEAN

GREENLAND
(Denmark)

Bering Strait

Bering Sea

Beaufort Sea

QUEEN ELIZABETH ISLANDS

ELLESMERE ISLAND

Baffin Bay

BROOKS RANGE

BANKS ISLAND

VICTORIA ISLAND

BAFFIN ISLAND

Arctic Circle

Yukon River

ALASKA RANGE

Fairbanks

Anchorage

KODIAK ISLAND

Gulf of Alaska

Mackenzie River

Great Bear Lake

Great Slave Lake

UNGAVA PENINSULA

Labrador Sea

ALEXANDER ARCHIPELAGO

QUEEN CHARLOTTE ISLANDS

COAST MOUNTAINS

LAURENTIAN SHIELD

Hudson Bay

LABRADOR

VANCOUVER ISLAND

Vancouver

Puget Sound

Seattle

ROCKY

CANADA

Edmonton

Calgary

Lake Winnipeg

NEWFOUNDLAND

CAPE BRETON ISLAND

PRINCE EDWARD ISLAND

Portland

Winnipeg

MOUNTAINS

Quebec

Montreal

Ottawa

St. Lawrence River

Bay of Fundy

San Francisco

COAST RANGES

SIERRA NEVADA

Great Salt Lake

Salt Lake City

BLACK HILLS

Minneapolis

Milwaukee

Chicago

Omaha

Missouri River

Lake Superior

Lake Michigan

Lake Huron

Toronto

Lake Erie

Lake Ontario

Detroit

Cleveland

Boston

Cape Cod

New York

Philadelphia

APPALACHIAN MTS.

Baltimore

Washington

ATLANTIC OCEAN

Los Angeles

San Diego

MOJAVE DESERT

GRAND CANYON

Denver

Colorado River

Kansas City

St. Louis

Ohio River

Indianapolis

Louisville

UNITED STATES

Nashville

Charlotte

Cape Hatteras

BERMUDA (U.K.)

Phoenix

Red River

Fort Worth

Atlanta

Birmingham

PACIFIC OCEAN

Ciudad Juárez

Chihuahua

BAJA CALIFORNIA

Rio Grande

Austin

San Antonio

Houston

New Orleans

Jacksonville

Cape Canaveral

Tropic of Cance

Cabo San Lucas

Gulf of California

Monterrey

SIERRA MADRE ORIENTAL

Miami

Nassau

BAHAMAS

Gulf of Mexico

Havana

CUBA

San VIRGIN ISLANDS (U.S., U.K.)

Juan ANGUILLA (U.K.)

DOMINICAN REPUBLIC

ANTIGUA AND BARBUD

GUADELOUPE (Fr.)

MEXICO

PLATEAU OF MEXICO

SIERRA MADRE OCCIDENTAL

Guadalajara

Santiago de Cuba

CAYMAN ISLANDS (U.K.)

JAMAICA

Port-au-Prince

HAITI

Kingston

PUERTO RICO (U.S.)

ST. KITTS NEVIS

Santo Domingo

Roseau

DOMINICA

MARTINIQUE (Fr.)

Castries ST. LUC

BARBADOS

Bridgetow

Mexico City

Veracruz

Puebla

YUCATÁN PENINSULA

Acapulco

ISTHMUS OF TEHUANTEPEC

Belmopan

BELIZE

GUATEMALA

Guatemala City

San Salvador

EL SALVADOR

HONDURAS

Tegucigalpa

NICARAGUA

MOSQUITO COAST

Managua

Lago de Nicaragua

Caribbean Sea

NETHERLANDS ANTILLES (Neth.)

ARUBA (Neth.)

Kingstown

ST. VINCENT AND THE GRENADINES

St. George's

GRENADA

Port of Spain

TRINIDAD AND TOBAGO

COSTA RICA

San José

PANAMA

ISTHMUS OF PANAMA

Panama City

SOUTH AMERICA

Equator

N
W · E
S

- ⊛ National capital
- • Major city
- — National boundary

0    400    800 mi.
0    400    800 km

Azimuthal Equal-Area Projection

# WORLD: *Religions*

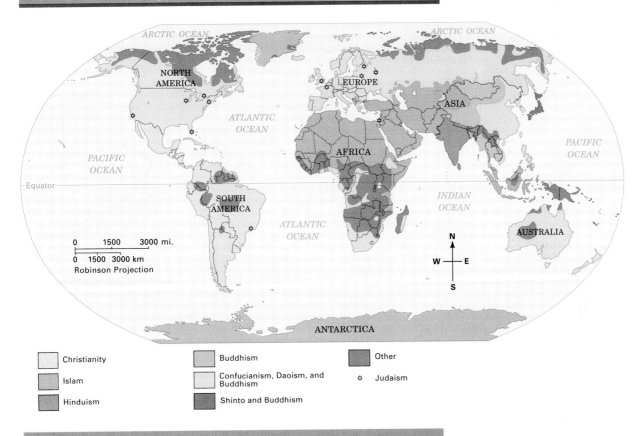

Christianity

Islam

Hinduism

Buddhism

Confucianism, Daoism, and Buddhism

Shinto and Buddhism

Other

☼ Judaism

# WORLD: *Languages*

Indo-European (includes English, Spanish, Hindi)

Sino-Tibetan (includes Chinese, Burmese)

Ural-Altaic (includes Finnish, Hungarian, Turkish)

Japanese and Korean

Dravidian

Malayo-Polynesian (includes Hawaiian, Pilipino)

Amerindian (includes Inuit, Iroquoian, Quechua)

African (includes Yoruba, Swahili)

Semitic (includes Hebrew, Arabic)

Other

# WORLD: *Vegetation*

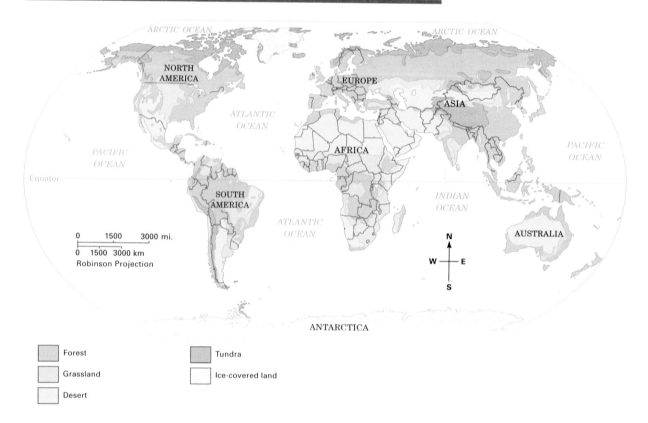

Forest

Grassland

Desert

Tundra

Ice-covered land

# WORLD: *Climate*

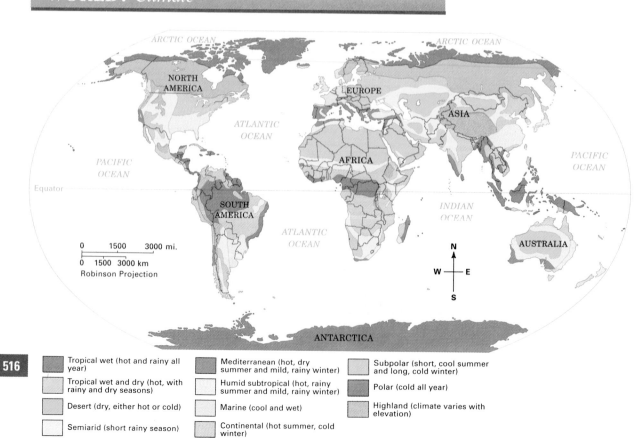

Tropical wet (hot and rainy all year)

Tropical wet and dry (hot, with rainy and dry seasons)

Desert (dry, either hot or cold)

Semiarid (short rainy season)

Mediterranean (hot, dry summer and mild, rainy winter)

Humid subtropical (hot, rainy summer and mild, rainy winter)

Marine (cool and wet)

Continental (hot summer, cold winter)

Subpolar (short, cool summer and long, cold winter)

Polar (cold all year)

Highland (climate varies with elevation)

| PLACE | LAT. | LONG. | PAGE |
|---|---|---|---|
| **Delphi** (ancient site of oracle in Greece) | 38°N | 22°E | **348** |

### E

| PLACE | LAT. | LONG. | PAGE |
|---|---|---|---|
| **Ecbatana** (ancient city of Iran; legendary site of tomb of Mordecai and Esther) | 35°N | 48°E | **81** |
| **Eleusis** (ancient Greek city) | 38°N | 24°E | **348** |
| **Ephesus** (ancient city near Athens) | 38°N | 27°E | **370** |
| **Euphrates R.** (in southwest Asia; along with Tigris R., site of several ancient civilizations) | 36°N | 40°E | **151** |
| **Everest, Mt.** (part of Himalaya range; highest mountain in the world: 29,028 ft.) | 28°N | 87°E | **223** |

### G

| PLACE | LAT. | LONG. | PAGE |
|---|---|---|---|
| **Gades** (Phoenician trading colony in Spain; modern Cádiz) | 37°N | 6°W | **39** |
| **Ganges R.** (in India) | 23°N | 91°E | **223** |
| **Gaul** (ancient Roman province; modern France) | 47°N | 1°E | **433** |
| **Gobi** (desert mostly in Mongolia) | 43°N | 103°E | **27** |
| **Guangzhou** (city in China) | 23°N | 113°E | **27** |
| **Gytta** (Phoenician colony on W. Africa coast) | 32°N | 9°W | **46** |

### H

| PLACE | LAT. | LONG. | PAGE |
|---|---|---|---|
| **Hadar** (site of discovery of australopithecine remains in Africa) | 10°N | 40°E | **93** |
| **Harappa** (site of ancient Indus Valley civilization in Pakistan) | 31°N | 73°E | **224** |
| **Hebron** (ancient town of Jordan; modern Al Khalīl) | 32°N | 35°E | **300** |
| **Hellespont** (narrow strait between Turkey and Egypt; modern Dardanelles) | 40°N | 26°E | **370** |
| **Himalayas** (mountain system in S. Asia) | 30°N | 85°E | **223** |
| **Hindu Kush** (mountain range in Central Asia) | 35°N | 69°E | **223** |
| **Hit** (town in Iraq; ancient Is) | 34°N | 43°E | **151** |
| **Huang He** (river in China; also known as Yellow R.) | 37°N | 117°E | **27** |

### I

| PLACE | LAT. | LONG. | PAGE |
|---|---|---|---|
| **Iconium** (ancient city in Turkey visited by Paul) | 37°N | 32°E | **461** |
| **Indus R.** (in Pakistan) | 24°N | 68°E | **223** |
| **Istanbul** (capital of Turkey; ancient Constantinople) | 41°N | 29°E | **508** |
| **Ithaca** (Greek island) | 38°N | 21°E | **329** |

### J

| PLACE | LAT. | LONG. | PAGE |
|---|---|---|---|
| **Jericho** (ancient city in Jordan; modern Arīhā) | 32°N | 35°E | **303** |
| **Jerusalem** (ancient city; capital of modern Israel) | 32°N | 35°E | **200** |
| **Jordan R.** (forms boundary between Israel and Jordan) | 32°N | 36°E | **300** |
| **Judea** (ancient Roman province in Palestine) | 31°N | 34°E | **465** |

### K

| PLACE | LAT. | LONG. | PAGE |
|---|---|---|---|
| **Kabul** (capital of Afghanistan) | 35°N | 69°E | **41** |
| **Kapilavastu** (town of ancient India; birthplace of the Buddha) | 27°N | 83°E | **251** |
| **Karnak** (part of site of ancient Thebes; village on E. bank of Nile) | 26°N | 33°E | **211** |
| **Kish** (ancient city of Sumer) | 33°N | 45°E | **151** |
| **Knossos** (royal city of ancient Crete) | 35°N | 25°E | **465** |
| **Kunlun Shan** (mountain range in China) | 35°N | 83°E | **27** |

### L

| PLACE | LAT. | LONG. | PAGE |
|---|---|---|---|
| **Lagash** (Sumerian city in Babylonia) | 32°N | 47°E | **151** |
| **Leptis** (ancient city of N. Africa) | 34°N | 14°E | **51** |
| **London** (capital of the United Kingdom) | 52°N | 0°W | **508** |
| **Luoyang** (city of E. China) | 35°N | 113°E | **277** |

### M

| PLACE | LAT. | LONG. | PAGE |
|---|---|---|---|
| **Macedonia** (ancient kingdom N.W. of Aegean Sea) | 41°N | 22°E | **370** |
| **Madeira Islands** (territory of Portugal off W. coast of Africa) | 33°N | 16°W | **46** |
| **Mediterranean Sea** (between Europe and Africa) | 36°N | 13°E | **433** |

This dictionary lists many of the important people introduced in this book. The page number refers to the main discussion of that person in the book. For more complete references see the Index.

## Pronunciation Key

This chart presents the system of phonetic respellings used to indicate pronunciation in the Biographical Dictionary and in the chapters of this book.

| Spellings | Symbol | Spellings | Symbol | Spellings | Symbol |
|---|---|---|---|---|---|
| pat | a | kick, cat, pique | k | thin, this | th |
| pay | ay | lid, needle | l | cut | uh |
| care | air | mum | m | urge, term, firm, word, heard | ur |
| father | ah | no, sudden | n | | |
| bib | b | thing | ng | valve | v |
| church | ch | pot, horrid | ah | with | w |
| deed, milled | d | toe | oh | yes | y |
| pet | eh | caught, paw, for | aw | zebra, xylem | z |
| bee | ee | noise | oy | vision, pleasure, garage | zh |
| life, phase, rough | f | took | u | | |
| gag | g | boot | oo | about, item, edible, gallop, circus | uh |
| hat | h | out | ow | | |
| which | hw | pop | p | butter | ur |
| pit | ih | roar | r | | |
| pie, by | eye, y | sauce | s | Capital letters indicate stressed syllables. | |
| pier | ihr | ship, dish | sh | | |
| judge | j | tight, stopped | t | | |

## A

**Abraham** c. 1900 B.C., first leader of Israelite nation (p. 299).

**Adad-Nirari** (*uh DAD nih RAH ree*) c. 911 B.C., king of Assyria (p. 176).

**Aeneas** (*ih NEE uhs*) c. 1200s B.C., Trojan hero in war against Greece; according to legend escaped to Italy where son, Romulus, founded Rome (p. 421).

**Alaric** c. 370–410, Visigoth king who conquered Rome in 410 (p. 475).

**Alexander the Great** 356–323 B.C., Macedonian king, 336–323 B.C., who conquered Greece, Persia, and Egypt (p. 378).

**Ambrose of Milan, Bishop** c. 340–397, bishop of Milan, 374–397 (p. 469).

**Antigonus** (*an TIHG uh nuhs*) 382–301 B.C., general of Alexander the Great who controlled Macedonia after Alexander's death (p. 381).

**Antiochus** (*ahn TEE uh kuhs*) ?–163 B.C., Syrian ruler, 175–163 B.C., whose order for Jews to worship Greek gods led to the Maccabean revolt (p. 313).

**Archytas** (*ahr KY tuhs*) 300s B.C., Greek who built wooden flying machine (p. 12).

**Aristarchus** (*ar ih STAHR kuhs*) 200s B.C., Greek astronomer who theorized that the earth revolved around the sun (p. 386).

**Aristides** (*air ih STY deez*) A.D. 100s, Greek writer (p. 449).

**Aristophanes** (*ar ih STAHF uh neez*) 400s B.C., Greek playwright (p. 385).

**Aristotle** (*AR ih staht l*) 384–322 B.C., Greek philosopher and teacher of Alexander the Great (p. 378).

**Aryabhata** c. 400s, Indian astronomer (p. 249).

**Asoka** (*ah SHOH kah*) 200s B.C., Buddhist ruler of Mauryan empire 269–232 B.C. (p. 239).

**Attila the Hun** c. 406–453, king of the Huns, a tribe of barbarians, and conqueror of Roman cities (p. 4).

**Augustine, Saint** 354–430, church leader, philosopher, and author of *The City of God* (p. 479).

**Augustus** (*aw GUHS tuhs*) 63 B.C.–A.D. 14, title meaning "respected one," given to Octavian, first Roman emperor, 27 B.C.–A.D. 14 (p. 431).

**Aurelius** *See* **Marcus Aurelius**

## B

**Brutus** c. 85–42 B.C., one leader of group of Roman senators which assassinated Julius Caesar in 44 B.C. (p. 430).

**Buddha, The** c. 565–c. 483 B.C., Indian philosopher, teacher, and founder of Buddhism (p. 236). *See also* **Gautama, Siddhartha**

## C

**Caesar, Julius** 100–44 B.C., Roman general who ended the Republic and ruled as dictator 46–44 B.C.; assassinated (p. 418).

## H

**Hellenistic** (hĕl´ə-nĭs´tĭk) Greek-like; relating to Greek history and culture from the time of Alexander's rule to 146 B.C. (p. 379).

**helot** (hĕl´ət) a state slave in ancient Sparta (p. 353).

**hieroglyphics** (hī´ər-ə-glĭf´ĭks) the ancient Egyptian writing system in which pictorial symbols stand for words or sounds (p. 196).

**Hinduism** (hĭn´dōō-ĭz´əm) the major religion and way of life in modern India (p. 245).

**history** (hĭs´tə-rē) a record of what happened in the past; the study of the past, including explanations of the events (p. 9).

**hunter-gatherer** (hŭn´tər-găth´ər-ər) a person who gets food by hunting wild animals and gathering wild plants, roots, nuts, and berries (p. 106).

## I

**inset** (ĭn´sĕt´) a small map that appears within another map and shows some of the same area in greater detail (p. 40).

**irrigation** (ĭr´ĭ-gā´shən) the act of supplying dry lands with water by means of canals, ditches, pipes, and streams (p. 136).

## J

**Judaism** (jōō´dē-ĭz´əm) the monotheistic religion of the Jewish people (p. 299).

## K

**kitchen midden** (kĭch´ən mĭd´n) a rubbish heap, including artifacts and bones, left in a settlement by people of the past (p. 73).

## L

**legend** (lĕj´ənd) a story handed down from earlier times; also on maps, an explanation of the symbols (p. 39).

**lyric poetry** (lĭr´ĭk pō´ĭ-trē) poems that express personal emotions, often having musical sound patterns (p. 384).

## M

**market** (mär´kĭt) a demand for goods; the opportunity to buy or sell (p. 449).

**martyr** (mär´tər) a person who chooses to die rather than give up religious beliefs (p. 467).

**megalith** (mĕg´ə-lĭth´) a very large stone used in various prehistoric buildings or monuments (p. 82).

**messiah** (mə-sī´ə) the hoped-for king who would free the Jewish people (p. 313).

**middleman** (mĭd´l-măn´) a trader who goes between two parties, buying from one and selling to another; a go-between (p. 286).

**migration** (mī-grā´shən) the permanent movement of people from one region and resettlement in another (p. 230).

**moderation** (mŏd´ə-rā´shən) the condition of not being excessive; not extreme (p. 238).

**monarchy** (mŏn´ər-kē) a system of government in which a monarch—a king, queen, or emperor—is the sole and absolute ruler (p. 339).

**monastery** (mŏn´ə-stĕr´ē) a dwelling place for persons living under religious vows (p. 481).

**monotheism** (mŏn´ə-thē-ĭz´əm) the belief that there is only one god (p. 299).

**monsoon** (mŏn-sōōn´) a wind system affecting the climate of India and southern Asia; reverses direction seasonally, producing a wet season and a dry season (p. 47).

**mummy** (mŭm´ē) a dead body embalmed in the manner of the ancient Egyptians (p. 192).

**myth** (mĭth) a traditional story about the origin and history of a people and their gods, ancestors, and heroes (p. 12).

## N

**nobility** (nō-bĭl´ĭ-tē) a class of people having high birth or rank; aristocracy (p. 271).

**nomad** (nō´măd´) one of a group of people who move with their flocks and herds as the seasons change to find water and pasture (p. 157).

## O

**obelisk** (ŏb´ə-lĭsk) a tall, four-sided stone pillar that tapers to a point like a pyramid (p. 200).

**oligarchy** (ŏl´ĭ-gär´kē) a system of government in which a few people rule (p. 339).

**omen** (ō´mən) a thing or event that is believed to foretell good or evil (p. 396).

**oracle** (ôr´ə-kəl) a prediction about the future; also, the person who makes such a prediction, believed to come from a god or an ancestor (p. 266).

**oral tradition** (ôr´əl trə-dĭsh´ən) the legends, myths, and beliefs that a culture passes from generation to generation by word of mouth (p. 57).

## P

**pagan** (pā´gən) to the early Christians, a person who is not a Christian or Jew (p. 469).

**papyrus** (pə-pī´rəs) a long, thin reed; also, the paper-like writing material made by Egyptians from the reed's pith (p. 189).

**parable** (păr´ə-bəl) a story that teaches a moral or religious lesson (p. 315).

**patrician** (pə-trĭsh´ən) a member of the small class of wealthy families in ancient Rome (p. 406).

**persecute** (pûr´sĭ-kyōot) to punish; to treat harshly or cruelly (p. 458).

**pharaoh** (fâr´ō) a ruler of ancient Egypt (p. 199).

**philosopher** (fĭ-lŏs´ə-fər) a person who seeks wisdom through intellectual means and moral discipline (p. 372).

**pictograph** (pĭk´tə-grăf´) a picture that stands for a word or idea; picture writing (p. 160).

**plague** (plāg) a highly contagious, widespread disease that is often fatal (p. 369).

**plain** (plān) a broad area of flat, open land (p. 151).

**plateau** (plă-tō´) an elevated area of flat land (p. 150).

**plebeian** (plĭ-bē´ən) in ancient Rome, a member of the large class of ordinary citizens (p. 406).

**polytheism** (pŏl´ē-thē-ĭz´əm) belief in more than one god (p. 158).

**prehistory** (prē-hĭs´tə-rē) the history of humans before the development of writing (p. 57).

**primary source** (prī´mĕr´ē sôrs) information about events recorded at the time of those events (p. 60).

**projection** (prə-jĕk´shən) a system for mapping the spherical earth on a flat surface (p. 44).

**prophet** (prŏf´ĭt) a person who expresses and explains the will of God (p. 310).

**province** (prŏv´ĭns) a territory governed as a unit within a country or empire (p. 277); in the ancient Roman Empire, any of the lands outside Italy conquered and ruled by the Romans (p. 432).

## R

**rabbi** (răb´ī) teacher; the leader of a Jewish congregation (p. 321).

**radiocarbon dating** (rā´dē-ō-kär´bən dāt´ĭng) a method for determining the age of once-living things, based on the fact that their radioactive carbon content decays at a regular rate (p. 68).

**rain forest** (rān fôr´ĭst) a dense evergreen forest in a tropical area with an annual rainfall of at least 100 to 140 inches (p. 16).

**region** (rē´jən) an area with similar features that set it apart from surrounding areas (p. 31).

**reincarnation** (rē´ĭn-kär-nā´shən) the belief in rebirth in another body; the belief that at death the soul enters the body of another living form (p. 238).

**republic** (rĭ-pŭb´lĭk) a nation in which political power lies with the citizens, who elect leaders and representatives; the head of state in a republic is not a monarch (p. 406).

**Resurrection** (rĕz´ə-rĕk´shən) the rising of Jesus on the third day after his death (p. 318).

**rhetoric** (rĕt´ər-ĭk) the art of effective writing and public speaking (p. 443).

**ritual** (rĭch´ōo-əl) a ceremony or rite; the prescribed form for a religious or solemn ceremony (p. 446).

## S

**sanctuary** (săngk´chōo-ĕr´ē) a place of worship such as a church, temple, or mosque (p. 347).

**sarcophagus** (sär-kŏf´ə-gəs) a stone coffin; any coffin (p. 71).

**scale** (skāl) the proportion that exists between information on a graph and the amount or measure it represents; also in maps, the relationship between the actual size of an area and its size as shown on the map (p. 35).

**scribe** (skrīb) a professional writer or record keeper; a person whose job is to copy documents and manuscripts (p. 161).

**secondary source** (sĕk´ən-dĕr´ē sôrs) information about events recorded after those events by people who have studied the primary sources (p. 60).

**sect** (sĕkt) a group of people who form a distinct unit within a larger group, as for example, within a religious group (p. 459).

**seismograph** (sīz´mə-grăf´) an instrument for detecting and determining the direction, strength, and length of earthquakes and other ground movements (p. 281).

**self-sufficient** (sĕlf´sə-fĭsh´ənt) able to provide for oneself without the help of others (p. 130).

**Senate** (sĕn´ĭt) in ancient Rome, the supreme council of state of the Republic and later of the empire (p. 397).

**shrine** (shrīn) a place where people worship, usually containing a sacred object or statue (p. 129).

**silt** (sĭlt) a fine-grained soil, often deposited on riverbanks during floods (p. 224).

**subcontinent** (sŭb´kŏn´tə-nənt) a large landmass, such as India, that is part of a continent but is separated from it in some way (p. 223).

**surplus** (sŭr´pləs) an extra amount; more than is needed (p. 121).

**synagogue** (sĭn´ə-gŏg´) a building or meeting place for Jewish worship and instruction (p. 321).

## T

**technology** (tĕk-nŏl´ə-jē) the tools, machines, and methods used to make products, save time, or in some way improve people's lives (p. 99).

**thematic map** (thĭ-măt´ĭk măp) a map that gives information on a particular theme or subject (p. 43).

**topography** (tə-pŏg´rə-fē) the physical features of a region, such as mountains, plains, and rivers (p. 27).

**tragedy** (trăj´ĭ-dē) a serious drama in which the hero is brought to defeat by a character flaw (p. 350).

**tribute** (trĭb´yōot) a gift or payment to show respect or admiration (p. 211).

**tyrant** (tī´rənt) a ruler who has total power, not limited by a constitution or by other officials; especially, one in ancient Greece (p. 340).